Law Enforcement Intelligence:

A Guide for State, Local, and Tribal Law Enforcement Agencies

Second Edition

David L. Carter, Ph.D.
School of Criminal Justice,
Michigan State University

This project was supported by Cooperative Agreement #2007-CK-WX-K015 by the U.S. Department of Justice Office of Community Oriented Policing Services. Points of view or opinions contained in this publication are those of the author and do not necessarily represent the official position or policies of the U.S. Department of Justice or Michigan State University. References to specific agencies, companies, products, or services should not be considered an endorsement by the author or the U.S. Department of Justice. Rather, the references are illustrations to supplement discussion of the issues.

Letter from the COPS Office

January 2009

Dear Colleague:

This second edition of *Law Enforcement Intelligence: A Guide for State, Local, and Tribal Law Enforcement* captures the vast changes that have occurred in the 4 years since the first edition of the guide was published in 2004 after the watershed events of September 11, 2001.

At that time, there was no Department of Homeland Security, Office of the Director of National Intelligence, Information-Sharing Environment, or Fusion Centers. Since the advent of these new agencies to help fight the war on terror, emphasis has been placed on cooperation and on sharing information among local, state, tribal, and federal agencies. The successes of community policing are evident, not just within law enforcement, but also through agencies' work with the community to protect civil liberties and civil rights. A strong foundation between the police and the community also yields valuable information for fighting crime and terrorist threats. Through community policing and the wide array of approaches that fall under its umbrella—hot spots, CompStat, problem-oriented policing, and Intelligence-Led Policing—law enforcement can gather and share information that will enhance public safety.

Years of partnership building and problem solving with the community, the private sector, nonprofit organizations, elected officials, social service providers, and other key stakeholders have created an environment in which Intelligence-Led Policing and information sharing is more viable because of the strong relationships established through community policing.

This *Guide* serves as a road map to understanding criminal intelligence and its related methodology, standards, processes, management, and resources. In fact, nearly 85 percent of the material in this second edition is new. I am proud to add this valuable publication to the COPS Office library. My thanks to Dr. David Carter for synthesizing the vast body of law enforcement information and intelligence into one volume that I know will be an indispensable knowledge resource for law enforcement agencies around the country. During these challenging times, community policing is more important than ever.

Sincerely,

Carl Peed
Former Director
Office of Community Oriented Policing Services

Preface

When the first edition of *Law Enforcement Intelligence* was published, it documented unprecedented changes in law enforcement intelligence that occurred largely in response to the September 11, 2001 terrorists' attacks. Indeed, the new initiatives reflected philosophical and operational changes that represented a geometric evolution in law enforcement intelligence in only 3 short years. The first edition of the *Guide* described a broad array of cutting-edge issues and practices. At the time, it seemed implausible that such dramatic changes would occur again. Nevertheless, since the publication of the first edition, a staggering number of significant developments affecting law enforcement intelligence have occurred:

- There were only a few Regional Intelligence Centers across the U.S. that are now evolving into a nationwide network of fusion centers.

- The *Fusion Center Guidelines* had not been written.

- There had been no national fusion center conferences and regional fusion center groups did not exist.

- The Fusion Process Technical Assistance Program, a joint Department of Justice and Department of Homeland Security project, did not exist.

- The Office of the Director of National Intelligence (ODNI) did not exist.

- The Information Sharing Environment did not exist.

- The FBI's Intelligence Directorate did not exist.

- The DEA's National Security Branch of the Office of Intelligence did not exist.

- The National Criminal Intelligence Resource Center did not exist.

- Many intelligence training programs that are now taken for granted did not exist.

- The Joint Regional Information Exchange System—which is now virtually gone— was "the system" for information sharing and analysis.

- "All-hazards" intelligence was not in our lexicon.

- Intelligence-Led Policing was in its infancy.

- What is now the expansive Open Source Center which, as part of the ODNI is aggressively reaching out to state, local, and tribal law enforcement was a narrowly focused program called the Foreign Broadcast Information Service operated by the CIA.

- Relatively few law enforcement agencies had any type of intelligence capacity.

- Suspicious Activity Reporting (SAR) was largely limited to "tips and leads" and there were no unified standards or formal processes to report suspicious activities.

This second edition of *Law Enforcement Intelligence* describes these and many more changes in the philosophy, national standards, and practice of law enforcement intelligence while maintaining the core goal of being a primer on "all things intelligence" for the law enforcement community.

The *Guide* is intended to support policy in law enforcement agencies and seeks to objectively provide the best knowledge and practice of law enforcement intelligence at the time of publication. It is not meant as an academic work nor does it look at theoretical issues or arguments. It is not directed as a guide to the intelligence community except to explain the roles, responsibilities, and restrictions of the intelligence community's state, local, and tribal law enforcement partners.

The Internet references cited in this publication were valid as of June 2009. Given that URLs and web sites are in constant flux, neither the author nor the Office of Community Oriented Policing Services can vouch for their current validity. Please note that some of the sites referenced require a user name and/or password to gain access.

Acknowledgments

In completing this second edition, first and foremost I want to thank Carl Peed, former Director of the Office of Community Oriented Policing Services (the COPS Office). Carl's support for both editions of *Law Enforcement Intelligence* was consistent, strong, and unwavering. Carl, I sincerely appreciate all you have done for this project.

I also thank the membership of the Criminal Intelligence Coordinating Council for taking the time to review the original draft of this *Guide* to ensure that it reflected the information needed by the law enforcement intelligence community. Many people assisted me in the preparation of this *Guide*. Their contributions, large and small, helped in developing the comprehensive contents. While I hope to not leave out anyone, I particularly want to thank: Bill Harris (Delaware Information Analysis Center), Bob Hipple (Indianapolis [Indiana] Metropolitan Police Department), Bruce Parker (Brevard County [Florida] Sheriff's Office, Retired), Ed McGarrell, Steve Chermak, Natalie Hipple, and Jeremy Carter (Michigan State University [MSU]), Hal Wilson (Drug Enforcement Administration), Kathy Suey (Las Vegas Metropolitan Police Department), Kelly Stone (North Central Texas Fusion Center), Lance Ladines (Washington Joint Analysis Center), Mark Johnson (Open Source Center), Merle Manzi (Florida Department of Law Enforcement, Retired), Norm Beasley (Maricopa County [Arizona] Sheriff's Office), Ray Guidetti (New Jersey Regional Intelligence Operations Center), Rick Stephens (FBI), Ritchie Martinez (Arizona High Intensity Drug Trafficking Area), Roger Bragdon (Chief, Spokane [Washington] Police Department, Retired), Sabra Horne and Craig Manly (Office of the Director of National Intelligence), Scott Whitney (Customs and Border Protection), and Tom Martinelli (Wayne State University).

I expressly want to thank those who volunteered to review the *Guide*: Dan Oates (Aurora [Colorado] Police Department), Bob Casey (FBI), Ed McCarroll (Department of Homeland Security [DHS]), Kevin Saupp (DHS), Lisa Palmieri (DHS and International Association of Law Enforcement Intelligence Analysts), Mark Gage (National White Collar Crime Center) and Michael Ronczkowski (Miami-Dade Police Department). I know you were all a little surprised when you discovered the size of the document.

I also had assistance from friends whose work went well beyond "a little help," particularly reading and reviewing drafts. I thank Russ Porter (Iowa Department of Public Safety) for not only his review but also for giving me ideas and perspectives on many issues. Larry Shaw (Florida Department of Law Enforcement) for helping me navigate through the maze of information systems and networks. I sincerely appreciate the extra time and work of Doug Bodrero and Phil Ramer (both of the Institute for Intergovernmental Research) for giving me ideas, reviewing materials, and providing me with comprehensive comments while they were traversing the country on various projects, all for the promise of a meal and a drink.

To Amy Schapiro, COPS Office Social Science Analyst: your constant support and facilitation to make the processes go smoothly are appreciated. To Josh Reinsch of the Michigan State University Intelligence Program, I thank you for your quick work and willingness to make the extra effort in all that you do for us. And to Robyn Nielsen, also of the MSU Intelligence Program, I truly appreciate your hard work, quick responses, unquestioned dedication, and support for this and other projects. You make my life a lot easier.

To my longtime friend and coconspirator Andi Bannister (Wichita State University): I cannot thank you enough for meticulously reviewing every word of this document and providing suggestions for content, wording, and presentation. As always, you made my work go much smoother (with fewer mistakes!) with all of the time and effort you put into reviewing this *Guide*.

Also important, I thank my wife Karen, children Hilary, Jeremy, and Lauren and son-in-law Joseph O'Donnell who put up with the time I worked on this and other projects—you are always in my thoughts.

Last, I dedicate this *Intelligence Guide* to a beautiful, smart, sweet, bundle of energy who always makes me smile: my granddaughter, Shey Catherine O'Donnell.

David L. Carter, Ph.D.
Michigan State University

Executive Summary

Law Enforcement Intelligence: A Guide for State, Local, and Tribal Law Enforcement Agencies is a policy oriented review of current initiatives, national standards, and best practices.

The first two chapters provide definitions and context for the current state of law enforcement intelligence. Chapter 2 also provides a discussion of homeland security—or "all-hazards"—intelligence. While more law enforcement agencies and fusion centers are embracing the all-hazards approach, its application remains somewhat unclear. This discussion provides a framework for homeland security intelligence policy.

Chapter 3 is a historical perspective that has multiple purposes. First, it provides a discussion of past abuses by law enforcement intelligence because it is important to understand the problems of the past in order to prevent them in the future. Next, the chapter provides a framework for national recommendations and professional standards for the practice of intelligence. Finally, the discussion identifies the various working groups and committees that are framing the current intelligence model and the relationship of those groups to federal agencies and professional law enforcement organizations.

Fundamental to all types of intelligence is a system for managing the flow of information for analysis. This is alternately called the Intelligence Process or the Intelligence Cycle. Chapter 4 is a descriptive discussion of the process as it applies to law enforcement agencies. While there are different models for the Intelligence Process, this discussion relies on the model used in the *National Criminal Intelligence Sharing Plan*.

Recommendations from both the *National Criminal Intelligence Sharing Plan* and the COPS Office-funded International Association of Chiefs of Police intelligence summits urge law enforcement agencies to adopt Intelligence-Led Policing (ILP). The challenge, however, is that there is no universally accepted definition or process for understanding and implementing ILP. Chapters 5 and 6 amalgamate the diverse literature on ILP to provide a holistic view. Chapter 5 focuses on the concept of ILP as it applies to American law enforcement, with a perspective on the British approach from which the concept originated. Chapter 6 focuses on the organizational and administrative processes for implementing ILP.

There is no issue more topical (or controversial) in law enforcement intelligence than the protection of civil rights and privacy. Chapter 7 is a broad examination of the issue identifying the concerns expressed by citizens and illustrating some of the problems faced with intelligence operations through the use of two federal civil rights cases. Integrated into the chapter is a detailed discussion of 28 CFR Part 23 and its application for placing information that identifies individuals or organizations in a criminal intelligence records system. The discussion expands the issues further with a detailed discussion of intelligence records and civil rights liability. The chapter ends with a discussion of how a law enforcement agency can immunize itself against civil rights lawsuits related to the intelligence function.

As a mechanism to enhance widespread information sharing among state, local, and tribal law enforcement agencies, the intelligence fusion concept grew rapidly. This growth was further spurred when fusion centers were embraced by the Information Sharing Environment (ISE) to be the critical information-sharing clearinghouse for terrorism information between law enforcement and other ISE information-sharing partners. Chapter 8 describes the fusion concept and the processes by which a fusion center operates. This chapter also addresses the concerns that critics have expressed about fusion centers.

Every major national standard for intelligence—the *National Criminal Intelligence Sharing Plan*, the *Fusion Center Guidelines*, the *Information Sharing Environment Implementation Plan* and the Department of Homeland Security's *Target Capabilities List*—has recommended establishing a public-private partnership for information sharing to support the intelligence function. Few, however, have established a substantive information-sharing relationship with the private sector. There are difficult hurdles to establishing such a relationship but it certainly is possible. Chapter 9 discusses the recommendations, the issues, and the processes for making public-private partnerships for intelligence a reality.

At the heart of all intelligence activities is the need to manage a wide array of information. A number of critical issues in this process are important to understand. Chapter 10 addresses these issues in a comprehensive manner, relying on best practices and national standards. In a logically organized approach, the key topics discussed are: *Suspicious Activity Reporting* (SAR); defining and using *intelligence requirements;* the *information collection process* including the development of a *collection plan;* the role of *analysis* (from a consumer's perspective); and *intelligence outputs and products.* With the increase of different information-sharing initiatives, one of the challenges has been to ensure that the right information gets in the hands of the right people who can use the information to develop policy and operational responses. This chapter includes a discussion of information-sharing practices to avoid.

A new initiative of the Office of the Director of National Intelligence is the National Open Source Enterprise. The goal of open source information and intelligence is to exploit open sources as "the source of first resort" in any intelligence endeavor. The reasons are that open sources are easier, faster, pose less risk to civil rights, and are less controversial for the agency. Part of this new initiative is to include law enforcement intelligence in open source information sharing. Chapter 11 provides a detailed discussion of open sources, the different types of information that can be obtained, how it can be obtained, and caveats for analysis.

A wide—and confusing—array of federal intelligence resources, including networks, systems, analytic services, applications and products, is available to state, local, and tribal law enforcement. Many have a specialized expertise or a limited area of application, while others are very broad in their application. Chapter 12 discusses federal intelligence resources, starting with a discussion of classified information, including a description of the process for a state, local, or tribal law enforcement officer to obtain a federal security clearance. Most law enforcement officers, however, will not have a clearance and will be dealing with Sensitive But Unclassified (SBU) information. A discussion is provided of the meaning and rules for SBU information sharing. Important to note: SBU information is going through a government-wide transition to become categorized as Controlled Unclassified Information (CUI) and has some distinct issues for sharing and storing the information. The chapter provides a detailed discussion of CUI and the guidelines imposed for its use. The last part of the chapter is an encyclopedic listing of diverse federal information and intelligence systems and resources.

One of the recommendations of the *National Criminal Intelligence Sharing Plan* is that every law enforcement agency, regardless of size, should develop an intelligence capacity. For some agencies this will be an entire unit, while for other agencies it will be a part-time assignment of one person. In either case, there are management concerns related to the intelligence function. Chapter 13 focuses on management concerns that have relative uniqueness to the intelligence function. It begins with a comprehensive list of factors to consider when developing the intelligence capacity. This is followed by a detailed description of developing a Concept of Operations (ConOps) that serves as the road map for developing and implementing the intelligence function. Finally, a wide range of management issues are discussed, ranging from developing policies to human resources concerns.

The final chapter examines critical issues and challenges for the future and a model for implementing change. The *Guide* also includes comprehensive resources for all aspects of intelligence, a glossary of intelligence terms, and appendixes to support the various discussions. Included in the appendixes are two intelligence audit checklists.

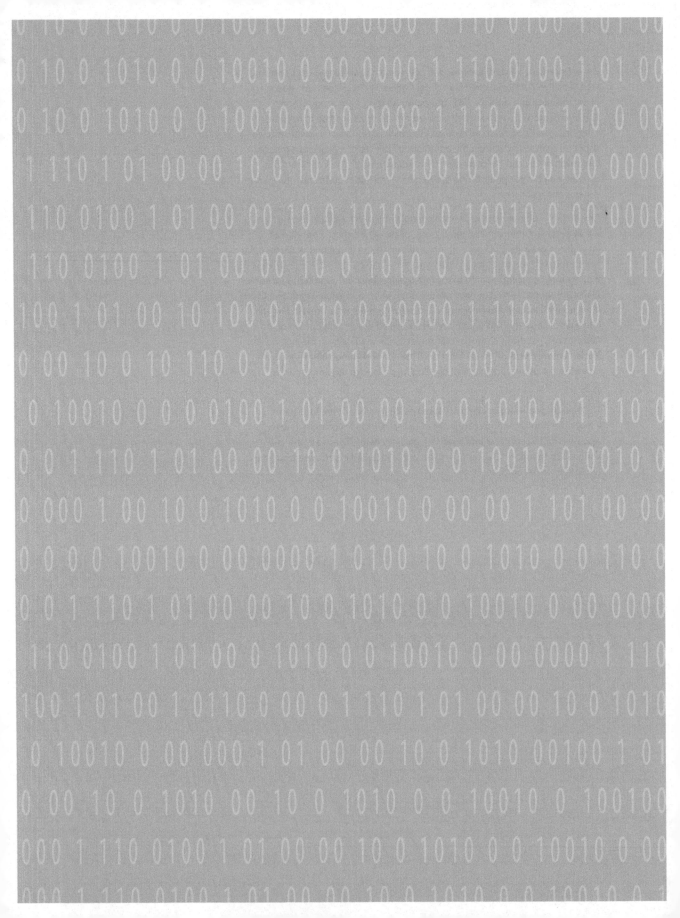

Contents

Chapter 1:
Introduction

Introduction

To protect the United States from threats to our security and sovereignty, current initiatives at the federal, state, local, and tribal levels seek to develop a "culture of information sharing."[1] This is a significant challenge that requires the integration of new law, policy, procedure, training, and organizational change.

The National Strategy for Information Sharing focuses on five core principles:

1. Effective information sharing comes through strong partnerships among federal, state, local, and tribal authorities, private-sector organizations, and our foreign partners and allies.

2. Information acquired for one purpose, or under one set of authorities, might provide unique insights when combined, in accordance with applicable law, with seemingly unrelated information from other sources. We, therefore, must foster a culture of awareness in which people at all levels of government remain cognizant of the functions and needs of others and use knowledge and information from all sources to support counterterrorism efforts.

3. Information sharing must be woven into all aspects of counterterrorism activity, including preventive and protective actions, actionable responses, criminal and counterterrorism investigative activities, event preparedness, and response to and recovery from catastrophic events.

4. The procedures, processes, and systems that support information sharing must draw on and integrate existing technical capabilities and must respect established authorities and responsibilities.

5. State and major urban area fusion centers represent a valuable information-sharing resource and should be incorporated into the national information-sharing framework. This will require fusion centers to achieve a baseline level of capability to gather, process, share, and utilize information, and operate in a manner that respects individuals' privacy rights and other legal rights protected by U.S. laws.[2]

To achieve the culture of information sharing, every law enforcement agency in the United States, regardless of size, must have the capacity to understand the implications of information collection, analysis, and intelligence sharing. Each agency must have an organized mechanism to receive and manage intelligence as well as a mechanism to report and share critical information with other law enforcement agencies. In addition, it is essential that law enforcement agencies develop lines of communication and information-sharing protocols with the private sector, particularly those related to the critical infrastructure, as well as with those private entities that are potential targets of terrorists and criminal enterprises.

Not every agency has the staff or resources to create a formal intelligence unit, nor is it necessary in smaller agencies. Even without an intelligence unit, a law enforcement organization must have the ability to effectively consume the information and intelligence products being shared by a wide range of

[1] Program Manager–Information Sharing Environment. *Information Sharing Environment Implementation Plan.* Washington, D.C.: Office of the Director of National Intelligence, 2006.

[2] *National Strategy for Information Sharing.* Washington, D.C.: Executive Office of the President, 2007, pp. 2–3.

organizations at all levels of government. State, local, and tribal law enforcement (SLTLE) will be most effective when a single source in every agency is the conduit of critical information, whether it is the Terrorist Intelligence Unit of the Los Angeles Police Department, the sole intelligence analyst of the Lansing (Michigan) Police Department, or the patrol sergeant who understands the language of intelligence and is the information-sharing contact in the Mercedes (Texas) Police Department. Each law enforcement agency must have an understanding of its intelligence management capabilities, regardless of its size or organizational structure.

This document describes common language and processes for developing and employing an intelligence capacity in SLTLE agencies across the United States as well as articulating a uniform understanding of concepts, issues, and terminology for law enforcement intelligence. While terrorism issues are the most pervasive, the discussion of intelligence in this *Guide* is directed toward "all crimes, all threats, and all hazards." As such, the principles of intelligence discussed in this document apply beyond terrorism and include organized crime and entrepreneurial crime in all forms.

Drug trafficking and the associated crime of money laundering, for example, continue to be a significant challenge for law enforcement. Transnational computer crime, particularly Internet fraud, identity theft cartels, and global black marketeering of stolen and counterfeit goods, are entrepreneurial crime problems that are increasingly relegated to SLTLE agencies to investigate simply because of the volume of criminal incidents. Similarly, local law enforcement is increasingly drawn into human trafficking and illegal immigration enterprises and the often-associated crimes related to counterfeiting of official documents, such as passports, visas, driver's licenses, social security cards, and credit cards. Even the trafficking of art and antiquities has increased, often bringing a new profile of criminal into the realm of entrepreneurial crime. Most recently, the application of intelligence to pervasive violence in America's communities is also an important focus. All require an intelligence capacity for SLTLE, as does the continuation of historical organized crime activities such as auto theft, cargo theft, and virtually any other scheme that can produce profit for an organized criminal entity.

To be effective, the law enforcement community must interpret intelligence-related language in a consistent manner. In addition, common standards, policies, and practices will help expedite intelligence sharing while at the same time protecting the privacy of citizens and preserving hard-won community policing relationships.

Perspective

At the outset, law enforcement officers must understand the concept of law enforcement intelligence, its distinction from national security intelligence, and the potential problems an SLTLE agency can face when the two types of intelligence overlap. A law enforcement executive must understand what is meant by an "intelligence function" and how that function can be fulfilled through the use of different organizational models. Related executive decisions focus on staffing, particularly when there are fiscal limitations. Complicating this mission are two new intelligence responsibilities that have emerged: 1. Information sharing with national security and homeland security partners as part of the Information Sharing Environment and 2. developing a capacity for Homeland Security—or "all-hazards"—Intelligence.

Another important—and pervasive—challenge is to ensure that all new intelligence initiatives fully protect the privacy and civil rights of all persons. Critical issues and new initiatives for this responsibility are discussed throughout the *Guide*, with one chapter devoted specifically to this topic.

These issues pose a wide range of important questions: What kinds of information does the law enforcement agency need (that is, what are its intelligence requirements) from the federal government to most effectively counter terrorism? How are those needs determined? How is the information requested? When and in what form will the information be received? Will a security clearance be needed to review the information that an executive requests? Beyond terrorism, what types of threats exist in a community? How are these threats identified? What kinds of threats are included in "all-hazards" intelligence? What are the best sources and methods (that is, a collection plan) for understanding these threats and developing actionable intelligence? How do we engage the community and private sector in the intelligence process? What are the limitations on collecting and disseminating information between law enforcement and the community and private sector? The answers are not easy, but they are attainable.

From a policy and process perspective, what is meant by information sharing? What information can be collected? What information can be retained in a criminal intelligence records system? How long may the records be retained? When does a person transcend the threshold of exercising his or her rights to posing a threat to community safety? What resources exist to aid an SLTLE agency in accomplishing its intelligence goals? How can the entire law enforcement agency be integrated into the intelligence function? If a law enforcement organization is to be effective, the answers to these questions must be a product of written policy.

The intent of this document is to provide answers—or at least alternatives—to these questions. To begin the process, every law enforcement administrator must recognize that intelligence and information sharing can be effective in preventing terrorism and fighting organized crime. To realize these ends, however, the intelligence process for law enforcement at all levels of government requires the following:

- Reengineering some of the organization's structure and processes so that they are consistent with national initiatives and national standards of good practice in law enforcement intelligence.

- Developing a shared vision of the terrorist or criminal threat.

- Establishing a commitment to participate and follow through with threat information.

- Overcoming the conceptual difficulty of intelligence processes that some personnel find difficult to grasp.

- Committing an agency's resources, time, and energy to the intelligence function.

- Establishing policies and practices that protect individuals' civil rights and privacy.

- Embracing and using contemporary technology, including electronic access to information and an electronic communications capability through a secure connection.

- Having proactive people using creative thought to identify "what we don't know" about terrorism and international organized crime.

- Requiring a law enforcement agency to think globally and act locally.

- Engaging in public-private partnerships for intelligence.

- Engaging the community to participate in the intelligence process.

- Being committed and patient.

Conclusion

The amount of change in the law enforcement intelligence process that has occurred during the past 4 years is unprecedented. The roles and responsibilities for state, local, and tribal law enforcement are challenging from operational, policy, and fiscal perspectives. Despite these challenges, comprehensive plans and new resources have become available to achieve the goal of protecting our communities.

Chapter 2:
Understanding Contemporary Intelligence for
Law Enforcement Organizations: Concepts and Definitions

Understanding Contemporary Intelligence for Law Enforcement Organizations: Concepts and Definitions

In the purest sense, intelligence is the end product of an analytic process that evaluates information collected from diverse sources; integrates the relevant information into a logical package; and produces a conclusion, estimate, or forecast about a criminal phenomenon by using the scientific approach to problem solving (that is, analysis). Intelligence, therefore, is a synergistic product intended to provide meaningful and trustworthy actionable knowledge to law enforcement decision makers about complex criminality, criminal enterprises, criminal extremists, and terrorists.

The law enforcement intelligence function has essentially two broad purposes:

1. Prevention involves gaining or developing information related to threats of terrorism or crime and using it to apprehend offenders, harden targets, and use strategies that will eliminate or mitigate the threat. Two generally accepted types of intelligence are specifically oriented toward prevention:

    a. Tactical Intelligence. Actionable intelligence about imminent or near-term threats that is disseminated to the line functions of a law enforcement agency for purposes of developing and implementing preventive, and/or mitigating, response plans and activities.

    b. Operational Intelligence. Actionable intelligence about long-term threats that is used to develop and implement preventive responses. Most commonly, operational intelligence is used for long-term inquiries into suspected criminal enterprises and complex multijurisdictional criminality.

2. Planning and resource allocation provides information to decision-makers about the changing nature of threats, the characteristics and methodologies of threats, and emerging threat idiosyncrasies for the purpose of developing response strategies and reallocating resources, as necessary, to accomplish effective prevention.

    a. This is known as strategic intelligence. It provides an assessment of the changing threat picture to the management of a law enforcement agency for purposes of developing plans and allocating resources to meet the demands of emerging threats.

While investigation[1] is clearly related to the information collection[2] and intelligence processes, the intelligence function is often more exploratory and more broadly focused than a criminal investigation, per se. For example, a law enforcement agency may have a reasonable suspicion to believe that a person or group of people have the intent, capacity, and resolve to commit a crime or terrorist act. Evidence, however, may fall short of the probable cause standard, even for an arrest for criminal attempt or conspiracy. Moreover, there may be a compelling community safety reason to keep an inquiry open to identify other criminal offenders—notably leaders—and weapons that may be used.

[1] "Investigation" is defined as the pursuit of information based on leads and evidence associated with a particularly defined criminal act to identify and apprehend criminal offenders for prosecution in a criminal trial.

[2] "Information collection" in the context of law enforcement intelligence is the capture of information and data to determine if suspicious activities have a criminal nexus and/or to understand the operation of crime phenomena.

Because of this broader role, the need to keep information secure, and the necessity of keeping records that identify individuals and organizations for whom evidence of criminal involvement is uncertain or tangential,[3] rigid guidelines must be followed. These guidelines are designed to protect the constitutional rights of citizens while at the same time permitting law enforcement agencies to proceed with an inquiry for purposes of community safety. The guidelines are also designed to facilitate accurate and secure information sharing between law enforcement agencies because the nature of terrorism and criminal enterprise threats are inherently multijurisdictional. Further, if law enforcement agencies at all strata of government subscribe to the same guidelines, information sharing can be more widespread because there is certainty that regardless of with whom the information is shared, the security and integrity of the records will remain intact.

Defining Intelligence

There are many misconceptions about the meaning and application of "intelligence;" not only among the lay public but also within law enforcement. Colloquial uses of the term provide an intuitive understanding, such as "Officer Jones collected some good intelligence." These uses, however, lack precision and are unable to account for the diverse applications and rules associated with the intelligence function.

As a primer, there are two broad classes of intelligence, as illustrated in Figure 2-1. The first category is the "discipline" of intelligence, which refers to the set of rules, processes, and lexicon of the intelligence function. This *Intelligence Guide* is solely about the discipline of intelligence. Within the framework of the discipline, there are three types of intelligence of concern for the present discussion:[4]

1. Law enforcement (or criminal[5]) intelligence, 2. Homeland security—also known as "all-hazards"—intelligence, and 3. National security intelligence. While there are important similarities across these three categories, there are also distinct differences. These critical factors are discussed throughout this *Guide* as they specifically relate to state, local, and tribal law enforcement (SLTLE) agencies.

Figure 2-1: Classes of Intelligence

Intelligence:
Analysis of raw information to provide synergistic knowledge about a threat

Discipline of Intelligence: Concepts, rules, processes, and law of the intelligence function

Application of Intelligence: Crimes/Targets

| Law Enforcement Intelligence | Homeland Enforcement Intelligence | National Enforcement Intelligence | Indicators, Motives, Methods of those Posing Threats |

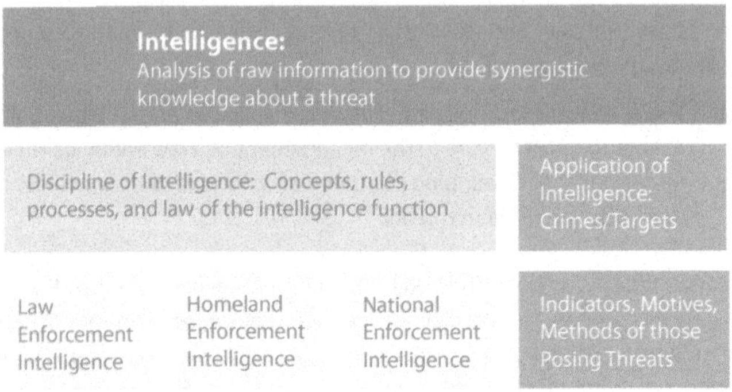

[3] This includes information that would be in the intelligence records system "Temporary File" as well as "Non-Criminal Identifying Information" as defined by 28 CFR Part 23.

[4] This is not an exclusive categorization of intelligence. The discipline of intelligence may be divided into other categories; for example, National Security Intelligence may be divided into "policy intelligence" and "military intelligence." One may also consider "business intelligence," "geospatial intelligence," or "cyber intelligence," among others. The categorization used above is the best model to illustrate critical points for the current discussion.

[5] The author uses the phrase "law enforcement intelligence" because a realm of study in the field of criminal psychology addresses "criminal intelligence" as it relates to the criminal personality and the propensity and processes by which criminals behave.

The second broad class is the "application of intelligence," which deals with knowledge related to a specific crime type. Intelligence analysis that produces information about new methods and indicators in the uses of improvised explosive devices (IED) by jihadists, for example, is the "application of intelligence." Another illustration would be indicators drawn from an analysis of international financial transactions that are characteristic of a money laundering enterprise. An essential ingredient for the application of intelligence is an understanding of the nature and constituent elements of the crime phenomenon of concern. For example, if a community is threatened by multijurisdictional gang activity that operates as a criminal enterprise, an understanding of the gang culture, signs, symbols, hierarchy, and other gang-specific characteristics is essential for analysts and officers to be effective in combating the crime problem. While the two classes of intelligence are inextricably linked for purposes of training and application, it is nonetheless essential to understand the unique aspects of each.

With an understanding of the classes of intelligence, attention will be directed toward the definitions of each.

Law Enforcement Intelligence

This *Guide* uses definitions based on generally accepted practice and standards by the law enforcement intelligence community at the local, state, and tribal levels. This does not mean that other definitions of terms are wrong, but this approach provides a common understanding of words and concepts as most applicable to the targeted audience of this *Guide*.

Before defining intelligence, it is essential to understand the meaning of "information" in the context of this process. Information may defined as "pieces of raw, unanalyzed data that identify persons, organizations, evidence, events or illustrates processes that indicate the incidence of a criminal event or witnesses or evidence of a criminal event."[6] As will be seen, information is collected as the currency that produces intelligence.

The phrase "law enforcement intelligence," used synonymously with "criminal intelligence," refers to law enforcement's responsibility to enforce the criminal law. Oftentimes, the phrase is used improperly, and too often, intelligence is erroneously viewed as pieces of information about people, places, or events that can be used to provide insight about criminality or crime threats. It is further complicated by the failure to distinguish among the different types of intelligence.

Figure 2-2: Diverse Information Collected for Intelligence Analysis

[6] Global Intelligence Working Group. *Criminal Intelligence for the Chief Executive. A Training Program for the Chief Executive. Glossary.* Washington, D.C.: Global Justice Information Sharing Initiative, U.S. Department of Justice, 2004.

Pieces of information gathered from diverse sources, such as wiretaps, informants, banking records, or surveillance (see Figure 2-2), are simply raw data that frequently have limited inherent meaning. Intelligence is when a wide array of raw information is assessed for validity and reliability, reviewed for materiality to the issues at question, and given meaning through the application of inductive or deductive logic. Law enforcement intelligence, therefore, is "the product of an analytic process that provides an integrated perspective to disparate information about crime, crime trends, crime and security threats, and conditions associated with criminality."[7] The need for carefully analyzed, reliable information is essential because both policy and operational decisions are made using intelligence; therefore, a vigilant process must be in place to ensure that decisions are made on objective, informed criteria, rather than on presumed criteria.

Often "information sharing" and "intelligence sharing" are used interchangeably by persons who do not understand the subtleties, yet importance, of the distinction. In the strictest sense, care should be taken to use terms appropriately because, as will be seen in later discussions, there are different regulatory and legal implications for "intelligence" than for "information" (See Table 2-1) As such, the subtleties of language can become an important factor should the management of a law enforcement agency's intelligence records come under scrutiny.

Table 2-1: Comparative Illustrations of Information and Intelligence

Information	Intelligence
• Criminal history and driving records • Offense reporting records • Statements by informants, witnesses, and suspects • Registration information for motor vehicles, watercraft, and aircraft • Licensing details about vehicle operators and professional licenses of all forms • Observations of behaviors and incidents by investigators, surveillance teams, or citizens • Details about banking, investments, credit reports, and other financial matters • Descriptions of travel including the traveler(s) names, itinerary, methods of travel, date, time, locations, etc. • Statements of ideologies, beliefs, and practices	• A report by an analyst that draws conclusions about a person's criminal liability based on an integrated analysis of diverse information collected by investigators and/or researchers • An analysis of crime or terrorism trends with conclusions drawn about characteristics of offenders, probable future crime, and optional methods for preventing future crime/terrorism • A forecast drawn about potential victimization of crime or terrorism based on an assessment of limited information when an analysts uses past experience as context for the conclusion • An estimate of a person's income from a criminal enterprise based on a market and trafficking analysis of illegal commodities

[7] Carter, David L. *Law Enforcement Intelligence Operations*. 8th ed. Tallahassee, Florida: SMC Sciences, Inc. 2002.

Definitions and Context

State and local law enforcement have consistently defined law enforcement intelligence as containing the critical element of "analysis" before any information can be characterized as "intelligence." For example, the International Association of Chiefs of Police *Criminal Intelligence Sharing* plan funded by the Office of Community Oriented Policing Services observes that:

> ...intelligence is the combination of credible information with quality analysis—information that has been evaluated and from which conclusions have been drawn.[8]

Similarly, the Global Intelligence Working Group, a project that is funded by the Office of Justice Programs and is part of the Global Justice Information Sharing Initiative, discusses law enforcement intelligence by observing:

> ...the collection and analysis of information to produce an intelligence end product designed to inform law enforcement decision-making at both the tactical and strategic levels.[9]

Following a consistent vision, the International Association of Law Enforcement Intelligence Analysts states that intelligence is an analytic process:

> ...deriving meaning from fact. It is taking information collected in the course of an investigation, or from internal or external files, and arriving at something more than was evident before. This could be leads in a case, a more accurate view of a crime problem, a forecast of future crime levels, or a hypothesis of who may have committed a crime or a strategy to prevent crime.[10]

In creating standards for state, local, and tribal law enforcement, the Commission on Accreditation for Law Enforcement Agencies (CALEA) seeks to provide specific guidance on policies and practices that ensures efficacy and protection from liability on all aspects of law enforcement duties. With respect to intelligence, CALEA's standards note:

> Certain essential activities should be accomplished by an intelligence function, to include a procedure that permits the continuous flow of raw data into a central point from all sources; a secure records system in which evaluated data are properly cross-referenced to reflect relationships and to ensure complete and rapid retrieval; a system of analysis capable of developing intelligence from both the records system and other data sources; and a system for dissemination of information to appropriate components.[11]

It is clear not only from these discussions, but also from the legacy of law enforcement intelligence from various national crime commissions examining intelligence-related activities at the state and local level, that a common thread is that information must be analyzed before it is classified as intelligence. Chapter 3 will show that there is a fundamental reason for this: regulations applying to state, local, and tribal intelligence records must[12] meet standards of assessment that do not apply to federal agencies.[13] As a consequence, the analytic component is essential for the definition.

[8] International Association of Chiefs of Police. *Criminal Intelligence Sharing: A National Plan for Intelligence-Led Policing at the Federal, State, and Local Levels.* A Summit Report. Alexandria, Virginia: IACP, 2002, p. v.

[9] Global Intelligence Working Group. *National Criminal Intelligence Sharing Plan.* Washington, D.C.: Office of Justice Programs, 2003, p. 6.

[10] International Association of Law Enforcement Intelligence Analysts. *Successful Law Enforcement Using Analytic Methods.* Internet-published document, undated, p. 2.

[11] Commission on Accreditation of Law Enforcement Agencies. *Standards for Law Enforcement Accreditation.* "Standard 51.1.1 – Criminal Intelligence." Washington, D.C.: CALEA, 2002.

[12] Most notably, 28 CFR Part 23 as well as various court decisions.

[13] These issues are described in detail, in both Chapter 3 and Chapter 7.

It is often stated that for every rule there is an exception. The definition of law enforcement intelligence fits this axiom. As a matter of functional practicality, the FBI Directorate of Intelligence (DI) categorizes intelligence somewhat differently. As observed by one FBI DI official in a confidential interview:

> In the law enforcement/national security business, [intelligence] is information about those who would do us harm in the form of terrorist acts or other crimes, be they property crimes or violent crimes. ... [The FBI DI] produces both "raw" (or unevaluated intelligence) and "finished" intelligence products (those that report intelligence that has had some degree of analysis).

Given the nature of the FBI DI's responsibilities and the need to get the critical threat information into the hands of the law enforcement community quickly, this definition is more appropriate for its role. Law enforcement executives need to be aware of the different roles and the different context when interpreting information. These differences are not in conflict; rather, they coexist to support the different missions and responsibilities of agencies at all levels of government. Similarly, the need for a different approach to the "Intelligence Cycle" exists for the FBI compared to SLTLE because of different intelligence demands.

The remedy is simple: Those responsible for the intelligence function need to understand these differences and apply policies and practices (described later) that are most appropriate for the types of intelligence being produced and consumed.

Homeland Security (All-Hazards) Intelligence

While the phrase "homeland security intelligence" is relatively new, it integrates well-established law enforcement responsibilities, most notably the "order maintenance" function of law enforcement.[14] These new intelligence responsibilities have emerged within the homeland security framework requiring that intelligence activities at the state, local, and tribal levels must assess threats posed by "all hazards." While there certainly are gray areas within this framework, the key factor for law enforcement agencies is to focus on threats posed by hazards that have implications for responsibilities for public safety and order maintenance. Within this context, the author defines homeland security intelligence as the collection and analysis of information concerned with noncriminal domestic threats to critical infrastructure, community health, and public safety for the purpose of preventing the threat or mitigating the effects of the threat.

A public health emergency or natural disaster, for example, will necessarily involve a law enforcement agency to assist in maintaining order and executing operations to maintain public order until the crisis is resolved. Homeland security intelligence may identify community safety vulnerabilities emerging from the emergency or disaster and give this information to law enforcement agencies so that appropriate precautions can be put into place. In yet other cases, information may begin as homeland security intelligence and become law enforcement intelligence, such as a general threat to critical infrastructure that evolves into a

[14] For a discussion of "order maintenance" responsibilities see Carter, David L. *Police and the Community.* 7th ed. Upper Saddle River, New Jersey: Prentice Hall, 2000.

threat where an individual is identified. If an individual is identified as related to a critical infrastructure threat, in all likelihood a criminal nexus has emerged and a law enforcement intelligence inquiry may proceed jointly with homeland security intelligence.

This form of intelligence presents many challenges because it is not purely criminal, yet addresses responsibilities that law enforcement agencies have to manage within their communities. Homeland security intelligence is not clearly delineated either as a matter of law or of policy, yet it is increasingly prevalent because of the impact of Department of Homeland Security (DHS) responsibilities, particularly in the arena of critical infrastructure.

As noted above, in some cases law enforcement intelligence and homeland security intelligence may overlap. This is illustrated by an actual case study appended at the end of this chapter related to a threat associated with zebra mussels that has both homeland security and criminal implications. The value of the case study is to illustrate not only homeland security intelligence but also law enforcement intelligence as applied to a nontraditional threat.

National Security Intelligence

In understanding the broad arena of intelligence, some perspective of national security intelligence (NSI) is useful for SLTLE agencies. This primer is meant to familiarize the law enforcement reader with basic terms, concepts, and issues, and is not intended as an exhaustive description.

NSI may be defined as "the collection and analysis of information concerned with the relationship and homeostasis of the United States with foreign powers, organizations, and persons with regard to political and economic factors as well as the maintenance of the United States' sovereign principles."[15] NSI seeks to maintain the United States as a free, capitalist republic with its laws and constitutional foundation intact, and identify and neutralize threats or actions that undermine United States sovereign principles.

NSI embodies both policy intelligence and military intelligence. Policy intelligence is concerned with threatening actions and activities of entities hostile to the U.S., while military intelligence focuses on hostile entities, weapons systems, warfare capabilities, and order of battle. Since the fall of the Soviet Union and the rise of threats from terrorist groups, both policy and military intelligence have evolved to grapple with the character of new threats. The organizations responsible for NSI are collectively known as the Intelligence Community (IC).

The IC is a federation of 16 executive branch agencies and organizations that work within their own specific mission as well as in an integrated fashion to conduct threat assessment and intelligence activities necessary for effective foreign relations and the protection of United States national security. These activities include the following:

- Collection of information needed by the President, the National Security Council, the Secretaries of State and Defense, and other Executive Branch officials for the performance of their duties and responsibilities

[15] Carter, David L. *Law Enforcement Intelligence Operations.* 8th ed. Tallahassee, Florida: SMC Sciences, Inc., 2002.

- Production and dissemination of intelligence related to national security and the protection of U.S. sovereign principles from interference by foreign entities
- Collection of information concerning, and the conduct of activities to protect against, intelligence activities directed against the U.S., international terrorist and international narcotics activities, and other hostile activities directed against the U.S. by foreign powers, organizations, persons, and their agents
- Administrative and support activities within the U.S. and abroad that are necessary for the performance of authorized activities such as foreign relations, diplomacy, trade, and the protection of interests of our allies
- Such other intelligence and activities as the President may direct as related to national security and the U.S. relationship with foreign entities.

The 16-member IC consists of the following organizations:[16]

1. Air Force Intelligence.
2. Army Intelligence.
3. Central Intelligence Agency.
4. Coast Guard Intelligence.
5. Defense Intelligence Agency.
6. Department of Energy.
7. Department of Homeland Security.
8. Department of State.
9. Department of the Treasury.
10. Drug Enforcement Administration.
11. Federal Bureau of Investigation.
12. Marine Corps Intelligence.
13. National Geospatial-Intelligence Agency.
14. National Reconnaissance Office.
15. National Security Agency.
16. Navy Intelligence.

As seen in the definition and descriptions of NSI, there is no jurisdictional concern for crime. As a result, constitutional restrictions that attach to criminal cases that law enforcement faces on information collection, records retention, and use of information in a raw capacity do not apply to IC responsibilities where there is no criminal investigation.

SLTLE agencies have no direct jurisdiction as related to NSI; however, this does not mean that they will not encounter NSI or receive collection tasks to support NSI. Indeed, given that the Federal Bureau of Investigation (FBI) is a member of the IC, there is a strong likelihood that SLTLE officers serving on a Joint Terrorism Task Force will encounter or be exposed to NSI. Similarly, since the Drug Enforcement

Administration (DEA) is also a member of the IC, officers working on an Organized Crime Drug Enforcement Task Force may also encounter this intelligence. In both instances the officers typically will have Top Secret or Secret security clearances that provide access to classified documents which may provide additional insights about the information, including the source of the information and the method of collection. Nonetheless, it is a slippery slope for SLTLE officers to rely on this information for a criminal investigation because there is a strong likelihood that the methods of collecting the NSI would not meet constitutional muster in a criminal trial.

Even if it appeared that constitutional standards may be met, there are other potential problems when using the information in a criminal enquiry. Since the accused in a criminal proceeding has the right to be confronted by his or her accusers, the exercise of this right could compromise sensitive sources and methods. While the Classified Information Procedures Act (CIPA) provides a mechanism to deal with the process, some find that it is cumbersome and may result in greater complications than would otherwise be necessary.[17]

The next issue deals with constitutional law. If the information was collected from NSI sources in a manner inconsistent with the Constitution, it is likely, based on the "Fruits of the Poisonous Tree Doctrine," that any subsequent evidence developed during the course of that investigation would be subject to the Exclusionary Rule. Consequently, the evidence would be inadmissible.

Liability is a final issue concerning state, local, and tribal officers' access to NSI. Specifically, in a criminal investigation, if SLTLE officers used NSI that was collected in a manner inconsistent with constitutional standards or if that information (including personal records) was kept as intelligence records that were under the custodianship of a state, local, or tribal law enforcement officer, it is possible that the officer(s) and the chain of command (through vicarious liability) of that officer's agency could be liable under 42 USC 1983, Civil Action for Deprivation of Civil Rights. Under this provision, as most officers are well aware, if a state or local officer, acting under the color of state law, violates the civil rights of a person, the officer and his or her chain of command may be sued in federal court. Even though that officer may be working on a federal task force under the supervision of a federal officer, such as an FBI Supervisory Special Agent, the applicable test is whether the officer is paid by and bound by the employment rules of his or her state or local employing jurisdiction.[18]

Based on authorities from the National Security Act of 1947; Executive Order 12333; various executive directives, and the U.S. Attorney General Guidelines, the FBI is the lead agency in domestic intelligence collection. It is important that SLTLE understand the distinction between the authority of IC agencies to collect and retain information and that of SLTLE agencies.

A new challenge emerges with the Information Sharing Environment (ISE) created by the Intelligence Reform and Terrorism Prevention Act of 2004. As will be discussed in the next chapter, the ISE seeks to share all information related to

[17] The author has elected not to discuss CIPA in any detail because it deals with federal investigations rather than state, local, and tribal criminal investigations. For the person interested in further exploring CIPA, see www.usdoj.gov/usao/eousa/foia_reading_room/usam/title9/crm02054.htm.

[18] The FBI and DEA may keep such records in their custody on the basis of their national security responsibilities. While it is possible to hold a federal officer liable based on what is known as a "Bivens Suit"—derived from the case of *Bivens* v. *Six Unknown Agents* 403 US 388 (1971)—it would be difficult, particularly under the conditions of counterterrorism.

threats to the homeland. The challenge arises particularly if SLTLE agencies collect or retain information related to a national security threat rather than to a crime. SLTLE agencies sole jurisdiction as related to intelligence is based in their statutory authority to enforce the criminal law. As such, there is extensive constitutional rigidity and judicial scrutiny of their processes as well as the information that is collected and retained in a criminal intelligence records system (See Figure 2-3). Conversely, constitutional protections do not attach in the same way to the collection and retention of information by the IC. As a result, these agencies have greater latitude in the types of information they possess.

The processes are complicated further regarding the collection of information domestically (within the territory of the United States) that is related to national security threats. The primary responsibility for collecting domestic information for national security falls within the authority of the DHS, the FBI, and the DEA, which can produce intelligence for dissemination to SLTLE. U.S. foreign intelligence agencies, however, are prohibited from working with state and local law enforcement in a manner that could be interpreted as "tasking intelligence collection." As a result, SLTLE agencies should rely on their relationship with the DHS, the FBI, and the DEA on matters of domestic intelligence, including when those matters involve international terrorism activity. (See Figure 2-3)

Figure 2-3: Law Enforcement and National Security Intelligence Authority Comparison

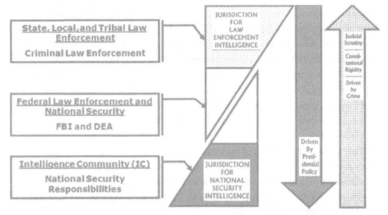

Effective policy and processes must be implemented and enforced to ensure that SLTLE agencies do not maintain improper information about individuals and organizations in their records system as a product of the ISE. These issues will be discussed in greater detail in the chapter on civil rights.

The lessons learned from this brief review of national security intelligence are threefold:

1. State, local, and tribal law enforcement officers have no jurisdiction to collect or manage NSI.

2. Use of NSI in a criminal investigation by a state, local, or tribal law enforcement officer could derail the prosecution of a case because of civil rights protections.

3. Use of NSI in a criminal investigation by an SLTLE officer and/or retention of NSI in a records system or in the personal records of an SLTLE officer could open the possibility of civil liability from a Section 1983 lawsuit.

Emerging Intelligence Initiatives Associated with Homeland Security/All-Hazards Intelligence

While the range of activities that could be encompassed by homeland security intelligence is broad, two initiatives are moving forward with greater rapidity: the Fire Service Intelligence Enterprise and Public Health/Medical Intelligence.

Fire Service Intelligence Enterprise

The Fire Service Intelligence Enterprise (FSIE), a new initiative that is in its infancy, is epitomized by this observation from *Fire Chief* magazine:

> Does the fire service, or emergency services in general, have a role in the world of intelligence? This question probably would never have been asked prior to Sept. 11, 2001, but it is being asked now. Given that firefighters are among the country's first responders to terrorist incidents, natural disasters, industrial accidents, and everyday emergencies, the answer is a resounding yes.[19]

Asking law enforcement about the fire service role in intelligence operations does not evoke a response with the same vigor. The reason, for the most part, is uncertainty: Law enforcement is uncertain about the types of information they can share with the fire service and whether the fire service holds a unique role beyond the private sector.

Exploration has resulted in the FSIE experimental initiative. Based on a test program from the Fire Department of New York (FDNY) along with joint efforts from within DHS—the Intelligence & Analysis Directorate (I&A) and the Federal Emergency Management Agency (FEMA)—the concept is being further explored.[20]

> Though not a federally sanctioned establishment or organization, its establishment by state and local fire service officials and industry groups was a result of advice and support provided by the State and Local Program Office to the FDNY and FEMA's United States Fire Administration. This relationship contributed to a draft approach for state and local fire services to share threat and related information among the country's nearly 1.2 million firefighters

[19] Pitts, Diane, "Getting the 411," *Fire Chief,* January 1, 2008. firechief.com/leadership/incident-command/intelligence-community-information-sharing-0101/index.html

[20] For a list of the intelligence and information requirements of the FSIE, see: Office of Intelligence and Analysis. *National Strategy for the Fire Service Intelligence* Enterprise. Washington, D.C.: U.S. Department of Homeland Security, 2008, pp.14–21.

and EMS customers. I&A continues working with the United States Fire Administration and the National Fire Academy in Emmitsburg, Maryland, to incorporate intelligence training into their course curriculum and ensure that our first responders better understand the events surrounding or leading up to their involvement in an incident.[21]

FSIE's objective is to establish a direct information conduit between the fire service and both DHS and local law enforcement, largely through a fusion center. The law enforcement agency would pursue a direct information-sharing relationship with the fire service per a directive of the National Response Plan. The National Response Plan mandates the alignment of federal coordinating structures, capabilities, and resources into a unified, all-discipline, and all-hazards approach to domestic incident management.[22]

Through sharing pre-incident information and intelligence and real-time incident updates, situational awareness will be enhanced to support the preparedness efforts of both local fire departments and the DHS. Rapid and comprehensive information sharing also is imperative to establishing a common operational picture on the local and national levels during a major incident.[23]

The difficulty for the FSIE concept is that it predominantly exists within the "all-hazards" framework of intelligence about which law enforcement is still attempting to identify and resolve its intelligence role. Further, the issues of information sharing and civil rights remain difficult to resolve unequivocally. Similarly, some members of the fire service are not overly enthusiastic about being associated with the law enforcement intelligence function.

Amalgamating the fusion concept with the all-hazards approach to intelligence requires a critical review of operating processes, responsibilities, and roles. The jury is out on whether the FSIE will be a fruitful initiative. Nonetheless, law enforcement executives and intelligence commanders should be aware of the FSIE concept and explore the role, if any, it holds in the local law enforcement intelligence structure.

Medical Intelligence: Protecting the Public Health

A growing component of the all-hazards responsibility in homeland security intelligence deals with public health threats. Medical intelligence assesses public health trends, organizations, and related events that can affect the health of a community. There has been significant growth in the military on medical intelligence where the focus is broader, notably looking at foreign medical trends. Comprehensive resources on medical intelligence can be found at these resources:

- The Armed Forces Medical Intelligence Center[24]
- The WWW Virtual Library collection on Epidemiology[25]
- The Biodefense and Public Health Database[26]
- The Centers for Disease Control and Prevention (CDC) WONDER Database of Health and Risks.[27]

[21] Tomarchio, Jack. " Focus on Fusion Centers: A Progress Report." Prepared statement before the Ad Hoc Subcommittee on State, Local and Private Sector Preparedness and Integration, Committee on Homeland Security and Government Affairs, United States Senate, April 17, 2008, p. 7.

[22] Ibid

[23] Pitts, Op. Cit.

[24] mic.afmic.detrick.army.mil (restricted access site).

[25] www.epibiostat.ucsf.edu/epidem/epidem.html

[26] www.biohealthbase.org

[27] wonder.cdc.gov

The significant points to note are these:

1. There is a distinct trend toward medical intelligence as a tool to assist in the protection of our communities.

2. Medical intelligence will become an increasingly important intelligence responsibility as a result of the all-hazards mandate.

3. There are resources to assist in identifying public health threats.

Gang Intelligence

Gang intelligence provides challenges to fully understanding the application of current law, regulation, policy, and practice for law enforcement intelligence. As noted previously, intelligence is the output of the analytic process; however, with those persons specializing in gang investigations, the term "intelligence" is commonly used more broadly. Typically, gang specialists include "indicators" under the rubric of intelligence; for example, information about gang behaviors, signs and symbols of different gangs ("colors" and "tagging"), the modus operandi of different gangs, and trends in the different gang activities. Frequently, much of this information is not analyzed, or at least not analyzed in the same sophisticated manner as the intelligence process. As a practical element of the discussion in this section, the recognition of this fact is functional; thus, when discussing gang intelligence, this common application of the term by gang investigators will be used.

Certainly there is an important role for analysis when dealing with gangs; however, gang data and information are not subject to analysis as frequently as they should be. This should change not only with the expansion of analytic expertise in law enforcement agencies, notably through fusion centers, but also as a result of approval of the *Guidelines for Establishing and Operating Gang Intelligence Units and Task Forces*[28] by the Global Intelligence Working Group.

The following is information from the FBI:
- "Today, gangs are more violent, more organized, and more widespread than ever before."
- "There are approximately 30,000 gangs, with 800,000 members, impacting 2,500 communities across the U.S."
- Latino gangs are sowing violence and crime in big cities like Los Angeles, Chicago, and New York, but are also spreading to rural and suburban areas.
- The violent gang MS-13—composed mainly of Central American immigrants from El Salvador, Honduras, and Guatemala—"has a significant presence in Northern Virginia, New York, California, Texas, as well as places as disparate and widespread as Oregon City, Oregon; and Omaha, Nebraska." MS-13 is estimated to have some 8,000 to 10,000 hard-core members—and is growing increasingly sophisticated, widespread, and violent.[29]

With many criminal gangs taking on the characteristics of transjurisdictional criminal enterprises, the need for information sharing and analysis of threats is essential. The tools and resources of intelligence can be important factors in effectively dealing with gang problems.

[28] Global Intelligence Working Group. *Guidelines for Establishing and Operating Gang Intelligence Units and Task Forces.* Washington, D.C.: Bureau of Justice Assistance, U.S. Department of Justice, 2008.

[29] www.fbi.gov/page2/april05/ swecker042005.htm

Gang intelligence provides challenges in the application of current law, regulation, policy, and practice for law enforcement intelligence. As noted previously, intelligence is the output of the analytic process. For those specializing in gang investigations, however, "intelligence" is commonly viewed more broadly, typically including information about gang behavior, indicators, modus operandi, and trends that are largely derived from raw information learned from investigations rather than analysis. As a practical element of this discussion, the subtle distinction between what is meant by "intelligence" by gang investigators as compared to the meaning of "intelligence" by those working in the law enforcement intelligence community should be recognized.

What Is a Gang?

The initial vision when hearing the word "gang" is a group of young males, typically in the inner city involved in "turf battles" and who spray paint gang symbols on property and is involved in violent, often deadly, confrontations with other collectives of young men. Typically, a vision of the well-known Los Angeles-based "Crips" and "Bloods" gangs is part of that picture. While these kinds of gangs certainly exist, gangs encompass a much larger population.

The National Gang Threat Assessment[30] divided gangs into six broad categories:

1. National and Regional Street Gangs.

2. Gangs and Organized Crime.
   - Asian Organized Crime
   - Russian Organized Crime

3. Gangs and Terrorist Organizations.
   - Domestic Terrorist Groups
   - International Terrorist Groups

4. Prison Gangs.

5. Hispanic Gangs.

6. Outlaw Motorcycle Gangs.

As can be seen from these categories, the line between gangs and organized crime may be blurred. Similarly, the line between gangs and terrorist organizations can also be difficult to discern because often both use the tactics of intimidation and fear to accomplish their goals.

While each state has its own statutory definitions of a gang, most use a model similar to that of the Violent Gang and Terrorist Organization File (VGTOF) of the National Crime Information Center (NCIC). According to VGTOF guidelines, a gang member must be characterized as, and have at least two of, the following criteria:
- Has been identified as a gang member by an individual of proven reliability.
- Has been identified as a gang member by an individual of unknown reliability, and that information has been corroborated in significant respects.

[30] National Alliance of Gang Investigators Associations. *National Gang Threat Assessment.* Washington, D.C.: Bureau of Justice Assistance, U.S. Department of Justice, 2005.

- Has been observed by law enforcement members to frequent a known gang's area, associate with known gang members, and/or affect that gang's style of dress, tattoos, hand signals, or symbols.
- Has been arrested on more than one occasion with known gang members consistent with gang activity.
- Has admitted membership in a gang at any time other than at the time of current arrest/incarceration.[31]

As can be seen, the value of intelligence and information sharing for both identifying and classifying a person as a gang member can be an important tool. This is particularly true because gangs are often transjurisdictional. Both tactical and strategic intelligence can provide important information to law enforcement agencies about gang threats and trends.

Two initiatives have been developed that serve to enhance the use of intelligence when dealing with the gang threat: The National Gang Intelligence Center and the *Guidelines for Establishing and Operating Gang Intelligence Units and Task Forces.*

National Gang Intelligence Center

The National Gang Intelligence Center (NGIC) integrates the gang intelligence assets of all Department of Justice agencies and has established partnerships with other federal, state, and local agencies that possess gang-related information, thereby serving as a centralized intelligence resource for gang information and analytical support. This enables gang investigators and analysts to identify links between gangs and gang investigations, further identify gangs and gang members, learn the full scope of their criminal activities and enterprises, determine which gangs pose the greatest threat to the United States, identify trends in gang activity and migration, and guide the appropriate officials in coordinating their investigations and prosecutions to disrupt and dismantle gangs. The NGIC's mission is to support law enforcement agencies through timely and accurate information sharing and strategic and tactical analysis of federal, state, and local law enforcement intelligence focusing on the growth, migration, criminal activity, and association of gangs that pose a significant threat to communities throughout the United States.[32]

The NGIC focuses on gangs operating on a national level that demonstrate criminal connectivity between sets of common identifiers. In addition, because many violent gangs do not operate on a national level, the NGIC will also focus on selected regional-level gangs. To maximize effectiveness, the NGIC produces intelligence assessments, intelligence bulletins, joint agency intelligence products, and other nonstandard intelligence products for its customers.[33]

Guidelines for Establishing and Operating Gang Intelligence Units and Task Forces

Developed by the Gang Intelligence Strategy Committee (GISC) of the Global Justice Information Sharing Initiative, the *Gang Guidelines* seek to develop an integrated strategy to deal with gangs by cohesively linking both intelligence and operational responses to gang threats through task forces. On the issue

[31] National Gang Center. *Brief Review of Federal and State Definitions of the Terms "Gang," "Gang Crime," and "Gang Member."* Undated and unpublished web document. www.nationalgangcenter. gov/documents/definitions.pdf.

[32] "Attorney General's Report to Congress on the Growth of Violent Street Gangs in Suburban Areas," Washington, D.C.: U.S. Department of Justice, 2008, p. 14. www.usdoj.gov/ndic/ pubs27/27612/27612p.pdf.

[33] www.usdoj.gov/criminal/ngic

of intelligence, the *Gang Guidelines* stress the importance of analysis and recommend the use of the intelligence process to manage and assess raw information. Similarly, the Gang Guidelines embrace the *National Criminal Intelligence Sharing Plan* as the intelligence model that should be used in all gang intelligence initiatives. Finally, the *Gang Guidelines* recognize the important role that intelligence can fulfill by more efficiently and effectively directing task forces responses to gang threats.

The *Gang Guidelines* are new, having been approved in late 2008; however, with their endorsement by the Criminal Intelligence Coordinating Council there will likely be widespread adoption by law enforcement agencies, fusion centers, and gang task forces.

Conclusion

The intent of this chapter was to provide the reader with insight into the meaning of intelligence, the diverse types of intelligence, its role, and some of the complications that emerge from using the term. Law enforcement intelligence, for example, is defined somewhat differently by the FBI and the DEA than it is by SLTLE agencies. The reason for the difference is based on the sources of information used by the FBI and the DEA as well as the responsibilities these federal law enforcement agencies hold for disseminating unique critical information in a timely fashion. The important point is that the consumer simply needs to know the different definitions and the different context. With this knowledge, information can be interpreted and used most effectively.

Also introduced in this chapter was the concept of homeland security intelligence and the unique role it fulfills for law enforcement agencies. While not a traditional activity for law enforcement, homeland security intelligence seeks to enhance public safety and order while protecting the community from nontraditional threats.

Finally, Chapter 2 addressed the meaning of NSI and the complications it conceivably can pose for SLTLE agencies. Once again, it is important to understand the issues and parameters of each type of intelligence. The proverbial bottom line is that understanding the definitions and their application is an essential foundation for the remaining topics discussed throughout this *Intelligence Guide*.

Chapter Annex 2-1: Law Enforcement and Homeland Security Intelligence Case Study

This illustration is based on an actual case. It demonstrates the interrelationship between the two types of intelligence.

Threats Posed by Zebra Mussels

A congressman from a Midwestern state was a vocal supporter of legislation to ban Internet gaming in the U.S. An individual who opposed this legislation made a threat to the congressman's office that if the congressman voted for the legislation, the individual would introduce zebra mussels into some of his state's lakes.

Zebra mussels (*Dreissena polymorpha*) are an invasive species native to the Black Sea and Caspian Sea regions of Eurasia. In 1988 they were introduced to U.S. fresh water in Lake St. Clair— between Lake Erie and Lake Huron on the Michigan, U.S.—Ontario, Canada, border— through ballast water discharged from transoceanic vessels. The zebra mussel competes with native species of mussels and is particularly prone to clogging pipes, valves, and drains that affect drinking water, hydroelectric plants, and a wide variety of manufacturing firms. According to the Nonindigenous Aquatic Species Program of the U.S. Geological Survey, "Zebra mussels can have profound effects on the ecosystems they invade…and represent one of the most important biological invasions into North America".[33] Zebra mussels are small and easily transported in a plastic bag, jar, or bucket. They can stay alive out of the water for several days in cool, humid conditions by simply closing their shell tight. Under the right environmental conditions, it would take as few as three zebra mussels to begin an "invasion" in a body of water.[34]

The congressman voted for the ban on Internet gaming. Recently, zebra mussels have been appearing in local lakes in the congressman's state. The immediate issue: Is the presence of the newly discovered zebra mussels in the congressman's state a product of the threat?

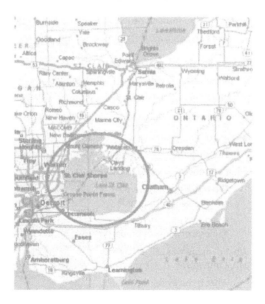

[33] See nas.er.usgs.gov/queries/FactSheet.asp?speciesID=5.

[34] Personal Correspondence, Nonindigenous Aquatic Species Program biologist, U.S. Geological Survey, Gainesville, Florida.

Criminal Intelligence

Zebra mussels are explicitly included in the United States Code (42 USC §42 and §43–the Lacey Act). Mere transportation of zebra mussels is a federal misdemeanor. If an individual intentionally causes damage or loss of property as a result of the introduction of zebra mussels, or conspires to do so, this can be the federal crime "Animal Enterprise Terrorism," punishable as a felony, depending on the value of property loss.

Other possible federal and state crimes include extortion, terroristic threat, and criminal environmental law violations.

Homeland Security Intelligence

A determination should be made of hazards posed to the community and economy by this threat. Are threats posed to other bodies of water as a result of this act? What preventive/protection measures should local critical infrastructure or key resources vulnerable from this threat take? Intelligence requirements need to identify persons with zebra mussels in their possession and determine the reason. Businesses and government entities whose operations could be affected by the zebra mussels must be identified and notified.

Case Intelligence Requirements

- What information is available about the individual who made the threat?
    - Has the congressman received threats in the past? If so, collect all related information.
    - Are there vocal activists against the ban on Internet gaming who could be reasonably tied to the congressman and/or the state?
    - Are there any links between these individuals and environmental issues?
- How can zebra mussels be introduced into a new environment?
    - What do zebra mussels look like?
    - What are the different methods/processes that might be used for introduction?
    - What are the indicators of zebra mussels being introduced?
- What evidence is needed to prove:
    - The zebra mussels were intentionally introduced?
    - There was intent to cause damage or a loss of property?
- What damage was caused by the zebra mussels?
    - What is the evidence that supports this?

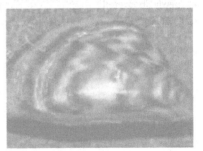

Standing Intelligence Requirements

- If someone is identified with zebra mussels in his or her possession:

    - Identify the individuals and the reasons for their possession of the zebra mussels.

    - Document precautions taken to avoid introduction of the zebra mussels to the local environment?

    - Document any evidence to support the elements of applicable state and/or federal laws?

        - What additional evidence may be needed?

Homeland Security Intelligence Requirements

- Is there a need for the fusion center to forecast their spread and impact or can this be handled more effectively by another agency?

    - If so, which agency?

    - Is there a memorandum of understanding in place to work with this agency?

- What are the characteristics of the new host environment that would help target places where the zebra mussels may be introduced and flourish?

- Do any of the identified host environments have characteristics that increase the seriousness of the invasion (for example, public water supply, hydroelectric plant, manufacturing, commercial, or recreational body of water)?

Chapter 3:
A Brief History of Law Enforcement Intelligence:
Past Practice and Recommendations for Change

A Brief History of Law Enforcement Intelligence: Past Practice and Recommendations for Change

Controversies have surrounded law enforcement intelligence because of past instances where the police maintained records of citizens' activities that were viewed as controversial, not traditional, suspicious, or perceived as anti-American, even though no crimes were being committed. This, of course, violates fundamental constitutional guarantees and offends the American sense of fairness concerning government intrusiveness. Unfortunately, the boundary is not precise about the types of information the police can collect and retain. Some legal guidelines lack clarity and the application of law to factual situations is often difficult. Beyond the legal ramifications, law enforcement's early intelligence initiatives often lacked explicit focus and typically maintained a shroud of secrecy. We can learn important lessons from these historical experiences that provide context and guidance for law enforcement intelligence today.

Aggravating these factors was an unclear relationship between law enforcement intelligence and national security intelligence that has changed continuously since the mid-20th century. The changes have been both politically and legally controversial as these initiatives sought to respond to changing sociopolitical events in American history, most recently through post-9/11 counterterrorism efforts. As a result, there is value in understanding selected portions of history from both types of intelligence to gain context and understand the lessons learned.

Law Enforcement Intelligence: The Years of Evolution

Early law enforcement intelligence units going back to the 1920s used a records process known as the "dossier system." Essentially, intelligence files were nothing more than dossiers—files containing a collection of diverse raw information—about people who were thought to be criminals, thought to be involved with criminals, or persons who were thought to be a threat to the safety and order of a community. Bootleggers during prohibition and many of the high-profile criminals of the early twentieth century—for example, Bonnie and Clyde, the Barker Gang, Machine Gun Kelly, Al Capone—were the typical kinds of persons about whom police agencies kept dossiers.

During the depression of the 1930s, little was done in the law enforcement intelligence arena. Other priorities were higher: the pervasive threat to the country was the economy, not criminality. Circumstances began to change in the latter part of the decade as communism —or the "Red Scare"—became predominant. The police relied on the only system they knew: the dossier.

In 1937, U.S. Representative Martin Dies (D-Texas) became the first chairman of the House Committee on Un-American Activities. Dies, a supporter of the Ku Klux Klan, fueled the fire of concern about communism in the United States, including labeling people as Communists who appeared "un-American," which often resulted in their loss of jobs and functional displacement from society. Concern about communism was pervasive, but was of secondary interest in the 1940s because of World War II. After the war, when the Soviet Union was formed and built its nuclear arsenal, the Red Scare reemerged with even greater vigor.

The fires were fanned significantly in 1950 by Senator Joseph McCarthy (R-Wisconsin) who was using this national concern as the foundation for his floundering reelection bid to the Senate. McCarthy railed against the American Communist Party and called for expulsion from government, education, and the entertainment industry anyone who was an avowed Communist or Communist sympathizer. Because of fear about the Soviet Union among the American public, the war on communism resonated well.

Responding to expressions of public and government concern, local law enforcement agencies began creating intelligence dossiers, known as "Red Files," on persons who were suspected Communists and Communist sympathizers. Law enforcement agencies, therefore, were keeping records about people who were expressing their political beliefs and people who were known to sympathize with these individuals. The fact that these people were exercising their constitutional rights and had not committed crimes was not considered an issue because it was felt that the presence of, and support for, communism within the nation was a threat to the national security of the United States.[1]

The dossier system had become an accepted tool for law enforcement intelligence; therefore, when new overarching challenges emerged, it was natural for law enforcement to rely on this well-established mechanism for collecting and keeping information. In the 1960s, law enforcement met two challenges where intelligence dossiers appeared to be an important tool: the Civil Rights movement and the anti-Vietnam War movement. In both cases, participants appeared to be on the fringe of mainstream society. They were vocal in their views and both their exhortations and actions appeared to many as being "un-American." This was aggravated by other social trends: World War II baby boomers were in their teens and 20s, exploring their own newly defined world of "sex, drugs, and rock n' roll" and contributing to the stereotype of the "long-haired, dope-smoking, commie-hippie spies"—a sure target for a law enforcement traffic stop.

An overlap among these social movements was viewed by many as conspiratorial. Moreover, rapidly changing values, stratified in large part along generational and racial lines, created a sense of instability that appeared threatening to the mainstream. Rather than being culturally unstable, as we have learned in hindsight, it was simply social evolution. Because of the dissonance in the 1960s and the largely unsupported assumption that many of the activists and protestors "might" commit crimes or "might" be threats to our national security, law enforcement agencies began developing dossiers on these individuals "just in case." Typically, dossier information was not related to specific crimes, rather, it was kept as a contingency should the information be needed in some future investigation. There is little doubt that law enforcement was creating and keeping these dossiers with good faith to protect the community from activities then viewed as threats; however, that faith does not mitigate unconstitutional practices.

[1] It was rationalized that such activities were warranted on the grounds of a "compelling state interest." This argument, however, did not meet political or constitutional scrutiny.

There was additional concern during this time because of the activist nature of the U.S. Supreme Court during the era of Chief Justice Earl Warren (1953–1969). Many of the "liberal decisions" of the Warren Court were met with disfavor and the often-expressed belief that the Court's decisions[2] were "handcuffing the police." With regard to the current discussion, perhaps most important was that the Warren Court led a generation of judicial activism and expanded interpretations of the Constitution. Moreover, it symbolically motivated activist attorneys from the 1960s to try new strategies for the protection of constitutional rights. Among the most successful was reliance on a little-used provision of the Civil Rights Act of 1871, codified as Title 42 of the U.S. Code, Section 1983–Civil Action for Deprivation of Rights.

Commonly referred to as "1983 suits," this provision essentially provides that anyone who, acting under color of state or local law, causes a person to be deprived of rights guaranteed by the U.S. Constitution or federal law may be civilly liable. The initial lawsuits focused on whether a city, police department, and officers could be sued for depriving a person of his or her constitutional rights. The Supreme Court held that they could. A significant aspect of the case was that the police could be sued if there was "misuse of power possessed by virtue of state law and made possible only because the wrongdoer is clothed with the authority of state law."[3] This opened the floodgates for lawsuits against law enforcement (and correctional institutions).

Initial lawsuits focused on various patterns of police misconduct such as excessive force and due process violations. The reach of lawsuits against law enforcement grew more broadly with decisions holding that the police chain of command could be held vicariously liable for the actions of those under their command, as well as their parent jurisdiction. Moving into the late 1960s and early 1970s, such lawsuits moved toward law enforcement intelligence units. It was increasingly discovered that law enforcement agencies were keeping intelligence files on people for whom there was no evidence of criminality. The practice of keeping intelligence dossiers on a contingency basis was found to be improper, serving no compelling state interest and depriving those citizens of their constitutional rights. As a result, the courts repeatedly ordered intelligence files to be purged from police records and in many cases police agencies had to pay damage awards to plaintiffs. The decisions also permitted citizens to gain access to their own records. Many activists publicized their intelligence files as a badge of honor, often to the embarrassment of the police.[4] Law enforcement intelligence operations were cut back significantly or eliminated as a result of the embarrassment and costs associated with these lost lawsuits. The lessons learned from this era suggest caution in the development of intelligence records—information must be collected, retained, reviewed, and disseminated in a manner that is consistent with legal and ethical standards.

This lesson is reinforced by the findings of the United States Senate Select Committee to Study Governmental Operations with Respect to Intelligence Activities[5]—the Church Committee, named after its chairman, Frank Church (D–Idaho)[6]—which held extensive hearings on domestic intelligence, most notably

[2] Among the most often cited are *Miranda* v. *Arizona* (police must advise arrestees of their Fifth and Sixth Amendment rights prior to a custodial interrogation); *Mapp* v. *Ohio* (applying the Exclusionary Rule to the states); *Gideon* v. *Wainwright* (right to appointed counsel); and *Escobedo* v. *Illinois* (right to counsel when the process shifts from investigatory to accusatory).

[3] *Monroe* v. *Pape* 365 U.S. 167 (1961).

[4] For example, it was not uncommon to find notations and even photographs of an "intelligence target" having dinner or attending a public event such as a movie or the theater. The citizen would then pose a rhetorical question, "Is this how you want your tax dollars spent?"

[5] United States Senate, Select Committee to Study Governmental Operations with Respect to Intelligence Activities. *Intelligence Activities and the Rights of Americans, Book II, Final Report*. Washington, D.C.: Library of Congress, 1976.

[6] Alternately known as the Church Commission.

the Federal Bureau of Investigation's (FBI) Counter Intelligence Program, which spanned the years 1959 to 1971. The committee's conclusion:

> Domestic intelligence activity has threatened and undermined the Constitutional rights of Americans to free speech, association and privacy. It has done so primarily because the Constitutional system for checking abuse of power has not been applied.

Concern was widespread about all aspects of intelligence. The combined effect of these diverse factors prompted the U.S. Department of Justice (DOJ) to develop guidelines for the management of criminal intelligence records that were maintained by state and local law enforcement agencies.

Codified as 28 CFR Part 23[7]—Criminal Intelligence Systems Operating Policies,[8] the regulation governs interjurisdictional and multijurisdictional criminal intelligence systems that are operated by or on behalf of state and local law enforcement agencies and that are funded with federal funds. The regulation, created in 1979, stemmed from an amendment to the Omnibus Crime Control and Safe Streets Act of 1968.

The Justice System Improvement Act of 1979 created significant changes in DOJ organizations and stimulated regulatory changes, including creation of this regulation by the DOJ Office of Legal Policy. The regulation arose out of concern about aggressive information collection and intelligence activities by state and local law enforcement agencies that frequently involved collecting and retaining information about citizens who were expressing unpopular beliefs but whose actions were not criminal.

Since the federal government cannot mandate policy to state and local governments, the only method by which such policy could be leveraged was to make the policy implementation a condition for the acceptance of federal funds. The regulation provides guidelines on the collection, retention, review, dissemination, and purging of criminal intelligence records. Essentially, the regulation requires that, before information that identifies an individual or an organization may be retained in the criminal intelligence records system of a state or local law enforcement agency, there must be sufficient evidence to establish a reasonable suspicion that the individual [or organization] is involved in criminal behavior. When the regulation was created, many viewed this as a significant barrier to effective intelligence operations. Hindsight, however, has proven that the regulation is an important tool for maintaining citizens' civil rights without placing an undue burden on intelligence activities.

Congressional Inquiries into Intelligence Activities

During this era, inquiries into the Intelligence Community (IC) moved away from assessing the efficiency of intelligence operations and toward assessing the legality and propriety of the actual operations conducted. As will be seen, the recommendations made by three congressional committees would result in major changes in both the jurisdiction and roles of IC members with respect to law enforcement and national security intelligence. This would lead to the separation

[7] Code of Federal Regulations.

[8] www.iir.com/28cfr

of the two types of intelligence activities—the so-called "wall between domestic and international intelligence."

In 1975, the Rockefeller Commission (Commission on CIA Activities within the United States) recommended limiting the Central Intelligence Agency's (CIA) authority to conduct domestic intelligence operations. Furthermore, the commission also recommended that the director of central intelligence and the director of the FBI set jurisdictional guidelines for their respective agencies. In 1976, the House Select Committee on Intelligence (the Pike Committee, chaired by Otis Pike, D–New York) also made recommendations to further limit the jurisdictional overlap between agencies responsible for national security intelligence and agencies primarily responsible for law enforcement intelligence. It was the recommendations of the Church Committee, however, that were the most profound in developing the wall of separation.

The Church Committee, an inquiry formed by the U.S. Senate in 1976, examined the conduct of the IC in a broader fashion than did the Rockefeller Commission.[9] The recommendations made by this inquiry led to jurisdictional reformations of the IC. Most of the recommendations were directed at developing new operational boundaries for the FBI and the CIA. Out of the committee's 183 recommendations, the following illustrate how law enforcement intelligence was separated from national security intelligence:[10]

- The committee recommended that agencies such as the National Security Agency, the CIA, and military branches not have the power to conduct domestic intelligence operations (that is, law enforcement intelligence functions). Specific attention was given to the role of the CIA, noting that "the CIA should be prohibited from conducting domestic security activities within the United States."[11]
- The committee recommended that the FBI have "sole responsibility" for conducting domestic intelligence investigations of Americans.
- The FBI should "look to the CIA as the overseas operational arm of the intelligence community."[12]
- All agencies should ensure against improper intelligence activities.

The recommendations of the Church Committee have been widely recognized as a primary reason for the separation of law enforcement intelligence from national security intelligence. The call for this separation, however, did not mean that the agencies should stop working with each other. In fact, the Church Committee also recommended that the FBI and the CIA continue sharing information and make a better effort to coordinate their initiatives. This was operationally complicated: How do the two agencies work together and coordinate initiatives when there are substantial limitations on the kinds of information that can be collected and shared? Moreover, what, if any, role did state, local, and tribal law enforcement (SLTLE) intelligence have in this arrangement? The result was increased compartmentalization both between the agencies and within each agency.[13] Recommendations to improve law enforcement intelligence, however, have not been limited to the federal level. Such recommendations have also been made for state and local law enforcement agencies.

[9] Johnson, L. *A Season of Inquiry: The Senate Intelligence Investigation.* Lexington, Kentucky: The University Press of Kentucky, 1985.

[10] For a complete review of the recommendations made by the Church Committee visit the Public Library tab on www.aarclibrary.org and click on "Church Committee Reports". For a more complete review of the formation of the Church Committee, see note 14.

[11] United States Senate Select Committee to Study Governmental Operations with Respect to Intelligence Activities. *Intelligence Activities and the Rights of Americans, Book II, Final Report.* April 26, 1976. Washington, D.C.: U.S. Government Printing Office, 1976.

[12] Ibid

[13] For example, because of the regulations—or at least the interpretation of the regulations—FBI agents working within the former Foreign Counter Intelligence Division were often barred from sharing information with agents working on criminal investigations.

National Crime Commissions and New Initiatives Influencing the Evolution of State, Local, and Tribal Law Enforcement Intelligence

Since 1931, 15 national crime commissions have examined a wide array of crime issues in the United States, ranging from street crime and drug trafficking to organized crime and terrorism. Most have included assessments and recommendations related to some aspect of law enforcement intelligence. Understanding the broad intent of the commissions, followed by those with specific intelligence recommendations, demonstrates a well-established legacy for establishing law enforcement intelligence operations that are objective, analytic, and respectful of privacy and civil rights. While the recommendations reflect forward thinking, not all recommendations were embraced immediately—largely because they represented a change in the police occupational culture of the era. Nonetheless, important concepts were established that served as the foundation for today's law enforcement intelligence practices.

The Commissions and their Purpose

The National Commission on Law Observance and Enforcement (known as the Wickersham Commission) issued a series of reports and memoranda from 1928 to 1931 examining all aspects of serious crime in the United States. The intent was to address the growth of organized crime (particularly that arising from Prohibition) and increases in violent crime that appeared to correlate with growing industrialization and urbanization. The Commission also sought to understand the failure of law enforcement, the courts, and corrections to manage America's crime problem effectively. For the next 3 decades there were no major national commissions examining crime, in large part, no doubt, because of Americans' preoccupation with the Great Depression, followed by World War II, and post-World War II concerns about the growing nuclear threat from the Soviet Union. Indeed, these global events were largely responsible for virtually none of the Wickersham Commission's recommendations being implemented.

In November 1963, the assassination of President John F. Kennedy prompted President Lyndon B. Johnson to create what came to be known as the Warren Commission (U.S. Supreme Court Chief Justice Earl Warren). While the Commission's goal was to determine the circumstances leading to the assassination, the less controversial results of the Commission examined the relationships among federal, state, and local law enforcement, their communications, and generally their ability to work together for a common purpose: protecting the President of the United States. Unbeknownst at the time, the assassination was a harbinger of a violent and paradigm-changing decade to come.

As the 1960s progressed, increased concern about crime was emerging because of the growth of violence, the increase in drug use, the greater awareness of organized crime, and concerns about inequities in the administration of justice, particularly as related to minorities. To address these concerns, in 1965 President Johnson created the President's Commission on Law Enforcement and

Administration of Justice, an inquiry that complemented President Johnson's domestic social agenda known as "The Great Society." The President's Commission investigated all aspects of the criminal justice system, as well as specific inquiries into narcotics and organized crime, in a series of task force reports that were released 1967.

Recognizing that the 1960s was the "decade of social revolution" on many fronts, there were concerns about problems ranging from violence, riots in our cities, increases in the use of narcotics, a growth of illegal dangerous drugs, to concerns about moral decay, often illustrated by the increasing presence of pornographic materials. In 1967, a series of violent demonstrations in cities throughout the U.S. spurred by the Civil Rights Movement led to the creation of the National Advisory Commission on Civil Disorders (known as the Kerner Commission, chaired by Governor Otto Kerner of Illinois) as an attempt to understand the dynamics of civil disobedience and civil disorders as well as to evaluate the government's response. The following year, 1968, saw the creation of two additional commissions: The National Commission on the Causes and Prevention of Violence and the U.S. Commission on Obscenity and Pornography.

The social upheaval of the 1960s was characterized by many factors, including a significant rise in the abuse of illegal drugs, as learned in earlier commission reports. As a result, a new inquiry was created specifically to examine this issue more closely; the U.S. Commission on Marihuana and Drug Abuse (1970).

One of the signature components of the 1967 President's Commission was the attempt to professionalize all aspects of the criminal justice system. Following this lead was the Justice Department's National Advisory Commission on Criminal Justice Standards and Goals (1973) as well as a series of reports from working groups of that commission known as the *National Advisory Committee on Criminal Justice Standards and Goals* (1976).

National inquiries, seeking to identify causes of various crimes as well as providing blue-ribbon advice on the best tactics, recommended strategies and programs to deal with crime. These included the Justice Department's National Advisory Committee for Juvenile Justice and Delinquency Prevention (1980); the Attorney General's Task Force on Violent Crime (1981); the President's Commission on Organized Crime (1983); and the Attorney General's Commission on Pornography (1986).

Throughout the 1990s there were no national commissions on crime issues as had been so prevalent in the previous 3 decades. There was, however, a significant increase in government-sponsored research and program development on a wide array of crime-related issues from the National Institute of Justice, the Bureau of Justice Assistance, the Bureau of Justice Statistics, the Office of Juvenile Justice and Delinquency Prevention; and the newest Justice Department agency, created in 1994, the Office of Community Oriented Policing Services (the COPS Office). In many ways, the products of these agencies were a surrogate for the national commissions.

Table 3-1: National Crime Commissions in the U.S., 1931–2004

- National Commission on Law Observance and Enforcement (Wickersham Commission), 1931.
- President's Commission on the Assassination of President Kennedy (Warren Commission), 1964
- President's Commission on Law Enforcement and Administration of Justice, 1967
- National Advisory Commission on Civil Disorders (Kerner Commission), 1967
- National Commission on the Causes and Prevention of Violence, 1968
- U.S. Commission on Obscenity and Pornography, 1968
- U.S. Commission on Marihuana and Drug Abuse, 1970
- National Advisory Commission on Criminal Justice Standards and Goals, 1973
- National Advisory Committee on Criminal Justice Standards and Goals, 1976
- National Advisory Committee for Juvenile Justice and Delinquency Prevention, 1980
- Attorney General's Task Force on Violent Crime, 1981
- President's Commission on Organized Crime, 1983
- Attorney General's Commission on Pornography, 1986
- Advisory Panel to Assess Domestic Response Capabilities for Terrorism Involving Weapons of Mass Destruction (Gilmore Commission), 1999
- National Commission on Terrorist Attacks Upon the United States (9/11 Commission), 2004

In the late 1990s, there was a growing concern about terrorism, particularly after attacks on the U.S. military and the U.S. embassy bombings in Africa, as well as a general increase in terrorist attacks throughout the Middle East. As a result, the U.S. Congress mandated a 5-year annual inquiry into the susceptibility of the U.S. to attacks using weapons of mass destruction (WMD). The Advisory Panel to Assess Domestic Response Capabilities for Terrorism Involving Weapons of Mass Destruction (known as the Gilmore Commission, chaired by former Virginia Governor James Gilmore) issued its first report in 1999.

In 2004, the latest significant commission, the National Commission on Terrorist Attacks Upon the United States (9/11 Commission), issued its report. It had implications for the criminal justice system but addressed much wider issues. They are discussed later in this chapter.

The National Crime Commissions and Law Enforcement Intelligence

Not all of these commissions addressed the issue of intelligence directly; however, all called for increased use of diverse analytic techniques to not only understand crime and criminal justice but also to aid in forecasting crime for purposes of prevention—a fundamental construct of the intelligence process.

The Wickersham Commission observed there was a need to study and understand the crime environment (that is, analysis) as an important tool for capturing criminal offenders. Thirty-three years later, one of the earliest explicit recommendations for intelligence and information sharing between federal agencies and state and local law enforcement came from the 1964 President's Commission on the Assassination of President Kennedy (the Warren Commission). While the majority of the Commission's recommendations were directed at federal agencies, notably the Secret Service and the FBI, it also recommended that these agencies work more closely with local law enforcement. Specifically, the Commission called for increased information sharing and stronger liaison between local and federal agencies.[14]

The 1967 reports of the President's Commission on Law Enforcement and Administration of Justice emphasized many of the same factors, but provided significantly more research, more detail, and explicit recommendations. Moreover, the year following the release of the President's Commission reports, Congress passed landmark legislation—the Omnibus Crime Control and Safe Streets Act of 1968—which, among other things, provided funding for implementing many of the Commission's recommendations. Within the intelligence arena, the President's Commission recommended:

> Police departments in every major city should have a special intelligence unit solely to ferret out organized criminal activity and to collect information regarding the possible entry of criminal cartels into the area's criminal operations.[15]

Interestingly, the President's Commission noted that "criteria for evaluating the effectiveness of the [intelligence] units, other than mere numbers of arrests, must be developed".[16] That debate remains. The President's Commission went on to recommend that the "…Department of Justice should give financial assistance to encourage the development of efficient systems for regional intelligence gathering, collection, and dissemination."[17] This would become a reality roughly a decade later when the Regional Information Sharing System (RISS) and its six regional intelligence centers were created by the Justice Department.[18]

While the intelligence focus of the President's Commission was largely on organized crime and to a lesser extent on narcotics control, the Kerner Commission's focus was on civil disobedience and violent civil disorders. With respect to the riots and civil disorders experienced by America's cities, the Kerner Commission made this observation:

> No particular control tactic was successful in every situation. The varied effectiveness of control techniques emphasizes the need for advance training, planning, adequate intelligence systems, and knowledge of the [inner city].[19]

Further, the Kerner Commission recommended that law enforcement agencies should do the following:

> Establish an intelligence system to provide police and other public officials with reliable information that may help to prevent the outbreak of a disorder and to institute effective control measures in the event a riot erupts.[20]

The National Commission on the Causes and Prevention of Violence made similar observations:

[14] The Warren Commission Report. *Report of the President's Commission on the Assassination of President John F. Kennedy.* New York: Barnes and Noble, Inc., 2003. [Originally published in 1964].

[15] President's Commission on Law Enforcement and Administration of Justice. *Task Force Report: Organized Crime.* Washington, D.C.: U.S. Government Printing Office, 1967, p. 20.

[16] Ibid.

[17] Ibid., p. 22.

[18] See www.riss.net.

[19] National Advisory Commission on Civil Disorders. *Summary Report.* Washington, D.C.: U.S. Government Printing Office, 1968, p. 6

[20] Ibid., p. 16.

A major weakness of many police departments is the absence of a reliable intelligence system. The absence has gravely handicapped police and public officials in anticipating and preventing trouble, and in minimizing and controlling a disorder that has broken out. In large part, this happens because of a failure to learn about and to understand neighborhood problems and grievances and to develop reliable information concerning community organizations and leaders. Related to this problem is the need for a reliable mechanism to monitor, to collect, and to evaluate rumors and also the need for an effective program to counter false and provocative rumors which can aggravate tension and incite violence.[21]

The recognition that intelligence could be a valuable tool for forecasting threats and dealing with complex criminality was growing slowly as a wide range of systemic crime-related social problems were examined by these national inquiries. Intelligence was being viewed more broadly as evidenced by the most comprehensive recommendation yet from the National Advisory Commission on Criminal Justice Standards and Goals. The National Advisory Commission developed a standard expressly for intelligence operations—ironically, it is Standard 9.11—that states, in part:

> Every police agency and every state immediately should establish and maintain the capability to gather and evaluate information and to disseminate intelligence in a manner which protects every individual's right to privacy while it curtails organized crime and public disorder.[22]

The standard is remarkably similar to a recommendation from the *National Criminal Intelligence Sharing Plan* that was released 31 years later. Interestingly, the standard notes that "information" is collected and "intelligence" is disseminated. This reference to analysis had not been articulated clearly in the previous commission reports. Moreover, the attention to individual privacy that was included in the standard is also an important ingredient that is critical to all law enforcement intelligence activities today.

Furthermore, included in the National Advisory Commission's report were recommendations directed at the structure and operations of the intelligence functions for state and local law enforcement agencies. These recommendations included the following:

Establishing Intelligence Functions
- Each state should develop a centralized law enforcement intelligence function with the participation of each police agency within the state.[23]
- States should consider establishing regional intelligence networks across contiguous states to enhance criminal information-sharing processes.[24]
- Every local law enforcement agency should establish its own intelligence function in accordance with its respective state's intelligence function.[25]

Intelligence Function Operations
- Each state and local intelligence function should provide support to federal agencies.

[21] National Commission on the Causes and Prevention of Violence. *Law and Order Reconsidered*. Washington, D.C.: U.S. Government Printing Office, 1968, p. 312

[22] National Advisory Commission on Criminal Justice Standards and Goals. *Police*. Washington, D.C.: U.S. Government Printing Office, 1973, p. 250.

[23] Ibid

[24] National Advisory Committee on Criminal Justice Standards and Goals. *Organized Crime–Report of the Task Force on Organized Crime*. Washington D.C.: U.S. Department of Justice, Law Enforcement Assistance Administration, 1976.

[25] Ibid

- Operational policies and procedures should be developed for each local, state, and regional intelligence function to ensure efficiency and effectiveness.[26]
- Each agency should have a designated official who reports directly to the chief and oversees all intelligence operations.
- Each agency should develop procedures to ensure the proper screening, securing, and disseminating of intelligence-related information.[27]

In 1976, the concept and operating policies for intelligence were expanded even further by the National Advisory Committee on Criminal Justice Standards and Goals. The Committee's publication, *Organized Crime–Task Force Report on Organized Crime* has a chapter on intelligence that provides more detail than that provided by any previous commission or inquiry. Beyond recommendations for the creation of an intelligence unit, the standards include recommendations for maintaining privacy, the use of the "need-to-know" and "right-to-know" standards for dissemination, standards for purging intelligence records, and the need to maintain individual and organizational accountability in the intelligence function.[28] While the recommendations focus on organized crime, including drug trafficking, compared to the "all crimes, all hazards" approach used by law enforcement in the post-9/11 environment, many of the 1976 standards and discussions of intelligence are consistent with today's vision of good practice in law enforcement intelligence.

Created in 1983, the President's Commission on Organized Crime was a comprehensive examination of all aspects of organized crime, ranging from "traditional" organization crime (that is, the Mafia, La Cosa Nostra) to drug trafficking cartels, sophisticated money laundering operations, and entrepreneurial crime of all types and commodities. The intent was to provide a comprehensive insight into organized crime, its structure, its effects, and how best to control it. It recognized that effective intelligence analysis was a critical tool to enable law enforcement to deal successfully with multijurisdictional complex criminality.[29]

By the mid-1980s, criminal enterprises had grown dramatically and encompassed a diverse array of illegal activities, from drug trafficking to counterfeiting consumer commodities. Investigators and intelligence units had neither the expertise nor the personnel to contain the problem effectively. This was aggravated by a failure of law enforcement to generally understand the nature of organized crime and by poor information sharing among law enforcement agencies at all strata of government.[30] Organized crime was characterized as a "rapidly changing subculture" that was outpacing the capability of law enforcement to control it. Increasingly, organized crime was viewed largely as a federal responsibility that would be supported by state and local law enforcement through information sharing and participation on task forces.

Similar to the issues of organized crime, the Attorney General's Commission on Pornography (1986) recognized that intelligence operations would be a useful tool for stopping interstate traffic in obscene and pornographic materials. However, state and local law enforcement tended to view this as a low priority and not a good investment of time and resources.

[26] Ibid

[27] National Advisory Committee on Criminal Justice Standards and Goals. *Disorders and Terrorism: Report of the Task Force on Disorders and Terrorism.* Washington, D.C.: U.S. Department of Justice, Law Enforcement Assistance Administration, 1976.

[28] National Advisory Committee on Criminal Justice Standards and Goals. *Organized Crime–Report of the Task Force on Organized Crime.* Washington, D.C.: U.S. Government Printing Office, 1976, pp. 121–135.

[29] President's Commission on Organized Crime. *Organized Crime and Money Laundering.* Washington, D.C.: U.S. Government Printing Office, 1984.

[30] President's Commission on Organized Crime. *Final Report.* Washington, D.C.: U.S. Government Printing Office, 1987.

In the 1990s, following an increased number of terrorist attacks in the Middle East and particularly after the bombings of U.S. embassies in Dar es Salaam, Tanzania, and Nairobi, Kenya, questions began to emerge about the United States mainland as a terrorist target and the ability of the U.S. to effectively forecast, manage, and respond to an attack "at home"—particularly an attack involving WMD. As a result, in 1999 the U.S. Congress mandated the creation of the Advisory Panel to Assess Domestic Response Capabilities for Terrorism Involving Weapons of Mass Destruction (the Gilmore Commission). The annual reports, issued between 1999 and 2003, went beyond WMD and explored terrorism more broadly—particularly after 9/11—and what the U.S. Government needed to do to effectively protect the homeland. In addition to recommending more robust intelligence and information sharing, the Gilmore Commission urged policymakers to move beyond simply reacting to the September 11 terrorist attacks and develop forward-thinking efforts by government at the federal, state, and local levels, and by the private sector as well. In its 2002 report, the Gilmore Commission stated the following:

> Intelligence—its timely collection, thoughtful analysis, and appropriate dissemination—is the key to effective prevention of terrorist attacks. From the inception of our deliberations, we have said that "more can and must be done to provide timely information—up, down, and laterally, at all levels of government—to those who need the information to provide effective deterrence, interdiction, protection, or response to potential threats."

While improvements have been made, that statement is still true today.[31]

That message was reinforced, particularly with regard to information sharing, in a staff report from the National Commission on Terrorist Attacks Upon the United States (the 9/11 Commission). One issue of concern was the effectiveness of information sharing by the FBI with state and local law enforcement. The commission's staff report stated, in part, the following:

> We heard complaints that the FBI still needs to share much more operational, case-related information. The NYPD's Deputy Commissioner for Counterterrorism, Michael Sheehan, speculated that one of the reasons for deficiencies in this information sharing may be that the FBI does not always recognize what information might be important to others. ... Los Angeles Police Department officials complained to us that they receive watered-down reports from the FBI. ... We have been told that the FBI plans to move toward a "write to release" approach that would allow for more immediate and broader dissemination of intelligence on an unclassified basis.[32]

These issues are being addressed through the *National Criminal Intelligence Sharing Plan* (NCISP) and, more specifically through the development of law enforcement intelligence "requirements" by the FBI. Moreover, former FBI Executive Assistant Director for Intelligence Maureen Baginski specifically stated in remarks at the 2004 COPS Office National Community Policing Conference that the initiatives of the FBI Office of Intelligence included a revised report-writing style that would facilitate information sharing immediately, including sharing with intelligence customers who did not have security clearances.[33]

[31] Advisory Panel to Assess Domestic Response Capabilities for Terrorism Involving Weapons of Mass Destruction. *Implementing the National Strategy.* Washington, D.C.: RAND Corporation, 2002, p.30.

[32] National Commission on Terrorist Attacks Upon the United States (2004). *Staff Statement No. 12: Reforming Law Enforcement, Counterterrorism, and Intelligence Collection in the United States,* 2004, p. 8. www.9-11commission.gov/staff_statements/staff_statement_12.pdf.

[33] Baginski, Maureen. Remarks in a keynote address at "Community Policing for America's Future: National Community Policing Conference," Office of Community Oriented Policing Services, Washington, D.C.: June 22, 2004.

Interestingly, the 9/11 Commission's staff report on reformation of the intelligence function included many of the issues and observations identified in previous commission reports during the previous 40 years. The difference, however, is that substantive change is actually occurring, largely spawned by the tragedy of September 11, 2001.

The 9/11 Commission Report issued a wide range of recommendations related to intelligence. Cooperative relationships, the integration of intelligence functions, and a general reengineering of the intelligence community were at the heart of their recommendations. In commentary, the Commission noted the role of state, local, and tribal law enforcement agencies:

> There is a growing role for state and local law enforcement agencies. They need more training and work with federal agencies so that they can cooperate more effectively with those authorities in identifying terrorist suspects.[34]

The 9/11 Commission went on to recognize the following:

> The FBI is just a small fraction of the national law enforcement community in the United States, a community comprised mainly of state and local agencies. The network designed for sharing information, and the work of the FBI through local Joint Terrorism Task Forces, should build a reciprocal relationship in which state and local agents understand what information they are looking for and, in return, receive some of the information being developed about what is happening, or may happen, in their communities.[35]

The 9/11 Commission also recommended creation of a new domestic intelligence entity that would need to establish "…relationships with state and local law enforcement…"[36] In proposing a new National Counterterrorism Center (NCTC), the Commission stated that the Center should "… [reach] out to knowledgeable officials in state and local agencies throughout the United States."[37] Implicit in the Commission's recommendations is that terrorism is a local event that requires critical involvement of state and local government in prevention and response.[38]

The inquiries into crime and justice from the Wickersham Commission through the 9/11 Commission have the same themes: Attack the root causes of crime; understand all aspects of the crime dynamic; attack crime from a holistic approach; work with and share information between agencies; move beyond traditional approaches; and protect the privacy and civil rights of individuals. Whether the crime is strong-armed robberies or terrorism, these principles run true. Certainly, the practice of law enforcement intelligence has listened to and learned from these lessons in a frenzy of change during the post-9/11 era.

Law Enforcement Intelligence Initiatives in the Post-9/11 Environment

Several important initiatives have been spurred by the terrorist attacks of September 11, 2001 that have had a significant and fast effect on the evolution of law enforcement intelligence. The more significant developments occurring during this time are listed in Table 3-2.

[34] National Commission on Terrorist Attacks Upon the United States. *The 9/11 Commission Report.* Washington, D.C.: U.S. Government Printing Office, 2004, p. 390. www.9-11commission.gov/report/911Report.pdf.

[35] Ibid., p. 427.

[36] Ibid., p. 424.

[37] Ibid., p. 404.

[38] Ibid.

In October 2001, about 6 weeks after the 9/11 attacks, the International Association of Chiefs of Police (IACP) held its annual meeting in Toronto, Ontario, Canada. There, the Police Investigative Operations Committee discussed the need for SLTLE agencies to reengineer their intelligence function as well as the need for national leadership to establish standards and direction for SLTLE agencies. From this meeting, the IACP, with funding support from the COPS Office, held the Intelligence Summit in March 2002. The summit developed a series of recommendations, a criminal intelligence sharing plan, and adopted *Intelligence-Led Policing*.[39]

The Global Justice Information Sharing Initiative (Global), a group funded by the U.S. Office of Justice Programs, was already in existence with the charge of developing processes and standards to efficaciously share information across the criminal justice system. In response to the IACP Intelligence Summit of 2002, Global created a new subgroup, the Global Intelligence Working Group (GIWG). The purpose of the GIWG was to move forward with the summit's recommendations. The first GIWG product was the *National Criminal Intelligence Sharing Plan*.

Table 3-2: Significant Post-9/11 Law Enforcement Intelligence Initiatives

- COPS/IACP Intelligence Summit, 2002
- Global Intelligence Working Group (GIWG)
- Counter-Terrorism Training Coordination Working Group (CTTWG)
- *National Criminal Intelligence Sharing Plan* (NCISP)
- Criminal Intelligence Coordinating Council (CICC)
- Minimum Criminal Intelligence Training Standards
- Fusion Center Guidelines
- Department of Homeland Security (DHS) Target Capabilities List (TCL)
- Intelligence Reform and Terrorism Prevention Act of 2004 (IRTPA)
  - Creation of the Office of the Director of National Intelligence (ODNI) and appointment of the Assistant Deputy Director of National Intelligence (ADDNI) for Homeland Security and Law Enforcement
  - Creation of the Directorate of Intelligence (DI) at the FBI
  - Creation of the National Counterterrorism Center (NCTC)
  - Creation of the Information Sharing Environment (ISE)
- Creation of the Interagency Threat Assessment and Coordination Group (ITACG)
- National Strategy for Information Sharing (NSIS)
- Second COPS/IACP Intelligence Summit

[39] International Association of Chiefs of Police. *Criminal Intelligence Sharing: A National Plan for Intelligence-Led Policing at the Local, State and Federal Levels.* Alexandria, Virginia: International Association of Chiefs of Police, 2002.

Formally announced at a national signing event in the Great Hall of the U.S. Department of Justice on May 14, 2004, the *National Criminal Intelligence Sharing Plan* (NCISP) signified an element of intelligence dissemination that is important for all law enforcement officials. With formal endorsements from the DOJ, DHS, and the FBI, the NCISP provided an important foundation on which state, local, and tribal law enforcement agencies could create their intelligence initiatives. The intent of the plan was to provide SLTLE agencies (particularly those that do not have established intelligence functions) with the necessary tools and resources to develop, gather, access, receive, and share intelligence.

The NCISP[40] established a series of national standards that have been formally recognized by the professional law enforcement community as the role and processes for law enforcement intelligence today. The plan is having a significant effect on organizational realignment, information-sharing philosophy, and training in America's law enforcement agencies.

The NCISP also recognized the importance of local, state, and tribal law enforcement agencies as a key ingredient in the nation's intelligence process and called for the creation of the Criminal Intelligence Coordinating Council (CICC) to establish the linkage needed to improve intelligence and information sharing among all levels of government. Composed of members from law enforcement agencies at all levels of government, the CICC was formally established in May 2004 to provide advice in connection with the implementation and refinement of the NCISP. Members of the CICC serve as advocates for local law enforcement and support their efforts to develop and share criminal intelligence for the purpose of promoting public safety and securing our nation. Because of the critical role that SLTLE play in homeland security, they must have a voice in the development of policies and systems that facilitate information and intelligence sharing. The CICC serves as the voice for all levels of law enforcement agencies by advising the U.S. Attorney General and the Secretary of Homeland Security on the best use of criminal intelligence as well as the capabilities and limitations of SLTLE agencies related to information sharing.[41]

During the same period that these initiatives were occurring, many states and regions somewhat independently were developing multijurisdictional intelligence capabilities intended to maximize the diverse raw information input for analysis and examine potential acts of terrorism that may occur within regions. The units, called "fusion centers," were embraced by the DHS, which began providing funding to enable some of the centers to operate. The concept of "intelligence fusion" caught on rapidly as an efficient and effective mechanism for developing intelligence products. With recognition that other crimes, such as financial crime and weapons offenses, may have a nexus with terrorism, the centers' foci broadened to "all crimes." Moreover, with the broad mission of the DHS, which was increasingly providing substantial amounts of funding, the fusion centers' focus broadened further to encompass "all crimes, all hazards, all threats."

Recognizing the benefits of standardization to enhance the quality of work being done by the fusion centers, the GIWG created the *Fusion Center Guidelines*[42] for developing a series of recommendations and good practices for law enforcement agencies that are participating in the intelligence fusion process. While primarily focusing on criminal intelligence, the *Guidelines* also give attention to the law enforcement information-sharing relationship with the private sector, as well as public safety issues related to homeland security intelligence. The fusion process

[40] it.ojp.gov/documents/NCISP_Plan.pdf

[41] www.iir.com/global/council.htm

[42] it.ojp.gov/topic.jsp?topic_id=209

seeks to have as many law enforcement agencies as possible as information-sharing partners. Analytic outputs will be more robust as law enforcement participation increases because there will be a wider array of diverse information being entered into the analytic process. The recommendation from the NCISP and the second COPS/IACP Intelligence Summit that all agencies, regardless of size, should develop an intelligence capacity is clearly an important ingredient for increased agency participation with fusion centers.

At virtually the same time, the DHS was developing plans to meet its mission, mandated in Homeland Security Presidential Directive-8 "…to prevent, respond to, and recover from threatened and actual domestic terrorist attacks, major disasters, and other emergencies…".[43] A critical part of this initiative was to define critical knowledge, skills, abilities, and processes (that is, "capabilities") that were necessary for law enforcement and emergency services personnel to perform these tasks. These capabilities have been articulated in detail in the *Target Capabilities List*[44] (TCL). Intended to protect the nation from all hazards, "…the TCL is a national-level, generic model of operationally ready capabilities defining all-hazards preparedness." [45] The list is broken down into different "areas" associated with prevention and response. The "Prevent Mission Area" has two specific intelligence-related target capabilities: "Information Gathering and Recognition of Indicators and Warnings" and "Intelligence Analysis and Production." The "information gathering" capability is focused on "…the continual gathering of only pure, unexamined data…" that can be used in the intelligence process to identify threats and indicators of threats. This is the type of information that is essential for effective analysis and is the currency that fusion centers rely on law enforcement agencies to submit to the fusion process, typically through tips, leads, suspicious activity reports, and observation of terrorism or criminal indicators.

> The "intelligence analysis" target capability involves "…the merging of data and information for the purpose of analyzing, linking, and disseminating timely and actionable intelligence with an emphasis on the larger public safety and homeland security threat picture. This process focuses on the consolidation of analytical products among the intelligence analysis units at the Federal, State, local, and tribal levels for tactical, operational, and strategic use. This capability also includes the examination of raw data to identify threat pictures, recognize potentially harmful patterns, or connect suspicious links to discern potential indications or warnings."[46]

The discussion of both of these target capabilities in the *Target Capabilities List* refers to both the *NCISP* and *Fusion Center Guidelines* as standards and processes to accomplish the capabilities. The integration of these initiatives strives to create a culture of information sharing that inextricably includes state, local, and tribal law enforcement.

Building on these initiatives—and on other new programs and activities in the Intelligence Community as well as recommendations from the 9/11 Commission—Congress passed the Intelligence Reform and Terrorism Prevention Act of 2004 (IRTPA). Among the many important aspects of this legislation are four particularly

[43] For more information on the National Preparedness Goal, Homeland Security Presidential Directive-8 and the *Target Capabilities List*, see the Fact Sheet at www.llis.dhs.gov/docdetails/details.do?contentID=14468. (must register to access)

[44] Available online at www.llis.dhs.gov/docdetails/details.do?contentID=26724.

[45] U.S. Department of Homeland Security. *Target Capabilities List. A Companion to the National Preparedness Guidelines.* Washington, D.C.: U.S. Department of Homeland Security, 2007, p. 1.

[46] Ibid., p. 91.

important factors that are significant for the current discussion: creation of the Office of the Director of National Intelligence (ODNI), creation of a Directorate of Intelligence (DI) in the FBI, creation of the National Counterterrorism Center (NCTC), and mandating the creation of the Information Sharing Environment.

The first factor of the IRTPA provisions related to SLTLE was creation of the ODNI. The Director of National Intelligence (DNI) serves as the head of the Intelligence Community and as a principal advisor to the President on issues related to national security. One of the unprecedented aspects of this office is the formal recognition that SLTLE has a role in both national security and homeland security. The staff of the ODNI includes an Assistant Deputy Director of National Intelligence (ADDNI) for Homeland Security and Law Enforcement. While the role and functions of this position are still evolving, essentially the ADDNI is responsible for policy issues related to information sharing between the Intelligence Community and SLTLE. Moreover, the ADDNI advises the Intelligence Community on law enforcement capabilities, operations, and restrictions related to national security.

The second factor was creation of the FBI Directorate of Intelligence (DI) to manage all FBI intelligence activities.[47] The DI is organized as part of the FBI's National Security Branch and is embedded in all investigative domains— counterterrorism, counterintelligence, WMD, cyber, and criminal inquiries.[48] A key responsibility of the DI is identifying threats and sharing threat information with SLTLE agencies and the Intelligence Community. The DI's goal is to be a "full and trusted partner who can be relied on to proactively bring FBI resources to the table to help resolve threats."[49] The IRTPA mandate firmly established and expanded the DI's authority over the management of the FBI's intelligence functions, including oversight of field intelligence operations and coordination of human source development and management.

The third factor was the creation of the National Counterterrorism Center (NCTC). The NCTC serves as the primary organization for integrating and analyzing all intelligence pertaining to terrorism with the exception of purely domestic terrorism. The NCTC also serves as the central knowledge bank on terrorism information and provides all-source intelligence support to government-wide counterterrorism activities. Its mission is essentially to "get the right counterterrorism information into the right hands of the right people" in DHS, the FBI, the Intelligence Community and, indirectly, SLTLE. The NCTC seeks to bring intelligence from across the federal government into one place to integrate and analyze it then disseminate the integrated intelligence to customers.[50]

The final IRTPA factor of concern to SLTLE is creation of the Information Sharing Environment (ISE). The IRTPA required the President to establish an ISE "for the sharing of terrorism information in a manner consistent with national security and with applicable legal standards relating to privacy and civil liberties." It also required designation of a program manager for the ISE who is charged with planning and overseeing the ISE's implementation and management.

[47] Rather than create a new domestic intelligence agency, as recommended by the 9/11 Commission, the legislation increased the intelligence authority and responsibilities of the FBI.

[48] www.fbi.gov/intelligence/intell.htm

[49] Statement by FBI Assistant Director Wayne Murphy, Directorate of Intelligence, at the 2007 IACP Intelligence Summit, Washington, D.C., November 27, 2007.

[50] www.nctc.gov/nic

[51] www.ise.gov/docs/ise-impplan-200611.
pdf

[52] Ibid. Program Manager's Office, p. 83.

[53] In November 2007 a letter, jointly
signed by the U.S. Attorney General and
Secretary of Homeland Security, was sent
to each state governor concerning the
designation of a primary fusion center.
The letter stated, in part, "…Guideline
2 states that DOJ and DHS will work
with governors or other senior state
and local leaders to designate a single
fusion center to serve as the statewide
or regional hub to interface with the
federal government and through which
to coordinate the gathering, processing,
analysis, and dissemination of terrorism,
law enforcement, and homeland security
information in an all-crimes approach.
… it is imperative for your office to
designate one fusion center to serve as
the statewide hub. … In designating
a single fusion center, please give
consideration to developing an inclusive
strategy that is consistent with the
federal efforts to constitute the ISE."

[54] www.whitehouse.gov/nsc/infosharing/
sectionIV.html

[55] Ibid.

The Information Sharing Environment Implementation Plan[51] is designed to increase the sharing of terrorism information among and between the 16-member Intelligence Community, law enforcement agencies at all levels of government, and the private sector as well as foreign partners. The ISE seeks to "…implement an effective, widespread culture of information sharing, balanced with a need for security and the protection of privacy and civil liberties…"[52] The Implementation Plan provides a detailed process and action steps that indicate significant expectations for state, local, and tribal law enforcement to be participants in the ISE. *The Implementation Plan* further stipulates that each state must identify a primary state fusion center that will be the information-sharing nexus between the federal ISE and SLTLE agencies.[53]

As is evident from the above initiatives, information sharing has become the fundamental principle for intelligence processes to protect the United States. Despite new programs, legislation, and regulations, information sharing across governmental levels was still problematic. In an attempt to remedy this, key decision-makers and representatives of all levels of the ISE were to meet on a consistent basis and resolve information-sharing problems as members of the new Interagency Threat Assessment and Coordination Group[54] (ITACG) within the NCTC. ITACG members include the DHS, the FBI, members of the Intelligence Community, and state and local law enforcement representatives. A key role of the ITACG is to support the efforts of NCTC to produce "federally coordinated" terrorism-related information products intended for dissemination to state, local, and tribal officials and private-sector partners.

ITACG members, particularly at the state and local levels, help define the intelligence products needed by each type of consumer. Because each level of government has different priorities, ITACG members provide advice, counsel, and subject matter expertise to the Intelligence Community regarding the operations of SLTLE agencies, including how such entities use terrorism-related information to fulfill both their counterterrorism responsibilities and their core mission of protecting their communities.

Beyond these responsibilities, a key role of the ITACG is to coordinate the production and timely dissemination of specific intelligence products to SLTLE officials. The intelligence products include the following:
- Alerts, warnings, and notifications of time-sensitive terrorism threats to locations within the United States
- Situational awareness reporting regarding significant events or activities occurring at the international, national, state, or local levels
- Strategic assessments of terrorist risks and threats to the United States.[55]

The ISE was evolving beyond a plan and moving into actual policy and processes. Taking the next step, in October 2007 the White House released the *National Strategy for Information Sharing* (NSIS).

> The Strategy will assist the Administration in ensuring that Federal, State, local, and tribal government employees responsible for protecting our Nation from future attacks or responding should an attack occur understand the

Administration's expectations and plans for achieving improvements in the gathering and sharing of information related to terrorism. [56]

The strategy goes on to note:

> The President's guidelines recognized that State, local, and tribal authorities are critical to our Nation's efforts to prevent future terrorist attacks ... The informational needs of State, local, and tribal entities continue to grow as they incorporate counterterrorism and homeland security activities into their day-to-day missions. Specifically, they require access to timely, credible, and actionable information and intelligence about individuals and groups intending to carry out attacks within the United States, their organizations and their financing, potential targets, pre-attack indicators, and major events or circumstances that might influence State, local, and tribal preventive and protective postures.[57]

The role of state, local, and tribal law enforcement intelligence is undeniable.

In many ways, post-9/11 intelligence developments came full circle with the second IACP/COPS Intelligence Summit. While many important and substantive changes have been made in law enforcement intelligence, the *2008 Summit Report* observed the following:

> The participants in the follow-up IACP Criminal Intelligence Sharing Summit nevertheless made it clear that many of the nation's law enforcement agencies do not participate in the criminal intelligence sharing plan. Too many state, local, and tribal agencies, it would seem, underestimate their importance to the criminal intelligence sharing process, overestimate the burdens of full participation, and/or remain unaware of how to contribute to the vital work of the plan.[58]

Clearly, challenges remain.

Collateral Developments

A number of other activities were either already in place or were in development concurrently with the above initiatives. The distinction of these activities is that they have helped facilitate the goals and processes of the strategies described above.

Counter-Terrorism Training Coordination Working Group (CTTWG)[59]

The CTTWG was formed in 2002 to facilitate interagency coordination, information exchange, and sharing of innovative training initiatives among federal agencies involved in terrorism and antiterrorism training. The group was later expanded to include representation from the major law enforcement and law enforcement training organizations. Further expansion of the CTTWG included policy-level agency representatives from a broad range of federal agencies; law enforcement organizations involved in federal, state, local, and tribal law enforcement training; and academe. The CTTWG recognized that, increasingly, training issues and programs being brought before them were focusing on the discipline of

[56] *National Strategy for Information Sharing.* Washington, D.C.: Executive Office of the President, 2007, p. 1.

[57] Ibid., p. 17.

[58] International Association of Chiefs of Police. *National Summit of Intelligence.* Washington, D.C.: Office of Community Oriented Policing Services, U.S. Department of Justice, 2008, p. 2.

[59] www.counterterrorismtraining.gov.

intelligence. As a result, greater attention was focused on intelligence training and how to maximize the use of limited resources by ensuring that the intelligence training conveys a consistent, quality message; is not duplicative; is consistent with national standards; and meets the needs of law enforcement. Among the new intelligence initiatives was the creation of an online Law Enforcement Intelligence Master Training Calendar.[60] The group also assumed responsibility for preparing Version 2.0 of the Minimum Criminal Intelligence Training Standards.

Minimum Criminal Intelligence Training Standards[61]

Recognizing that the intelligence capacity of America's law enforcement community could not be realized without effective training, the CTTWG developed the *Minimum Criminal Intelligence Training Standards*. The standards identify six law enforcement focal areas— Chief Executive, Intelligence Commander/Manager, Intelligence Analyst, Criminal Intelligence Officer, General Law Enforcement Officer, and Train-the-Trainer— critical to successful intelligence activities. For each area, a group of experienced law enforcement intelligence professionals articulated learning objectives and identified key knowledge, skills, and abilities that are needed to execute intelligence responsibilities. With position-specific knowledge of the intelligence process increased within the law enforcement community, the willingness and ability to proactively contribute to the ISE increases significantly. Version 2.0 of the standards was approved in October 2007.

Global Justice Extensible Markup Language Data Model (GJXDM)

Because of the administrative independence among and between each component of the criminal justice system, many criminal justice information systems evolved in a manner that would not easily permit electronic information sharing. Frequently relying on proprietary data models from vendors, information often had to be exchanged in hard copy or be reentered. The Global Justice Information Sharing Initiative took on the task of developing a common data model that could serve as a standard used by all system components. The GJXDM is an Extensible Markup Language (XML) standard designed specifically for criminal justice information exchanges, providing law enforcement, public safety agencies, prosecutors, public defenders, and the judicial branch with a tool to share data and information effectively and in a timely manner.[62] There are three primary parts to GJXDM: the Data Dictionary (identifying content and meaning), the Data Model (defining structure and organization), and the Component Reuse Repository (a database). While the intent of the data model was to enhance criminal justice information sharing, the model has been embraced as a means of enhancing electronic sharing of criminal intelligence data. As a result, the GJXDM serves as an important technological component to support the ISE.

National Information Exchange Model[63] (NIEM)

A joint initiative of the DOJ and the DHS, NIEM embraced the GJXDM data model and built an information-sharing policy framework that met the mandates of the Homeland Security Act of 2002, the Intelligence Reform and Terrorism Prevention Act of 2004, and Homeland Security Presidential Directive 5 (HSPD-5).

[60] The Intelligence Master Training Calendar is available on the public side of the National Criminal Intelligence Resource Center web site: mastercalendar.ncirc. gov.

[61] The standards are available at: www. it.ojp.gov/documents/min_crim_intel_ stand.pdf.

[62] it.ojp.gov/topic.jsp?topic_id=228

[63] See www.niem.gov.

Rather than nationwide integration of all local, state, tribal, and federal databases, NIEM focuses on cross-domain information exchanges between key domains and communities of interest across all levels of government—whether between individual local law enforcement agencies, law enforcement and emergency service agencies, and other domains, or between local, state, tribal, regional, and federal agencies.[64]

The development of a common data standard and data-sharing model is clearly an important thread that permeates the culture of information sharing.

Grants for Training, Technical Assistance, and Technology

Various agencies and bureaus within both the DOJ and the DHS have been committed to providing grant support to further the intelligence mission. A wide variety of intelligence training programs have been supported, special activities to provide technical assistance, and assistance in purchasing technology and information systems— consistent with GJXDM and NIEM—have been critical to the development of the information-sharing culture. A factor that is particularly important to note is that many of the intelligence-related initiatives have been collaborative partnerships between the DOJ and the DHS. Beyond the support these initiatives have provided, this collaboration demonstrates information sharing in practice.[65]

Implications

The ISE *Implementation Plan* states that there is a need to "promote a culture of information sharing across the Information Sharing Environment." While a great deal of work and resocialization remains, a review of the initiatives discussed above demonstrates that significant strides have been made. While the ISE will face challenges to meet its ultimate goal, the changes that have been made in a comparatively short amount of time represent important milestones and are a significant leap forward.

Collectively, these initiatives have changed the philosophy of law enforcement intelligence that reflects the following:

- A commitment to information sharing both within and between law enforcement agencies
- The need to establish an objective, thoughtful intelligence function that has consistent national professional standards
- The recognition that state, local, and tribal law enforcement agencies have an important role in both homeland security and national security
- A process committed to preventing terrorism and multijurisdictional criminality
- A commitment to pursuing the intelligence function in a manner that is consistent with privacy and civil rights protection.

[64] *Introduction to the National Information Exchange Model.* Washington, D.C.: NIEM Program Management Office, February 12, 2007, p. 3.

[65] Sources to gather information about grants, training, and technical assistance from both the DOJ and the DHS include: www.counterterrorismtraining.gov, www.ncirc.gov, www.llis.dhs.gov, www.iir.com, and www.fema.gov/emergency/nims/compliance/grants.shtm.

Law Enforcement Intelligence at the State, Local, and Tribal Levels

Although the recommendations provided by the various national crime commissions were designed to strengthen law enforcement's capabilities to fight organized crime, by the mid-1980s, criminal enterprises had grown dramatically and encompassed such a diverse array of illegal activities, that the ability of SLTLE agencies to deal with these problems was limited. Investigators and intelligence units had neither the expertise nor the personnel to contain the problem effectively. This was aggravated by a failure of law enforcement to generally understand the nature of the problem and by poor information sharing among law enforcement agencies at all strata of government.[66] Organized crime was characterized as a "rapidly changing subculture" that was outpacing the capability of law enforcement to control it. As a result, law enforcement intelligence units were often relegated to being little more than an information clearinghouse or, in some cases, viewed as a failed initiative.[67]

Despite the lack of success, many within the law enforcement community still viewed the intelligence function as important to law enforcement agencies. A primary limitation of state and local intelligence units, however, was their inability to move beyond the collection of information to a systematic method of analyzing the collected data. The solution, then, was to have "the analytical function… guides the data collection [procedure]" rather than vice versa.[68]

Another limitation of law enforcement intelligence was that many law enforcement executives either did not recognize the value of intelligence and/or did not have the skills necessary to use intelligence products effectively. Furthermore, intelligence personnel did not possess the analytic (and often reporting) skills needed to produce meaningful intelligence products. The need for training was considered an important solution to this problem, and still is.

A historical issue was that intelligence units tended to be reactive in nature, often viewed as a repository of sensitive information rather than a proactive resource that could produce information critical for preventing crime and apprehending offenders. Similarly, intelligence units tended not to produce consistent, specifically defined products. Instead, intelligence reports tended to be written on an ad hoc basis to address critical matters.

A final limitation was that intelligence products were not disseminated in a timely or comprehensive manner. This, perhaps, was the greatest setback because the character of organized crime was constantly changing: different commodities were being trafficked, methods of operations tended to change, and participants in the operation of the enterprise changed. The need for timely and relevant information was seen as a necessary component for improving law enforcement intelligence operations.

While the majority of the past recommendations focused on the development and operations of intelligence units, recommendations have also been made regarding the ethical issues associated with state and local intelligence operations.

[66] President's Commission on Organized Crime. *Final Report.* Washington, D.C.: U.S. Government Printing Office, 1987.

[67] Martens, F., "The Intelligence Function," in *Major Issues in Organized Crime Control: Symposium Procedings, Washington, D.C.,* September 25–26, 1986. ed. Herbert Edelhertz, Washington, D.C.: U.S. Department of Justice, National Institute of Justice, Government Printing Office, 1987.

[68] Ibid.

Similar to the concerns that led to the formation of the Church Committee at the federal level, potential abuses of power was also a concern at the state and local levels. Accordingly, recommendations were made to ensure that citizens' civil rights remain intact.

For example, the *Law Enforcement Intelligence Unit File Guidelines*[69] were created to provide a practical policy and procedures that were intended to facilitate an effective intelligence process that was compliant with 28 CFR Part 23 and protected citizens' rights. Similarly, the Commission on Accreditation for Law Enforcement Agencies (CALEA) has recommended that every agency with an intelligence function establish procedures to ensure that data collection on intelligence information is "limited to criminal conduct that relates to activities that present a threat to the community" and to develop methods "for purging out-of-date or incorrect information."[70] In other words, the CALEA standard identified the need for law enforcement agencies to be held accountable for abuses of power associated with their intelligence activities. The latest revision of the CALEA intelligence standard embraces the *National Criminal Intelligence Sharing Plan* and its recommendations.

As will be seen later, the development of the Intelligence-Led Policing concept and the creation of the *National Criminal Intelligence Sharing Plan* have been important milestones in the evolution of law enforcement intelligence. By creating both an overarching intelligence philosophy and a standard for operations, state, local, and tribal law enforcement intelligence is becoming more professional. It is embracing more sophisticated tools, developing greater collaboration as one voice from the law enforcement intelligence community, and moving with a greater sense of urgency because of 9/11.

Conclusion

While we have evolved in our expertise and professionalism, many of the same issues remain. What are the lessons learned from history?
- Building dossiers full of raw, diverse information provides little insight— analysis is needed to give meaning to the information.
  - The improper collection of information can have a negative impact on our communities, including a chilling effect on the constitutional right of freedom of speech.
- To be effective, intelligence units must be proactive by developing unique products and disseminating the products to appropriate personnel on a consistent and comprehensive basis.
- A clear distinction is needed between law enforcement intelligence and national security intelligence. While some information can support the goals of both forms of intelligence, the competing methodologies and types of information that may be maintained in records mandates that the distinction remain clear and that overlap occurs only for clear purposes of public safety, including the apprehension of offenders and prevention of criminal and/or terrorists' acts.

[69] it.ojp.gov/process_links.jsp?link_id=3773

[70] Commission on Accreditation for Law Enforcement Agencies. *Standards for Law Enforcement Agencies.* 4th ed., 1998.

- Targeting people is unlawful without some evidence of a criminal predicate.
  - If the reason for the target is their support of an unpopular cause.
  - If they are being targeted because of their political beliefs, religion, race, ethnicity, or other attribute or characteristic (such as people who are perceived to be Muslim).
  - Targeting without lawful justification can result in civil rights suits and vicarious liability lawsuits, which can be both costly and embarrassing to the police department.
- The need to institute a privacy policy and civil rights protections are essential professional objectives.
- Monitoring an individual's behavior is proper if reasons can be articulated that reasonably support the notion that…
  - The person may be involved in criminality now or in the future.
  - There is a reasonable threat to public safety.
- Retaining information in intelligence files about an individual or an organization is improper if there is no reasonable suspicion of his or her criminal involvement, unless that information is used only as noncriminal identifying information and is labeled as such.
- A full-time law enforcement intelligence function should be organized professionally and staffed with personnel who are specifically trained in analysis and intelligence product preparation.
- There must be clear lines of communication between the intelligence unit and decision-makers.
- Law enforcement intelligence units must be evaluated regularly to ensure functional utility and operational propriety.
- Information sharing remains an important priority.

While past abuses of the intelligence function were no doubt done in a good faith effort to protect the community, nonetheless they were abuses. The changes that have occurred, particularly in the post-9/11 environment, and the professional development of the law enforcement intelligence function have demonstrated a respect for civil rights, a reliance on the scientific approach to problem solving, and a commitment to keeping America's communities safe.

Chapter 4:

The Intelligence Process (Cycle)
for State, Local, and Tribal Law Enforcement

The Intelligence Process (Cycle) for State, Local, and Tribal Law Enforcement

Regardless of the type of intelligence, the single function that permeates all activities is the Intelligence Process (also known as the Intelligence Cycle). This process provides mechanisms to ensure the consistent management of information that will be used to create intelligence. This chapter is an overview of the Intelligence Process. Many of the issues introduced here will be discussed in detail in the remaining chapters of this *Guide*.

The Intelligence Process has been depicted in a variety of ways throughout the intelligence literature. The number of phases in the process may differ, depending on the model used, but the intent of each model of the Intelligence Process is the same:

> To have a systemic, scientific, and logical methodology to comprehensively process information to ensure that the most accurate, actionable intelligence is produced and disseminated to the people who provide an operational response to prevent a criminal threat from reaching fruition.

The process applies to all crimes, whether terrorism, drug trafficking, gangs, or any other criminal enterprise. Indeed, the process also helps identify circumstances where there is a nexus among these different types of crimes.

National Criminal Intelligence Sharing Plan: Training Recommendation for the Intelligence Process
Recommendation 18: Training should be provided to all levels of law enforcement personnel involved in the criminal Intelligence Process. The training standards, as contained within the *National Criminal Intelligence Sharing Plan*, shall be considered the minimum training standards for all affected personnel. Additionally, recipients of criminal intelligence training, as recommended in the *National Criminal Intelligence Sharing Plan*, should be recognized and awarded certificates for successful completion of training.

To be consistent with established national standards, the model used in this discussion is the one prescribed in the *National Criminal Intelligence Sharing Plan* (NCISP). While often depicted as "steps," in practice the different components of the process are phases, and there is a constant ebb and flow of information between phases as information is processed and shared. The Intelligence Process, therefore, is not a series of independent steps that are mechanically processed in an unbending sequential order; rather, they represent a recipe for intelligence and information sharing that will frequently change according to the availability of "ingredients" and the "nutritional needs" of the consumer.

The model of the Intelligence Process used in the NCISP (Figure 4-1) has six phases:

1. Planning and Direction.
2. Collection.
3. Processing/Collation.
4. Analysis.
5. Dissemination.
6. Reevaluation.

Each phase may be broken down into subprocesses (Figure 4-2) that collectively contribute to an effective information management and analysis system.

Figure 4-1: Intelligence Process, NCISP

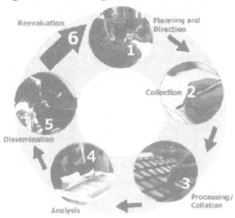

In many ways, the Intelligence Process acts like a radar sweep across a community. The process seeks to identify potential threats, determine the status of suspicious activity, and provide indicators of criminality so that operational units can develop responses. An illustration of the ebb and flow of the Intelligence Process: An intelligence bulletin may describe certain indicators. An officer observes behaviors that are consistent with these indicators, collects further information that is processed through the cycle, thereby providing an analyst with more raw data to help refine the analysis. When a more refined analysis is once again disseminated back to operational units, the likelihood increases of providing more explicit intelligence that operational units may use to prevent a crime or a terrorist attack.

Figure 4-2: Intelligence Process and Subprocesses

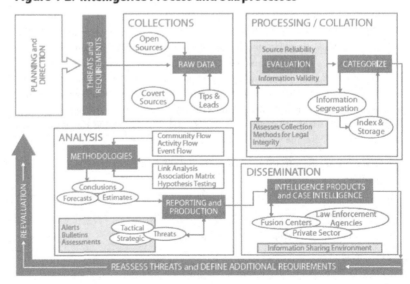

As an illustration, an intelligence bulletin describes an emerging threat of Eastern European organized crime operating protection rackets in a major midwestern city. A police officer working neighborhoods with large populations of Russian immigrants has noticed an increase in thefts and property damage to small businesses largely operated by immigrants. In light of the intelligence bulletin, the officer provides information to the intelligence unit that crimes reported as simple thefts and property destruction within this area of the city may, in reality, be symptoms of "enforcer" activities of Eastern European organized crime protection schemes. The analyst corroborates the information with practices of the organized crime group in other cities and provides the additional information to officers in a revised bulletin. To be most effective, the Intelligence Process requires this ongoing two-way flow of information.

Planning and Direction

The intelligence function involves the coordination of many activities. Similar to intermeshed gears, there must be a plan for how each moving part will operate in concert with other elements and how the gears will collectively manage a change in the environment. The gears of the Intelligence Process are prioritized and synchronized in the first phase of the cycle: Planning and Direction.

Former FBI Executive Assistant Director for Intelligence Maureen Baginski often stated, "The absence of evidence is not the absence of a threat." As part of the Planning and Direction process, it is important to recognize not only the threats that have been identified, but also dynamic threats where evidence indicating their presence may appear serendipitously. A threat may emerge within a jurisdiction or region for a wide variety of reasons; therefore, personnel must be trained to be vigilant in looking for evidence of threats (that is, indicators). This, however, must be a pragmatic process.

While a common perspective is that the Intelligence Process should take an "all-crimes/all-threats approach," pragmatically, these threats are not "equal" and must be prioritized considering the probability of their presence and the nature of the harm they pose to a community. This process is described in detail in Chapter 6. Threat prioritization is part of the "Direction" component of the first phase. This is done through ongoing threat assessments that are constantly refined by information that is processed through the Intelligence Cycle. A threat must be assessed on multiple criteria as illustrated in Figure 4-3.

The first threat component is threat identification. When evidence of a threat is identified, the Intelligence Process must assess where the threat lies on a multivariate continuum of probability. While quantifying a threat would add an element of precision, typically the variables related to a threat can be measured only on an ordinal scale:[1] for example, based on qualitative data a judgment can be made on the relative value of a threat variable on a scale of 1 to 10. As illustrated in Figure 4-4, the first two variables (A and B) measure the quality of the information. The second two variables (C and D) measure the probable outcome of the threat. Combined, they provide guidance for decision-making. A moderate assessment of the quality of information may produce a different operational

[1] An "ordinal scale" is a scale of measurement whereby data are put in a rank order, but where there is no fixed amount of difference between the points on the scale. For example, college sports rankings will rate the top 20 teams. The ranking, however, does not mean that the team ranked first is 20 times better than the 20th-ranked team.

response as the severity of the threat increases. As severity decreases, a higher quality of information may be desired before an operational response is made. This is basically a method to weigh risk/outcome tradeoffs.

Figure 4-3: Threat Assessment Components for Planning and Direction

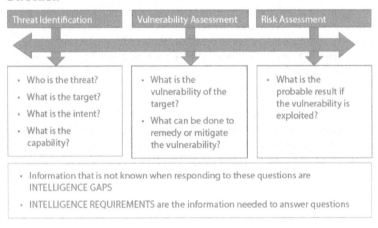

The next step is a vulnerability assessment of probable targets. When a threat is identified, the universe of targets is typically narrowed. Regardless if the probable number of targets is large or small, some judgments can be made on how vulnerable the targets are. As vulnerability increases, so does the seriousness of the threat. As an example, assume that a small group of eco-terrorists plans on fire-bombing the sales inventory of various automobile dealers who sell large trucks. Most dealership sales lots are easily accessible 24 hours a day. As such, their vulnerability increases and so does the threat. In a different scenario, assume that the same group of eco-terrorists plans to fire-bomb tanks at a military installation to protest fuel consumption and damage done to the environment by the tanks traversing their training range. In this case, target vulnerability is low because of the inaccessibility to the tanks on the military base and the ability of the tanks to withstand Molotov cocktails should the intruders get near them. As should be apparent, target vulnerability is an important variable in any threat assessment.

Figure 4-4: Simplified Threat Assessment Illustration[2]

Making Threats										Posing Threats
Low										High
1	2	3	4	5	6	7	8	9	10	

Variable A — Reliability and Validity of Information on Threat

Low										High
1	2	3	4	5	6	7	8	9	10	

Variable B — Weight of Evidence of Threat

Low										High
1	2	3	4	5	6	7	8	9	10	

Variable C — Severity of Threat

Low										High
1	2	3	4	5	6	7	8	9	10	

Variable D — Probability of Occurrence

Once threats and target vulnerability have been identified, a risk assessment is made. Risk is epitomized by the question: "What is the probable result if the vulnerability is exploited?" In the above illustration, the risk to the automobile dealers may be high and the risk to the military installation may be low; however, before a conclusion may be drawn on risk, more information is needed to corroborate judgments and determine if there are other, previously undiscovered, compounding factors. This process helps define further intelligence requirements—information that needs to be collected to better understand the threat.

Essentially, the threat assessment process seeks to make a distinction on whether an intelligence target is "making a threat" or "posing a threat." This is obviously subjective; hence, as much information as practicable should be collected and analyzed on these three factors. In most instances, there will be insufficient information to make a meaningful assessment of each component of the threat assessment model. As a result, answers to the "requirements" questions will help clarify the threat picture. Obtaining additional information will increase the quality of intelligence by identifying and eliminating error.

It should also be recognized that previously undefined threats may also emerge. Changes in the character of a community may stimulate new threats, the presence of a particular target may draw a threat, or the threat simply may appear as a result of the combined effect of many factors. The point to note is that law enforcement personnel must be trained to identify behaviors that are more than merely suspicious, record the behaviors with as much detail as possible, and forward this information to the intelligence analysts.

The importance of the threat assessment model in Planning and Direction lies within the ability to maximize resources and operational initiatives for those crimes and circumstances which pose the greatest risk to public safety and

[2] This scale is not intended to be a threat assessment tool, but an illustration of the threat assessment concept in the discussion.

security. In many ways, the Intelligence Process looks for images through a lens that is out of focus. The two-way exchange of information helps focus the lens to understand if a threat is present and the degree of risk it poses. The Planning and Direction process constantly monitors changes in the environment and helps define changing priorities as well as new two-way information sharing needs.

Beyond resource issues, Planning and Direction requires the identification of threat priorities to focus awareness training for officers on how to recognize all threats. It also requires policy and procedural mechanisms to make the organization sufficiently nimble to respond effectively to the changing threat environment. Just like the Intelligence Process itself, the Planning and Direction phase is characterized by an ebb and flow of information that provides insight so that the evolving threat environment can be managed efficaciously.

Collection

Collection is the gathering of raw information that will be used by analysts to prepare intelligence reports and products. As a way to better envision the Collection phase of the process, law enforcement personnel typically will gather information in five basic forms:

1. A response to *intelligence requirements*.

2. A response to terrorism or criminal *indicators*.

3. *Suspicious Activity Reports* (SAR) of activities observed by or reported to officers.

4. *Leads* that officers develop during the investigation of unrelated cases.

5. *Tips* that may come from citizens, informants, or the private sector.

The response to *intelligence requirements* is information that is intentionally and specifically sought to answer certain questions. That information may be sought from open sources or may be a product of law enforcement methods, such as interviews, surveillance, undercover operations, or other law enforcement processes. A response to *indicators* would be law enforcement officers collecting information based on their observation of circumstances or behaviors they recognize because of information they gained from training and/or intelligence bulletins that describe such indicators. Typically, indicators will include the signs and symbols of criminal activity such as graffiti, the symbol of an extremist group on a wall or a car, or unusual activity at a location that is consistent with threat activity described in an intelligence report.

Typically, information collected from *SARs* is based on behavior observed by law enforcement officers who, relying on their training and experience, believe the individual may be involved in criminal activity, in the past or the future, although a specific criminal nexus is not identified. The term *leads* refers to information that officers develop about a probable emerging threat that is largely unrelated to the current investigation but comes to light during the inquiry. *Tips* reflect information that has been observed by citizens and submitted to a law enforcement agency for further inquiry.

The collection process must seek to establish a criminal nexus with any person or organization that is identified in criminal intelligence records. This nexus is referred to as a *criminal predicate.* The standard for that criminal predicate is reasonable suspicion that is more than mere suspicion that the identified person is committing or is about to commit a crime. In practice, law enforcement agencies collect information on individuals where no criminal predicate exists. Examples are SARs, tips, and leads. This may appear to be a contradiction, but it is an inherent part of the Intelligence Process that has a remedy. The law enforcement agency has an obligation to determine if there is veracity to the criminal allegations found in SARs, leads, or tips. This is the purpose of the two-tiered "Temporary File" and "Permanent File" records system used for intelligence records. In practice, *retention* of collected information becomes the critical issue for demonstrating the criminal predicate.

The reader should note that care was taken to specify that the criminal predicate must be established when collecting and retaining information that *identifies people or organizations.* The critical point to note is that constitutional rights attach when identity is established.

The Intelligence Process will also seek to collect information about crime trends, methods of criminal operations, ideologies of extremists groups, and other nonidentifying information that helps describe and understand criminal phenomena. The criminal predicate rule does not apply to these types of information because individuals are not identified.

A final issue of Collection—and the entire Intelligence Process—is operations security (OPSEC). OPSEC focuses on identifying and protecting information that might provide an intelligence target with clues to an inquiry, and thereby enable the target to thwart the inquiry.[3] To protect the integrity of the intelligence inquiry, it is essential to maintain the security of collection sources, methods, and content.

Processing/Collation

This phase of the Intelligence Process, Processing/Collation, has four distinct activities, as illustrated in Figure 4-5. The first is to evaluate raw data from the collection phase to determine its utility for analysis. An assessment should first examine the *reliability* of the source of the information. Ideally, the individual who was the primary collector should record a statement of reliability. The importance of this assessment relates to the confidence level an analyst will give the information when making judgments during the analysis. The conclusion drawn by an analyst when using information derived from a completely reliable source will be different from a source deemed unreliable.

The next assessment during evaluation examines the *validity* of the raw information. Validity is epitomized by the question: "Does the information actually portray what it seems to portray?" Validity assessment may be done by the collector and/or the analyst. The collector may believe that if information comes from a reliable source and it is logical, then validity is high. Conversely, the analyst may have competing information that questions the validity. In such cases, the analyst should define intelligence requirements to collect additional information in order to gain the most accurate raw information for a robust analysis. The Intelligence Cycle, therefore, starts over, even though this is only the third phase.

Source reliability and information validity are often initially assessed using the ordinal scales similar to those depicted in Figure 4-6. These rudimentary scales nonetheless provide important fundamental guidelines for intelligence assessments. As such, law enforcement personnel should be trained to provide these assessments when collecting information for the Intelligence Cycle.

A next form of evaluation is to assess the *method* by which the information was collected to ensure that it meets constitutional standards. Recommendation 6 of the NCISP states:

> All parties involved with implementing and promoting the *National Criminal Intelligence Sharing Plan* should take steps to ensure that the law enforcement community protects individuals' privacy and constitutional rights within the Intelligence Process.[4]

[3] See www.belvoir.army.mil/dptms/opsec. asp

[4] Global Intelligence Working Group. *National Criminal Intelligence Sharing Plan.* Washington, D.C.: Global Intelligence Working Group, 2003, p. 21.

Figure 4-5: Processing and Collation Activities

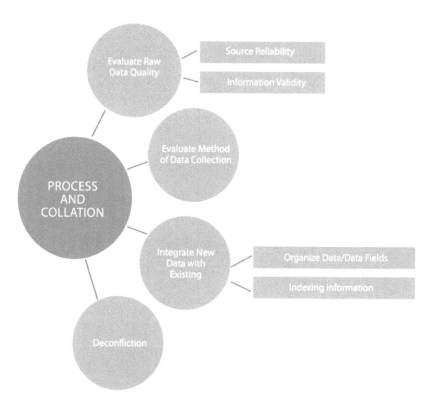

Figure 4-6: Example of Reliability and Validity Rating Scales

Source Reliability

| A
Completely Reliable | → | • No doubt of trustworthiness, authenticity
• The source is competent
• History of the source is completely reliable |

| B
Usually Reliable | → | • Some doubt of trustworthiness, authenticity
• Some doubt about competence
• Majority of the time a reliable source |

| C
Fairly Reliable | → | • Usually some doubt of authenticity, trust
• Usually some doubt about competence
• Reliable source some of the time |

| D
Not Usually Reliable | → | • Definite doubt about authenticity, trust
• Define doubt about competence
• History of occasional reliability |

| E
Unreliable | → | • Great doubt about authenticity, trust
• Great doubt about competence
• History of unreliable information |

| F
No Judgment | → | • Cannot be judged
• No information to base decision |

Information Validity

| 1
Confirmed | → | • Confirmed by other independent sources
• Logical in itself
• Agrees with other information on subject |

| 2
Probably True | → | • Not confirmed
• Logical in itself
• Agrees with other information on subject |

| 3
Possibly True | → | • Not confirmed
• Reasonably logical in itself
• Agrees somewhat with other information |

| 4
Doubtfully True | → | • Not confirmed
• Not illogical in itself
• Not believed when received, but possible |

| 5
Improbable Report | → | • The contrary is confirmed
• Is illogical in itself
• Contradicted by other information |

| 6
No Judgment | → | • Cannot be judged
• No information to base decision |

One of the first issues of information collection is the assessment of the *method* used to collect the data. When a law enforcement agency is collecting information, it must follow lawful processes; for example, information collected about a person should be consistent with constitutional standards (including the four exceptions[5] to the Fourth Amendment search warrant requirement). The issue of lawful collection methods is important for three reasons: First, it is a constitutional guarantee that law enforcement officers have sworn to uphold. Second, if there is a criminal prosecution of the intelligence target, critical evidence could be excluded from trial if the evidence was not collected in a lawful manner. Third, if a pattern emerges that information about individuals was collected on a consistent basis that does not meet constitutional standards, this may open the agency to civil liability for civil rights violations.

Not only is this assessment a professional obligation, it also is particularly important should the intelligence target be prosecuted. Once again, training should seek to ensure that the information was lawfully collected and the facts of the collection are carefully documented.

The third activity in the collation/processing phase is to integrate the new information with existing data. During this process, in consideration of all other information that has been collected, the following questions may be asked:

- Does it meet the criminal predicate test?
- Is the information relevant and material (as opposed to being just "interesting")?
- Does the information add new questions to the analysis?
- Does the information need corroboration?
- Does the information support the working hypotheses of the inquiry or does it suggest a new or alternative hypothesis?

The answers to these questions will help define requirements and directions for the inquiry. This process also includes organizing and indexing the data to standardize the data fields and enhance the ability to make accurate data comparisons.

A final activity during this phase is "deconfliction," the process or system used to determine whether multiple law enforcement agencies are conducting inquiries into the same person or crime. This is accomplished in several ways, including using deconfliction information systems such as the National Drug Pointer Index (NDPIX) managed by the Drug Enforcement Administration (DEA). The deconfliction process not only identifies if multiple inquiries exist, but a system like NDPIX also notifies each agency involved of the shared interest in the case and provides contact information. This is an information- and intelligence-sharing process that seeks to minimize conflicts between agencies and maximize the effectiveness of the inquiry.

In sum, the Processing/Collation phase of the Intelligence Cycle is important for two reasons: 1. It seeks to provide quality control of information through the process and 2. It provides important insights into defining intelligence requirements.

[5] These are: 1. Consent; 2. the Plain View Doctrine; 3. A search incidental to a lawful arrest; and 4. Exigent circumstance.

Analysis

Analysis is the heart of the Intelligence Process. Entire books have been written on analytic methodologies and the critical thinking process. The intent of the current discussion is not to repeat this information, but provide some insights into analytic responsibilities that will be of benefit to the intelligence consumer.

The analytic process is essentially the scientific approach to problem solving. It is the use of established research methodologies—both quantitative and qualitative—that seek to objectively integrate correlated variables in a body of raw data in order to derive an understanding of the phenomena under study. It is synergistic in nature; the completed analysis provides knowledge rather than a simple recitation of facts. The outcome, however, is only as good as 1. The quality of the raw information submitted for analysis and 2. The quality of the analysis. Effective training, policy direction, supervision, and an operational plan for the intelligence function are essential for the analytic process to produce robust and actionable intelligence.

The phrase "actionable intelligence" has two fundamental applications for law enforcement. The first is tactical, wherein the output of analysis must provide sufficient explicit information that operational units can develop some type of response. In some cases that response is minimal, such as providing indicators of terrorism or criminal activity for patrol officers to observe. In other cases, it may involve a complex operational activity to make arrests. The second application of actionable intelligence is strategic, describing changes in the threat picture of a jurisdiction or region; that is, the intelligence may describe changes in crime types, crime methodologies, or both.

The output of the analytic process is reports, referred to as *intelligence products.* During the course of the analysis, the intelligence analyst will prepare explicit inferences about the criminal enterprise in order to understand its effects. These are typically expressed in the form of *conclusions, forecasts,* and *estimates* that are explained in the products.

A *conclusion,* as the term infers, is a definitive statement about how a criminal enterprise operates, its key participants, and the criminal liability of each. A forecast[6] describes the expected implications of the criminal enterprise, the future of the enterprise, changes in the enterprise or its participants, and threats that are likely to emerge from the enterprise. An *estimate* focuses on monetary effects, changes in commodity transactions, and/or likely future effects of the criminal enterprise; for example, profits from a new criminal enterprise, economic losses associated with a terrorist attack, or the increase of contraband if new smuggling methods are used.

There are different consumers of intelligence, each of whom has somewhat different needs. Line officers need to have information that concisely identifies criminal indicators, suspects, addresses, crime methodologies, and vehicles thought to be associated with a criminal enterprise. Administrators and managers need information about the changing threat environment that has implications

[6] Sometimes the word "prediction" is used instead of forecast. Prediction is a definitive statement of the future that in reality is virtually impossible to determine. Intelligence analysis is probabilistic in nature; hence the term "forecast" is used to describe what is likely to occur in light of the currently known facts.

for the deployment of personnel and expenditure of resources. Analysts need a comprehensive package of information that includes raw data sources, methods, and intelligence requirements. Intelligence reports that contain little more than suppositions, assumptions, rumors, or alternative criminal scenarios are not "actionable."

Dissemination

An intelligence product has virtually no value unless the system is able to get the right information to the right people in a time frame that provides value to the report's content. Dissemination—or information sharing—seeks to accomplish this goal. Many issues could be discussed related to dissemination, including the various intelligence and information records systems, privacy issues, information system security issues, operations security of shared information, the means of dissemination, interoperability issues, and the *Global Justice Data Standards*.[7] However, the intent of the current discussion is to describe the general philosophy and rules of intelligence dissemination.

Pre-9/11, the general philosophy of intelligence dissemination tended to focus on "operations security;" that is, intelligence records were not widely disseminated out of the concern that critical information would fall into the wrong hands, thereby jeopardizing the inquiry as well as possibly jeopardizing undercover officers, informants, and collection methods. While these issues still remain important, the post-9/11 philosophy is radically different. Indeed, law enforcement seeks to place as much information in the hands of as many authorized people who need it to prevent threats from reaching fruition. Basically, the idea is that the more people who receive the information the greater the probability of identifying and interrupting a threat. Perhaps the critical question is, "Who is considered an authorized person?"

Right to know and need to know

Even with this changed philosophy, important rules of dissemination seek: 1. to protect individuals' civil rights and 2. maintain operations security as needed. To accomplish these goals, the first rules of dissemination provide criteria to determine who should receive the intelligence. The accepted standard has a two-pronged test:

1. Does the individual to which the information is to be disseminated have the *right to know* the information? This is determined by the recipient's official capacity and/or statutory authority to receive the information being sought.

2. Does the recipient have a bona fide *need to know* the information? The information to be disseminated is pertinent and necessary to the recipient in order to prevent or mitigate a threat or assist and support a criminal investigation.[8]

Intelligence products that provide information about criminal indicators and methodologies are intended to receive wide distribution so that officers are aware of these factors during the course of their daily activities. As a general rule, it can be assumed that anyone working in law enforcement meets the right-to-know and need-to-know tests for these types of intelligence. However,

[7] As a comprehensive resource, see it.ojp. gov.

[8] Adapted from: Law Enforcement Intelligence Unit. *Criminal Intelligence File Guidelines, Section IX: File Dissemination.* Sacramento, California: Law Enforcement Intelligence Unit, revised 2002.

intelligence reports related to a specific criminal inquiry that identifies individuals or organizations would have a significantly more limited dissemination. While all law enforcement officers would have the right to know this information, only those officers working on some aspect of the inquiry have the need to know the information.

With the changing intelligence philosophy and the recognized need to involve the private sector and nonlaw enforcement government personnel in the ISE, the application of *right to know* and *need to know* has changed somewhat from the pre-9/11 era.[9] For example, anyone in law enforcement has the *right to know* intelligence (by virtue of his or her employment). Similarly, a member of the National Guard or a Department of Homeland Security (DHS) intelligence analyst working in a state fusion center would also have the *right to know* intelligence by virtue of his or her assignment, even though he or she is not a law enforcement employee. In yet a different application, the corporate security director of a nuclear power plant would have the right to know intelligence that is related only specifically to the security director's responsibilities of protecting the plant.

Once again, because of the new intelligence philosophy a significantly broader range of law enforcement officers have the *need to know* intelligence. The rationale, as stated previously, is that all officers need to be aware of threats to increase the probability of stopping the threat. The need to know certain intelligence by nonlaw enforcement personnel should be determined on a case-by-case basis. For example, in all likelihood there is no need for a DHS analyst to know intelligence related to auto thefts; however, the DHS analyst would need to know the information related to a criminal enterprise smuggling cocaine from Colombia because of the value of communications between the DHS analyst and other federal agencies such as the DEA or Immigration and Customs Enforcement.

Third Agency Rule

Another information-sharing restriction is found in what is commonly called the Third Agency Rule. Essentially, if an officer receives intelligence from an intelligence source (such as a fusion center), that officer cannot disseminate the intelligence to a third party without permission from the original source. As an example, Officer Adam receives intelligence from the Central Fusion Center. Officer Adam cannot give the intelligence directly to Officer Baker without first gaining permission from the Central Fusion Center. This is a general rule—with some exceptions that will be discussed later—and it will be stated or applied differently between agencies. Consumers of intelligence need to be aware of the local applications of the Third Agency Rule.

There are two types of intelligence: case intelligence and intelligence products. Case intelligence identifies people; intelligence products provide general information about threats and indicators. For case intelligence, it should be assumed that the Third Agency Rule is intact, while for intelligence products, it may be assumed that the Third Agency Rule is waived. Fundamentally, the reason is that when individuals or organizations are not identified in intelligence products, civil rights do not attach. Again, a review of agency policy will determine the exact applications of the rule locally.

[9] A review of the goals and action steps in the *Information Sharing Environment Implementation Plan* clearly demonstrates the mandate for these additional intelligence consumers. See www.ise.gov/docs/ise-impplan-200611.pdf.

It should be reinforced that in law enforcement intelligence, both the right-to-know and need-to-know provisions as well as the Third Agency Rule, serve two purposes: 1. To protect individuals' civil rights and 2. To maintain operations security of intelligence inquiries.

Classified Information[10]

A great deal of detailed information has been written about classified information. For the most part, these regulations apply to the intelligence community and federal law enforcement. As a rule, unless working in a fusion center or assigned to a Joint Terrorism Task Force, most state, local, and tribal law enforcement (SLTLE) officers will not have security clearances or access to classified information; however, having a basic understanding of information classification provides perspective for the following discussion. Essentially, classified information is a designation of information that is critical to the security of the United States. Explicit processes and procedures for classifying, storing, providing access, and generally handling this information have sanctions, including federal criminal violations, if the processes are violated.

There has been a great deal of debate about the need for security clearances for SLTLE personnel. Law enforcement executives and managers argue that they need a security clearance to have access to information about threats within their jurisdiction. On this same theme, a report from the Congressional Research Service stated the following:

> … these officials might need some access to classified information, for example, "real time" intelligence information concerning terrorism threats, to adequately plan, coordinate, and execute homeland security activities.[11]

Federal authorities respond that they will provide all information needed to SLTLE personnel about threats within a community—a response met with some skepticism.[12]

Another issue to be aware of is that federal security clearances are not universal; for example, if a law enforcement executive has a security clearance from the Department of Defense as a result of his or her military reserve status or if an officer has a DEA clearance that was investigated by the U.S. Office of Personnel Management as part of a Organized Crime Drug Enforcement Task Force, those clearances often are not recognized by the FBI for having access to classified information for which the FBI is the custodian. These are issues about which the reader should be aware—they remain to be resolved.

Chapter 10 discusses a range of issues related to classified information and security clearances. Suffice it to note at this point that classified information may be disseminated only to an individual who has the appropriate type of security clearance, which establishes the right to know. The need to know still must be determined before dissemination, even if the individual has the appropriate level of clearance.

[10] For detailed information on classified information see the Information Security Oversight Office at www.archives.gov/isoo/policy-documents/eo-12958-amendment.html#1.2.

[11] Reese, Shawn. State and Local Homeland Security: Unresolved Issues for the 109th Congress. Washington, D.C.: Congressional Research Service, Library of Congress, 2005, p. 11.

[12] In a joint publication by the Major Cities Chiefs Association and the Major County Sheriffs' Association, a resolution to handle the backlog of security clearances applications for SLTLE personnel was offered as follows:

Chiefs and sheriffs will join with DHS to implement a comprehensive plan to eliminate the backlog of pending applications and expedite the security clearance process. Features of the plan include:

1. Reduction in requests for TOP SECRET/Sensitive Compartmented Information (TS/SCI) clearances and accesses.

2. Focus primarily on faster and more useful SECRET-level clearances.

3. Law enforcement agencies propose to conduct background investigations and expedite adjudication of SECRET level clearances.

4. DHS agrees to provide training on clearance process.

5. DHS agrees to assist major law enforcement agencies in expediting priority security clearances.

6. Per federal statutes/regulations, DHS commits to accept clearance granted by other agencies.

Source: Intelligence and Information Sharing: DHS and Law Enforcement. Major Cities Chiefs Association and Major County Sheriffs' Association, 2007, p. 3. (Unpublished report.)

Sensitive But Unclassified Information (SBU)/Controlled Unclassified Information (CUI)

SBU—or "tear line"[13]—Information does not have any formal restrictions, clearances, or sanctions as found with classified information. Rather, the SBU designation is more akin to a professional responsibility that is expected to be honored in light of one's professional obligations. While most SLTLE officers will not have a security clearance, virtually all will have access to SBU information. SBU information may have been previously classified but typically "sources" and "methods of collection" have been removed, thereby declassifying the information and rendering it SBU. In other cases, the inherent sensitivity of the information based on its character, such as an analysis of terrorists' tactics that produces indicators of terrorist activity, may warrant the SBU label.

Among the many forms of SBU labels, particularly at the federal level, the two most commonly used in law enforcement are *Law Enforcement Sensitive* (LES) and *For Official Use Only* (FOUO). As a general rule, LES information may be shared with anyone in the law enforcement community (sworn or nonsworn) who has the right to know and a need to know the information. FOUO means that the information may be shared with anyone who has the right to know and the need to know. For example, information about a threat to a nuclear power plant would be shared with the corporate security director and manager of the plant. These are general rules which, in practice, have no enforceable sanctions should they be violated. Rather, they provide guidance on disseminating sensitive information and rely on the professional decisions of those who receive the information to maintain security.

Because of the lack of explicit guidance and the wide range of SBU dissemination labels, there is both uncertainty and inconsistency in dissemination processes. As a result, one of the mandates of the Intelligence Reform and Terrorism Prevention Act of 2004 was to develop the ISE which included, as one of the ISE program manager's responsibilities, the creation of a labeling protocol for SBU information that had a consistent meaning and application across the entire ISE. This is particularly true given the important role of sharing unclassified terrorist information with state, local, and tribal law enforcement. There is a need to disseminate information; that is, share important information with others, but that information sharing must be controlled—protecting information and ensuring that it is not disseminated inadvertently.

As a result, the federal government is in the process of changing SBU label markings with a new information control model called *Controlled Unclassified Information* (CUI). A number of new factors with CUI provide more specific and universal direction than has existed with SBU labels. Although Chapter 10 contains a discussion of these details, it should be noted for purposes of dissemination in the Intelligence Process that there are controls for establishing the right to know for unclassified information that need to be safeguarded.

[13] The "tear line" refers to a classified report where there is a summary of the report at the bottom that excludes information about the sources of information and/or methods of information collection. This summary may be torn off the report; hence, it is referred to as tear line information and it is SBU.

Reevaluation

The classic definition of a "system" is a series of interconnected component processes that have an interrelated purpose of which a change in one component will affect the other components. The Intelligence Process is indeed a system. As each component—or phase—processes information, it will affect the body of knowledge in the other components as related to the intelligence inquiry. Just like any system, homeostasis—that is, a "steady state" of the system—must be maintained. This is the purpose of reevaluation: To ensure that all information is being processed in a comprehensive manner, the Intelligence Process must be ongoing with each new piece of information in the process being added to the full body of new knowledge to aid in developing the most precise intelligence possible. Reevaluation also serves as a measurement to determine if the intelligence products created by this process have value. Are threats accurately identified? Are all components of the Intelligence Process functioning as intended? Are effective operational interventions able to be developed based on the intelligence?

Conclusion

This chapter described the Intelligence Process (or cycle) as depicted in the *National Criminal Intelligence Sharing Plan*. The introduction of key terminology and concepts provides perspective on how they relate to the Intelligence Process and, as will be seen, the role of the Intelligence Process in other intelligence initiatives, including Intelligence-Led Policing.

Chapter Annex 4-1: Federal Bureau of Investigation Intelligence Cycle

This illustration is based on an actual case. It demonstrates the interrelationship between the two types of intelligence.

The FBI Intelligence Cycle

The Federal Bureau of Investigation (FBI) Directorate of Intelligence (DI) has significantly different intelligence responsibilities than state, local, or tribal law enforcement agencies. This difference is a result of its national criminal intelligence responsibilities and the FBI's national security responsibilities. One model of the Intelligence Cycle is not "better" than the other; rather, they are just slightly different approaches based on different operational responsibilities. The following brief description of the FBI DI Intelligence Cycle will provide an understanding of the FBI's approach and terminology that can be valuable for SLTLE personnel when they are communicating with the FBI's intelligence personnel.

The Intelligence Cycle is the process of developing unrefined data into polished intelligence for use by policymakers. It consists of the six steps described in the following paragraphs. The graphic below shows the circular nature of this process, although movement between the steps is fluid. Intelligence uncovered at one step may require going back to an earlier step before moving forward

Requirements are identified information needs—what we must know to safeguard the nation. Intelligence requirements are established by the Director of National Intelligence according to guidance received from the President and the National and Homeland Security Advisors. Requirements are developed based on critical information required to protect the United States from national security and criminal threats. The Attorney General and the Director of the FBI participate in the formulation of national intelligence requirements.

Planning and Direction is management of the entire effort, from identifying the need for information to delivering an intelligence product to a consumer. It involves implementation plans to satisfy requirements levied on the FBI, as well as identifying specific collection requirements based on FBI needs. Planning and direction also is responsive to the end of the cycle, because current and finished intelligence, which supports decision-making, generates new requirements. The Executive Assistant Director for the National Security Branch leads intelligence planning and direction for the FBI.

Collection is the gathering of raw information based on requirements. Activities such as interviews, technical and physical surveillances, human source operation, searches, and liaison relationships collect intelligence.

Processing and Exploitation involves converting the vast amount of collected information into a form usable by analysts. This is done through a variety of methods including decryption, language translations, and data reduction. Processing includes entering raw data into databases where the data can be used in the analysis process.

Analysis and Production is the conversion of raw information into intelligence. It includes integrating, evaluating, and analyzing available data, and preparing intelligence products. The information's reliability, validity, and relevance are evaluated and weighed. The information is logically integrated, put into context, and used to produce intelligence. This includes both "raw" and finished intelligence. Raw intelligence is often referred to as "the dots"—individual pieces of information disseminated individually. Finished intelligence reports "connect the dots" by putting information into context and drawing conclusions about its implications.

Dissemination—the last step—is the distribution of raw or finished intelligence to the consumers whose needs initiated the intelligence requirements. The FBI disseminates information in three standard formats: *Intelligence Information Reports*, *FBI Intelligence Bulletins*, and *FBI Intelligence Assessments*. FBI intelligence products are provided daily to the Attorney General, the President, and to customers throughout the FBI and in other agencies. These FBI intelligence customers use the information to make operational, strategic, and policy decisions that may lead to the levying of more requirements, thereby continuing the FBI Intelligence Cycle.

Chapter 5:
The Concept of Intelligence-Led Policing (ILP)

The Concept of Intelligence-Led Policing (ILP)

Participants in the International Association of Chiefs of Police (IACP)/Office of Community Oriented Policing Services (the COPS Office) 2002 intelligence summit recommended the adoption of Intelligence-Led Policing (ILP) by America's state, local, and tribal law enforcement (SLTLE) agencies in the post-9/11 era. ILP was envisioned as a tool for sharing information that would aid law enforcement agencies in identifying threats and developing responses to prevent those threats from reaching fruition in America's communities.[1] This was reinforced by a recommendation in the *National Criminal Intelligence Sharing Plan*[2] (NCISP) to adopt ILP and has been echoed broadly by law enforcement leaders and reflected in new programming by the U.S. Department of Justice and the U. S. Department of Homeland Security.

The challenge, however, is that there are differing views of the ILP concept and its application. Indeed, there is a movement toward the adoption of ILP without a universally accepted definition or a manual of practice. The intent of the discussion in this chapter is to provide a perspective of ILP in the context of contemporary developments in law enforcement intelligence, integrating the more commonly accepted applications of ILP, and particularly focusing on the processes required to implement the concept.

Implementation of ILP requires a realistic understanding of the current intelligence capacity across the spectrum of American law enforcement and a flexible approach to meet the capabilities and needs of major cities and counties as well as small departments and rural communities.

Conceptual Foundations

The NCISP states, "The primary purpose of *Intelligence-Led Policing* is to provide public safety decision-makers [with] the information they need to protect the lives of our citizens."[3] How is this accomplished? There is no manual of practice for ILP because, like community policing, it must be tailored to the characteristics of the individual agency. ILP may be characterized as follows:

> …an underlying philosophy of how intelligence fits into the operations of a law enforcement organization. Rather than being simply an information clearinghouse that has been appended to the organization, ILP provides strategic integration of intelligence into the overall mission of the organization.[4]

The concept of ILP must be created through an inclusive development process to ensure that it is integrated with an agency's goals and functions, its capabilities, and the characteristics of both the agency and the jurisdiction it serves. It is not an add-on responsibility of the agency but an adaptation to more efficiently and effectively deal with multijurisdictional threats and serious crime that touch communities. There are no shortcuts in the process—it requires creativity, organizational introspection, and a willingness to adapt the organization. The following discussions provide a framework for understanding the diverse aspects

[1] www.theiacp.org/Portals/0/pdfs/ Publications/intelsharingreport.pdf

[2] Global Intelligence Working Group. *National Criminal Intelligence Sharing Plan.* Washington, D.C.: U. S. Office of Justice Programs, 2003.

[3] Ibid. p. v.

[4] Carter, David L. *Law Enforcement Intelligence: A Guide for State, Local and Tribal Law Enforcement Agencies.* Washington, D.C.: Office of Community Oriented Policing Services, U.S. Department of Justice, 2004, page 41.

of the ILP concept. Building on this understanding, the next chapter (Chapter 6) discusses the policy and organizational dynamics necessary to effectively implement ILP.

Defining ILP

There is no universally accepted definition of ILP, although the components of most definitions are the same, or at least similar. In 2009, the Bureau of Justice Assistance (BJA), in partnership with the Global Justice Information Sharing Institute, produced two definitions of ILP in which the conceptual foundation was articulated as building on the lessons of Problem-Oriented Policing and CompStat and applying these principles to a threat-based environment of multijurisdictional complex criminality. The conceptual foundation embraces recent initiatives in law enforcement intelligence, ranging from the operation of the Regional Information Sharing System (RISS), to the products of the Global Justice Information Sharing Initiative, to the development of the National Information Exchange Model.

In the document, the BJA states that ILP is:

> ILP can be defined as a collaborative law enforcement approach combining problem-solving policing, information sharing and police accountability, with enhanced intelligence operations.

However, for the purposes of their document, BJA narrowed the definition to the following:

> ILP is executive implementation of the intelligence cycle to support proactive decision making for resource allocation and crime prevention.[5] In order to successfully implement this business process, police executives must have clearly defined priorities as part of their policing strategies.

Building on these foundations, this author proposes an operational definition of ILP as follows:

> The collection and analysis of information related to crime and conditions that contribute to crime, resulting in an actionable intelligence product intended to aid law enforcement in developing tactical responses to threats and/or strategic planning related to emerging or changing threats.

Breaking the definition down to its critical components will provide a better understanding.

Collection

An essential part of the intelligence process is the collection of raw information that may be used in the analysis. Collection should be focused to identify and understand threats that emerge in a jurisdiction. This focus, often determined by an analyst who will define intelligence requirements, is based on information received from officers, confidential sources, and citizens in the form of tips, leads, and Suspicious Activity Reports. The key point is that collection seeks raw information within defined parameters that is essential for effective analysis.

Analysis

Analysis is the scientific approach to problem solving. It relies on deductive and inductive reasoning to define requirements and forecast threats. Analysis may be

[5] Global Justice Information Sharing Initiative. Navigating Your Agency's Path to Intelligence-Led Policing. Washington, DC: U.S. Department of Justice, Office of Justice Programs, Bureau of Justice Assistance, 2009, p. 2.

quantitative, notably for strategic analysis, but frequently it is qualitative, for both tactical and strategic analysis. The Office of the Director of National Intelligence (ODNI) has stated that analysis is "a process in the production of intelligence in which intelligence information is subjected to systematic examination in order to identify significant facts and derive conclusions."[6] The ODNI goes on to make the following distinctions between raw information and analyzed information (that is, intelligence):

- Raw information:
    - Provides input
    - Builds awareness
- Analyzed information (intelligence):
    - Provides understanding
    - Reduces uncertainty
    - Enables better decisions

The analytic process is synergistic, providing integrated meaning and deriving knowledge from diverse raw facts. Moreover, analysis is used to define "intelligence gaps" and articulate "requirements."

Crime and Conditions that Contribute to Crime

ILP focuses on threats and it becomes essential to identify variables within a community and the surrounding region that support the generation and maturation of crime. These variables can be wide-ranging: The emergence of organized criminal elements within the region who traffic in drugs or guns; the emergence of an extremist group that articulates hate or violence; conflict within a region that may be a breeding ground for violence between racial, ethnic, or religious groups; and a variety of unique characteristics that are idiosyncratic to a given community, such as proximity to an international border. It is important that the information collected provide insight into the existence of the conditions, factors that will exacerbate the conditions and individuals who may be instrumental in exploiting the conditions to commit terrorism or crime.

Actionable Intelligence

Paraphrasing former FBI Executive Assistant Director for Intelligence Maureen Baginski, intelligence helps law enforcement officers make decisions. Essentially, for intelligence to be useful it must provide direction for developing and executing plans. A law enforcement agency must be able to take an intelligence report and implement some type of activity that will prevent or mitigate crime. This means that the intelligence produced by an analyst will drive operational responses to, and strategic planning for, threats.

With actionable intelligence, a law enforcement agency has sufficient information to develop preventive interventions to threats. The report may describe either imminent threats to a community or region, wanted persons who may pose threats, or threat methodologies about which law enforcement officers should be aware. The basic premise is that the agency must be able to use the information in some manner. Moreover, actionable intelligence should ensure that the right information is placed into the hands of the people who can do something about the threat.

[6] Ramsey, Theresa. *Global Maritime Intelligence Integration (GMII) Enterprise.* PowerPoint Presentation. Washington, D.C.: Office of the Director of National Intelligence, May 9, 2007.

Tactical Responses to Threats

Both tactical and strategic intelligence are extensions of actionable intelligence. Depending on the nature of the threat, a wide array of tactical responses may be deemed appropriate, ranging from increasing mass transit security procedures to being aware of suspicious activities at a potential intelligence target. Tactical intelligence is all about prevention: Using information related to terrorism and crime threats for strategies that will eliminate or mitigate short-term and immediate threats. Tactical intelligence is epitomized by the question, "What type of operational response can be developed using this intelligence?"

Strategic Planning Related to Emerging or Changing Threats

Threats within a community typically change over time. Strategic analysis is used primarily for planning and resource allocation to understand the changing nature of the threat picture. Information is provided to decision-makers about the changing nature, characteristics, and methodologies of threats and emerging threat idiosyncrasies so that they can develop response strategies and reallocate resources. If, for example, a community has never had a problem with right-to-life extremists and a new clinic opens that offers abortion procedures, a strategic analysis may provide insight into whether the clinic and its personnel will be subject to any type of threat by extremist groups.

By using strategic analysis, plans may be developed to either prevent a threat from maturing or mitigate the threat should it emerge. It is epitomized by the question, "What future plans and resources must be configured, and how must they be configured, to meet threats defined in the strategic analysis?"

Fundamental Perspectives on the History of ILP: The British Experience

To refine our vision of ILP, context is needed. Specifically, one needs to understand the dynamics within the American law enforcement environment that will influence the implementation of ILP as well as limitations to adopting the British National Intelligence Model for U.S. law enforcement.

Perspective 1: The Current State of American Law Enforcement Intelligence

Some evidence suggests that ILP can provide an important element to community security to prevent (or at least mitigate) terrorism, violence, criminal extremism, and complex criminality. This author agrees. The concern, however, is how ILP is implemented. At one meeting, a strong ILP advocate urged law enforcement leaders to take the Nike® approach and "just do it." The problem is that American law enforcement is neither structurally nor substantively ready to support the ILP infrastructure. Just like a building, the foundation must first be in place—most American law enforcement agencies have gathered some bricks, but they are a long way from completing the foundation.

[7] Also, as a means of comparison, this author has provided intelligence training to law enforcement agencies in Europe, Asia, and Australia.

During the past 20 years, this author has provided intelligence training to literally thousands of law enforcement personnel representing hundreds of agencies at all levels of government from every state and most territories.[7] Yet this is a small proportion of American law enforcement. What has been learned is that agencies that have an intelligence capacity are the exception, rather than the rule. Moreover, what is commonly called an intelligence unit or capacity in most agencies is, in practice, more of a hybrid organizational entity that may be doing crime analysis and/or investigative support. In many cases, there is also the integration of crime analysis and intelligence analysis despite the fact that these are different.[8] In other cases, there may be multiple intelligence capacities that are function-specific, such as gang intelligence, drug intelligence, and/or organized crime intelligence. Once again, many of these activities are more akin to investigative support than to intelligence.

Historically, the vast majority of American law enforcement agencies have had no intelligence capacity or training on the intelligence function and processes—typically, they were viewed as something needed only by the largest agencies. Of the agencies that had an intelligence capacity, the legacy has been somewhat problematic. Early law enforcement initiatives typically did not conduct analyses. Instead, they kept dossiers on individuals who were "suspicious" or were deemed to be threats of some sort, often based on intuitive, rather than empirical, threat criteria. In the 1960s and 1970s, many agencies were sued under federal civil rights legislation[9] for maintaining intelligence records on people who had not committed crimes but were engaged in behaviors and ideologies that were deemed to be unconventional or un-American. While these practices generally no longer exist, the legacy lives on, with many members of the public remaining suspicious of current law enforcement intelligence activities.

Beyond the civil rights issues, the intelligence function was often ill-defined, typically remaining out of the mainstream of state and local law enforcement activities. There were few analysts and many were poorly trained, often inheriting the title of "analyst" as a result of longevity, not expertise. It was often difficult to distinguish what the intelligence unit, as an organizational unit, contributed to the total law enforcement mission. While there were certainly exceptions to such a characterization, it was the status quo for most American law enforcement intelligence initiatives. Although this has changed dramatically, the history remains a difficult obstacle to overcome.

This change began in the post-9/11 era, leading to an increased awareness of intelligence and growing intelligence capacities, In particular, this was the result of the IACP/COPS Office intelligence summit; the efforts of the Global Intelligence Working Group (GIWG); the release of the NCISP; the creation of the Criminal Intelligence Coordinating Council (CICC); the growth of intelligence fusion centers; and the wide array of new law enforcement intelligence training programs typically available at no charge to SLTLE agencies. Nonetheless, this is a long way from being comprehensive. The next step of being active participants in the Information Sharing Environment (ISE) is, in reality, barely on the horizon for most SLTLE agencies.

Increasing numbers of agencies have some form of intelligence capacity, yet comparatively, the numbers are still small. Moreover, many agencies—even

[8] Crime analysis assesses the interactive effects and covariance of explicit variables of crimes that have occurred in order to determine a perpetrator's methodologies with the intent to clear the crimes and prevent future incidents by apprehending the perpetrator. Intelligence analysis deals with threats, whether from terrorism, criminal extremism, or organized crime, through the analysis of information that suggests a threat, the identification of intelligence requirements, and the use of both target and vulnerability assessments, with the intent of preventing the threat from reaching fruition.

[9] Specifically, 42 United States Code, Section 1983—Civil Action for Deprivation of Civil Rights.

moderate-sized departments—either do not see the need for an intelligence capacity or feel they cannot justify devoting resources to develop an intelligence capacity because of competing demands, notably, increasing violent crime rates and managing calls for service. For the vast majority of these agencies, the chief executive—as well as others in the chain of command—typically relies on historically based assumptions about intelligence and does not understand the rapid evolution and value of the modern law enforcement intelligence function. In light of these factors, there is limited motivation for such agencies to adopt ILP. The issue is not that agencies do not want to participate in fusion centers and the ISE; they often do not see the value in light of other responsibilities.

Based on these issues, an earlier point warrants repeating: Most American law enforcement agencies do not have the foundation to implement ILP. An intelligence foundation must first be constructed.

Perspective 2: The British National Intelligence Model and Challenges in Adapting It to U.S. Law Enforcement

When seeking to make use of a new concept, we often look to other models in an attempt to learn what works and adopt (or adapt) that practice. The British have a longer and more sophisticated legacy in law enforcement intelligence than U.S. law enforcement. All provincial British constabularies have had some form of a fairly long-standing intelligence unit to deal with organized crime, drugs, and other complex crimes unique to their jurisdictions. As an example, many of the British constabularies have a Football Intelligence Unit to deal with hooliganism at soccer matches. At a national level, the National Drugs Intelligence Unit was created in the 1980s to deal with the significant increase in transnational drug trafficking and associated crime, such as money laundering. The service relied on personnel assigned (that is, "seconded") from police forces throughout England and Wales. In 1992, the unit was expanded and renamed the National Criminal Intelligence Service (NCIS) to deal with all forms of organized crime. In particular, the NCIS evolved in response to the changing political environment associated with the European Union (EU), where, among other factors, immigration and customs checkpoints were eliminated for persons traveling between the EU member countries. In 2006, a new agency was created, the Serious Organised Crime Agency (SOCA), that integrated the NCIS along with a national investigative body, the National Crime Squad, and the drug enforcement functions of Her Majesty's Revenue and Customs Service.[10]

[10] SOCA is an intelligence-led agency responsible for dealing with major organized crime. The United Kingdom (U.K.) Security Service (MI5) is responsible for dealing with threats to U.K. national security with the greatest emphasis on terrorism, but also espionage, including domestic intelligence. The Secret Intelligence Service (MI6) is responsible for collecting intelligence outside of the U.K.

In the 1990s, the British government began implementing a business plan philosophy for all elements of government service. It had two fundamental initiatives: either "privatise" portions of government service, or apply a business model to the remaining government services. The move had wide-ranging effects: for example, the British National Rail Service—BritRail— was sold in pieces to various private companies. Similarly, local governments "privatised" such functions as vehicle maintenance and the janitorial service. The national police training function in England and Wales was also changed to a quasiprivate organization called CENTREX, which in April 2007 evolved to be part of the

National Police Improvement Agency (NPIA). The point is that the mandate to use business processes permeated virtually every aspect of British government, including the police.

As part of this movement, in the late 1990s, NCIS, with advice from Her Majesty's Inspectorate of Constabulary[11] (HMIC), developed the British National Intelligence Model[12] (NIM), which was initially released in 2000 and formally adopted in 2002 as accepted policy by the British Association of Chief Police Officers (ACPO), which is a national police policymaking body. The NIM followed the government policy of using a business process model to deal with crime control.

The adoption of the NIM by ACPO meant that the chief constables of the 43 provincial police forces in England and Wales agreed to adopt the NIM and adapt it to meet the needs of their policing area.[13] The intelligence function within the constabularies largely deals with violent crime, football hooliganism, nonserious (local) organized crime, and unique local recurring crime problems.

The British police movement to ILP in accordance with the NIM has not been easy. Many did not understand the concept because it required a reallocation of resources and added a significant analytic component to each police force. The NIM was criticized by many as being an esoteric model that created a great deal of data and new processes that were not providing good value for money. Its full implementation has been much slower than anticipated, and as one might assume, some of the police forces have embraced the concept much more openly than others, who, in some cases, are using the NIM largely in name only.

Despite these problems, there have also been important successes as a result of the NIM. Many lessons learned from the NIM can be adopted in the United States, and a unique body of model practices, including analytic models, are available from the HMIC[14] (of course, needing adaption to the United States). American law enforcement agencies, however, have a significantly different experience in law enforcement intelligence that prohibits wide-scale adoption of British ILP, with some notable exceptions in the predominantly larger U.S. major cities and counties. Some perspective will provide greater understanding.

As mentioned previously, England and Wales have 43 police forces, the result of the amalgamation of many smaller police agencies in the 1960s. The smallest of these constabularies has around 900 sworn constables who are policing sizeable geographic areas that have both urban and rural characteristics. Most of the agencies have 1,200 to 1,600 sworn personnel. While not a national police force, national standards apply to all agencies for training, promotion, operations, and salary. Indeed, personnel may transfer laterally between the constabularies.

Given the size of these police forces and their reasonable operating budgets,[15] all have the resources to hire analysts and the flexibility to reassign personnel to meet the needs of a comprehensive new initiative such as ILP. This is not meant to infer that the constabularies are flush with money and people; rather, one finds significantly more flexibility, resources, and diverse expertise in large agencies than in the small departments typically found in the United States. Moreover,

[11] The HMIC is an organization in the British Home Office responsible for inspecting the British police forces to ensure that they are efficient organizations using "good practice" and providing "good value for money" in their service.

[12] More detail on the National Intelligence Model can be found in the ACPO document at www.acpo.police.uk/asp/policies/Data/nim2005.pdf.

[13] England and Wales have 43 provincial constabularies, whose chief constables are responsible to the local police authority (somewhat akin to a board of police commissions). The commissioner of the London Metropolitan Police reports to the British Home Secretary and has much broader authority and flexibility. While ACPO policy is not binding on the London Metropolitan Police, it has also adopted the NIM. An additional police service, the City of London Police, which is the smallest police agency in the U.K., is responsible for a small geographic area known as "the square mile" that largely encompasses the London financial district.

[14] Go to the HMIC web site at inspectorates.homeoffice.gov.uk/hmic and search for "intelligence."

[15] The national budget, through the Home Office, provides 51 percent of the funding for each provincial police force; 49 percent comes from local funds. This permits the Home Office to exert greater influence for national standards and priorities, although in practice, each chief constable retains significant autonomy.

having a solid history of sophisticated law enforcement intelligence analysis, the British police service was able to adopt the NIM and ILP with greater ease.

Comparing U.S. and U.K. Law Enforcement Intelligence

Compared with the British police structure, America's roughly 18,000 law enforcement agencies, most of which have 10 or fewer sworn officers, have diverse policing standards both between and within states. They often have limited budgets, all of which typically come from local funds, with some exceptions in the form of short-term federal grants. Federal standards and recommendations are largely unenforceable unless tied explicitly to special conditions in a grant.

In light of these radical differences and the significantly different history of law enforcement intelligence, when one compares U.S. and U.K. policing, it is unreasonable to assume that the basic practices of the NIM, as found in the United Kingdom, and, by extension, ILP, can be implemented effectively in the United States on a short-term wholesale basis. In America, we need to start at a far more basic level. A functional model of ILP must be developed that has both the flexibility and applicability to the American law enforcement landscape.

At the outset, ILP should be viewed as a philosophy, not a process. Indeed, American law enforcement agencies should rely on this philosophy to develop new intelligence-based processes that functionally balance each agency's jurisdictions, characteristics, and resources. The lessons learned from community policing can be a valuable guide.

Developing ILP in a law enforcement agency requires two developmental activities: 1. Devising the information collection framework to manage threats within a jurisdiction and 2. Developing the organizational infrastructure to support the ILP initiative. These will be discussed in detail in Chapter 6.

ILP And Community Policing, Problem Solving, and CompStat

A common concern expressed by police executives is that the shift toward ILP—largely the result of increased counterterrorism responsibilities—may require a shift of resources away from community policing. It becomes a question of how community policing and ILP are integrated. As will be seen, there are more commonalities between the two than one may intuitively expect. Indeed, new dimensions of ILP depend on strong community relationships. Crime will continue to be a critical responsibility for the police as will the need for community support. Moreover, with increased social tension resulting from the homeland security environment, the need is even greater to maintain a close, interactive dialog between law enforcement and the community.

Community policing has developed skills in many law enforcement officers that directly support new ILP responsibilities: The scientific approach to problem solving, environmental scanning, effective communications with the public, fear reduction, and community mobilization to deal with problems are among the important attributes community policing brings to this challenge. The NCISP observed these factors, noting the following:

> Over the past decade, simultaneous to federally led initiatives to improve intelligence gathering, thousands of community-policing officers have been building close and productive relationships with the citizens they serve. The benefits of these relationships are directly related to information and intelligence sharing: COP officers have immediate and unfettered access to local, neighborhood information as it develops. Citizens are aware of, and seek out COP officers to provide them with new information that may be useful to criminal interdiction or long-term problem solving. The positive nature of COP/citizen relationships promotes a continuous and reliable transfer of information from one to the other. It is time to maximize the potential for community-policing efforts to serve as a gateway of locally based information to prevent terrorism, and all other crimes.[16]

Furthermore, the Office of Domestic Preparedness Guidelines for Homeland Security describe the roles community policing has in the intelligence process. These include the following:

- Providing examples and materials that may aid in the recognition of terrorism to community policing contacts to make members of the community aware of those actions, behaviors, and events that constitute "suspicious."

- Organizing community meetings to emphasize prevention strategies, vigilance, and public awareness.

- Ensuring that members of the community are aware of the means of, and processes for, relaying observed data to police officers and police organizations, just as they are, or should be, aware of methods to relay information to community policing officers.

- Encouraging prevention, proactive policing, and close working relationships between the police and the community.[17]

These factors precipitated the development of ILP as an underlying philosophy of how intelligence fits into the operations of a law enforcement organization. Rather than being simply an information clearinghouse that has been appended to the organization, ILP provides strategic integration of intelligence into the overall mission of the organization. In many ways, ILP is a new dimension of community policing, building on tactics and methodologies developed during years of community policing experimentation. Some comparisons illustrate this point. Both community policing and ILP rely on these activities:

- Information Management

    - Community policing—Information gained from citizens helps define the parameters of community problems.

    - ILP—Information input is the essential ingredient for intelligence analysis.

- Two-way Communications with the Public

    - Community policing—Information is sought from the public about offenders. Communicating critical information to the public aids in preventing crime and reducing fear.

[16] it.ojp.gov/ncisp

[17] www.ojp.usdoj.gov/odp/docs/ODPPrev1. pdf

- ILP—Communications from the public can provide valuable information for the intelligence cycle. When threats are defined with specific information, communicating critical information to citizens may help prevent a terrorist attack and, like community policing, will reduce fear.

- Scientific Data Analysis
  - Community policing—Crime analysis is a critical ingredient in the CompStat[18] process.
  - ILP—Intelligence analysis is the critical ingredient for threat management.
- Problem Solving
  - Community policing—Problem solving is used to reconcile community conditions that are precursors to crime and disorder.
  - ILP—The same process is used for intelligence to reconcile factors related to vulnerable targets and trafficking of illegal commodities.

The importance of these factors is illustrated in the comments of FBI Director Robert Mueller in announcing an increased concern for terrorism at major national events during the summer of 2004. When referring to the photographs of seven terror suspects believed to be in the United States, Director Mueller stated:

> We need the support of the American people … to cooperate when called upon, as agents will be reaching out to many across the nation to help gather information and intelligence … to be aware of your surroundings and report anything suspicious … to "BOLO" [Be On the Lookout] for those pictured above. … Have you seen them in your communities? Have you heard that someone might be helping them to hide? Do you have any idea where they might be? If so, we need you to come forward.[19]

These words reflect the operational essence of the interrelationship of law enforcement intelligence and community policing. Like community policing, ILP requires an investment of effort by all components of the organization as well as the community. Gone are the days when intelligence units operated in relative anonymity. Based on the precepts of the ILP philosophy and the standards of the NCISP, law enforcement intelligence is an organization-wide responsibility that relies on a symbiotic relationship with residents.

Comparing ILP and CompStat

The CompStat process, with its origins in the New York Police Department, has been an important tool for law enforcement agencies to effectively deal with crime trends on a timely basis. The process has been adopted in varying forms and with consistent success by many midsized and large law enforcement agencies across the United States and in several foreign countries. A solid foundation of research supports CompStat as a crime-management tool that demonstrates the value of innovative approaches to law enforcement problems.[20]

As law enforcement personnel grapple with understanding ILP, many have suggested that it is the same as CompStat. Certainly, there are important similarities that will help in the adoption of ILP; however, there are also important substantive differences that must be recognized. At the heart of the matter is

[18] For a good contemporary discussion of CompStat, see: Shane, Jon, "CompStat Process." *FBI Law Enforcement Bulletin* 73 (2) (April 2004): 12–23.

[19] www.fbi.gov

[20] A great deal of research and literature can be found at www.ncjrs.org. Use the search utility for "CompStat."

the fact that CompStat and ILP are different because of a number of functional variables that are illustrated in Figure 5-1.

As can be seen, ILP is concerned with "all crimes and all threats," not just terrorism; however, the nature of crime that ILP focuses on typically is multijurisdictional and often complex criminality, such as criminal enterprises.

The value of CompStat is its identification of emerging, significant crime series or serious crime within a jurisdiction (that is, hot spots), based on a timely analysis of incident reports. The analysis of data captured by crime reporting can provide important information—such as geographical parameters and modus operandi—that can be used to forecast continued criminal incidents in the immediate future, aid in problem solving, and provide descriptive information, such as behaviors, targets, and criminal instruments that operational units may use to apprehend perpetrators, disrupt criminal activity, or alter crime-generating environments.

Conversely, ILP focuses on threats rather than crimes that have occurred (although a threat may also include a threat emerging from a crime series, such as a serial murder). The threat information may be derived from Suspicious Activity Reports filed by an officer, tips and leads submitted by community members, significant changes in sociodemographics within a region or other indicators (some of which may be collateral crimes) that reasonably suggest the presence or emergence of a serious multijurisdictional crime problem. Rather than analyze information and evidence derived from incident reports, the intelligence analyst must define intelligence requirements consisting of information that the analyst needs to more definitively identify the threat and factors that are contributing to the threat's evolution.

Similarly, to be effective, both community policing and ILP require feedback on information analysis—whether it is crime analysis or intelligence analysis—to be consistently informed of potential problems or threats that may be encountered during the course of a shift.

In this regard, what kind of information do street officers need from the intelligence unit? Ideally, intelligence analysis should address four broad questions:[21]

1. Who poses threats? This response identifies and describes people in movements or ideologies who pose threats to community safety.

2. Who's doing what with whom? This includes the identities, descriptions, and characteristics of conspirators or people who provide logistics in support of terrorism and criminal enterprises.

3. What is the modus operandi of the threat? How does the criminal enterprise operate? What does the terrorist or extremist group typically target and what are the common methods of attacking? How do members of the extremist group typically integrate with the community to minimize the chance of being discovered?

4. What is needed to catch offenders and prevent crime incidents or trends? What specific types of information are being sought by the intelligence unit to aid in the broader threat analysis?

[21] On a related note, following the terrorists' attacks of September 11, 2001, the FBI developed a series of interview questions for persons who may have knowledge about terrorism. State and local law enforcement were asked to participate in the questioning of some persons who were in the U.S. on visas. There was a mixed response, largely based on the perspective of local government leaders. Despite this, the questions were also intended to provide insight and information for officers. More information, as well as the protocol questions, can be found in: General Accounting Office. Homeland Security. *Justice Department's Project to Interview Aliens After September 11, 2001.* Report to Congressional Committees. Report Number GAO-03-459, April 2003. www.gao.gov.

Both CompStat and ILP are prevention-oriented and are driven by an information flow coming from the line level upward. Intelligence awareness training for street officers recognizes that officers on patrol have a strong likelihood of observing circumstances and people that may signify a threat or suggest the presence of a criminal enterprise. The patrol officer must be trained[22] to regularly channel that information to the intelligence unit for input into the Intelligence Cycle for analysis. Like community policing, this requires new responsibilities for patrol officers and organizational flexibility to permit officers to explore new dimensions of crimes and community problems that traditionally have not been part of their responsibilities.

While there are fundamental similarities, the methodology and focus of ILP is notably different from, and more difficult than, CompStat because of the differences in the raw data. Understanding these differences and, more important, the role ILP fulfills is an important foundation for the following discussions.

Figure 5-1: Comparison of CompStat and Intelligence-Led Policing

Similarities of CompStat and Intelligence-Led Policing: Important Lessons Learned from CompStat Can Be Applied to ILP
✓ Both have a goal of prevention
✓ Commitment to the concept by the chief executive is essential
✓ Analysis serves as the basis for operational responses
✓ Processes for constant raw information flow for analysis must be in place
✓ Community engagement is critical for reporting suspicious activities
✓ Intervention activities are driven by definable evidence of crime and threats
✓ Administrative and organizational flexibility are required
✓ Research and lessons learned serve as the basis for creative intervention
✓ Managers and supervisors are held demonstrably accountable

While principles and processes are similar, there are also substantive differences	
CompStat	Intelligence-Led Policing
• Intrajurisdiction	• Multijurisdiction
• Incident-driven	• Threat-driven
• Analysis based on known facts from reported crime data and investigations	• Analysis-based tips, leads, suspicious activity reports, and information collection
• Focuses on crime sprees and incident trends with intent to apprehend specific offenders	• Focuses on root causes and conditions that contribute to serious crime and terrorism
• Relies on crime mapping, incident analysis, modus operandi analysis	• Relies on link analysis, commodity flow, transaction analysis, association analysis
• Time-sensitive (24 hour feedback/response)	• Strategic (inherently long-term)
• Predominant focus on street crime (burglary, robbery, homicide, assault, theft, etc.)	• Predominant focus on criminal enterprises (terrorism, organized crime, violence, etc.)
• Reported criminal incidents drive collection and analytic parameters	• Intelligence requirements drive collection and analytic parameters

[22] Training—including line officer training—is discussed in detail, including line officer training, in a later chapter.

Ethical Issues

Another important characteristic similar to both community policing and ILP is the emphasis on ethical decision-making. In community policing, the need for ethical decision-making was based on the need to develop trust between the police and community, among other reasons. Without this trust, the public would not provide the critical information needed for crime control. The need for ethical decision-making in ILP is similar, but goes a step further. Because of concerns about the types of information being collected by law enforcement and how that information is retained in records, concerns have been expressed that law enforcement may violate citizens' rights in the quest for terrorists. As a result of these concerns, the aura of ethical decision-making and propriety of actions must be unquestioned in the law enforcement intelligence function.

Civil Rights and ILP

A unique challenge in dealing with ILP is maintaining privacy and protecting individuals' civil rights. CompStat and crime analysis each have an entirely different set of legal rules. Typically, CompStat deals with aggregate data of criminal incidents and the attributes of those incidents. In those types of analysis, individuals are not identified; therefore, civil rights do not attach to the data. If the crime analysis focuses on the identification of individuals, the identification is a result of evidence obtained during the criminal investigation leading to probable cause for arrest. The law of criminal evidence and procedure applies to the further collection of evidence, and the information is retained in the law enforcement agency's records management system (RMS), which has rules of wide latitude for keeping information about criminal suspects, witnesses, and victims.

Conversely, as noted previously, ILP deals with threats and conditions that may facilitate the threats. At this point, there are no civil rights issues of consequence. However, as the intelligence process identifies individuals and organizations for which there is only a reasonable suspicion that they may take advantage of the conditions to commit criminal acts in the future, the information is classified as "criminal intelligence information." As such, this information may only be entered into a separate "criminal intelligence records system," not the RMS. Consequently, there must be adherence to the guidelines of 28 CFR Part 23.[23] Failure to do so could open the law enforcement agency to civil liability.

For the current discussion of ILP, the point to note is simply this: There are significantly different rules for the collection, retention, and dissemination of "criminal intelligence information" compared to "criminal investigation information." Beyond the information management differences, there are conceivable differences in the method of analysis that is performed when individuals are identified as either intelligence targets or witnesses. As such, there must be a separate records system and supporting policies developed for ILP as well as training on the proper method of processing information used in ILP.

[23] Technically, 28 CFR Part 23 applies only to federally funded multijurisdictional criminal intelligence records systems operated by state, local, and tribal law enforcement agencies. In practice, however, it must be assumed that 28 CFR Part 23 applies to all state, local, and tribal agencies for two reasons: 1. The NCISP recommends that all agencies adopt these guidelines as a national standard of good practice and 2. Precedent in federal civil rights cases suggests that adherence to the federal guidelines can be an affirmative defense should a civil rights case be brought against an agency for the types of information being retained in a criminal intelligence records system.

Public Education

As noted previously, public education is critical for effective ILP. The lessons learned from community policing provide important insights. The public encompasses many different groups and different public education initiatives need to be provided to each constituent group. For example, what does the agency want to accomplish with a public education program: Reducing fear? Developing volunteers for the police department? Resolving community tensions, such as demonstrated resentment toward the Muslim community? Is the goal simply to give citizens information about terrorism indicators to aid in prevention? The important point to note is that a specific goal should be related to the public education initiative.

Such a program may also stratify the community in order to give specific types of information to different targeted audiences. Who in the community should be targeted for an education program: The business community? Civic and church groups? Graduates of the Citizens' Police Academy (CPA)? Nonlaw enforcement government employees? Teachers and students? The general community? Demographically defined segments of the community?

Different segments of the community may have different needs. For example, since approximately 85 percent of America's critical infrastructure is owned by the private sector, a special public education program may focus on threat-related issues for this narrowly defined community. Conversely, a completely different kind of public education may be directed toward graduates of the CPA who may be trained to work as volunteers during crises or a heightened alert status. Yet a different public education agenda would be directed toward a particular ethnic or religious community within a city. Each segment of the community has a different goal. In this case, the business sector to harden potential targets, the CPA graduates to aid the police in response to increased service demands, and the ethnic community to gain information about suspicious persons and their actions.

These segments may be further divided, particularly if there are unique targets within the community. The business community, for example, may be broken down into different segments: Different threats may target a nuclear plant or telecommunications switching station (both are critical infrastructure) or a meat processing plant or university genetic research laboratory (both of which may be a target of domestic environmental extremists).[24] The law enforcement agency will have to conduct a threat assessment to fully understand the character of the threat within the community as well as to understand the agency's intelligence requirements.[25] Collectively, these elements have a symbiotic relationship to aid in the development of a public education program.

[24] At times, targets may not be readily apparent in a community. Does East Lansing, Michigan, appear to be a terrorist target? In 1992, the Animal Liberation Front started a fire in the Michigan State University (MSU) mink research facility and caused more than $2 million in damages. On December 31, 1999, a fire in MSU's Agricultural Hall caused $700,000 in damages and destroyed years of research. Earth Liberation Front claimed responsibility, targeting genetic research.

[25] The threat assessment and intelligence requirements will be discussed in a later chapter.

Community education programs should also intend to have a specific outcome. Whether it is to reduce fear or to enlist support for volunteer efforts, all public education initiatives should incorporate five factors related to the intelligence function:

1. Know how to observe.

2. Know what is suspicious.

3. Know how to report.

4. Know what to report.

5. Know what happens next.

To maximize the quality and quantity of information provided by the community, law enforcement must provide a framework of knowledge. The more that law enforcement can educate the community, the more robust the feedback from the community.[26] In this regard, Tables 5-1 and 5-2 illustrate a range of items that may be incorporated into a public education program from both a topical and an outcome perspective.

Community Members as Law Enforcement Volunteers

Oftentimes, community members ask what they may do to aid in counterterrorism. One important element is serving as a volunteer for the law enforcement agency. Experience has shown that community volunteers can save the agency money as well as often provide unique expertise. Money can be saved when citizens are able to perform tasks that would otherwise have to be performed by a law enforcement employee; for example, the Austin (Texas) Police Department uses volunteers as part of its Civil Defense Battalion to accomplish these goals.

Obviously, an agency needs to develop some means of screening volunteers as well as provide structure for their work agreement and for administrative controls when they are performing activities on behalf of the law enforcement agency. In this regard, an important resource is Volunteers in Police Service (VIPS).[27] The VIPS web site provides a wide array of resources, documents, policies, and tips that can make a law enforcement volunteer program functional and easy to manage.

Volunteers with unique occupational experience may be particularly valuable to the intelligence function. An attorney, accountant, people with experience in researching land titles, and academic researchers and scholars are illustrations of professional volunteers who could provide important assistance to the intelligence function. Of course, background checks and nondisclosure agreements must be required of all such volunteers.

[26] www.policevolunteers.org

[27] Ideally, the law enforcement agency would be able to provide feedback to the citizen about information that was reported. Many times this is not feasible in the intelligence environment; however, it serves as positive reinforcement to the citizen when feedback is provided.

Table 5-1: Examples of Topics in a Public Education Program

• Understanding terrorism
• What is terrorism (defined/explained)
• Why people commit terrorist acts
• Perspectives of terrorism
• Asymmetric warfare
• An act of terror is defined by the victim
• How terrorism can touch a community…
   » As a target
   » Logistics and support provided to terrorists
   » Activities that fund terrorist organizations
• New preparedness resources for local emergency services
	• What is being done at the national level
	   » National strategies developed
	   » National threat assessment by FBI
	   » FBI reprioritized and reorganized to aid state and local law enforcement
	• What is being done at state and local levels
	   » Participation in Joint Terrorism Task Forces
	   » Officers receiving antiterrorism training
	   » New communications and information sharing (Automated Trusted Information Exchange, RISS, Law Enforcement Online) that give local law enforcement more access

Table 5-2: Examples of Actions the Public Can Take

• Keep informed to know what to look for and report to the police
   » Law enforcement must be prepared to share information with public
• Be aware, yet be fair
• Be cognizant of threats, but avoid stereotyping and hyperbole
• Information on how to talk/deal with children regarding terrorism
   » www.ed.gov/admins/lead/safety/emergencyplan/index.html
   » www.fema.gov/kids/
   » www.atf.gov/kids/index.htm
	• Information on how to protect family www.ready.gov
	• Safety checklist
	• Communications information
	• What "awareness" means
	• Explain the Alert System
	• How to help children cope with fear
	• Safety issues
	• Equipment and resource checklist
	• Understand the Homeland Security Advisory System and its effect

Conclusion

As noted in a recent publication from the Office of Community Oriented Policing Services:

> For the past 20 years, community policing has encouraged law enforcement to partner with the community to proactively identify potential threats and create a climate of safety. Its emphasis on problem-solving has led to more effective means of addressing crime and social disorder problems. In the 21st century the community policing philosophy is well-positioned to take a central role in preventing and responding to terrorism and in efforts to reduce citizen fear.[28]

The prudent executive will explore these avenues as part of a comprehensive, community wide homeland security strategy. Because of the concern for terrorism and Islamic extremism, the need to embrace all elements of the community becomes an even higher priority. As noted by the Muslim Public Affairs Council: "Ultimately, U.S. counterterrorism efforts will require a partnership between policymakers and the American Muslim community…".[29]

[28] Scheider, Matthew, Robert Chapman, and Michael Seelman, "Connecting the Dots for a Proactive Approach." *Border and Transportation Security.* Washington, D.C.: Office of Community Oriented Policing Services, 2004. www.cops.usdoj.gov/RIC/ResourceDetail.aspx?RID=245.

[29] Muslim Public Affairs Council. *A Review of U.S. Counterterrorism Policy: American Muslim Critique and Recommendations.* Washington, D.C.: Muslim Public Affairs Council, 2003, p. 8.

Chapter 6:
Developing and Implementing Intelligence-Led Policing

Developing and Implementing Intelligence-Led Policing

Chapter 5 established the concept and issues associated with Intelligence-Led Policing (ILP). Building on those concepts, this chapter will identify the processes and elements required to implement ILP in a state, local, and tribal law enforcement (SLTLE) agency. Because of the conceptual nature of ILP, it must be designed to meet the explicit needs of a given agency. This is complicated by the fact that there are a wide range of resource and environmental variables that will also influence implementation.

The important point to note is that there is not a single model of ILP that can be plugged into an agency. Rather, as will be seen, there are tools that can be used to identify the intelligence needs of an agency and then craft the policies and processes to make ILP functional for each department.

Essentially, intelligence is about managing information; specifically, the information that is needed to identify threats of concern to a community, and having sufficient information about the threat to develop operational responses to prevent or mitigate the threat. As depicted in Figure 6-1, this is a three phase-process as related to the integration of ILP into a law enforcement organization. The first phase examines the elements necessary for the information management process to be effective and it begins with developing the information management plan. The second phase is creating the organizational infrastructure to make the information management plan functional. The third phase is implementation. The following discussions address these three phases.

Figure 6-1:
Three Phases of ILP Development in an SLTLE Organization

Phase 3: Implementation of Intelligence-Led Policing

Phase 2: Creating the Organizational Infrastructure

Phase 1: Information Management Plan

Establishing a Framework for Strategic Priorities and Information Processing: The Information Management Plan

The information management framework is a business plan that guides a focused series of processes for the intelligence function. This plan identifies priority problems and institutionalizes a process for monitoring the problems through the application of seven critical components. A rudimentary approach is used in Table 6-1 to explain each component by indicating the kinds of questions each component is intended to answer and the organizational positions most likely to be responsible for answering the questions.

Table 6-1: Seven Components of the Information Management Plan

The Concept...	Asks the question...	Responsibility...
Strategic Priority	What problems are important to me?	Executive
Intelligence Requirements	What additional information do I need to better understand each problem, its causes, and its effects?	Executive, Commander, and Analyst
Collection Plan	Where (sources) and how (methods) will I get the additional information that I need to better understand the problem?	Commander and Analyst
Analysis	Collectively, what does the new information mean and what new insights does it provide about the problem?	Analyst with review by Supervisor
Intelligence Products	What actionable information do I need to tell other people in order to prevent or control the problem?	Analyst with Commander's Advice
Operational Responses	What explicit operational activities may be implemented to prevent or mitigate the priority problems? What resources are needed?	Intelligence and Operations Commanders
Process Review	From this process: • Was the information accurate and useful? • Could the problem be altered as a result of the information? • What will make the process better?	Intelligence and Operations Commanders with Feedback to Executive

Integrated within the information management plan is the Intelligence Process (discussed in Chapter 4). The six phases of the Intelligence Cycle operationalize the acquisition and processing of information needed for the intelligence function. The information management components collectively create the information management plan; the Intelligence Cycle is the mechanism for ensuring that information is collected, assessed, and processed in a manner that is scientific and consistent with accepted practice.

As illustrated in Figure 6-2, the Intelligence Process is a critically important subsystem of the information management plan. The current discussion, however, focuses on the essential components necessary develop and implement the plan. It lays the foundation for operationally responding to threats as well as providing a quality control mechanism for both information management and information processing.

Figure 6-2: Structure of the Information Management Plan

The Information Management Plan

The seven core components of the management plan integrate the intelligence function with all other agency responsibilities. It should be emphasized that these are management components, not functional components, per se. For example, the "analysis" component of the management plan focuses on the role analysis plays in information management. Conversely, the analysis phase of the Intelligence Process is focused on developing intelligence from raw data. The following discussions provide a brief description of each of the plan's components.

Establishing Strategic Priorities for Intelligence-Led Policing

Intelligence strategic priorities are the articulated criminal and terrorist threats that must be monitored and managed by a law enforcement agency in light of the impact these threats have on public safety and security. A strategic priority must be specified in the context of the local community and the law enforcement agency's intent to manage that priority.

Defining intelligence priorities can become a complex process because law enforcement organizations have a wide range of potential responsibilities ranging from traffic control to counterterrorism. Pragmatically, because of resource limitations, these different responsibilities cannot be treated equally. Each responsibility must be given a priority that will guide the allocation of resources and the amount of organizational effort that will be devoted to addressing it.

Even within each responsibility there will be additional prioritization. To use a familiar example, it is inescapable that virtually every SLTLE agency will have a strategic priority related to traffic control. Within the traffic control strategic priority there will be subpriorities such as these:

- Traffic accident investigation
- Driving under the influence enforcement
- Speed enforcement
- Vehicle registration and regulatory enforcement
- Parking enforcement.

This does not mean there will be no parking enforcement, but under normal circumstances parking enforcement may occur only when there is a complaint. Priorities can also change with circumstances. As an example, parking enforcement may be given a high priority when vehicles have to be moved from an emergency snow route or a hurricane evacuation route when warranted by the weather conditions. It is essential, therefore, that a law enforcement agency identify priorities within a dynamic framework that prescribes the conditions under which priorities will change and how the priority will be addressed (for example, parking enforcement only on the emergency routes but no attention to parking enforcement in commercial loading zones).

Strategic priorities are influenced by the systemic influence of several environmental factors. These include the following:

- Known public safety threats

- The seriousness of each threat

- Political priorities within a community

- Resources of the law enforcement agency

- Expertise of the law enforcement agency

- Special funding obligations (such as the conditions of a grant award or legislative mandates)

- Obligations in partnership agreements with other law enforcement agencies, public safety agencies, or the private sector

- Personal/professional priorities of the law enforcement executive.

These are legitimate factors because their effects on organizational prioritization are a product of an interactive balance among the factors. This process applies throughout the law enforcement organization, including intelligence.

Obviously, there are many different foci that ILP may address, particularly in light of the "all-crimes, all-threats, all-hazards" approach to intelligence. Important information must be gained by executives, both empirically and ideologically, that will help focus the prioritization process. In setting strategic priorities for ILP, the law enforcement executive may seek answers to a variety of questions, such as the following:

- ILP and the Overall Agency Mission

    - What is the priority of ILP in relation to the mission, responsibilities, and other strategic priorities of the law enforcement agency?

        - What proportion of the agency's work force will be exclusively dedicated to ILP?

        - What facility, equipment, supply, and service needs are required to support the various ILP full-time assignments?

        - What are the time and resource requirements to support personnel who devote a portion of their time to ILP (including training)?

- Threat-Related Assessment Factors

    - What known threats to public safety exist within the jurisdiction?

    - What threats may emerge?

    - What critical infrastructure is in the jurisdiction?

    - What key resources are in the jurisdiction?

    - What unique characteristics exist within the community that may heighten or aggravate either a criminal or homeland security threat? (For example, proximity to an international border, ports, refineries, geographic area that is disproportionately susceptible to natural disasters.)

    - What unique crime problems in the community need to be addressed? (For example, firearms violence, gangs, drug trafficking.)

- Administrative and Environmental Factors
  - What political mandates exist that are related to real or perceived threats that must be addressed?
  - What resources and expertise does the agency have or have access to that will support ILP? (For example, analysts, analytic software, fee-based information systems.)
  - What intelligence-related agreements has the agency entered into that obligates the agency and its resources? (For example, fusion center, Joint Terrorism Task Force, regional task forces.)
  - What obligations does the agency have to focus on specific intelligence-related initiatives, processes, and/or outcomes as a result of grants or special funding (such as a crime-control tax)?
- Executive Prerogatives
  - What personal and/or professional commitments and/or philosophies of the chief executive must be addressed in establishing strategic priorities?

The answers to these and other questions unique to the jurisdiction will provide the framework within which strategic priorities for ILP may be articulated and prioritized. The next phase is to operationalize the priorities. For example, assume that a law enforcement agency identified four ILP strategic priorities, in no particular order of importance, as the following:

1. Terrorism.
2. Homeland security.
3. Violence by firearms.
4. Gangs.

Within each of these priorities there will be a subset of priorities that must be operationally defined as they apply to the agency. For example, the FBI's definitions of international and domestic terrorism are as follows:

> International terrorism involves violent acts or acts dangerous to human life that are a violation of the criminal laws of the United States or any state, or that would be a criminal violation if committed within the jurisdiction of the United States or any state.

> Domestic terrorism is the unlawful use, or threatened use, of force or violence by a group or individual based and operating entirely within the United States or Puerto Rico without foreign direction committed against persons or property to intimidate or coerce a government, the civilian population, or any segment thereof in furtherance of political or social objectives.[1]

[1] Federal Bureau of Investigation. Counterterrorism Division. *Terrorism: 2002–2005.* Washington, D.C.: Federal Bureau of Investigation, undated, p. v.

While suiting the FBI's needs, these definitions are not likely to be as useful for a state, local, or tribal law enforcement agency that is defining its strategic priorities. Rather, an agency may use a more simplified definition to meet its needs; for example, the strategic priority of terrorism may be articulated simply as this:

- Terrorism[2]
    - Internationally affiliated terrorist groups
    - Individual radicals who support the ideology of internationally based terrorist groups
    - Right-wing criminal extremist
    - Environmental criminal extremists
    - Right-to-life criminal extremists.

With respect to the strategic priority of homeland security,[3] a state, local, or tribal law enforcement agency should define the priority within the context of unique characteristics of a jurisdiction. For example, the homeland security priority of an agency located near the U.S.-Mexico border may include strategic awareness of tuberculoses; a community where there is a high density of cattle raised for beef processing may include mad cow or hoof-and-mouth disease; an agricultural community that raises crops may focus on the accidental or intentional introduction of a communicable crop disease such as soybean rust. The significant point to note is that with the current all-hazards approach to homeland security intelligence, factors beyond the traditional expertise of law enforcement need to be explored when identifying threats (hazards) and defining strategic priorities for homeland security.

In light of the "all-crimes, all-threats, all-hazards" approach used in contemporary intelligence activities, the strategic priorities for intelligence will tend to be broader than was historically the case. Strategic priorities for the law enforcement agency will be defined throughout the organization and take many different forms (see Chapter Annex 6-1 for selected, and diverse, statements of strategic priorities from three law enforcement agencies). Specifically for ILP, an example of strategic priorities may be simply listed as illustrated in Table 6-2.

Within the framework of strategic priorities, an assessment must be made of what information is already known about the nature of each priority. Gaps in the information are then articulated as intelligence requirements.

[2] Note that each subcategory specifically includes the conditional modifier of "terrorist" or "criminal." This is an important factor because state, local, and tribal law enforcement agencies may collect and retain only information that identifies individuals and organizations where there is a criminal nexus, not just an extreme ideology.

[3] The reader should recall that homeland security intelligence deals with all hazards that have implications for law enforcement public safety and order maintenance functions.

Table 6-2: Examples of ILP Strategic Priorities

The Anytown Police Department's strategic priorities for Intelligence-Led Policing are:

- Terrorism
  - » Internationally affiliated terrorist groups
  - » Individual radicals who support the ideology of internationally based terrorist groups
  - » Right-wing criminal extremists
  - » Environmental criminal extremists
  - » Right-to-life criminal extremists
- Homeland Security
  - » Critical Infrastructure
    - Anytown water treatment plant
    - Anytown Naval Air Station
    - Anytown electrical substation
  - » Key Resources
    - FastCar Assembly Plant of Anytown
    - Anytown Grain Elevator Complex
    - GoodBeef Stockyards and Auction Barn
- Violence by Firearms
  - » Homicide by firearm
  - » Robbery by firearm
  - » Assault by firearm
- Gangs
  - » All criminal gang activity
- Organized crime activity
  - » Loan sharking
  - » Credit card fraud

Intelligence Requirements

While the use of intelligence requirements has been a long-standing practice of the Intelligence Community, it is a relatively new practice for law enforcement. Again, because of jurisdictional differences, requirements have slightly different applications for the law enforcement community.

Information that is missing but needed to understand a threat, target, or suspect is an "intelligence gap." Information that is identified to fill this gap is an "intelligence requirement." Requirements help administrators make decisions, and those decisions vary widely, such as these examples:

- Determining if a reasonable suspicion exists
- What resources to deploy
- Whether to prepare for a new threat
- Determining if a new target exists within a community
- Alternatives for preparing for a new threat or hazard
- Determining if new partnerships need to be developed to manage a change in the threat picture
- Determining if a new expertise needs to be developed to manage a threat
- Identifying new training personnel that an agency will need to deal with the changing threat picture.

The significant point to note is that requirements define the types of information that has to be collected to address the strategic priorities. Collecting information to fill the intelligence requirement requires a proactive deployment of resources. This may include open sources, law enforcement and intelligence information systems, human sources, undercover officers, patrol officers, informants, community partnerships, public-private partnerships, or the use of technical surveillance resources. These are articulated in the collection plan.

Collection Plan

The collection plan is a systematic procedure for gathering relevant information from all lawful sources that responds to intelligence requirements to produce an intelligence product. Usually the collection plan includes a specified time frame; although in the case of a standing intelligence requirement that time frame may be ongoing. The collection plan is related to the strategic priorities via the intelligence requirements by collecting targeted information about threats from both strategic and tactical perspectives. Some factors to be considered in the collection plan include the following:

- Is the requirement sufficiently clear to locate and identify the specific information that is needed?
- Have open sources been used as the "source of first resort"?
- Has any portion of the information already been collected in the form of tips, leads or Suspicious Activity Reports (SAR)?
- Do partnerships exist that can assist in responding to the intelligence requirement? (For example, private sector partnerships, the fusion center, community partnerships, and so forth.)

- If not available from open sources or previously collected information, what method(s) will be used to collect the information?
- What sources will be used to collect the information?
- What unique technological methods, if any, are needed to collect the information?
- Are there legal and/or administrative restrictions on collecting the information?
- Are there explicit notifications or approvals required for the collection of specific types of information?
- Can source validity and information reliability be accurately assessed? If not, other collection sources and methods should be explored.

Collected information is processed using the constructs of the Intelligence Cycle. As sufficient valid and reliable information is collected and analyzed, intelligence products are developed to monitor the strategic priorities and determine what, if any, operational responses are needed to address threats in each priority area.

Analysis

Raw data collected in accordance with the collection plan has little value until it has been analyzed. Relying on the scientific approach to problem solving, logical reasoning, and objective interpretation of data, the analytic process gives an integrated meaning to diverse individual pieces of information. Analysis establishes connections between the different data, cause and effect, and correlations of activities and behaviors. The new knowledge derived from analysis can provide insights into imminent and emerging threats, as well as potential intervention methods.

Certainly a goal of effective analysis is to ensure that the conclusions drawn from the process are "actionable"; that is, when the information from the analysis is given to operational units in the law enforcement agency, there is sufficient detail that enables the operational units to develop specific plans to prevent and/or mitigate threat. This actionable information is presented in a written form known as the intelligence products.

Intelligence Products

Intelligence products are the reports and delivery mechanisms that convey the findings of the analytic process. Ideally, an intelligence unit or fusion center will establish a menu of products that meet the specific needs of its various consumers. The products should have a consistent format and appearance (that is, a "brand") that will aid consumers in selecting the products most applicable to their responsibilities. For example, when a threat is identified and reported, managers will need different types of information than line officers will need. Situational awareness, a strategic assessment, and tactical indicators represent intelligence products that have a different focus on the same threat.

Each intelligence unit and fusion center will determine the types of intelligence products it will produce. Important, the products are the primary methods that the intelligence function will communicate with their customers. The overall utility of the intelligence unit will be judged by the intelligence products it disseminates. The products must be of sufficient quality, substance, and utility that operational units of the agency are able to develop tactics and strategies to prevent threats from reaching fruition.

Ensuring that these characteristics are embodied in each intelligence product will maximize the utility of the product which, in turn, contributes to public safety and security.

Operational Responses

Identifying threats through the Intelligence Process is an important ingredient for public safety. Intelligence, however, is only part of the security equation: the critical next element is for operational commanders to develop intervention activities that will stop or mitigate the threat. Some of the operational responses will be fairly simple, such as providing indicators of the threat so that officers will be aware of them while carrying out their daily responsibilities. Other interventions may be more sophisticated such as using suppression tactics (saturation patrol, for example), proactive intervention (such as consistent car stops and field interviews of persons and their associates reasonably believed to part of the threat), target hardening, community education, development of a task force, and aggressive use of traditional investigative tactics that may serve to identify and apprehend offenders. It is important to note that operational units should rely on the intelligence function as a resource when developing intervention strategies. The analyst has the most comprehensive insight into the threat and may provide valuable feedback to operational planning.

Implementing operational responses inevitably requires the expenditure of resources. While resource allocation is part of the operational commander's responsibility when developing intervention methods, the intelligence function can assist in prioritizing and focusing strategies. This can translate to a more efficient use of resources.

Review of the Process

A final step of the information management plan is to review the process to establish what intelligence was developed and if any new gaps have emerged. It should ask such questions as these:
- Was the information or intelligence accurate?
  - Was the threat accurately identified?
  - Was the nature of the threat and its characteristics accurately identified?
- Was the target accurately identified?
  - Were the vulnerabilities of the target accurately identified?
- What was learned from victims, witnesses, offenders, and locations?
- Was there useable intelligence from any technical or surveillance activity?
- What was learned about intelligence gaps and is there information that can be collected on a standing basis to prevent future intelligence gaps?

- Did the threat change after the operational response? If so, why?
- Did the operational activity cause displacement which, in turn, will cause new threats to emerge in a different geographic area?
- What operational responses were used and are the threats vulnerable to the same approach in the future?
- Have new threats been identified or have new threats emerged?
- Were partner agencies (include private sector) involved in any aspect of collection or response?
  - What were the benefits?
  - What feedback have they provided?
  - What feedback have they received?
- What measures have been put in place to minimize the possibility of the threats arising again?[4]

The review is an important tool for evaluating the information management plan, Intelligence Process, operational responses, and the status of strategic priorities. Indeed, the review can also be critical for defining new intelligence requirements and reordering the priorities.

Summary

The information management plan is like a skeletal structure linking the components together. It serves as the framework to make the organizational components functional for ILP.

Organizational Infrastructure for ILP

Before the ILP concept can be introduced into a law enforcement agency, a number of components (see Figure 6-3) must be developed, each of which complements the definition of ILP provided in Chapter 5. The complexity and detail of these ingredients vary widely between agencies, depending on such factors as these:

- Size of the agency
- Resources
- Demographics of the jurisdiction
- Location of the jurisdiction
- Character of the jurisdiction (industrial, commuter population, central city, suburb)
- Relationship with the community (supportive, conflictive, large undocumented population)
- Perspective on intelligence by elected officials and community leaders.

An assessment of these variables—many of which will be intuitive to the agency—will help guide the development of each ILP component.

[4] Based on: National Centre for Policing Excellence. *Guidance on the National Intelligence Model.* London, U.K.: Association of Chief Police Officers, 2005, p. 94.

Figure 6-3: Components of ILP

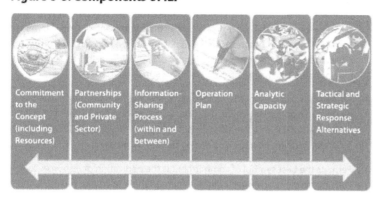

| Commitment to the Concept (including Resources) | Partnerships (Community and Private Sector) | Information-Sharing Process (within and between) | Operation Plan | Analytic Capacity | Tactical and Strategic Response Alternatives |

Commitment

The change to ILP must start with the chief executive because if the leadership of a law enforcement agency does not understand and buy in to the concept, it will never be functionally adopted. The law enforcement executive's commitment must be demonstrated through allocation of personnel and resources to develop and implement the concept. If agency personnel do not believe the leader is committed to the new program, implementation efforts will not be effective.

An excellent example of a leader's demonstration of commitment is seen in the following experience:

> When Dr. Gerry Williams was chief of police in Aurora, Colorado, in the late 1980s, he decided to implement community policing. There was a great deal of resistance, and he recognized the need to educate Aurora police personnel on the concept. He asked that a team from the National Center for Community Policing at Michigan State University prepare a 4-hour awareness program that would be mandatory for all Aurora police employees to attend on the change in policing philosophy. He also asked the team to offer the training at 12 different times throughout the day (over a 2-week period) that would cover every shift so all personnel would have the opportunity to attend the mandatory training on their regularly scheduled duty time. At each of the 12 sessions—whether offered in the middle of the night or the middle of the day—Chief Williams opened the training by making a firm statement that the movement to community policing was going to be the unquestioned policing philosophy to be used by the Aurora Police Department and that resources would be committed to ensure the change would take place. Chief Williams then sat down in the middle of the front row where everyone was certain to see him and sat through every one of the 12 sessions. It did not take long for the word to spread through the department that "the chief is serious about this" because he set other duties aside to attend the entirety of all the sessions. This was an important sign of commitment. Moreover, the chief answered questions during the sessions and interacted with officers on the breaks to reinforce his commitment.

Commitment begins with the chief executive's true understanding of the concept. In some cases, this has occurred after the chief executive has attended a training program developed exclusively from the executive's perspective (such as the BJA program, "Criminal Intelligence for the Chief Executive"). A program such as this provides fundamental concepts that show the value of intelligence, demonstrates how intelligence integrates with the department's overall mission, and permits the chief to interact with others who may not only provide reciprocal support but also may permit an exchange of ideas on how ILP may be used.

The chief executive should also formally articulate his or her support of the concept in a policy statement. The policy statement provides the organizational parameters of ILP and gives all members of the agency a tangible reference point for understanding how ILP is to be implemented and used.

Perhaps the best symbol of commitment is the dedication of resources to ILP. Training agency personnel, assigning them to the intelligence function, and dedicating funding to the development and execution of ILP sends a strong message to agency personnel about the executive's commitment.

It is also critically important to gain commitment to the concept from commanders and managers because they are responsible for the actual execution of ILP. If commanders and managers have neither a clear understanding of how ILP can benefit the agency nor of their ILP responsibilities for directing personnel under their command, full implementation will not occur, regardless of the chief executive's support. In all types of organizations, there have been instances in the management process in which middle managers have defeated a new initiative simply by not thoroughly ensuring that personnel under their command perform the duties necessary to make the initiative work. This reflects an old adage in management: "Managers may not be able to turn the water on, but they can easily turn it off."

Component 1—Key Takeaways
- The chief executive must understand and support the concept of ILP:
    - How ILP fits into the department's mission
    - Articulated commitment to the concept
- Commitment of people and resources:
    - Training
    - Infrastructure development
- Commitment must extend throughout the chain of command

Partnerships

Effective ILP requires the development of a range of partnerships. There are good examples of this in the counterterrorism area (such as the Terrorism Early Warning Groups) as well as the precedent established in community policing. The range of partnerships includes the private sector, nonlaw enforcement government service, and the community. Each can be an important source of information for the intelligence process. The fundamental rationale for public-private partnerships is based on the fact that when more people know what to observe and how to report it to law enforcement, the greater the probability of collecting information that may be used to stop a terrorist attack or criminal enterprise.

There is a precedent of success for including community members as part of the information-collection process, as seen in programs used by the Turkish National Police, Israeli Police, and the London Metropolitan Police. Each has developed programs aimed at the community to report specific types of information— essentially, "intelligence requirements"—to the police to aid in preventing terrorism. Certainly, if community partnerships are effective in these diverse cultures, they can be effective in the United States. Moreover, public-private partnerships are a simple extension of many current programs used throughout the United States that deal with crime, ranging from Neighborhood Watch to Volunteers in Police Service.

One question that emerges is whether the average community member is interested in participating in ILP programs. A pilot program offered by the Regional Community Policing Institute at Wichita State University extended an open invitation to local residents in Wichita, Manhattan, and Topeka, Kansas, to attend a public awareness session on citizen reporting of suspicious activities possibly related to terrorism. More than 600 people attended the sessions in the heartland because of their concern about the threat and their desire to contribute to counterterrorism initiatives.

Engaging the community can significantly increase the information-collection parameters for the intelligence process. Several key factors make these partnerships work effectively for ILP.

- The law enforcement agency must establish trusted relationships with people through local law enforcement officers. Typically, a "meet and greet" alone will not suffice. Information that may be sensitive, confidential, or even fearful may need to be exchanged. As a lesson learned from community policing, the bond of trust established through an ongoing dialog becomes a critical element.

- Once trust is established, an effective means of two-way communication must be established with each individual. In some cases, this may be technological, such as e-mail or telephone. In other cases, individuals may feel comfortable sharing the information only on a one-to-one basis with their trusted law enforcement partner.

- Just as with officers, training—or public awareness—about the signs and symbols of terrorism and organized crime is important for enabling the partner to identify substantive information that should be reported. For example, a community partner may see a symbol, tattoo, or foreign word that is symbolic of a terrorist or criminal entity, but if he or she has not been trained to recognize these symbols, the information will not be reported. Similarly, community and private partners should receive information about behaviors that are unusual and which suggest criminality in order to enhance their specific awareness.[5]

[5] A good example of behaviors is found in the Michigan State Police video, *Seven Signs of Terrorism*, which is available for public distribution. www.michigan.gov/msp/0,1607,7-123-1564-155763--,00.html.

- Partner training should also include instruction on the type of information that should be documented for reporting to law enforcement. While documentation of behaviors, evidence, vehicles, and personal descriptions are second nature to law enforcement officers, it is not a customary practice for nonlaw enforcement personnel. Explaining what kinds of information should be reported—along with date, time, and location—is an important element in partner training.

- The agency should develop a policy and process to protect the privacy and safety of community partners. As will be discussed in detail in a subsequent chapter, there should be a privacy policy to protect business partners' proprietary information that may need to be disclosed during the information-sharing process. Partners need to be informed of these policies in order to reinforce the trusted relationship.

Illustrations of Partnerships in Other Countries

Israel. During the height of the Al-Aqsa Intifada, the Israeli Police sought alternative methods for gaining information about planned terrorist attacks. One technique was to establish community partnership patrols that worked with the residential Palestinian population is such cities as Tel Aviv and Jerusalem. The Israeli community partnership officers developed trusted, often confidential, relationships with many Palestinian citizens in these cities with the expressed intent to gain information or indicators about possible terrorist attacks. The motives of the Palestinians were quite simple: Many of the Palestinians who worked and resided in Israeli cities had been victims of terrorists' attacks alongside the Israeli victims.

Turkey. After a series of terrorists attacks in Istanbul in November 2003, the Turkish National Police (TNP) interviewed captured terrorists to learn how they were recruited into the PKK (Kurdistan Workers' Party) and the Turkish al-Qaida. It was learned many were recruited in high school and often initially participated with the group out of social pressure rather than commitment to the group's cause. As a result, the TNP began outreach and education programs in the high schools both to dissuade young people from joining these groups and to gain information that could be used in the intelligence process.

A number of good partnerships have emerged, notably in larger law enforcement agencies. The New York (City) Police Department's SHIELD[6] is a comprehensive information-sharing and public information program. The Delaware Information Analysis Center[7] has established formal relationships with nonlaw enforcement government organizations and targeted private-sector entities for information sharing over the secure Automated Trusted Information Exchange network. The Nassau County (New York) Police Department created the Security/Police Information Network as a comprehensive public-private information-sharing network that is stratified by sectors and divided between vetted and nonvetted information-sharing partners using e-mail and periodic meetings. There are certainly other examples, but the point is clear: Partnerships are critical, there are models to provide guidance, and partnerships must be established throughout America's communities, not just in major metropolitan areas.

[6] See www.nypdshield.org.

[7] See dsp.delaware.gov/ Intelligence.shtml.

As may be expected, the development process and expected outputs differ somewhat between community partners and private sector partners

Community Partnerships

Just as with any other crime or community problem, it is important to enlist the support of the community. In the intelligence arena, two factors make community partnerships more challenging. First, the agency is concerned about threats, and second, many community members are uncomfortable with the intelligence role in law enforcement. On the issue of threats, it is insufficient to simply tell citizens to be aware of suspicious activities. More guidance is needed. In many instances, citizens have reported something to this effect: "A man who looks like he's from a Middle-Eastern country is taking a picture of a bridge." In such cases, whether intentional or not, citizens are often falling prey to a stereotype. Beyond this factor, there is virtually no value to such information alone. Citizens need to be given guidance about looking at behaviors that are suspicious and instruction on how to document those behaviors when reporting the information to a law enforcement agency. This reduces the possibility of stereotyping people and provides more valuable information to the law enforcement agency.

With respect to the intelligence role, many people have expressed concern that forming community partnerships for intelligence is akin to turning citizens into informants on their neighbors. This belief goes hand in hand with the belief that many people hold that law enforcement agencies are collecting as much information as possible on all citizens—or at least on citizens who do not share "law enforcement beliefs." Many individuals assume that intelligence activities routinely violate citizens' privacy and civil rights. The challenge is to educate skeptics about the process and the importance of citizen involvement in ILP simply because citizens are often in a place to observe suspicious behaviors more often than are law enforcement officers. The notion of citizen participation goes back to one of the most fundamental principles of modern law enforcement articulated by Sir Robert Peel in developing the London Metropolitan Police in 1829: "The police are the public and the public are the police."

As noted previously, training sessions for citizens can be quite helpful in this process. In a number of communities, both in the United States and abroad, citizen training programs have resulted in reasonable degrees of success. The programs should tell citizens 1. What to look for, 2. What kind of information they should document, and 3. How to report the information to a law enforcement officer or agency.[8] Providing such information increases efficiency and decreases the possibility of stereotyping.

Component 2a—Key Takeaways
- Enlist community support
- Establish trusted lines of communication with community members
- Provide community training so community members will recognize the signs and symbols of terrorism, crime, and other threats facing the community
- Tell the community what kinds of information are needed by the agency
- Tell the community how to report information

[8] Chapter Annex 6-1 is a community handout used by the Wichita State University Regional Community Policing Institute to emphasize these points.

Public-Private Partnerships

Public-private partnerships are more structured than community partnerships. While all businesses are subject to partnerships, those that are prone to threats (in light of specific threats that are identified in a region) should be given the highest priority. The private sector has a great deal to offer in information sharing—many have global contacts and communications systems that can also be of value to a law enforcement agency. Whether it is the use of delivery persons who can be alert to suspicious behaviors, security personnel at corporate facilities, or salespersons who can be aware of unusual or suspicious purchases, the value of raw information exchanged with the private sector can be robust.

In some cases, a law enforcement agency may develop an intelligence liaison contact with a company to serve as the primary two-way point of contact between the company and the law enforcement agency. Such a partnership will increase the efficiency and effectiveness of the information-sharing process. As with community partnerships, the law enforcement agency will need to train appropriate company personnel and in some cases, special training may be provided that is unique to a given corporate sector. This is conceptually similar to the terrorism early warning (TEW) group concept that has been instituted in many communities throughout the United States.[9] Given that law enforcement intelligence focuses on all crimes and all threats, the intelligence liaison contact will be concerned with threats broader than terrorism.

When law enforcement agencies work more closely and have more detailed information exchanges with the private sector, two issues of particular importance must be addressed. The first is protection of citizens' privacy. Instances occur in which a citizen's or lawful U.S. resident's identity may be provided to the private sector, for example, between law enforcement agencies and the airline industry. While there are bona fide reasons for providing information about individuals, care must be taken to ensure accuracy of the information provided and protect the individuals' privacy. The second issue is protecting the proprietary information of companies. In some instances, a company may provide information about its products or business processes to a law enforcement agency as a means of identifying and mitigating threats. It is incumbent on the law enforcement agency to ensure that any such proprietary information is protected.

Component 2b—Key Takeaways

- Enlist support of the private sector:
    - Give priority to threat-prone sectors, particularly in light of regional threats
- Create an intelligence liaison contact
- Provide training to recognize the signs and symbols of terrorism, crime, and other threats that may be encountered
- Tell the partners the types of information the agency needs
- Protect citizens' privacy
- Protect proprietary information

[9] A wide range of information on TEW groups may be found by using the search utility on www.llis.gov.

Information-Sharing Processes

The heart of effective intelligence is the capture and sharing of critical raw information. It is logical that each law enforcement agency must develop an effective mechanism to record and manage this array of information that is distinct from or segregated from other records in the agency's records management system. This mechanism will have a significantly different structure between law enforcement agencies, depending on the agency's size and resources. Despite these differences, a number of questions must be answered when developing an intelligence or sensitive information records capability in a U.S. law enforcement agency. Among these are the following:

- Where and how will this information be stored? It should be noted there are still agencies in American law enforcement that, because of their small size and rural—sometimes remote—locations, do not have networking capabilities. Some still operate with paper records, photocopies, and faxes.

- How will SARs, tips, and leads be assessed, managed, and stored?

- How will source reliability and information validity be evaluated?

- How will overall accuracy of information (including the documentation trail) be ensured?

- Who has the authority to enter information into the system, and how will entries be audited?

- How will the information be secured?

- Who will have access to the information, and under what circumstances is access permitted?

- Is the records system meant for raw information storage or for criminal intelligence records? If the latter, a 28 CFR Part 23-compliant policy should be developed.

- What are the information-sharing rules, and who makes the dissemination decisions?

- Have adequate measures been taken for security of information?

- For electronic systems, are data compatibility standards in place? Are data standards consistent with the Global Justice Extensible Markup Language Data Model[10] and the National Information Exchange Model?[11]

While each question could be discussed at length, for the current discussion it must be recognized that all of these issues must be addressed as part of building an ILP structure. For large agencies, these issues typically have been resolved, but for the majority of law enforcement agencies, many of which have only a few police officers, this is new ground. Yet if they are expected to collect raw information for the fusion centers and the Information Sharing Environment (ISE), the questions must be addressed.

Finally, as a result of articulated national standards and precedence in civil law, every agency that develops a criminal intelligence records system should ensure that it meets accepted regulatory and legal standards.[12]

Component 3—Key Takeaways

- Explicit processes and policies must be developed to ensure that the right information is disseminated to the personnel who need it

- Ensure that information-sharing mechanisms are two-way

- Policies must address both intra- and extradepartmental processes

[10] See it.ojp.gov.

[11] See www.niem.gov.

[12] In particular, the records system should be 28 CFR Part 23-compliant and a privacy policy should be in place. See it.ojp.gov/privacy/206/28CFR Part_23.PDF and it.ojp.gov/default. aspx?area=privacy&page=1260, respectively.

Operational Plan

Most law enforcement agencies have an operational plan in place that includes a mission statement, goals, objectives, and a system of directives. Many of these elements apply directly to ILP without any change; for example, standards of personnel conduct or officer safety guidelines apply uniformly. Elements of a departmental operational plan, however, typically are directed toward criminal investigation and apprehension. Consequently, the ILP operational plan must deal with the operational components of managing threats. The goals and objectives of ILP should be clearly articulated. Operational differences between intelligence and investigations should be spelled out, as should the relationship of ILP to the agency's criminal apprehension mission. Even such issues as personnel evaluation will differ in ILP compared with traditional performance measures.

The operational plan is the road map to executing ILP as an agency strategy.

Component 4—Key Takeaways

- The *National Criminal Intelligence Sharing Plan* states, "For *Intelligence-Led Policing* to be effective, the process must be an integral part of an agency's philosophy, policies, and strategies and must also be integral in the organization's mission and goals" (p. 7)

- Each element of the agency's operational plan should be coordinated to include the ILP mission

- An ILP operational plan should be developed to guide the agency's intelligence activities

Analytic Capability

Without analysis, there is no intelligence; however, most American law enforcement agencies do not have an analyst because they simply do not have the budget. In addition, political and collective bargaining implications often need to be addressed if a chief executive explores the hiring of an analyst. On the political side, it is often difficult for lay citizens—including city council members—to understand why funding should be allocated in a small law enforcement agency for an analyst when there is an increase in crime. Unfortunately, in many communities, it would be more difficult to add a police employee who was a nonsworn analyst than to add another sworn officer. Furthermore, in states where there is mandatory collective bargaining, such as Michigan, it is difficult to add positions that are law enforcement-related without either obtaining concessions from the collective bargaining unit or a renegotiated collective bargaining agreement.[13] As a result, many agencies need to explore options for developing an analytic capability. An agreement with the fusion center, a shared analyst between agencies, the use of volunteer analysts, or the use of college interns as analysts are among the alternatives that an agency may use to develop an analysis capability.

While not perfect, creative options may be the only recourse; for example, a fundamental analysis performed by officers may be the only alternative. There is precedent for this with officers using problem analysis as part of problem-oriented policing. The Center for Problem-Oriented Policing[14] offers a downloadable model

[13] The strength of collective bargaining units and contents of collective bargaining agreements vary widely, even in states with binding arbitration. As a result, each collective bargaining agreement must be examined separately.

[14] www.popcenter.org

problem-oriented policing curriculum that provides instruction on analysis. While not designed for ILP, it can assist in developing the analytic skills that officers need for threat analysis.

The point to note is that rather than relying on intuition, agencies should use an objective assessment of facts to provide a stronger foundation for ILP.

Component 5—Key Takeaways
- Analysis is the key to effective intelligence:
  - Of necessity, the analytic capability of agencies varies widely, ranging from sophisticated to simple
- Sometimes the analytic process is similar to the basic analysis individual officers do in problem-oriented policing
- An important element is to develop the analytic mindset

Tactical and Strategic Response Alternatives

The distinction between tactical and strategic analysis was discussed earlier. Developing response alternatives to criminal threats represents a different way of thinking about crime. The FBI Counterterrorism Division, for example, historically worked cases with the intent of making an arrest as soon as probable cause was developed. The intelligence-led approach now used in FBI counterterrorism is to gain as much information as possible about all investigative targets rather than making immediate arrests. One approach may be to "turn" a target to become an informant, permitting the informant to continue to operate. In other cases, a target may remain under constant surveillance, despite the presence of probable cause, so that the agency can identify as many associates as possible, as well as understand the way the targets communicate, finance, and generally operate their enterprise, with the goal of disrupting the criminal organization. While many of these targets will eventually be arrested—as is often the case in ILP—arrest is not the only goal. Rather, an important goal is to dismantle the criminal organization to eliminate the threat. As noted by Ratcliffe and Guidetti,

> Intelligence-led policing is a conceptual framework for conducting the business of policing. It is not a tactic in the way saturation patrolling is, nor is it a crime-reduction strategy in the way situational crime prevention is. Rather, it is a business model (John and Maguire, 2003) and an information-organizing process that allows police agencies to better understand their crime problems and take a measure of the resources available to be able to decide on an enforcement tactic or prevention strategy best designed to control crime.[15]

Component 6—Key Takeaways
- Unlike operational activities used to suppress crime or apprehend offenders, new tactics must be used to deal with threats
- Instead of immediately arresting criminal suspects, the agency may monitor the suspects' behavior for further intelligence value
- Depending on the nature of threats, creative new initiatives need to be developed to prevent threats; often this may not involve arrests

[15] Ratcliffe, J.H. and R. Guidetti. "State Police Investigative Structure and the Adoption of Intelligence-Led Policing." *Policing: An International Journal of Police Strategies and Management*, 2007. www.jratcliffe.net, under research publications, "State Police Investigative Structure and the Adoption of Intelligence-Led Policing"

Next Steps: Implementation

Often, agencies will ask for a template on how to implement ILP. The fact is that there is no universal template. Rather, each agency must examine the ILP philosophy and critical components, design an implementation scheme in light of the needs, resources, and articulated goals, and tailor the practice of ILP to those requirements. The implementation process is an exercise in organizational change to place the components "in action."

Self-Assessment of the Agency's Intelligence Capacity

In examining the intelligence capabilities of American law enforcement agencies, the author developed a four-point qualitative scale to describe the intelligence capacity based on policies, expertise, and information sharing capabilities.[16] As illustrated in Figure 6-4, the categories are as follows:

- No Intelligence Capacity
- Basic Intelligence Capacity for Information Sharing
- Advanced Intelligence Capacity Including Records Systems
- Mature Full-Service Intelligence Capacity.

While information sharing and connectivity have increased in recent years, most American law enforcement agencies have a minimal intelligence capacity. Time and resources—including specialized expertise—are needed to develop the infrastructure and knowledge within the agency to enable the agency to have a functional intelligence operation. Resources and external assistance include assistance with policy development, training, access to critical information systems, and other infrastructure components.

Figure 6-4: ILP Continuum of Variables

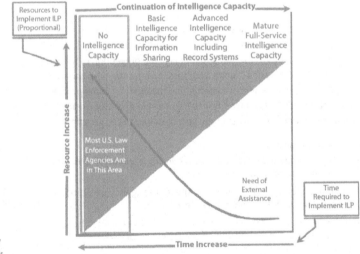

[16] As part of Department of Homeland Security-funded intelligence training programs, the author and his colleagues developed a comprehensive self-assessment tool that measures organizational variables across seven dimensions, providing a refined measurement of a law enforcement agency's ILP capacity. Agencies can access this self-assessment at no cost by enrolling in the training. For more details about the training, see intellprogram. msu.edu.

The categories describing the intelligence capacity are not dichotomous, but exist on a continuum. That is, depending on the operational characteristics of the agency's intelligence function, the intelligence capacity will be somewhere on a continuum within that category (see Figure 6-5). As might be expected, the lower on the continuum, the greater the need for external assistance and resources to develop the capacity to a level that is needed for the agency

Figure 6-5: ILP Subcontinuums of Variables

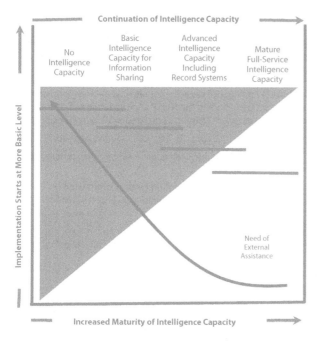

In determining the level of the intelligence capacity, and the place to start for developing or reengineering the intelligence function, a law enforcement agency must conduct a self-assessment of critical variables. Table 6-3 illustrates the operational characteristics that describe the four levels. Below each operational characteristic are action steps that should be taken to at least maintain the current level or move forward.

Certainly the "operational characteristics" and the "action steps" are not absolutes for determining a law enforcement agency's intelligence capability. Rather, they represent important milestones that can be identified and assessed in the implementation process.

The Implementation Starting Point

Any new initiative must have a starting point that provides an accurate picture of the organization's current state of knowledge and capabilities. In the United Kingdom, when the National Intelligence Model was introduced to the provincial constabularies, the starting point was fairly unified across all police forces with a strong foundation, given their history. In the United States, the starting point is at a significantly more fundamental level. To determine this starting point, several questions must be answered in each law enforcement organization:

- What is the knowledge level of the chief executive and command staff regarding the current philosophy and practice of law enforcement intelligence, including ILP?

- Is there an intelligence unit or intelligence capacity in the law enforcement agency?

  - Does the current intelligence capacity operate in a manner consistent with current practice, including the NCISP and the Minimum Standards set by the Counterterrorism Training Coordination Working Group?[17]

  - Has the current intelligence capacity developed a privacy policy?

  - What processes have been addressed and considered in extending the current intelligence capacity to ILP?

  - Is the law enforcement agency accredited by the Commission on Accreditation for Law Enforcement Agencies (CALEA)? If so, what compliance commitments and policies have been put in place to meet the CALEA standard for intelligence?

- What is the level of general awareness and knowledge of all law enforcement personnel concerning law enforcement intelligence?

- What internal resources are available to assist in developing and implementing ILP?

- What external resources are available to assist in developing and implementing ILP?

- Has the law enforcement agency established a particular relationship and/or processes related to the state or regional fusion centers?

  - Does the agency have someone assigned full- or part-time to a fusion center?

- Are there particular obstacles or challenges that must be resolved before implementing ILP?[18]

The intent of these questions is to collectively establish a profile of the agency's intelligence capacity, if any, so that the law enforcement agency has a clear picture of its starting point. This assessment will help guide the agency toward the next step in the implementation process.

As noted previously, a critical tool for socialization is providing fundamental knowledge to personnel. The need for training cannot be overemphasized, particularly awareness training for line personnel. New policies and procedures will have little meaning if personnel do not understand the concepts. Once again, the vast majority of America's uniformed law enforcement officers simply are unaware of the intelligence process and their role in it because our pre-9/11

[17] www.it.ojp.gov/documents/criminal_intel_training_standards.pdf

[18] These can be wide-ranging. For example, some agencies that operate under binding collective bargaining may have to resolve duty changes and training in a new collective bargaining agreement. Another example is that in some localities, the city council has forbidden a law enforcement agency from developing an intelligence capacity because of privacy and civil rights concerns. In yet other agencies that are operating under an intelligence-related court order or consent decree, changes may need to be made in the order prior to developing and implementing ILP.

Table 6-3: Organizational Self-Assessment Factors of an Intelligence-Led Policing Capacity

No Intelligence Capacity	Basic Intelligence Capacity for Information Sharing	Advanced Intelligence Capacity Including Intelligence Records Systems	Mature Full-Service Intelligence Capacity
Operational Characteristics: • No systematic intelligence training has been provided to personnel. • No intelligence policy or procedures. • No connectivity to intelligence records systems. • No systematic intelligence initiatives in the agency beyond sharing some intelligence products received from FBI, Department of Homeland Security, fusion center, etc.	**Operational Characteristics:** • Limited intelligence training, typically an investigator. • Generic intelligence policy. • No criminal intelligence records system. • No or minimal connectivity to intelligence records systems. • Intelligence activity limited to an individual or two identifying and sharing intelligence products and some BOLOs (be on the lookout).	**Operational Characteristics:** • One or two criminal intelligence analysts. • A formal criminal intelligence records system. • Connectivity to RISS.net (Regional Information Sharing System), LEO and/or LEIU (Law Enforcement Intelligence Unit).	**Operational Characteristics:** • Multiple analysts • Multisource connectivity • Advanced analyst training • Comprehensive records system
Action Steps: • Develop intelligence capacity as per *National Criminal Intelligence Sharing Plan* (NCISP) standards • Awareness training for all agency personnel as per the Minimum Criminal Intelligence Training Standards for United States Law Enforcement and Other Criminal Justice Agencies (Minimum Standards). • Develop operational plan • Establish logistics to receive and store Controlled Unclassified Information (CUI) • Develop privacy policy • Designate intelligence liaison officer (ILO) for fusion center • Establish community partnerships • Establish connectivity with RISS.net and/ or Law Enforcement Online (LEO)	**Action Steps:** • Review policies related to intelligence operational plan • Awareness training for all agency personnel as per the Minimum Standards • Establish public-private partnerships • Establish community partnerships • Ensure that CUI meets security standards • Ensure that privacy policy is in place or create one • Establish an ILO	**Action Steps:** • Ensure that intelligence records are 28 CFR Part 23-compliant • Write/review privacy policy for consistency with ISE guidelines • Ensure that all officers have received intelligence awareness training • Review operational plan as per the NCISP • Ensure that analyst training is compliant with the Minimum Standards • Identify a fusion center liaison • RISS, LEO, and LEIU memberships • Community partnerships established • Public-private partnerships established	**Action Steps:** • Ensure that all processes are NCISP-compliant • Advanced analyst training • ILO training program • Fusion center liaison • RISS, LEO and LEIU Memberships • Community partnerships established • Public-private partnerships established • Review privacy policy with ISE guideline

Assumption for all four categories: The Global Intelligence Working Group and ISE standards and guidelines are sufficiently new that most agencies have not fully addressed the standards, if at all.

philosophy that intelligence was to have very limited information sharing for operational security purposes. The paradigm has shifted dramatically, and local American law enforcement has a significant learning curve ahead of it.

When a commitment has been made to implement ILP, one of the top priorities is to provide training at two cognitive levels.[19] The first is awareness, which in reality, is more like education than training because the intent is to understand the concept of intelligence, how it works, and how it will contribute to the law enforcement mission. The second level is the development of skills and applications of intelligence, such as information collection, reporting processes, and proper use of intelligence reports. Beyond the cognitive-level training, there must be training that is explicitly directed to the different organizational levels and assignments within an agency that need the knowledge and skills to effectively perform in the ISE. The Minimum Standards provide the critical foundation content that is needed in any of these training initiatives. Moreover, the flexibility inherent in the Minimum Standards permits each agency to tailor the training program to its particular needs.

Change is a difficult process that most people initially resist; therefore, an early step in the process to introduce ILP is to overcome this resistance or dogmatism. The most effective way to accomplish this is by developing an understanding of ILP and demonstrating the benefits the change will produce for the individual and the organization. In a nutshell, people at all levels of the organization must be sold on the new concept—in this case, ILP. Changing attitudes, values, and beliefs—that is, resocializing people—is a difficult process requiring proactive initiatives, vigilance, patience, and the recognition that some people will never accept the change.

One of the key methods to help the socialization process is to demonstrate commitment and allocate resources to ILP.

With the resocialization process under way in a law enforcement agency, an operational plan must be developed that articulates the mission and processes of the agency's intelligence capacity. Indeed, the first recommendation of the *National Criminal Intelligence Sharing Plan* addresses the need for an intelligence infrastructure for all American law enforcement agencies regardless of size.[20] Once again, the operational plan will be unique to each agency. While there are certain components that can be modeled, the vast differences between agencies minimize the ability to use a true model operational plan. Instead, assistance should be provided in the process of developing an operational plan that meets the needs and capabilities of each SLTLE agency.

After training has been provided and the operational plan developed and disseminated throughout the agency, the plan should be implemented through a formal notification to all personnel. Regardless of the level of planning, some aspects of the plan simply will not work. The need to obtain feedback from personnel to determine what works and what does not is essential. Plans that do not work should not be viewed as failures but as part of the fine-tuning process to make the plan work as effectively as possible.

[19] Government-sponsored or -endorsed intelligence training can be found on the Intelligence Master Training Calendar at www.ncirc.gov.

[20] Global Intelligence Working Group. *National Criminal Intelligence Sharing Plan. Recommendation 1.* Washington, D.C.: Office of Justice Programs, 2003, page v.

Finally, an important, yet often overlooked tool for effective ILP is a performance evaluation system that recognizes and rewards those individuals who are practicing ILP, as well as a performance assessment of the entire ILP initiative.

If a traditional evaluation system for assessing individual performance is in place that is based purely on quantitative variables—number of citations issued, number of reports written, number of arrests made, number of calls answered, and so forth—then the largely qualitative character of an officer's activities will not be considered in the performance evaluation system. Employees know that organizational success is inextricably tied to the evaluation process; therefore, if success in ILP is going to be achieved, there must be a personnel assessment system that values the practice.

Similarly, the agency's overall success in effectively implementing ILP must be measured, as well. Goals from the operational plan should be stated in a measurable form so that ongoing assessments may adjust the components and modify implementation as necessary to ensure efficient and effective practice of ILP.[21]

Conclusion

A theme that has permeated this discussion is that the introduction of ILP is an exercise in organizational change—a process that is always difficult. While important lessons can be learned from the British National Intelligence Model as well as from other countries that have experimented with ILP, such as Australia, American law enforcement agencies have a significantly different experiential and structural demography that prevents a comprehensive adoption of the model at this point. Most law enforcement agencies in the United States are just beginning to enter the intelligence arena and, therefore, the introduction of ILP must start at a basic level.

In summary, as agencies begin to introduce ILP, a number of important lessons from the organizational change process can help guide this transformation:[22]

- There must be a stimulus for change. There must be a leader with a vision willing to take the first step in challenging the status quo—a change agent. Important, this stimulus must be ongoing and widespread. Given this, a change agent must address two significant elements: 1. vigilance in effort and 2. diversity in focus.

- There must be administrative commitment. The effective administrator must provide ongoing support for a new initiative or program; that is, provide consistency between what is said and what is done. If administrators are not willing to try such things as reallocation of resources, amending policies and procedures, or experimenting with new ideas, then there is little reason to believe the sincerity of their pronouncements. If commitment is not shown to either employees or politicians, the probability for success will be reduced significantly.

[21] One method for monitoring implementation status and success is to use the ILP Self-Assessment Tool prepared as part of the Michigan State University (MSU) "Sustaining Intelligence" training program funded by the U.S. Department of Homeland Security. More information on this tool may be obtained by contacting the MSU School of Criminal Justice Intelligence Program – intellprogram.msu.edu.

[22] Modified from: Carter, David L. *The Police and Community.* 7th ed. Upper Saddle River, New Jersey: Prentice Hall, 2002, chapter 9.

- <u>Any change must be grounded in logical and defensible criteria.</u> While it is somewhat of a cliché, it is worth noting that changing to simply shake up the organization would be dysfunctional rather than productive. If politicians and employees are going to tie their professional fortunes to change, they must be given good evidence to support the change. Moreover, since change consumes resources, it is wasteful to pursue it unless this change is well-grounded in logic and evidence.

- <u>People at all levels must be able to provide input.</u> For a new endeavor, the importance of team-building cannot be understated. Any initiative must have participation from as many people as possible. Not only will this diverse input provide new insights, but team-building provides ownership and, hence, a sense of investment and responsibility by members of the team.

- <u>There must be sufficient time for experimentation, evaluation, and fine-tuning of any new program or idea.</u> When a new initiative is started, it will inherently contain bugs because not every malady or problem can be anticipated, and some ideas will not work as originally conceived. Just because operational problems arise, it does not mean the idea was bad. Administrators, politicians, and employees must be flexible, adjusting their activities until there has been sufficient time to actually evaluate the initiative's true effects.

- <u>Before change is introduced, the plan must be communicated to all persons and their support must be enlisted.</u> Politicians, citizens, and employees alike must understand clearly what is being done and why. There is a tendency to assume that everyone knows and understands the issues of a new endeavor to the same extent as those who are immersed in the planning. Lack of communication is something that can destroy a new activity but, fortunately, is fairly easy to avoid. Remember that communication is more than sending messages; it also involves gaining feedback from the messages. Be cognizant of the issue, recalling the admonishment, "Don't leave people in the dark."

- <u>Change takes time in order to have an effect; major change may take a generation.</u> Americans are generally a short-term and impatient culture. When implementing major organizational and behavioral change such as ILP, a key ingredient is resocialization of employees, citizens, and political leaders. This is inherently a long-term endeavor that requires patience and stamina before positive results can be seen. This sense of time must be instilled in all involved in order to minimize frustration and impatience.

- <u>Recognize that not everyone will buy in to new ideas.</u> For virtually any endeavor that is proposed, we must recognize that complete support is improbable; it is the nature of the human psyche. One must take care, however, to not discount people who oppose new initiatives as being "lost causes" or who are obstructionists. Listen to their concerns—they may raise some valid issues that need to be addressed. If their ideas are used positively, people who oppose a new initiative may become part of the team. Realism dictates, however, that there will still be those who oppose the new system (frequently for personal reasons). In these cases, an administrator's options are: 1. continue to try to convince them to change; 2. Ignore or avoid them; 3. Place employees in an assignment where they can do little damage; 4.

Increase the quality of the relationship with those political leaders and employees who support the initiative; or 5. Tolerate employees or politicians until they resign, retire, or lose their influence.

- Be flexible and open in your view of organizational, philosophical, and programmatic change. No matter how much thought is given to a new initiative and how much effort is invested in planning, we still must recognize that many ideas are losers. We often will not know this until the idea has been tried and evaluated. Even in failure, we can learn something. Unfortunately, given the culture of our political environment, there is a tendency to mandate success—a practice that is tantamount to a search for mediocrity. Both within the police organization and the broader political system, we must maintain the freedom to fail. Without this, creative new ideas will be few and far between.

- The chance always exists that one may be placed on the hot seat from a political perspective. It cannot be denied that any attempt at change carries risks—the more massive the change, the greater the risk. Questioning traditional orthodoxy is not easily accepted by organizations, particularly bureaucratic organizations typically found in government. Proponents of new initiatives must understand that when they are on the forefront of change, their political necks are on the line. In light of this, administrators must be supportive and empathic with the politicians and employees supporting the change.

- Change requires challenging conventional wisdom or, at least, traditions. Debating the value of traditions has not been a politically popular avenue for people to follow, yet it is a necessary one for new ventures to be undertaken. When conventional wisdom is challenged, it will be met with resistance, criticism, and, perhaps, ridicule from doubters, dogmatists, and traditionalists. The astute leader must be prepared to deal with these reactions both personally and professionally. Important, when those who support the leader's ideas of change are attacked, the leader has the obligation to reassert that person's value and contributions to the organization.

- The organization's personnel evaluation system must measure and reward effective involvement in change. Since change requires a personal commitment or investment, there must be some individual benefits that can be accrued from one's participation. Benefits do not have to be monetary, but they can include such things as positive reinforcement, job perquisites, creative freedom, recognition, and awards or commendations. Similarly, awards and expressions of appreciation must also be afforded to those who substantially help usher change. In essence, without rewards, failure is ensured.

ILP holds great potential for American law enforcement. For success, however, the change process to implement ILP must begin at the most fundamental level; it must be deliberate and be tailored to the needs and resources of the agency.

Chapter Annex 6-1:
Community Education Handout

Wichita State University
Regional Community Policing Institute

The Citizens' Role in Counterterrorism

OBSERVE	RESOURCES
• Be aware of potential attackers who may be conducting surveillance of a target	
• Behaviors include unusually long observation of a target, including taking notes, photographs, drawing schematics, and similar documentation, recording or monitoring activities, drawing diagrams, making notes on maps, using vision enhancing devices, possessing floor plans or blueprints	Office of Community Oriented Policing Services www.cops.usdoj.gov Terrorism Answers www.terrorismanswers.com United For a Stronger America www.weprevent.org
• Be aware when a stranger attempts to gain information about an important place or potential target	U.S. State Department, Counterterrorism Office www.state.gov/s/ct/
• Questions may include the schedule and types of deliveries, security, and operations that go "beyond curiosity"	National Center for Disaster Preparedness www.ncdp.mailman.columbia.edu
• Potential attackers may "test security"	National Academies Press, Terrorism and National Security Collection
• These include walking or driving into prohibited areas as an "accident" to determine the type of security or police response	stills.nap.edu/collections/terror/index.html
• Be aware of strangers acquiring unusual quantities and kinds of supplies that could facilitate an attack	Department of Homeland Security Preparedness Web Site www.ready.gov/
• This could include law enforcement, military or security supplies, uniforms, identification badges, explosives, weapons, chemicals; false identities, etc.	FirstGov for Citizens www.firstgov.gov/Topics/Usgresponse.shtml
• Be suspicious of people who "don't belong" and/or whose behavior is unusual	Citizens Corps www.citizencorps.gov
• For example, furtive conduct, the appearance of a "dry run" of an attack, the deployment of assets or supplies to commit the attack.	Federal Bureau of Investigation www.fbi.gov
DOCUMENT	
• Jot down descriptions of people and vehicles	
• People – race/ethnicity, sex, age, complexion, height, weight, clothing	
• Vehicles – "CYMBAL" – Color, Year, Make, Body and License	
• Make a note of both:	School of Criminal Justice
• The behaviors that drew your attention to the individuals	Michigan State University
• The types of behavior you observed	
REPORT	Regional Community Policing Institute Wichita State University www.wsurcpi.org
• Call the local police	
• Remember…	Intelligence Program/School of Criminal Justice Michigan State University intellprogram.msu.edu
• What may seem to be inconsequential may be an important piece of information in a larger puzzle	
• Follow your intuition	

Chapter 7:
*Civil Rights and Privacy in the
Law Enforcement Intelligence Process*

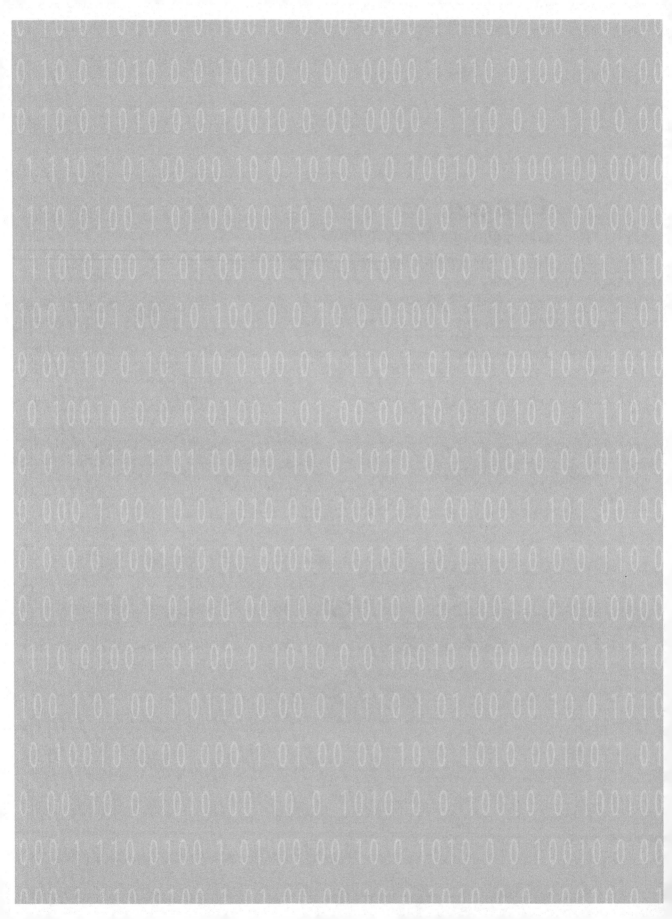

Civil Rights and Privacy in the
Law Enforcement Intelligence Process

In the process of providing public safety, an inherent responsibility of all law enforcement agencies is the protection of citizens' civil rights—intelligence activities are no exception. One of the most important and fundamental aspects of American life is the freedoms afforded to every citizen through civil rights protections. Despite the perceptions of some, law enforcement officials accept this responsibility. They understand that the protection of civil liberties is just as important as protecting the community from crime and terrorism. While this is a fundamental truth, there is debate on where the line should be drawn with respect to the degree of intrusion allowed to the government on privacy and personal liberty in order to protect America's citizens and the country's sovereignty from external threats, such as terrorism.

One question that has been debated is whether some civil liberties should be reduced to protect America from terrorism. This issue is embodied in the philosophical question of which is more important—protecting Americans from a terrorist attack that may kill thousands of people or protecting individual civil liberties which are the lifeblood of America's most sacred principles? In truth, when examined objectively, there is no unequivocal right or wrong answer to this question because it is philosophical in nature and depends on each individual's personal philosophy and life's experiences.

Fortunately, the working law enforcement officer does not have to deal with this philosophical debate. Rather, the officer must focus on fairly explicit rules that ensure that constitutional protections for citizens remain intact. These include the following:

- Law enforcement cannot collect information on individuals for intelligence activities unless there is a criminal predicate. The law enforcement officer must have reliable, fact-based information that reasonably infers that a particularly described intelligence subject has committed, is committing, or is about to commit a crime.

- All information collected about an individual for intelligence purposes must be done in a manner that is consistent with the law of criminal procedure.

- Collected information cannot be retained indefinitely. Instead, it may be retained only if there is reliable information that provides sustained evidence of a criminal predicate.

- The law enforcement agency has the responsibility of protecting the privacy of information they collect about individuals in the course of intelligence operations. This protection of privacy extends to the dissemination of information only to officials who have the right to know and a need to know the information to further a criminal inquiry.

- When there is no evidence of a sustained criminal predicate, all intelligence records about an individual must be purged (destroyed).

Each issue will be discussed in the coming pages. Because of the importance and emotions on both sides of the debate, there has been a significant increase in the scrutiny of law enforcement intelligence activities to ensure that information is being collected, used, retained, and disseminated in a proper manner. Indeed, many law enforcement agencies have been criticized for their intelligence function, not only because of perceived abuses, but even for the potential for abuse. This last point deserves special attention.

The "potential for abuse" does not mean abuse will occur, rather it means that the opportunity for abuse exists if there are no control factors in place to prevent abuse. The three most salient factors are these:

1. Policy.
2. Training.
3. Supervision and accountability.

Policy establishes the agency philosophy, standards, expectations, and decision-making boundaries of any organizational task and responsibility.

Training provides the knowledge, skills, and abilities to perform any particular occupational task. It specifies the method of performing, what must be done, how it should be done, and what should not be done. It demonstrates the application of policy and typically informs personnel of implications and sanctions if the task is not performed correctly.

Supervision and accountability are organizational mechanisms to ensure that policy is followed and performed in the manner specified by the training. Subordinates' activities and behaviors are monitored by a supervisor to hold the individuals accountable for performing their responsibilities only in a manner that is sanctioned by the agency.

With clearly defined policy, effective training, and responsible supervision, the potential for abuse is dramatically reduced. Two additional factors that can also affect the potential for abuse are systemic to the organization. First is the type of people the agency employs. What are the requirements? What characteristics are sought in new employees? What factors in the selection process shape the type of person who is hired? The clay used to mold the law enforcement officer will significantly influence the effectiveness of policy, training, and supervision.

The second factor is agency leadership. The tone that the leader establishes for the department, as well as expectations of the leader, will be reflected in the behaviors of the employees. A leader who establishes clear expectations of personnel performance and supports those expectations with both rewards and sanctions, as appropriate, will also significantly lower the probability of abuse from occurring.

The potential for abuse exists with all types of law enforcement assignments, not just intelligence. Modern law enforcement seeks to perform all law enforcement responsibilities in a lawful, professional manner. To conclude that the law enforcement intelligence unit or an intelligence fusion center is inherently flawed simply because of the potential for abuse is a fallacious argument.

Privacy and Civil Rights: A Foundation

To begin, some basic definitions are in order. The term privacy refers to individuals' interests in preventing the inappropriate collection, use, and release of personally identifiable information. Privacy interests include privacy of personal behavior, privacy of personal communications, and privacy of personal data.[1] The U.S. Constitution does not explicitly use the word privacy, but several of its provisions protect different aspects of this fundamental right. Although an explicit federal constitutional right to an individual's privacy does not exist, privacy rights have been articulated in different contexts by the U.S. Supreme Court.[2] Privacy protections are numerous and include protection from unnecessary or unauthorized collection of personal information (e.g., eavesdropping), public disclosure of private facts, and shame or humiliation caused by release of personal information."[3]

Recommendations from the National Criminal Intelligence Sharing Plan (NCISP)

Recommendation 6: All parties involved with implementing and promoting the National Criminal Intelligence Sharing Plan should take steps to ensure that the law enforcement community protects individuals' privacy and constitutional rights within the intelligence process.

Recommendation 9: In order to ensure that the collection or submission, access, storage, and dissemination of criminal intelligence information conforms to the privacy and constitutional rights of individuals, groups, and organizations, law enforcement agencies shall adopt, at a minimum, the standards required by the Criminal Intelligence Systems Operating Policies federal regulation (28 CFR Part 23), regardless of whether or not an intelligence system is federally funded.

The term civil rights is used to imply that the state has a role in ensuring that all citizens have equal protection under the law and equal opportunity to exercise the privileges of citizenship regardless of race, religion, sex, or other characteristics unrelated to the worth of the individual. Civil rights, therefore, are obligations imposed on government to promote equality. More specifically, they are the rights to personal liberty guaranteed to all United States citizens by the Thirteenth and Fourteenth Amendments and by acts of Congress. Generally, the term civil rights involves positive (or affirmative) government action, while the term civil liberties involves restrictions on government.[4] As such, civil liberties refers to fundamental individual rights derived from the Bill of Rights, such as freedom of speech, press, or religion; due process of law; and other limitations on the power of the government to restrain or dictate the actions of individuals. Civil liberties offer protection to individuals from improper government action and arbitrary governmental interference.

Privacy, civil rights, and civil liberties have important implications for the law enforcement intelligence process, particularly in light of past abuses. Critics claim that law enforcement has not changed its intelligence practices and that post-9/11 counterterrorism initiatives have made law enforcement agencies even more intrusive. Understanding this concern and the consequent scrutiny of law enforcement intelligence activities by those concerned about civil rights abuses provides an important perspective.

[1] For a comprehensive review of privacy issues, particularly related to various types of electronic information collection, including the Internet and e-mail, see: Lilly, Jacob R. "National Security at What Price?: A Look Into Civil Liberty Concerns in the Information Age Under the USA PATRIOT Act Of 2001 and a Proposed Constitutional Test For Future Legislation." *Cornell Journal of Law and Public Policy.* 12 (Spring) (2003): 447.

[2] Several state constitutions contain explicit language regarding a right to privacy.

[3] NCISP, p. 5

[4] NCISP, p. 6

Increased Scrutiny of Law Enforcement Intelligence: The Challenge of Balancing Civil Liberties and Community Safety

Why is there increased scrutiny and criticism of law enforcement intelligence activities when there is a demonstrable threat of terrorism that can cause catastrophic effects, as evidence by the human, social, and economic impact of 9/11? There appear to be several factors.

Perhaps at the top of the list are abuses in the past. Unfortunately, there is a documented history of law enforcement (and other government agencies) that improperly collected, retained, and/or disseminated information and behavior about individuals whose public statements and actions were controversial, but not criminal. While in many of those instances law enforcement agencies believed that the intelligence target was undermining American sovereignty,[5] the fact remains that the agencies had no authority to collect or retain the information because it was a noncriminal expressive activity. It must be emphasized that law enforcement authority to perform any kind of intelligence activity is based solely in the statutory authority to enforce the criminal law, hence the obligation to follow the law of criminal procedure. As such, collecting information about citizens without an articulable criminal nexus is improper. Law enforcement agencies remain under scrutiny and are still paying the price for past abuses.

A second reason has its foundation in the civil rights revolution that had its birth in the 1960s and is exemplified by Supreme Court decisions under Chief Justice Earl Warren that expanded the application of civil rights and liberties.[6] The era experienced, for the first time, citizens overtly exercising and testing their rights in the form of public demonstrations and civil disobedience on a major scale as part of the civil rights movement and Vietnam War protests. This atmosphere prompted lawsuits by a new breed of activist civil rights attorneys against police departments and corrections agencies. These actions largely brought a long-standing statute, 42 USC 1983—Civil Action for Deprivation of Civil Rights, out of dormancy. Collectively, these events placed a new emphasis on the rights of Americans and added a new lexicon to the American citizenship experience.

A third factor is that many persons do not understand the distinction between law enforcement intelligence and national security intelligence. As such, they assume that actions of the intelligence community may also reflect actions of a local law enforcement agency. For example, the National Security Agency's capture of international telephone conversations or the FBI monitoring a suspicious person entering the United States identified by the CIA as a possible threat are examples of information collection that a state, local, or tribal law enforcement agency will neither perform nor typically have access to. Yet, there often is an assumption that law enforcement agencies are involved in such activities and, as such, must be monitored in order to protect civil rights.

Fourth, the 24-hour news cycle and evolving news outlets have also contributed to the increased scrutiny of law enforcement operations, including intelligence.

[5] This was particularly true with the fear of communism and members of the Communist Party in the United States, and their sympathizers during the 1950s and 1960s.

[6] As an example of how law enforcement adapts to change, when many of the Warren Court decisions expanded civil rights protections for the criminally accused, there was a loud cry by many that the Court was "handcuffing the police" and that this would lead to more crime. (The *Miranda* v. *Arizona*, 348 U.S. 436 (1966), decision was a particularly significant decision influencing the sentiment at that time.) Sentiments ran so strong that "Impeach Earl Warren" billboards appeared all across America. As new policy and training were put in place in law enforcement agencies, and particularly as new officers were hired, most of whom were college educated, the Warren Court decisions were embraced as "simply the rules we have to follow." It became, in a comparatively short amount of time, a nonissue.

Notwithstanding some changes in the print media, the evolution of the electronic media—both broadcast and Internet—have contributed significantly to the scrutiny of government activities. The increased electronic outlets have added spirited competition to news organizations, increasing competition to capture news stories that will pique the interests of consumers and meet the need for content on a 24/7/365 basis. As a result of these factors, there is more competition for controversial stories that will uniquely resonate with consumers. Moreover, because of the need to fill every hour with content, stories receive greater depth and are often repeated many times throughout a day. The consequent effect is a bombardment of news on a given topic that gives an impression of an issue that is somewhat disproportionate.

A fifth factor contributing to the scrutiny of law enforcement intelligence appears to be the increased partisanship among both elected officials and the electorate. This has developed a dichotomous environment on virtually every social, political, and economic issue where attitudes and behaviors tend to be drawn exclusively along partisan lines with extreme criticism and little conciliation toward opponents' views. Virtually any factor at issue—including law enforcement intelligence—can be caught in some type of partisan dispute.

Next, the growth of civil rights advocacy groups[7] has also clearly influenced public scrutiny of law enforcement. These groups identify incidents and trends that heighten their concerns about privacy protections. Through press releases, white papers, public presentations, and lawsuits, these groups publicize government behaviors they feel are improper. While not always publicly popular, these groups nonetheless bring the issue to the table to open a public debate and, oftentimes, seek to change public policy through litigation or political influence.

Finally, the movement of "open government" invites public scrutiny. Largely beginning in the 1970s with Watergate, a grassroots movement known as "open government" began slowly. The essential concern was that public officials were abusing the authority of their offices and had the obligation to demonstrate that actions of government officials were lawful and in the best interests of all citizens. The movement continued to gain widespread support with government officials slowly responding. Open records acts and open meetings acts were increasingly being passed, federal and state freedom of information acts (FOIA) were expanded, and judicial interpretations of FOIA legislation became increasingly broad. As a result of public demands, elected officials were required to issue financial disclosure statements and public watchdog groups began issuing reports on various actions of officials at all levels of government. Essentially, the movement seeks accountability in government.

Collectively, these factors have contributed to the public expectation of the right to know what's going on in government activities and have increasingly sought explanations and accountability through lawsuits. In recent years, fueled by the growth of the Internet and 24-hour news channels, accountability has grown to second-guessing many government decisions. For example, the recent publication of some classified documents by the media is one artifact

[7] See: Bill of Rights Defense Committee, www.bordc.org; American Civil Liberties Union, www.aclu.org; Electronic Frontier Foundation, www.eff.org; or Center for Democracy and Technology, www.cdt.org. Each has particular areas of concern about privacy, civil rights, and civil liberties as related to all types of governmental policy and actions, not just law enforcement. Each organization provides an important watchdog role, albeit oftentimes with controversy. Of course, an important watchdog or advocacy organization that stimulates controversy is probably not taking much action.

of this movement. As a general rule, mainstream open government advocates recognize the need to maintain secrecy of "content;" however, they expect openness as it relates to processes. That is, the public recognizes the need to keep explicit information confidential, but wants assurances that information is being collected, retained, used, and shared in a manner that protects their rights. These ideals affect law enforcement intelligence activities at all levels of government and necessitate the need to have open processes and privacy policies in place. The ideal that government is "of the people, by the people, for the people" is being increasingly demanded, and must be taken seriously by policymakers. Intelligence is no exception. Indeed, the inherent threat-based confidential nature of the intelligence process invites even more scrutiny. As evidence of this, the American Civil Liberties Union (ACLU) has stated:

> No American is beneath the law's protection. And no one ... is above the law's limits. Our system of checks and balances must be maintained if American democracy is to be preserved.[8]

Similarly, the Bill of Rights Defense Committee has stated as its mission...

> ... to promote, organize, and support a diverse, effective, nonpartisan national grassroots movement to restore and protect civil rights and liberties guaranteed to all U.S. residents by the Bill of Rights. Our purpose is to educate people about the significance of those rights in our lives; to encourage widespread participation; and to cultivate and share the organizing tools and strategies needed for people to convert their concern, outrage, and fear into debate and action to restore Bill of Rights protections.[9]

It is important to recognize the need for accountability and the ramifications on a law enforcement agency if accountability is dismissed or ignored. Collectively, these factors represent a significant sociopolitical change in American life and, consequently, emerging law enforcement intelligence initiatives.

Consent Decree Defined

A consent decree is a settlement that is contained in a court order. The court orders injunctive relief against the defendant and agrees to maintain jurisdiction over the case to ensure that the settlement is followed. (Injunctive relief is a remedy imposed by a court in which a party is instructed to do or not do something. Failure to obey the order may lead the court to find the party in "contempt of the court" and to impose other penalties.) Plaintiffs in lawsuits generally prefer consent decrees because they have the power of the court behind the agreements. Defendants who wish to avoid publicity also tend to prefer such agreements because they limit the exposure of damaging details. A court will maintain jurisdiction and oversight to make sure the terms of the agreement are executed.

From Lexis-Nexis Legal, www.lexisnexis.com

---

[8] From www.aclutx.org/files/ACLU%20 of%20TX%20DISPATCH%2002-2006.pdf, click Safe and Free, and from that page click Surveillance.

[9] www.bordc.org/about

Lawsuits and Decrees Related to Law Enforcement Intelligence Activities

Perhaps the most controversial area of information-gathering by law enforcement agencies deals with cases where individuals are involved in "expressive activity" that is often controversial, even extreme. People who express extreme views related to animal and environmental protection, antigovernment sentiments, anarchy, white supremacy, or any other belief system are often viewed as a threat, even though their specific actions are not criminal. Indeed, evidence has shown that there is an area of behavior between "extreme" and "criminal" that is dynamic and often difficult to define. The distinction between making a firm statement of belief and making a threat is often a matter of interpretation. In the post-9/11 environment we, as a country, have become hypersensitive about threats, which appears to be leading toward less tolerance of diverse, even extreme, views. The challenge for law enforcement is to make that distinction. The intelligence process seeks to collect information about individuals who pose threats to the community, but the behavior a law enforcement officer may define as having a criminal nexus may be behavior a civil libertarian calls a freedom of expression.

The need to understand the subtleties in these distinctions is important to ensure that law enforcement officers are performing their function lawfully while simultaneously protecting the community from harm. Unfortunately, as noted previously, there is a legacy of law enforcement abuses where agencies have collected information on individuals simply as a result of their political beliefs.[10] While law enforcement agencies have changed significantly during the past several decades, this legacy is difficult to overcome.

The Supreme Court's broad interpretation of the First Amendment-based right of association, as originally defined in *NAACP* v. *Alabama*[11] and most recently in *Boy Scouts of America* v. *Dale*,[12] can protect groups engaged in First Amendment conduct from unjustified political or religious surveillance that causes them cognizable harm. As a result, the state's interest in protecting the community may, in many instances, be outweighed by the protections afforded to expressive activity found in these court decisions. While limitations on surveillance cannot unduly restrict the government's ability to conduct necessary information-gathering, requiring a reasonable suspicion of criminal activity before investigating First Amendment activity can help achieve a suitable balance between public safety interests and associational rights.[13] This evidence of criminal activity, that is, the criminal predicate, establishes the compelling state interest that justifies law enforcement intelligence inquiries.

Two particularly noteworthy court cases concern expressive activity and the law enforcement intelligence function. Understanding the lessons learned from these cases provides insight useful for decision-making related to information collection and retention.

[10] See: Chevigny, Paul G., "National Security and Civil Liberties: Politics and Law in the Control of Local Surveillance." *Cornell Law Review* 69 (April) (1984): 735.

[11] *NAACP* v. *Alabama*, 357 U.S. 449 (1958).

[12] Boy Scouts of America, et al v. Dale, 530 U.S. 640 (2000).

[13] Fisher, Linda E., "Guilt by Expressive Association: Political Profiling, Surveillance and the Privacy of Groups." *Arizona Law Review* 46 (Winter) (2004): 621.

New York:

Handschu v. *Special Services Division,* 605 F. Supp. 1384(S.D.N.Y. 1985), affirmed, 787 828 (2d Cir. 1986). In the 1960s, the New York Police Department (NYPD) increased surveillance and other investigations to include:

> …more undercover and other surveillance of "groups that because of their conduct or rhetoric may pose a threat to life, property, or governmental administration"; of "malcontents"; and of "groups or individuals whose purpose is the disruption of governmental activities" for the peace and harmony of the community.[14]

While many activists maintained that the NYPD was collecting information on various activists who held nontraditional views but were not committing crimes, they had difficulty demonstrating evidence of this.

During a 1971 trial of 21 Black Panthers charged with attempting to blow up several police stations, information made public through the discovery process, evidence, and testimony revealed that the NYPD kept dossiers on groups defined as radical and activist, as well as others including gay groups, educational reform advocates, and some religious and civic groups.[15] As a result of this new information, the Handschu case was filed as a class action lawsuit against NYPD surveillance activities[16] by 16 individuals affiliated with various ideological associations and organizations.

> In the suit, plaintiffs contended that "informers and infiltrators provoked, solicited, and induced members of lawful political and social groups to engage in unlawful activities"; that files were maintained with respect to "persons, places, and activities entirely unrelated to legitimate law enforcement purposes, such as those attending meetings of lawful organizations"; and that information from these files was made available to academic officials, prospective employers, and licensing agencies and others. In addition, plaintiffs identified seven specific forms of police conduct: 1. the use of informers; .2. infiltration; 3. interrogation; 4. overt surveillance; 5. summary punishment; 6. intelligence-gathering; and 7. electronic surveillance. The complaint alleged, inter alia, that these police practices had had a "chilling effect" on the exercise of freedom of speech, assembly, and association; that they also violated constitutional prohibitions against unreasonable searches and seizures; and that they abridged rights of privacy and due process. The suit requested declaratory and injunctive relief to curtail these practices.[17]

Police officials conceded that their activities included information-gathering for the intelligence process and was "not limited to investigations of crime, but related to any activity likely to result in 'a serious police problem.'"[18] Essentially, the police department asserted that it had a need to collect information about people and their activities which, although absent a criminal predicate at the time, held a demonstrably strong potential for criminal activity and the information collection was necessary for community safety.

[14] *Handschu* v. *Special Services Division,* 605 F. Supp. 1384 at 1396 (S.D.N.Y. 1985).

[15] Lee, Chisun, "The NYPD Wants to Watch You." *The Village Voice.* Series of articles December 18–24, 2002.

[16] Specifically identified for these activities was the Special Services Division of the NYPD Intelligence Bureau.

[17] Koehnlein, Bill. *The History of the Handschu Decree.* New York Civil Liberties Union, 2003.

[18] Handschu, Ibid. p., 1396.

The consent decree in *Handschu* v. *Special Services Division*, which included what is referred to as the Handschu Settlement agreed to in 1985, governs NYPD investigations of groups or individuals engaging in various forms of political activity. The settlement established the Handschu Authority[19] to oversee the activities of the Public Security Section (PSS) of the Intelligence Division.[20] The NYPD could not engage in any investigation of political activity that the settlement defined as "the exercise of a right of expression or association for the purpose of maintaining or changing governmental policies or social conditions."[21] The settlement authorized the PSS to commence an investigation only after the NYPD established the following:

> … specific information [that] a person or group engaged in political activity is engaged in, about to engage in, or threatened to engage in conduct which constitutes a crime.[22]

Information obtained during investigations of individuals, groups, or organizations could be collected or maintained only in conformity with the settlement. Information "from publicly available sources" could not be maintained with the PSS. Officers were allowed to collect only certain, general information about a planned noncriminal event "in order to preserve the peace, deploy manpower for control of crowds, and protect the right[s] of individuals to freedom of speech and assembly."[23] The settlement prohibited developing a file on an individual or group based solely on that individual's or group's "political, religious, sexual, or economic preference." In sum, these are the five key elements of the Handschu consent decree:

1. Political groups can be investigated only when suspected criminal activity is alleged.
2. The NYPD must obtain a written authorization from a three-person panel—the Handschu Authority—after presenting its suspicions.
3. The NYPD is prohibited from videotaping and photographing public gatherings where there is no indication that any criminal activity is present.
4. The NYPD must obtain written agreement from any agency with which it intends to share this information, acknowledging that it will abide by the terms of the Handschu Agreement.
5. The court ordered the panel to prepare annual reports, open to the public, demonstrating the NYPD's requests for surveillance and the number of requests the panel granted.

In light of the threat environment after the 9/11 attacks—an environment which, of course, was particularly pronounced in New York—the NYPD sought and obtained modification of the consent decree.[24] While the NYPD requested fairly broad latitude for information collection about activities of persons who were likely political extremists, the court's modification of the consent decree was narrower, yet still permitting some expansion of the original restrictions. The court acknowledged that there was a change in the public safety environment in New York following the 9/11 attacks and modified the Handschu consent decree to be consistent with the FBI Guidelines[25] issued by the U.S. Attorney General.

[19] The Handschu Authority, similar to an oversight board, consisted of the First Deputy Commissioner of the Police Department, the Deputy Commissioner for Legal Affairs, and a civilian member appointed by the mayor for a term that was revocable at will.

[20] The Public Security Section (PSS) of the NYPD Intelligence Division was the new name of what had been the Special Services Division of the Intelligence Unit when the original class action lawsuit was filed.

[21] Steigman, Jerrold L., "Reversing Reform: The Handschu Settlement in Post-September 11 New York City." *Brooklyn Journal of Law and Policy* 11 (2003): 759.

[22] Ibid.

[23] Ibid., p. 760.

[24] Steigman, Ibid. p. 746.

[25] The Guidelines are available at: www. justice.gov/ag/readingroom/guidelines. pdf.

The FBI Guidelines provide for three graduated levels of investigative activity: 1. [permit] checking initial leads [when] information is received of such a nature that some follow-up as to the possibility of criminal activity is warranted; 2. a preliminary inquiry [is] authorized when there is information or an allegation which indicates the possibility of criminal activity and whose responsible handling requires some further scrutiny beyond checking initial leads; and 3. a full investigation [is] authorized when facts or circumstances reasonably indicate that a federal crime has been, is being, or will be committed.[26]

The modification authorized by the court was viewed as a "mixed bag" by both the NYPD and civil libertarians; hence, one may conclude that it was a reasonable compromise. The Handschu Authority for oversight was retained in the modified consent decree. Another motion related to the consent decree requested the court to enjoin enforcement of New York City Police Department Interim Order 47 which established procedures and guidelines for the police department's use of photographic and video equipment, arguing that it was incompatible with NYPD guidelines, violated the plaintiff's First Amendment rights, and violated previous Handschu judgments.[27]

In February 2007, the court rejected the motions on the grounds that the investigations in question are not politically motivated. The court also stated that, since Order 47 did not constitute a First Amendment violation, it would not grant the plaintiffs' injunctive relief. Later in the year, the court further modified its February decision on the enforceability of the consent decree, requiring that plaintiffs show a systemic pattern of violations before the court will enjoin any police department policy.

The lessons learned from Handschu are that, regardless of the threat environment facing a community, surveillance of individuals by a law enforcement agency—including photographs, video, and collecting identities—still requires a criminal nexus. While some flexibility may be given in the post-9/11 environment, the constitutional guarantee of free speech and the freedom of expression remain paramount and must be respected by law enforcement agencies.

Denver:
American Friends Service Committee, et al v. City and County of Denver, 2004 U.S. Dist. LEXIS 18474. On March 11, 2002, the ACLU of Colorado publicly disclosed documents demonstrating that the Denver Police Department's (DPD) Intelligence Bureau had been monitoring and recording the peaceful protest activities of Denver-area residents and keeping files on the expressive activities of advocacy organizations about whom there was no evidence of criminal activity. In a letter dated March 11, 2002 to the Denver mayor, the ACLU asked the mayor to take immediate steps to stop the DPD's practice of keeping files on peaceful protest activities and to take four additional actions:

1. Prohibit the police from sharing their criminal intelligence information with other law enforcement agencies.

2. Order a full public accounting about the criminal intelligence information that would answer a number of questions.

[26] *Handschu v. Special Services Division,* 71 Civ. 2203 (Feb. 11, 2003) Slip Op. at 33–34.

[27] www.nyclu.org/node/1084, "*Handschu v. Special Services Division*"

3. Notify individuals named in the criminal intelligence information and permit them to review the information about them in the files.

4. Preserve the criminal intelligence information because it might be evidence in any forthcoming lawsuits. [20]

At a March 13, 2002 news conference, the Denver mayor made the following statement:

> After a preliminary review of the policy and reviewing a sampling of the files that have been kept on individuals and organizations, it is our conclusion that there was an overly-broad interpretation of the policy that resulted in cases where it may not have been justifiable to include certain individuals or organizations in our· intelligence-gathering activities.[29]

The plaintiffs filed a class action civil rights suit[30] against the DPD for violating U.S. and Colorado constitutional protections by not adhering to police department intelligence records policy and failing to manage its criminal intelligence records system in line with the guidelines in 28 CFR Part 23. The Plaintiffs' Class Action Complaint for Declaratory and Injunctive Relief[31] initially filed on March 28, 2002, challenged a practice of the Denver Police Department of monitoring the peaceful protest activities of Denver-area residents when there was no evidence of criminal activity; maintaining criminal intelligence records files[32] on...

> ...the expressive activities of law-abiding individuals and advocacy organizations, many of which the Department has falsely branded with the label of "criminal extremist;" and providing copies of certain Spy Files to third parties.[33]

The complaint further alleged that the DPD had...:

> ...singled out and selected the Plaintiffs and the plaintiff class for surveillance and monitoring based upon their advocacy of controversial or unpopular political positions and opinions.[34]

The plaintiffs also expressed concern that individuals would be less likely to join a rally or to participate in other expressive activities if they feared being photographed by the police or that their identities would appear in police criminal intelligence files. The complaint goes on to state that the criminal intelligence records on the plaintiffs...

> ... contain nothing but identifying information and facts that show that the targets of the surveillance are engaged in peaceful and legitimate educational activities, political expression, petitioning the government, and political association. The pages contain no facts that suggest that any of the named plaintiffs are involved in criminal activity.
>
> The Department has recorded false and derogatory information about the Plaintiffs. It has mischaracterized the goals and purposes of the Plaintiffs' expressive activity and smeared their personal, political, and professional reputations.
>
> The Department has disseminated the information in the Spy Files to third parties."[35]

[28] *American Friends Service Committee, et al v. City and County of Denver,* Class Action Complaint for Declaratory and Injunctive Relief, p. 4.

[29] Ibid.

[30] 42 U.S.C. §1983 – Civil Action for Deprivation of Civil Rights

[31] www.aclu-co.org/Spyfiles/ Documents/203SpyfileComplaint.pdf

[32] The criminal intelligence files in the complaint and subsequent news releases by the ACLU were referred to as the "Spy Files."

[33] American Friends Service Committee, Ibid. p. 2.

[34] Ibid.

[35] Ibid. p. 6.

Supporting their claims, the plaintiffs demonstrated practices in the department, including memoranda to officers from supervisors, that explicitly contradicted the DPD's criminal intelligence records policy, 28 CFR Part 23 and/or constitutional standards. One memorandum from the Intelligence Bureau commander to subordinates stated, in part:

> Please purge, i.e., shread, [sic] toss, or take home, ALL references and files earlier than a 1994 date. The heart of an Intelligence Bureau lies with the ability to maintain integrity of all files and references in the likely event of litigation by political or subversive groups.[36]

In light of the evidence presented in this case, while not admitting "...any fault or liability to Plaintiffs, nor any violation of law,"[37] the City of Denver entered into a Settlement Agreement with the plaintiffs. As part of the Settlement Agreement[38] the department established a new, more restrictive intelligence records policy,[39] created an oversight board, purchased a new computerized intelligence records system, and agreed to semiannual audits of compliance with the Settlement Agreement for 5 years.

The lessons learned from this case reinforces the requirement of a criminal predicate. Beyond this, the Denver case illustrates 1. The importance of supervision to enforce currently existing policy, 2. The importance of using the right-to-know and need-to-know standards of dissemination, and 3. The importance of complying with the 28 CFR Part 23 guidelines.

Implications from Handschu (New York) and American Friends (Denver)

At the heart of civil rights issues related to law enforcement intelligence are collection, retention, and dissemination of information which identifies individuals and organizations whose expressions and expressive activities pose a threat to public safety and security. The proverbial bottom line that is clear from these two cases reinforces the premise that any collection, retention, and dissemination of such information may occur when there is nexus between the behavior and a crime. Simply unpopular, unusual, or extreme expressions, along with assumptions that persons making such expressions may eventually lead to a crime, do not alone meet the test. There must be demonstrable evidence of a crime. Law enforcement officers should be trained to understand the issues associated expressive activity and a criminal predicate.

It is also clear from these cases that simply having a policy on criminal intelligence records is not enough, even if the policy is compliant with 28 CFR Part 23. There must also be supervision to ensure that the policy is followed. Law enforcement personnel must have explicit direction on their information-collection activities, and that direction must be consistent with standards that are characteristic of both professional good practice and the protection of civil rights and liberties. Similarly, it is important to reinforce that the dissemination of any such criminal intelligence information must meet the right-to-know and need-to-know standards.

[36] Denver Police Department Intelligence Bureau, Interoffice Correspondence to "All Troops" from the Intelligence Bureau Commander, Subject: Purge Days, November 2, 1998. www.aclu-co.org/spyfiles/Documents/MemoJoeBlack110298.pdf

[38] *American Friends Service Committee, et al v. City and County of Denver*, Settlement Agreement, April 17, 2003, p. 5, Section 7.3.

[39] www.aclu-co.org/spyfiles/Documents/SettleAgreement.pdf

[40] www.aclu-co.org/spyfiles/Documents/SettleAgreementExh1.pdf

These factors will be discussed in detail later. The important point to note is the role these factors played in these two important cases and the subsequent effects which resulted when the standards were not met.

Civil Rights Example: First Amendment Free Expression—Two Views

A common point of conflict over civil rights is found in actions related to free expression by persons involved in protests or demonstrations. Civil rights advocates maintain that their demonstrations are expressive activity protected by the First Amendment. As such, it is improper for law enforcement agencies to collect and retain information about persons who are involved in planning and participating in demonstrations, as well as about advocates of those individuals.

Law enforcement agencies maintain that the only information they collect and retain is that related to persons who commit crimes or pose threats to community safety. Civil rights advocates respond that minor crimes, such as trespassing or minor property destruction, are of such low magnitude that they do not counterbalance the violation of the broader First Amendment guarantees and that law enforcement uses minor crimes as an excuse to collect information about those with whom it disagrees. Law enforcement counters that it has the responsibility to protect the property of all victims and that any demonstration that permits property destruction can quickly spin out of control and result in even greater threats. The debate continues, often with opposing arguments, as illustrated in Table 7-1.

Table 7-1: Counterpositions on First Amendment Information Collection

Position of Protestors	Response of Law Enforcement
1. Government should not attempt to regulate expressive activity, no matter how repugnant, as long as the activity is done without committing a crime.	1. Often, it is difficult to determine, during the course of a protest or rally, if a crime is being committed or going to be committed. Anarchists, for example, have frequently spray-painted private property or have broken windows during the course of a protest. Spray-painting the property of another is "destruction of property," not an expressive activity.
2. Expressive activity is a fundamental right that is essential to the fabric of American life. As such, law enforcement should take no action to repress expressive activity.	2. Law enforcement has the obligation to protect the rights of all Americans, not just those engaged in expressive activity. As such, law enforcement agencies have the responsibility to take reasonable restrictive actions to protect the rights of others as well as to maintain community safety and security.
3. There should be no expressly defined "protest zones" that favor one group over another.	3. Some groups have a history of committing crimes during a protest, more so than others. Protest zones are used only in those cases where there is a history of crime or information that reasonably suggests a crime will be committed during a protest.
4. Law enforcement should not use pens, barricades, or force to regulate expressive activity.	4. In some cases, pens and barricades are used to protect the protestors or to prevent a conflict between protestors and those opposed to the group's expressive activity (e.g., Ku Klux Klan rallies).
5. Law enforcement should not use surveillance and infiltration of political or social groups involved in expressive activity.	5. Where there is reasonable suspicion to believe a crime will occur, the use of surveillance and infiltration is an accepted and lawful method to gather evidence for developing a criminal case for prosecution.
Believe these actions are required to protect civil rights	Balance is required to protect both	Believes this information is required to protect community

These are essentially diametrically opposed positions on the same issue. Which positions are correct? Like most issues where there are clear dichotomous perspectives, truth is somewhere in the middle of the continuum. The reality is that the burden typically falls on the law enforcement agency to show that its actions and the information collected was done in a manner that protects both civil rights and community safety. To minimize allegations of negligence and impropriety, as well as to demonstrate good faith actions by the law enforcement agency, a number of action steps could be performed, such as these:

1. Review the evidence and determine if there is trustworthy information on which a reasonable person would conclude that a crime may occur.

2. Use the least-intrusive means of information collection.

3. Provide specific direction on the types of criminal behavior that is suspected and types of information that needs to be collected to support the criminal predicate.

4. Ensure that supervision is present to monitor the law enforcement officers' information-collection activities.

5. When possible and appropriate, communicate with the protesting group to express concerns about crimes and the procedures that will be followed should a crime occur.

6. Ensure that all personnel understand the policy for information collection.

7. Ensure that all law enforcement activities are documented and explained as a matter of record.

8. Provide information and training to officers about the elements of crimes for which there is specific concern.

9. When the demonstration is over, review all information collected and destroy all information that is not needed to support a criminal case.

10. Prepare an after-action report that reviews processes, issues, and concerns—preferably with assistance from legal counsel—and amend processes that may place the agency in legal jeopardy.

The Need for More Controls of Intelligence Inquiries than Criminal Investigations[40]

At the heart of the diverse reasons why information collection by law enforcement agencies for the intelligence process is met with skepticism and suspiciousness is the belief by many that intelligence inquiries are more dangerous to liberty than criminal investigations. An intelligence inquiry attempts to assess the presence of a threat and the determination if a threat is real, unlike a criminal investigation that occurs after a crime has been discovered. Moreover, intelligence inquiries often engage First Amendment expression, they are more secretive, and they are less subject to after-the-fact scrutiny. Civil rights activists, therefore, argue that intelligence activities should require stronger compensating protections and remedies for violations. Three primary factors support these notions.

First, intelligence inquiries are broader. While they are limited by the criminal code, their breadth goes beyond crimes that have been committed and moves into the arena of threats. An explicit concern of civil rights activists is when law

[40] Based on a policy statement posted by the Center for Democracy and Technology, entitled "Bill Introduced to Reform FBI Data Demands", which can be found at www.cdt.org/publications/policyposts/2007/5

enforcement collects information about First Amendment activities. There often is disagreement about the interpretation of language and behaviors and whether the activity is the exercise of free speech or the exhortation of a threat.

Second, intelligence inquiries are conducted in much greater secrecy than criminal cases, even perpetual secrecy. When a person is accused in a criminal case, normally that person can make public statements about his or her innocence and publicly rebut the criminal assertions in open court proceedings. Moreover, in a criminal investigation the suspect is often aware of the investigation while it is underway. Similarly, most searches in criminal cases are carried out with simultaneous notice to the target. In intelligence cases, by contrast, the target and the individuals scrutinized because of their contacts with the target are rarely told that the government is collecting information about them. While the presumption of evidence is clearly respected in a criminal investigation, it is sometimes argued that there is a presumption of guilt in an intelligence inquiry. This perspective must change.

Third, in a criminal investigation almost everything the government does is ultimately exposed to scrutiny. A prosecutor knows that, at the end of the criminal process, his or her actions will be in public. If the prosecutor is overreaching or is on a fishing expedition, it will be aired with the prosecutor facing public scrutiny, ridicule, and perhaps disbarment.[41] That is a powerful constraint. Similarly, a police department must ultimately account to the public for crime rates and disorder in a community. Most intelligence inquiries never result in a trial or other public proceeding. The evidence may be used clandestinely. Sometimes the desired result is the mere sense that the government is watching.

Intelligence inquiries are broader, more secretive, and subject to less after-the-fact scrutiny; therefore, protections must be built in at the beginning. One important protection is a federal regulation related to criminal intelligence records that are held by state, local, and tribal law enforcement agencies.

Maintaining Privacy in the Intelligence Process

The concept of privacy is broad, encompassing different personal values and interests. A number of privacy-related factors become relevant in the current law enforcement intelligence environment and are intended to address "all crime and all threats."[42] Privacy interests may be characterized as representing a diverse array of issues, such as privacy of a person's beliefs, personal behavior, personal communications, personal attributes (such as health or handicaps), and personal data (information privacy). Private information includes not only information that a law enforcement agency may be collecting about a person's possible involvement in a criminal act, but also information relating to the following:

- Name, address, telephone number, or e-mail
- Race, national, or ethnic origin
- Religion
- Gender
- Marital status
- Fingerprints, blood type, or DNA

[41] This occurred with North Carolina prosecutor Michael Nifong in the allegations of sexual assault against Duke University lacrosse players. For more information, see "Duke Lacrosse Prosecutor Disbarred." CNN. www.cnn.com.

[42] Portions of this discussion are based on information in: National Criminal Justice Association (NCJA). *Justice Information Privacy Guide.* Washington, D.C.: NCJA, 2002, 12–13.

- Financial status, history, or credit condition
- Psychiatric or psychological conditions and history
- Criminal history
- Age
- Sexual orientation
- Education
- Medical history or conditions
- Employment history, including employment dispositions
- Identifying number, symbol, or other character assigned to identify a person (such as a social security number, driver's license number or university student identification number).

In the course of an intelligence inquiry, the law enforcement agency will collect different types of personal information, but has the obligation to maintain the privacy of the information regardless of whether the person is an intelligence target, witness, informant, or information provider (such as a citizen).

> Privacy of personal data (information privacy) is described as when, how, and to what extent you share personal information about yourself. Information privacy involves the right to control one's personal information and the ability to determine if and how that information should be obtained and used. It entails restrictions on a wide range of activities relating to personal information: its collection, use, retention, and disclosure.[43]

The law enforcement organization has an obligation to protect the privacy of all persons about whom the agency collects personal identifying information, including those suspected of committing crimes. Two primary methods are used: security and confidentiality.

Security of personal information means that mechanisms and processes have been put in place to ensure that there is no unauthorized access to private information. Whether the private information is in a computer system or in paper records, there must be an adequate mechanism in place to ensure that the information is not obtained by persons who do not have lawful access to them.

Confidentiality, particularly as related to information sharing, includes behaviors and processes that seek to prevent unauthorized disclosure of the information to third parties. After private information has been collected, the custodian of the information has the obligation to protect it from being shared with others unless there is a bona fide reason for a third party to receive the information. Once again, the standard of sharing personal information to others based on their right to know and need to know the information. This is an illustration of processes to ensure confidentiality. Moreover, there is an expectation that those who receive private information will maintain the confidentiality of personal information entrusted to them. Confidentiality is about limiting access to personal information 1. To those having specific permission for access[44] to the records and 2. Preventing its disclosure to unauthorized third parties.

[43] NCJA, 2002, p. 12.

[44] "Permission to access" private records can include consent by the individual and permission as provided through lawful regulatory procedures and/or the legal process.

To maximize privacy protection, law enforcement agencies should ensure that privacy protections are in place. The *National Strategy for Information Sharing* emphasized this by establishing core privacy principles that all agencies are required to adopt. These are:

- Share protected information only to the extent that it is terrorism information, homeland security information, or law enforcement information related to terrorism.
- Identify and review the protected information to be shared within the Information Sharing Environment (ISE).
- Enable ISE participants to determine the nature of the protected information to be shared and its legal restrictions (e.g., "this record contains individually identifiable information about a U.S. citizen").
- Assess, document, and comply with all applicable laws and policies.
- Establish data accuracy, quality, and retention procedures.
- Deploy adequate security measures to safeguard protected information.
- Implement adequate accountability, enforcement, and audit mechanisms to verify compliance.
- Establish a redress process consistent with legal authorities and mission requirements.
- Implement the guidelines through appropriate changes to business processes and systems, training, and technology.
- Make the public aware of the agency's policies and procedures, as appropriate.
- Ensure that agencies disclose protected information to nonfederal entities—including state, local, tribal, and foreign governments—only if the nonfederal entities provide comparable protections.
- State, local, and tribal governments are required to designate a senior official accountable for implementation.[45]

Protecting privacy is accomplished through the implementation of a privacy policy,[46] along with effective training and supervision.

A privacy policy is a written, published statement that articulates the policy position of an organization on how it handles the personally identifiable information that it gathers and uses in the normal course of business. The policy should include information relating to the processes of information collection, analysis, maintenance, dissemination, access, expungement, and disposition.

The purpose of a privacy policy is to articulate publicly that the agency will adhere to legal requirements and agency policy determinations that enable gathering and sharing of information to occur in a manner that protects personal privacy interests. A well-developed and implemented privacy policy uses justice entity resources wisely and effectively; protects the agency, the individual, and the public; and promotes public trust.[47]

State, local, and tribal law enforcement (SLTLE) agencies have a mandate to establish a privacy policy not only from the NCISP, but also to participate in the ISE. It is clear that there are unequivocal expectations for law enforcement agencies

[45] *National Strategy for Information Sharing.* Washington, D.C.: Executive Office of the President, 2007, 27–28.

[46] The *Privacy Policy Development Guide* may be downloaded at it.ojp.gov/documents/ Privacy_Guide_Final.pdf.

[47] Global Justice Information Sharing Initiative. *Privacy Policy Development Guide.* Washington, D.C.: Bureau of Justice Assistance, Office of Justice Programs, U.S. Department of Justice, 2006, 4–1.

to meet national professional standards for privacy and civil rights protections. As such, the obligation is to not only implement the policy, but to also provide training and supervision to ensure that the policy is effectively applied.

28 CFR Part 23 – Criminal Intelligence Operating Policies

As is evident from the preceding discussions, at the heart of the civil rights issues is whether law enforcement agencies are collecting and retaining personal identifying information of persons who are involved in expressive activity. Often, it is difficult to distinguish between expressive activity and activity that is a precursor to a crime. If certain behaviors suggest that a crime is being planned, the law enforcement agency has the responsibility to collect information to verify this and take action, as appropriate. It is not always immediately clear if a crime is in the preparatory stage, so criminal intelligence records are retained until the veracity of the threat is verified or dismissed. Because of this fine line, guidelines must be established as a matter of policy to ensure the information is weighed and appropriately retained or destroyed, depending on what additionally collected information suggests about criminal liability.

The guiding regulation for managing a criminal intelligence records system for SLTLE agencies is the federal regulation entitled Criminal Intelligence Systems Operating Policies codified in the Code of Federal Regulations at 28 CFR Part 23.[48] The regulation was created largely as a response to past practices of law enforcement agencies collecting and retaining information about people based on their activities and/or expressed nontraditional beliefs that were often extreme or unpopular, but not criminal. The regulation seeks to provide procedural guidance for the management of criminal intelligence records systems that is consistent with constitutional guarantees. The federal government, however, cannot mandate this regulation to independently governed state and local governments. Nevertheless, adoption of the regulation is a condition that SLTLE agencies must agree to in order to receive certain federal grant funds. If a local police department, for example, accepted federal funds to purchase a computer system that would be used to maintain a criminal intelligence records system, adoption of 28 CFR Part 23 is a requirement for receiving the funds.

This regulation was the only clear guideline for managing criminal intelligence records and it became the de facto standard that most agencies adopted, whether federal funds were received or not. Broad adoption of the regulation gained further momentum when the NCISP recommended that all law enforcement agencies adopt 28 CFR Part 23. As a result, the regulation became a recognized national professional standard.

Although agencies that embraced the regulation understood the regulatory language, it was not easily translated to policy. Moreover, the regulation had some operational gaps. The Law Enforcement Intelligence Unit (LEIU), therefore, developed a model operational policy and procedures that translated both the language and spirit of the regulation to be more easily adopted by a law enforcement agency. This practical interpretation of 28 CFR Part 23 is known as the LEIU File Guidelines.[49]

[48] The Bureau of Justice Assistance has developed an online training about 28 CFR Part 23 which can be accessed through the secure National Criminal Intelligence Resource Center (www.ncirc. gov) web site, accessible through HSIN Intel, LEO, and RISS.

[49] The LEIU File Guidelines can be found at it.ojp.gov/documents/LEIU_Crim_Intell_File_Guidelines.pdf.

The LEIU File Guidelines represent an important step in the management of criminal intelligence records systems to ensure constitutional integrity. Based on litigation, experience, and concern expressed by civil libertarians, the management of a criminal intelligence records system must also consider elements beyond this practical interpretation of 28 CFR Part 23; therefore, the current best practice is an amalgamation of different sources relying on a conservative integration of accepted practice and regulation. Those sources include 28 CFR Part 23, the LEIU File Guidelines, established law of criminal evidence and procedure, and precedent from lawsuits arising from civil rights lawsuits involving criminal intelligence records. It should be noted that this information reflects general practice, not unique state laws which may have different effects. The decision tree in Figure 7-1 is a visual representation of the following discussion concerning factors that should be considered before entering information into a criminal intelligence record system. This is a conservative interpretation of these factors in order to provide the safest guidance on retaining information in a criminal intelligence records system.

When information is collected, one of the first issues is to determine whether the information identifies either a person or an organization. Identity is not limited to a name but can include any descriptive information from which a person may identify an individual to the reasonable exclusion of others; for example, providing an address and physical description of a person living at that address may constitute identity. Determining if the information identifies an organization is somewhat more challenging because 28 CFR Part 23 includes organizations as protected criminal intelligence information but does not explicitly define organization. Based on precedent and experience, an organization is a distinguishable entity that has a definable purpose, an identifiable organizational leadership structure, and a process or method for members to affiliate with the organization, albeit informal. Certain entities exist, such as anarchist collectives wherein people tend to affiliate with each other around a common belief; however, they do not have the explicit characteristics defined above. In this illustration, the group is more of a movement than an organization. A movement that simply has a discernable ideology that people support, even as a collective, is not an organization.

A common question is why can information be retained in a criminal intelligence records system without establishing reasonable suspicion (i.e., a criminal predicate) if it does not identify a person or organization? Constitutional rights attach to individuals, not aggregate data, philosophical movements, criminal methods, or other information that is descriptive and useful for intelligence analysis but does not explicitly identify a person. Building on the concept from *Katz* v. *U.S.*[50] that the Fourth Amendment protects people, not places, logic says that constitutional protections are afforded to individuals, not aggregate behaviors or other information that are not explicitly linked to individuals. 28 CFR Part 23 explicitly extends protection to organizations as well as individuals.

If the information identifies an individual or organization, the next step is to determine if the information was collected in a manner consistent with lawful

[50] 389 U.S. 347 (1967)

criminal procedure. While this is not a requirement of 28 CFR Part 23, precedence in both criminal and civil law suggests that this is good practice for an agency to follow in the process of deciding what information should be included in a criminal intelligence records system. There are several reasons. First, it is a constitutional protection that should be afforded to individuals; it is part of the fundamental fairness that the American justice system affords to individuals under the due process clauses of the Fifth and Fourteenth Amendments. Second, the sole authority for law enforcement to have criminal intelligence and investigative functions is based in the statutory authority to enforce the criminal law. As such, there is a reasonable probability that criminal intelligence and investigative inquiries may lead to prosecution. If there are violations of criminal procedure, the evidence will likely be excluded from trial. Third, it strengthens the legal integrity of the intelligence or investigative inquiry, thereby reducing the probability of civil liability. Processes that carefully adhere to constitutional guarantees demonstrate good faith and, conversely, are an affirmative defense to negligence by the agency. Fourth, given the scrutiny of law enforcement intelligence and investigative practices by many in the civil rights community, having this step in the process reduces criticism of law enforcement activities. Finally, the practice is consistent with the Privacy Guidelines of the Information Sharing Environment, which state, in part:

i.   Seek or retain only protected information that is legally permissible for the agency to seek or retain under the laws, regulations, policies, and executive orders applicable to the agency.

ii. Ensure that the protected information that the agency makes available through the ISE has been lawfully obtained by the agency and may be lawfully made available through the ISE.[51]

[51] Program Manager for the Information Sharing Environment (PM-ISE). *Guidelines to Ensure that the Information Privacy and Other Legal Rights of Americans Are Protected in the Development and Use of the Information Sharing Environment.* Washington, D.C.: PM-ISE, Office of the Director of National Intelligence, Guidelines 2.b.(i) and (ii), September 4, 2006.

Figure 7-1: Intelligence Records Submission Decision Tree

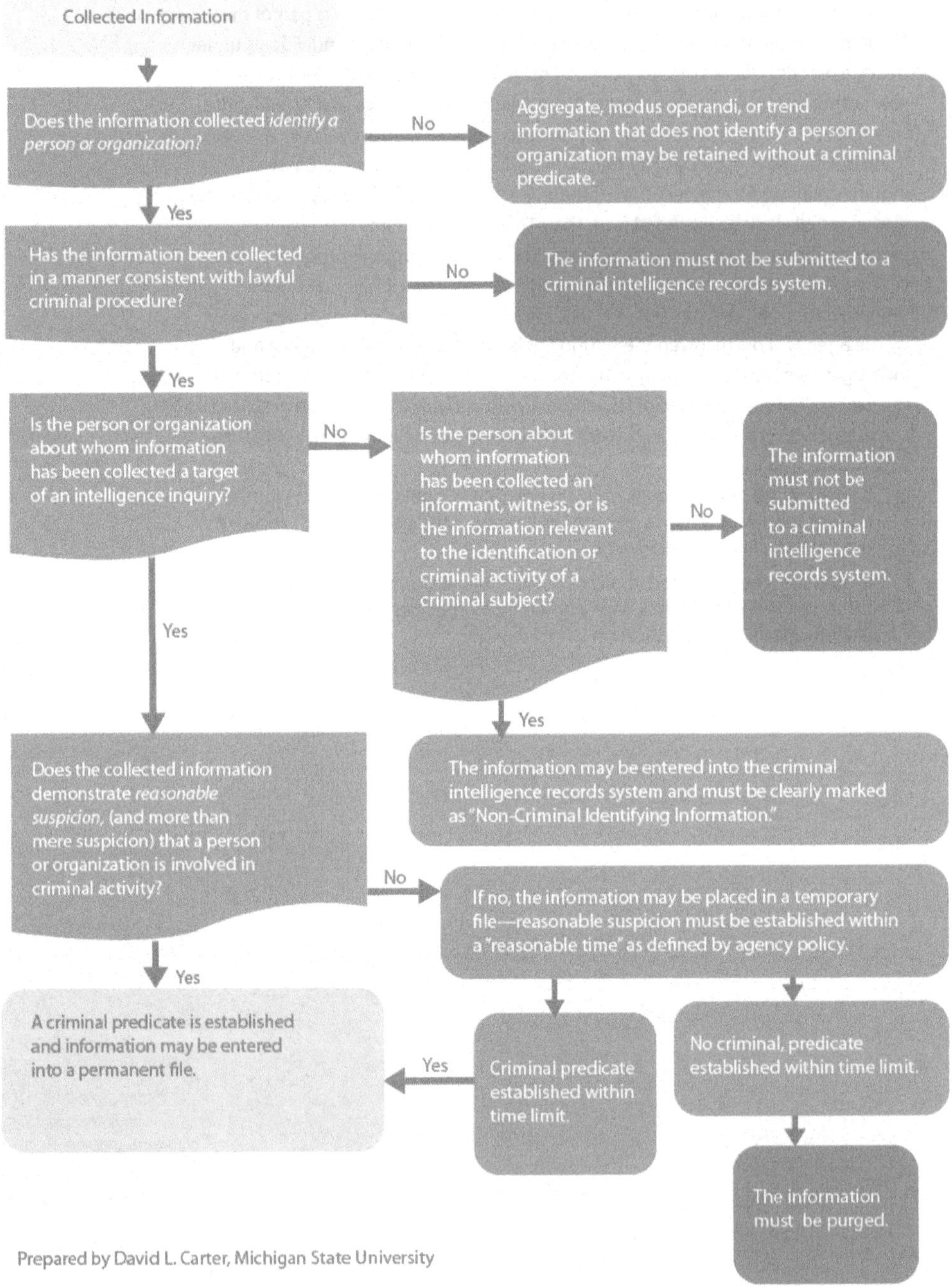

Collected Information

Does the information collected *identify a person or organization?* — No → Aggregate, modus operandi, or trend information that does not identify a person or organization may be retained without a criminal predicate.

Yes ↓

Has the information been collected in a manner consistent with lawful criminal procedure? — No → The information must not be submitted to a criminal intelligence records system.

Yes ↓

Is the person or organization about whom information has been collected a target of an intelligence inquiry? — No → Is the person about whom information has been collected an informant, witness, or is the information relevant to the identification or criminal activity of a criminal subject? — No → The information must not be submitted to a criminal intelligence records system.

Yes ↓ (from target question)

Yes ↓ (from informant/witness question) → The information may be entered into the criminal intelligence records system and must be clearly marked as "Non-Criminal Identifying Information."

Does the collected information demonstrate *reasonable suspicion,* (and more than mere suspicion) that a person or organization is involved in criminal activity? — No → If no, the information may be placed in a temporary file—reasonable suspicion must be established within a "reasonable time" as defined by agency policy.

Yes ↓

A criminal predicate is established and information may be entered into a permanent file. ← Yes — Criminal predicate established within time limit.

No criminal, predicate established within time limit. ↓ The information must be purged.

Prepared by David L. Carter, Michigan State University

If information is collected about a person in the intelligence process and done so in a manner that is consistent with constitutional standards, the agency needs to have a reason for collecting it. That reason is to further an inquiry about threats to the community in the hopes of preventing that threat from reaching fruition. As a result, information is collected about individuals because they are either a target of an intelligence inquiry or have some type of information about the threat, even if they are not suspected of a crime. There is a need to lawfully retain both types of information in a criminal intelligence records system.

If a person is not the inquiry's target but has critical information, "Non-Criminal Identifying Information" (NCI) may be entered into a criminal intelligence information file if it is relevant to the identification of the subject or the subject's criminal activity, provided that: 1. Appropriate disclaimers accompany the information, noting that it is strictly identifying information carrying no criminal connotation; and 2. If the information pertains to the political, religious, or social views, associations, or activities of the criminal subject, it must relate directly to criminal conduct or activity. For example, if a criminal subject is known to attend a particular church, synagogue, or mosque, the inclusion of the religious affiliation in the system as NCI Information would be permitted only if it is directly related to the criminal conduct or activity, such as where the evidence indicates that the church, synagogue, or mosque is the site of the criminal activity. If an individual has material information about an acquaintance that supports the intelligence inquiry, this individual may also be entered into the criminal intelligence records system with a clear NCI identifier.

If the person about whom the information has been collected is the target of the inquiry, that information may be retained only if a *criminal predicate* is established. Determining a criminal predicate is a two-fold process. First, there must be a nexus between a person's behavior and a crime or an organization's operations and involvement in criminal activity. Second, for information to be submitted to a criminal intelligence records system as criminal intelligence information, the level of proof is "reasonable suspicion." Under 28 CFR Part 23, "Reasonable Suspicion or Criminal Predicate" is established when information exists that establishes sufficient facts to give a trained law enforcement or criminal investigative agency officer, investigator, or employee a basis to believe that there is a reasonable possibility that an individual or organization is involved in a definable criminal activity or enterprise. Reasonable suspicion is more than "mere suspicion;" that is, a person's behavior may seem suspicious; however, that information must meet the criminal nexus and level of proof tests prior to being retained in a criminal intelligence records system.

Often, intelligence personnel will receive a tip from the public or perhaps a Suspicious Activity Report (SAR) from a patrol officer. Typically, there is no criminal predicate documented in such information. Practically speaking, the intelligence officer should not simply dismiss the information; indeed, the officer has the responsibility to determine the veracity of the information as it relates to a criminal threat. The challenge to resolve is how the information can be lawfully retained if there is no criminal predicate. Since the 28 CFR Part 23 guidelines do not address this circumstance, a practical interpretation of the regulation, which has been accepted by the courts, was created in the LEIU File Guidelines.[52] The guidelines recommend establishing two types of intelligence files: Temporary files and permanent intelligence files.

A *temporary file* is for information that does not rise to the level of reasonable suspicion but references an event or activity that indicates the possibility of criminal activity, such as a tip, lead, or SAR, none of which constitute criminal intelligence information under 28 CFR Part 23. Since this information is not criminal intelligence information, it must be clearly labeled as such in a temporary file (and defined by policy), whether stored in the same database or accessed or disseminated with criminal intelligence information. The temporary file must have a policy-defined time limit for retaining information in the file (a generally accepted time limit is 60 days). The purpose of the temporary file is simply to have a place to store raw information while an inquiry is made to determine if a criminal predicate can be established. If the criminal predicate is not established within the policy-defined time limit, the information should be purged.

Once a criminal predicate is established, the information is considered criminal intelligence information and may be stored in a *permanent file*. While it is commonly accepted phrasing, the term permanent file is somewhat misleading because the information in this file is subject to the 28 CFR Part 23 5-year review and purge requirement.

It should be stressed that these processes and rules apply only to a criminal intelligence records system that is managed by an SLTLE agency. The guidelines of 28 CFR Part 23 do not apply to a law enforcement agency's investigative records nor to a law enforcement agency's Records Management System[53] (RMS). Sometimes questions about different types of records law enforcement agencies maintain appear to be intelligence-related but are often kept separately from the RMS. The most common questions are associated with Field Interview records and gang records. Because law enforcement agencies vary widely in these types of records, some general questions (Table 7-2) can be asked to reasonably determine if the records are criminal intelligence information for purposes of 28 CFR Part 23.

This discussion was intended to provide general information about the management and use of criminal intelligence records. Often, there are explicit questions about specific systems of a given agency. The best resource for these questions is the 28 CFR Part 23 Training and Technical Assistance program funded by the Bureau of Justice Assistance.[54]

[52] See www.it.ojp.gov/documents/LEIU_Crim_Intell_File_Guidelines.pdf.

[53] The RMS typically stores information such as offense reports, arrest records, traffic accident records, miscellaneous investigations, and similar types of records kept on the daily operations of managing and responding to calls for service and crime.

[54] For more information about this program see www.iir.com/28cfr, or visit www.ncirc.gov for BJA's online 28 CFR Part 23 Training.

Table 7-2: Questions to Determine if Records Must Comply with 28 CFR Part 23 Regulations

If the answer is "Yes" to any of the following questions, the records are criminal intelligence information and should be compliant with 28 CFR Part 23 regulations.	If the answer is "Yes" to any of the following questions, the records are most likely not criminal intelligence records for purposes of 28 CFR Part 23 regulations.
1. Are the records expressly called "intelligence records"?	1. Are the records kept for investigative support of known crimes?
2. Are the records retained in the same records system as criminal intelligence records?	2. Are the records kept in support of an active criminal investigation of a crime that has occurred and/or a known continuing criminal enterprise?
3. Are the records kept primarily to assess threats with limited or no known criminal history of the intelligence targets?	3. Are the records kept to monitor the behavior of convicted criminal offenders (e.g., sex offenders), including persons on probation or parole, who are reasonably believed to pose a hazard to public safety?
4. Are records being retained that identify individuals or organizations suspected of criminal activity but are not the subject of a current criminal investigation?	4. Are the records kept to identify individuals who are affiliated with a known crime group (e.g., persons who have tattoos known to be affiliated with a criminal gang)?

Federal Civil Rights Liability and Intelligence[55]

As evidenced by myriad lawsuits, such as the New York and Denver cases previously discussed, intelligence abuses have occurred. Unfortunately, critics often do not recognize the many changes that have occurred in law enforcement practices, coupled with the more specific professional direction of law enforcement intelligence. Higher educational standards, better training, adoption of ethical standards, and inculcation of law enforcement as a profession, are indicative that the culture of law enforcement has changed, rejecting past practices that contributed to the aforementioned abuses.

Beyond this history, the public generally has a misconception about the law enforcement intelligence function, envisioning it as involving spying, surreptitious activities, and acquisition of information by stealth. The public and media need to be reassured that law enforcement intelligence processes will strictly subscribe to individual constitutional protections when collecting, retaining, and disseminating information. Moreover, the public needs to understand that intelligence analysis is simply the scientific approach to problem solving, similar to the way analysis has been effectively used in community policing. The difference, however, is that community policing focused on crime and community disorder, while intelligence focuses on threats and methods that may be used to prevent such threats from reaching fruition. Generally speaking, critics are not against using information gathering and analysis to combat terrorism or solve crimes; rather, they simply demand that it be conducted in accordance with the constitutional parameters that law enforcement officers are duty-bound to follow.

[55] Based in part on: Carter, David L. and Thomas Martinelli. "Civil Rights and Law Enforcement Intelligence." *The Police Chief*, June 2007.

Because of the importance of protecting citizens' civil rights in all law enforcement activities, including intelligence operations, a remedy is available to citizens when an employee of a state, local and, in some cases, tribal law enforcement agency violates individual civil rights guarantees under the color of law. As noted earlier, this remedy is Title 42 of the United States Code, Section 1983 – Civil Action for Deprivation of Civil Rights (frequently referred to simply as Section 1983).

Section 1983 lawsuits provide civil action for the deprivation of constitutional and federal statutory rights by persons acting under the color of law. This statute was originally created as part of the Civil Rights Act of 1871, which was intended to curb oppressive conduct by government and private individuals participating in vigilante groups, such as the Ku Klux Klan. Section 1983 experienced a period of dormancy until 1961 and the landmark Supreme Court case, *Monroe* v. *Pape*, 365 U.S. 167 (1961) gave individuals a federal court remedy as a first resort rather than only in default of (or after) state action. Today, Section 1983 lawsuits against law enforcement agencies most commonly involve First Amendment issues such as freedom of speech, Fourth Amendment issues like search and seizure or use of force, and Fourteenth Amendment claims of due process violations.

The key elements of the statute:
- Was the individual deprived of a constitutional or federally protected right?
- Did the law enforcement employee act under color of state law?
- Did the law enforcement employee fail to provide the standard of care owed to the individual?
- Was the law enforcement employee's conduct the cause of the individual's deprivation of constitutional right or federal statutory protection?
- Did the law enforcement agency fail to provide due diligence to ensure that agency policy and personnel practices protect civil rights?

For a successful civil rights case to occur, the plaintiffs must show that the law enforcement agency was negligent and that there was a pattern of misconduct associated with that negligence. Typically, this is achieved by providing evidence that the law enforcement agency failed to provide due diligence in protecting individuals' civil rights. To accomplish this, the plaintiffs typically will attempt to demonstrate that the law enforcement agency showed deliberate indifference toward the protection of individuals' privacy and civil rights. In intelligence-related cases, this deliberate indifference may be a product of such things as these:
- Failure to train—the agency does not provide intelligence training to all law enforcement personnel in line with the recommendations of the Minimum Criminal Intelligence Training Standards that have been promulgated by the Global Advisory Committee.
- Failure to direct— the agency does not provide clear policy and procedures on criminal intelligence information collection, retention, review, and dissemination.
- Failure to supervise— the agency does not adequately monitor the intelligence- related activities of personnel and/or does not enforce intelligence policy.

- Failure to establish a privacy policy—the agency does not articulate a clear policy to protect the privacy, civil rights, and civil liberties of citizens as related to intelligence and records management activities.

- Failure to adopt accepted professional standards of good practice— the agency does not adopt the recommendations of the National Criminal Intelligence Sharing Plan or the Intelligence Standards of the Commission on Accreditation for Law Enforcement Agencies.

Hypothetical Example: Federal Civil Rights Liability and Intelligence Records

How could a state or local law enforcement agency be held liable in a federal civil rights lawsuit (42 U.S.C 1983 – Civil Action for Deprivation of Civil Rights) for improperly retaining personal identifying information in a criminal intelligence records system if the system's policies are 28 CFR Part 23 compliant?

- If the officers who were entering personal identifying information on suspicious persons in the criminal intelligence records system did not know that this information could not be entered because there was no criminal nexus, then there is a potential for negligence for failure to train.

- If a law enforcement employee did not understand that people involved in a protest were exercising their First Amendment rights to expressive activity, then there is a potential for negligence for failure to train.

- If the training was not adequate to teach the officers to do the job properly, there could also be negligence by failure to train.

- If a supervisor did not monitor the information being entered into the system or did not take corrective action for improperly entered information, then there is a potential for negligence for failure to supervise.

- If a law enforcement employee who clearly did not understand the policies of the intelligence unit or did not respect/follow the policies of the intelligence unit or if the person was unable to adequate apply the policies, then there is a potential for negligence for negligent retention.

- If command-level personnel learn of improper information being collected and retained and did not take actions to correct the problem, then there is a potential for negligence for failure to direct.

The resulting deliberate indifference is behaviors and processes that cause ongoing negligence in the protection of civil rights and liberties. The following are examples of behaviors or activities that are evidence of ongoing negligence.

- Retaining information that identifies people or organizations where there is no reasonable evidence supporting a criminal nexus.

- Profiling based solely on attributes such as race, religion, ethnicity, or country of origin rather than behaviors where there is a criminal nexus.

- Insinuating guilt by association or guilt based on mere suspicion.

- Inappropriate surveillance and information collection about an individual or organization.

- Knowingly keeping inaccurate information or information that should have been purged.

- Sharing information with other law enforcement agencies that identifies people or organizations with the inference of a criminal involvement when a criminal predicate does not exist and/or without establishing the recipient's right to know and need to know the information.

As noted in the New York and Denver cases, the loss of a civil rights lawsuit can be costly, embarrassing, disruptive of operations, and provide significant new restrictions on intelligence activities. As will be seen, this can be easily avoided with proper policy, training, and supervision in place.

Providing a Transparent Process

An important tool for gaining citizen support for the intelligence function while at the same time minimizing accusations of impropriety is to ensure that the intelligence process is public and transparent. Providing some insight into the need for transparency was a press release by the ACLU of Massachusetts commenting on the opening of the Massachusetts intelligence fusion center. The statement expressed concern about the center's role and activities, specifically stating the following:

> We need a lot more information about what precisely the fusion center will do, what information they will be collecting, who will have access to the information, and what safeguards will be put in place to prevent abuse.

These are reasonable and easily answerable questions. By simply providing this information to the community through a public information document or in town hall presentations, a great deal of conflict, criticism, and cynicism can be avoided. Uncertainty generates citizen consternation that translates into mistrust and allegations of impropriety. Educating the community about the intelligence process can reduce these tensions.

Hypothetical Example: Court Determination of a Criminal Intelligence Records System

A municipal law enforcement agency has a SAR records system that was developed using a federal grant. The agency states, as a matter of policy, that the SAR system is not a criminal intelligence records system. Is it conceivable that this SAR records system could be subject to the 28 CFR Part 23 guidelines?

It is possible that this could occur as a result of a lawsuit. For example, a plaintiff files a federal civil rights lawsuit (42 U.S.C. Section 1983) against a law enforcement agency alleging that the agency is collecting, retaining, and disseminating personal identifying information that is criminal intelligence. The complaint goes on to allege that the new records system is actually a criminal intelligence records system under the guise that the information is "only in SARs."

In its response to this complaint, the agency will no doubt say 28 CFR Part 23 applies only to the criminal intelligence records system and that the SAR records are not criminal intelligence records.

If the plaintiffs successfully argue that, since the primary persons accessing the SAR system are intelligence analysts and personnel assigned to the intelligence unit, this might be persuasive. Moreover, if the law enforcement agency employs an Intelligence-Led Policing philosophy wherein intelligence analysis permeates law enforcement operations and operational decision-making, this could be further evidence supporting the notion that the SAR system is indeed criminal intelligence. The argument would continue that it is irrelevant what the law enforcement agency called the system; rather, the single issue of determination is how the system is used.

If these arguments were successful, the court could rule that the SAR system is, indeed, a criminal intelligence records system irrespective of what the law enforcement agency called it. Consequently, as part of a settlement or injunctive relief, the guidelines of 28 CFR Part 23 could be applied to the SAR system.

In the last few years, many SLTLE agencies have reengineered their intelligence capacity largely through guidance provided by the National Criminal Intelligence Sharing Plan, the Law Enforcement Intelligence Unit File Guidelines, and various intelligence training programs developed under the sponsorship of the Bureau of Justice Assistance[56] and the Department of Homeland Security Training and Exercise Integration.[57] These intelligence programs include instruction on the constitutional guidelines regarding civil rights protections; however, new challenges are emerging that pose renewed concern about abuses.

In particular, there is increasing concern about the ISE[58] that is the product of the Intelligence Reform and Terrorism Prevention Action (IRTPA) of 2004. Largely based on the recommendations of the 9/11 Commission Report, the executive implementation of IRTPA is designed to maximize information-sharing between all levels of government, including sharing terrorism information between the Intelligence Community and SLTLE agencies. The reason, of course, was to ensure that America would be able to have the information and ability to connect the dots when a terrorism threat emerged. Despite this noble goal to protect America from terrorism, many critics felt the legislation went too far.

To address these diverse issues, three fundamental areas emerge where civil rights issues are of concern:

1. Ensure that the collection and retention of information in a criminal intelligence records system are done in a proper manner, both legally and ethically.

2. Ensure that individual privacy rights are protected for all information that has been collected and retained.

3. Ensure the integrity of data quality and data security.

While there are additional intelligence issues that have civil rights implications, these are among the most fundamental and challenging. It bears repeating that these issues are applicable to information and records that identify individuals.

Ensure that the collection and retention of information in a criminal intelligence records system is done in a proper manner, legally and ethically. As noted previously, the authority for SLTLE agencies to perform any type of intelligence operations lies in their statutory authority to enforce the criminal law. As such, any information that is collected and retained in a criminal intelligence records system must be based on a criminal predicate; that is, it must be demonstrated that there is a relationship between the person(s) identified in criminal intelligence records and criminal behavior. The level of that relationship is more than mere suspicion—there must be reasonable suspicion articulated to link the suspected individual to specific criminal behavior.

Ensure that privacy is protected for all information that has been collected and retained. Ensuring that information about individuals is collected and retained with proper legal basis is only one aspect of ensuring that citizens' civil rights are protected.

> A privacy and civil liberties policy is a written, published statement that articulates the policy position of an organization on how it handles the personally identifiable information it gathers and uses in the normal course of business.[59]

[56] These include the Criminal Intelligence for the Chief Executive (CICE) course, the State and Local Anti-Terrorism Training (SLATT) program, and the Criminal Intelligence Commanders course that is in preparation as of this writing. See www.slatt.org.

[57] Most notably the Intelligence Toolbox course. See intellprogram.msu.edu.

[58] See www.ise.gov.

[59] Global Justice Information Sharing Initiative. *Privacy and Civil Liberties Policy Development Guide and Implementation Templates.* Washington, D.C.: Office of Justice Programs, U.S. Department of Justice, rev. 2008, 4–1.

Law enforcement agencies must have mechanisms in place—including proper training, policies, procedures, supervision, and discipline—to make certain that this information is not disseminated to persons who do not have the right to know and the need to know the information. A privacy policy must be developed and implemented with proper safeguards in place. Incorporated within this policy must be a clearly defined process of discipline, demonstrating strict, swift, and certain sanctions for sworn members who fail to strictly comply with the policy's provisions.

Ensure the integrity of data quality and data security. Data quality refers to procedural mechanisms that ensure that raw information is collected and recorded in a valid, reliable, and objective manner. Its intent is to maximize the accuracy of raw information that will be used in the intelligence records system. Security includes processes and mechanisms to ensure that information is not accessed by, or disseminated to, persons who do not have the lawful right and need to know the information. Such security measures reinforce the procedural processes of individual privacy protections without divulging the substance of the intelligence gathered. Procedure over substance is a broad policy philosophy that can be shared with the community to quell mistrust and yet, it does not jeopardize an agency's efforts to protect data quality.

Steps to Ensure Protection of Citizens' Civil Rights

A wide range of issues has been discussed that represent legal flash points related to law enforcement intelligence activities. There are a number of mechanisms that may be easily implemented to ensure that civil rights protections remain intact while addressing the concerns of intelligence critics (See Figure 7-2).

1. <u>Policy Implementation.</u> Every law enforcement agency should implement a privacy policy, security policy, and accepted records management policy, such as the LEIU crimminal intelligence file guidelines.[60] Relying on policy models and policy development processes recommended by the Global Intelligence Working Group provides a solid foundation on which to demonstrate that the agency is following accepted national standards. This has a twofold advantage: First, it demonstrates to the community that the law enforcement agency has an intelligence policy foundation that is consistent with nationally recognized standards. Second, in case of a lawsuit, it can be used as an affirmative defense that the agency's policies are consistent with professionally recognized good practice.

2. <u>Training.</u> Training has three fundamental levels. First, every agency should follow the training recommendations of the NCISP and the Minimum Criminal Intelligence Training Standards,[61] which includes an intelligence awareness training program for all officers.[62] Second, beyond these training standards, appropriate personnel within the agency need to receive training on agency policy and fusion center policy related to all aspects of the intelligence function. Special attention should be devoted to collection, retention, and dissemination of intelligence as well as special issues such as SARs, intelligence related to juveniles, and other unique forms of information. Last, as mentioned earlier, sworn personnel need to appreciate the gravity associated with constitutional rights violations as they pertain to intelligence

[60] www.it.ojp.gov/documents/LEIU_Crim_Intell_File_Guidelines.pdf

[61] https://it.ojp.gov/documents/min_crim_intel_stand.pdf

[62] Intelligence training resources can be found at: www.slatt.org, www.counterterrorismtraining.gov, and intellprogram.msu.edu.

gathering. Not unlike other critical issues in policing, a zero tolerance policy toward such infractions is mandatory. This policy demonstrates to law enforcement personnel, as well as to the community, that civil rights violations will not be tolerated and immediate disciplinary action will be taken.

3. Supervision. Good policy and training are only part of the equation; an agency must ensure that policies and procedures are being complied with as intended. If personnel are not following policy or are misinterpreting it, there exists a lack of systemic accountability and uniformity when it comes to meting out appropriate discipline. Street-level supervisors must be vigilant in their agency's commitment to constitutional policing and must hold their subordinates to the highest standards of the profession, specifically when dealing with intelligence gathering. When patterns and practices of civil rights violations are uncovered over a period of time, plaintiff attorneys simply have to demonstrate to juries that street-level supervisors and their bosses knew or should have known of these violations and deliberately chose not to take disciplinary action. Deliberate indifference has proven to be very costly for law enforcement agencies that have opted to look the other way when citizens or fellow officers have reported possible civil rights violations.[63]

Figure 7-2: Strategies to Ensure Civil Rights Protections

[63] Martinelli, T.J. and Joycelyn M. Pollock. "Law Enforcement Ethics, Lawsuits, and Liability: Defusing Deliberate Indifference." *The Police Chief* 67 (October, 2000) 10: 52–57

4. <u>Public Education.</u> A critical element of success for law enforcement intelligence is informing the public of law enforcement intelligence initiatives. Once again, there are two critical reasons for this. The first, as noted earlier regarding the ACLU's concerns, is to simply educate the public about the intelligence process. This eliminates erroneous assumptions and second-guessing. Much of the lay public assumes law enforcement agencies perform some type of widespread clandestine information collection and operate in a manner similar to the Intelligence Community. Correcting this misperception can go a long way toward developing positive support for the Intelligence Process. The second benefit to public education is to inform citizens of the signs and symbols of terrorism to assist in the information-collection process. For example, a trial program by the Regional Community Policing Institute at Wichita State University, in association with various police departments in Kansas, provided community training on terrorism and intelligence to educate the community on what to look for and how to report the information. Those attending the training were provided with a document called *Observe – Document – Report* and received instruction regarding the indicators of behavior that were considered suspicious, what kind of information needed to be documented, and how to report their observations to law enforcement. This model also helps citizens feel like they are contributing to the security of their own community and helps minimize the level of distrust toward their agency's efforts to combat crime and terrorism.

5. <u>Transparent Processes.</u> The intelligence function, like all other aspects of an American law enforcement agency, should have clearly understood and transparent processes. While certain information used in the intelligence function must be secured, the process that is used must be open. Critics of law enforcement intelligence argue that the Intelligence Process is secretive and that there is widespread spying on citizens.[64] This argument can be successfully countered by an agency that is open and transparent about how the Intelligence Process works, including relationships of an agency with other organizations, such as a fusion center. Without divulging the substance of intelligence records, an agency's efforts to educate its citizens about the procedural steps taken for information gathering and its data storage policies can go a long way toward achieving buy-in by the citizenry policed.

6. <u>Accountability Audits.</u> It should be a mandatory practice to have periodic internal audits of the intelligence processes within an agency. A two-step process may be involved. First, a supervisor or manager must review and document the intelligence processes following a recognized checklist of variables[65] written in the form of an inspection report. This would be followed by an external auditor, a balanced independent person such as a retired judge or other respected individual, who could review the report and ask challenging questions of both the auditor and chief executive. Important too, the audit should be viewed as a positive process designed to identify weaknesses or concerns that can be remedied. Taking proactive action such as an audit can ensure that all aspects of the process are operating as constitutionally mandated. It can identify unforeseen problems and serve as affirmative evidence that the agency is operating in good faith and without malice.

[64] As an illustration, the reader is urged to conduct an Internet search of the phrase "spy files." The results will provide insight on the breadth of concern about the intelligence process, as well as the issues of concern by many citizens.

[65] Two examples of Intelligence Audit checklists can be found at https://intellprogram.msu.edu/Carter_Intelligence_Guide.pdf and www.it.ojp.gov/documents/LEIU_audit_checklist.pdf.

7. <u>Always Act in Good Faith.</u> All actions of the agency and its personnel should clearly demonstrate that the decisions made in the intelligence process are expressly intended to meet lawful standards. Good faith can be demonstrated in a variety of ways including the implementing policies and procedures, providing training to personnel, and ensuring that appropriate supervision is being performed. Many areas of discretion in the intelligence process often lack definitive legal guidance. If the framework is in place to aid personnel in making the best discretionary decision that protects individuals' rights while maintaining community safety, then the probability of negligence is reduced through these good faith activities.

8. <u>Assistance of Legal Counsel.</u> The case law, as it pertains to police misconduct, relies on best police practice concepts such as good faith, reasonableness, and discretion without malice when judging an officer's conduct in hindsight. Juries typically do not want to find officers guilty for their alleged misdeeds or policy violations and, more times than not, will give the officers the benefit of the doubt. But without clearly drafted policies, in-depth training scenarios, and evidence of an organization's strict compliance with constitutional law issues, an agency's legal counsel may find it difficult to defend one of its own against an allegation of civil rights violations in a court of law. Competent legal counsel may be the best preventive measure that agencies can use to prepare for litigation involving allegations of civil rights violations. Whether it is a sole practitioner or an insurance carrier's legal counsel, an attorney well-versed in municipal law, Section 1983 actions, and police misconduct cases, can assist in drafting an agency's privacy and security policies, as well as formulating the process for gathering and analyzing intelligence data.

With this approach, an agency can be assured that every conceivable step has been taken to comply with the latest Supreme Court rulings pertaining to best police practices in accordance with society's increased need for vigilant police protection in this post-9/11 era. In the past, police ethics trainers have used case law examples and arbitration awards to demonstrate examples of police misconduct that resulted in suspensions or terminations. A municipal legal expert can draft street-level scenarios that engage police trainees in dialog that addresses both best police practices and the need to strictly adhere to the constitutional parameters of police work.

Conclusion

In the evolving world of information sharing that is increasingly being driven by intelligence fusion centers and the information-sharing environment, law enforcement executives face new challenges in managing sensitive information and intelligence. Professional law enforcement accepts the responsibility for protecting citizens' civil rights while protecting the community. Moreover, this same environment will draw greater scrutiny from civil rights activists to ensure that the types of information collected, retained, and disseminated by law enforcement agencies is done so in a lawful manner. We have the knowledge and tools to protect both the community and citizens' rights. The intent of this discussion was to ensure that these tools are accounted for and placed in perspective.

Chapter Annex 7-1:
Protecting Civil Rights and Immunizing an Agency from Liability in the Law Enforcement Intelligence Process

The following is a series of action steps and policy actions to ensure that the law enforcement agency protects privacy and civil rights. These same actions will also help protect the agency from a civil rights lawsuit.

Many citizens do not understand the law enforcement intelligence process and express concerns often based on erroneous assumptions. As a foundation, the law enforcement agency should have a publicly available information document that answers these questions:

- What precisely does the intelligence unit or fusion center do?
- What type of information will be collected and retained in the intelligence records system by the law enforcement agency?
- Who will have access to the information?
- What safeguards are in place to ensure proper and lawful use of the information?

Law enforcement agencies can take a number of actions to ensure the protection of citizens' civil rights. The application of some of these items will be dependent on the specific agency, its size, its jurisdiction, and whether it has a full-time intelligence unit or a part-time intelligence capacity. The items below provide a framework for ensuring that civil rights are protected and, consequently, limiting a law enforcement agency's civil liability.

- Adopt the *National Criminal Intelligence Sharing Plan* (NCISP).
  - it.ojp.gov/ncisp
- Adopt and adhere to the Guidelines of 28 CFR Part 23.
  - www.iir.com/28cfr click on "Guidelines"
- Implement court-tested policies and procedures.
  - www.fas.org/irp/agency/doj/lei/app.pdf
- Provide a regular internal audit of the intelligence unit.
  - www.iir.com, under Information Sharing, Global Justice Information Sharing Initiative, National Criminal Intelligence Plan, "Law Enforcement Intelligence Unit (LEIU): Audit Checklist for the Criminal Intelligence Function." www.it.ojp.gov/documents/LEIU_audit_checklist.pdf
- Adopt a privacy policy.
  - it.ojp.gov/documents/Privacy_Civil_Rights_and_Civil_Liberties_Policy_Templates.pdf
- Adopt the IACP Oath of Honor and IACP Model Policy on Standards of Conduct as standards for ethical behavior.
  - www.theiacp.org/PoliceServices/ExecutiveServices/ProfessionalAssistance/Ethics/tabid/140/Default.aspx
  - www.theiacp.org/PoliceServices/ExecutiveServices/ProfessionalAssistance/Ethics/ModelPolicyonStandardsofConduct/tabid/196/Default.aspx

- Appoint an external auditor to regularly review intelligence processes.
- Clearly identify lines of authority and responsibility for intelligence records management, including a two-stage review and approval process for records entry.
- Use the law of criminal evidence and procedure as a guideline for information management whenever in doubt.
- Have a documented process for right to know and need to know.
- All personnel should sign a nondisclosure agreement related to information contained in the criminal intelligence records system.
- Always act in good faith: When a decision is made about information collection, retention, or dissemination where there is a lack of clarity caused by unusual circumstances, write a justification for the decision and the rationale as part of the case file. This memo to the file ensures clarity of the facts and circumstances at the time for the decision in case that decision is challenged or reviewed.
- Review federal and state FOIA and Privacy Act Guidelines and Exemptions. Have a clear policy and procedure to handle FOIA requests particularly related to the intelligence function.
- Provide training for all of the above.

Chapter 8:
The Intelligence Fusion Process

The Intelligence Fusion Process

The intelligence fusion process represents a new chapter in the evolution of law enforcement intelligence. Fusion centers represent a new intelligence structure for most state, local, and tribal law enforcement (SLTLE) agencies to understand and with whom they can interact. Contrary to intuition, the fusion process (developing intelligence from diverse resources) and the creation of fusion centers (the physical plant) is more involved than merely changing the organizational functions of an existing law enforcement intelligence unit. It typically involves either reengineering the entire conceptual framework of the intelligence function in an agency or creating an entirely new entity. It requires engaging a wide array of people and organizations to be contributors and consumers of the intelligence function; it involves changing attitudes and processes of personnel; it requires establishing new functional and information-sharing processes among SLTLE partners; it involves the development of new agreements and functional relationships; the development of new policies and processes; and the inculcation of the Intelligence Led-Policing[1] philosophy.

The challenges are multifold, not the least of which is opening oneself and one's agency to organizational change. Most humans are dogmatic, resisting change; however, if incongruent past practices and erroneous assumptions are not eliminated from intelligence processes, the likelihood of success is diminished. The following discussion is intended to provide insight into different dimensions of the fusion process as well as concerns that have been expressed about intelligence fusion.

Historical Perspective

Initially, intelligence fusion centers were generally referred to as Regional Intelligence Centers (RIC). They took different forms throughout the United States, with no single model for what the intelligence center did or how it should be organized. They evolved largely through local initiatives as a response to perceived threats related to crime, drug trafficking, and/or terrorism within a geographic region. The intent was to marshal the resources and expertise of multiple agencies within that region to deal with cross-jurisdictional crime problems. In some cases, a region was defined as a county (e.g., Rockland County, New York Intelligence Center[2]); as a major urban area (e.g., Los Angeles Joint Regional Intelligence Center[3]); a portion of a state (e.g., North Central Texas Fusion Center[4]), or an entire state (e.g., Minnesota Joint Analysis Center[5]).

The earliest RICs began as the product of counterdrug initiatives in the 1980s. Indeed, the High Intensity Drug Trafficking Area (HIDTA) intelligence centers[6] served as models for successful structures and initiatives as well as for identifying systemic issues that had to be overcome to make the intelligence center functional.[7] In the late 1990s, the Bureau of Alcohol, Tobacco and Firearms (ATF) developed a number of programmatic activities to reduce gun violence. Emerging from these initiatives were ATF Regional Crime Gun Centers. The centers, in some cases, were colocated with the HIDTA RIC and had a number of intelligence-related roles including "…analyzing trace data to identify gun traffickers,

[1] See www.theiacp.org/PublicationsGuides/NationalPolicySummits/tabid/298/Default.aspx or www.it.ojp.gov/documents/ncisp

[2] www.co.rockland.ny.us/DA/RC_DA_Programs.html

[3] www.llis.dhs.gov/channel/channelContentListing.do?channelId=90287&categoryId=5525 (must register)

[4] www.fusionsystem.us

[5] www.llis.dhs.gov/channel/channelContentListing.do?channelId=90287&categoryId=5912 (must register)

[6] www.whitehousedrugpolicy.gov/hidta/newyork_newjersey.html

[7] The Counterdrug Intelligence Executive Secretariat (1331 F Street, N.W., Suite 700, Washington, DC 20530; Telephone: 202.353.1875; Fax: 202.353.190), has an insightful unpublished report on *Metropolitan Area Consolidation/Collocation of Drug Intelligence Elements* that describes success and challenges for Regional Intelligence Centers.

disseminate investigative leads, and coordinate with the HIDTA RIC to identify drug traffickers and their sources of guns."[8] In virtually all cases, both the HIDTA and ATF intelligence centers had a great deal of interaction with SLTLE agencies. The intent was to integrate, that is, fuse, information from diverse sources to better understand and prevent multijurisdictional crime problems.

This laid the foundation for intelligence centers, but beyond idiosyncratic local crime issues, there was little incentive to expand the centers. Of course, this changed after September 11, 2001.

Because of their demonstrated successes and the information-sharing challenges of counterterrorism, additional state and local entities embraced the concept and began developing their own centers. These centers were initially developed by state and local governments. The federal government, at first by the Department of Homeland Security (DHS), saw the value of these initiatives and began providing funding support. Fusion centers were about to experience an expanding role.

> Recognizing that state and local fusion centers represent a critical source of local information about potential threats and a mechanism for providing terrorism-related information and intelligence from federal sources, the Program Manager for the ISE (PM-ISE), the Department of Homeland Security (DHS), and the Department of Justice (DOJ) are taking steps to partner with and leverage fusion centers as part of the overall information-sharing environment.[9]

Building on this observation, a report by the Government Accountability Office (GAO) documented a number of federal efforts underway designed to support fusion centers and address challenges or obstacles identified by fusion center directors. These include the following:

- The DHS, the FBI, and the PM-ISE have taken actions to assist fusion centers in gaining access to, and managing, multiple federal information systems, including classified systems.

- Both the DHS and the FBI have committed to providing security clearances to state, local, and tribal fusion center personnel and reducing the time it takes to process a clearance.

- The DHS and the FBI are assisting fusion centers in obtaining and retaining qualified personnel, both through assignments of federal employees to state fusion centers and through some DHS funding support.

- Federal funds in support of fusion centers have become more readily available and streamlined in operation to make grant awards faster and easier.

- Both the DOJ and the DHS have provided training and technical assistance in support of fusion center development and maturation.[10]

While progress has been made, many of the fusion centers and their governing officers appear to believe that there is still a long way to go before fusion centers will fulfill their envisioned role seamlessly.

[8] www.atf.gov/field/newyork/rcgc

[9] Government Accountability Office. *Homeland Security: Federal Efforts Are Helping to Alleviate Some Challenges Encountered by State and Local Information Fusion Centers.* Washington, D.C.: Government Accountability Office, GAO-08-35 Homeland Security, October 2007, p. 2.

[10] GAO, Ibid., pp. 23–39.

Refining the Fusion Center Concept

It was clear after the 9/11 terrorists' attacks that there had been poor information sharing among and between all levels of law enforcement (and the Intelligence Community). As more information was learned about the terrorists and their minor encounters with state and local law enforcement in the weeks and months before the attacks, it was painfully evident that current information systems and processes were simply inadequate to deal with threats of this nature. It was also evident that if a diverse array of raw information was collected by different agencies, it would be essential to have a mechanism to provide data integration and analysis so its meaning would be of value to operational law enforcement personnel.

Increasingly, state and local law enforcement leaders recognized that the experiences of the HIDTAs and RICs could be applied to counterterrorism. Because of the need to have two-way information-sharing directly with federal law enforcement and indirectly with the Intelligence Community, the fusion centers, the FBI, and the DHS reached out to each other to develop fusion centers more holistically. Indeed, "federal departments and agencies—including DHS, FBI, and DOD [Department of Defense]—launched efforts to develop strategies to incorporate these fusion centers into their information and intelligence activities."[11]

The argument that fusion centers represent a vital part of our nation's homeland security relies on at least four presumptions:

1. Intelligence and the Intelligence Process play a vital role in preventing terrorist attacks.

2. It is essential to fuse a broader range of data, including nontraditional source data, to create a more comprehensive threat picture.

3. State, local, and tribal law enforcement and public-sector agencies are in a unique position to make observations and collect information that may be central to the type of threat assessment referenced above.

4. Having fusion activities take place at the subfederal level can benefit state and local communities, and possibly have national benefits, as well.[12]

The initial focus of many new fusion centers was exclusively on terrorism; indeed, that still remains the case for a few of the centers such as the Georgia Information Sharing and Analysis Center.[13] Most of the centers broadened their focus to embrace "all crime and all threats" for two reasons. First, it was recognized that most terrorist acts had a nexus with other crimes, and focusing exclusively on terrorism may miss some important indicators. Second, because there is a wide variety of crime, notably criminal enterprises, that were transjurisdictional and represented complex criminality,[14] it was recognized that the fusion process would be of value in dealing with these crimes.

Further evolution of fusion center responsibilities has moved into the arena of an all-hazards focus (in addition to "all crimes, all threats"). Inclusion of the all-hazards approach has come from two sources: One is a result of the special conditions on some DHS grants to fusion centers that specify all hazards. The second source is from state or fusion center governing board mandates.

[11] Program Manager-Information Sharing Environment. *Information Sharing Environment Implementation Plan*. Washington, D.C.: PM-ISE, Office of the Director of National Intelligence, 2006, p. 18.

[12] Masse, Todd and John Rollins, "A Summary of Fusion Centers: Core Issues and Options for Congress." *CRS Report for Congress*. Washington, D.C.: Congressional Research Service, United States Congress, September 19, 2007, p. 3.

[13] www.llis.dhs.gov/channel/channelContentListing.do?channelId=90287&categoryId=5546 (must register).

[14] "Complex criminality" refers to criminal enterprises that are involved in a wide range of criminal activities in support of their core enterprise. A drug trafficking organization, for example, may be involved in drug production, drug trafficking, money laundering, smuggling, corruption of public officials, fraud, and other offenses.

Recognizing that fusion centers were increasingly integrating the concepts of established law enforcement intelligence activities with the "all-crimes, all-threats, all-hazards" model of intelligence, the Homeland Security Advisory Council made the following observation:

Although the primary emphasis of intelligence/information fusion is to identify, deter, and respond to emerging terrorism-related threats and risks, a collateral benefit to state, tribal, and local entities is that it will support ongoing efforts to address nonterrorism related issues by:

- Allowing state and local entities to better identify and forecast emerging crime, public health, and quality-of-life trends

- Supporting targeted law enforcement and other multidisciplinary, proactive, risk-based and community-focused, problem-solving activities

- Improving the delivery of emergency and nonemergency services.[15]

There is no single model of a fusion center because of the diverse needs and environmental characteristics that will affect the structure, processes, and products of a center. In states such as Texas and California with their large land mass, large populations, and international borders, the structure and processes of fusion centers will be significantly different than predominantly land-locked rural states such as Wyoming or Nebraska.

A Congressional Research Service (CRS) report observed that questions have arisen regarding the current and/or potential efficacy of fusion centers. The report notes that in light of the growth of the fusion centers in state and local jurisdictions without a coordinated national plan, "…there appears to be no 'one-size-fits-all' structural or operational model for fusion centers."[16] From a centralized federal perspective—as reflected in the CRS report—the lack of a uniform model is assumed to be a significant flaw. The state and local perspective is somewhat different. Indeed, the ability to build a fusion center around grassroots needs is preferred because this permits state and local agencies to mold the fusion center into a model that best suits the needs and challenges that are idiosyncratic to each jurisdiction. As noted by Johnson and Dorn, describing the New York State Intelligence Center:

> Creating one center for intelligence and terrorism information— to combine and distribute that information to law enforcement agencies statewide— prevents duplication of effort by multiple agencies. Additionally, one state fusion center serving the entire New York law enforcement community provides a comprehensive picture of criminal and terrorists networks, aids in the fight against future terrorists events, and reduces crime.[17]

Within this same line of thought, fusion centers are also structured differently because of legislative or executive mandates. Montana's fusion center (Montana All Threat Intelligence Center), for example, is mandated to focus on "all threats;" the New Jersey Regional Operations Intelligence Center includes emergency operations as well as fusion; the Massachusetts Commonwealth Fusion Center focuses on all crimes; and the Oregon Terrorism Intelligence Threat Assessment

[15] Homeland Security Advisory Council. *Intelligence and Information Sharing Initiative: Homeland Security Intelligence and Information Fusion.* Washington, D.C.: U.S. Department of Homeland Security, 2005, p. 2.

[16] Masse and Rollins, Ibid., p. 18.

[17] Johnson, Bart R. and Shelagh Dorn. "Fusion Centers: New York State Intelligence Strategy Unifies Law Enforcement." *The Police Chief.* (February 2008): 38.

Network limits its focus to terrorism. The variability of fusion center structures is broad because of functional necessity and the inherent nature of local control and states' rights perspectives.

While the structure and operational processes of fusion centers may be different, national professional standards have nonetheless been articulated that outline good practice in critical administrative areas, regardless of the center's mission. That is the intent of the *Fusion Center Guidelines*.[18] See Table 8-1.

Table 8-1: Topics in the Fusion Center Guidelines

- The National Criminal Intelligence Sharing Plan and the Intelligence Process
- Mission Statement and Goals
- Governance
- Collaboration
- Memoranda of Understanding (MOU)
- Database Resources
- Interconnectivity
- Privacy
- Security
- Facility, Location and Physical Infrastructure
- Human Resources
- Training of center Personnel
- Multidisciplinary Awareness and Education
- Intelligence Services and Products
- Policies and Procedures
- Center Performance Measurement and Evaluation
- Funding

Despite some criticisms, the fact that fusion centers are structured differently is not a weakness, but a strength. It exemplifies that each center is designed to meet local and regional needs and to best integrate the fusion center with existing organizational components (and priorities).

The Michigan State Police, for example, have widespread responsibility for both traffic and criminal law enforcement throughout the state. As such, the Michigan Intelligence Operations Center is organizationally placed in the state police. Florida, however, has two predominant state law enforcement organizations: the Florida Highway Patrol, responsible for traffic law enforcement, and the Florida Department of Law Enforcement (FDLE), responsible for criminal law enforcement. As a result, the Florida Counter Terrorism Intelligence Center is organized as part of the FDLE Office of Statewide Intelligence. The two states structured their fusion center in a manner that best fits existing organizational structures and functional responsibilities.

[18] The *Fusion Center Guidelines* are often referred to as federal guidelines because they are a product of the Global Intelligence Working Group (GIWG) of the Global Justice Information Sharing Initiative (Global), which is funded by, and advisory to, the Bureau of Justice Assistance, Office of Justice Programs, U.S. Department of Justice. It should be noted that the vast majority of GIWG members are from SLTLE agencies. Similarly, the group of subject matter experts assembled to develop the *Fusion Center Guidelines* also comprised predominantly state, local, and tribal representatives.

The point to note is that there are different operational and functional models of law enforcement throughout the United States. Fusion centers are no different because they are an element of state or local government and will have challenges to meet the unique needs of the jurisdiction they serve. As observed in one study:

> Fusion centers [must identify] their mission and their customers, at what level of analytic product they will produce, and to whom. Not all fusion centers will need the same amount of strategic analysis or tactical analysis, but, in order to determine what to produce, they will have to understand their customers' needs and ensure they are educated so they understand the difference between the two products. Fusion centers will also need to determine how they will integrate the emergency responder community.[19]

It is, perhaps, this last point that will be the most challenging to define because all-hazards intelligence and meeting the needs of the emergency responder community are not traditional roles for the law enforcement intelligence function. Some guidance to assist fusion centers in this area is being developed through the identification of "baseline capabilities."

Baseline Capabilities for Intelligence Fusion Centers

As a result of national plans that seek to increase the efficiency and effectiveness of information-sharing efforts, fusion centers will serve as the interlink between SLTLE and the federal Information Sharing Environment for the exchange of terrorism information. As such, it was recognized that there was a need to define fundamental baseline operational capabilities that should be used by fusion centers and major urban area intelligence units to meet the information needs of all consumers of the various intelligence centers. A joint project of the Global Intelligence Working Group, U.S. Department of Justice, U.S. Department of Homeland Security, and the Program Manager-Information Sharing Environment is currently working on the project. The end result will be a companion document to the *Fusion Center Guidelines* that will identify elements that serve as the foundation for integrating state and major urban area fusion centers into the national Information Sharing Environment. The project is based on the fusion process capabilities outlined in the 2007 Fusion Center Assessment and the 2007 and 2008 Homeland Security Grant Program, Fusion Capability Planning Tool Supplemental Resource. In addition to the 2007 Assessment, the baseline operational standards that will be outlined in the project are being developed using guidance provided in the *Fusion Center Guidelines,* the *National Criminal Intelligence Sharing Plan,* the *Information Sharing Environment Implementation Plan,* and the U.S. Department of Homeland Security's *National Preparedness Guidelines* and *Target Capabilities List.* Relying on the guidance of these national standards, development of the baseline capabilities for fusion centers will be guided by the requirements of the National Strategy for Information Sharing.

[19] Nenneman, M. *An Examination of State and Local Fusion Centers and Data Collection Methods.* Monterey, California: A thesis prepared for the Naval Post Graduate School, 2008, p. 109.

The baseline capabilities follow the structure of the *Fusion Center Guidelines* and represent a comprehensive articulation of functional standards and performance expectations. As a supplement to the *Baseline Capabilities for State and Major Urban Area Fusion Centers,* baseline capabilities have been prepared for Critical

Infrastructure and Key Resources, although at this writing the capabilities had not been approved for use. In addition, baseline capabilities for public health and for the Fire Service Intelligence Enterprise have been developed. These additional documents support the all-hazards responsibilities of fusion centers. The reader should monitor the Global Justice Information Sharing Initiative web site[20] and/or the National Criminal Intelligence Resource Center (NCIRC)[21] for the final approved supplement to *Baseline Capabilities for State and Major Urban Area Fusion Centers.*

What Is Intelligence Fusion?

The GIWG national *Fusion Center Guidelines* define a fusion center in the following manner:

> … a collaborative effort of two or more agencies that provide resources, expertise, and/or information to the center with the goal of maximizing the ability to detect, prevent, apprehend, and respond to criminal and terrorist activity. The intelligence component of a fusion center focuses on the intelligence process, where information is collected, integrated, evaluated, analyzed, and disseminated. Nontraditional collectors of intelligence, such as public safety entities and private sector organizations, possess important information that can be "fused" with law enforcement data to provide meaningful information and intelligence about threats and criminal activity.[22]

The fusion process is an overarching methodology of managing the flow of information and intelligence across levels and sectors of government to integrate information for analysis.[23] The process relies on active involvement of state, local, tribal, and federal law enforcement agencies—and sometimes nonlaw enforcement agencies—to provide the raw information for intelligence analysis. As the array of diverse information sources increases, there will be more accurate and robust analysis that can be disseminated as intelligence. Information fusion utilizes the intelligence process[24] for information management and analysis. The fusion center is the physical location where the fusion process occurs.[25]

While the phrase "fusion center" has been used widely, often there are misconceptions about the function of the center. Perhaps the most common misconception is that the center is a large room full of workstations where the staff are constantly responding to inquiries from officers, investigators, and agents. This vision is more accurately a "watch center" or "investigative support center," not an intelligence fusion center. Another common misconception is that the fusion center is minimally staffed until there is a crisis wherein representatives from different public safety agencies converge to staff workstations to manage the crisis. This is an "emergency operations center," not an intelligence fusion center.

In the purest sense, the fusion center is not an operational center, but a support center. It is analysis-driven. The fusion process proactively seeks to identify criminal and homeland security threats and stop them before they occur. Prevention is the essence of the intelligence process. The distinction, however, is that the fusion center is typically organized by amalgamating representatives from different federal, state, local, and tribal law enforcement agencies (and, in

[20] www.it.ojp.gov/global

[21] The NCIRC is accessible through the RISS. NET portal and the FBI's LEO.

[22] Global Intelligence Working Group. *Guidelines for Establishing and Operating Fusion Centers at the Local, State, Tribal and Federal Level.* Washington, D.C.: U.S. Department of Justice and U.S. Department of Homeland Security, 2005, p. 8.

[23] *Local Anti-Terrorism Information and Intelligence Sharing: Information Sharing Overview.* Lessons Learned Information Sharing, U.S. Department of Homeland Security, 2005. www.llis.dhs.gov.

[24] The Intelligence Process, also known as the Intelligence Cycle, involves the systemic steps for collecting, assessing, analyzing, and disseminating intelligence.

[25] Global Justice Information Sharing Initiative. *Fusion Center Guidelines: Executive Summary.* Washington, D.C.: U.S. Department of Justice and U.S. Department of Homeland Security, 2006. it.ojp.gov/documents/fusion_center_executive_summary.pdf.

some cases, the private sector) into one physical location. Each representative is intended to be a conduit of raw information from his or her agency who can infuse that agency-specific information into the collective body of information for analysis. Conversely, when the fusion center has intelligence requirements,[26] the representative is the conduit back to the agency to communicate, monitor, and process the new information needs. Similarly, the agency representative ensures that analytic products and threat information are directed back to the parent agency for proper dissemination. Agency representatives may be physically assigned to the center, but a more common arrangement is for the agency representative—often called a terrorism liaison officer[27] or intelligence liaison officer—to performs his or her fusion center responsibilities along with the officer's other assignments at his or her home agency.

In short, an intelligence fusion center must be able to: 1. Access and explore all government databases, including intelligence, regulatory, and law enforcement; 2. Integrate the information found in those databases; 3. Make independent judgments about that information; and 4. Provide warning.[28]

[26] "Intelligence requirements" are information that is needed to help make a comprehensive and accurate analysis of a threat. See: Global Intelligence Working Group, Intelligence Requirements Subcommittee Report. *Recommendations for Intelligence Requirements for State, Local and Tribal Law Enforcement Agencies.* (October 2005).

[27] For example, see Arizona Counter Terrorism Information Center, Terrorism Liaison Officer Program, https://www.llis.dhs.gov/docdetails/detailsProfile.do?contentID=26251 (must register).

[28] Wortzel, Larry, *Creating an Intelligent Department of Homeland Security. Executive Memorandum 828.* Washington, D.C.: The Heritage Foundation, 2002. www.heritage.org.

[29] RISS.NET, www.riss.net.

[30] LEO (operated by the FBI), www.fbi.gov/hq/cjisd/leo.htm

[31] HSIN, www.gao.gov/new.items/d07822t.pdf.

[32] International Justice and Public Safety Network, www.nlets.org.

[33] ATIX, www.riss.net/Atix.aspx.

Delaware Information Analysis Center use of ATIX

The Delaware Information Analysis Center (DIAC) takes a proactive approach to information sharing and homeland security. To maximize timely, secure, two-way information exchange, the DIAC communicates with all of its local law enforcement partners and private sector critical infrastructure partners through the Internet using the Automated Trusted Information Exchange (ATIX) portal. ATIX provides a wide array of diverse threat and homeland security information as well as content and secure e-mail. A service provided at no charge by RISS.net, ATIX simply requires an Internet connection and the secure ATIX/RISS.NET software. Users, like DIAC, are also able to have secure information exchange "communities" to ensure that only DIAC and its partners have access to specified information. As the fusion center for Delaware, DIAC's proactive approach to local law enforcement through the use of ATIX has been a significant tool for success.

www.riss.net/atix.aspx
dsp.delaware.gov/Intelligence.shtml

Obviously, not every law enforcement agency can contribute a person to work in the fusion center. Instead, the center must develop mechanisms for two-way information sharing that captures information from the nontraditional collectors and provides threat-based intelligence and intelligence requirements back to those who have the need to know. As a result, multiple strategies and technologies need to be developed for diverse two-way information sharing.

Electronic two-way information sharing through various secure electronic information systems—Regional Information Sharing System Network (RISS. NET),[29] LEO,[30] Homeland Security Information Network (HSIN),[31] National Law Enforcement Telecommunications System (NLETS)[32] (now the International Justice and Public safety Network), or ATIX[33]—can be very effective. In the case of ATIX, individuals beyond the law enforcement community who have a demonstrated need—including some private sector persons—may also have access to the system and use it for secure two-way information sharing. Another example is the New York Police Department's Operation Nexus:

> The New York City Police Department's [NYPD] Operation Nexus is a nationwide network of businesses and enterprises joined in an effort to prevent another terrorist attack against our citizens. Our detectives [visit] firms that have joined us in this mutual effort. Members of Operation Nexus are committed to reporting suspicious business encounters that they believe may have possible links to terrorism. The NYPD believes terrorists may portray themselves as legitimate customers in order to purchase or lease certain materials or equipment, or to undergo certain formalized training to acquire important skills or licenses. … Through Operation Nexus, the NYPD actively encourages business owners, operators and their employees to apply their particular business and industry knowledge and experience against each customer transaction or encounter to discern anything unusual or suspicious and to report such instances to authorities.[34]

Another model has emerged that is being increasingly adopted throughout the United States. Developed in Los Angeles, the Terrorism Early Warning (TEW) group has multiple functions, including supporting the intelligence fusion center.

> The Los Angeles TEW includes analysts from local, state, and federal agencies to produce a range of intelligence products at all phases of response (pre-, trans-, and post attack) specifically tailored to the user's operational role and requirements. The TEW bridges criminal and operational intelligence to support strategic and tactical users. As part of this process, the TEW seeks to identify emerging threats and provide early warning by integrating inputs and analysis from a multidisciplinary, interagency team. Toward this end, the TEW has developed a local network of Terrorism Liaison Officers at law enforcement, fire, and health agencies, formed partnerships with the private sector to understand threats to critical infrastructure, and has developed and refined processes to analyze and synthesize threat data to support its client agencies.[35]

Regardless of the method of information-sharing, the key factors are: 1. There must be diverse raw input; 2. It must be analyzed; and 3. Actionable intelligence output must be shared with appropriate consumers.

Why Fusion Centers?

The heart of good intelligence analysis is a diverse array of valid and reliable raw information. The more robust the raw information, the more accurate the analytic output (i.e., intelligence). If one thinks of information input in terms of bandwidth, the typical law enforcement intelligence unit has a narrow bandwidth; that is, information is gathered from a fairly narrow array of sources, thereby limiting both the quality of the analysis and the ability to see the big picture of a criminal enterprise. Quite simply, the more limited the input of raw information, the more limited the quality of intelligence, but if the number of sources is broadened to include a wide range of agencies representing much broader geographic

[34] www.nypdshield.org/public/nexus.nypd

[35] Sullivan, John P. *Terrorism Early Warning and Co-Production of Counterterrorism Intelligence.* A paper presented at the Canadian Association of Security and Intelligence Studies. Montreal, Canada, 2005, p. 1.

and jurisdictional parameters, then the bandwidth is much wider. With wider bandwidth, there is a greater and more diverse information flow. With greater information flow, the analysis becomes more accurate and utilitarian. As the quality of analysis increases, the ability to prevent or mitigate the operations of a terrorist or criminal organization increases exponentially.

Recent analyses of both law enforcement and national security intelligence operations found a problem that has been referred to as the stovepipe of information in agencies.[36] That is, each agency would develop a large body of information and analytic products that it would retain and rarely share with other agencies. Analysis was generally limited to the information that came from internal sources and its dissemination was also largely internal. As a result, while agencies were developing information it was simply being stacked and stored in isolation, metaphorically as in a stovepipe. Current thought recognizes that far more value can be derived from information that is widely shared for analysis. Information from one agency may be a key in learning about a threat when integrated with information another agency: there was a need to fuse as much information as possible.

As noted in a report from The Heritage Foundation, the fusion center would not simply duplicate the activities of existing agencies, but would enhance and improve their efforts by providing a service that does not yet exist.[37] Another perspective on their development observed the following:

> Conceptually, fusion centers differ from [state police intelligence units] in that they are intended to broaden sources of data for analysis and integration beyond criminal intelligence, to include federal intelligence as well as public and private sector data. Furthermore, fusion centers broaden the scope of state and local analysis to include homeland security and counterterrorism issues.
>
> Despite being an expansion of existing subfederal intelligence/information activities, fusion centers represent a fundamental change in the philosophy toward homeland defense and law enforcement. The rise of fusion centers is representative of a recognition that nontraditional actors—state and local law enforcement and public safety agencies—have an important role to play in homeland defense and security.[38]

In exploring the need and structure of fusion centers, a project by the Police Executive Research Forum identified five critical questions:[39]

1. **Why do we need a fusion center?** Fusion centers embody the core function of collaboration, and as demands increase and resources decrease, fusion centers serve as an effective tool to maximize available resources and build trusted relationships. What distinguishes fusion centers from intelligence units within local law enforcement agencies is that fusion centers synthesize data gathered from multiple sources and disciplines.

2. **What is a fusion center's mission?** While opinions on the topic vary, many

[36] As an illustration see, Kindsvater, Larry C., "The Need to Reorganize the Intelligence Community". *Studies in Intelligence.* Vol. 47, No. 1, 2003. www.cia.gov

[37] Dillon, Dana R. "Breaking Down Intelligence Barriers for Homeland Security." *Backgrounder #1536.* Washington, D.C.: The Heritage Foundation, 2002. www.heritage.org.

[38] Masse and Rollins, Ibid., p. 2.

[39] *What is a Fusion Center?* Washington, D.C.: Police Executive Research Forum, 2008. Brochure available from www.llis. dhs.gov (Must register to access).

in the law enforcement community believe it makes more sense to establish a fusion center with a broader mission and scope, i.e., implement an all-crimes or all-hazards approach, while still maintaining the unique capability to monitor terrorist activity. The value of an all-crimes center is that it increases the ability of law enforcement to detect the traditional crimes that ultimately may be precursors of terrorist activity. The underlying purpose and goal of a fusion center is to provide law enforcement agencies with analyses of local, state and regional activities. Local law enforcement agencies, however, must do their part by feeding information to the center.

3. **Who governs the fusion centers?** Most fusion centers established memoranda of understanding with participating agencies and appointed a governing board of representatives from these agencies to provide oversight and ensure adherence to policies, as per the recommendations put forth in the *Fusion Center Guidelines*.

4. **What major functions and services do fusion centers perform?** Fusion centers are intended to be analytical support centers for law enforcement and other public safety agencies. A fusion center serves as a repository for all information available from open-source and law enforcement agencies throughout the state or region. Fusion centers and the agencies they serve work together to determine the best method for disseminating center analysis and products.

5. **How does law enforcement define value in its relationship with fusion centers?**
   - Providing daily information to law enforcement agencies
   - Interpreting diverse threat information from a local perspective
   - Providing timely actionable intelligence.
   - Connecting the dots from diverse jurisdictions that affect a local area
   - Serving as a one-stop shop for threat information.
   - Managing diverse pieces of information in a coherent form for local law enforcement agencies.

Fusion Centers and the Crime Laboratory: An Analogy

The relationship of the fusion center to a law enforcement agency may be seen in a somewhat familiar analogy: the crime laboratory. The vast majority of law enforcement agencies do not have a crime lab, just as they do not have an intelligence unit; however, they periodically need forensic analysis of evidence for a case. To use the crime lab effectively, each agency must have some type of forensic capacity so that physical evidence can be collected properly (i.e., prevent contamination and maintain the integrity of the chain of custody). The agency must also have established a relationship with the crime lab and know the processes for submitting evidence for analysis.

Most agencies use a state crime lab. While a small agency may use the laboratory only periodically, in those few times forensic analysis is needed. It is essential that the local agency has trained personnel and has access to appropriate resources to use the crime lab's services expeditiously and effectively. Table 8-2 provides a comparative series of factors that are analogous between crime laboratories and fusion centers.

This analogy illustrates that there is a precedent for many organizational processes and practices that are required for fusion centers. Building on these experiences can make integration of the fusion center into law enforcement agency operations much easier.

Table 8-2: Analogy of a Crime Lab and a Fusion Center

Crime Laboratory	Fusion Center
• Central laboratory operated by the state.	• Fusion center operated by the state.
• In each law enforcement agency there must be a capacity to collect physical evidence to prevent contamination.	• In each law enforcement agency there must be a capacity to lawfully collect raw information, building on the criminal predicate.
• Retain physical evidence to meet chain-of-custody requirements.	• Retain information to meet 28 CFR Part 23 guidelines.
• Certified agency participant with crime laboratory in order to submit evidence for analysis.	• Certified as a fusion center participant to establish right to know and need to know to receive intelligence product.
• Forensic analysis is performed by specifically trained analysts.	• Intelligence analysis is performed by specifically trained analysts.
• Crime lab provides analytic results of physical evidence.	• Fusion center provides intelligence products.

Fusion Centers and the Information Sharing Environment

The *Information Sharing Environment (ISE) Implementation Plan* embraced the growth of fusion centers as a critical linchpin serving as information clearinghouses between federal entities (both federal law enforcement and the Intelligence Community), nonfederal law enforcement, and the private sector.

> [M]any states and localities emphatically moved to create and invest in fusion centers in the post-9/11 environment. These fusion centers now play a prominent role in collecting, analyzing, and sharing terrorism information. Individually, these centers represent vital assets for collecting terrorism-related information. Collectively, their collaboration with the Federal Government, with one another (state-to-state, state-to-locality), and with the private sector represents a tremendous increase in both the nation's overall analytic capacity and the multidirectional flow of information. It is important to note that these centers are not homogenous—considerable variations exist in terms of operations and mission focus (e.g., homeland security, law enforcement, emergency response). To date, more than 40 such centers have been established across the United States, and significant effort has gone into developing and adopting standards to facilitate easier information access, sharing, and use.[40]

[40] PM-ISE, (2006). Ibid, pp. 7–8.

To further this plan, the PM-ISE has established a National Fusion Center Coordination Group (NFCCG), led by DHS and DOJ, to identify federal resources to support the development of a national, integrated network of fusion centers. Moreover, the ISE…[41]

> …recognizes the "all-crimes and all-hazards" nature of State and local sharing, where SLT organizations may share and fuse together multiple types of information to address a variety of needs including law enforcement, preparedness, and response and recovery. In many instances, this information may not initially be recognized as terrorism information, but may be information that could ultimately prove crucial in preventing, preparing for, or responding to terrorism. The ISE focus on terrorism information will not impede or interrupt these additional fusion center functions.[42]

Operationalizing the Fusion Process

As depicted in Figure 8-1," three critical focal areas make the integrated information-sharing strategy functional. While all the factors are essential, the fusion center plays a uniquely critical role.

The process begins with the fundamental step of developing an intelligence capacity in all SLTLE agencies, regardless of size, as per Recommendation 1 in the *National Criminal Intelligence Sharing Plan*.[43] The intelligence capacity must be integrated with a law enforcement agency's proactive participation with the fusion center. The more agencies that participate as a fusion center partner, the greater the value of the center. As noted by the PM-ISE, "state and major urban area fusion centers will be central to implementation at the state and local levels…".[44] Creation of the fusion center, therefore, is only one ingredient; it is essential to have widespread participation.

The outer band of Figure 8-1 is the federal ISE, which consists of both the Intelligence Community and federal law enforcement. Both deal with national security and homeland security from a broad perspective and typically at a classified level. The challenge is to share appropriate threat information with local law enforcement. Similarly, when local law enforcement discovers information that is valuable to the ISE, there must be a mechanism to effectively share the information. The primary state fusion center is intended to fulfill these roles.

Figure 8-1: Organizational Interrelationships and Responsibilities for the Fusion Process and ISE

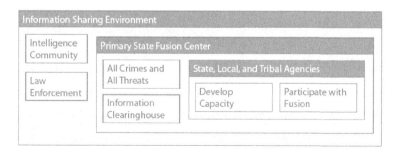

[41] GAO, Ibid., p. 12.

[42] PM-ISE, (2006). Ibid., p. 11.

[43] Global Intelligence Working Group. "*Recommendation 1.*" *National Criminal Intelligence Sharing Plan*. Washington, D.C.: Bureau of Justice Assistance, Office of Justice Programs, U.S. Department of Justice, 2003, p. 21.

[44] Program Manager-Information Sharing Environment. *Common Terrorism Information Sharing Standards (CTISS) Program Manual*. Washington, D.C.: PM-ISE, 2007, p. 18.

The fusion center is envisioned as serving as an information clearinghouse between the ISE and local law enforcement. Generally speaking, the center will have representatives from all levels of government, experienced analysts, personnel with federal security clearances, and access to a wide range of information systems, sometimes including classified systems. With this foundation, the fusion center can disseminate critical intelligence to local and tribal partners as well as pass critical raw information to the federal ISE that is collected at the local, tribal, and private levels.

A simplified version of the fusion process to accomplish these objectives is depicted in Figure 8-2. A fundamental objective is to gain buy-in by all critical sectors within a state: law enforcement, federal partners within the state, the Intelligence Community[45] as applicable to each state and the private sector. The fusion process receives input (both raw data and intelligence as indicated in the block arrows of Figure 8-2) from a variety of agencies. The analysts integrate the diverse data and provide analytic output that may include information for prevention, target hardening, or threat assessment. In addition, the analysts may also define further intelligence requirements. After analyzing and redefining intelligence requirements, the fusion center disseminates relevant information and intelligence to its participants in the form of actionable intelligence.

It cannot be overemphasized that for intelligence fusion to be successful, as many law enforcement agencies as possible must participate in the process. Every nonparticipating agency represents a weakness in the ability to identify and prevent threats.

Figure 8-2: The Fusion Process

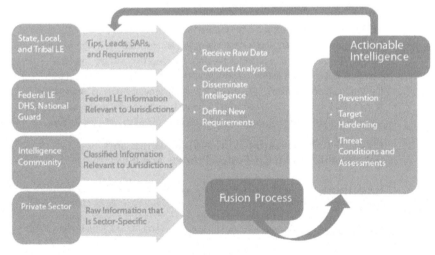

[45] The 16-member Intelligence Community (IC), which includes the FBI and the Drug Enforcement Administration, has a presence in every state; however, the specific IC agencies represented in each state, and consequently each fusion center, will vary widely. States with large international ports of entry or military bases, for example, will have a greater IC presence. See www.odni.gov/who_what/061222_DNIHandbook_Final.pdf.

Is there a Role for the Private Sector?

Often overlooked, the private sector can be a rich resource of information that adds a broadened dimension to information collection. Many large corporations have sophisticated security operations that monitor global threats to their facilities, products, and personnel posed by organized crime and criminal extremists, as well as predatory criminals. This type of information is often different from that collected by law enforcement organizations and can add a unique, and more insightful, component to the body of information being analyzed by the fusion center.

Similarly, the private sector is often a legitimate consumer of law enforcement intelligence meeting the right-to-know and need-to-know information-sharing standards. Eighty-five percent of the U.S. critical infrastructure is owned by the private sector. Moreover, the private sector has a large personnel force who, if given the proper information, can significantly increase the "eyes and ears on the street" to observe individuals and behaviors that pose threats. As noted in a "Best Practices" paper produced by the DHS, "a jurisdiction's analysis and synthesis entity [such as a fusion center], should also establish processes for sharing information with the local private sector."[46]

Of course, there are information-sharing issues that need to be resolved. For example, certain types of personal identifying information may be inappropriate for law enforcement to release to the private sector. Conversely, the private sector will be reluctant to share proprietary information related to corporate products and processes. Despite these limitations, the private sector has a legitimate role in fusion centers. Just as in the case of law enforcement partners, memoranda of agreement need to be in place that include provisions on information-sharing processes and restrictions.

[46] Lessons Learned Information Sharing Best Practices. *Local Anti-Terrorism Information and Intelligence Sharing: Dissemination.* Washington, D.C.: U.S. Department of Homeland Security, 2006. https://www.llis.dhs.gov/member/secure/detail.cfm?content_id=13091 (Must register to access).

Concerns About Fusion Centers

As might be expected, centralized intelligence fusion centers have heightened the concerns of some citizens who fear that the centers will collect, retain, and disseminate information that will further erode the privacy of law-abiding citizens who express support for unpopular or controversial causes. In some cases, a dialog with the community will reduce the concerns; in other cases, it will not. It is nonetheless important to understand these points of conflict. The following discussion presents the more common concerns expressed about fusion centers followed by the law enforcement response. The intent is to provide insight and communications between fusion centers and critics.

Concern: "There is a lack of an underlying philosophy. In the absence of a common understanding about what constitutes intelligence, fusion center development and progress may be impeded."[47]

Response: The purpose of a philosophy is to establish the underlying purpose, processes, and parameters in the execution of an enterprise. The philosophy of law enforcement intelligence, and by extension intelligence fusion centers, has never been clearer than it is today. The philosophy is being molded quite effectively, with a clear articulation of roles and responsibilities as found in the *National Criminal Intelligence Sharing Plan,* with further support provided by the *Information Sharing Environment Implementation Plan* and the DHS *Target Capabilities List.* Indeed, Fusion Center Guideline 1 states, "Adhere to the *National Criminal Intelligence Sharing Plan* and perform all steps of the intelligence process."[48] The *Guidelines* established the NCISP and the standards contained therein as an unequivocal philosophy.

Concern: "…arguably, the *2006 Fusion Center Guidelines* have the following limitations: 1. They are voluntary; 2. The philosophy outlined in them is generic and does not translate theory into practice; and 3. They are oriented toward the mechanics of fusion center establishment."[49]

Response: The *Fusion Center Guidelines* cannot be viewed in isolation, but must be viewed in the context of the other national standards described above. While they are voluntary—the federal government has no authority to mandate all state and local fusion centers to follow the guidelines—the guidelines nonetheless represent accepted national professional standards that are adopted for two reasons. First, the philosophical reason is to ensure ongoing professional practice. The second, more pragmatic reason, is that adoption of the *Guidelines* represents good faith and a component of due diligence that helps protect the fusion center from civil liability. While voluntary, the *Fusion Center Guidelines* represent the de facto national standard for state, local, and tribal law enforcement.

[47] Masse and Rollins, Ibid., p. 4.

[48] Global Intelligence Working Group (2005), Ibid., p. 25.

[49] Masse and Rollins, Ibid.

With respect to the philosophy, the *Guidelines state*, "…a fusion center is defined as a collaborative effort of two or more agencies that provide resources, expertise, and/or information to the center with the goal of maximizing the ability to detect, prevent, apprehend, and respond to criminal and terrorist activity."[50] These are explicit, practical objectives, not generic ones.

Finally, the criticism that the Guidelines "…are oriented toward the mechanics of fusion center establishment" is puzzling. The philosophy has been clearly established, as described above: It is a responsible, proactive, and effective fact that national standards for the mechanics of fusion centers have been established to help ensure consistency, efficiency and effectiveness. Indeed, the Guidelines represent important control mechanisms for fusion centers to help ensure adherence to the rule of law.

Concern: "Arguments against fusion centers often center on the idea that such centers are essentially preemptive law enforcement—that intelligence gathered in the absence of a criminal predicate is unlawfully gathered intelligence."[51]

Response: The fallacy of this argument rests on erroneous or misinformed assumptions about the law enforcement intelligence function. The first is that *information* is collected; *intelligence* is the output of the analytic process. This is an important distinction.

Certainly intelligence is preemptive. The intent of intelligence is to *prevent* crime. All crime-prevention programs are a form of preemptive law enforcement. The rationale of the criticism is inherently illogical. A cornerstone of law enforcement for decades has been a preemptive approach toward crime whenever possible. Indeed, this preemptive philosophy is the reason that the National Crime Prevention Council was created. Law enforcement intelligence is simply another dimension of prevention.

With respect to the concern about "unlawfully gathering" information, law enforcement personnel at all levels of government are acutely aware of the criminal predicate standard for intelligence. They adhere to privacy and civil rights standards in the intelligence process just as they adhere to constitutional standards of criminal procedure in the course of criminal investigations. Law enforcement organizations have privacy policies, intelligence records policies, and training, all of which meet constitutional and regulatory requirements. Law enforcement understands these obligations and fulfills them.

Concern: "Ambiguous lines of authority allow for 'policy shopping'. … Fusion centers … exist in a no-man's land between the Federal Government and the states, where policy and oversight is often uncertain and open to manipulation."[52]

[50] Global Intelligence Working Group. *Fusion Center Guidelines.* Washington, D.C.: Bureau of Justice Assistance, Office of Justice Programs, U.S. Department of Justice, 2005, p. 5.

[51] Masse and Rollins, Ibid., p. 5.

[52] German, Michael and Jay Stanley. *What's Wrong with Fusion Centers?* New York American Civil Liberties Union, 2007, p. 9.

Response: All state and regional fusion centers are a part of state or local government; therefore, they have a chain of command and accountability to their parent governmental authority. All fusion centers have a policy manual that establishes, among other things, authority and responsibility. In some cases, fusion centers may be colocated with federal agencies, most notably with the FBI; however, there are clear lines of authority and responsibility for the management and accountability of the fusion center to the state or local government. Some have governing boards, others have direct lines of command to a state or local law enforcement organization or state office of homeland security. While there are different organizational configurations of fusion centers, the lines of authority are unequivocally clear. The practice of policy shopping simply does not occur.

Concern: "Private sector participation in fusion centers risks privacy and security. Fusion centers are poised to become part of a wide-ranging trend of recent years in the United States: the creation of a 'Surveillance-Industrial Complex' in which security agencies and the corporate sector join together in a frenzy of mass information gathering, tracking, and routine surveillance."[53]

Response: All nonlaw enforcement personnel in fusion centers, including public and private partners, must pass a background investigation before they are given access to information. Most have security clearances, which make them subject to federal laws governing the handling of classified and sensitive information and state and local privacy protection laws. In addition, private-sector representatives do not represent a single company, but the entire sector. The Washington Joint Analysis Center (WAJAC), for example, reached an agreement with The Boeing Company to assign a Boeing intelligence analyst to WAJAC. The analyst has a Defense Department security clearance and will represent aircraft manufacturers and their suppliers in the fusion center.

Information-collection for the intelligence process is a product of explicit procedures that are dictated by law and the scientific approach to problem solving—it is not collected in a frenzy. Indeed, mass information-gathering is avoided because it makes the intelligence process more difficult since it means that a greater mass of information would have to be sorted through to identify a threat. Indeed, the purpose of *intelligence requirements* is to identify and collect only that information which is needed for analysis.

The *National Criminal Intelligence Sharing Plan*, the *Fusion Center Guidelines*, the *Information Sharing Environment Implementation Plan*, and the DHS *Target Capabilities List* describe the importance of private-sector involvement in law enforcement intelligence.

[53] Ibid., p. 11.

Certainly there is sensitivity to the types of information to which the private sector participants have access; therefore, each fusion center has a privacy policy to which private-sector participants agree to adhere. Moreover, private-sector partners have to sign a memorandum of understanding (MOU) and a nondisclosure agreement, all of which help to protect individual privacy.

Concern: "Military participation in fusion centers violates fundamental tenets of liberty. Officials who regard American communities as battlegrounds in a 'war' can be tempted to dispense with 'inconvenient' checks and balances."[54]

Response: While the public may not be aware, both law enforcement agencies and military representatives in the law enforcement intelligence arena are hypersensitive to these issues.

Law enforcement does not have this war perspective, nor is law enforcement influenced by the military. Law enforcement agencies are acutely aware of the distinctions and simply use the military as a lawful support resource in the fusion centers just as the military has been used for years as a lawful resource in drug enforcement initiatives. Analysts, not information collectors or operational personnel, are assigned to fusion centers from the military; most typically, they are from the National Guard.

Concern: "Data fusion = data mining, which is bad for privacy and bad for security."[55]

Response: These two forms of research and analysis are *not* the same. *Data mining* (also known as Knowledge Discovery) has been defined as "the nontrivial extraction of implicit, previously unknown and potentially useful information from data".[56] It uses machine learning and statistical and visualization techniques to discover and present knowledge in a form which is easily comprehensible to humans.[57] *Data fusion* is the process of integrating information obtained from many heterogeneous sources into a single composite picture of the environment.[58]

Data mining is a proactive process using sophisticated software and mathematical models to develop new knowledge about an entity. Data fusion is an integration and analytic technique that increases the accuracy of analysis by relying on a wide array of diverse information sources. Generally speaking, law enforcement agencies and fusion centers have neither the resources nor the expertise for data mining activities; however, the inclusion of different agencies from different levels of government establishes the heterogeneous information sources characteristic of data fusion. Analysis is performed on this diverse data using the scientific approach to problem solving as is characteristic of all types of intelligence analysis.

[54] Ibid., p. 15.

[53] Ibid., p. 11.

[54] Ibid., p. 15.

[55] Ibid., p. 15.

[56] Frawley, W., G. Piatetsky-Shapiro, and C. Matheus. "Knowledge Discovery in Databases: An Overview." *Artificial Intelligence Magazine* (Fall 1992), 213–228.

[57] www.the-data-mine.com, *Introduction to Data Mining*.

[58] www.cas.edu.au/content.php/260.html

Concern: "Excessive secrecy undermines the mission of fusion centers."[59]

Response: Fusion centers operated by state and local law enforcement should have transparent processes; however, the content of much of their work must remain largely secret both to protect privacy and protect the integrity of inquiries. Some levels of secrecy increase when the fusion center is accredited as a Sensitive Compartmented Information Facility (SCIF).[60] In these cases, there will be more secrecy, as a matter of federal law, because the facility will contain classified information. While there are instances of excessive secrecy, the fundamental issue is that "excessive" will be interpreted differently, depending on one's position and perspective.

For many people, the past abuse of law enforcement intelligence will be the lens through which all law enforcement intelligence activities will be judged. The ongoing skepticism, while frustrating, is a reminder of the need to remain vigilant in training, supervising, and managing the intelligence process.

Similarly, critics need to realize the radical changes that have occurred in law enforcement organizations during the past 5 decades. Officers are significantly more educated, training has increased dramatically, and professional leadership has embraced modern management techniques, values, and responsibilities. This underlying fabric serves as an important foundation for the law enforcement intelligence function.

Fusion Centers and Civil Rights Issues

There is a concern among many privacy advocates that the growth of fusion centers will increase the jeopardy to citizens' civil rights and privacy. As noted in a National Governors Association best practices paper, "The risks to individuals' privacy begin when personal information of any kind is entered into criminal justice information systems."[61] Criminal intelligence records systems are certainly included in this description and warrant special attention because of the low level of proof— i.e., reasonable suspicion—required to enter personal identifying information into the system.

Complicating this issue is the fact that by not understanding the concept of the fusion process, many privacy advocates fear that the centers are the next iteration of centralized surveillance of citizens.

Perhaps the greatest concern of a fusion center in this regard is the participation of federal law enforcement agencies whose jurisdiction for information collection and retention is different from SLTLE agencies. Certainly, when an SLTLE agency is the custodian of an intelligence records' system, care must be taken to exclude information from the fusion center that does not meet the standards of 28 CFR Part 23.

Fundamentally, the privacy and civil rights issues of citizens related to fusion centers are the same as any other aspect of the intelligence process. Those relevant standards of the NCISP apply in the same manner and should be fully

[59] German and Stanley, Ibid., p. 9.

[60] For more information on SCIFs, see www.fas.org then search for "Physical Security Standards for Sensitive Compartmented Information Facilities"

[61] MacLellan, Thomas. *Protecting Privacy in Integrated Justice Systems.* Washington, D.C.: National Governors Association Center for Best Practices, 2006, p. 4

- **Recognize the importance of information sharing.** Encourage the practice of sharing information with other law enforcement and public safety agencies. Use the guidelines and action steps of the NCISP to implement or enhance your organization's intelligence function.

- **Improve information flow.** Ensure that channels of communication exist to efficiently share information and intelligence, including Suspicious Activity Reports. Work with the fusion center to agree on a common lexicon and the most effective and efficient methods for the transfer of this information.

- **Support an information-sharing culture through training initiatives.** Provide training programs for everyone and explain intelligence, why it is valuable, and how it benefits the department.

- **Train new recruits.** Provide training to new recruits on the role of fusion centers, why the mission is important, what information to collect, and how to send information to the fusion center.

- **Communicate your needs to the fusion center or governing board.** Constantly communicate your information needs and requirements to the fusion center and offer definitions for actionable information. Ensure that your agency provides feedback on the value of products disseminated and offers recommendations for improvement when necessary.

- **Assign personnel to the fusion center.** Depending on the center, officers, investigators, and analysts may all be assigned and have skills and knowledge to contribute. There are many models for assignment—some agencies choose to assign personnel on a part-time basis (e.g., 1 day a week)—while others serve full-time for a 3- or 6-month rotation.

- **Establish or participate in a terrorism liaison officer (TLO) program.** For departments who cannot afford to lend personnel to a center, participate in a TLO program or intelligence liaison officer programs. Their purpose is to disseminate information distributed by the center to the "boots on the ground" and ensure that all appropriate information collected by his or her agency is effectively shared with the fusion center.

- **Educate political leaders.** Educating political leaders about fusion centers, their value, and their needs may encourage them to demonstrate commitment to the fusion concept and, thus, support your agency and that commitment through appropriate funding. Join the governing board of the fusion center, if one exists. Participating on an interagency governing board will demonstrate the importance of collaborating with the fusion center and allow for a greater understanding of the capabilities and products the center has to offer law enforcement.

- **Hire analysts, if possible.** Both intelligence and crime analysts require different skill sets than those required for patrol officers and investigators. Analysts can make officers work smarter, providing for both increased efficiency and effectiveness.

Based on: *10 Ways to Engage and Support Your Fusion Center.* Washington, D.C.: Police Executive Research Forum, 2008. https://www.llis.dhs.gov (Must register to access).

adhered to. Further, *Guideline 8* of the *Fusion Center Guidelines* states that the management of the fusion center should: "Develop, publish, and adhere to a privacy and civil rights policy."[62] Commentary on this guideline goes on to note the following:

> …one of the critical issues that could quickly stop intelligence sharing is the real or perceived violation of individuals' privacy and constitutional rights through the use of intelligence sharing systems. In order to balance law enforcement's ability to share information while ensuring that the rights of citizens are upheld, appropriate privacy policies must be in place.[63]

As a consequence, civil rights issues for fusion centers have components related to policy, training, supervision, and public information that must be addressed in the development and implementation stages.

Developing the Fusion Center

As noted previously, a fusion center's operations should be consistent with the recommendations of the *NCISP*[64] and the *Fusion Center Guidelines*[65] of the Global Intelligence Working Group. The *NCISP* provides standards for all aspects of the intelligence function to ensure best practices, effective operations, and adherence to civil rights. The *Fusion Center Guidelines* are designed to ensure the following:

> Information and intelligence sharing among states and jurisdictions will become seamless and efficient when each fusion center utilizes a common set of guidelines. The complete support of public safety leaders at all levels is critical to the successful implementation and operation of fusion centers.[66]

Adherence to established national standards will increase the quality of information sharing both within the fusion center's participants' jurisdictions, with intelligence entities outside of the region, and with the Information Sharing Environment. Further, the standards will institutionalize a consistent approach to information collection, retention, analysis, and dissemination that represent recognized and accepted processes as defined by the consensus of intelligence subject matter experts who helped design the standards.

Beyond relying on national standards, consideration must be given to defining who the center's stakeholders are and determining what it will take to get the stakeholders' buy-in to the center's operations. It is this simple: There is a direct correlation between stakeholders' (or consumers') participation in the fusion center and the success of the center. Similarly, stakeholders will not participate in the center unless the products they receive are useful.

To assist in the development and utility of fusion centers, the following common themes, and more important, common questions, should be examined:

- Do fusion centers solve the pre-9/11 information-sharing problems, and as such, make Americans safer?
- Can fusion centers work if they are not part of an integrated philosophy of intelligence and security?
- Who benefits from fusion centers?

[62] *Fusion Center Guidelines*, Ibid., p. 49.

[63] Ibid.

[64] See it.ojp.gov/documents/ncisp.

[65] See www.iir.com/global/guidelines.htm.

[66] Global Intelligence Working Group, 2005., Ibid., p. ii.

- Who should staff, fund, and oversee them?
- What role, if any, should fusion centers play in the Intelligence Community?
- What role should federal agencies play in fusion centers, including funding?
- Do fusion centers represent a shift in the security versus civil liberties pendulum?
- How active and proactive, if at all, should fusion centers be in the collection of intelligence that is not directly tied to a specific and identifiable criminal act?
- Is the current configuration of 40-plus fusion centers, in some cases several operating within one state, the most efficient organizational structure?
- Is the current approach to creating, authorizing, funding, and supporting fusion centers sustainable?
- What are the risks to the fusion center concept and how have those risks been specifically weighed and balanced against the stated goals of fusion center operations?[67]

The answers to these questions provide the foundation for shaping the guiding principles related to the creation and management of fusion centers:

1. Adhere to the tenets contained in the *NCISP*.
2. Collaboratively develop and embrace a mission statement.
3. Create a representative governance structure.
4. Use an MOU or other type of agreement, as appropriate.
5. Integrate SLTLE agencies.
6. Create an environment in which participants can seamlessly communicate.
7. Develop, publish, and adhere to a policies and procedures manual.
8. Develop, publish, and adhere to a privacy policy.
9. Ensure that appropriate security measures are in place for the facility, data, and personnel.
10. Integrate sworn and nonsworn personnel and ensure that all personnel are properly trained.
11. Leverage existing systems and databases and allow for future connectivity.
12. Offer a variety of intelligence services and monitor outputs and outcomes.[68]

[67] Masse and Rollins, Ibid., pp. 3—4.

[68] Modafferi, Peter and Kenneth Bouche. "Intelligence Sharing: Efforts to Develop Fusion Center Intelligence Standards." *The Police Chief* Vol. 7, No. 2, February 2005.

From an *operational* perspective, the experience of the North Central Texas Fusion Center has defined five guiding principles in support of the fusion center's performance:

Guiding Principle 1:   Processing tools and the aggregation of data across jurisdictions and across disciplines are required to achieve the benefits of fusion.

Guiding Principle 2:   Visualization and analysis tools are essential for "connecting the dots."

Guiding Principle 3:   The most important objective is disaster prevention, early warning, and mitigation.

Guiding Principle 4:   The more data the better.

Guiding Principle 5:   Cross-disciplinary analyst(s) need to be assigned to constantly explore the data and test hypotheses.[69]

Building on these principles, three broad phases, each with specific focal areas, are envisioned to accomplish the fusion center's development.

Phase 1. The foundation phase includes these components:

- **Reeducation.** Stakeholders must understand the contemporary role of law enforcement intelligence and the capabilities of the fusion center. Just as important, stakeholders must understand their role in making the intelligence function succeed at preventing acts of terrorism, prevent the occurrence of organized crime, and manage homeland security threats that may affect public safety. As recommended by the *NCISP* and the *Minimum Criminal Intelligence Training Standards,* personnel at all levels of the organization, from executives to line personnel, must receive awareness training as intelligence relates to their role.

- **Developing a mission, goals, and objectives.** What should the fusion center do? How will it operate? What crimes will it address? What will it produce? What is its role and relationship with its consumers? What are the priorities of the fusion center? These questions must be resolved and articulated in the mission, goals, and objectives. It is a laborious process requiring input from executives to stakeholders. It cannot be done effectively, however, until after the training component is completed because all personnel must understand the contemporary law enforcement intelligence function and ensure that their vision of the fusion center is consistent with contemporary standards.

- **What the fusion center will not do.** Just as important as what the fusion center will do, is some discussion of what the fusion center will not do. There will likely be changes in the historic intelligence activities of agencies that will not be continued in the fusion center; for example, many activities of state police intelligence units tended to be more akin to investigative support rather than intelligence activities. For the center to function most effectively, these factors must be clear. Similarly, stakeholders and consumers must understand what the fusion center will not do to avoid erroneous expectations.

[69] Stone, Kelly. *Deploying and Operating an Effective Regional Fusion System: Lessons Learned from the North Central Texas Fusion System.* Unpublished policy paper prepared by the North Central Texas Fusion System, McKinney, Texas, 2006, p. 5.

Phase 2. Proactive developmental activities that must be overtly addressed in this phase include the following:

- **Developing relationships.** Two critical elements to the success of any intelligence activity are information collection and information dissemination. Both must have detailed elements to ensure that everyone does his or her job with respect to intelligence activities. The fusion center must rely on management support from partnering agencies to support the fusion center. It must also rely on personnel to collect needed information, document it, and forward it to the fusion center. Similarly, to succeed, dissemination of information and products from the fusion center must be done in an effective manner that is easily accessible by consumers, in a format that is easy to use, and consistently contain useful information. To accomplish this, there must be overt initiatives to develop relationships among stakeholders within the fusion center and with its external constituency by developing commitments to participate in the center's activities.

- **Outputs/products.** The fusion center must identify specific outputs and products that will be produced on a regular basis. These are among the questions that need to be addressed and articulated as the fusion center's development process moves forward: Will both tactical and strategic reports be produced? Will bulletins and advisories be produced? Will summaries be produced? What is the schedule for outputs? How will responses to specific inquiries be produced? What is the process for determining *right-to-know* and *need-to-know* standards for products and outputs?

Phase 3. The third phase involves moving Phase 1 and Phase 2 activities into operational form, including everything from facilities and staffing to developing memoranda of agreement (see Chapter Annex 8-1), to the actual implementation of the fusion center's operations. This phase can consume a massive amount of time and logistics, particularly when the intelligence function is not only being revised, but reengineered, as well. Other activities in this phase include melding agencies and their data, protecting each agency's data, standardizing data for incorporation into a single system, ensuring quality control (i.e., accuracy) of data, security of the data, and establishing processes for auditing and accountability.

Outputs of the Fusion Center

The fusion center is not designed to respond to ongoing calls or inquiries about individuals or threats. While this will no doubt occur occasionally, if it happens too frequently the staff will be overwhelmed and unable to perform their analytic responsibilities. The most important output of the intelligence fusion center is actionable intelligence, meaning that the intelligence produced by the center will drive operational responses and a strategic awareness of threats.

An operational response occurs when the analysis determines that there is a threat against a specific type of target. Operationally, the law enforcement agency may then take necessary actions to harden the target or intercept the threat. Strategic awareness is broader information that provides information about threats and methodologies or indicators of terrorists and criminals.

The specific kinds of output from fusion centers are not universal. Different regions of the country, the character of targets in a region, and the unique character of threats must be taken into consideration when output is being designed. In a given geographic region, for example, there may be a large presence of active right-wing extremists and, therefore, the fusion center would focus a significant amount of attention on their activities. Similarly, the U.S. border with Mexico would receive significant attention devoted to drug smuggling and human trafficking. Thus, while all fusion centers should have an all-crimes approach, strategic priorities within those crime categories would be appropriate.

In light of this, the fusion center's substantive outputs should be based on three basic factors:

1. Defined threats based on comprehensive and ongoing threat assessments within the jurisdiction of the fusion center.
2. Information and intelligence needs defined by stakeholders.
3. National priorities, including those of external funding, such as the National Preparedness Goal[70] or FBI intelligence requirements.

Beyond the substantive content, the format and frequency of outputs need to be identified, specifically in light of the types of analysis and products that are produced and the frequency of which they are produced. In some cases, the format of the output may be dependent on unique characteristics of the fusion center's jurisdiction. E-mail alerts, for example, may not be feasible in regions where there is limited electronic connectivity among law enforcement agencies. Similarly, intelligence alerts and bulletins that are designed as briefings and handed out at roll calls would not be feasible for rural or decentralized law enforcement agencies. Types of output may include any or all of the following:

- Summary briefs—incidents and activities, globally or locally, that may have some correlation to threats, particularly if the incidents reflect a trend.
- Threat assessment—a detailed description of threats, targets, the likelihood of an attack against a defined target, and the potential methods of attack.
- Situational awareness reports—the current status of known threats or changes in the status of known threats.
- Information bulletin—information on new or emerging threats, including threat indicators and methodologies.
- Intelligence assessments—comprehensive analysis, usually of a strategic nature, about a threat.
- Raw intelligence—information that is derived from a source deemed to be reliable but that has not been corroborated or analyzed. Typically, the threat is time-critical and potentially severe, hence the dissemination of the information.

In addition to these intelligence products, the fusion center will also produce case intelligence, which is intelligence related to specific threats, targets, and suspects. Case intelligence is produced and disseminated on a timely basis as facts warrant rather than on a fixed schedule. Dissemination is narrower and goes only to persons who have a demonstrable *right to know* and *need to know* the information.

The different intelligence outputs may use a variety of analytic techniques such as link analysis, financial analysis, association matrices, visual investigative analysis, threat profiling, and pattern analysis. Typically, a fusion center would also be

[70] www.llis.dhs.gov/member/ secure/dynamicpage. cfm?pagetitle=Preparedness (Must register to access)

involved in other processes that enhance the criminal inquiries of intelligence targets, such as deconfliction, case correlation (particularly between jurisdictions), and intelligence support of investigations related to criminal enterprises and terrorism.

Conclusion

The intelligence fusion process holds a great deal of promise for effective intelligence operations. This is particularly true, given the multijurisdictional character of terrorists' operations and criminal enterprises, as well as hazards that will require public safety operations. The four greatest challenges are: 1. Develop a cooperative and committed relationship between all stakeholders; 2. Ensure privacy and protection of personal identifying information; 3. Establish policies and processes that support efficient, effective, and lawful intelligence operations; and 4. Stay on message as an analytic center.

Chapter Annex 8-1: Developing a Memorandum of Understanding[71]

Fusion centers inherently require the sharing of information and, oftentimes, resources between law enforcement agencies. In either case, there are important obligations on the part of the fusion center and each agency that enters into an agreement with the fusion center. An agreement needs to be in place to formalize and institutionalize obligations and responsibilities of all parties involved. These agreements have different names: memorandum of understanding (MOU), memorandum of agreement, letter of understanding, or statement of understanding. Regardless of the name, all refer to a written agreement between two or more parties that articulates a specific relationship.

Because the nature of the agreements will vary widely, this description focuses on the basic principles and types of content that should be included in an MOA.

Guiding Principles of an MOU:

- *The MOU Is a Statement of Commitment*—The MOU defines the actual agreements and responsibilities in the relationship. The commitment statement can set the context, quality, or sentiment behind the relationship.

- *The MOU Requires Explicit Statements of Expectations and Obligations*—Specific activities, expertise, and resources need to be articulated in the agreement with as much detail as possible.

- *The MOU Must State What Is Not Intended To Be Covered*—If there are specific activities and responsibilities that might be assumed to be covered by the MOU but are not intended to be covered by the agreement, they should be spelled out.

Contents of an MOU:

1. Introduction

   a. What is the intent, capability, or resource for which the MOU is being created?

   b. Specify the agencies that are participating in the MOU. An MOU may between two entities, such as the fusion center and a single law enforcement agency, or it may include multiple parties.

   c. Provide a statement of why the MOU necessary. This is essentially the spirit of the agreement, which can be useful if questions of interpretation later arise about certain provisions in the agreement.

   d. What agreements are set forth by this MOU?

2. Purpose

   a. To what capability does the MOU apply? When answering this question, consider these questions:

      i. What is the intended level of commitment?

      ii. What is the command structure that will make decisions about, and enforce components of, the agreement?

[71] For further information see: 1. Office for Interoperability and Compatibility. *Writing Guide for a Memorandum of Understanding (MOU)*. Washington, D.C.: U.S. Department of Homeland Security, undated. www.safecomprogram.gov/SAFECOM/library/default.htm 2. *Partnering for Strength: Getting your Relationships in Print*. Collaborating Agencies Responding to Disasters (CARD), undated. www.cardcanhelp.org/resources.html.

3. Scope
   a. Who are the public safety, public service, and other governmental and nongovernmental agencies that will use the capability/resource?
   b. Are there organizations or agencies that must be excluded that would otherwise be a participant?
4. Definitions
   a. What are the technical and operational aspects of responsibilities, capabilities, and resources? Consider including definitions for each.
   b. Be certain to define/explain acronyms that may be commonly used.
5. Policy
   a. Specify the circumstances for use of fusion center resources, including special requests.
   b. Specify authorization required for contacting and use of the fusion center.
   c. Specify the operating procedures associated with the fusion center as related to the parties of the MOU.
6. User Procedure Requirements
   a. What are the training, exercise, and equipment requirements associated with participating in this MOU?
7. Financial Relations
   a. If the MOU includes a fee-for-service arrangement or other financial obligations, a method for determining financial payments should be clearly established. Any and all financial commitments should be spelled out clearly, with appropriate approvals and monitoring systems in place.
   b. Articulate any financial obligations that must be considered.
      i. What is going to be done?
      ii. Who is going to do it?
      iii. Under what conditions and when will it happen?
      iv. Who pays for what?
8. Maintenance
   a. What are the maintenance requirements associated with participating in this MOU?
   b. If any licenses are required for activities (e.g., software licensing) who will own the licenses?
   c. Who will maintain the equipment?
9. Oversight
   a. What governance structure oversees the fusion center?
   b. What is the relationship of the governance structure to the parties of the MOU?
   c. What are the participation requirements in this governance structure of agencies entering this MOU?
   d. How are issues affecting policy, recommendations, and/or subsequent change implemented by the governance structure?

10. Responsibility For Standard Operating Procedure (SOP) Compliance

   a. Who is responsible for ensuring that the SOPs associated with this capability/resource are followed and that individual agency personnel are trained appropriately?

   b. How will compliance be carried out?

11. Updates To The MOU

   a. Who has the authority to update or modify this MOU?

   b. How will this MOU be updated or modified?

   c. Will updates or modifications require this MOU to have a new signature page verifying the understanding of changes by each participating agency?

12. Separation From The MOU

   a. Under what circumstances may a signatory agency withdraw from the MOU?

   b. What are the penalties or obligations (both funding and other resources), if any, for separation prior to the termination date of the MOU?

13. Authorized Signatures and Dates

   a. All parties to the MOU must have a signature of agreement and commitment by an individual who has the authority to make such commitments.

   b. Explicit dates should be specified as to when the MOU goes into effect.

Chapter Annex 8-2: Common Terrorism Information-Sharing Standards Program

Program Manager/Information-Sharing Environment

Common Terrorism Information-Sharing Standards (CTISS) Program

The Program Manager-Information Sharing Environment released standards that state, local, and federal law enforcement officials must follow when they share information about suspicious activity that could have links to terrorism. Those standards define fusion centers as central nodes for sharing information. The role of fusion centers in collection, integration, analysis, and redistribution of incident information is envisioned to follow these processes:

1. **Observation.** A person witnesses suspicious activity and reports it to a law enforcement agency.

2. **Initial response and investigation.** A law enforcement officer collects additional information from interviews and databases.

3. **Local and regional information processing.** The reporting agency stores that information in its records management system.

4. **Creation of a Suspicious Activity Report (SAR).** A person assigned to the intelligence fusion center assesses the information using standards developed by Office of the Director of National Intelligence (ODNI). If the reported activity could have links to terrorism, the official creates an Information Sharing Environment Suspicious Activity Reporting (ISE-SAR) record.

5. **Information sharing and dissemination.** That ISE-SAR record is shared with FBI and Homeland Security Department employees who work at the fusion center. The employees enter the information into FBI and DHS databases.

6. **Information processing at the federal headquarters level.** The ISE-SAR record is combined with information from other state and local authorities to create an agency-specific national threat assessment, which is shared with agencies that participate in the ISE.

7. **National Counterterrorism Center (NCTC) analysis.** The ODNI's NCTC analyzes the data using information from the intelligence, defense, law enforcement, foreign affairs, and homeland security communities.

8. **NCTC threat alerts and warnings.** The NCTC products are shared with all appropriate federal departments and agencies and with SLT through the state or major urban area fusion centers. The sharing with state, local, and tribal entities and the private sector occurs through the federal departments or agencies that have been assigned the responsibility and have connectivity with the state or major urban area fusion centers.

9. **Focused collection.** The information has come full circle and the process begins again, informed by an NCTC or other federal organization's product and the identified information needs of state, local, and tribal entities and federal field components.

www.ise.gov/pages/ctiss.html

Chapter 9:
Developing Public-Private Partnerships for Law Enforcement Intelligence

Developing Public-Private Partnerships for Law Enforcement Intelligence

Conceptually, it could be argued that the idea for public-private partnerships in law enforcement goes back to one of the most fundamental principles of policing articulated by Sir Robert Peel in 1829 in the United Kingdom. Peel noted that the government alone could not perform all policing duties—assistance was needed by members of the public and, by extension, the private business sector, to help keep communities safe from crime. Indeed, Peel argued that in a democratic society, the police derived its authority from the public; hence, the public had an obligation to assist the police on matters of public safety. His principle, "The police are the public and the public are the police" infers a reciprocal responsibility. In the 21st century, this can be inferred to include two-way information sharing and joint public safety initiatives—responsibilities that both law enforcement and the private sector should embrace.

Reinforcing this notion was an observation reported in a study by the Vera Institute of Justice, which concluded:

> The police depend on citizens to assist in almost every aspect of crime prevention and investigation. Mobilizing that public support is essential to the core mission.[2]

Traditionally, the relationship between law enforcement and the private sector concerning crime control and community safety initiatives has been relatively superficial. Typically, such initiatives have been related to crime issues that were largely idiosyncratic to a given community. In some cases, the law enforcement-private sector relationship has even been contentious. For example, alarm companies and law enforcement have often had problems related to responses to false alarms just as law enforcement and private investigators or security guards have been at professional odds, often with law enforcement viewing these two groups despairingly as "police wannabes."

In other cases, new law enforcement-private sector relationships have been derailed by legitimate obstacles such as civil rights and privacy concerns by law enforcement or the potential to undermine profit and investments by private entities. While not insurmountable, resolution of these issues requires creativity and innovation, both of which are often labor-intensive. All too often the initiative has dwindled away, with both groups saying "we tried" rather than forging forward to resolve the barriers. In some cases, it was perceived that the potential outcomes were not worth the time and resource investment needed to make the initiative work. These perspectives are beginning to be reshaped in the post-9/11 era, albeit slowly.

[1] Carter, David L. *Police and the Community.* 7th ed. Englewood Cliffs, New Jersey: Prentice Hall, Inc., 2000.

[2] Bhanu, Chitra and Christopher Stone. *Public-Private Partnerships for Police Reform.* New York: Vera Institute of Justice, 2004, p. 3.

Working cooperatively with the private sector to accomplish functional goals can be highly productive. As observed by the Vera Institute:

> Perhaps the most promising but least studied source of external support for police reform is the private business community. Not only do private sector companies command political attention, they hold talent, dynamism, creativity, and a wealth of resources that can be useful to reformers within police agencies.[3]

Similarly, a study by the RAND Corporation found the following:

> Private organizations also have proved to be a good source of information for local police. Private security officers, reservation and store clerks, and baggage handlers are good examples of private sources with helpful information; they are much more likely than an officer to see or sense something suspicious. Some agencies are trying to develop such relationships by creating seminars to teach businesses about the kinds of information that are most helpful. These seminars have the twofold objective of easing the anxiety of participants while enhancing the likelihood that they will call the police with information.[4]

As law enforcement reengineers its intelligence initiatives for homeland security, it has become obvious that the need for effective public-private partnerships is more important than ever. Moreover, the partnerships need to be configured in an array of different models depending on the threat picture within a region. The obstacles still remain; however, increasingly it is understood that the value derived from such relationships is indeed worth the investment of time and resources. While there are many programmatic approaches related to the private sector associated with prevention, disaster preparedness, incident management, and response, the current discussion will be limited to public-private partnerships for intelligence (P3I).

Background and Perspective

Much of the current thought on public-private partnerships has been shaped by initiatives related to the development of the European Union. A brief look at this history provides some perspective.

As a means to increase their economic strength on a global basis, 13 Western European countries developed an agreement that was originally known as the European Economic Commonwealth. It evolved into the European Community and, as it is known today, the European Union.[5] One of the foundations of developing a viable and economically strong union of diverse, multilingual governments was to embrace public-private partnerships. The conceptual framework developed by the European Union has broad applicability to the U.S.

> A public-private partnership is an agreement of cooperation between autonomous private and public parties working together to achieve joint objectives, on the basis of a clear division of responsibilities, tasks and authority, and with no hierarchy amongst the parties. The most important preconditions for the success of a public-private partnership are mutual trust and recognition of the possibilities for the future.[6]

[3] Bhanu and Stone. Ibid., p. 1.

[4] Riley, K. Jack, Gregory Treverton, Jeremy Wilson, and Lois Davis. *State and Local Intelligence in the War on Terrorism*. Santa Monica, California: RAND Corporation, 2005, p. 40.

[5] The current European Union membership is 27 countries, with three candidate countries awaiting admission. The history of the European Union is too complex and unnecessary for the current discussion. A good history, including milestone events, can be found at europa.eu/abc/history/index_en.htm.

[6] European Commission. *Report of the Seminar on Public Private Partnerships*. The Hague, Netherlands: 2003, www.theccv.eu/binaries/English_documents/Crime_prevention/seminar_ppp.pdf, p. 6.

In expanding the concept of public-private partnerships to public safety and security issues, the European Commission report stated the following:

Security—or safety—is a fundamental right, … meaning that the State bears responsibility for the preservation of this right. Four notions are important in this respect:
1. The State cannot solve the security problems in society alone.
2. When there is a specific risk, the people in charge must take the necessary measures.
3. Repression is not the only solution; there is a need to develop prevention.
4. The problems on a local level must be tackled by a common endorsement of all the participants [public and private alike].[7]

Three conditions for effective partnerships were articulated for public-private partnerships to be functional:
1. Effective cooperation, which includes the willingness to listen, to get to know each other, to respect each other, to recognize the limits of each partner, to share useful information, leading to discretion, confidentiality and the willingness to share information.
2. Working methodically: which means not to wait for a crisis before working together, to meet regularly, to plan processes of meeting, to use tools agreed on by all the partners to collect information.
3. Strengthening and a territorial disposition adapted to the history of the [community] and to its administrative and social reality.[8]

On the last point, for P3I in the U.S., this would include consideration of civil rights and privacy issues, protection of corporate proprietary information, adherence to national standards for security of sensitive information, and participation in the Information Sharing Environment (ISE).

U.S. National Standards and Recommendations for Public-Private Partnerships

In the U.S., the need to proactively incorporate the private sector as a functional partner in the information/intelligence-sharing process has been consistently recognized by a wide range of inquiries. The *9/11 Commission Final Report* noted this:

> The mandate of the Department of Homeland Security does not end with the government; the department is also responsible for working with the private sector to ensure preparedness. This is entirely appropriate, for the private sector controls 85% of the critical infrastructure in the nation. Indeed, unless a terrorist's target is a military or other secure governmental facility, the "first" responders will almost certainly be civilians. Homeland security and national preparedness therefore often begins with the private sector.[9]

[7] European Commission. (2003). Op. cit., p. 15.

[8] European Commission. (2003). Op. cit., p. 15\6.

[9] National Commission on Terrorist Attacks upon the United States. *9/11 Commission Final Report.* Washington, D.C.: 2004, 397–398.

There is no more critical need for information-sharing with the private sector than to develop intelligence to prevent terrorists' attacks from touching U.S. soil. The 9/11 Commission goes on to observe the following on the matter of public-private information sharing:

> The necessary technology already exists. What does not [already exist] are the rules for acquiring, accessing, sharing, and using the vast stores of public and private data that may be available. When information sharing works, it is a powerful tool.[10]

In examining the successes of government information-sharing, the Government Accountability Office made the following observation:

> One of the challenges in securing our homeland is ensuring that critical information collected and analyzed by the Department of Homeland Security (DHS) and Department of Justice (DOJ) is shared in a timely and secure manner with a variety of parties within federal, state, and local governments, as well as the private sector.[11]

To deal with these issues, the *National Strategy for Homeland Security* stated, "Government at the federal, state, and local level must actively collaborate and partner with the private sector…".[12] Similarly, the *National Strategy for Information Sharing* observed, "Private sector information represents a crucial element in both understanding the current threat environment and protecting our nation's critical infrastructure from targeted attacks."[13]

The Global Intelligence Working Group recommended that law enforcement include the private sector in the law enforcement intelligence mission. Recommendation 7 of the *National Criminal Intelligence Sharing Plan*, for example, states the following:

> Local, state, tribal, and federal law enforcement agencies must recognize and partner with the public and private sectors in order to detect and prevent attacks to the nation's critical infrastructures. Steps should be taken to establish regular communications and methods of information exchange.[14]

Similarly, the *Fusion Center Guidelines* observed:

> The public safety and private sector components are integral in the fusion process because they provide fusion centers with crime-related information, including risk and threat assessments, and subject.

As evidence by the various reports cited thus far, it is clear that public-private information-sharing is critical for homeland security. It is recommended in virtually every inquiry and assessment of intelligence effectiveness, yet in the years since the 9/11 attacks, accomplishments have not reached the magnitude that was envisioned. As noted by a 2005 Bureau of Justice Assistance report exclusively devoted to public-private relationships in homeland security, "Barriers to information sharing between law enforcement and private security clearly exist."[15] The report goes on to conclude:

[10] Ibid., p 419.

[11] Government Accountability Office. *TECHNOLOGY: Numerous Federal Networks Used to Support Homeland Security Need to Be Better Coordinated with Key State and Local Information-Sharing Initiatives.* Washington, D.C.: Government Accountability Office, 2007, p. 9.

[12] *National Strategy for Homeland Security.* Washington, D.C.: Executive Office of the President, 2002, p. 33.

[13] *National Strategy for Information Sharing.* Washington, D.C.: Executive Office of the President, 2007, p. 4.

[14] Global Intelligence Working Group. *National Criminal Intelligence Sharing Plan.* Washington, D.C.: Bureau of Justice Assistance, Office of Justice Programs, U.S. Department of Justice, 2003, p. 27.

[15] Morabito, Andrew and Sheldon Greenberg. *Engaging the Private Sector to Promote Homeland Security: Law Enforcement-Private Security Partnerships.* Washington, D.C.: Bureau of Justice Assistance, 2005, p. 4.

[16] Ibid., p. 7.

The lifeblood of any policing agency is information; thus, information sharing (and its analyzed counterpart, intelligence sharing) should be a central component of any law enforcement-private security partnership.[16]

Not only has the DOJ noted the importance of public-private information sharing, a recent array of DHS inquiries has also emphasized the importance of this relationship. For example, one of the objectives of the DHS Intelligence Enterprise Strategic Plan is as follows:

> Objective 1.4: Reporting: Manage Homeland Security intelligence-related information reporting, seamlessly linking all levels of government and the private sector.[17]

Similarly, one of the DHS Lessons Learned/Best Practices papers, states:

> A jurisdiction's analysis and synthesis entity should also establish processes for sharing information with the local private sector. Private businesses and public safety agencies can provide each other with valuable threat and vulnerability information. However, public and private entities often have restrictions on information sharing with each other because of concerns over the release of sensitive or proprietary information.[18]

Yet another DHS Lessons Learned/Best Practices document recommends: "Local businesses and industries should also be incorporated into any local information sharing network".[19] One of the caveats, however, is that, "Public safety and private security officials should cooperatively establish guidelines that strike a balance between the need to inform the private sector of potential threats and the need to ensure that proprietary information is not improperly disseminated".[20] Another report addressed this issue, noting:

> Currently, no formal process exists for state, local, tribal, and private sector entities to task federal agencies with specific intelligence requirements. Failing to understand these entities' requirements inhibits the federal government's ability to understand the threats facing the Nation, much less provide actionable, timely, preferably UNCLASSIFIED, and frequently updated homeland security information and intelligence to those on the front lines of the domestic War on Terrorism.[21]

It is clear from these recommendations and assessments that the private sector must be integrated into information-sharing partnerships. Despite this plethora of recommendations, integration has been surprisingly limited. Moreover, the economic lifeblood of many communities lies in the corporate sector. Many corporations and industries—beyond those that are part of the critical infrastructure—have been identified as targets of terrorist attacks. Information-sharing between public and private entities simply has not evolved as recommended and expected. It is incumbent upon law enforcement leaders to develop a process and training to remedy that problem.

[17] Office of the Chief Intelligence Officer. *DHS Intelligence Enterprise Strategic Plan*. Washington, D.C.: U.S. Department of Homeland Security, 2006, p. 7.

[18] Lessons Learned Information Sharing Best Practices. *Local Anti-Terrorism Information and Intelligence Sharing: Dissemination*. 2006. www.llis.dhs.gov/member/secure/detail.cfm?content_id=13091. (Must register to access)

[19] Lessons Learned Information Sharing Best Practices. *Local Anti-Terrorism Information and Intelligence Sharing: Information Sharing Networks*. 2006. www.llis.dhs.gov/member/secure/detail.cfm?content_id=13088. (Must register to access)

[20] Ibid.

[21] Lessons Learned Information Sharing Best Practices. *Homeland Security Intelligence Requirements Process*. 2006. www.llis.dhs.gov/member/secure/detail.cfm?content_id=15327. (Must register to access)

P3I and the Intelligence Process

The current model of intelligence, related particularly to homeland security, addresses "all crimes, all hazards and all threats." From this perspective, state, local, and tribal law enforcement agencies are concerned with two types of intelligence: law enforcement and homeland security.

As a brief review, law enforcement intelligence is the analytic output of raw information that describes threats to a community that have a nexus with crime. This traditional form of intelligence focuses on criminal behaviors such as those related to terrorism or criminal enterprises. The less-traditional homeland security intelligence is the analytic output of raw information that describes noncriminal threats to the critical infrastructure, public health, or community safety for which a law enforcement agency will have some type of public order, public safety, and/ or order-maintenance responsibility. If a pandemic flu strikes a community, for example, law enforcement agencies will likely have to assist with victims, aid in quarantines, and assist in expediting and protecting medical supplies. As another illustration, homeland security intelligence may determine that, as a result of new industry, larger barges will travel a major waterway near a community which, in turn, increases the likelihood of a barge striking a major bridge. As a result, law enforcement strategic planning would have to deal with rescue and recovery plans, traffic control plans, and security of the accident scene.

Linking both types of intelligence into a targeted capability outcome, the DHS *Target Capability List* states the following:

> Effective and timely sharing of information and intelligence occurs across Federal, State, local, tribal, territorial, regional, and private sector entities to achieve coordinated awareness of, prevention of, protection against, and response to a threatened or actual domestic terrorist attack, major disaster, or other emergency.[22]

Some challenges for P3I may occur for health professionals with unique types of personal identifying information (such as information on public health and the Health Insurance Portability and Accountability Act of 2006).[23] Plans and processes for lawfully dealing with sharing this type of information and avoiding barriers should a public health tragedy emerge are much easier to resolve before a crisis than during a crisis. If a public health emergency occurs, it would be essential for health care professionals to identify individuals to law enforcement who pose a risk or who are at risk. If processes are put in place with both law enforcement and public health professionals trained, conflict resolution and service delivery will be expedited.

The intent of this discussion has been to place some basic definitions and concepts in context to provide perspective for the P3I. A transitional issue is the relationship of public-private partnerships to the ISE from the context of state, local, and tribal law enforcement agencies.

[22] National Preparedness Directorate. *Targeted Capabilities List.* Washington, D.C.: U.S. Department of Homeland Security, 2007, p. 69.

[23] See the Office of Civil Rights, U.S. Department of Health and Human Services, www.hhs.gov/ocr/hipaa, for more information.

The Information-Sharing Environment and the Private Sector

A new challenge for both law enforcement and the private sector results from the creation of the ISE. The ISE is a formal set of guidelines and processes to enhance the sharing of intelligence across five critical sectors: 1. The Intelligence Community; 2. Federal law enforcement; 3. State, local, and tribal law enforcement; 4. The private sector; and 5. Foreign partners.

> Recognizing the need to go beyond individual solutions to create an environment—the aggregation of legal, policy, cultural, organizational, and technological conditions—for improving information sharing, Congress passed and the President signed the landmark Intelligence Reform and Terrorism Prevention Act of 2004 (IRTPA). The Act requires the President to establish an Information Sharing Environment (ISE), "for the sharing of terrorism information in a manner consistent with national security and with applicable legal standards relating to privacy and civil liberties."[24]

Based on this legislative mandate, the program manager for the ISE guided the development of an implementation plan to provide the mechanism by which the ISE would accomplish its legislative mandate. A critical starting point was defining a vision that has essentially become the ISE's ultimate goal:

> We envision a future ISE that represents a *trusted partnership among all levels of government in the United States, the private sector, and our foreign partners, to detect, prevent, disrupt, preempt, and mitigate the effects of terrorism against the territory, people, and interests of the United States of America.*[25] (Emphasis in original.)

Key to realizing this vision was to create a culture of information sharing among the Intelligence Community, law enforcement agencies, and the private sector. This ambitious plan includes developing the willingness among all entities to be involved proactively in two-way information sharing, increasing technological connectivity between the entities to appropriately and lawfully share information and to develop a common lexicon to increase the quality of information while maintaining security.

As part of this challenge, the *ISE Implementation Plan* stated that the private sector should be part of "… a coordinated [information sharing] source … for access to terrorism information, alerts, warnings, and situational awareness".[26] The *Implementation Plan* went on to note that private-sector information represents a crucial element in both understanding the current threat environment and preventing the nation's critical infrastructure from being the target of attacks.

> Protecting the interconnected and interdependent U.S. infrastructure also requires a robust public-private partnership that provides the private sector with information on incidents, threats, and vulnerabilities, as well as protects private-sector information in such a way that the private sector is willing to share it with government partners.[27]

[24] Program Manager–Information Sharing Environment. *Implementation Plan for the Information Sharing Environment.* Washington, D.C.: PM–ISE, Office of the Director of National Intelligence, 2006, p. xiii.

[25] Ibid.

[26] Ibid., p. 12.

[27] Ibid., p. 19.

While going beyond the needs of the intelligence process, the primary conduits for sharing terrorism information currently are the Sector Coordinating Councils (SCC) and sector-specific Information Sharing and Analysis Centers established by the *National Infrastructure Protection Plan* (NIPP) and the National Infrastructure Coordination Center. To date, however, sharing through these mechanisms has yielded mixed results. One of the reasons stems from the ambiguity inherent in the public-private relationship. Another important factor is that the private-sector participants report the demand from federal, state, and local governments for critical infrastructure and other information since 9/11 has multiplied many times over, imposing more demands on industry to collect information and report it. Added to the complexity of these factors is that requests for private-sector information are rarely coordinated or consistent, resulting in duplicative requests.[28] If P3I is going to be successful, a consistent collection plan needs to be established. The NIPP[29] articulated six objectives that can serve as guideposts for the collection plan:

1. Sharing information to manage risks to business enterprises and in a manner that protects the information privacy and other legal rights of Americans.

2. Creating a national framework and culture for sharing information that rationalizes requests for terrorism information to the private sector and that adequately protects the risks and proprietary interests of corporations.

3. Creating an integrated, trusted environment in which information can be shared, maintained, and protected.

4. Ensuring access to the integration and analysis of data from multiple sources to provide industry with indicators of impending threats or current attacks.

5. Receiving actionable alerts and warnings concerning specific industries that improve their situational awareness of terrorist threats and enable them to prioritize risks and security investments, and shape the development of plans to ensure the security, continuity, and resiliency of infrastructure operations.

6. Implementing policies and mechanisms that provide liability and antitrust protections to the private sector in connection with sharing information in good faith.[30]

One initiative that is intended to help facilitate these initiatives is the United States Public Private Partnership (USP3). USP3 was designed to serve as a coordination conduit for private and public outreach programs creating a national cross-sector membership. Members in USP3 are involved in information sharing among the partnership.[31] While the concept is sound and there has been good support for the initiative, notably by the DHS, the project has had limited participation. Nonetheless, USP3 should be monitored and supported by local law enforcement as a foundation for developing solid partnerships with the private sector.

The challenge is to understand the complete character of P3I, defining the critical issues that must be resolved, and achieving these objectives in a manner that protects the critical interests of both private entities and law enforcement organizations. These are often competing interests; however, some principles can be relied on to guide both types of organizations through this largely uncharted territory.

[28] Ibid.

[29] The NIPP can be downloaded at www. dhs.gov/xlibrary/assets/NIPP_Plan.pdf.

[30] Ibid., p. 20.

[31] www.usp3.org

Fundamental Principles of Public-Private Partnerships for Intelligence

The P3I is intended to prevent or mitigate criminal and homeland security threats to a community through a two-way flow of raw information and intelligence. In its Homeland Security Policy Statement, the National Governors Association observed that:

> …private sector partners play a key role in providing experts, technology, and infrastructure resources to establish and maintain our nation's security. The role of the business community and the impact on the economic viability of a community when faced with [the prospect of] a terrorist attack must be considered.[32]

One perspective of understanding private-sector targets within a community is to use the framework on which the DHS relies for identifying critical infrastructures and key resources. Certain national infrastructures are so vital that their incapacity or destruction would have a debilitating impact on the defense or economic security of the United States.

- Telecommunications
- Electrical power systems
- Gas and oil storage and transportation
- Banking and finance
- Transportation
- Water supply systems
- Emergency services (including medical, police, fire, and rescue)
- Continuity of government.[33]

These elements of the critical infrastructure affect every community in the United States and, therefore, are of primary national concern.

The term "key resources" means publicly or privately controlled resources essential to the minimal operations of the economy and government.[34] A key resource can vary between communities. Hallmark Cards, for example, is not part of the U.S. critical infrastructure; however, the company employs more than 4,000 competitively paid workers at its Kansas City, Missouri, headquarters and, therefore, is a key resource for the economy of Kansas City. A key resource may also go beyond a single business and include an entire sector within a community. For example, the beef cattle industry in Dodge City, Kansas, includes cattle feed lots owned by a wide array of individuals and businesses, a cattle auction house, and multiple beef processing companies. Collectively, these businesses are the economic engine, hence key resources, for southwestern Kansas. (See Chapter Annex 9-1 for a public-private case study of this in Dodge City.)

As noted previously, while there are many roles the private sector may fulfill in homeland security, the current discussion is focusing solely on the intelligence role for prevention. As such, both private critical infrastructures and knowledge resources should be identified by their likelihood of becoming a target in light of the reasonable threats within the region.

[32] National Governors Association. "Section 5.5 – Coordination with the Private Sector." *Policy Position: EC-05. Homeland Security Policy.* Washington, D.C.: National Governors Association, 2007.

[33] *Executive Order No. 13010. Critical Infrastructure Protection.* See 42 U.S.C. 5195c(e).

[34] Homeland Security Act of 2002 codified as 6 U.S.C. 101(9).

One might also consider the nonlaw enforcement public sector within the same framework as private because much of its information processing and roles are more like the private sector than law enforcement. Moreover, these organizations will have access to unique types of information; for example, public health, agriculture and veterinary medicine, mass transportation, and aviation departments possess a significant amount of information that could provide value to both law enforcement and homeland security intelligence.

Intelligence relies on raw information. From this perspective, an important element to consider is that the private sector has access to raw information not readily available to law enforcement that can be important for responding to intelligence requirements related to threats within a community or a region. This information may come from independent sources (domestically or internationally) that a corporate security organization has developed through its own sources. These are some examples:

- An automobile manufacturer's corporate security division learns through an investigation of trans-shipment thefts from an overseas parts supplier that the same criminals are smuggling explosive components to a person within the U.S.

- Corporate security of a multinational banking firm learns of suspicious financial transactions originating in your city that involve transferring funds to a bank in Iran suspected of hosting bank accounts of persons suspected of terrorism.

- Corporate security of a large retail company discovers that drugs being smuggled from Thailand to your community are hidden in legitimate shipments of merchandise.

Information from the private sector may also be developed as the result of a request from law enforcement to be on the look out (BOLO) for certain terrorism or criminal indicators. Examples:

- Law enforcement intelligence provides training on criminal indicators to freight or package delivery companies and asks their delivery persons to report suspicious activities based on those indicators.

- Law enforcement intelligence asks retailers to notify it if certain commodities known to be used in terrorism financing or part of another type of criminal enterprise are being sold in, or stolen from, their stores (e.g., Enfamil infant formula[35]).

- Law enforcement intelligence asks a representative of large corporate retailers of certain chemicals to report unusual purchases of selected products that could be used to commit a terrorist attack.

"Business leaders often ask what—other than extra funds—they can contribute to effective police reform. One answer is skills."[36] The private sector has expertise not readily available in law enforcement. This can range from unique technologies, international audio and video communications, abilities to assess hazardous materials, and access to a wide array of equipment ranging from chemical detectors to satellites.

[35] See www.ice.gov/pi/news/newsreleases/articles/babyformula.htm.

[36] Bhanu and Stone, Op. cit., p. 3.

Types of Partnerships

Partnerships may be developed in different forms according to resources, threats, and information needs. They will be determined by such factors as the nature of threats within a community; the types of critical infrastructures and key resources in a region and their vulnerability; and the willingness of public and private organizational leaders to enter into an information-sharing partnership.

Full Partnerships through Personnel Assignment

Full partnerships occur when a person from the private sector is assigned full-time to a fusion center or intelligence unit. Typically, the individual will represent a business sector, not just the company where he or she is employed. The Boeing Corporation, for example, has assigned an intelligence analyst (who has a Department of Defense security clearance) full-time to the Washington Joint Analysis Center (WAJAC). The Boeing employee represents the entire aircraft manufacturing industry (including suppliers), not just the Boeing Corporation. The criterion for a private sector representative to be assigned to WAJAC is stipulated in its operations manual:

> "Private Entities: WAJAC shall consider the assignment of personnel from privately owned corporations who have a stake in homeland security and meet the approval of the WAJAC Advisory Board." (p. A-4).

Having a private-sector employee represent an entire sector, with the approval of the WAJAC Advisory Board, avoids allegations of playing favorites to any specific company. Moreover, it is simply more efficient and effective to have one sector representative rather than multiple representatives from one sector. Of course, a challenge is to ensure that the sector representative has an agreement with other members of the sector to share needed information.

A full partnership assignment should include, at the minimum: 1. A background investigation of the person being assigned; 2. A memorandum of agreement (MOA) between the public and private entities that spells out duties, responsibilities, and processes of both parties as related to the employee's assignment; and 3. A signed nondisclosure agreement.

The law enforcement intelligence entity needs to assess the sectors in its region to determine the most critical to have represented in the fusion center or unit. Of course, those which have major installations in the region are the most likely candidates. Table 9-1 lists the range of sectors that may provide value to an intelligence unit.

Table: 9-1: Sectors of Private Industry

• Agriculture, food, water, environment	• Postal and shipping
• Banking and finance	• Private security
• Chemical industry and hazardous materials	• Public works
• Criminal justice (nonlaw enforcement)	• Real estate
• Education	• Retail
• Emergency services (nonlaw enforcement)	• Transportation – Aviation (all commercial)
• Energy	• Transportation – Aviation (general)
• Government	• Transportation – Buses and light rail
• Health and public health	• Transportation – Maritime
• Hospitality and lodging	• Transportation – Rail
• Information and telecommunications	• Transportation – Roads and bridges
• Military facilities and defense industrial base	

Full-time Information-Sharing Partnership

Under a full-time arrangement there is two-way information sharing between law enforcement and private sector partners that occurs on an ongoing basis, just as the agency does with law enforcement partners. The distinction between this and the full partnership is that in the current case a person is not assigned to a fusion center or intelligence unit—he or she remains at his or her place of employment. This is particularly valuable when standing intelligence requirements are related to the private sector. The most common model where this is used is when an intelligence liaison officer[37] (ILO) program has been established.

The ILO concept establishes a formal relationship with the private-sector organization designating an individual who will be the contact point on all two-way information-sharing. Typically, the ILO is vetted for security purposes; receives training along with law enforcement officers on intelligence, counterterrorism, and homeland security intelligence issues; is given defined areas of responsibility for information-sharing; and is often given access to a secure e-mail system, such

[37]This concept is used in a variety of different agencies and has different names: Terrorism liaison officer (TLO) and industry liaison officer (ILO) are common examples. Regardless of the name of the program, the concept is the same. Similarly, the concept is not limited to the private sector. A state fusion center, for example, may designate an ILO from different law enforcement agencies throughout the state.

as the Automated Trusted Information Exchange (ATIX). ILOs should also meet regularly with the intelligence group to discuss issues and processes in order to maximize effectiveness as well as to maintain a strong relationship that is essential for sustaining the ILO program. As was the case with the full partnership, all participating organizations should sign an MOA and the ILO should sign a nondisclosure agreement.

Since the ILO will physically remain at his or her place of employment, information security becomes a greater issue for both parties. Information security processes, therefore, should be outlined in the MOA.

The ILO program is a functional option when the private sector does not have sufficient personnel to assign a person to the law enforcement agency, yet its information is critical for community safety.

The ILO fulfills a number of important roles which include, but are not limited to these:[38]

- Collect, report, retrieve, and share training materials related to threats faced by the sector.

- Serve as a source person for internal and external inquiries from the fusion center or intelligence unit.

- Collect, report, retrieve, and share information and intelligence related to potential threats to the sector.

- Identify, communicate, and serve as a liaison with stakeholders in the sector.

- Serve as the contact person for persons in the sector who have questions about, or information to share about, a threat.

- Conduct, coordinate, and/or facilitate training regarding threats in the sector. The training should be for law enforcement and/or the sector.

- Serve as the designated sector representative for meetings, associations, task forces, or any other entity related to sector threats.

- Monitor and share information with the fusion center or intelligence unit about the existence and/or changes of sector critical infrastructure and key resources.

- Conduct and maintain threat and vulnerability assessments for the sector.

- Keep up to date on terrorist and criminal threats to the sector by monitoring all sources, including open sources.

- Familiar with all law and national standards related to the intelligence function.

- Serve as a sector subject matter expert on all technical and industry-specific language, equipment, and processes for the sector.

Ad Hoc Partnerships

The ad hoc partnership is used on an as-needed basis. This is a particularly viable alternative when no standing intelligence requirements are needed from a particular industry in the private sector. When threat circumstances arise relating to the sector or organization, a mechanism is in place for rapid information-sharing. In extreme cases, a private-sector representative may be placed on a

[38] Based on the Arizona Counterterrorism Information Center bulletin on the terrorism liaison officer program.

temporary duty assignment to the law enforcement agency. Similar vetting processes should be used as in the case of the ILO as well as the memorandum of understanding (MOU) and nondisclosure agreement.

Obstacles to Law Enforcement-Private Partnerships

The inherent nature of P3I requires the open two-way exchange of threat-based information and intelligence between law enforcement agencies and the private sector for both law enforcement and homeland security purposes. As such, processes need to ensure that the exchange is open and that both law enforcement and the private sector receive the information they need. Unfortunately, this is not easy. In exploring the law enforcement-private sector relationship, the Bureau of Justice Assistance (BJA) identified three key obstacles that must be overcome when establishing effective partnerships.[39]

Obstacle 1: Barriers to Information-Sharing. A number of information-sharing barriers must be overcome by both law enforcement and the private sector if effective information sharing is to take place.

The barriers emanating from a law enforcement agency to the private sector include the following:

- Uncertainty about what types of information may be shared with the private sector because of privacy and civil rights concerns.

- Uncertainty about how to share information designated for law enforcement distribution only. In this regard, one question to resolve is whether the assignment of a private-sector representative in a formal arrangement under the authority of an MOU establishes that person as an agent for the law enforcement organization. In many cases, this will be largely influenced by state law.

- Determination of an acceptable method to share sensitive information and intelligence. (Once again, ATIX may provide the best answer.)

Conversely, private-sector barriers to law enforcement include these:

- The reluctance to share proprietary information even if related to a potential threat.

- Foreign-owned companies are reticent to share any information with the government in the U.S.

- As a rule, the private sector does not want to risk information becoming public that could harm profits.

While these information-sharing barriers are not insurmountable, they require nontraditional and creative resolution to address legal controls, information security concerns, and legitimate corporate interests.

Obstacle 2: Lack of Trust. Surveys by the Justice Department[40] have consistently found that the level of trust between law enforcement and private sector security is quite low. The two sectors often view each other as having separate goals and different constituencies. The law enforcement agency's constituency is the community it serves, whereas the constituency of the private sector includes

[39] Morabito, Andrew, and Shelton Greenberg. *Engaging the Private Sector to Promote Homeland Security: Law Enforcement-Private Security Partnerships.* Washington, D.C.: Office of Justice Assistance, U.S. Department of Justice, 2005, p. 4.

[40] Ibid.

not only a broader community but also its investors who go far beyond the local community. There is also an often unstated belief by both law enforcement and the private sector that if one cooperates, the other may not reciprocate. Contributing to the distrust is that, in some instances, private security is seen as not being equal to sworn law enforcement. Of course, private security capability is quite broad, ranging from security guards to sophisticated investigators and analysts.

BJA noted that to develop trust, law enforcement executives and their staffs must do the following:

- Create a vision and passion that brings workers together.

- Deliver what is promised.

- Ensure consistency. Constant change or change that is not understood destroys credibility.

- Communicate.

- Draw out and address past suspicions and concerns.

- Pay attention to detail.

- Train law enforcement personnel and private-sector partners together.

- Ensure equity and equality. Both sides must produce their share of work and be recognized for it.

- Reinforce the importance of the partnership (with an emphasis on sharing the credit for successes).

- Admit mistakes and learn from them. Both sides will make errors.

Obstacle 3: Misinformation and Misunderstanding. Among the major causes of lack of trust are misinformation and misunderstanding. Often, neither law enforcement nor the private sector has a complete understanding of what the other does or can do. Collectively, these have often been viewed as insurmountable by both parties. Successful partnerships demonstrate that the barriers can be overcome, but it requires leadership, commitment, and work to resolve the barriers.

How can these obstacles be overcome? BJA recommends use of the "4 C's":[41]

- Communication—Goals, plans, the types of information to be shared, and concerns should be clearly and unequivocally stated by both parties.

- Cooperation—Overt efforts must be made to reach out to the other. Each party will have wins and losses. The need to develop creative ways to share information should be paramount to establishing a trusting relationship.

- Coordination—Be certain that the actions and responsibilities of each party are clearly articulated to ensure there is no duplication and that all activities mesh well in a seamless public-private Information Sharing Environment.

- Collaboration—Not only work together, but plan together. Each should rely on the expertise and strengths of the other.

---

[41] Morabito and Greenberg, Ibid., p. 5.

Two Critical Issues to Resolve: Sharing Criminal Information and Private Proprietary Information

Sharing criminal information with a private partner has concerns and restrictions that are related to civil rights, state law, criminal intelligence records regulations and policy, and operational security. Most issues can be resolved but they will require carefully crafted policies, MOU provisions, and training. A critical issue for law enforcement is the sharing of information when individuals or organizations are identified: this is the point where constitutional protections attach.

Perhaps the easiest issue is how to share information related to criminal intelligence when individuals and organizations are *not* identified. This may be information about threat conditions, threat indicators, and advisories related to unspecified threats. In these cases, the information-sharing restrictions essentially focus on the right-to-know and need-to-know requirements. The MOA between both parties should be written in such a manner as to make the private-sector representative an agent of the law enforcement entity, thereby giving him or her the right to know. The need to know is determined on a case-by-case basis, just as it should be for law enforcement personnel.

The greater challenge is how to lawfully share information with private-sector partners that identifies individuals and organizations. When a person or organization is identified, constitutional rights and more stringent restrictions attach to the information and information-sharing process. The ability to share this information with private-sector personnel hinges on two important concerns. The first is how state law deals with privacy issues and, in particular, whether a private-sector partner is deemed to be an agent of the law enforcement agency. The second issue is the right-to-know and need-to-know standards that apply in the same manner as described above. Essential to success is the careful crafting of the MOA, training for all parties, and a secure information-sharing process.

Just as there are legal and operational restrictions on sharing criminal information, there are corporate restrictions on sharing proprietary information that belongs to private entities.

- Do you know the private-sector entities in your jurisdiction that should be involved?

- Do you have an established contact with any of these private-sector entities?

- Have representatives of these entities been vetted?

- Do you have an MOA with any of these entities?

- Have the entities with which you have a relationship signed a nondisclosure agreement?

Proprietary information is information that is patented, copyrighted, and/or trademarked, and describes a product, process, design and/or formula that was developed or purchased by a private organization and is part of that organization's business processes. It includes, but is not limited to: financial information; data or statements; trade secrets; product research and development; existing and future product designs and performance specifications; marketing plans or techniques; schematics; client lists; computer programs; processes; and know-how that have been clearly identified and properly marked by the company as proprietary information, trade secrets, or company confidential information

To be proprietary, the information must have been developed by the private entity and is not available to the government or to the public without restriction from another source. The formula for a soft drink, software code, the business plan of a company, a business marketing list ,or the components of a computing device are examples of proprietary information. The nature of proprietary information can range on a very broad spectrum. Essentially, every product and every business in the world conceivably has some form of proprietary information that typically is not shared because of concern over aiding competitors or undermining one's success in the marketplace.

In some cases, proprietary information may be relevant to the prevention or mitigation of a criminal incident or emergency; for example, the design of a production or shipping facility, the location of storage and backup sites, the compounds in a chemical product, or the process to disable some type of device. In such a circumstance, it is hoped that the private entity would share proprietary information with law enforcement. To accomplish this, the law enforcement agency must recognize the magnitude that such a request holds. The disclosure of the information could undermine the success of the company. While the law enforcement agency sees the value of learning such information, it must also be cognizant of the risk that it poses to the private-sector partner. It is good practice to have a procedure for the release of proprietary information and a statement of release and nondisclosure that is signed by both parties. Examples of components of such a document are listed in Table 9-2.

Table 9-2: Sample Components of a Release and Nondisclosure Agreement Regarding Proprietary Information

- Identify the specific type of proprietary information needed.
- Provide a clear state of justification of why the information is needed to prevent or mitigate terrorism or criminal offense or the public safety need for such information.
- Define the conditions under which the private-sector entity would release the information.
- Articulate any unique stipulations to the distribution of the information.
- Define the information security requirements for protecting the proprietary information.
- Describe the time frame, if any, for which the information release is authorized.
- Describe how the information is to be handled after the threat requiring the information has passed.
- Stipulate sanctions, processes, or other remedies to impose should the information be inappropriately disclosed or disseminated.
- Signed and dated by both the public sector and private sector authorizing agents.

Developing the Message to Private-Sector Partners
- There should be a consistent message to private-sector partners, but recognize the following:
- Different types of substantive information may be disseminated to the different partners.
  » Somewhat different information will be sought from the different partners.
- The message should emphasize their responsibility to contribute to community safety.
  » This is somewhat of a parallel to Neighborhood Watch or Business Watch.
- Key components of the message:
  » We need your help to protect our community by reporting suspicious activity that you observe.
  » We will provide information on what to look for.
  » We will provide you with details on the reporting process.
  » The process is designed to protect the rights of innocent persons.
- Goal: To convey to partners their obligation to community safety through a structured process that protects citizens civil rights.

Developing a Successful Public-Private Partnership for Intelligence

Successes in P3I require a collaborative effort and an effective plan. In its study of public-private relationships, the Bureau of Justice Assistance identified 12 essential components to develop. These components can be used as a road map for creating a public-private partnership. To begin, the law enforcement agency must articulate its vision and responsibilities for each of the factors listed below (See Figure 9-1). The response to each factor is reviewed and refined by those responsible for establishing and managing the partnership. The final implementation plan, including commitments of personnel and resources, is reviewed, refined (as necessary), and affirmed by the chief executive. The critical factors to be addressed in this process are the following:

- Negotiate and develop common goals.
- Identify and develop common tasks for both law enforcement and private-sector personnel.
- Develop knowledge of the capabilities and goals of participating agencies and businesses.
- Articulate well-defined projected outcomes.
- Establish a reasonable timetable for implementation.
- Provide training on the concepts, purpose, and tasks for all involved.
- Clearly identify the tangible purposes of the partnership.
- Clearly identify leaders and those responsible for tasks and goals.
- Create an operational guide on how the partnership will function after it is implemented.
- Secure an agreement by all partners about how the partnership will proceed, including resources and responsibilities.
- Articulate a mutual commitment to providing necessary resources.
- Establish an assessment and reporting process.[42]

Denver Police Department Public-Private Partnership (DP3)
The acronym DP3 stands for Denver Public-Private Partnership. DP3 represents the Denver Police Department's effort at forming a partnership with private security professionals in the City and County of Denver.

The centerpiece of DP3 is a broadcast alert communication network whereby DP3 members receive up-to-the-minute information regarding security threats, crime trends and incidents-in-progress, upcoming major events, BOLO announcements, and the like.

Additionally, DP3's web site will post crime-prevention information and have links to partner organizations' web sites. These sites have many valuable resources relating to security, domestic preparedness, and major incident planning.

Benefits of Membership
The DP3 homepage will post public information and links, but members will have additional privileges. DP3 members, after a limited background and records check, will receive e-mail or text messages and alerts. Members will also have access to the DP3 archives of past alerts and the document library.

Who Should Join
Eligibility for membership in DP3 is limited to security directors and supervisors having an established proprietary or contractual security force within the City and County of Denver. They may also designate members of their staff as being eligible for membership. Access to the DP3 site, however, is open. A brief e-mail to DP3@ci.denver.co.us expressing interest in membership is all that is required, and you will be contacted with instructions and an application. Applicants will undergo a brief computer records and background check as part of the application and approval process.

www.denvergov.org/DP3

[42] Adapted from: Morabito and Greenberg, Ibid, pp. 5–6.

Following this process provides a solid foundation and a clear purpose for the partnership with a demonstration of support and commitment by the chief executive. Collectively, this represents an explicit development plan that may be submitted to potential private-sector partners. If the partnership is going to move forward, the private sector must review, refine, and agree to its responsibilities associated with the above factors. There may need to be a negotiation process on certain elements of the plan, which the law enforcement agency must reasonably consider. In the end, each party must agree to its responsibilities and commitments before the partnership is finalized. The development and implementation plan should then move into a joint operational plan with a signed MOA, as appropriate (see Figure 9-1 again).

It is a recipe for failure if either the law enforcement agency or private entity attempts to implement critical factors without input from the other party. Remember that in many cases, the private partner will often have to sell the partnership to a larger corporate structure. As such, demonstrating substantive input into the partnership development process by the private entity can be an important factor in securing corporate commitments.

In developing a public-private partnership in support of the intelligence function, Matthew Simeone of the Nassau County, New York, Police Department identified several key factors executives should consider:

- First who, then what: Make sure the right people were in the right positions in the organization before they decide on strategy.

- Tipping Point Leadership: Within every organization there are people, acts, and activities that exert a disproportionate amount of influence on performance. Consequently, focusing efforts on identifying and then leveraging these factors can enable great change.

- Instilling a Need for Change: An initiative involving the private sector and information sharing is likely to bring about debate within the agency regarding the type of information that will be shared. Preparing an internal campaign that addresses the anticipated concerns of officers and the value they will receive from the partnership is essential for the partnership to be effective.

- Committing the Resource: As has been discussed on previous issues, the failure to commit resources to the partnership is essentially condemning the partnership to failure.

- Leveraging the Natural Leaders: The person responsible for developing and implementing the public-private partnership must believe in the concept, understand the concept, have the interpersonal and intellectual skills to move the partnership forward, and be respected within the agency as an informal leader.

- Be Open to Innovation: Agencies should be open to user innovation and should encourage creativity and sharing within the agreed-on guidelines. Just because something has not been done before does not mean it is a bad idea or that it will not work.

- Build on Established Experiences: While public-private partnerships for intelligence may be new, the agency may have previous public-private experiences related to crime prevention or community policing that can serve as a springboard for the intelligence initiative.[43]

Some examples of different law enforcement-private partnership models will provide additional insight.

[43] Adapted from: Simeone, Matthew J. *The Integration of Virtual Public-Private Partnerships in Law Enforcement to Achieve Enhanced Intelligence-Led Policing.* Monterey, California: A thesis prepared for the Naval Postgraduate School, 2007, 103–108.

Figure 9-1: Establishing a Public-Private Partnership for Intelligence

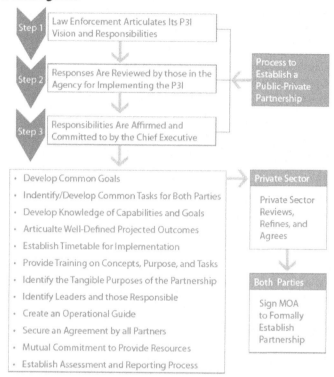

- Develop Common Goals
- Indentify/Develop Common Tasks for Both Parties
- Develop Knowledge of Capabilities and Goals
- Articualte Well-Defined Projected Outcomes
- Establish Timetable for Implementation
- Provide Training on Concepts, Purpose, and Tasks
- Identify the Tangible Purposes of the Partnership
- Identify Leaders and those Responsible
- Create an Operational Guide
- Secure an Agreement by all Partners
- Mutual Commitment to Provide Resources
- Establish Assessment and Reporting Process

Step 1 Law Enforcement Articulates Its P3I Vision and Responsibilities

Step 2 Responses Are Reviewed by those in the Agency for Implementing the P3I

Step 3 Responsibilities Are Affirmed and Committed to by the Chief Executive

Process to Establish a Public-Private Partnership

Private Sector Private Sector Reviews, Refines, and Agrees

Both Parties Sign MOA to Formally Establish Partnership

InfraGard[44]

In the 1990s, with the rapid growth of computer networking and reliance on computerization for managing many aspects of government and commerce, it was recognized that the U.S. cyber infrastructure responsible for sustaining the fundamental elements of American life was increasingly vulnerable to terrorist attacks, criminal incursions, and natural disasters. To address this issue, a new initiative in critical infrastructure protection was developed by the Federal Bureau of Investigation (FBI) with the expressed purpose of understanding potential threats and developing ways to prevent or mitigate threats. The greatest emphasis was focused on cyber threats and cyber security.

As this initiative developed, it became apparent that a significant portion of the critical infrastructure was owned by the private sector. As such, it was concluded that critical infrastructure could be adequately protected only by developing a two-way information-sharing partnership between the government and the private sector. It was in this environment that InfraGard was developed.

InfraGard is an information-sharing and analysis effort serving the interests and combining the knowledge base of a wide range of members. At its most basic level, InfraGard is a partnership between the FBI and the private sector. It is an

[44] For more information about InfraGard see www.infragard.net/about.php?mn=1&sm=1-0.

association of businesses, academic institutions, state and local law enforcement agencies, and other participants dedicated to sharing information and intelligence to prevent hostile acts against the United States. InfraGard chapters are geographically linked with FBI Field Office territories, with an FBI special agent coordinator assigned to it. The FBI coordinator works closely with program managers in the Cyber Division at FBI Headquarters.

In its early development, InfraGard was under the direction of the National Infrastructure Protection Center (NIPC) with its focus on cyber infrastructure protection. After September 11, 2001, NIPC expanded its efforts to include physical as well as cyber threats to critical infrastructures. InfraGard's mission expanded accordingly.

In March 2003, the NIPC was transferred to the DHS, which now has responsibility for Critical Infrastructure Protection (CIP) matters. The FBI retained InfraGard as an FBI-sponsored program and works with DHS in support of its CIP mission, facilitating InfraGard's continuing role in CIP activities. In addition, the FBI has further developed InfraGard's ability to support the FBI's investigative mission, especially as it pertains to counterterrorism and cyber crimes.

The goal of InfraGard is to have ongoing, two-way, substantive information sharing between the FBI and its private-sector critical infrastructure partners. InfraGard members gain access to information that enables them to protect their assets and, in turn, give information to the government that facilitates its responsibilities to prevent and address terrorism and other crimes. This information exchange occurs at both the national and local levels for a more comprehensive approach to infrastructure protection.

To accomplish its goal, the FBI established the following objectives:
- Increase the level of information and reporting between InfraGard members and the FBI on matters related to counterterrorism, cyber crime, and other major crime programs.
- Increase interaction and information-sharing among InfraGard members and the FBI regarding threats to the critical infrastructures, vulnerabilities, and interdependencies.
- Provide members with value-added threat advisories, alerts, and warnings.
- Promote effective liaison with local, state, and federal agencies including the DHS.
- Provide members with a forum for education and training on counterterrorism, counterintelligence cyber crime, and other matters relevant to informed reporting of potential crimes and attacks on the nation and U.S. interests.

InfraGard is a solidly conceived and developed program. As might be expected, more substantive information exchanges tend to occur at the local level, while the national level initiatives are important for setting the tone for the public-private partnership. Critical to the success is having a special agent coordinator who fully understands the concept and its value and immerses himself or herself in the partnership to ensure that it is a productive relationship.

Security/Police Information Network:
Nassau County, New York

The Nassau County Security/Police Information Network (SPIN) is a dynamic, multidimensional crime-prevention partnership between the Nassau County Police Department and the private sector that seeks to increase public safety through the sharing of important and timely information. This program is designed to promote homeland security initiatives and business continuity, as well as to foster the exchange of information that is critical to the success of protecting Nassau County residents and businesses.

The goals of SPIN are to share information, identify and discuss crime trends and solutions, and work together toward the common goal of protecting persons and assets. SPIN enables the police department or any other county agency to send information to the general distribution group or to a specific sector (i.e., colleges/ universities, hospitals, schools, malls/retail, utilities, petroleum, technology, hotels/ motels, financial institutions, corporate security, and civic leaders). In addition, SPIN connects local, state, and federal law enforcement agencies operating in Nassau County, as well as public transportation and other government agencies. As a result, SPIN's multitiered approach allows messages to be tailored to law enforcement, vetted security directors, or chambers of commerce and civic organizations.

SPIN members are contacted by e-mail of unfolding situations as they occur. Messages include notifications of bank robberies, major road closings, disruptions in public transportation, major fires or explosions, civil disturbance, public health or weather-related emergencies, or any other situations involving public safety or affecting continuity of business. In addition, Sex Offender Registry notifications are sent to vulnerable entities using SPIN. Members can use SPIN to share information or inquire about safety matters or concerns.

The establishment of such a comprehensive network has applications that are far-reaching in scope, such as: aiding in the capture of felony suspects; notifying participants of the latest crime trends; helping the continuity of business through traffic delay notifications; and facilitating the large-scale exchange of information. The network also provides the police department with the ability to provide training materials to participants that will enhance the safety of all who live and work in Nassau County. Informational meetings are held as necessary to discuss timely security-related issues. Meeting topics have included domestic terrorism, the Republican National Convention, gang awareness, and the *National Response Plan*.

Recognizing the vast amount of knowledge, expertise, and resources in the private sector, SPIN recently expanded the scope of its public-private partnership with the formation of a Security Advisory Council. Utilizing the expertise of security professionals and police officers, the Council is focused on the establishment of guidelines promoting homeland security, crime-prevention and crime-reduction techniques, as well as working toward a coordinated response to critical incidents. The Security Advisory Council's first project, *Digital Video*

Surveillance Guidelines, was recently completed. The guidelines were presented at a SPIN meeting and then posted to the departmental web site.

SPIN, in partnership with the Nassau County Office of Emergency Management, has the ability to send out information to the entire SPIN membership, or to any specific sector of private industry, which are sorted into their own e-mail distribution groups.

The design of SPIN (see Figure 9-2) is not only logical; it is easily adaptable and scalable to meet the needs of agencies of diverse sizes.

Surrounding its law enforcement core are nonlaw enforcement government agencies and responsibilities that are among the easiest with which to establish a partnership, as well as to meet and communicate on a regular basis.

Relying on e-mail and a web portal, SPIN has been comparatively inexpensive to implement, it is less labor-intensive than face-to-face initiatives, it is fast, and it is easier for many private-sector entities, particularly those with a small workforce, to participate. Yet, it has empirically been demonstrated to be highly effective.[45]

Jani-King Janitorial Services Terrorism Awareness Program

Dallas-based Jani-King International, Inc., the world's largest commercial cleaning franchisor, has announced a training program for its franchisees and employees to provide an additional level of security to the more than 50,000 buildings that Jani-King cleans. Some 10,000 franchisees will be trained to assess potential building and workplace security threats and report them to authorities.

Jani-King believes that an aggressive and proactive approach to terrorism prevention is critical and of benefit to everyone. "The key word here is prevention," says Jani-King President Jerry Crawford. "We want to create a security force multiplier to help reduce the risk of terror threats."

"Jani-King is one of the only businesses where banking institutions, major corporations, educational facilities, nuclear power plants, and utilities literally hand over the keys to their buildings and provide access to secure areas," says Crawford. "We feel an obligation to put into action additional measures to help keep these buildings safe."

Crawford explained that Jani-King's training program would specifically educate employees and franchisees on three key areas that are important to terror prevention: awareness, identification, and reporting. "The training will consist of awareness of potential security threats, recognition skills, and proper reporting channels," says Crawford. "Franchise owners will not be trained to confront suspicious persons." Crawford gave an example. "Our crews clean the same buildings night after night. We see the normal activity. We want our employees to understand how to spot suspicious activity and then how to report it."

www.bizjournals.com/dallas/stories/2004/09/13/daily13.html

---

[45] For a comprehensive discussion of SPIN, see: Simeone, 2007, Op. cit.

Homeland Security, Information-Sharing, and the Private Sector

While there is an important role in all aspects of the intelligence process for public-private partnerships, it has been most comprehensively structured through initiatives of the DHS. Directed by legislation, Executive Orders, and Homeland Security Presidential Directives, DHS has developed a comprehensive structure for information sharing. Each holds potential for the intelligence process.

The DHS model has established different formal mechanisms to address its relationship with the private sector. These mechanism are intended to reach beyond the intelligence process and include the diverse elements of the *National Strategy for Homeland Security,* that include processes "to protect, prevent, respond to and recover from" terrorism and other man-made or natural threats to the homeland. The focus of the current discussion is to examine these processes from an intelligence perspective.

Figure 9-2: Nassau County (New York) Police Department SPIN Project Diagram

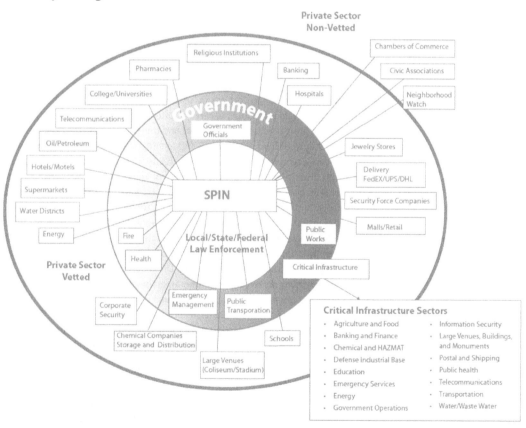

Critical Infrastructure Sector Partnership[46]

Critical infrastructure protection is a shared responsibility among federal, state, local, and tribal governments and the owners and operators of the nation's critical infrastructure and knowledge resources. Partnership between the public and private sectors is essential for three interactive reasons:

1. The private sector owns and operates approximately 85 percent of the nation's critical infrastructure.

2. Government agencies have access to important information about threats that may disable or destroy the critical infrastructure.

3. Both the private sector and the government control security programs, research and development, and other resources that may be more effective if discussed and shared, as appropriate, in a partnership setting.

Many factors inhibit information sharing for critical infrastructure protection, ranging from limitations by the government for sharing certain types of sensitive information to reservations by the private sector about making business processes available to persons outside of the corporate structure. Because of the important, yet tentative, understanding by both parties, mechanisms had to be put in place to enhance the sharing of important information, yet protect the responsibilities of each. *Homeland Security Presidential Directive 7* and the *NIPP* provide the overarching framework for a structured partnership between government and the private sector for protection of the CI and KRs. This sector partnership structure encourages formation of Sector Coordinating Councils and Government Coordinating Councils to facilitate communications and enhance information-sharing policies and practices.

Sector Coordinating Councils. A "sector" refers to businesses that share a common or closely related product or service. Often, members of a sector are business competitors—such as Delta Airlines and United Airlines in the aviation sector— yet they also share common risk and security problems. In the case of homeland security, sectors are identified as they relate to the protection of U.S. sovereignty and citizens, ranging from the provision of important services to the continuity of both government and the economy. The Sector Coordinating Councils (SCC) foster and facilitate the coordination of sector-wide activities and initiatives designed to improve the security of the nation's critical infrastructure. They are self-organized, self-led, broadly representative of owners and operators (and their associations) within the sector, and are focused on homeland security and critical infrastructure protection. The DHS has a strong preference that each SCC be chaired by an owner and/or operator. Government agencies may suggest the inclusion of various parts of a sector, but it is the responsibility of each SCC to identify the sector's boundaries, establish the criteria for membership, seek broad participation and representation of the diversity of the sector, and establish the governance, business case, and work processes of the sector's SCC.

Government Coordinating Councils. The Government Coordinating Councils (GCC) bring together diverse federal, state, local, and tribal interests to identify and develop collaborative strategies that advance the protection of critical infrastructures. GCCs serve as a counterpart to the SCC for each critical

[46] www.dhs.gov/xprevprot/partnerships/ editorial_0206.shtm

infrastructure and key resource sector. They provide interagency coordination around CI and KR strategies and activities, policy, and communication across government and between government and the sector to support the nation's homeland security mission. GCCs coordinate with, and support the efforts of, the SCCs to plan, implement, and execute sufficient and necessary sector-wide security to support the CI and KR sector. GCCs can leverage complementary resources within government and between government and CI and KR owners and operators.

Critical Infrastructure Partnership Advisory Council

The DHS established the Critical Infrastructure Partnership Advisory Council (CIPAC) to facilitate the effective defense of our nation's critical infrastructure by coordinating federal infrastructure protection programs with the infrastructure protection activities of the private sector and of state, local, territorial, and tribal governments.

CIPAC membership encompasses CI and KR owner/operator institutions and their designated trade or equivalent organizations identified as members of existing SCCs. The GCC members of CIPAC are representatives of federal, state, local, and tribal government entities.

CIPAC provides the framework for members of SCCs and GCCs to engage in intragovernment and public-private cooperation, information sharing, and engagement across the entire range of critical infrastructure protection activities. It enables them to interact freely and share sensitive information and advice about threats, vulnerabilities, protective measures, mutual actions, and lessons learned. CIPAC, therefore is exempt from the requirements of the Federal Advisory Committee Act that require public disclosure of an advisory committee's activities.

CIPAC consists of Joint Sector Committees in which GCC and SCC members participate. The Food and Agriculture Joint Sector Committee, for example, comprises food and agriculture GCC and SCC members. The CIPAC also includes one Joint Cross-Sector Committee consisting of the designated private-sector and agency leads from each Joint Sector Committee. The 16 sectors and 7 subsectors of CIPAC are as follows:

- Chemical Sector
- Commercial Facilities Sector
- Communications Sector
- Dams Sector
- Defense Industrial Base Sector
- Emergency Services Sector
- Energy Sector
    - Electricity Subsector
    - Oil and Natural Gas Subsector
- Financial Services Sector
- Food and Agriculture Sector

- Health Care and Public Health Sector
- Information Technology Sector
- Nuclear Sector
- Postal and Shipping Sector
- State, Local, Tribal, and Territorial Government Coordinating Council
- Transportation Sector
  - Aviation Modal Subsector
  - Highway and Motor Carrier Modal Subsector
  - Maritime Modal Subsector
  - Mass Transit Modal Subsector
  - Railroad Modal Subsector
- Water Sector

Special Note: Terrorism Early Warning Group

While the structure and processes of the Terrorism Early Warning (TEW) groups concept go far beyond both private-sector and intelligence issues, it is important to note the private-sector role.[47] TEW groups include analysts from local, state, and federal agencies as well as input from the private sector and the nonlaw enforcement public sector to produce a range of intelligence products at all phases of response (pre-, trans-, and post-attack) specifically tailored to the user's operational role and requirements. TEW groups seek to identify emerging threats and provide early warning by integrating inputs and analysis from multidisciplinary, interagency teams. Using all-source/all-phase fusion, where intelligence is derived from all potential sources (classified, sensitive but unclassified, and open sources), provides information and decision support at all phases of a threat or response to a threat.[48]

In many ways, a TEW epitomizes the concept of thinking globally, acting locally because it seeks to identify global-distributed threats and achieve an understanding of their impact on a local community. This requires more than simple information sharing: it demands collaborative information fusion and the production of intelligence among cooperative nodes that are distributed among locations where terrorists operate, plan, or seek to attack.[49] As a result, there is a need to develop a diverse array of intelligence in a collaborative and integrated process that encompasses multiple sources, including the private sector.

The TEW concept and approach are based on the recognition that local and regional agencies are producers as well as users of intelligence. The following precepts form a foundation for both individual TEWs and the need to link these TEWs into a national network.

- Intelligence for domestic civil protection (homeland security) is not solely a top-down, federally-driven process.
- Intelligence must move top-down, bottom-up, and laterally. There is also a need for bilateral police information sharing and cooperation, independent of federal agencies.

[47] The "Lessons Learned Information Sharing" web site operated by the DHS has extensive resources on all aspects of the TEW. For more information search "TEW" at www.llis.gov.

[48] TEW Information based on: Sullivan, John P. *Terrorism Early Warning and Co-Production of Counterterrorism Intelligence.* Paper presented at the Canadian Association for Security and Intelligence Studies, Montreal, Quebec, Canada, 2005.

[49] Ibid.

- Local police and public safety and health agencies may be first to observe indicators.

- The need for local responsibility to protect public and craft response.

- There is a need for accountability, structure, and guidelines (i.e., doctrine) for access to national intelligence products.

- Regional entities (such as TEW groups) are partners in processing and disseminating intelligence (including providing local context and analyzing products). Local knowledge adds significant value.

Further, while an emphasis on prevention and deterrence is a critical aspect to TEW operations, the domestic intelligence effort is not exclusively related to supporting criminal investigations or pre-attack, pre-event prevention. Intelligence sharing and access to a wide range of intelligence products is needed during attacks in order to develop effective consequence management efforts.[50]

Anecdotal evidence suggests the TEW is an effective process for managing complex diverse information, particularly in large, multijurisdictional areas. As mentioned previously, the TEW concept encompasses far more than the intelligence process. As such, it requires greater degrees of collaboration among partners. Nonetheless, it is an initiative that should be explored when considering any aspect of public-private partnerships for counterterrorism.

Conclusion

The intent of this discussion was to emphasize the importance of P3I and the value such partnerships can bring to the intelligence process. Processes were described on how to develop and implement a public-private partnership as well as challenges that will be encountered. Even with the value of P3I, such partnerships nonetheless require creativity, collaboration, and flexibility by all parties to be developed effectively. There will be challenges which lack clear direction to resolve and new relationships that alter the status quo. Nonetheless, the value gained can be of significant importance for the protection of our communities.

[50] Sullivan, John P., et. al. (undated). *Los Angeles TEW Concept of Operations*, p. 10. www.llis.dhs.gov.

Chapter Annex 9-1:
Public-Private Partnership Exercise

Sudden Impact: Threat Planning for Infectious Disease in Cattle
Communicable Cattle Disease Exercise
Dodge City, Ford County, Kansas
(Funded by the National Institute of Justice)

Intelligence Case Study
The following is an actual case study from Ford County (Dodge City) Kansas. Ford County is one of the largest cattle production areas in the U.S. Tens of thousands head of cattle are raised and processed here every year. Because of the critical role cattle play in the American food supply as well as the economic impact of the cattle industry in Kansas, the Kansas Bureau of Investigation (KBI) and the Ford County Sheriff's Office developed a program, with funding support from the National Institute of Justice, to determine how public safety organizations could best work with the private-sector cattle farms, sale barns, and processing plants in case an infectious disease was introduced either intentionally or through natural causes.

Particular challenges:
- Information sharing

    - Would the cattle producers provide sufficient critical information, including proprietary information, to public safety officials related to the identification or discovery of an infectious disease and the status of cattle from feedlots to processing to shipping?

    - What kind of information could the public safety sector provide to the cattle industry regarding threats, particularly concerning sensitive information and with consideration of privacy issues?

    - What kind of public health information would be needed and how could it be shared, particularly related to health privacy laws (notably the Health Insurance Portability and Accountability Act)?

- Interruption of operations

    - How would the cattle industry respond to public safety requests to reduce or stop operations should an emergency occur?

    - What authority does public safety agencies have to mandate the closure of private-sector operations in such an emergency?

    - At what point is the public safety threat sufficient to warrant a halt in cattle production operations?

    - What effect would such actions have on the local economy and to what extent should such factors be considered in halting operations?

While there were many other aspects, particularly related to emergency responses, these emerged as the most critical for the current illustration. Following a comprehensive simulation exercise, it was apparent that the private-sector businesses and public safety officials had distinctively different perspectives on these issues, despite the fact that extensive meetings and agreements had taken place prior to the simulation.

Some of the issues that emerged:

- Law enforcement tended to take an aggressive stance and gave orders rather than working cooperatively.

- Law enforcement was reluctant to share certain types of information about threats, suspects, and associated facts under the assumption it was improper to share this information with the private sector.

- The private companies tended to withhold certain types of critical information under the assumption it would not be understood by public safety officials.

- Private companies resisted shutting down all operations because of the economic impact of such actions.

- Private companies argued against stop orders of cattle that were already in shipment because of the economic impact. Conversely, law enforcement tended to dismiss the economic variables.

The lesson learned from this exercise was that despite extensive planning by a wide variety of people who had the intent to find the best method to handle an emergency, additional planning was necessary. Both groups viewed the issues from significantly different perspectives.

Public-private partnerships are necessary and can be effective, but they are not easy. The stress and disagreement that arose from an exercise would be magnified under the conditions of an actual threat. Hence, the need for extensive planning, communications, training, and exercising is essential.

Chapter 10:

Managing Information: A Closer Look at Suspicious Activity Reports, Intelligence Requirements, Collection, Analysis, and Products

Managing Information: A Closer Look at Suspicious Activity Reports, Intelligence Requirements, Collection, Analysis, and Products

It is all about the information. Raw information is the fuel that drives the intelligence process. The information flow should be constant, bidirectional, and originate from a diverse array of sources. Managing this information relies on a number of processes that have been introduced in previous chapters. The intent of this chapter is to build on the discussions of these processes with more detail, providing insight into current intelligence applications for information management. Because of the rapid evolution of law enforcement intelligence— particularly as influenced by fusion center development, Intelligence-Led Policing (ILP) and the Information Sharing Environment (ISE)—there is value in a closer examination of these integrated processes as tools for both the information collector and the intelligence consumer.

Suspicious Activity Reporting

Law enforcement intelligence has long used information, both solicited and unsolicited, to learn about criminal threats. Traditionally referred to as "tips and leads," this information was most commonly provided to the intelligence function by officers, informants, and sometimes by the community. In some cases, intelligence personnel would disseminate specific types of information that was needed to answer specific questions about national threats; i.e., intelligence requirements. While criminal investigators and patrol officers rely on the public as a source of information, through Neighborhood Watch or Crime Stoppers, this practice is not as common for the intelligence function.

As the philosophy and processes of intelligence have changed, so have the processes related to tips and leads. It has been recognized that there is value in a proactive approach to generate more of this type of information for the intelligence function. Beyond simply capturing more information, a more structured process was needed to capture, evaluate, store, and share this information. The process is evolving with coordinated development by the Global Intelligence Working Group (GIWG) on behalf of the Department of Justice (DOJ), the Program Manager's Office for the Information Sharing Environment (PM-ISE), and the Intelligence and Analysis Directorate (I&A) of the Department of Homeland Security (DHS). These new initiatives collectively refer to the management of suspicious behaviors through the use of Suspicious Activity Reports (SAR).[1]

[1] There are two types of SARs: one type deals specifically with financial transactions where financial institutions must report large cash transactions as suspicious activity. For more information about the financial SAR see www.fincen. gov/reg_sar.html. Another type of SAR pertains to criminal behavior.

Suspicious Activity Reporting for a Law Enforcement Agency

A further description of suspicious activity reporting gives perspective as described in a project by the Major Cities Chiefs Association:

> The Suspicious Activity Report (SAR) process,… focuses on what law enforcement agencies have been doing for years—gathering information regarding behaviors and incidents associated with crime—and establishing a process whereby information can be shared to detect and prevent criminal activity, including that associated with domestic and international terrorism.[2]

Suspicious activity reporting is a formalized process to *document* and *share* observed behaviors which are indicative of criminal activity. Information— including "tips and leads"—may come from law enforcement personnel, private-sector partners, or citizens. This information should be placed in written form and processed through the agency in order to have the SAR integrated into the analytic process of the intelligence function.

There are three types of Suspicious Activity Reports. The first is the *financial* SAR. This was mandated by the Bank Secrecy Act wherein a wide range of financial institutions must report certain types of transactions to the Treasury Department. The suspicious activity most commonly associated with financial SARs is money laundering or trafficking in unlawful commodities.

The second is the *all-crimes* SAR. This is simply the documentation and reporting of suspicious activity related to any crime. The activity may be observed by a law enforcement officer or reported to an officer. This is similar to what many law enforcement agencies have used, traditionally known by various names such as a Field Intelligence Report, Field Interview Report or Miscellaneous Investigation Report.

The third type is the *Information Sharing Environment Suspicious Activity Report* (ISE-SAR). This is the documentation of suspicious activity specifically related to terrorism or crimes that support or facilitate terrorist planning and acts. As will be described later, an all-crimes SAR and an ISE-SAR are handled differently.

At a law enforcement agency, the form and processes for line officers are typically the same for both the all-crimes and ISE-SARs; however, when the SAR is processed through the intelligence unit or fusion center, the ISE-SAR is processed and shared differently. The reason for the different processing is based on the responsibility of the ISE to deal with terrorism and crimes supporting terrorism.

The first step for a law enforcement agency is to have an intelligence policy to manage suspicious activity reporting. Several organization components need to be in place to have an effective suspicious activity reporting process. Included are:

1. *An agency-wide process for documenting suspicious activity.* A policy guiding the format, use of case numbers, and processing of the SAR must be a formal part of the agency's records system.

2. *An agency-wide process of sharing SARs with other components of the agency and shared externally with other agencies— such as a fusion center—as appropriate.* A report of suspicious activity is of little value if it is just recorded, but not shared.

[2] *Suspicious Activity Report Support and Implementation Project. Final Report.* Washington, D.C.: Major Cities Chiefs Association; U.S. Department of Justice and U.S. Department of Homeland Security, 2008, p 1.

3. *Training personnel on the indicators of the crimes of concern.* Indicators are the signs, symbols, material, and behaviors that are known to be linked to crimes. For example, certain symbols are known to be linked expressly to right-wing extremist groups just like the possession of certain precursor chemicals are known to be associated with "cooking" methamphetamine. Virtually any type of crime will have some type of indicators. As a result, personnel must be trained to recognize these indicators to support suspicious activity reporting. Important, training should include the fact that activities should be viewed as suspicious in light of the "totality of the circumstances," not just on the observation of an indicator alone.

4. *A SAR review and purge process.* Not all activities that initially appear suspicious are criminal. Consequently, the SAR policy should have a process to review the SAR, and ensure there is a reasonable criminal nexus. If not, the SAR should be purged. Important, the agency's privacy policy should be a key component in the review and purge process

---

Financial SAR

To assist law enforcement agencies in its efforts to combat money laundering, terrorist financing, and other financial crimes, the Bank Secrecy Act (BSA) requires financial institutions to file SARs to inform the federal government of transactions related to possible violations of law or regulation. The financial SAR was created replace multiple reports required by different financial regulatory agencies to report, and subsequently investigate, financial transactions that may have a criminal nexus. To further increase efficacy of criminal financial investigations, all financial SARs are filed through the Financial Crimes Enforcement Network (FinCEN).

While it is the financial institutions' responsibility to file the financial SAR, law enforcement intelligence units deal with these reports extensively in the course of identifying illegal activity, identifying offenders, developing cases against continuing criminal enterprises and identifying emerging threats based on trend and pattern analysis of reported financial irregularities.

The financial SAR can be an important resource for the intelligence process because virtually every criminal enterprise has to have a financial network. The SAR is an important tool for tool for intelligence analysis because it reaches into a wide variety of financial institutions and processes, including:"

- Depository institutions, e.g., banks, credit unions, and thrifts
- Brokers or dealers in securities and/or futures
- Money services businesses, e.g., sellers of money orders and travelers' checks; check cashers and currency exchangers
- Casinos and card clubs
- Insurance companies
- Mutual funds
- Individual(s) transporting more than $10,000 in currency or other monetary instruments into/out of the U.S.
- Shippers/receivers of more than $10,000 in currency or other monetary instruments into/out of the U.S.

SARs are a critical source of information for the intelligence cycle. Oftentimes, the reports identify behavior related to previously unknown threats. In other cases, the SAR provides information about an inquiry that helps more clearly understand a known threat or new dimensions of a known threat. The SAR also aids in defining new intelligence requirements. While the SAR is certainly not the only source of new information for the intelligence cycle, it fulfills a critical role, particularly when supported by officers who are comprehensively trained on terrorism and crime indicators and who consistently report that suspicious activity.

Suspicious Activity Reporting Processes

An important part of the suspicious activity reporting process is the underlying assumption that many people observe suspicious activity in their daily lives but either do not recognize it or think the suspicious behavior is not of sufficient consequence to report. As will be seen, a goal is to generate increased reporting of suspicious activity with the belief that as these reports increase, the probability of gaining critical threat information will also increase. The keys to success are the following:

- Recognize "focused" suspicious activity
- Capture substantive information about suspicious activity
- Ensure that all activity is reported through the proper internal intelligence channels or external channels, such as a fusion center (instead of simply being recorded in a law enforcement agency's records management system)
- Review and analyze the information and, if creditable, share it or store it in a searchable database.

This new vision of suspicious activity reporting has two integrated dimensions. The first dimension is development of a model for refining suspicious activity processes. The second dimension is broadening the scope of persons who are encouraged to report suspicious activity, such as community members and private-sector partners.

With the first dimension, "suspicious activity" can encompass a broad array of behavior. Moreover, what a person defines as suspicious will vary, depending on a person's life experiences, values, and other social factors. Direction must be given so that suspicious activity is defined (and viewed) in the context of the types of information that is needed for the intelligence process. To accomplish this, a three-part model can be used: Observe, Document, and Report (see Figure 10-1).[3]

[3] This model is based on a community training model for counterterrorism developed by the Regional Community Policing Training Institute at Wichita State University, Dr. Andra Katz-Bannister, Director.

Figure 10-1: Suspicious Activity Reporting Model

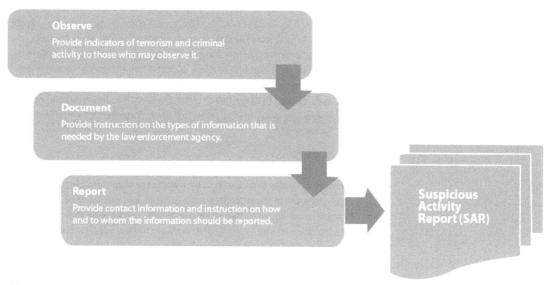

Observe

People must be observant, but observations need to be targeted. Awareness training is needed to ensure that the behavior that is observed has a potential criminal nexus. Often, training includes providing information about "indicators"—behaviors that are reasonably linked to potentially criminal activities. There are two critical components of indicators: First, the focus must be on *behavior*— not the attributes of an individual. Moreover, there must be a reasonable likelihood that the behavior could be related to a crime; that the behavior is not just "odd" or "unusual." "Attributes of an individual" would include perceived[4] race, ethnicity, gender, religion, and so forth. That is, a person *should not* be deemed "suspicious" simply because he or she possesses these attributes— suspicion must be based on *behavior*. If suspicious behaviors are observed and documented as they relate to the preparation or commission of a crime, then the attributes can be properly used as part of the description of the suspicious person. Of course, these guidelines are general and must be applied in light of circumstances and other information the observer has.

The second critical component is for the observer to understand the *types of behaviors and symbols* (e.g., gang markings, tattoos, slogans of criminal extremists, etc.) that are particularly indicative of criminal activity. This means that observers can benefit from some type of training or information about suspicious activities.

For law enforcement officers, training programs are available, both in class and online, that can provide important contemporary information about threat indicators. One such program has been the *State and Local Anti-Terrorism Training (SLATT)* program funded by the U.S. Bureau of Justice Assistance (BJA). SLATT training provides detailed information to officers on indicators of both international and domestic terrorism/criminal extremism from the perspective

[4] The word "perceived" is used here because often an observer sees a characteristic that is mistaken for an attribute. For example, an untrained observer may see a person that the observer concludes is from the Middle East when, in fact, the person is of a different ethnicity.

of how patrol officers, for example, may encounter and observe such behaviors during their regular work shift.[5]

Communities Against Terrorism (CAT), also funded by the BJA, is a program directed toward the nonlaw enforcement community to provide suspicious activity indicators The CAT program assists law enforcement in the development of partnerships with community members because when community members are aware of potential indicators of terrorism activities, they may provide law enforcement with valuable information. To assist law enforcement in the outreach effort, the CAT offers has templates of flyers containing potential indicators that law enforcement can distribute to specific industries.[6]

Document

When suspicious activity is observed, the value of the SAR is increased if the observer provides explicit information about the suspicious persons and the specific nature of the suspicious activity. While law enforcement officers are trained to collect such information, the public, which reports a significant amount of suspicious activity, typically does not have this knowledge. Public education programs need to inform community members of the kinds of information that are most valuable: Detailed descriptions of the suspicious persons and their vehicles, location of the activity, the actions that appeared suspicious, and any objects the person might have that added to the suspicious activity are all types of information that must be documented. Once again, the CAT program provides the details that are specific to different kinds of businesses.

Report

For law enforcement officers, new processes—described later as the Nationwide SAR Initiative—are being developed to establish common standards for capturing and reporting SARs that will enhance SAR information-sharing. At the outset, the process has a particular focus on terrorism because it is being driven by the ISE.[7] However, since the standards are being prepared with support from the GIWG and the Criminal Intelligence Coordinating Council (CICC), the framework for suspicious activity reporting is envisioned to eventually apply to "all crimes and all threats". A goal is to have the reporting of suspicious activities become more standardized, with officers using a consistent reporting process.

Reporting suspicious activities has been more problematic for community members. In many cases, information has not been reported because the community simply did not know how or to whom to report this information. Law enforcement agencies have been improving their capacity to assist citizen reporting; for example, increasing numbers of law enforcement agencies have developed SAR web sites, special telephone numbers, and initiatives related to agencies' community-based programming.

[5] See www.slatt.org. The web site not only provides training schedules but also online training and a wide range of resource materials. For full access to the web site, one must register with employment verification that the user has a bona fide need for access to the site. Because the program is funded by BJA, there is no charge for the training.

[6] CAT brochures may be downloaded by registered users of slatt.org at www.slatt.org/secured/cat.aspx.

[7] See www.ise.gov/pages/ctiss.html for more information on the ISE initiatives and standards related to SARs.

The goal is to educate and encourage people to be aware of behavior that is likely to be criminal, capture critical facts about the behavior, and submit the information to a law enforcement agency. In many cases, the information can provide important missing puzzle pieces to the intelligence analyst. In other cases, the information may inform the law enforcement agency about potential criminal activity about which the agency was previously unaware.

As initiatives are developed to encourage people to report suspicious behavior, law enforcement is more likely to identify and mitigate threats. A significant element of this process is to ensure that suspicions are based *on behavior* and that the observer captures as much accurate information as possible to report the suspicious activity. Once this information is in the hands of the intelligence function, it must be integrated to learn what else is known about the suspicious activity and to define future information needs to clearly understand if a threat exists and, if so, how it can be stopped.

SARs and Personal Identifying Information

An important issue related to SARs is whether the report contains Personal Identifying Information (PII). PII may be defined as any information or data from which a reasonable person may identify a specific individual. When PII is collected, civil rights protections and privacy standards must be applied.

A PII-SAR is a report that names an individual or provides sufficiently specific information where identity could reasonably be established, such as the physical description of an individual and the address where the person lives. In these cases, retention, security, and dissemination guidelines must be restrictive, with the safest approach of using information management standards that are consistent with the 28 CFR Part 23 guidelines.[8] It should be stressed that SARS typically are not defined as criminal intelligence and the 28 CFR Part 23 guidelines are not required for SARs. However, the guidelines serve as a good model to use for protecting privacy and civil rights. In addition, several agencies are developing SAR-specific guidelines to ensure the protection of privacy and civil liberties. A non-PII-SAR is a report that describes suspicious circumstances, indicators, and/or behaviors of unknown persons. If PII is not included in the report, then the law enforcement agency has significant latitude for retaining and disseminating the information.

Regardless of the SAR model used by a law enforcement agency, distinct policies with respect to the handling of SARs that have PII and those that do not should be made.

Establishing Controls on Suspicious Activity Reports/ Information

Information contained in SARs is sensitive for several reasons: The basis or motivation for reporting the information and the inherent accuracy of the information is often unknown. As such, law enforcement must determine whether lawful activity was misperceived as being criminal and whether the information was reported accurately. Despite these potentially limiting factors, when suspicious activity is reported to law enforcement, the agency has a public

[8] The reader is reminded that 28 CFR Part 23 applies only to criminal intelligence information. Even if the SAR is not retained as part of the criminal intelligence records system, the guidelines afford recognized civil rights and privacy standards to demonstrate that the law enforcement agency is doing due diligence in protecting individuals' rights. Actual policies should be reviewed by counsel with specific reference to the laws of each state.

safety responsibility to determine if there is a reasonable suspicion that a crime is being planned or has been committed. If so, the information should be retained and serve as the basis for a further criminal inquiry and operational planning to protect the public.

Because of this sensitivity, the Global Justice Information Sharing Initiative's Privacy Committee identified six critical factors, or points in the SAR process, wherein information management controls should be implemented to ensure the security and privacy of PII while at the same time permitting the agency to further its inquiry into the behavior. These controls are based on the same principles of information management used to protect information in a criminal intelligence records system. With some modification from the Privacy Committee's report, the six controls include the following:

1. Receipt/Collection. At the time of receipt or collection, suspicious activity information should be assessed and reviewed for sensitivity and confidentiality using corroborative information, if possible. Every effort should be made to validate or refute the information in order to resolve as quickly as possible whether there is a criminal predicate or whether the SAR is unfounded. Collecting information that is purely expressive activity protected by the First Amendment should be prohibited.

2. Storage. Storage of suspicious activity information should be handled similarly to data that rise to the level of reasonable suspicion. Those requirements should include an audit and inspection process, supporting documentation, and logical separation or labeling of the unconfirmed SAR from other information.

3. Access. Because of uncertainty about the information's credibility and/or accuracy, access to suspicious activity information should be handled similarly to access to information that rises to the level of reasonable suspicion. Access should be allowed only where there is a right to know and a need to know the information in the performance of a law enforcement, homeland security, or public safety activity.

4. Dissemination. Suspicious activity information, if systematically collected and stored for interagency distribution, should be disseminated primarily in response to an inquiry, and only for law enforcement, homeland security, and public safety purposes. Uncorroborated suspicious activity with PII should not be regularly disseminated in bulletins or other similar products, but it may be included in secure information databases and disseminated to relevant law enforcement, homeland security, and public safety agencies that have the right to know and need to know the information for public safety purposes.

5. Retention. The retention period for suspicious activity information should be established by policy and be of sufficient time to determine the veracity of the information in light of the agency's expertise and resources. Suspicious activity records should have a "disposition" label, such as "undetermined/unresolved" or "cleared/unfounded," to clearly notify the user of the information's status. Agencies should also consider the need for maintaining some type of suspicious activity data for purposes of statistical reporting and performance measurement when setting retention and purge procedures.

6. Security. Physical and electronic security measures should be similar to those used for information that is rising to the level of reasonable suspicion.[9]

[9] These factors are based on the following document with some modification: Global Intelligence Working Group. *Privacy Committee Report: Tips and Leads Issues Paper*. Washington, D.C.; Global Justice Information Sharing Initiative, U.S. Department of Justice, 2007, pp. 7–8.

Permeating each factor in this process should be constant attention to privacy, accuracy, and corroborating the information in the SAR, as reinforced by a report to Congress by the PM-ISE:

> Protecting the information privacy and legal rights of Americans is a top priority: At the local level, SARs will be incorporated into existing processes and systems used to manage other crime-related information and criminal intelligence so as to leverage existing policies and protocols utilized to protect the information privacy, civil liberties, and other legal rights of the general public. Multiple levels of review and vetting will be established to ensure that information is legally gathered and managed, and reports containing personally identifiable information that are unfounded, or that cannot be reasonably associated with criminal activity, will not be shared beyond the originating entity.[10]

Complicating these processes among many law enforcement officers is that all information may be useful sometime in the unknown future. This belief produces a great reluctance to destroy any information or reports. Iit must be remembered that SARs are largely unsolicited tips and leads from sources that have a wide range of credibility. If the follow-up shows that the allegation in the SAR is unfounded, there is no reason to retain any PII.

Policy Recommendations for Developing and Managing a Suspicious Activity Reporting System

As has been evident in this discussion, law enforcement agencies are increasingly developing a more comprehensive system to stimulate the reporting of suspicious activity as well as to have a more structured process to manage SAR records. The Major Cities Chiefs Association and the Global Justice Information Sharing Initiative approached this task with support from the Department of Justice (DOJ) and the Department of Homeland Security (DHS). A number of substantive recommendations were made from this project including, in part, the following:

- Agencies should educate and gain the support of policymakers about issues and processes related to suspicious activity reporting.

- All privacy and civil liberties policies and training should be reviewed to verify that they are consistent with current law and national standards.

- Information management of the SARs process should be integrated with existing processes and systems that manage criminal investigative information and criminal intelligence, thereby leveraging existing policies and protocols to protect privacy and civil rights.

- The SAR policy should be communicated to the public because transparency is the key to acceptance.

- Gathering, processing, reporting, analyzing, and sharing suspicious activity information is critical to preventing crimes, including those associated with domestic and international terrorism. The SAR process should have an all-crimes orientation.

- The SARs process should use criminal information management processes, applying SARs to the appropriate criminal records management system or criminal intelligence records system.

[10] McNamara, Thomas E. *Annual Report to the Congress on the Information Sharing Environment.* Washington, D.C.: Program Manager–Information Sharing Environment, 2008, p. 29.

- Suspicious activity submissions should not bypass the local law enforcement agency or agency of original jurisdiction and the standard 911 reporting systems.
- When an agency receives information that affects another jurisdiction, it is the responsibility of the receiving agency to immediately notify the affected agency and discuss coordination, deconfliction, investigation, and vetting procedures with the affected agency. Once vetted, further dissemination of the information would be the responsibility of the affected agency.
- A process should be established to ensure that SARs are made available to fusion centers and local Joint Terrorism Task Forces (JTTF) in a timely manner.
- An ongoing emphasis should be placed on defining and communicating trends in terrorism activity, geographically-specific threat reporting, dangers to critical infrastructure, and general situational awareness.
- There is a need for a common national methodology, including common data codes, for sharing suspicious activity data in order to discern patterns across the country.
- Training is a key component of the SAR process. All relevant agency personnel must be trained to recognize behavior and incidents indicative of criminal activity associated with international and domestic terrorism.
- Incorporating outreach to the public, law enforcement, and the private sector in the collection process is important to the success of the program.
- Develop a common national methodology to horizontally and vertically share SAR data in a timely manner that is consistent with privacy and civil liberty guarantees.
- Develop a standardized training program to provide consistent nationwide SAR training.[11]

The intent of these recommendations is to maximize the utility of suspicious activity information while at the same time protecting civil liberties. While these recommendations are intended to bring about standardization of the SAR process, the report notes that every jurisdiction will have to develop policies and procedures that take into account the unique circumstances and relationships within that community.[12]

The Nationwide Suspicious Activity Reporting Initiative

The Nationwide Suspicious Activity Reporting (SAR) Initiative (NSI) directly supports efforts to protect local communities from terrorism and other violent crime while at the same time protecting the privacy and civil liberties of Americans. An outgrowth of a number of separate but related activities during the last several years, the NSI responds directly to the mandate to establish unified, standardized, and integrated process to gather, document, process, analyze, and share information regarding circumstances potentially associated with terrorism-related criminal activity in a manner that rigorously protects the privacy and civil liberties of Americans, as called for in the National Strategy for Information Sharing (NSIS). The NSI process is a cycle of 12 interrelated operational activities that address the requirements outlined in the NSIS. The NSI long-term

[11] *Suspicious Activity Report Support and Implementation Project*, Op. cit., 2008, pp 2–5.

[12] Ibid., p. 6.

goal is that most federal, state, local, and tribal law enforcement organizations will participate in a standardized, integrated approach to gathering, documenting, processing, analyzing, and sharing information about suspicious activity.

Suspicious activity is defined as "observed behavior reasonably indicative of pre-operational planning related to terrorism or other criminal activity."[13] Although the Nationwide SAR Cycle was developed to enhance our abilities to identify, document and share terrorism-related suspicious activity, the process and technological concepts can be applied to address any emerging crime problem. The NSI cycle intentionally used this approach because individuals and groups involved in terrorism may engage in broad range of criminal activity as they plan, prepare for, and carry out a terrorist attack.

The Challenge. The lack of unified operational processes and a standardized technological approach for gathering, handling, and sharing terrorism-related suspicious activities has impeded the use of locally generated information to identify and mitigate emerging crime trends, including those potentially related to terrorism. Furthermore, the lack of standardized privacy and civil liberty rules can lead to the inappropriate collection and retention of data, and potentially infringe on the privacy and civil liberties of Americans.

The Solution. The NSI builds on what law enforcement and other agencies have been doing for years—gathering information regarding the behaviors and incidents reasonably indicative of criminal activity. As part of this standardized process, frontline and analytic personnel are trained to identify and distinguish between legal and illegal behaviors. Furthermore, through the establishment of clearly defined business rules, potential SARs are reviewed and vetted before they are made available to other analytic and investigative personnel. The use of common data and technical architecture standards enable terrorism-related SARs to be accessed by fusion centers, authorized federal, state, local, and tribal law enforcement agencies, DHS Headquarters, and the FBI's JTTFs and Field Intelligence Groups, thereby enabling the discovery of patterns and trends by analyzing information at a broader level than typically recognized within a single jurisdiction, state, or territory.

The NSI cycle (Figure 10-2) accommodates the specific risks and threats of local, state, and tribal law enforcement agencies. The first part of the cycle encourages jurisdictions to conduct risk assessments and use that information to identify and document priority information needs for that jurisdiction. Those information needs are guide the training provided to frontline law enforcement officers and analysts regarding those behaviors and incidents reasonably indicative of pre-operational planning related to criminal activity—including those potentially related to terrorism. So whether the identified risk is related to illegal drugs, violent gang activity, terrorism or other crime—the NSI process and technological concepts can be applied to address any emerging crime problem.

[13]Information Sharing Environment, Functional Standard, Suspicious Activity Reporting. ISE-FS-200, Version 1.5, 2009, Section 5, h. See www.ise. gov/docs/ctiss/ISE-FS-200_ISE-SAR_ Functional_Standard_V1_5_Issued.pdf.

<u>The Benefit.</u> Better recognition by law enforcement of behaviors and incidents indicative of criminal activity in a manner that more effectively protects privacy and civil liberties. Investigators, analysts, and homeland security professionals have improved access to critical information, enabling more rapid identification of emerging threats facing our local communities. Preliminary results have already proven value to local counterterrorism efforts. For example, in one jurisdiction during a 12-month period, 1,500 SAR were documented, and of those 1,500 more than 65 have been referred to the JTTF, resulting in 21 prosecutions and convictions in state court for terrorism-related offenses.

While there is widespread recognition of the importance of identifying and reporting suspicious activities, the initiative is not without its critics. The American Civil Liberties Union made the following comment about suspicious activity reporting:

> This overbroad reporting authority gives law enforcement officers justification to harass practically anyone they choose, to collect personal information, and to pass such information along to the intelligence community. Suspicious activity report (SAR) policing opens the door to racial profiling and other improper police behavior, and exposes law-abiding people to government prying into their private affairs without just cause.[14]

Because of these concerns, training is essential. It must be emphasized that the focus is on collecting information about behaviors that represent pre-operational indicators of criminal activity. Unusual or odd behavior or circumstances would not be included unless there is some articulable relationship between that behavior and a potential crime. Beyond training, it is essential to have ongoing supervision and a substantive assessment mechanism to document the effectiveness of the process.

Summary

Suspicious activity reporting is being embraced as a key element in the contemporary intelligence process. With appropriate methods and systems in place, it serves as a valuable tool for gaining critical raw information. The reader is cautioned that the processes are still in development. Moreover, SARs are sensitive from a civil rights perspective and require careful development and controls. While noteworthy progress has been made, challenges remain. The PM-ISE has noted the following:

> Fostering an information-sharing culture may be the most formidable challenge confronting the ISE. In the post-9/11 world, a predisposition to share the right information with those who need it is not merely an option but a fundamental principle firmly grounded in law and regulation. The goal is clear, but achieving it will take dedicated effort. The NSIS states "We will…change government culture to one in which information is regularly and responsibly shared and only withheld by exception." ISE cultural change initiatives aim to ensure that this principle is clearly understood and that managers are held accountable for driving change in their agencies.[15]

[14]German, Mike and Jay Stanley. *Fusion Center Update.* Washington, D.C.: American Civil Liberties Union, 2008, p. 2.

[15] McNamara, *Annual Report to the Congress,* Op cit., 2008, p. 47.

1. RECOGNIZE the importance of SAR, understand your role in the SAR process, and know that your involvement makes a difference. Strong leadership is an essential element. Gain support from personnel, leadership, and policymakers both internally and externally.

2. DEVELOP a data-collection process and secure standardized reporting format for sharing suspicious activity. Define and communicate trends in terrorism-related activity, geographically specific threat reporting, dangers to critical infrastructure, and general situational awareness.

3. LEVERAGE and adopt the use of common national standards to enhance the capability to quickly and accurately analyze suspicious activity data such as the ISE Functional Standard for Suspicious Activity Reporting, the State and Local Agency Information Exchange Package Document (IEPD) for SAR Reporting, the National Information Exchange Model (NIEM), and the Records Management System (RMS) and Computer Aided Dispatch (CAD) functional standards.

4. INCORPORATE appropriate guidelines and concepts into your operations, such as Intelligence-Led Policing, the *National Criminal Intelligence Sharing Plan, the Fusion Center Guidelines, the Findings and Recommendations of the Suspicious Activity Report (SAR) Support and Implementation Project,* and privacy and civil liberties templates. Use the IEPD for the *SAR for Local and State Entities* to establish and integrate the SAR process.

5. IMPLEMENT and adhere to your agency's privacy policy and ensure that the privacy and civil liberties of citizens are protected. Evaluate and update, if necessary, your privacy and civil liberties policy to ensure that the gathering, documenting, processing, and sharing of information regarding terrorism-related criminal activity is specifically addressed. Communicate the policy to the public.

6. TRAIN personnel and institutionalize the SAR process within your agency. Ensure that law enforcement and public safety personnel understand the SAR process and what internal policies or protocols exist to share appropriate information. Learn about available training to increase or enhance abilities, such as the State and Local Anti-Terrorism Training (SLATT) Program.

7. INSTITUTIONALIZE the gathering of suspicious activity information at the street level and standardize the reporting of such data so that it may be shared with other appropriate public safety partners, such as your criminal intelligence unit, state or regional fusion center, Joint Terrorism Task Force (JTTF), and other law enforcement and public safety partners.

8. EDUCATE citizens, businesses, and partners on suspicious activity reporting and how to report activity to appropriate officials. Integrate programs such as the Communities Against Terrorism (CAT) program in your community. Develop outreach materials to educate the public on recognizing and reporting behaviors and incidents indicative of criminal activity associated with international and domestic terrorism.

9. PARTNER with other law enforcement, public safety, private sector, and state or major urban area fusion centers. Foster interagency collaborations to maximize each other's resources and create an effective and efficient information sharing environment.

10. CONNECT to a major information sharing network, such as the Regional Information Sharing Systems (RISS), the Federal Bureau of Investigation's Law Enforcement Online (LEO), and the U.S. Department of Homeland Security's Homeland Security Information Network (HSIN). Leverage proven and trusted technology to share information, communicate, and access additional resources.

From: *10 Ways to Integrate Suspicious Activity Reporting into Your Agency's Operations.* Washington, D.C.: Bureau of Justice Assistance, U S. Department of Justice, 2008. (Brochure)

Figure 10-2: Nationwide Suspicious Activity Reporting Cycle

Federal agencies produce and make available intelligence and other informational products to support the development of geographic risk assessments by state and major urban area fusion centers

State and major urban area fusion centers, in coordination with local-feds, develop risk assessments

State and major urban area fusion centers, in coordination with local Feds, develop information requirements based on risk assessments

Frontline law enforcement personnel (federal, state, local, and tribal) trained to recognize behavior and incidents indicative of criminal activity associated with terrorism. Community outreach plan implemented.

Observation and reporting of behaviors and incidents by trained law enforcement personnel during their routine activity

Supervisory review of the report in accordance with department policy

Nationwide SAR Cycle

National coordinated information needs on annual and ad hoc basis

Authorized ISE participants access and retrieve ISE-SAR

ISE-SAR posted in an ISE Shared Space

Determination and documentation of an ISE-SAR

At fusion center or JTTF, a trained analysis or law enforcement officer determines, based on information availble, knowledge, experience, and personal judgement, whether the information meeting the ISE-SAR criteria may have a terrorism nexus

SAR made available to fusion center and/or JTTF

In major cities, SAR reviewed by trained counter-terrorism expert

Suspicious Activity Processing Steps

● Planning   ■ Gathering and Processing   ▲ Analysis and Production   ◆ Dissemination   ⬡ Reevaluation

Intelligence Requirements

With the growth of the ISE and fusion centers, law enforcement is increasingly relying on the use of intelligence requirements as a method for defining the types of raw information that are needed to develop a more robust analysis of threats. An "intelligence gap" is missing information that is needed for effective intelligence analysis. An "intelligence requirement" is the information needed to fill the gap. When managing information, both the gaps and requirements must be identified and defined.

To illustrate requirements, a statement by former Secretary of Defense Donald Rumsfeld, which was panned by many pundits as being nonsense, demonstrates the concept when dissected. Secretary Rumsfeld stated the following:

> "There are known knowns. There are things we know that we know. There are known unknowns. That is to say, there are things that we now know we don't know. But there are also unknown unknowns. There are things we do not know we don't know."[16]

Table 10-1 illustrates Secretary Rumsfeld's statement as applied to different intelligence challenges—international terrorism (such as al-Qaeda) and violent crime within a community—followed by a statement of the intelligence action related to requirements which must be taken.

Table 10-1: Interpretation and Illustration of the Rumsfeld Quote

	Al-Qaeda Example	Violent Crime Example	Intelligence Action
There are known knowns	We know that al-Qaeda's intent is to commit more terrorist attacks against the U.S. and U.S. interests.	We know there is an increase in violent crime using guns within a community.	The information we know must be consistently monitored and verified (i.e., "standing requirements") to determine any changes in the status of the information we know.
There are known unknowns	We know that al-Qaeda has plans for future terrorist attacks, but the timing, method, and locations are unknown.	We know there is an increase in black market guns, but it is unknown who the supplier is, where the guns come from, or how the transactions are made.	We know that we have intelligence gaps. Intelligence requirements, sources, and methods must be defined so that we may learn the currently unknown information.
There are unknown unknowns	If al-Qaeda has developed new alliances or new methods to commit attacks, these are unknown to us.	There are factors driving the increase in violence beyond the availability of guns; however, these other factors are unknown to us at the time.	Information must be collected from all sources and analyzed in an attempt to identify new threat information.

[16] Department of Defense News Briefing, February 12, 2002. See www.slate.com/id/2081042.

The intelligence analyst must integrate currently held information to determine what we know about a threat: these are the "known knowns." Because the threat environment is dynamic, these known factors must be constantly monitored to verify the threat and determine if a change is occurring to the threat picture. In many instances, while we know that a general threat exists, the specific character of the threat—the method of attack, specific target of attack, and when the attack may be attempted—is unknown. These are "known unknowns." Finally, there are threats which may be developing, either by a known suspect or a suspect completely unknown to us, that we are simply unaware of—these are the "unknown unknowns." The goal is to continually monitor suspicious activities and collect information from diverse sources that may give us an indicator of a new threat. When these new indicators are learned, requirements are defined to better identify the threat and those who pose the threat.

One can understand how the layman may interpret Secretary Rumsfeld's statement as nonsense, but he was essentially describing intelligence gaps and intelligence requirements.

The use of intelligence requirements is a concept that is largely new to law enforcement intelligence, although it has long been used in national security intelligence to specify information needs about threats. It is a holistic approach to collecting and analyzing information so that the most comprehensive picture of a threat emerges, as well as alternatives for countering the threat. The use of requirements also increases the efficacy of the intelligence process by expressly focusing on information needs rather than using a broad dragnet approach to information collection or simply awaiting the serendipitous discovery of critical data.

To use an analogy, the job of an intelligence analyst is akin to putting together a jigsaw puzzle without knowing what the final picture in the puzzle looks like. Each piece of information is like a puzzle piece and the analyst must see where it fits to create a discernable image. The missing pieces are information gaps; the intelligence requirements are to identify and collect the missing pieces, filling gaps, to make the picture more complete. As more pieces are identified, new requirements often emerge. Once sufficient information has been collected, the picture becomes clear and the threat is more clearly understood. Of course, in practice it is not that simple; therefore, there is the need to elaborate on the issues and processes related to requirements-driven intelligence.

Filling Gaps/Fulfilling Requirements

The information-collection process has to be focused so that specific information needs are fulfilled. This increases the efficiency of the process and ensures that the right information needs are being targeted. Historically, law enforcement used an approach that was based largely on intuition of what was suspicious. Often it was mere suspicion based on statements or behaviors that seemed out of the norm, extreme, or unusual. This process was neither objective nor scientific and was often influenced by bias (typically, unintended bias) imposed by the officer's attitudes, values, and beliefs. This process collected volumes of diverse raw information that was forwarded to analysts and investigators who could examine the information in hopes of discovering that substantive threat information may emerge. As illustrated in Table 10-2, there are a number of differences between this tradition-driven approach and the requirements-driven approach to information collection. In essence, the requirements-driven approach is more scientific and, therefore, more objective, more focused, more efficacious, and less problematic on matters related to civil rights. On this last point, given that intelligence requirements are often the product of an ongoing criminal inquiry, the criminal predicate is more easily articulated.

Essentially, the tradition-driven approach is like throwing out a net, seeking to collect as much information as possible under the assumption that threat information and evidence of crime will emerge from the vast body of information. It is less efficient, less effective, and more likely to lead to civil rights liability. Requirements-driven intelligence is more laser-like. It focuses specifically on the types of information we need to give us an understanding about a narrowly defined area of threat.

Table 10- 2: Traditional Collection versus Requirements-Driven Collection

Tradition-Driven	Requirements-Driven
• Data-driven	• Analysis-driven
• Exploratory	• Specifically focused
• Emphasizes amassing data	• Emphasizes a focused, selective approach to information collection and analysis
• Assumes collected information will identify criminals	• Analytic inference of criminal suspects from collected information
• An aggregate approach to information collection (dragnet); even mere suspicion	• Targeting/specificity on information regarding reasonable suspicion of crimes
• Explores all general inferences about potential criminality	• Selectively explores crime and threat leads based on priorities and evidence
• Explores collected information to see if there are questions to answer	• Answers questions by collecting and analyzing specifically collected information
• Develops intelligence records for contingency needs, (i.e., just in case information is needed)	• Develops intelligence records in support of active threats and criminal enterprises

Applying the Concept to Law Enforcement

As part of the FBI Intelligence Directorate's reengineering process, former Executive Assistant Director Maureen Baginski used requirements-driven intelligence. This concept is epitomized by the statement frequently made by Baginski, and previously referenced in Chapter 4's discussion of the intelligence process, "The absence of evidence is not the absence of a threat."

This is an insightful observation for understanding why requirements-driven intelligence is important. Let us say that a law enforcement executive asks the Regional Intelligence Fusion Center if there is a terrorism threat within the agency's region. The response may be, "There is no evidence to suggest a terrorist threat within the region." However, there may be an unknown threat in the community for which no evidence has been discovered (e.g., "unknown unknowns"). One such unknown threat in the community was Timothy McVeigh who placed the bomb at the Murrah Federal Building in Oklahoma City. Another unknown threat was Muhammad Atta, who had a base of operations within U.S. communities to aid in planning the attacks of September 11, 2001. These were both clear threats to their communities but the evidence of these threats had not been discovered.

We must have a means of identifying these unknown threats, assessing the danger posed, and taking appropriate action to prevent or mitigate the threat. The process is not easy, especially for a state, local, or tribal law enforcement (SLTLE) agency that may have limited information-collection and analytic capabilities. Identifying evidence of such threats is both labor-intensive and resource-intensive, requiring good information-sharing, effective linkages with intelligence networks, constant monitoring and exchange of information, and ongoing information collection, assessment, and analysis within an agency's jurisdiction. These needs reinforce the value of fusion centers, which will have all of these characteristics, and the need for agencies to be a fusion center partner. The fusion process is particularly structured to use the intelligence requirements model effectively.

While requirements-driven intelligence will work well for a law enforcement agency, it requires a commitment of time and resources to accomplish its goals. At the very least, a law enforcement agency needs a minimalist intelligence capacity to contribute to the process at a state or regional level, particularly to be an effective intelligence fusion center partner.

Comparing Intelligence Requirements and Crime Analysis

Intelligence requirements may be conceptualized as information that is needed to make decisions on how to best protect a community from threats posed by organized crime and terrorism. When requirements are filled, executives and managers have sufficient reliable information to direct an operational response to a threat.

As an illustration, SLTLE agencies often make operational decisions related to incidents of predatory crime based on crime analysis requirements. Indeed, this is the fuel of the CompStat process. Specifically, as a result of the timely analysis of reported crime, certain types of crime trends emerge. Relying on information derived from that analysis such as type of crime, modus operandi, time and geographic factors, suspect descriptions, etc., response strategies are developed to deal with the crimes that have occurred and the likely forecast (i.e., future) of crime that will occur if the crime series is left unchecked. The agency may use saturation patrol, undercover officers, decoys, surveillance, or a combination of strategies to capture these repeat offenders. Without the information from the crime analysis output, the most effective operational decisions cannot be made.

Of course, crime analysis requirements are much easier to provide than intelligence requirements because of the inherent differences between criminal investigation and criminal intelligence. Essentially, investigations are crime-driven while intelligence is threat-driven. Thus, investigations are reactive, responding to crimes that have occurred and a known quantifiable universe of data that have been identified through the investigation. Conversely, intelligence is proactive by intervening when a threat is identified. Essentially, intelligence is pre-crime and far more probabilistic—factors that pose both operational challenges and civil rights issues.

Requirements and Strategic Priorities

Intelligence activities should be based on the mission of the unit or fusion center; for example, the mission of a High Intensity Drug Trafficking Area intelligence center would be focused on the production and distribution of illegal drugs. Similarly, intelligence activities of the Immigration and Customs Enforcement service of the DHS are focused on smuggling humans and contraband across U.S. borders. Most state, local, and tribal intelligence activities, however, have adopted an all-crimes, all-threats, all-hazards approach. In reality, all-crimes for intelligence purposes is somewhat of a misnomer. Because this encompasses a wide breadth of crime types, pragmatically, even an all-crimes intelligence operation must prioritize the types of crime that will be the focus of intelligence activities. As noted in the Chapter 6 discussion of strategic priorities, this priority will be based on geography, criminal history of the region, and special issues that help facilitate organized crime and terror threats, such as the presence of seaports, international airports, or unique commercial industries, such as critical infrastructure or key resources.

Intelligence requirements should also be mission-related. Known as *priority intelligence requirements,* the intent is to maintain focus on crime and threats that have been assessed as having the impact of greatest concern in the jurisdiction. We know, however, that crimes and threats change over time. In the case of drugs, for example, trends change in different geographic areas of the country quite frequently. In some areas, methamphetamines are a major problem, in another region the drug problem may be crack cocaine. In both cases, the primary drug problem will evolve. As a result of such changes in crime problems, reprioritizing intelligence targets should be part of the reevaluation component of the intelligence process, as well as of strategic intelligence analysis.

Typologies of Requirements

There are various ways to describe intelligence requirements, meaning that there is no uniform standard for describing the different types of requirements used by law enforcement agencies. This discussion seeks to take the different models and terms currently used and not only explain them, but also illustrate their relationships.

Requirements may be characterized in different ways based on their role. These different characterizations are not mutually exclusive. Indeed, as illustrated in the Venn diagram of Figure 10-3, there is a nexus among the different types, with the various characterizations fundamentally relating to their purposes.

Functional requirements are defined by the intelligence unit or fusion center for the purpose of learning about different dimensions of a threat. Information is collected through SARs and the collection plan associated with ongoing inquiries to help the analyst understand the functional evolution of threats. This is often a systemic process wherein as more information is received and analyzed, a better understanding of the threat emerges which, in turn, helps define additional requirements. This is an iterative process that continues to refine the threat picture until the threat is compromised or until it dissipates.

There are four types of functional requirements:

1. Analyst defined. During the course of the analysis the intelligence analyst discovers a gap in the information that needs to be filled for a comprehensive and accurate analysis to be completed. An analyst has three SARs that suggest an interrelationship among the three as preparation to commit a crime. The intelligence requirements are information that is needed to confirm this linkage.

2. Threat defined. Known threats within the jurisdiction that are monitored on a consistent basis to continually assess the threat. For example, if a jurisdiction has a known white supremacist group that has made criminal threats, monitoring that group to understand changes in its structure, membership, and/or activities can help identify imminent threats.

3. Target defined. Based on the nature of known threats, targets are monitored to assess vulnerability and risk. The Earth Liberation Front threatens to burn down houses and destroy construction equipment in a new subdivision that it says is in an environmentally sensitive area. The requirements would be to collect information on the vulnerability of the targets for a threat assessment.

4. Incident/event defined. If an event is planned or an incident occurs, requirements will be defined to determine potential threats associated with the event or future implications of the incident. For example, if the president of the World Bank is invited to give the commencement address at a local university, there is a high likelihood that anarchists will attend the commencement to demonstrate their disdain for the World Bank. Some anarchists will lawfully demonstrate while others are likely to commit property crimes and disrupt the event. The intelligence requirements are derived from the fact that the event was scheduled.

Figure 10-3: Characterizations of Law Enforcement Intelligence Requirements

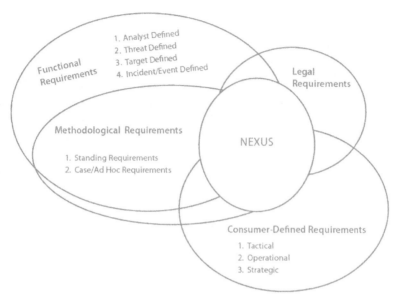

For each type of functional requirement, there are critical information needs to enable an understanding of all dimensions of a threat. Threat requirements apply to both law enforcement and homeland security/all-hazards intelligence. As the name implies, these are information needs that help an analyst define a threat with as much precision as possible. Whether the threat is from a terrorist group or from pandemic flu, the analyst needs a wide array of valid information from reliable sources that can provide as much insight as possible about the threat picture.

The method by which the information is solicited is referred to as the methodological requirements. Generally speaking, there are two types:

1. Standing requirements. Information that needs to be collected on an ongoing basis to monitor known and consistently present threats within a community.

2. Case (or ad hoc) requirements. Information that is needed by analysts to determine the existence and character of a threat that is based on unsolicited tips, leads, suspicious activity reports, and/or other information developed through the intelligence process.

Another dimension of requirements is based on an analysis request by intelligence consumers; for example, a partner agency in a fusion center may request a certain type of analysis for its jurisdiction. This request, therefore, will drive the requirements process. These are the types of requirements:

1. Tactical. What information is needed to prevent or mitigate an imminent or short-term threat?

2. <u>Operational.</u> What information is needed to prevent or mitigate a developing or long-term threat?

3. <u>Strategic.</u> What changes in the threat picture exist in the coming months or years that can have an impact on operational planning and resource allocation?

Overlapping these is a type of requirement that is unique to law enforcement: *legal requirements.* Recall that the sole authority for law enforcement agencies to have an intelligence function is their statutory authority to enforce the criminal law. As a result, conceptually all information collected must be viewed as if it may eventually result in a criminal prosecution. Consequently, information is needed, at the least, to aid in establishing the criminal predicate and eventually sufficient evidence to establish the burden of proof in a trial. Requirements will need to be defined that help establish the corpus delecti or the elements of a specific crime as it relates to the intelligence targets.

Requirements and Criminal Evidence

This issue warrants special attention because it is unique to law enforcement intelligence. In the national security intelligence community, requirements serve as information to help make decisions about threat prevention, policy development, and strategic responses. In law enforcement intelligence, however, while many of these same needs are fulfilled, there is the added dimension that information collected from requirements may also be used as criminal evidence. Given the civil rights responsibilities that law enforcement officers must uphold, intelligence requirements for a law enforcement agency must also ensure that information collected during the requirements process follows the law of criminal procedure.

This can be a challenging process for law enforcement because there is a constant balancing process. In some cases, information collected about an individual must be balanced and documented with the threat to public safety. In other cases, the officers may be following up on a SAR to determine the veracity of the lead and establish both a criminal predicate and determination of a threat. There are many scenarios where decisions are made about information collection and retention that are in the arena of uncertainty. Relying on a cautious perspective, some fundamental guidelines should help guide the information collection process for legal requirements:

• Follow the law of criminal evidence and procedure.

• Always act in good faith with documented evidence and rationale that are the basis for information-collection and retention.

• If there is a threat to community safety, document the evidence and rationale associated with that threat and corroborate it to the extent possible.

Summary

Information is needed to make decisions: the higher the quality and the more comprehensive the information, the more sound the decision. Similarly, information that answers a specific question is more useful than information that is general. If an executive is going to make a decision about implementing a new program, he or she needs information about the specific costs, benefits, and risks of the program as well as the more difficult dimension of what benefits will be lost if the program is not implemented. Typically, the information sought is not conclusive, but based on probability, the experience of others, experimentation, logic or, sometimes, an educated guess. Not having sufficient reliable information makes the decision process more difficult and risky.

The same process applies to the operational environment of criminal intelligence. To adequately assess the threats from a terrorist group or criminal enterprise, information is needed for a comprehensive analysis. Often during the course of the analytic process, critical information is missing that prevents a complete and accurate assessment of the issue. The collection process focuses on collecting the specific information identified in the requirement in order to answer questions related to criminal or terrorist threats.[17] The fulfillment of the intelligence requirement provides critical information for making strategic or operational decisions about how to respond to the threat.

The intent of this discussion was to provide some perspective of intelligence requirements as specifically related to law enforcement intelligence. Once those information needs are identified, the next step is to collect them.

Collection

Collection of information has been discussed in the context of the intelligence process (Chapter 4) and information needs for ILP (Chapter 6). The current discussion builds on the previous by looking at information from a broader perspective. Collection refers to information that is brought into the intelligence process for analysis. It is the generation of raw data and, as will be seen, it is not always an overt action by the law enforcement agency to reach out and gather information.

Essentially, information enters the intelligence process in one of three ways:
1. It is deliberately sought out and collected—tasked collection.
2. It is collected as a result of another law enforcement activity—routine collection.
3. It is given to law enforcement—volunteered information.

Tasked collection is in response to intelligence requirements and is typically gathered as a result of a collection plan, defined as follows:

> A plan for gathering information from all available sources to meet an intelligence requirement. Specifically, a logical plan for transforming the essential elements of information into orders or requests to sources within a required time limit.[18]

[17] FBI Office of Intelligence. *The FBI Intelligence Cycle: Answering the Questions. A Desk Reference Guide for Law Enforcement.* (Pamphlet), July 2004.

[18] www.acpo.police.uk/asp/policies/Data/nim2005.pdf

The collection plan, previously referred to in Chapter 6, typically will be determined by an analyst, sometimes with input from a supervisor, to determine what types of information are needed, where (sources) the information may be obtained, and how (methods) the information will be gathered. The analyst will have an array of options from which to choose, ranging from open sources (discussed in detail in Chapter 11) to restricted databases,[19] to interviewing people, and more. The key lies in the question: "Where might I find this information and how will I get it?" The collection plan is the road map to answering this question.

In some cases, the assistance of operational units will be needed. In these circumstances, intelligence personnel should coordinate with operational managers or supervisors to explain what information is needed, why it is needed, and the role of the operational units in collecting the information. Even in cases where the "why" must remain confidential, a general description of the "why" will help in gaining cooperation and commitment.

When operational units assist in collection, explicit descriptions of the types of information needed should be provided. Similarly, time constraints for when the information is needed should be established. Operational units should also be provided with precautions, if any, during the collection process. In some cases, precautions may be related to officer safety; in other cases, the precaution may be to collect the information in a subtle manner so as not to tip off an inquiry. The key, of course, is effective communications between intelligence personnel and operational personnel.

The second method, *routine collection*, refers to the collection of information as part of routine operational and law enforcement activity. It focuses on the standing intelligence requirements or other issues of intelligence significance that are known and require a constant input of raw information. Information collected in this way usually is submitted as an information/intelligence report, but it may also be recorded elsewhere such as information within or from the following:

- Crime reporting
- Criminal investigations, including stand-alone proactive or reactive operational databases/case management systems
- Firearms licensing to monitor trends and to flag names of known offenders
- Community and partnership activities and meetings
- Custody records.

Routine collection can take many forms. As one example, the intelligence commander in one state has configured e-mail notification from the Open Source Center[20] (OSC) so that whenever any kind of information naming his or her state is entered into the OSC, the commander routinely receives an e-mail about the entry. In many cases, the information would have limited or no value from a criminal intelligence perspective, but where there is value, the information may have been missed without routine collection.

[19] Chapters 12 and 13 will discuss these in detail.

[20] OSC is an information system operated by the Office of the Director of National Intelligence. Open source information is the topic of the following chapter.

Volunteered information is offered to law enforcement by the general public, community contacts, and private partners. Its collection is focused (but not exclusively based) on the intelligence requirement. Information obtained usually is recorded and submitted on a SAR or some form of information report, depending on the nature of the information.

Collecting Information from Corrections Agencies

Correctional agencies are an often overlooked source of information in the collection process. Increasingly, corrections departments are creating and using a Security Intelligence Threat Group, an intelligence-based approach to information collection and analysis to determine threats that reside in prison facilities.

Despite common misperceptions, many inmates retain strong connections with criminal groups on the outside during their incarceration. There is ample evidence that gangs and drug traffickers as well as radical ideological groups (such as the Aryan Brotherhood or Islamic extremists) have outside connections and tend to know, and sometimes have influence on, the criminal organization's activities. Corrections agencies have greater breadth for information collection and can be an important data source for the intelligence process.

> Significant elements of nontraditional information and intelligence resides within corrections IT systems. In fact, corrections is uniquely positioned to gather information that other law enforcement entities are not able to gather. Information like inmate visitor data, criminal associate data, and telephone record data are but a few of the intelligence sources that have the potential to provide valuable insight to law enforcement and homeland security agents seeking to develop a framework for social networking to better determine the synergistic relationship between the criminal enterprise and the terrorist network(s) that threaten our country.[21]

The types of information that correctional agencies are able to collect and retain are invaluable. While the information has often been successfully exploited for dealing with gangs, such initiatives need to be broadened. The National Institute of Justice has established the Corrections/Law Enforcement Intelligence Gathering and Sharing Project[22] as a means of enhancing threat identification. Beyond working with corrections agencies within a law enforcement agency's region, monitoring projects such as this can provide additional value for developing information-sharing.

Summary

Regardless of the method that is used to collect information, it is important to remember for law enforcement intelligence that there is a different standard for information that is collected for use in a criminal intelligence records system between information that identifies individuals and groups and information that contains no identifying information. (These differences are discussed in detail in Chapter 7.)

[21] Herzog, Thomas J. *Integrating Correctional Authorities into the Fusion Center Rubric.* Palm Coast, Florida: Corrections Technology Association, 2007, p. 4.

[22] www.justnet.org/TechBeat%20Files/ DataMining.pdf

Analysis

Without analysis, there is no intelligence. No single methodology is used for intelligence analysis; rather, various approaches and analytic tools are used, depending on the type of data/information that are available and the type of analysis (tactical or strategic) that is being performed.

The intent of this discussion is not to teach analytic methods, but to provide the consumer of analysis with insights into the process. Such insights should make the end-user a more enlightened consumer. Moreover, with a better understanding of analysis, a law enforcement officer will have better insights when responding to intelligence requirements.

Intelligence analysis is often referred to as a unidimensional activity that is the central step in the intelligence process. When examining the analysis function more closely, one finds that it is a process that requires three broad skill sets. (See Figure 10-4) As such, the development of knowledge, skills, and abilities (KSA) must correlate with these skill sets.

The first skill, *research,* involves collecting diverse pieces of information and assessing the value (validity and reliability), as well as the relevancy and materiality to the assessment. Research is somewhat different from collection. Research involves gaining information that clarifies issues and provides perspectives on an issue of interest. Examples: searching the web blogs of anarchists to learn more about their beliefs and train of thought; reviewing research on the characteristics and common processes of human smuggling; reviewing reports and articles on a specific issue, such as the behavioral characteristics of a person planning a suicide attack; or any other type of data collection that provides insight—as opposed to evidence— about a targeted issue. Certainly there could be an overlap between research and collection; however, the roles are more complementary than duplicative. Analysts' KSAs must include both research and assessment methodologies. The analyst must be aware of the diverse sources of information—both open source information and law enforcement proprietary information—and know how to gain access to them. While collection of information will occur from a wide array of sources beyond the analyst, the need for research skills to be able to drill down into the information is essential.

The intelligence analyst must be more than a recipient of information. The analyst must be proactive in two methods: The first is to define and disseminate intelligence requirements to fill gaps in the information in order to have a more comprehensive and robust analysis of a threat, individual, or target. The second method is to elicit information from diverse sources. Whether this is a data base, a fusion center, a private partner, or an investigator, the analyst must proactively seek the information. Information-sharing systems and practices have increased dramatically as a result of post-9/11 intelligence reengineering. Nonetheless, no system or process can ensure that all the needed information will reach the analyst's desk. Proactive efforts by the analyst will add redundancy to the collection process to ensure that it is as comprehensive as possible. This is reinforced by the *Law Enforcement Analytic Standard #11–Collection Follow-Up Standard:*

In the course of collection by investigators and others, analysts shall evaluate the progress of the collection to determine if the collection plan/requirements are being met and shall identify additional sources of information, as well as identify information that may be useful to other cases or activities. Where possible, analysts shall relay that information to an appropriate body for follow-up.[23]

Figure 10-4: The Analytic Process

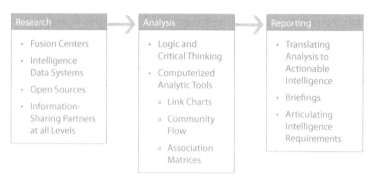

An important part of this process is that policies and procedures must give analysts the authority to seek needed information and have some type of accountability mechanism to ensure that the information is being provided. An unfortunate reality in many law enforcement organizations is that the intelligence analyst is often viewed as having a lower professional status than a sworn officer, sometimes making it difficult for analysts to give direction to investigators. While this artifact of organizational culture is slowly changing as analysts are increasingly viewed as practicing professionals, remnants of this perspective remain. Consequently, it is important for the intelligence process to ensure that analysts have the organizational authority to gain the information they need.

The second skill set, *analysis,* is essentially the scientific approach to problem solving. It relies on inductive and deductive reasoning; a balanced assessment of raw data; objectivity in the interpretation of facts; hypothesis testing; critical thinking; and decision making based on evidence. The late Carl Sagan, a world-renowned astrophysicist, explained the scientific process this way:

Science is a way of thinking much more than it is a body of knowledge. Its goal is to find out how the world works, to seek what regularities there may be, to penetrate to the connection of things—from subnuclear particles, … to living organisms, the human social community, and thence to the cosmos as a whole. Our intuition is by no means an infallible guide. Our perceptions may be distorted by training and prejudice or merely because of the limitations of our sense organs, … Science is based on experiment, on a willingness to challenge old dogma, on an openness to see the universe as it really is. Accordingly, science requires courage—at the very least the courage to question the conventional wisdom. … [T]he scientific cast of mind examines

[23] Global Justice Information Sharing Initiative and the International Association of Law Enforcement Intelligence Analysts, Inc. *Law Enforcement Analytic Standards.* Washington, D.C.: Global Justice Information Sharing Initiative, 2004.

the world critically as if many alternative worlds might exist. ... If you spend any time spinning hypotheses, checking to see whether they make sense, whether they conform to what else we know, thinking of tests you can pose to substantiate or deflate your hypotheses, you will find yourself doing science.[24]

This process described by Sagan is essentially what intelligence analysts do when attempting to derive meaning from a diverse array of facts. Sagan noted that science seeks to determine "…what regularities there may be…". In law enforcement, we seek to identify criminals' modus operandi because these regularities in criminal processes are important for forecasting crime and determining prevention strategies. Similarly, Sagan observed that science seeks "…to penetrate to the connection of things." Law enforcement intelligence analysts seek to find the connection between criminal conspirators (e.g., via link analysis), between different types of evidence (e.g., via association matrices) and between criminal transactions (e.g., via commodity flow diagrams).

Intelligence analysis is an intellectual exercise that has pragmatic applications. For most people, it does not come easily. It requires *structure, critical thinking, self-discipline,* and *strong substantive knowledge of the target.* "Structure" refers to the ability to be organized and follow accepted analytical methods without taking shortcuts and ensuring that all information and evidence is included in the analysis. "Critical thinking" means that the analyst will follow the rules of logical reasoning, not intuition. It also means that the analyst will draw conclusions based on the known evidence, not assumed evidence. "Self discipline" is essential for the analyst to remain objective and not be influenced by emotion or external pressures. This objectivity also means that the evidence is considered with respect to its "weight" (reliability, validity, and corroboration). Beyond having the analytic KSAs, the analyst needs to have "substantive knowledge" of the targeted crime(s). Whether the target is a Jihadist network, drug trafficking cartel, or money laundering network, the analyst needs to understand the terminology, beliefs, and mechanics associated with the criminal enterprise.

Training, programs, continuing education, and self-directed education are valuable for developing the substantive knowledge needed for effective analysis; however, the thinking skills, which must be integrated with the substantive knowledge, are more challenging. A person can be taught the processes and tools of analysis, but critical thinking is most effectively produced through "mental calisthenics" and experience. Mental calisthenics refers to series of written exercises or problems that challenge a person to find a solution. There may be multiple solutions, of which the next challenge is to find the best or most probable solution. This process is frequently used in Problem-Based Learning, which is a strategy that builds a curriculum around a central question. The question may force the student to either solve a problem or make a decision.[25] The analytic skill set is the most difficult to effectively develop in an analyst; it is also the most critical.

The third skill set is *reporting.* Throughout the analytic process, there are stages where the findings must be reported to decision-makers and investigators.

[24] Sagan, Carl. *Broca's Brain: Reflections on the Romance of Science.* New York: The Ballantine Publishing Group, 1979.

[25] Friedman, Robert S. and Fadi Peek, "Problem-Based Learning and Problem-Solving Tools: Synthesis and Direction for Distributed Education Environments," *Journal of Interactive Learning Research* 13,(3)(2002): 239–257.

Reporting is translating the analytic output into descriptive status reports or actionable intelligence. A descriptive status report essentially describes the character and process of an intelligence target, probable effects, and probable future activities. The report may also include evidence currently possessed, intelligence requirements, and unexplained crime-related phenomena that need closer assessment. Typically, these reports are designed to assist in planning and directing an inquiry, allocating resources, assessing risk to potential victims, gaining insights about threat timetables, planning for intervention and mitigation strategies. In contemporary intelligence, the reporting process is when the analyst develops "intelligence products." This will be discussed in detail in the next section of this chapter.

Suggested Software Needed for Effective Analysis
- Word processing program
- Spreadsheet program
- Relational database
- Presentation software
- Flowcharting software
- Link analysis software
- Database reporting/visualization software
- Mapping software
- Photo enhancement software
- Telephone analysis software
- Portable Document Format (PDF) creation software
- Security software (virus, adware, spyware software; firewall and Virtual Private Network [VPN] security)
- Publication software
- Statistical analysis software
- Text mining software

Resource: *The Analyst Toolbox*, Global Intelligence Working Group. it.ojp.gov/documents/analyst_toolbox.pdf

---

With actionable intelligence, a law enforcement agency has sufficient information to develop an operational response to threats. Within this framework, three factors contribute to effective analysis:

1. The overall quality of the information used to make a decision. Accuracy of information is essential. When information is analyzed, conclusions are drawn based on the facts that the analyst has. If the information is wrong or biased, this will inherently affect the quality of the analysis.

2. An increased body of information to make the information more comprehensive; hence, corroborating other facts. As the volume of high-quality information increases, the more accurate the analysis. Raw information is clarified and the quality of analysis will increase as volume increases. The key is to ensure that the quantity of information is accurate and relevant, a factor that is at the heart of the fusion process.

3. Increased specificity of the information. The more detailed the raw information, the greater the likelihood of identifying subtle factors about a threat.

Figure 10-5: Critical Characteristics of Information Quality

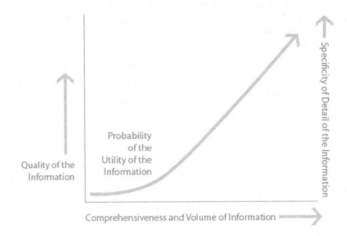

As illustrated in Figure 10-5, as each factor increases, the value of the analysis increases. Regardless of the skill of the analyst and the analytic tools available, the character of the raw information is fundamental to actionable analysis.

Analytic Tools

A number of analytic tools are available to the intelligence analyst. "Tools" essentially refers to methodological techniques that help *organize, integrate, compare, correlate,* and *illustrate* a body of raw information. None of the analyst tools will produce actionable intelligence alone; each adds a component of new knowledge—or at least new insight—about the data which, collectively, contribute to the analysis and/or lead to the definition of new intelligence requirements.

The actual analysis relies on the critical thinking skills of the analyst along with his or her ability to integrate the output of these diverse methodologies into a cohesive, actionable intelligence product. These products may include portions of the analytic tools output to illustrate complex relationships, such as an illicit commodity flow chart or a link analysis chart showing the relationships and hierarchy of people involved in a criminal enterprise.

While the intelligence consumer does not need to know how to perform these various types of analyses, there is value in understanding the different analytic tools available and the types of information they provide. While not an exhaustive list, the more common tools[26] an intelligence consumer may encounter include the following:

- Activity flow. Similar to a modus operandi or method of operation, the activity flow shows the steps a criminal enterprise uses, indicating exact incidents, dates, and a description of the activities that occurred. The incidents are linked in a flow chart to help understand the progression of the enterprise. The activity flow pieces together a complex criminal organization and may be used for intervention in the enterprise as well as to determine where gaps exist. If gaps are identified, intelligence requirements will be used to fill the gaps so that the activity of the enterprise can be fully mapped to aid in prevention and in prosecution.

- Association matrix. This matrix seeks to correlate two or more factors in a criminal enterprise, documenting the frequencies with which certain factors (e.g., persons, organizations, phone numbers, addresses, and similar variables) occur at the same time in order to isolate the correlating factors that are instrumental in the criminal enterprise operations and eliminate factors that have no correlation. The factors may be alike, such as correlating a series of telephone numbers. The factors may also be inherently independent but provide insight when they are correlated, such as charting the travel patterns of two intelligence targets when a telephone call or bank transaction precedes the travel.

- Commodity flow/visual investigative analysis. A diagram that illustrates how an unlawful commodity is moved through a criminal enterprise and the transactions that are made in the commodity movement. For example, the commodity flow of Afghan heroin would show each transaction and method of smuggling, along with the transaction costs, from Afghanistan to a city in Middle America.

- Communications traffic analysis. Important information can be gained from a traffic analysis of telephones, text messaging, and e-mail. By identifying with whom intelligence targets are communicating, the frequency of the communications, their origins and destinations, length of the communications, and whether there were attachments to e-mails, an analysis can provide significant corroboration and evidence of criminality. While the content of communications, obviously, will provide important information, an analysis of communications traffic can also be valuable.

- Crime pattern analysis. A generic term for a number of related disciplines such as crime or incident series identification, crime trend analysis, hot spot analysis, and general profile analysis and can include mapping.

- Criminal business profiles. Such profiles contain detailed analyses of how criminal operations or techniques work, in the same way that a legitimate business might be explained.

- Demographic/social trends analysis. An analytic method centered on demographic changes and their impact on criminality. It also analyzes social factors such as unemployment and homelessness, and considers the significance of population shifts, attitudes, and activities as they may affect crime.

[26] Many of these analytic tools are illustrated in: Peterson, Marilyn, et al. *Successful Law Enforcement Using Analytic Methods.* South Florida, Florida: International Association of Law Enforcement Intelligence Analysts, Inc., 1996.

- Event flow analysis. Charts that provide a visual depiction of a series of important occurrences or incidents (such as a criminal transaction) and the sequential relationship of these occurrences, such as travel of a criminal participant, monetary transactions, or other events that are critical in facilitating the crime.

- Financial analysis. There are a variety of financial analysis techniques that collectively seek to correlate diverse financial transactions including the nature of the transactions; parties involved; origin, intermediary, and destinations of transactions; and comparative analysis of income and expenditures. Collectively, the intent is to document transaction trends of intelligence targets (both individuals and organizations) and identify discrepancies or suspicious financial activities. Given that virtually all crimes have some form of financial element, financial analysis is an important tool.

- Hypothesis testing. The analyst will make a hypothesis about the linkages of people and organizations in the criminal enterprise, necessary transactions for the enterprise to operate, and critical commodities or resources necessary for the enterprise to be successful. Unlike the previous items in this list, which are visual depictions of various elements of the enterprise, hypothesis testing uses the depictions to determine if all the elements in the enterprise have been identified that can be used to prevent the enterprise from continuing and, ideally, determining the criminal liability of participants.

- Link Analysis. A chart that identifies all confirmed and suspected persons and organizations in the criminal enterprise and illustrates their relationship to each other.

- Market profiles. The profiles are assessments that survey the criminal market around a particular commodity in an area, such as drugs or stolen vehicles, or of a service, such as prostitution. They are continually reviewed and updated.

- Network analysis. This analysis not only describes the links between people who form criminal networks, but also the significance of the links, the roles played by individuals, and the strengths and weaknesses of a criminal organization.

- Operational intelligence assessment. Such an assessment evaluates incoming intelligence to maintain the focus of an operation on previously agreed objectives, particularly in the case of a sizeable intelligence collection plan or other large-scale operation.

- Results analysis. An analysis that evaluates the effectiveness of law enforcement activities; for example, the effectiveness of patrol strategies, crime-reduction initiatives, or a particular method of investigation.

- Risk analysis. An analysis that assesses the scale of risks posed by individual offenders or organizations to individual potential victims, the general public, and to law enforcement agencies.

- Target profile analysis. An analysis that embraces a range of analytical techniques to describe criminals, their criminal activity, lifestyle, associations, the risk they pose, and their strengths and weaknesses to give focus to the investigation targeting them. Profiles may also focus on victims and vulnerable persons.

Each of these techniques is used to better understand raw information and its relationships and to illustrate a criminal phenomenon. Figure 10-6 presents examples of two kinds of analytical charting.

Figure 10-6: Illustrations of Analytical Charting[27]

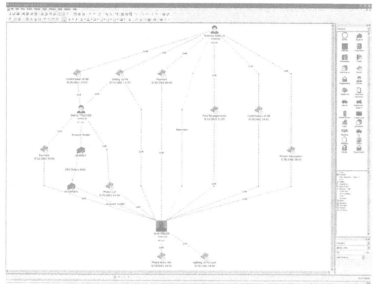

Link Analysis Chart

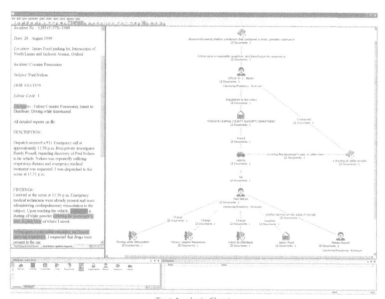

Text Analysis Chart

[27] The charting illustrations are from i2's Analyst Notebook software. Images courtesy of i2.

Predictive Analysis

Predictive analysis has become increasingly popular as a tool for intelligence analysis; therefore, a brief description of the concept can be of value to the intelligence consumer. Predictive analysis is borrowed largely from the private sector where econometric models are used to forecast market changes. By analyzing economic factors in a current market, buoyed by analysis of known trend data—such as changes in a sector's economics during different times of the year—a manufacturing firm may alter its production, workforce size, and supply chain to enable it to continue profitable operations while meeting supply demands throughout varying conditions. In that situation, the analysis provides strategic direction for both management and operations to make decisions about alternative futures that will help them avoid unnecessary profit losses while still fully serving customer needs.

Can such a quantitative-based approach work in the largely qualitative world of law enforcement intelligence analysis? While predictive analysis has important applications to intelligence analysis, it will not provide an analysis as robust as in more quantitative fields that have more predictable change cycles, such as in the business world. Nonetheless, it has important applications to intelligence, but will require a diverse and often labor-intensive research effort; a multifaceted analytic methodology, and a broadened method of reporting that offers differential outcomes based on the evolution of social and political trends. As time passes, these trends can be monitored by the intelligence analyst to refine the status and threat implications of the trends being observed.

Predictive analysis is a critical-thinking methodology that integrates known quantitative and qualitative variables—including incidents, events, and political and social dynamics—into a logical forecast of threat parameters. In many ways, the label "predictive" is misleading because it is virtually impossible to truly predict events that are based on human behavior and the infinite number of variables that can influence that behavior. The process is a probabilistic analytic exercise that gathers diverse data, constantly monitors changes in the data, and refines the forecast based on the new inputs. Just like the intelligence process itself, predictive analysis is reiterative, constantly seeking new inputs of information to refine the forecast.

The reiterative nature of predictive analysis complements requirements-driven intelligence. This process continuously seeks to identify information to fill intelligence gaps or voids in our knowledge base about threats, and then identify, collectand analyze information to fill those gaps. Intelligence requirements—the information that is required to fill a gap—provides constant input into the intelligence cycle to help ensure that there is a base of knowledge that is as comprehensive as possible.

Predictive analysis in law enforcement can have the greatest impact on strategic intelligence, although it can also have an application to aid in defining standing intelligence requirements. This analytic technique will not forecast threats, per se, but it can forecast changes in the environment that may alter conditions that contribute to threats.

Critical Variables for the Analysis of a Threat

Critical to analytic techniques that seek to help us understand any kind of threat, is the ability to collect information about a series of key variables related to the intelligence target(s). Once again, each variable has significant implications for intelligence requirements.

- Intent. What is the stated intent of the intelligence target? Has it changed? How might any of the current events or activities influence the stated intent of the target?

- History. What has the intelligence target or group done in the past? Often, history can provide insight into future behaviors, methods, and targets. This includes identifying and assessing triggering events from previous attacks or violent behaviors of the intelligence target.

- Capability. What capabilities does the target or group have? Have they been trained to execute terrorist attacks or crimes? Do they have critical assets available, including people, munitions, money, documents, and travel to commit the crime?

- Opportunity. Are there any unusual or unique opportunities arising that will help facilitate an attack? If so, what kind of access to that opportunity will the intelligence target have? Is there evidence to suggest that planning for an attack or crime to coincide with an opportunity has occurred?

- Resolve. Does the intelligence target or group actually have the commitment to execute the attack? Is the intelligence target simply making a threat or does the target actually pose a threat? Are there insights into how the resolve to commit an attack may be mitigated? Particularly in the case of ideological groups, a critical variable related to "resolve" is learning the characteristics of the leader. If the group has a charismatic leader, then the likelihood increases that the group will act on its intent.

Intelligence requirements and analysis are inherently related to threat assessments. The interrelationship is systemic: a change in one component will affect the others.

> Intelligence analysis is a complex task involving the examination and assessment of information to draw conclusions about a particular topic. It is not an academic exercise because it does not involve philosophical theories. Instead, intelligence analysis is a function heavily dependent on realism and requires an objective approach to thinking. It is predominantly process driven, and it requires continuous exhaustive research using information from a variety of classified and nonclassified sources. Analysis also involves the collation of information to identify relationships, expose indicators and filter factual evidence. This is a process that forces the questioning of information to confirm truths and probabilities. The next process is to scrutinize the information to recognize trends that will lead to an event or pattern. Once a conclusion about the information has been formed, an assessment is made which is then presented to customers so they can make well-informed decisions based on our findings.[28]

[28] Australia's Defence Intelligence Organisation, www.defence.gov.au/dio/analysis.html.

Summary

Intelligence analysis is both the development of cognition and a cognitive process. It is a cognitive process because the analyst is learning as he or she conducts the analysis. But it is also the development of cognition because the output of the analysis— conclusions, estimates, and forecasts—is new knowledge that will be shared with others in reports and briefings. Effective analysis, therefore, should serve the law enforcement agency in the following ways:

- Identifying points of opportunity for intervention that might change the state of affairs in some way, especially before a conflict occurs

- Helping states attain a comparative advantage in decision-making, thus the term "actionable intelligence"

- Protecting the state and its citizens to maximize security

- Optimizing resources

- Integrating information to enhance understanding of threat environments.

Analysis is a critical factor in information management because it provides the intelligence that describes criminal threats and the alternatives to manage those threats. This information must be expressed in the form of intelligence products.

Intelligence Outputs and Products

The output of analysis, that is, intelligence, must be placed in a reporting format that maximizes the consumption and use of the information. This is referred to as the intelligence product. In describing the relationship of analysis to products, Ratcliffe, in *Integrated Intelligence and Crime Analysis,* observed the following:

> …criminal intelligence is the creation of an intelligence knowledge product that supports decision-making in the areas of law enforcement, crime reduction, and crime prevention. In this context, an intelligence knowledge product is a product that can influence the thinking of a decision-maker. It is the result of a criminal intelligence analysis and could be a written bulletin, a presentation, a verbal report, or some combination of these in a briefing. An intelligence knowledge product could even be a brief telephone conversation if the intelligence is timely and has an effect on the decision-making of the recipient of the intelligence.[29]

Typically, different types of products are developed to meet the needs of different consumers and different types of analysis. A tactical analytic product will differ from a strategic analytic product. The product developed for a comprehensive assessment of a targeted criminal enterprise will differ from a product intended to make officers aware of criminal indicators. An executive briefing of a criminal threat will differ from a patrol briefing of a criminal threat. Regardless of the type of product, all should contain five fundamental elements in the context of the product's intent:

1. Identify the targeted consumer of the information (patrol officers, administrators, private sector, others).

2. Convey clearly the critical information needed by the intended consumer.

[29] Ratcliffe, Jerry H. *Integrated Intelligence and Crime Analysis: Enhanced Information Management for Law Enforcement Leaders.* Washington, D.C.: Office of Community Oriented Policing Services, U.S. Department of Justice, 2007, p. 8.

3. Identify time parameters wherein the intelligence is actionable.

4. Define additional intelligence requirements, if needed.

5. Provide operational recommendations in light of the analysis.

Ideally, products are a series of regularly produced intelligence reports that have a specific format and type of message to convey. They are most useful when each product has a specific purpose; is in a consistent, clear, and aesthetic format; and contain all critical information the consumer needs with no superfluous information. As a general rule, at least three types of products should be developed by an intelligence unit or fusion center:

1. Products directed toward the prevention of known threats.

2. Products that provide threat advisories which provide indicators of threatening behaviors and threatened targets.

3. Products that describe changes of the terrorist or criminal threat picture to a jurisdiction.

While most law enforcement officers are very familiar with investigative reports and records, they are less familiar with intelligence products. As indicated in Table 10-3, there are notable differences that are important for the consumer to understand. With a clear understanding of the distinction, there will be greater use of the products.

Table 10-3: Differences between Investigation and Intelligence Reports

Criminal Investigation Reports and Records	Law Enforcement Intelligence Reports, Records, and Products
• Primary goal is prosecution	• Primary goal is threat-based prevention
• Report is documentation of a criminal incident that occurred	• Report focuses on suspected criminal threats
• Report is an official record and is evidentiary	• Report documents information associated with a threat inquiry
• Motive is irrelevant as a legal element of the crime	• Motive is an important tool for forecasting
• Evidence is documented to prove the corpus delicti	• Information is documented to build hypotheses about criminal threats

Two broad distinctions in law enforcement intelligence outputs are characterized in Table 10-4. The first is "case intelligence." A critical characteristic of case intelligence is that it identifies individuals or organizations. Conceptually, its ultimate goal is arrest and prosecution of particularly-described persons as a means of preventing a threat from reaching fruition.[30] An important factor to note is that with case intelligence, civil rights attach to individuals who have been identified in any type of intelligence report. The second type, "intelligence advisory products," describes (i.e., advises) general indicators of crime and threats for which officers must be aware. The goal is for law enforcement personnel to be

[30] It should be remembered that the only authority for law enforcement agencies to be in the "intelligence business" is based on their statutory authority to enforce the criminal law; therefore, development of a criminal case is a sound model to follow.

aware of the indicators and, if observed, take appropriate action to ensure public safety and prevent a criminal incident from occurring. As a general rule, there are no explicit civil rights issues of advisory products until a person or organization is identified as related to the criminal indicators.

Table 10-4: Case Intelligence versus Intelligence Products

Case Intelligence	Intelligence Advisory Products
• Individuals are identified • Specific offenses are identified • Intelligence develops evidence of criminal liability • The goal is to develop a criminal case for prosecution	• Trends in crime and/or their methodologies are identified • A change in criminal trends is forecast • Indicators of the new crime types are identified for awareness by law enforcement personnel • The goal is to prevent the crime from occurring

Any intelligence unit or fusion center can determine the type of products it needs to develop based on the administrative mandate of the unit. Some are designed to meet unique jurisdictional needs, such as a transit law enforcement agency. As a general rule, law enforcement intelligence reports may be in a typology with two broad components: 1. The nature of the report and 2. The nature of the analysis.

Nature of the Intelligence Report

Different kinds of intelligence reports are created to meet the needs of specific audiences. An "Intelligence Alert" may be a short report giving the basic facts about indicators or persons related to a threat that is time-critical. An "Intelligence Bulletin" may provide more detailed information about indicators or threats that are not imminent but those which personnel may encounter. An "Intelligence Assessment" typically provides a historical perspective of a threat and how the current status of the threat has changed. At this point there are no uniform classifications of intelligence reports across all agency types and levels of government; rather each agency or fusion center produces reports that tend to meet these general guidelines. Law enforcement personnel should receive training on the types of products that are used in their jurisdictions and the intent of each report type.

Nature of the Analysis

Perhaps adding confusion to the universe of intelligence reporting is that some terminology has different meaning to the intelligence community, the military, and federal law enforcement when compared to state, local, and tribal law enforcement. The current discussion is directed toward the latter. Previously, the differences between tactical analysis and strategic analysis were described from the law enforcement perspective. Again, while there are no uniform categories of specific report types based on the kinds of analysis that was performed, suffice it to note that intelligence consumers should be aware that some report outputs will describe threats in need of an operational response (tactical) while other reports will describes changes in the threat picture (strategic).

Other report types exist or will emerge. Intelligence briefings are oral summaries of analyses that require yet a different approach to reporting that pay homage to the often repeated comment of Sgt. Joe Friday in the old television series Dragnet: "I want the facts, just the facts." We are increasingly seeing new report types emerging that are based on technology and range from text messaging to Podcasts. Regardless of the method of reporting, it is essential that each report type contains the information that is needed for the intended consumer to be effective in fulfilling his or her responsibilities.

Figure 10-7: Characteristics of Intelligence Products

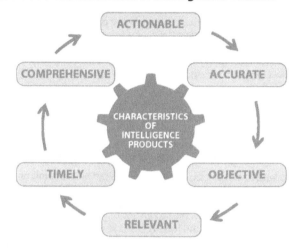

As illustrated in Figure 10-7 and discussed below, regardless of the type of product, each should reflect six core characteristics.

1. Actionable. The product should provide sufficiently definitive information that some kind of operational activity or response may be developed from the intelligence.

2. Accurate. The nature of the analytic process is often probabilistic; therefore, concrete conclusions and forecasts can rarely be made. Despite this, every effort should be made to be as accurate as possible, with weaknesses in the conclusions clearly documented.

3. Objective. Intelligence products should be free of bias. All information should be provided in a balanced manner clearly articulating knowns and unknowns as well as strengths and weaknesses in the analysis.

4. Relevant. The analysis, and the products, should focus on threats that are part of the strategic priorities and/or emerging threats that could have a significant effect on public safety in the region.

5. Timely. Timeliness has two components. First, the intelligence product should be of a threat that is of current concern. Second, when practicable, the product should be made available to maximize the time permitted for operational units to develop a response and put it in place.

6. Comprehensive. The intelligence product should provide as much information as possible about all dimensions of the threat.

Practices to Avoid with Intelligence Products

In the post-9/11 environment where the critical phrase is "information sharing," some practices related to intelligence products have emerged that create more problems than solutions. Information should be "targeted," that is, useful information needs to be shared with people who can use it. Unfortunately, this axiom has gone unheeded too frequently.

Three fundamental practices related to analysis and intelligence products should be avoided. They might be expressed as the "three don'ts of information sharing."

1. Don't repackage the intelligence products of another organization. Most agencies will have received the original product; hence, repackaging it is duplicative and can be confusing. A repackaged product adds little value and may have a misleading effect if the same information is distributed as the product of two different agencies. Further, if another agency's product is simply repackaged, the agency will not be able to provide any follow-up detail should inquiries be made.

2. Don't disseminate everything to everybody. Receiving too much information can be just as ineffective as receiving no information. If personnel are inundated with a cascade of information that has little value to them, they tend to pay little attention to any information. The intelligence function, not the consumer, must separate the wheat from the chaff. Targeted dissemination of information to people who need it is critical.

3. Don't develop a "publish or perish" attitude. This can be a systemic problem. Managers want to see productivity by intelligence analysts; however, productivity is difficult to quantify in the intelligence function. One activity which can be easily counted is the production of intelligence products and some intelligence units and fusion centers have used "products" as a measure of effectiveness. While it is understandable how this has evolved, the publication of products alone is not a measure of success. Even if the product is "interesting" it provides little value unless it is actionable. It is not the quantity of products that should be measured, but their *quality* and *utility*. Of course, this is difficult and somewhat subjective. The evaluation process is often difficult to perform effectively.

Figure 10-8 summarizes what intelligence products should and should not contain.

Figure 10-8: Attributes of Intelligence Products

Intelligence Products Should *Include*

- Applicable to the Jurisdiction
- Original Analysis
- Actionable/Utilitarian

Intelligence Products Should *Avoid*

- Repackaging Other Products
- Disseminating Everything
- "Publish or Perish" Attitude

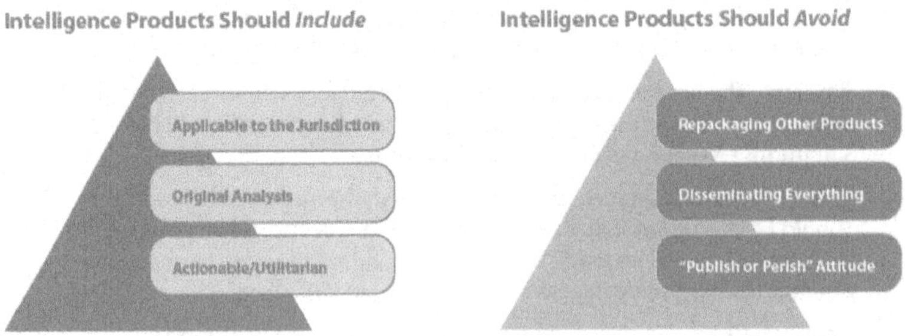

To avoid the problems embodied in the "don'ts" of intelligence products, those responsible for the intelligence function should answer these questions affirmatively as they relate to intelligence products:

1. Tactical and Operational Intelligence. Does the intelligence product provide sufficient detail about a threat within your region or service area so that operational personnel can develop tactical plans or activities to prevent or mitigate an identified threat?

2. Strategic Intelligence. Does the intelligence product describe the characteristics, modus operandi, or change in the threat picture in sufficient detail as related to your region or service area so that effective decisions can be made about strategic priorities and resource allocation?

3. Actionable Dissemination. In light of the nature of the threat and content of the intelligence product, who within your region or service area has the right to know and need to know this information for threat prevention, mitigation, and/or planning?

Summary

Intelligence products are the means by which critical threat information reaches the street. The importance of developing the kinds of products of greatest use to an intelligence unit or fusion center's consumer and placing the right product in the hands of the people who need it is a critical process.

Conclusion

As specified in the *National Strategy for Information Sharing* (NSIS), two fundamental objectives are related to SLTLE agencies with respect to sharing information from the federal government:[31]

1. Ensuring that the Federal Government provides information in ways that better meet the needs of SLT partners through the establishment of an Interagency Threat Assessment and Coordination Group (ITACG) within the National Counterterrorism Center (NCTC). This integrated approach allows Federal agencies to work together to disseminate a federally-validated perspective on available threat information.[32]

2. Supporting improved collaboration at the State and local levels by designating fusion centers "as the primary focal points within the State and local environment for the receipt and sharing of terrorism-related information" and by establishing and sustaining a national integrated network of these centers.[33]

In July 2007, Congress passed the 9/11 Commission Act of 2007 that statutorily created the ITACG and designated the PM-ISE "to monitor and assess" the ITACG's efficacy.[34] The Act also called for a DHS State, Local, and Regional Fusion Center Initiative which, among other requirements, must "support efforts to include state, local, and regional fusion centers into efforts to establish an information sharing environment."[35] The NSIS further advanced these initiatives by providing a detailed description of the role of the ITACG and the roles and responsibilities of Federal and SLTLE agencies. Significant advances have been made in implementing the NSIS objectives[36] at all levels of government; however, there is variability of successes around the U.S. at the state, local, and tribal levels.

[31] National Strategy for Information Sharing, 2007, p. 30.

[32] NSIS, p. 18.

[33] NSIS, p. 20.

[34] 9/11 Commission Act of 2007 (P.L. 110-53), §521(c). The ITACG was established as part of the ISE Implementation Plan and Guideline 2, but the statute strengthened several of its functions and provided for additional oversight.

[35] 9/11 Commission Act of 2007, Op cit. §511(b)(2).

[36] McNamara, *Annual Report to the Congress on the Information Sharing Environment*, 2008, Op cit., p. 24.

For effective information management in the intelligence process there must be a common foundation and ideological thread permeating the law enforcement organization. To meet the needs of contemporary law enforcement intelligence, including newly established national standards, the management of information requires the following:

1. Reengineering some of the organization's structure and information processes. SLTLE agencies should examine their current intelligence processes, if any, to determine if they are consistent with the NCISP and currently accepted national standards for law enforcement intelligence. If not, adjustments should be made to the organization and/or processes. This consistency is important so that there is a common understanding and acceptance of information validity, reliability, and consistency with civil rights standards. A common perspective of the intelligence process and a body of policies and procedures, all of which meet the same national standards, greatly enhances two-way information-sharing—an essential element of requirements-driven intelligence.

2. Developing a shared vision of the terrorist or criminal threat. All agencies at all levels of government must define and understand the threats that face them. This does not mean that all communities are threatened in the same way, but that all agencies understand the common enemies. This includes a common understanding of threats and general agreement on the types of threats facing America. Important strides have occurred as cooperative initiatives and information sharing have taken place: for example, the growth of the Intelligence Fusion Centers, and initiatives such as the Global Intelligence Working Group, Criminal Intelligence Coordinating Committee, the Information sharing Environment, and the Counterterrorism Training Coordination Working Group. With diverse membership from law enforcement agencies at all levels of government, the common lexicon is growing and communication is increasing.

3. A commitment to participate and follow through with threat information. Effective information sharing can exist only if there is a true commitment by an agency to participate, not just lip service to intelligence initiatives. To enhance output of these different national initiatives, an executive must ensure that personnel are trained in the intelligence process and that policies are in place for effective, lawful, and reliable information collection and sharing (in accordance with standards in the NCISP). Commitment also means that the chain of command reinforces the need for employee information collection and sharing processes. Too often the policies that are in place are irregularly applied. When this occurs, the intelligence process breaks down and the ability to connect the dots is jeopardized.

4. The commitment of an agency's resources, time, and energy to the intelligence function. A commitment to participate necessarily requires a commitment of resources. Intelligence is prevention-oriented. Often, it is difficult to see what has been prevented. Similarly, a great deal of information that is collected and shared leads to nothing—a fact of life in the intelligence enterprise—but the critical few pieces of information that lead to the prevention of a terrorist attack are well worth the investment. The intelligence function should be a budget line in the agency's regular budget, not an activity that is relegated to soft money or piggy-backed on other agency activities. The lack of a budget line for intelligence is tantamount to the lack of full commitment.

5. <u>Proactive people using creative thought to identify what we don't know about terrorism and organized crime.</u> Requirements-driven intelligence seeks to fully understand the environment of a community and how changes in that environment may influence threats or crime. Creativity requires viewing community conditions and potential threats through a lens that seeks to interpret information in different ways. Terrorists and criminals have shown they can be creative in the planning and execution of their crimes. Law enforcement must be similarly creative to identify changes in the threat environment and develop proactive operational initiatives to prevent threats from reaching fruition.

6. <u>A law enforcement agency to think globally and act locally.</u> Most people view issues in life from a provincial perspective. This is normal because our greatest concerns are those that affect us in the most direct manner. Unfortunately, the provincial view does not always serve us well when we view events around the globe with the mistaken belief that they won't affect us. Global events in terrorism and crime can affect us on local basis just as global economic events have an influence in our communities. As a simple example, terrorist events, war, economic markets, and political conflicts in OPEC will have an effect on the prices we pay at our local gas pumps. We must recognize that international planning, financing, and logistical support of terrorism, and criminal incidents can have an impact on our communities. Thus, local intelligence analysts must consider the extended effect of global incidents, such as the conflict between Israel and Hezbollah, and how that can be translated to local and regional reactions to those who support Islamic extremism. If the analyst does not have this information, then these are intelligence gaps that must be filled and applied locally.

Chapter 11:

Open Source Information and Intelligence:
A Perspective for State, Local, and Tribal Law Enforcement Agencies

Open Source Information and Intelligence: A Perspective for State, Local, and Tribal Law Enforcement Agencies[1]

When considering the collection of information for the intelligence process, a historically undervalued resource has been open sources of information.[2] In many ways, open source information holds some of the greatest value for intelligence because of the vast array of diverse, reliable information available for analysis. This is particularly true with the rapid growth of networking. A great deal has been written about open source information,[3] particularly as it is used in business intelligence, and increasingly for its use in national security intelligence. The current discussion will provide perspective for open source application in the law enforcement community, including important limitations that may be imposed on the retention of certain types of open source information.

It should go without saying: The growth of technology has radically changed the character of open source information. To provide perspective, as the public embraced the World Wide Web en mass beginning in the mid-to-late 1990s, the Internet emerged as the primary source to search for all types of information. As computer memory and processing speeds increased, more information was being stored and processed, including audio and video files. The integration of computing into nearly every aspect of daily life, spurred by the prevalence of wireless computing has caused the development of faster, more discriminating search software. Similarly, content providers have increased the type and mass of content available. Collectively, technological development and the willingness of the public to embrace this technology have contributed dramatically to the ease and value of open source information.

There is a caveat, however: Quantity of information does not equal quality of information. Open source users must take care by assuring that the information collected from open sources for use in decision-making is accurate and dependable. Information absent quality control is of little value. The challenge, particularly when massive amounts of information are at one's fingertips, is to make good end-user decisions about what information should be kept and which information should be discarded.

Understanding "Open Source"

The concept of open source information and intelligence is in a state of renewed interest, particularly as applied to the intelligence community and law enforcement. A brief discussion on the concept and its application in the current context will provide perspective.

Why Is there Value in Open Source Information?

Open source information has often held a second-class status in the intelligence world because of the erroneous assumption that people, movements, and conditions that pose threats would not have information that is available about their intent, characteristics, or behavior in the open.

[1] For an effective discussion of open source information, certain topics are most effectively illustrated using examples from commercial services and web sites. Attempts were made to be objective in the illustrations and where possible use multiple sources. References to businesses and web sites are for illustration purposes only and should not be construed as an endorsement in any form.

[2] Best, Richard and Alfred Cumming. *Open Source Intelligence (OSINT): Issues for Congress.* Washington, D.C.: Congressional Research Service, 2007, p. 4.

[3] For example, see www.oss.net/extra/document/?module_instance=3 and www.firstmonday.org/issues/issue76/stalder.

This assumption is erroneous for six fundamental reasons.

- First, individuals and groups who pose threats because they have an extremist ideology—even those who support violence to fulfill their ideological goal— and typically want to share their beliefs and goals, usually with the intent of persuading others to adopt their beliefs. They often post such information on web sites, in print, in broadcast media that are sympathetic to their cause, and via shortwave broadcasts.[4]

- Second, criminals use the web as a largely anonymous instrumentality to traffic in contraband. Offenders can easily reach a U.S. market from overseas and use techniques to make them difficult to track, both of which add to the lure.[5]

- Third, certain types of information that are useful for the intelligence process, including information that identifies individuals, are openly available because policy, regulation, or law permits the custodian of such information to make it publicly available in some states; for example, public databases contain information about motor vehicle licenses, property ownership, voter registration, sex offenders, salaries of public employees, and a wide array of other information for which an individual has little, if any, control over its public release.[6]

- Fourth, people want selected information to be public. This can occur for a multitude of reasons: telephone numbers, business names and addresses, various reports of research, and marketing are but a few examples. Not only do the individual pieces of information provide insight, surprising amounts of new knowledge can be gained when such information is analyzed in the aggregate.[7]

- Fifth, nonlaw enforcement entities, such as the news media or advocacy groups, may conduct inquiries that become open sources. These sources may provide personal information, descriptions of behavior, personal relationships, activities of a given group, and descriptions of an incident to satisfy the purpose of their business or cause.[8]

- Finally, information often becomes openly available because of an individual's carelessness. A politician making an embarrassing statement in the presence of an open microphone in a public venue or a person writing incriminating information in a blog are examples. In these cases, valuable information that may be used in the intelligence process is often available through open sources.[9]

Definitions and Categories

Open source information is any type of lawfully and ethically obtainable information that describes persons, behaviors, locations, groups, events, or trends. The Office of the Director of National Intelligence (ODNI) simply defines open source information as follows:

> Publicly available information that anyone can lawfully obtain by request, purchase, or observation.[10]

As can be seen by either of these definitions, the array of information that falls within the open source arena is very broad. From a law enforcement perspective, one of the values of open source information is that it can be searched for and collected without legal process. As will be described later, civil rights issues emerge related to the retention of open source information for the intelligence process.

[4] For example, see media files supporting the World Jihad at www.memri.org.

[5] For example, see the Drug Enforcement Administration's Operation Cyber-Chase arrests of illegal web-based pharmacies at www.usdoj.gov/dea/pubs/pressrel/pr042005.html.

[6] For example, see the Michigan Internet Criminal History Access Tool (ICHAT) at apps.michigan.gov/ICHAT/Home.aspx.

[7] For example, see the aggregated data base to locate people and businesses at www.switchboard.com.

[8] For example, NBC's news stories on pedophiles – see www.msnbc.msn.com/id/6083442.

[9] One source for inadvertently released information, among a wide array of other information, is www.cryptome.org.

[10] Intelligence Community Directive, Number 301. National Open Source Enterprise. Section F(3), July 11, 2006.

As one should assume, when raw open source information is evaluated, integrated, and analyzed it provides new insight about intelligence targets and trends—this is open source intelligence.

Open source information is wide-ranging. To provide perspective, examples of categories of open source information include these:

- All types of media.[11]
- Shortwave broadcasts and conversations.[12]
- Publicly available databases.[13]
- Directories.[14]
- Databases of people, places, and events.[15]
- Open discussions, whether in forums, classes, presentations, online discussions on blogs, or general conversations.
- Government reports and documents.[16]
- Scientific research and reports.[17]
- Statistical databases.[18]
- Commercial vendors of information.[19]
- Web sites that are open to the general public even if there is an access fee or a registration requirement.[20]
- Search engines of Internet site contents.[21]

The main qualifier that classifies information as open source is that no legal process or clandestine collection techniques are required to obtain the data. While open source data has virtually always existed, networking has increased its accessibility significantly. For example, if an analyst was preparing a strategic intelligence report on trends in international terrorism, he or she may go to the U.S. Department of State Counterterrorism Office[22] web site, the FBI terrorism reports[23] web site, the Department of Homeland Security-funded terrorism database,[24] and the Israeli Defense Forces terrorism statistics center web site[25] to download the various reports and data. If the analyst was preparing a report on right-wing extremists, he or she may visit the Southern Poverty Law Center[26] web site to download reports or go to a white supremacy web site, such as Stormfront,[27] to read materials and then conduct further research by following hyperlinks to gain more raw data to prepare an independent report.

Source of First Resort

Open sources are increasingly referred to as the source of first resort. This means that analysts and information collectors should exploit open sources of information as the first step in the information-collection process. Particularly when intelligence gaps, whether tactical or strategic, are identified, open sources can provide important insights which may give functional direction to a line of inquiry.

If a unique crime trend emerges within a community, for example, an open source search of newspapers nationwide can identify other locations where crimes with similar modus operandi have occurred.[28] Similarly, unknown graffiti or a unique

[11] See www.newslink.org.

[12] See www.shortwave.be and www.blackcatsystems.com/radio/shortwave.html.

[13] See as an example www.searchsystems.net and www.factfind.com/database.htm.

[14] One of the most extensive directories is in www.yahoo.com. However, other sources of directories exist, such as www.mypeoplesearch.com.

[15] See as an example www.namebase.org, www.searchsystems.net and www.blackbookonline.info.

[16] See www.thecre.com/links/fedgov-links.html, www.firstgov.gov/Topics/Reference_Shelf.shtml and www.firstgov.gov/Citizen/Topics/PublicSafety.shtml.

[17] See www.fas.org.

[18] See www.lib.umich.edu/govdocs-stats-pilot and www.ojp.usdoj.gov/bjs.

[19] See as an example www.accoleads.com.

[20] As an example, Islamic radical web sites can be found at www.e-prism.org.

[21] Beyond the commonly used Internet search engines such as Google, Lycos, Yahoo, Ask, and others, a unique web search site is www.itools.com.

[22] www.state.gov/s/ct

[23] www.fbi.gov/terrorism/terrorism.htm

[24] www.start.umd.edu

[25] dover.idf.il/IDF/English

[26] www.splcenter.org

[27] www.stormfront.org

tattoo may be searched via image files.[29] A blog search can provide unique insights about virtually any extremist group just as information may be obtained about a unique problem.[30] Similarly, insightful information about Hezbollah[31] can be found on YouTube and information about the MS-13 gangs[32] can be found on MySpace.

Similarly, because of the threat posed by jihadists, there is value in knowing the beliefs, language, arguments, and perspectives of jihadists to:

> …improve strategic understanding of the of the jihadist threat by more effectively mining the Internet and other open sources for information. Such an effort, it is suggested, also will enable … a better tactical understanding of how jihadists use the Internet's web-television capabilities, chat rooms, and "news" sites, to train forces and raise money. Ultimately, these observers suggest, the United States must develop the capability to understand and influence foreign populations — "not in their council of states but in their villages and slums" — if it is to effectively counter the threat posed by jihadists. In such circumstances, it is argued, the information that should matter most to policymakers can be derived from open sources.[33]

The value of open sources as the first resort is multifold. When an issue or threat emerges, open sources can often provide an efficient, effective, and fast insight into the issue that may often validate the need for further inquiry. Similarly, open sources can provide a broad view of a person or threat as a means of establishing context and perspective. Moreover, open sources can often provide insights and relationships that may be missed by the inherent nature of many closed sources.

> Allen Dulles estimated in 1947 that over eighty percent of the "information required for guidance of our national policy" was available in open sources. George Kennan revised the estimate to upwards of ninety-five percent in a 1997 *New York Times interview*.[34]

With this estimated amount of valuable information available through open sources, it is only reasonable to use these sources as a starting point in a line of inquiry. The application to law enforcement is just as valid as it is for national security. The below scenarios, all of which are based on actual cases, illustrate this point:

- A land developer reports that he has received a threat from an obscure radical environmental group saying that if he does not stop construction of condominiums at an environmentally sensitive location, "he will pay the price". A quick search of news stories identifies the presence of the environmental group in other locations, its past activities and attacks, and the methods of attack. This can be an important element for defining specific intelligence requirements and methods of prevention in the current case.
- A tip is provided to law enforcement that a radical Islamic cleric who preaches violence is going to be in its community to speak to a local group. An open source search provides information about the individual's past speeches, the content of the speeches and any public safety issues that emerged associated with the speech.

[28] For example, one such source is library. pressdisplay.com which can be accessed at no charge through www.opensource. gov.

[29] All major web search engines include an image search capability. In addition, there are specialized image search engines such as www.picsearch.com and www.thrall.org/proimage.html.

[30] For example, if protestors from the Westboro Baptist church are anticipated at a funeral for an American service veteran, information about tactics, can be found at www.godhatesamerica.com and their protest schedule can be found at www.godhatesfags.com.

[31] See youtube.com/watch?v=P28KJvu46DY .

[32] See profile.myspace.com/ index.cfm?fuseaction=user. viewprofile&friendid=91546354.

[33] Ibid., Best and Cumming, 2007, p. 2.

[34] Office of the Director of National Intelligence. *National Open Source Enterprise.* Washington, D.C.: Office of the Director of National Intelligence, 2007, p. 3.

- The manager of a nursery reports that a man driving a rental van just purchased an unusually large quantity of fertilizer. While a criminal history check was negative, an open source search of a commercial integrated database identified the individual's address and persons known to use the same address. An Internet search engine identifies some of the man's associates on a right-wing extremist web site.

- A confidential informant states that members of a violent gang are slowly moving into the region. An intelligence analyst conducts an open source search to learn more about the gang, identify gang characteristics, and locates samples of the gang's graffiti and tattoos and distributes the information to patrol officers so they can record the presence of gang symbols in the community.

- A group of anarchists announce that they are going to demonstrate against the president of the World Bank who is speaking at the commencement exercise at a local university. A search of anarchist blogs finds a discussion of plans by the anarchists to cause major disruption during the protests by destroying targeted property and resisting arrest.

In each case, the initial tip or lead was followed by a quick open source search to gather more information. Not only did the open source information provide more insight about the threat, the information aided analysts in defining explicit intelligence requirements to help in fully articulating the threat picture.

As a source of first resort, open sources are not only fast; they also represent a minimal intrusion on civil liberties. Furthermore, open sources are less expensive than traditional law enforcement information-collection methods.

National Initiatives: The National Open Source Enterprise

The Office of the Director of National Intelligence (ODNI) was created by the Intelligence Reform and Terrorism Prevention Act (IRTPA) of 2004. Among the mandates for the ODNI was the development of a comprehensive National Intelligence Strategy; including development of an Information Sharing Environment (ISE) that maximizes intelligence and information sharing among the Intelligence Community, law enforcement, the private sector, and foreign partners. The ISE includes development of a consistent intelligence lexicon and standardized information-sharing and security standards. To maximize efficient, effective, and comprehensive information collection in support of the intelligence process, one strategy of the ODNI was to create the National Open Source Enterprise (NOSE).[35]

In the development of this enterprise, the ODNI notes:

> Given the challenges and threats the United States faces in the 21st century, it is essential our decision-makers, war-fighters, law enforcement, and homeland security authorities receive accurate, actionable and timely intelligence support. … Part of this new approach to intelligence is the collection of national intelligence via an integrated collection enterprise, fundamental to which is a robust, distributed, open source exploitation capability, known as the National Open Source Enterprise (NOSE).[36]

[35] See *Intelligence Community Directive, No. 301, National Open Source Enterprise* (July 11, 2006).

[36] Office of the Director of National Intelligence, p. 3.

The NOSE builds on observations from *The Commission on the Intelligence Capabilities of the United States Regarding Weapons of Mass Destruction* (2005) which observed:

> The need for exploiting open-source material is greater now than ever before…The ever-shifting nature of our intelligence needs compels the Intelligence Community to quickly and easily understand a wide range of foreign countries and cultures…information often detailed in open sources…"[37]

Based on *Intelligence Community Directive 301*, which created NOSE, the following are among the new responsibilities of Intelligence Community members:

- Conduct acquisition, analysis, and dissemination of open source materials.
- Make all open source information, products, and services available across the Intelligence Community (unless expressly prohibited by law).
- Coordinate all open source resources and activities through the Assistant Deputy Director of National Intelligence for Open Source.
- Designate a primary open source coordinator in each department or agency.
- Support staffing requirements of the Director of National Intelligence's (DNI) Open Source Center.
- Make full use of open source information, expertise, and capabilities to conduct analysis and inform collection strategies.
- Use a formal intelligence requirements mechanism for open sources.[38]

These responsibilities represent a major commitment to open source activities. A significant initiative in this regard was creation of the OSC,[39] formerly the Foreign Broadcast Information Service of which the CIA serves as the Executive Agent.

> OSC offers extensive coverage of open source intelligence information monitored worldwide on topics such as military affairs, politics, the environment, societal issues, economics, and science and technology. The information is obtained from radio, television, press, periodicals, books and other sources of unrestricted information such as databases and gray literature (open source information not available by subscription).

The web site has a massive amount of information, in both text and multimedia, and is accessible through a standard Internet connection. State, local, and tribal law enforcement (SLTLE) personnel can gain access to the web site by registering, which includes verification of employment (i.e., right to know) and that the requester has the need to know sensitive homeland security information. While there is a great deal of information at the OSC that will be of interest, although marginally relevant to many SLTLE agencies, the greatest value of the OSC to law enforcement is the free access to many commercial databases.

The direction of these and additional open source activities demonstrate the importance and value that are being committed to the development of a new open source capability. Moreover, in light of the implementation of the ISE, the goals of information sharing across the Intelligence Community and with SLTLE and the private sector,[41] the NOSE takes on even greater meaning.

[37] *The Commission on the Intelligence Capabilities of the United States Regarding Weapons of Mass Destruction*, 2005

[38] *Intelligence Community Directive 301. National Open Source Enterprise.* Section E(6), July 11, 2006.

[39] www.opensource.gov

[40] infoserve.sandia.gov/electronic/fbis.html

Open Source and Law Enforcement Intelligence (Tradecraft)

"Tradecraft" is a collective term used by the Intelligence Community to refer to the methods used in the Intelligence Process, particularly collection and analysis, on both broad and specific scales. While the term is rarely used in law enforcement, it is useful to understand its meaning in light of developments in the ISE.

Therefore, open source tradecraft has two meanings for law enforcement. At the macro level, it broadly refers to how open sources can be used in the Intelligence Process. At the micro level, it means the explicit procedures in conducting open source searches as well as capturing and interpreting raw open source information. The remaining discussions deal with open source tradecraft for law enforcement at both levels.

The fact that information is collected from an open source should not dissuade a law enforcement officer or analyst from using it. Indeed, there is often high-quality, insightful evidence available from open sources. So much so, that the 9/11 Commission's Final Report recommended that a new "Open Source Agency" be added to the U.S. intelligence structure.[42] This is essentially being implemented with NOSE. However, like virtually every other aspect of intelligence issues, the use of open sources in law enforcement intelligence has unique applications and parameters that vary somewhat from open source exploitation by Intelligence Community agencies. Fundamentally, the distinction lies in the fact that the SLTLE agency should be collecting and retaining only open source information identifying individuals and/or organizations where there is a criminal nexus. As will be described below, a great deal of open source applications for law enforcement intelligence should be incorporated as standard protocol in the intelligence process.

Criminals Also Use Open Source

A 15-year-old Sierra Vista High School student who was shot October 13, 2007 in front of his southwest Las Vegas home was a key witness in a 2006 Crips gang-related double slaying in Riverside County. Prosecutors in California think another teen shot Demontre Carroll in the back to silence him. The teen, who had relocated to Las Vegas from Southern California because of threats on his life, was located by the assailant using the victim's MySpace page.

Las Vegas Review Journal, November 7, 2007, p. 1A.

---

[41] See: Program Manager-Information Sharing Environment. *ISE Implementation Plan*. Washington, D.C.: Program Manager-Information Sharing Environment, 2006, at www.ise.gov.

[42] National Commission on Terrorist Attacks Upon the United States. *The 9/11 Commission Report*. Washington, D.C.: U.S. Government Printing Office, 2004, p. 413. Also online at www.9-11commission.gov/report/911Report.pdf.

Law Enforcement Applications of Open Source

There are both tactical and strategic applications of open source for law enforcement intelligence, such as the following:

- *Identifying and verifying facts.* Perhaps one of the most common uses of open sources in law enforcement is to identify and verify a wide range of facts. Personal identity information, addresses and phone numbers, e-mail addresses, vehicles known to have been used, property records, are among a wide variety of other facts can easily be identified through open source public and commercial databases and directories.

- *Social networking.* Social networking sites such as MySpace, provide a wealth of information about individuals and persons with whom they interact. Social networking web sites contain identity information of the user and his or her friends, often with photographs, as well as private messages and statements about beliefs and behavior. Likes and dislikes are often enumerated, ranging from entertainment to politics to people, as well as contact information. While some information, such as a private message, is subject to legal process, a great deal of information is available as an open source.

- *Identifying criminal offenders.* In a surprising number of cases, people will make incriminating statements in open sources. It has occurred in media reports but most commonly in either social networking sites or on web sites devoted to a particular deviant or unlawful behavior. Sexual predators, drug traffickers, persons trafficking in stolen property, and criminal extremists are all examples that have been found in the "deep web." While incriminating statements alone will not meet the burden of proof for conviction, they clearly establish a criminal predicate and basis for further inquiry.

- *Understanding and interpreting ideologies.* An important element of analysis that aids in defining and forecasting threats is to understand the motivation or rationale of individuals involved in criminal behavior. Particularly in the case of ideological extremists, web sites can be a valuable source. Extremist web sites typically articulate their beliefs as well as what behaviors or changes their movement will cause. Moreover, drilling down and reading blogs can provide more information about individuals' beliefs and behaviors, including incriminating statements.

- *Identifying criminal methodologies.* Collecting information from media sources, web sites, and/or blogs can provide important insight into methods and targets of criminal acts. The modus operandi of violent serial offenders, criminal extremists, and criminal enterprises can be identified readily in many cases. This can be valuable information for developing preventive strategies; for example, a technique used by anarchists is the "black bloc" that includes property destruction and other activities that could be criminal. The tactics can be learned through various open sources.[43]

- *Identifying emerging crime issues and trends.* Just as criminal methodologies can be learned from open sources, so can new and emerging crime trends. In many cases, certain types of crime will disperse geographically in a consistent pattern. Drug trafficking and gang activity serve as good

[43] flag.blackened.net/revolt/rbr/rbr6/black.html

examples. Monitoring new and emerging crimes or changes in crimes on a broad geographic basis can often provide insight about crime problems that are on the horizon for a community. Methamphetamine hydrochloride, for example, first emerged in urban areas on both coasts of the United States. Its movement to rural areas and to the midwest was on a fairly definable path permitting forecasting. Much of the information was easily identifiable through media reports.

An Example of "Pushed" Open Source Information

In March 2008 there was a series of direct action demonstrations in San Francisco. Predominantly focused on the war in Iraq, other issues were also being expressed by demonstrators including opposition to the U.S. policy toward Israel, economic issues, and global warming. Some demonstrators stated on "direct action" web sites they would be involved in civil disobedience and arrests were anticipated.

To learn more about the protests and the plans, the author searched several direct action web sites related to the demonstration. One web site provided cell phone text messages on plans and events throughout the day. The author signed up for the text service and had information on the demonstration "pushed" to his cell phone, therefore not only monitoring the events, but arriving at locations where civil disobedience was planned prior to most demonstrators.

The texts were open sources in near real time and it illustrates that with technology, open source information can take diverse forms.

An important word of caution: Just as law enforcement seeks information that provides insights into criminal behavior, individuals who are involved in criminal behavior may also attempt to provide disinformation on their web sites in an attempt to mislead law enforcement authorities. This is of particular concern regarding ideological groups who may seek to either induce law enforcement into some form of unjustified action or to simply distract law enforcement away from the heart of a group's real activities. This reinforces the need to verify sources and content.

Open Sources and Civil Rights

Unlike Intelligence Community agencies and the private sector, SLTLE agencies must be vigilant in the management of open source information because of unique rules that apply to information retention in a criminal intelligence records system.

Raw information obtained from open sources tends to fall into two categories that have important significance for an SLTLE agency: 1. Information about individuals and organizations and 2. Aggregate nonidentifying information. As a general rule, when a law enforcement agency conducts an open source search for information, the agency should assumed that civil rights protections attach to any information that identifies individuals or organizations, no matter how innocuous that individual piece of information appears to be. Conversely, as a general rule, no civil rights attach to aggregate information or descriptions of issues, trends, ideologies, and so forth that does not identify an individual or organization.

Of particular importance is when the information involves expressive activity that is protected by the First Amendment. It is easy to find information posted on blogs and web sites that express extreme statements about a diverse array of behavior, such as support for international terrorism, advocacy of legalization of drugs, vehement opposition to policies of government officials, advocacy of pedophilia, racist beliefs, and so forth. The difficulty is to distinguish between extreme expressive beliefs and statements that have a criminal nexus.

The statements in Table 11-1 illustrate expressive beliefs (left column) and statements with a likely criminal nexus (right column). Assume that the statements are made by a person who has been identified by an SLTLE officer.

Table 11-1: Comparison of Expressive Statements and Statements with a Criminal Nexus

Expressive Statement	Statement with Criminal Nexus
• "All politicians are corrupt and ought to be shot."	• "The only way to stop this war is for us to kill the President."
• "Doctors who perform abortions are committing murder and must be stopped."	• "The only way to stop that doctor from performing abortions is for us to blow up his clinic."
• "Everyone should smoke marijuana."	• "I can get you some marijuana to smoke."
• "Violence is the only message they understand."	• "I urge you to kill our oppressors."

The differences are often subtle. The expressive statements, while extreme, are less explicit. Moreover, even in these illustrations, additional facts and circumstances would be needed to establish a criminal predicate.

It is good practice to assume that any information identifying individuals or organizations collected from open sources must be 28 CFR Part 23-compliant.[44] Thus, there must be evidence establishing a reasonable suspicion that there is a nexus between the person or organization identified in the open source and a crime; that is, the "criminal predicate test." The essential principle is not the source of the information, but *what information is being retained* by a law enforcement agency in its criminal intelligence records system. Illustrations of open source applications include the following:

- If information is being collected from open sources as part of the criminal investigation of a crime that has already occurred, the criminal predicate test for intelligence records typically does not apply. Information from a criminal investigation would be placed in the law enforcement agency's Records Management System, rather than the criminal intelligence records system.

- If a group plans a protest or demonstration in a jurisdiction, open source information may be used to determine how past protests or demonstrations have been conducted, tactics used in other protests and demonstrations, outcomes and behaviors of the protesters and demonstrators with no criminal predicate required.

[44] The reader is reminded that 28 CFR Part 23 applies only to information that is placed in a criminal intelligence records system.

- While there is some debate, the general rule is that an open source inquiry identifies people who have been arrested during a protest or demonstration; this information may be retained without a separate criminal predicate being established. If a person has been arrested, probable cause has been established, which is a higher standard than the "reasonable suspicion" required for the criminal predicate.

- If the law enforcement agency receives a Suspicious Activity Report that an identified person may commit a crime during the course of the protest or demonstration, that information may be retained in a temporary criminal intelligence file in order to collect further information to verify the veracity of the suspicious activity information. In these cases, the law enforcement agency's criminal intelligence records policy should be followed.

• Descriptive information about extremist ideological beliefs, behaviors of those supporting those beliefs, changes and trends in extremists beliefs or collective behavior, methods advocated for accomplishing the goals of the extremist ideology, and potential targets of the extremists' actions may all be collected, analyzed and retained by a law enforcement agency without a criminal predicate as long as specific individuals or organizations are not identified.

Creating intelligence dossiers on persons who are merely suspicious is both tempting and easy using open source data. Similarly, exploring a social networking site through its search utility to determine if something interesting is located about a person is similarly easy. Nevertheless, law enforcement personnel must follow 28 CFR Part 23-compliant procedures for collecting and retaining open source information in a criminal intelligence records system just as it would for any other form of criminal intelligence information. It warrants repeating: The issue is not whether the information is from an open source, but whether a law enforcement agency can properly keep the information. Decisions must focus on the reason for which information is being retained, not the source of the information.

An important point to remember is that laws vary by state and locality, whether it is intelligence records laws, open records legislation, a state freedom of information act, or state privacy act. There is sufficient variability among the states to warrant a careful review of state law as it relates to criminal intelligence records.

Working with Internet Service Providers and Web-Based Companies

Often, open source searches will lead to the need to use the legal process to gain further information about an inquiry. Of course, when a law enforcement agency seeks information about the specific behaviors of an individual who is a customer or client of a private company, significant privacy concerns arise.

While this process moves beyond open sources, it should be noted that Internet service providers and companies that operate social networking web sites typically have a published policy and guide to work specifically with law enforcement agencies. While it is important for the reader to be aware of this, since legal process has to be used and information is being sought that is not openly available, it is not open source information when the process goes beyond information that is openly available on the Internet.

Attribution and Copyrighted Materials in the Intelligence Process and Reports

Much of the open source information acquired through the intelligence process is in the public domain, that is, information for which no copyright is claimed. In other cases, as with certain commercial databases, rights to the information have been obtained by contract in accordance with usual government procurement procedures. In many other cases, however, agencies acquire copyright information without the authorization of the copyright holder.[45]

Too often products from law enforcement agencies, ranging from intelligence products to training materials, contain information that is drawn from other sources; however, there is no attribution to the original source. Attribution is important for four basic reasons:

1. It gives corroboration and support for the line of logic, inference, or conclusion that is presented in the report.

2. It permits the consumer to go to the original source for further information on the subject as well as giving the consumer the opportunity to independently evaluate the original source.

3. Attribution will typically meet the standards of law for copyrighted materials.

4. Attribution is the ethical and correct method of operation by giving appropriate recognition to the thoughts, ideas, creativity and work of others.

The importance for attribution has been reinforced by the ODNI through Intelligence Community Directive (ICD) 206, *Sourcing Requirements for Disseminated Analytic Products*.[47] The Directive states:

> Source reference citations shall be included as endnotes in disseminated analytic products. These endnotes shall be provided for all significant, substantive reporting or other information upon which the product's analytic judgments, assessments, estimates, alternative hypotheses and views, or confidence levels depend.[47]

The importance of attributing information to the original source is based on the following notion:

> Thorough and consistent documentation enhances the credibility and transparency of intelligence analysis and enables consumers to better understand the quantity and quality of information underlying the analysis.[48]

Of course, not all attributed material is copyrighted work, particularly in the case of public records. Most public documents and information that have been originally collected by the law enforcement agency are not copyrighted. In these cases, attribution is important for validity purposes.

Beyond public records there is information that should be attributed, particularly if it is from a copyrighted source. For example, information in a strategic

[45] Weimer, Douglas R., *The Copyright Doctrine of Fair Use and the Internet: Case Law*. Washington, D.C.: Congressional Research Service, 2005, pp.1–2.

[46] www.fas.org/irp/dni/icd/index.html

[47] Office of the Director of National Intelligence. ICD 206. *Sourcing Requirements for Disseminated Analytic Requirements*. Paragraph D.2, October 17, 2007, p. 2.

[48] Ibid., Paragraph B., p. 1.

intelligence product is drawn from a book on terrorism, a video from a television network that is used to illustrate terrorist attack methods, or the original concept and ideas of a consultant that is used in an intelligence report. All should be considered as copyrighted materials and attributable to the original source.

A copyright is a form of protection provided by the laws of the United States[49] to the authors of original works, including not only written materials, both published and unpublished, but also video and audio materials. Under the protection of federal copyright law,[50] the owner of copyright has the exclusive right of use, distribution, limitation to distribution, and to authorize others to reproduce copies; use the copyrighted material; prepare derivative works based on the original; and rent, sell or transfer the copyright.

Law enforcement agencies are obliged to follow copyright law just as any other individual or organization. While it is important to understand and respect copyrighted works, the "fair use" exemption permits use of the materials without seeking permission of the copyright owner.[51]

> The fair use of a copyrighted work, including such use by reproduction in copies or phonorecords[52] or by any other means specified by that section, for purposes such as criticism, comment, news reporting, teaching (including multiple copies for classroom use), scholarship, or research, is not an infringement of copyright. In determining whether the use made of a work in any particular case is a fair use the factors to be considered shall include:
> 1. The purpose and character of the use, including whether such use is of a commercial nature or is for nonprofit educational purposes.
> 2. The nature of the copyrighted work.
> 3. The amount and substantiality of the portion used in relation to the copyrighted work as a whole.
> 4. The effect of the use upon the potential market for or value of the copyrighted work.
>
> The fact that a work is unpublished shall not itself bar a finding of fair use if such finding is made upon consideration of all the above factors.[53]

With specific reference to copyright law and open source intelligence, a Congressional Research Service report stated:

> In using such copyrighted information, intelligence agencies, like other users of public information, are governed by the doctrine of "fair use" (based on common law and codified in the Copyright Act of 1976 (17 USC 107)).[54]

Clearly, law enforcement agencies are also obliged to conform to copyright law. Beyond the legal requirements, it is simply good practice to offer attribution of information where applicable.

Copyright and attribution issues are complicated when law enforcement agencies use the services of a commercial vendor whose work product has copyright protection. Care must be taken to ensure that users of the information understand the copyright implications in the service contract.

[49] United States Code, Title 17.

[50] United States Code, Title 17, Section 106 with reference the Copyright Act of 1976.

[51] Ibid., Section 107.

[52] "Phonorecords" is language from the 1976 law and has been interpreted to include all forms of audio and video media that meet the other standards for copyright protection. Similarly, digital materials such as web pages are also included.

[53] www.copyright.gov/title17/92chap1.html#107

[54] Weimer (2005), Ibid.

In the process of collecting information and preparing intelligence reports, law enforcement personnel should always include copyrighted material in their searches, be certain to provide proper sourcing[55] of the information, and be aware of the proper procedures in the fair use exemption.[56]

Metrics for Open Source Use

A great deal of information has been discussed about the effectiveness of open source information; however, the only true measure of effectiveness is to ensure that it is designed and evaluated to specifically meet the needs of the intelligence environment in which it is being used. A challenge, however, is the absence of widely accepted measurements or metrics related to open source intelligence. Responsible managers must develop outcome measures for intelligence practices to ensure they are accomplishing their intended goals (i.e., effectiveness) and are doing so in a manner that does not waste resources (i.e., efficiency).

Simple open source metrics may include the following:
- A count of open sources attributed in intelligence reports
- The proportion of all analysis where open sources are used
- Proportion of time when open sources are the source of first resort for intelligence requirements
- Time requirements for locating needed information in the open source environment versus the closed source environment.

While somewhat superficial, these metrics represent more than is currently used. Moreover, inasmuch as open source information is used by all-source analysts in connection with information from closed sources, it is difficult to measure how much open source information contributes to a specific intelligence product.

> It is anticipated that open source information will increasingly be relied upon given its greater availability, the nature of issues that today's analysts must cover, and the heavier emphasis placed on it by senior intelligence leaders.[57]

The ultimate open source metric is the qualitative contribution open sources make to the analysis. While this is difficult to measure, long-term evaluative assessments should be developed in order to focus the type of open sources and the methodology of their inclusion in the intelligence process which is most productive.

Open Source Content for the Intelligence Process

While open sources include information beyond the web, it is apparent that information about virtually any topic can be found on the Internet. Indeed, the quantity of information can be overwhelming. Having some perspective about different kinds of open source content that have particular value for law enforcement intelligence can begin to make the navigation and collection process more manageable.

[55] *Intelligence Community Directive 206* provides a significant amount of detail of information that should be included in the attribution.

[56] The United States Copyright Office web site, www.copyright.gov is very comprehensive and should provide answers to most copyright questions, including the fair use doctrine.

[57] Ibid. Best and Cumming, 2007, p. 17.

Open Source Information Identifying People and Organizations from Subscription Services and the Media

Two open sources that frequently identify people and organizations that warrant special attention are subscription database services and media reports. These are often subject to question about the propriety of their use. Both may be used properly and can be of great value to law enforcement intelligence. Just as in the case of any open source, the nature of the sources must be understood and the regulations concerning retention in criminal intelligence records systems must be applied in the same manner as any other information.

Searching media sources[58] can also provide a significant amount of information about individuals, organizations, trends in crime, movements, and criminal extremist ideologies. News services have global networks of sophisticated communications and informants with trained staff to conduct research and investigate virtually all issues that would be of interest to a consuming public. As a general rule, responsible news organizations also have editorial policies to ensure that the information used in news stories is valid, reliable, and corroborated (i.e., "well-sourced"). Crime and criminal extremism are important news; hence, journalists often seek to learn as much as possible about these incidents. The depth of information frequently includes details that are useful in the intelligence process. The news media can openly identify individuals and organizations involved in criminal incidents and often link similar individuals and incidents in diverse geographic locales. A search of news stories can provide both important leads and important undiscovered detail about a line of inquiry. A word of caution, however: not all media sources adhere to the same high standards. The practices and reputation of the media source must be evaluated just as any other source.

A number of companies have developed systems that permit a search for information from public and commercial databases using proprietary data integration software. Examples of the types of data that may be obtained are listed in Table 11-2. Companies such as AutoTrack,[59] Accurint,[60] Lexis-Nexis,[61] and RiverGlass[62] permit the development of extraordinarily detailed information about people into a summary report. Even though a fee is charged for these services, they are still open source because anyone can purchase the data and neither a legal process nor surreptitious collection methods are used.

Since both subscription services and media sources can provide a significant amount of detail about individuals and organizations, it is important to repeat once again that the criminal predicate rule is still applicable for information placed in law enforcement intelligence records.

National Media Exploitation Center

On a related point, initiatives by the Intelligence Community related to media information are worthy of note. Because of the vast amount of information that is available and easily accessible from the global news media, the National Media Exploitation Center (NMEC) was established in late 2001 at the Central Intelligence Agency[63] (CIA). NMEC's role is to coordinate FBI, CIA, the Defense Intelligence

[58] Such as News Directory www.newsdirectory.com or World: News, Media and Communications www.geocities.com/albaruthenia/AW/news.html.

[59] www.autotrack.com

[60] www.accurint.com

[61] www.lexisnexis.com

[62] www.riverglassinc.com

[63] Don Cryer, Special Assistant to the Director of Central Intelligence for Diversity Management. (November 5, 2003). *Prepared Statement, Hearing before the Permanent Select Committee on Intelligence, 108th Congress.*

Agency, and National Security Agency efforts to analyze and disseminate information gleaned from millions of pages of paper documents, electronic media, videotapes, audiotapes, and electronic equipment.[64]

Table 11-2: Examples of Information Obtainable from Subscription Database Services

- Full names
- Date of birth
- Place of birth
- Parents, spouses, siblings, and children
- Known associates
- Known addresses associated with all the names
- Social security numbers
- Mortgage and lien information
- Credit report
- Credit cards and credit card usage
- Professional affiliations
- Occupations and employers
- Licenses of all types
- Vehicle, watercraft, and aircraft registrations

In this venue, exploitation refers to the collection of open source information relevant to defined requirements, integrating it with other known information and deriving new knowledge from this process; that is, developing open source intelligence. The NMEC has a great deal of expertise and resources. SLTLE agencies may take advantage of the NMEC through federal partners—typically the FBI or DHS—at the primary state fusion center.

The Social Networking Concept and Issues for Open Source

A social network is a linked, interactive structure of people consisting of "nodes" that may be either an individual or group. The basis of the linkage is a shared interest of virtually any definable character—music, occupation, personal philosophy, political affiliation, sexual orientation, hobbies, and so forth. Each node may have multiple connections based on the different variables. For example, one person (i.e., a node) may be a member of multiple social networks. A person who is an accountant may also be a motorcycle enthusiast, enjoy country music, and be an avid fantasy football player. Each variable could represent membership in different social networks. Similar social network models can be defined for people who support extremist ideologies, are gang members, or are involved in illegal activities, such as drug use or pedophilia.

While social networks have existed in some form since the dawn of humankind, the growth of the Internet has resulted in new social networks that are virtual, notably represented by web sites such as MySpace,[65] FaceBook,[66] Bebo,[67] Twitter,[68]

[64] Federal Bureau of Investigation. "The FBI's Counterterrorism Program Since September 2001." *A Report to the National Commission on Terrorists Attacks Upon the United States.* Washington, D.C.: Federal Bureau of Investigation, undated, p. 16.

[65] www.myspace.com

[66] www.facebook.com

[67] www.bebo.com

[68] www.twitter.com

and SocialGrid.[69] Other social networking web sites not as sophisticated or widely known also represent diverse interests. Ironically, social network members will frequently post information that is incriminating or, at the least, sufficiently strong to establish a criminal predicate as related to their behavior. While in some cases one may find gang members or supporters of the Earth Liberation Front on popular web sites such as MySpace, there are many more underground web sites that will have postings indicating criminal behaviors. That is why creative search strategies become important. Typically, intuitive search criteria will not produce the results being sought; rather, use of terms and phrases unique to the social structure are required. As a result, background research to understand a social network becomes an important starting point.

A different form of social networking is found in YouTube.[70] As most readers will know, individuals may post videos on this web site for public viewing. The videos range from humor to personal statements about all kinds of issues. Included are videos related to Hamas,[71] Hezbollah,[72] MS-13[73] and others. In some cases, the videos are critical while in other cases, they are supportive of the cause. Reviewing the videos can provide unique insights and images, including signs and symbols of the group being examined.

To be most successful in searching a social network, the user must create an identity and become a member of the network. For purposes of intelligence inquiries, a false identity and e-mail address should be created by the law enforcement user.[74] Important, there are certain ethical and legal limits that should be fully explored before going forward. Of particular concern is the need to be certain that statements and actions by a law enforcement employee do not induce a person to commit an act that the person would not have otherwise done without the inducement. That is entrapment. A law enforcement agency should develop a policy and procedures to guide the use of creating a false identity and using that identity for intelligence inquiries including social networking.[75] Despite the caveat, the value of using the search engine of each social networking web site should not be underestimated.

Newsletters and Blogs

Monitoring a variety of variables related to a threat is an important part of strategic intelligence. Essentially, these are standing intelligence requirements. Open source materials that are particularly useful for this purpose are newsletters and blogs. While newsletters exist in both printed and electronic form, the latter is increasingly prevalent because they are more timely and frequently provide hyperlinks leading the reader to sources that will provide greater detail about the subject.

Newsletters are designed to highlight issues, trends, and developments within a specific topic area. Blogs are web-based opinion discussions also typically focused on a specific topic area where writers and readers express opinions, perspectives, and beliefs. In many cases, a single source will have both a newsletter and a blog; for example, a particularly useful newsletter and blog for intelligence issues is *Secrecy News*[76] from the Federation of American Scientists.[77]

[69] www.socialgrid.com

[70] www.youtube.com

[71] www.youtube.com/ watch?v=TrieBhaGgHM

[72] www.youtube.com/ watch?v=P28KJvu46DY

[73] www.youtube.com/ watch?v=MDUIxJJbP00

[74] The processes and "lessons learned in the creation of a false identity for law enforcement inquiries will not be discussed because this is a publicly available document.

[75] As a technical point, searching a social networking site is an open source. Establishing a false identity on the site to lure an individual into making incriminating statements is surreptitious and, therefore, not an open source.

[76] See www.fas.org/sgp/news/secrecy and www.fas.org/blog/secrecy, respectively.

[77] The Federation of American Scientists web site contains a great deal of interesting and useful information related to intelligence issues, including downloadable documents, many of which are often difficult to gain access to. See www.fas.org.

Generally speaking, there are four broad categories of newsletters and blogs:

1. *Professional/academic and government.* These sources tend to be among the most objective, although never rule out the ideological influence, even if unintentional, of an author or editor. Despite this caveat, these sources are most likely to make statements based on corroborated information and use an approach to analysis and conclusion based on logic and the scientific method rather than emotional arguments. Typically, these sources report facts and data more objectively and most commonly include attribution of facts and data.

2. *Commercial sources.* As the name implies, these are profit-driven sources often intended to provide information that supports the sale of products or services. Despite the fact that the motive of the source is to make a profit, the sources can nonetheless be very reliable. Indeed, the reliability of these sources is often an important selling point for the business. While the information is typically accurate, information about alternatives is not likely to be included.

3. *Advocacy groups.* These sources are agenda-driven based on the ideology and goals of the source. A newsletter from a right-wing extremist source will reflect information that supports that ideology. Similarly, discussions in a blog on environmental extremism will support the goals of that group. The reader should recognize where they are coming from and factor that into one's analysis. Using this approach, these sources can be quite insightful for understanding an ideology or advocacy position.

4. *Pundits.* A wide range of individuals blog on the web as critics and commentators on virtually every subject. Pundits work for a wide variety of organizations—news, entertainment media, professional organizations, etc.—and some are independent commentators working only for themselves, oftentimes not as a source of income, but as a means to discuss an interest or belief. What is important to recognize is that pundits typically do not seek to be objective, but to comment on a topic of interest from their particular ideology or perspective. This is also true for pundits who blog for news organizations. Often their arguments and observations are persuasive and useful, but typically they are not objective. Pundits tend to be news and policy wonks; hence, their research will often identify issues and sources of information that might otherwise be easily missed. As such, they are often good sources of raw information that can be corroborated through objective sources.

Subscribing to newsletters and monitoring blogs on a consistent basis can provide a wealth of information about trends, issues, and anomalies. When a new issue of concern begins to emerge on a consistent basis, and particularly if it is reflected in multiple sources, the issue should be proactively explored through other information sources to determine its reliability and validity and to assess the probable impact on one's area of responsibility.

The number of blogs and newsletters on the web is unknown; moreover, they are dynamic in both their presence and content; as a result, there is value in relying on web sites that aggregate blogs, newsletters, and news. These sites typically organize their content into broad categories and have search engines that limit queries to the site's contents. Both factors aid in narrowing the breadth of a search. Two such sites that are comprehensive in their aggregation are

BlogRunner[78] and TalkDigger.[79] Each uses a slightly different approach, thereby providing a more comprehensive search methodology.

Wikis

A wiki is software that allows users to easily create, edit, and link pages. Wikis are often used to create collaborative web sites and to power community web sites, often also referred to as wikis. These collaborations are increasingly being used by businesses to provide affordable and effective Intranets and for knowledge management.[80] More specifically, the collective business knowledge of all members of an organization can be documented, refined, and shared in a dynamic virtual environment.

Wikis generally are designed with the philosophy of making it easy to correct mistakes, rather than making it difficult to make them. Thus, while wikis are open, they provide a means to verify the validity of recent additions to the body of pages. The most prominent, on almost every wiki, is the "Recent Changes" page—a specific list numbering recent edits, or a list of all the edits made within a given time frame.

Critics of publicly-editable wiki systems argue that these systems could be easily tampered with, while proponents argue that the community of users can catch malicious content and correct it. The safe lesson on a public wiki is to use it as a pointer system and corroborate the content of interest.

Perhaps the best known wiki is the online encyclopedia *Wikipedia*;[81] however, there are many types of wikis, some with a very specific focus.[82] For example, the ODNI OSC provides access to a wiki that is specifically focused on intelligence called *Intellipedia*.[83] While primarily focused on the Intelligence Community, it contains information that is also useful to SLTLE. Wikis can be a valuable source when dealing with a topic or issue about which the information collector has limited information. Most wikis include external references to materials which helps in the corroboration process.

From an intelligence perspective, the wiki can provide subject matter knowledge on an issue as well as direction to more information.[84]

RSS Feeds

RSS (Really Simple Syndication) is a family of web feed formats used to publish frequently updated content including, but not limited to, blog entries, news headlines, and podcasts. An RSS document (which is called a feed, web feed, or channel) contains either a summary of content from an associated web site or the full text. RSS makes it possible for people to keep up with web sites in an automated manner that can be sent to the subscriber.[85]

From an open source perspective, the value of RSS feeds, when available on a web site, is that any new information or changes in content are sent to those registered for the service without the need to check each site. It increases both the efficiency and timeliness of information for the user.[86]

[78] www.blogrunner.com

[79] www.talkdigger.com

[80] en.wikipedia.org/wiki/Wiki

[81] en.wikipedia.org/wiki/Main_Page

[82] A wide variety of wikis can be searched through www.wiki.com.

[83] www.opensource.gov/providers/ intelinku/wiki/Main_Page (access only)

[84] For example, see the crime wiki at unclesam.pbwiki.com/Crime.

[85] en.wikipedia.org/wiki/RSS_(file_format)

[86] As an example, see the terrorism news and analysis RSS feeds at www.2rss.com/ rss_5352.html.

Gray Literature

Gray literature is open source information that typically is not published but made openly available, usually to a specific audience. While it is open, the information is often not easily identified or retrieved. The American Library Association observes:

> The greatest challenges involved with [gray literature is] the process of identification, since there is limited indexing, and acquisition, since availability is usually marred with uncertainty. Added to this is the absence of editorial control, raising questions about authenticity and reliability.[87]

Traditionally, gray literature was defined as any documentary material that is not commercially published and is typically composed of technical reports, working papers, business documents, and conference proceedings. More of these types of documents are becoming available online, but often are not discovered by traditional search engines.

This author views the concept of gray literature more broadly, particularly as applied to the law enforcement intelligence process. The basic idea of gray literature has three components: 1. Documents of interest that exist; 2. The information is open; and 3. The information is not widely distributed and therefore difficult to locate. The concept of gray literature, therefore, should not be limited to academic or scientific works, but applied to any documents characterized by these three elements.

Brochures printed by a right-wing extremist are handed out a local gun show or fliers printed by anarchists and distributed at a demonstration could also be considered gray. In both cases, the documents are not commercially published but are intended to be disseminated openly and as broadly as possible (the limitation often being a budgetary one). The limited supply of these unpublished materials makes them difficult to identify or locate. Collecting gray literature is a challenge and must be explored in light of the types of potential literature that exist and where they might be located, most likely by a human collector rather than by networking.

The Deep Web

The web is a complex entity that contains widely diverse information in a variety of formats. Most people tend to view the web in the context of web sites with a combination of fixed and dynamic content. The fixed content tends to have minimal change and is the most common content found in standard searches. The dynamic content on many web sites is far larger than the fixed documents and is more likely to be missed in standard searching, with the exception of file names and file extensions.

[87] www.ala.org/ala/mgrps/divs/acrl/publications/crlnews/2004/mar/graglit.cfm

The deep web or invisible web refers to the following:

> …the vast repository of information that search engines and directories don't have direct access to, like databases. Unlike pages on the visible Web (that is, the Web that you can access from search engines and directories), information in databases is generally inaccessible to the software spiders and crawlers that create search engine indexes.[88]

Common estimates suggest that the deep web contains 500 times the content that is found in the visible web. Five broad types of content[89] constitute the invisible web:

1. *The content of web-based databases.* Information stored in databases is accessible only by query to the database and are not picked up by the web crawlers used by search engines. This is distinct from static, fixed web pages, which contain documents that can be accessed directly. A significant amount of valuable information on the web can be generated from databases.

2. *Nontextual files.* These include multimedia files, graphics files, software, and documents in formats such as Portable Document Format (PDF). Web crawling has a limitation in searching the content of these types of files. Web crawlers can identify file names and extensions (e.g., .jpg, .wmv, .pdf, etc.) of such files, but cannot identify the content of these files during the web crawling process. Essentially, they are files that are not in HTML[90] format, therefore, a great deal of information and data are not picked up from these files by traditional searches.

3. *Script-based web pages.* These are web pages that are written in script coding, other than HTML and/or those with URLs[91] that contain a "?".

4. *Content available on sites protected by passwords or other restrictions.* The content of web sites protected by some degree of access through rigorous password protection or a Virtual Private Network (VPN) will not be identified by search engines. There is a continuum of identifiable and nonidentifiable information from these types of web sites depending on what types of information the site owners elect to be publicly accessible (often for marketing purposes) as well as the degree of security applied to the site (in some instances the web site's security is limited and some data can be identified). Suffice it to note, a significant amount of information from these sites is not identifiable through traditional search engines.

5. *Pages deliberately excluded by their owners.* A web page creator who does not want his or her page captured in search engines can insert special meta tags that will cause most search engines' crawlers to avoid the page.

Obviously, a great deal of open source information from the deep web could be valuable to the intelligence process if it could be identified and retrieved. The deep web is searchable, but not using standard search techniques. The goal is to find tools that can locate valuable open source deep web information.[92] The most effective ways to search the deep web is to use search utilities that are designed to explore specific databases. While this still reaches only a portion of the deep web, the information gained from these databases can be extremely valuable, although not necessarily convenient. Deep web searching of databases typically requires accessing a variety of web sites to search for the desired information.

Language Distribution on the Internet	
According to one web-based study, languages were distributed among web pages in these percentages:	
English	56.4%
German	7.7%
French	5.6%
Japanese	4.9%
Spanish	3.4%
Chinese	2.4%
Italian	2.0%
Other	17.6%

If an information collector is searching only in English, then the search has immediately eliminated 43.6 percent of the visible web.

Source: www.netz-tipp.de/languages.html

[88] websearch.about.com/od/invisibleweb/a/invisible_web.htm

[89] See www.internettutorials.net/deepweb.asp.

[90] HTML is Hypertext Markup Language.

[91] A URL is Uniform Resource Locater, which is the web address.

[92] For a guide to assist your search strategy, see: www.lib.berkeley.edu/TeachingLib/Guides/Internet/Strategies.html.

Both as a resource and as a means to illustrate the breadth of databases in the deep web, the following is a list of deep web/database search utilities. It is not a comprehensive list; rather, the sites are among those most likely to have some form of utility for law enforcement intelligence.

1. Clusty[93]—A metasearch engine that combines the results of several top search engines.

2. Intute[94]—A searchable database of trusted web sites reviewed and monitored by subject specialists.

3. Infomine[95]—A virtual library of Internet resources relevant to university students and faculty. Built by librarians from the University of California, California State University, the University of Detroit–Mercy, and Wake Forest University.

4. Librarians Internet Index[96]—A search engine listing sites deemed trustworthy by human librarians, not just an Internet bot.

5. Internet Archive[97]—A database of tens of thousands of movies, live music, audio, texts, and home of the Wayback Machine that allows you to find old versions of web pages, more than 55 billion.

6. Direct Search[98]—A list of hundreds of specialty databases and search engines. No longer maintained, but still perhaps the most complete list of the deep web.

7. Scitopia.org [99]—A federated search engine that consists of a real time search through a disparate group of databases. The user enters a set of query parameters, which are broadcast to the selected databases; the results are collated and presented back to the user in a unified format.

8. Science.gov [100]—A search engine for government science information and research results. Launched in February 2002, it is in its fourth generation, providing a search of more than 50 million pages of science information with just one query, and is a gateway to more than 1,800 scientific web sites.

9. Pipl[101]—As an alternative method to search for people, Pipl searches databases for names of individuals rather than names that are simply incorporated on web pages.

10. StumbleUpon[102]—Using the technique of web harvesting, this deep web search engine relies on a combination of human opinions and machine learning to immediately deliver relevant content.

11. GPO's Catalog of U.S. Government Publications[103]—A searchable database of federal publications, with links to those available online.

12. Smithsonian Institution Libraries[104] —A collection of 20 libraries from the world's largest museum complex.

13. The National Archives[105]—A list of all National Archives research tools and databases.

14. HighWire Press[106] —A searchable catalog of the largest repository of free full-text, peer-reviewed content, from more than 900 journals.

15. Education Resources Information Center (ERIC) [107]—A catalog of more than 1.2 million bibliographic records, providing links to the full text where available. Sponsored by the U.S. Department of Education and the Institute of Education Sciences.

16. Encyclopedia Britannica[108]—The authoritative encyclopedia searchable with full text online.

[93] www.clusty.com

[94] www.intute.ac.uk

[95] infomine.ucr.edu

[96] www.lii.org

[97] www.archive.org/index.php

[98] www.freepint.com/gary/direct.htm

[99] www.scitopia.org

[100] www.science.gov

[101] www.pipl.com

[102] www.stumbleupon.com

[103] catalog.gpo.gov

[104] www.sil.si.edu

[105] www.archives.gov/research/tools/index.html

[106] highwire.stanford.edu

[107] www.eric.ed.gov/ERICWebPortal/Home.portal

[108] www.britannica.com

17. Topix.net [109]—A news search engine.
18. Internet Public Library[110]—The Internet's public library, which is fully searchable.
19. The Online Books Page[111]—A searchable database of more than 25,000 English works with full text available free online.
20. ebrary[112]—A searchable database of more than 20,000 full-text books.
21. Hoover's[113]—A searchable database of businesses.
22. ThomasNet[114]—An industrial product search directory.
23. GuideStar.org[115]—A searchable database of nonprofit organizations.
24. American FactFinder[116]—A repository of aggregate census bureau data searchable by city, county, or ZIP Code.
25. FedStats[117]—A gateway to statistics from more than 100 U.S. federal agencies.
26. United States Government Printing Office (GPO)[118]—A search engine for multiple government databases, including U.S. budgets, campaign reform hearings, code of federal regulations, congressional bills, unified agendas, and more.
27. CIA Electronic Reading Room[119]—A searchable database of declassified CIA documents.
28. International Data Base (IDB)[120]—A computerized data bank of statistical tables and demographic information for 228 countries and areas.
29. FIRST[121]—A database of military aggression and weapons holdings.
30. CIA Factbook[122]—A reference material published by the CIA, containing information on every country in the world.
31. THOMAS (Library of Congress)[123]—A searchable database of legislative information from the Library of Congress.
32. Law Library of Congress[124]—The largest collection of legal materials in the world, containing more than 2 million volumes.
33. Global Legal Information Network[125]—A searchable public database of laws, regulations, judicial decisions, and other legal sources.
34. FindLaw[126]—A free legal database with searchable collections of cases and codes, legal news, and an online career center.
35. Bureau of Justice Statistics[127]—A directory of legal and judicial statistics, ranging from crime to law enforcement, to courts and sentencing.
36. Library of Congress[128]—A searchable catalog of the world's largest library, containing more than 130 million items.
37. Library of Congress Digital Collections[129]—A searchable database of Library of Congress items that have been digitized and fully available online.
38. Library of Congress Prints and Photographs Reading Room[130]—A searchable catalog of Library of Congress prints and photographs including thumbnail reproductions of the items.
39. National Institutes of Health[131]—A searchable encyclopedia of health topics.
40. FAA Flight Delay Information[132]—A map of the United States with flight delay information from the nation's largest airports.
41. National Highway Traffic Safety Administration[133]—A database of car and car part defects, searchable by item number or car make and model.

[109] www.topix.net

[110] www.ipl.org

[111] digital.library.upenn.edu/books/search.html

[112] shop.ebrary.com

[113] www.hoovers.com

[114] www.thomasnet.com/index.html

[115] www.guidestar.org

[116] factfinder.census.gov/home/saff/main.html?_lang=en

[117] www.fedstats.gov

[118] www.gpoaccess.gov/multidb.html

[119] www.foia.cia.gov

[120] www.census.gov/ipc/www/idb/index.php

[121] first.sipri.org/index.php

[122] www.cia.gov/cia/publications/factbook/index.html

[123] thomas.loc.gov

[124] www.loc.gov/law/index.php

[125] www.glin.gov

[126] www.findlaw.com

[127] www.ojp.gov/bjs

[128] www.loc.gov/search/new

[129] www.loc.gov/library/libarch-digital.html

[130] www.loc.gov/rr/print/catalog.html

[131] health.nih.gov

[132] www.fly.faa.gov

[133] www-odi.nhtsa.dot.gov/cars/problems/tsb/tsbsearch.cfm

Beyond these diverse resources, a number of fee-based deep web search utilities are available. The advantage to these search utilities is that they identify and seek information from multiple databases without the need to make separate inquiries, and proactively search for data in non-HTML formats (beyond databases). The following are among the most comprehensive::

1. Xrefer[134] —A searchable database of 236 titles and more than 2.8 million entries.

2. LexisNexis[135]—The world's largest collection of public records, unpublished opinions, forms, legal, news, and business information. More than 35,000 sources are searchable with full-text available online.

3. Forrester Research[136]—An independent technology and market research company publishing in-depth research reports on a variety of subjects.

4. Factiva[137] —A searchable collection of more than 10,000 individual sources.

5. Copernic[138]—Provides indexing, searching, and tracking of databases and deep web resources by using software that seeks and identifies web resources beyond those in HTML.

6. BrightPlanet[139]—Searches, harvests, consolidates, indexes, merges, analyzes, and categorizes documents and associated metadata in any format and language, from visible and deep sources on the web and from inside and outside the firewall.

   Both the BrightPlanet and Copernic utilities are particularly comprehensive deep web search tools that go beyond databases that are useful for law enforcement intelligence.

What should be apparent is that much of the deep web is not hidden in a surreptitious manner. Rather, it is hidden because it contains information in formats or architectures that are not readily identifiable by standard search engine technologies. As a result, it takes specially designed search utilities and greater effort by the user to identify and capture deep web information.

The Underground Web

The underground web is a cultural dynamic that has evolved on the Internet, just as it has in the physical society. An article in *Business Week* described it this way:

> Warning: You are about to enter the dark side of the Internet. It's a place where crime is rampant and every twisted urge can be satisfied. Thousands of virtual streets are lined with casinos, porn shops, and drug dealers. Scam artists and terrorists skulk behind seemingly lawful Web sites. And cops wander through once in a while, mostly looking lost.[140]

Many visible web sites reflect the underground culture where transactions constantly traverse the line between lawful and unlawful behavior. While they are virtually impossible to police, these visible sites—whether trafficking in illegal commodities or purveying any other kind of illegal activity—are often relatively

[134] www.xrefer.com

[135] www.lexisnexis.com

[136] www.forrester.com

[137] www.factiva.com

[138] www.copernic.com

[139] www.brightplanet.com and www.completeplanet.com

[140] www.businessweek.com/magazine/content/02_35/b3797001.htm

easy to find through diligent standard search techniques. Often operated offshore, the sites' owners do not want to be overly visible drawing attention to their activities, but they need to be found with relative ease to make a profit for their operations.

Other types of underground deep web sites exist with the intent to keep their activities as secret as possible from the visible web world. Nonetheless, they must be accessible for their clientele, with URLs often passed between individual referrals by those who are participants in the underground activities. Identity thieves selling stolen credit card information, pedophiles exchanging photographs, traffickers unlawfully selling controlled substances, and criminal extremists planning an event are examples of open source information that exist in the underground deep web.

While this kind of information is of great interest to law enforcement intelligence, it is difficult and time-consuming to locate. Painstaking searches of the deep web and labor-intensive reading of deep web content and blogs can produce evidence and leads for a criminal inquiry. Nonetheless, this process will be faster and more effective in identifying criminal threats than traditional methods of inquiry.

There is some optimism that this process could become easier. In mid-2006 the Symantec Corporation beta-tested new software called Dark Vision that mines underground web sites and chat rooms for sensitive information that is being sold.[141] The original plan was to target carder web sites—deep underground web sites where identity thieves sell stolen credit card information. While Symantec is uncertain when or if the software will be rolled out, it nonetheless represents a breakthrough that could be applied to other criminal activity.

A vast amount of open source incriminating information is available in the deep underground web. The challenge is to develop the searching expertise and investing the time to find this critical information.

A Broadened Perspective of Open Source for Law Enforcement

The value of many web resources, such as directories, extremist web sites, and social networking sites, for law enforcement intelligence is evident; however, there is a wide array of data that have value for the intelligence process that are less intuitively evident, for example:

- Information about a possible threat that includes the name of an unknown geographic feature.
- Information about the demographic characteristics in a geographic area that is needed in a strategic intelligence assessment.
- Information from a foreign source about money, distance, weight, temperatures or the size of clothing (among other things) that needs to be converted to U.S. standards.
- Real time information to track either a commercial flight or private aircraft.
- Legal description of the GPS coordinates and/or image of a house in question.
- A satellite image of a given location.
- The need to convert a digital video so it can be viewed on a law enforcement computer.
- The need to identify relatives of an intelligence target.

[141] www.infoworld.com/article/07/07/31/Symantec-Dark-Vision-mines-sites_1.html

These requirements, and much more, can be found in an eclectic array of web-based open sources. (See Chapter Annex 11-1 for the descriptions and locations of these web sites.)

The point of note is simple: One of the important values of online open sources is easy access to information that is unique yet critical to a comprehensive analysis.

Homeland Security Intelligence and Open Sources

Beyond enforcing the criminal law, America's law enforcement agencies have a wide range of well-established responsibilities related to public safety and order maintenance. Whenever there is a natural disaster, such as a flood, tornado, or hurricane, law enforcement has the responsibility to aid in the rescue and recovery of victims, protect unharmed citizens from injury and protect property. Similarly, in a catastrophe, such as the crash of an airliner or the collapse of a building or a public health emergency, law enforcement agencies have historically had significant responsibilities for public safety and order maintenance.

With the creation of new national initiatives related to homeland security after 9/11, many of these public safety responsibilities have become more structured. Particularly with the growth of intelligence fusion centers that have an operating philosophy of all crimes, all hazards and all threats, a new form of noncriminal intelligence has emerged: homeland security intelligence.

It should be reinforced that intelligence is based on prevention and is inherently a pre-incident function; whether that incident is criminal or all hazards/noncriminal. To reiterate, homeland security intelligence may be defined as "the analytic output of raw information that describes noncriminal threats to critical infrastructure, public health or community safety." Law enforcement needs to obtain a wide range of information to effectively prepare for homeland security threats identified through analysis. Open sources can be particularly valuable to aid in the intelligence process and to understand the characteristics and threats posed by pandemic flu, hazardous materials, or other direct or incidental threats posed by a homeland security emergency.

A wide range of information related to hazardous materials may be found at Environmental Chemistry;[142] information on threats to public health can be obtained from the Centers for Disease Control;[143] and a wide range of diverse useful information is available from a collection of online searchable databases provided by the National Center for Biotechnology Information of the National Institutes of Health.[144]

The broad range of homeland security threats is too exhaustive for a comprehensive discussion. The point to note is essentially this: Since the responsibility for homeland security intelligence has become a part of the law enforcement intelligence process, particularly at the state fusion center level, analysts and information collectors should aggressively use open sources as the first step in collecting this critical information.

[142] www.environmentalchemistry.com

[143] www.cdc.gov

[144] www.ncbi.nlm.nih.gov/sites/gquery

Open Source Processes and Protocols

A number of tools and techniques may be relied on to make the open source collection process more productive as well as to enhance the quality of information. The following discussion is a primer for insights into the process.

Using an Open Source Collection Plan

As anyone knows who has browsed the Internet, the ability to search diverse information and travel down an unanticipated path of hyperlinks can easily draw one away from their original line of inquiry into an area of often interesting but frequently irrelevant information. From an intelligence perspective, this is unproductive and risks the collection of unneeded and sometimes distracting information. The user is urged to develop an open source collection plan when using networking to seek open source information.

A collection plan is essentially a research methodology that seeks to focus the open source information collection process. Rather than relying on a dragnet approach, the collection plan focuses on source searching that is defined by specifically identified agenda items, such as the following:

- Intelligence requirements
- Research an identified emerging threat issue
- Identifying information in support of tips and leads that have been received
- Research information about a known local threat to determine its presence and effects in other geographical areas
- Research diverse and creative tactics for managing threats
- Gain a body of information about a specific intelligence target
- Gain knowledge about the current and changing nature of threat conditions in your region.

The plan should include the following:

- Specific types of information needed (i.e., names, locations, characteristics, or indicators of the threat or criminal behavior, signs and symbols of the threat, effects of the threat).
- Identification of the sources where the specified information is most likely to reside.
- Critical information associated with a given threat (e.g., methods, geography, modus operandi, and so forth).
- Logistical information associated with threats.
- Materiel used in the commission of a crime or terrorist act and how that materiel is used.
- Unique characteristics related to the intelligence target (i.e., important dates, times, symbolism, and so forth).

The significant point to note is that open source information collection through networking can be of the greatest utility when it has a specifically directed agenda.[145]

[145] See Chapter Annex 11-1 for a series of questions and methodology to help form a precise search plan.

Techniques and Tools

Perhaps the most important foundation skill to develop for any type of networking environment is to become adept at searching. The most common approach is to open one's search engine of choice and use the default search utility for the information that is needed. Some successes are achieved with this method, but the results often can provide a large quantity of related information that often lacks the specificity needed. Narrowing the search can be more productive in seeking the information that is needed. The first step is to develop a pre-search plan to focus on search requirements (See Chapter Annex 11-2). Beyond this plan, here are some tips for narrowing the search:

- Understand the culture of the intelligence target to both identify and accurately interpret relevant information. With a clear understanding of the culture of the target or the information that is being sought, a wider array of search terms and phrases can be developed. Moreover, narrowing the terms may assist in defining the sources or search engine to use.

- Based on the cultural assessment, carefully define the types of information that is being sought. To do this, rely on the concept of being collectively exhaustive; that is, make an attempt to search all derivative terms that describe the data or phenomenon being sought in the search.

- Once the information is defined, dissect it to develop alternative terms, synonyms, jargon, symbols, abbreviations, and alternative spellings.

- Examine different formats of the information being sought. For example, if searching for the name John Alexander Doe, the search should take several forms, such as:

  - John Doe
  - J Alexander Doe
  - J. Doe
  - J. Doe
  - Johnny Doe
  - Alexander Doe
  - J.A. Doe
  - J. "Alex" Doe

This is particularly important for deep web searches.

- Specialty search engines[146] can help focus a search by limiting searches to explicitly defined areas. Using a search engine that focuses only on news web sites[147] can pick up useful information from trends in terrorism or crime to the names of individuals or organizations that may be associated with threats. Moreover, news web sites often make an assessment of the quality of information easier than many other sites.

- Language translation from multiple languages to English is increasingly available at no charge online. These sites typically will permit the entry of text for translation or entry of a web site address to translate the information contained in the URL.

National Virtual Translation Center

Building on this last point, when foreign language translations are necessary, the National Virtual Translation Center[148] (NVTC) may be an additional resource to explore. Established by Congress in 2003, the NVTC role is to provide timely and accurate translations of diverse raw information for all elements of the Intelligence Community. A virtual workplace, NVTC personnel and linguists are located throughout the United States and connect through various networks with the NVTC program office in Washington, D.C. As a member of the Intelligence Community, the NVTC is part of the ISE and, therefore, may become a resource

[146] A wide variety of general and specialty Internet search engines can be found at www.searchengineguide.com/searchengines.html.

[147] An example is NewsDirectory at www.newsdirectory.com.

[148] www.nvtc.gov

for SLTLE, and particularly fusion centers, on inquiries that may coincide with Intelligence Community concerns. SLTLE agencies should work with their FBI or DHS fusion center partners to secure assistance with the fee-based NVTC.

The Need to Determine Accuracy, Reliability, and Validity

As is the case with any information collected for the Intelligence Process, it is essential to evaluate the accuracy of facts, the reliability of the source of information and validity of the information's content. These concepts are the same as for any type of information in the Intelligence Process:

- *Accuracy:* The information is true and may be corroborated.

- *Source Reliability:* The source of the information is dependable for providing accurate information.

- *Information Validity:* The information actually depicts or portrays what it purports.

A good method for measuring these standards in open sources is to seek multisource reporting of information for validity. It is important to ensure that multisource reporting is not merely repetitive reporting; for example, *USAToday*, CNN, Fox News, and MSNBC may report the same news story. If all of these news outlets are simply reporting the same facts derived solely from an Associated Press story, then this is not multisource validity. This is referred to as the echo chamber, which is described as follows:

> …a group of media outlets that tend to parrot each other's uncritical reports on the views of a single source, or that otherwise relies on unquestioning repetition of official sources.[149]

In the example above, if each network reports the Associated Press story and independently confirms it relying on its own reporters, then this is multisource validation. A useful tool for assessing validity and reliability can also be found online through web sites such as Truth or Fiction,[150] About.com: Urban Legends,[151] or Snopes.[152] These web sites contain surprisingly comprehensive and well-sourced information about rumors, legends, and information that has been quoted as fact. The web sites typically describe the veracity of the story, with some form of explanation.

Web content is bursting with hyperbole, innuendo, and false information. One must be diligent to ensure that collected information is accurate, reliable, and valid.[153]

[149] www.sourcewatch.org/index. php?title=Echo_chamber

[150] www.truthorfiction.com

[151] urbanlegends.about.com

[152] www.snopes.com

[153] For a comprehensive discussion of reliability, particularly as related to the web and open source information, see sourcesandmethods.blogspot. com/2008/10/how-to-determining-source-reliability.html.

Avoiding Traffic Analysis: Becoming Anonymous on the Web

Online intelligence and investigation procedures should mask the Internet Protocol (IP) address of the computer being used. This can easily be accomplished in two ways. One way is simply to have a stand-alone computer that is generically registered using a false identity with an Internet Service Provider (ISP).[154] The computer should not be connected to any other network and not used for personal activities, such as accessing accounts requiring a user name and password.

Another method is to use a proxy server that will mask the IP address of the computer being used.[155] There are commercial enterprises that will provide this service for a fee, such as Anonymizer[156] or The Cloak.[157] There are also free methods such as using a free proxy web site as found on Proxify[158] or ProxyIndex.[159] Another method is to identify anonymous server IP addresses and insert the IP number and port number into the proxy server option in your web browser. The process is actually quite simple. First go to a web site that lists proxy servers, such as Public Proxy Servers,[160] and select a server from the list. In your Internet browser, go to the proxy settings dialog box. In Microsoft Internet Explorer[161] (IE), the path is usually the following:

Tools > Internet Options > Connections > LAN Settings

In LAN settings, check the proxy server box and enter the IP address and port number (both will be on the proxy server list). Figure 11-1 illustrates how a proxy server from the Russian Federation (highlighted at the bottom of the image) was entered into the proxy server option in Microsoft IE.

The reason that the IP address should be masked is because tools are available on the Internet to trace domain names, IP addresses, connection routes, e-mail addresses, general geographic locations of the computer, and other electronic transaction information. These tools can also be used effectively by law enforcement and can be found at such web sites as DomainTools,[162] Better-WhoIs,[163] and Geektools.[164] It should be noted that different WhoIs web sites will have different databases to search and multiple sources may need to be used. If, however, the IP being searched for has been cleaned through a proxy server, the WhoIs search will not be fruitful.

Finally, the computer's cookies and Internet cache should be cleaned regularly. This will help ensure anonymity, particularly in light of the inevitable fact that someone will use the computer for personal business. While cookies and the cache can be cleaned manually, the most effective way is to use software designed for that purpose.[165]

[154]This is sometimes referred to as a "hello computer" much like and generically registered "hello telephone" used in law enforcement undercover operations.

[155]To maximize safety, use a proxy server even on a hello computer.

[156]www.anonymizer.com

[157]www.the-cloak.com/pay-terms

[158]www.proxify.com

[159]www.proxyindex.com

[160]www.publicproxyservers.com

[161]The path to LAN settings may differ somewhat between versions of IE. Other Internet browsers such as Netscape and Firefox, will have a similar ability to create a proxy server.

[162]whois.domaintools.com

[163]www.betterwhois.com

[164]www.geektools.com

[165]Effective software is available at no charge on the Internet for cleaning cookies and the cache. See a discussion of cookies, caches, avoiding spyware, maintaining your computer's registry, recommendations for software, and additional useful information at the nonprofit site www.instant-registry-fixes.org.

Figure 11-1: Example of Entering Proxy Server in MS Explorer

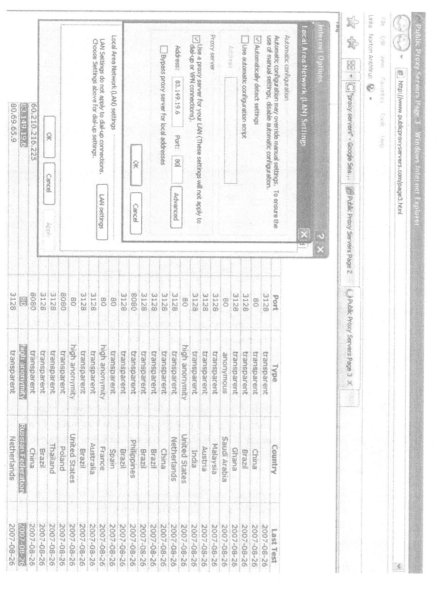

Port	Type	Country	Last Test
3128	transparent	China	2007-08-26
80	transparent	China	2007-08-26
3128	transparent	Brazil	2007-08-26
3128	transparent	Ghana	2007-08-26
80	anonymous	Saudi Arabia	2007-08-26
3128	transparent	Malaysia	2007-08-26
3128	transparent	Austria	2007-08-26
3128	transparent	India	2007-08-26
80	high anonymity	United States	2007-08-26
3128	transparent	Netherlands	2007-08-26
3128	transparent	China	2007-08-26
3128	transparent	Brazil	2007-08-26
3128	transparent	Brazil	2007-08-26
8080	transparent	Philippines	2007-08-26
3128	transparent	Brazil	2007-08-26
80	transparent	Spain	2007-08-26
80	high anonymity	France	2007-08-26
3128	transparent	Australia	2007-08-26
80	high anonymity	United States	2007-08-26
8080	transparent	Poland	2007-08-26
3128	transparent	Thailand	2007-08-26
3128	transparent	Brazil	2007-08-26
8080	transparent	China	2007-08-26
80	anonymous	Russian Federation	2007-08-26
3128	transparent	Netherlands	2007-08-26

The Investment in Critical Thought and Time

Despite the ease and speed of the Internet, two of the most important open
source tools are critical thought and time. Both are needed to define search terms
and phrases, develop the collection plan, identify critical information needed in
an inquiry verify the information, and interpret it. Often, this information will lead
to other sources and critical thought is needed to dissect the additional source
alternatives, weighing the value of each, and moving the search and collection
processes forward.

The process can be laborious, particularly as one sifts through diverse blogs.
Reading, consuming, interpreting, and collecting important information from
the overwhelming quantity of information is labor-intensive, but valuable for
discovering information that can be essential in identifying and preventing
threats.

Information collectors and analysts must have the wherewithal to push the
process forward, particularly during searches that seem to be unproductive.
Managers and administrators must develop the patience to understand these
unique performance characteristics when evaluating personnel.

Conclusion

This discussion was an overview of the open source concept, the current
philosophy and application of open source information as part of the National
Open Source Enterprise, the role of open sources in law enforcement intelligence,
and a primer on the use of open source techniques and tools for the intelligence
process. The web sites listed in this discussion are intended to serve as illustrations
and are not meant to be a comprehensive list nor an endorsement of any
particular commercial or open application. They were accurate at the time of
publication of this *Guide*.

As the source of first resort, open source information and intelligence provides
tremendous potential for law enforcement that should be exploited to increase
the efficiency and effectiveness of the intelligence function.

Chapter Annex 11-1: Eclectic Web Sites Sometimes Found Useful for Intelligence

The Intelligence Process sometimes needs information that intuitively would not seem to be part of a law enforcement inquiry. The sites can be accessed at no charge.

- According to the National Counterterrorism Center definition, terrorism occurs when groups or individuals acting on political motivation deliberately or recklessly attack civilians/noncombatants or their property and the attack does not fall into another special category of political violence, such as crime, rioting, or tribal violence. The incidents may be tracked on the Worldwide Incidents Tracking System: wits.nctc.gov.

- The Geographic Names Information System (GNIS), developed by the U.S. Geological Survey in cooperation with the U.S. Board on Geographic Names, contains information about physical and cultural geographic features in the United States and associated areas, both current and historical (not including roads and highways). The database holds the federally recognized name of each feature and defines the location of the feature by state, county, USGS topographic map, and geographic coordinates: nhd.usgs.gov/gnis.html.

- The National Geospatial-Intelligence Agency (NGA) GEOnet Names Server (GNS) provides access to the National Geospatial-Intelligence Agency's (NGA) and the U.S. Board on Geographic Names' (US BGN) database of foreign geographic feature names. The database is the official repository of foreign place-name decisions approved by the US BGN: earth-info.nga.mil/gns/html/index.html.

- The Statistical Abstract of the United States is the authoritative and comprehensive summary of statistics on the social, political, and economic organization of the United States. Sources of data include the Census Bureau, Bureau of Labor Statistics, Bureau of Economic Analysis, and many other federal agencies and private organizations: www.census.gov/compendia/statab.

- The U.S. Census Bureau FactFinder user can obtain comprehensive population, housing, economic, and geographic data in the form of maps, tables, and reports from a variety of Census Bureau sources: factfinder.census.gov.

- Sometimes simple information is needed:
    - The geographic location of an area code: www.areadecoder.com.
    - Social Security numbering scheme: www.ssa.gov/history/ssn/geocard.html.
    - Geographic, social, and economic information about a ZIP Code: www.zipskinny.com.
    - The definition of a word: thesaurus.reference.com.

- A Librarians Internet Index is comprehensive portal of links to web sites on virtually every topic. The unique aspect of this portal is that the web sites which have direct links have been reviewed as being trustworthy sites: www.lii.org.

- The How Stuff Works web site covers a very wide array of topics and explains the components and processes that make the topic functional: www.howstuffworks.com.

- Significant weather events always hold the potential for law enforcement activity. Two good and slightly different sources for weather are:
  - National Weather Service www.nws.noaa.gov.
  - The Weather Channel www.weather.com.
- At times there is a need to convert U.S. dollars to a foreign currency or vice versa. To do this easily at current rates, use the FX Currency Converter: www.oanda.com/convert/classic.
- The need to convert information in a variety of ways often becomes essential, but difficult. Online Conversion has made it simply by providing conversion calculators for length, temperature, speed, volume, weight, cooking, area, fuel economy, clothing, area, angles, frequency, distance, and much more: www.onlineconversion.com.
- Real time tracking of both commercial and private flights: www.flightware.com.
- Scalable satellite imagery can be used to see the layout of a target location (different sites will provide slightly different satellite images):
  - TerraServer www.terraserver.com.
  - Google Maps maps.google.com.
  - Digital Globe www.digitalglobe.com.
- Cyberhomes provides images and/or aerial views and maps of property throughout the U.S., GPS location, legal description of the property, and other information: www.cyberhomes.com.
- Genealogy web sites have become very popular as people seek to learn more about their family tree. Many of these web sites have a surprisingly wide range of information useful for law enforcement: www.ancestry.com.
- In some instances, information such as images, audio, video, word processing, etc., that are in a different format that cannot be opened on the law enforcement computer. These files can be converted online to a different format so they can be opened on your computer at: www.media-convert.com.
- Voicemail menus can often be frustrating, particularly when one needs to talk with a person. The Get Human web site identifies the shortcut codes in a large number of voicemail systems to avoid voice mail prompts and to reach a person: www.gethuman.com.
- A wide range of unique information searches: www.blackbookonline.info.
- Junk science is faulty scientific data and analysis used to advance special and, often, hidden agendas. Junk science is debunked at: www.junkscience.com.
- A guide to medical quackery and health fraud: www.quackwatch.com.

Chapter Annex 11-2: The Pre-Search Development Plan

The Pre-Search Development Plan[154]

1. What unique words, distinctive names, abbreviations, or acronyms are associated with your topic?

   The value of starting with these search elements is that they help define your search parameters. Be certain to include synonyms and professional terminology.

2. Can you think of societies, organizations, or groups that might have information on your subject on their pages?

   Search these as a "phrase in quotes," looking for a home page that might contain links to other pages, journals, discussion groups, or databases on your subject. You may require the phrase in quotes to be in the documents' titles by preceding it by title:[no space]

3. What other words are likely to be in any web documents on your topic?

   You may want to require these by joining them with AND or preceding each by +[no space].

4. Do any of the words in 1, 2, or 3 belong in phrases or strings, together in a certain order, like a cliché?

   Search these as a "phrase in quotes". (e.g., "world jihad" or "Aryan nation").

5. For any of the terms in #4, can you think of synonyms, variant spellings, or equivalent terms you would also accept in relevant documents?

   You may want to allow these terms by joining them by OR and including each set of equivalent terms in ( ). As an example of synonyms: "terrorists" and "jihadis". As an example of alternate spellings: "Osama" and "Usama".

6. Can you think of any extraneous or irrelevant documents these words might pick up?

   You may want to exclude terms or phrases with -[no space] before each term, or and not

7. What broader terms could your topic be covered by?

   When browsing subject categories or searching sites of webliographies or databases on your topic, try broader categories.

[154] Adapted from the Regents of the University of California. Copyright 2004 All Rights Reserved. Created by Joe Barker, Teaching Library, UC Berkeley.

Chapter 12:
Federal and National Law Enforcement Intelligence Resources, Networks, and Systems

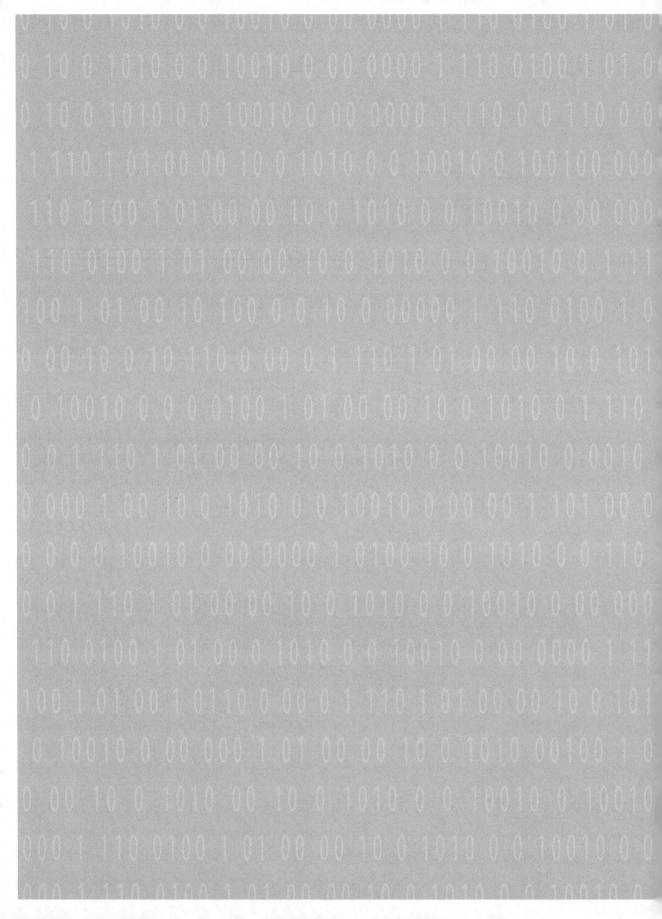

Federal and National Law Enforcement Intelligence Resources, Networks, and Systems

Legislation, mission-related responsibilities of federal agencies, and the need to develop programs and products that have interstate utility have led a wide variety of federal agencies to develop resources and systems that support law enforcement intelligence at the state, local, and tribal levels. Some resources are designed to meet specific needs, such as financial crimes investigations, while others are intended to support broad law enforcement needs, such as the FBI's Law Enforcement Online (LEO). Although in most cases, the resources are provided by a federal agency, some resources are national, but are provided by an entity other than the federal government. The value of these diverse resources and systems to state, local, and tribal law enforcement (SLTLE) will vary according to agency size, geographic location in the U.S., and unique crime problems facing a jurisdiction.

This chapter identifies the various resources, giving the greatest attention to those that have the most value for the broadest range of law enforcement agencies. Unlike previous chapters which sought to provide a discussion of integrated issues surrounding the chapter's topical theme, this chapter is more like a catalog. The goal is to identify the most relevant resources for SLTLE and provide insight into what the resources or systems can provide to a law enforcement agency.

Many resources are also available at the state and local levels, but there was no attempt to document them because of their limited national applicability and the volume of information involved. In some instances, the chapter discusses specific state resources for the purpose of illustration. Information about law enforcement intelligence resources within each state can be found at these sources:

1. *National Criminal Intelligence Resource Center* (NCIRC) operated by the Bureau of Justice Assistance, U.S. Department of Justice.[1]

2. Fusion Center Technical Assistance Program of the Lessons Learned Information Sharing (LLIS) online information system operated by the U.S. Department of Homeland Security (DHS).[2]

As will be seen, there is some overlap between resources and systems; nonetheless, exploring the materials in the following pages should provide valuable direction for the law enforcement intelligence consumer.

[1] The public side of this resource is at www. ncirc.gov. The public NCIRC site has a limited amount of information; however, it provides access to the Criminal Intelligence Master Training Calendar. The greatest value of this site is on the secure side of NCIRC that is accessible through the RISS.NET portal and LEO.

[2] Users must first register for access to this web site at www.llis.dhs.gov. After registering, the user must e-mail a request for access to the Fusion Center Technical Assistance Program channel on LLIS.

What Is Needed to Start?

From a basic perspective, certain fundamental elements need to be in place to enable access to, and use many of, these resources and systems.

- Access to the Internet through a security controlled computer(s) designated exclusively for law enforcement use (excluding undercover computers).
- The computer should have a firewall and virus and spyware protections.
- A privacy policy must be in place that is consistent with the federal privacy guidelines.[3]
- A security policy should be in place that is consistent with the Global Justice Information-Sharing Initiative security policy.[4]
- An additional fair use operating policy for the agency's law enforcement computers may be implemented describing both accepted and prohibited use of the law enforcement agency's computers.
- Supervisory accountability should be in place to monitor and supervise access to systems and resources.

Most systems that a user will access will have additional requirements, but they are simply the minimum requirements needed before gaining access to systems and resources.

Federal and National Law Enforcement Intelligence Resources

Many federal agencies have reengineered their intelligence function since 9/11 to make their intelligence products more accessible and useful to SLTLE. Intelligence products have been redesigned or new products developed, dissemination methods have been revised, greater attention has been given to providing critical information that is unclassified for wide consumption by SLTLE, and new offices and initiatives have been developed. More information is being produced and disseminated more widely than in the history of law enforcement. Among the challenges that law enforcement now faces is accessing the needed information and using it with efficacy.

Many federal intelligence resources are in a dynamic state responding to changes in threats as well as changes in policy. It is virtually impossible to provide an exhaustive discussion of them all. This discussion, therefore, will identify the federal intelligence resources that are of greatest use to SLTLE, their intelligence products, and the agencies' contact or access information. In addition, a broader discussion of the FBI than of other agencies will be provided because of the comparatively more frequent interaction on intelligence matters between SLTLE and the FBI.

While federal agencies have attempted to provide more unclassified information to America's law enforcement agencies, a significant amount of classified information remains relating to terrorism. The FBI and the DHS, therefore, have made a commitment to increase security clearances for SLTLE officers. Despite this, controversies and questions remain. Dealing with the issue of classified and sensitive information is the first place to start when discussing federal information sharing.

[3] it.ojp.gov/default.aspx?area=globalJustice&page=1151

[4] it.ojp.gov/global

When dealing with classified information, the following terms and concepts are often used as related to SLTLE:

Tear Line or Tear Line Report: The place on an intelligence report (usually denoted by a series of dashes) at which the sanitized version of a more highly classified and/or controlled report begins. The sanitized information below the tear line should contain the substance of the information above the tear line, but without identifying the sensitive sources and methods. This will permit wider dissemination of the information below the tear line, in accordance with the right-to-know and need-to-know principles.

Write for Release (Write for the Consumer): Preparing intelligence reports and products at the unclassified level to the greatest extent possible or using tear line reporting to facilitate the dissemination of releasable information to individuals who do not have a clearance.

Markings. Classified Information and information that has been declassified have an explicit set of comprehensive rules for the proper marking of documents to ensure notice is given about classification and safeguarding. The extensive set of markings guidelines are available from the Office of the Director of National Intelligence in the document entitled *Authorized Classification and Control Markings Register* (available on the Office of the Director of National Intelligence (ODNI) web site in the "Electronic Reading Room" at www.dni.gov/electronic_reading_room.htm).

Sources and Methods: This refers to how information was obtained. "Sources" refers to from whom or where the information was collected (for example, a confidential informant) and "methods" refers to the means used to collect the information (for example, an electronic intercept).

Classified Information

A mystique often surrounds classified information, leading most people to ask, "That's it?" after seeing a collection of classified documents. While a number of explicit elements are required for information to be classified, often the distinction between classified and unclassified information with respect to the law enforcement community is that the classified information contains information about the sources and methods used in the collection of information. Extensive rules and processes are associated with all aspects of classified information. The following discussion addresses only the fundamental issues of classification that are most pertinent to enabling law enforcement intelligence personnel to understand the process.

Some of the rules governing classified information are unique to the specific mission of some federal agencies, their responsibilities, and the types of information they collect and retain. The current discussion is limited to issues and questions that typically arise about classified information specifically related to how SLTLE agencies will most typically interact with the classified information environment.

Table 12-1: Information Categories for Classified Information[5]

Information To Be Classified Must Fall within One or More of the Following Prescribed Categories:
• Military plans, weapons systems, or operations
• Foreign government information
• Intelligence activities (including special activities), intelligence sources or methods, or cryptology
• Foreign relations or foreign activities of the United States, including confidential sources
• Scientific, technological, or economic matters relating to the national security, which includes defense against transnational terrorism
• United States Government programs for safeguarding nuclear materials or facilities
• Vulnerabilities or capabilities of systems, installations, infrastructures, projects, plans, or protection services relating to the national security, which includes defense against transnational terrorism
• Weapons of mass destruction.

The federal agency responsible for managing the classified information environment is the Information Security Oversight Office[6] (ISOO) of the National Archives and Records Administration (NARA). The ISOO is responsible to the President for policy and oversight of the government-wide security classification system and the National Industrial Security Program. The ISOO receives its authority from *Executive Order 12958, Classified National Security Information*[7] and *Executive Order 12829, National Industrial Security Program.*[8]

The classified information environment is highly controlled. Certain explicit categories of information are subject to classification (see Table 12-1), while other categories of information are subject to prohibitions or limitations concerning classification (see Table 12-2). Despite these regulations, antisecrecy advocates,[9] law enforcement officials, and members of Congress,[10] among others, have expressed concerns that the federal government tends to over classify too much information. Suffice it to note for the current discussion that the debate on over-classification between federal law enforcement and SLTLE is often heated.

[5] www.archives.gov/isoo/pdf/appropriate-classification.pdf

[6] www.archives.gov/isoo

[7] www.archives.gov/isoo/policy-documents/eo-12958-amendment.html

[8] www.archives.gov/isoo/policy-documents/eo-12829.html

[9] See, for example, www.fas.org/blog/secrecy/2007/12/classification_reform_bill_int.html.

[10] For example, in the 110th Session of the United States Congress, Rep. Jane Harmon introduced H.R. 4806 "To require the Secretary of Homeland Security to develop a strategy to prevent the over-classification of homeland security and other information and to promote the sharing of unclassified homeland security and other information, and for other purposes."

Table 12-2: Information Categories Prohibited or Limited for Classification[11]

Information That Is Subject to Prohibitions or Limitations with Respect to Classification:

- Is the information classified to conceal violations of law, inefficiency, or administrative error?
- Is the information classified to prevent embarrassment to a person, organization, or agency?
- Is the information classified to restrain competition?
- Is the information classified to prevent or delay the release of information that does not require protection in the interest of national security?
- Does the information relate to basic scientific research not clearly related to national security?
- If the information had been declassified, released to the public under proper authority, and then reclassified:
  » Was the reclassification action taken under the personal authority of the agency head or deputy agency head based on his or her determination that the reclassification was necessary in the interest of the national security?
  » Was that official's determination in writing?
  » Was the information reasonably recoverable?
  » Was the Director of the Information Security Oversight Office notified of the reclassification action?
- If the information had not previously been disclosed to the public under proper authority but was classified or reclassified after receipt of an access request:
  » Does the classification meet the requirements of this order (to include the other elements of this methodology)?
  » Was it accomplished on a document-by-document basis with the personal participation or under the direction of the agency head, the deputy agency head, or the senior agency official?
- If the classification decision addresses items of information that are individually unclassified but have been classified by compilation or aggregation:
  » Does the compilation reveal an additional association or relationship that meets the standards for classification under this order?
  » Was such a determination made by an Original Classification Authority in accordance with the other elements of this methodology?
  » Is the additional association or relationship not otherwise revealed in the individual items of information?

[11] www.archives.gov/isoo/policy-documents/eo-12829.html

According to Executive Order 12958,[12] information at the federal level may be classified at one of three levels:

1. "Top Secret" shall be applied to information, the unauthorized disclosure of which reasonably could be expected to cause exceptionally grave damage to the national security that the original classification authority is able to identify or describe.

2. "Secret" shall be applied to information, the unauthorized disclosure of which reasonably could be expected to cause serious damage to the national security that the original classification authority is able to identify or describe.

3. "Confidential" shall be applied to information, the unauthorized disclosure of which reasonably could be expected to cause damage to the national security that the original classification authority is able to identify or describe.

Classified Information, including computers that contain classified information or are connected to a classified information system, must be located in a Sensitive Compartmented Information Facility (SCIF). A SCIF is an accredited area, room, group of rooms, or installation where Sensitive Compartmented Information (SCI) may be stored, used, discussed, and/or electronically processed. SCIF procedural and physical measures, which are explicitly stipulated in federal government regulations, prevent free access to persons unless they have been authorized with an appropriate security clearance.

Security Clearances for SLTLE Personnel

Before an individual is given access to classified information, he or she must have the appropriate clearance level. Beyond the clearance levels of Top Secret, Secret, and Confidential, "highly sensitive programs" require a clearance addendum to the Top Secret clearance, such as SCI, Special Access Programs, Q Clearances, and other similar programs. Beyond the clearance levels and special conditions that establish a person's right to know, an individual must also have the need to know the classified information. Just because a law enforcement employee has a security clearance does not mean that he or she will be given broad access to classified information.

Beyond access to classified information, security clearances are also often required for access to certain facilities. Employees working in a SCIF must have at least a Secret clearance. Similarly, certain intelligence training programs require people to have clearance before attending the training, either because of the location for the training (i.e., in a secured facility) or content of the training.

A number of federal agencies can authorize clearances. The process begins with the applicant completing a comprehensive questionnaire—Form SF-86 Questionnaire for National Security Positions[13]—wherein he or she must provide extensive information about his or her personal background. The information is used by the federal agency to conduct a comprehensive personal security investigation. Fingerprints must also be submitted and privacy waivers signed. Following the investigation, the findings are adjudicated by a separate body that determines whether to issue a clearance. The adjudication process is an administrative examination of a sufficient period of a person's life to make an

[12] www.archives.gov/isoo/policy-documents/eo-12958-amendment.html amends a previous Executive Order on classified information.

[13] Form SF-86 is available as a form which may be filled out on the computer from the General Services Administration at www.opm.gov/Forms/pdf_fill/sf86.pdf. Applicants should check with the agency from which they are seeking the clearance for special instructions; for example, the SF-86 asks for the applicant's employment history during the past 7 years, while other agencies request the employment history for the past 10 years.

affirmative determination that the individual, based on his or her past behavior and associations, is eligible for a security clearance. The process is the careful weighing of a number of variables. In particular, a person's conduct is reviewed to make a determination that he or she has high integrity and is reliable and trustworthy. When questionable conduct is identified, the adjudication will consider the following factors:

- The nature, extent, and seriousness of the conduct
- The circumstances surrounding the conduct, including knowledgeable participation
- The frequency and how recent the conduct occurred
- The individual's age and maturity at the time of the conduct
- The voluntariness of participation
- The presence or absence of rehabilitation and other pertinent behavioral changes
- The motivation for the conduct
- The potential for pressure, coercion, exploitation, or duress
- The likelihood that the conduct will continue or recur.

The factors are balanced to determine if the clearance should be granted. Once a clearance is issued, the applicant must be briefed on the regulations associated with the clearance and sign a nondisclosure agreement.[14]

As noted previously, different agencies issue clearances, with some variability in processes. The most common clearances for SLTLE are from the FBI and the DHS. The clearance process is labor-intensive and expensive. For these reasons, as well as some operations security concerns, there must be a substantial reason for issuing a clearance to an SLTLE employee. Moreover, conducting an excess number of clearance investigations slows the process, thereby taking longer to process clearances for those persons who may be in more critical positions. Not all SLTLE requests for clearances will be honored by the federal agency.

In most cases, the FBI will begin consideration of a clearance investigation for an SLTLE officer by examining local issues on a case-by-case basis[15] (See Figure 12-1 for the steps in the FBI process.). For those who seek to apply for a security clearance, the appropriate forms and fingerprint cards can be obtained from the local FBI Field Office.

[14] The general nondisclosure agreement can be found at contacts.gsa.gov/webforms.nsf/0/03A78F16A52271678525 6A69004E23F6/$file/SF312.pdf.

[15] The FBI provides the following guidance: Most information needed by state or local law enforcement can be shared at an unclassified level. In those instances where it is necessary to share classified information, it can usually be accomplished at the Secret level. Local FBI Field Offices can help determine whether a security clearance is needed, and if so, what level is appropriate.

Figure 12-1: Steps in the FBI Security Clearance Process for SLTLE Personnel[16]

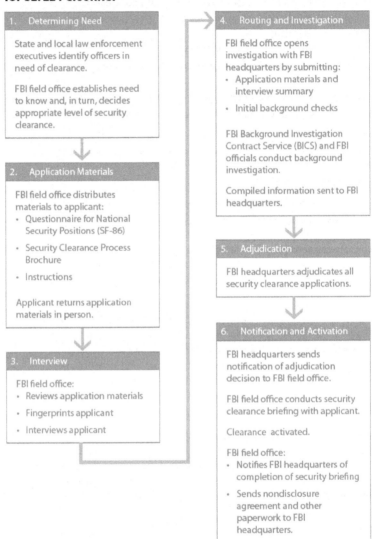

1. **Determining Need**

State and local law enforcement executives identify officers in need of clearance.

FBI field office establishes need to know and, in turn, decides appropriate level of security clearance.

2. **Application Materials**

FBI field office distributes materials to applicant:
- Questionnaire for National Security Positions (SF-86)
- Security Clearance Process Brochure
- Instructions

Applicant returns application materials in person.

3. **Interview**

FBI field office:
- Reviews application materials
- Fingerprints applicant
- Interviews applicant

4. **Routing and Investigation**

FBI field office opens investigation with FBI headquarters by submitting:
- Application materials and interview summary
- Initial background checks

FBI Background Investigation Contract Service (BICS) and FBI officials conduct background investigation.

Compiled information sent to FBI headquarters.

5. **Adjudication**

FBI headquarters adjudicates all security clearance applications.

6. **Notification and Activation**

FBI headquarters sends notification of adjudication decision to FBI field office.

FBI field office conducts security clearance briefing with applicant.

Clearance activated.

FBI field office:
- Notifies FBI headquarters of completion of security briefing
- Sends nondisclosure agreement and other paperwork to FBI headquarters.

Sensitive but Unclassified and Controlled Unclassified Information

Dissemination refers to the types of information about threats, suspects, and indicators of criminality that a law enforcement agency or government entity wants to purposely share. Because of the sensitivity of the information, controls are put in place to protect the information and prevent inadvertent information sharing with persons who do not have the right to know and need to know.

[16] From: U.S. General Accounting Office. *Security Clearances.* GAO-04-596. Washington, D.C.: U.S. General Accounting Office, 2004, p. 8.

The management of information that is deemed sensitive but does not meet the requirements for classification is going through a significant change process at this writing. The changes are predicated on new initiatives of the Information Sharing Environment (ISE) to be compliant with provisions of the Intelligence Reform and Terrorism Prevention Act of 2004. Because a multiyear transition process is in place transitioning Sensitive But Unclassified (SBU) to Controlled Unclassified Information (CUI), this chapter discuss both.

Sensitive but Unclassified Information

It is not feasible for every law enforcement officer to have a security clearance and not all information meets the standards for classification. A mechanism exists to get critical information into the hands of officers that does not involve the classified information framework. The traditional approach has been to use markings designating the information as SBU. A wide variety of SBU labels are placed on intelligence products and other information by the originator of the information to indicate that the information should not be shared broadly and that dissemination should be limited only to those indicated by the SBU label.

There are no national standards or guidelines for SBU information; rather, each agency has developed its own policies and procedures to identify and safeguard SBU information. Generally, this unclassified information is withheld from the public for a variety of reasons, but has to be accessible to law enforcement, private security, or other persons who have a responsibility to safeguard the public. Agencies have discretion to define SBU in ways that serve their particular needs to safeguard information. Since there is no uniformity in implementing rules throughout the federal government on the use of SBU, the specific meanings of the markings are often unclear.[17] There have been even fewer efforts to define and safeguard the information at the state, local, and tribal levels. There is an intuitive understanding, but no formal process to control the information. Some guidance has been provided by the DHS, which issued a directive in 2004 on "For Official Use Only" information.

For Official Use Only Information

The For Official Use Only (FOUO) label is used within the DHS "…to identify unclassified information of a sensitive nature, not otherwise categorized by statute or regulation, the unauthorized disclosure of which could have an adverse impact on a person's privacy or welfare, the conduct of a federal program, or other programs or operations essential to the national interest."[18] FOUO is not classified information, but information that should be distributed only to persons who need to know the information to be aware of conditions that will help keep the United States and local communities secure. Within DHS, the caveat For Official Use Only will be used to identify SBU information that is not otherwise governed by statue or regulation. In sum, FOUO information may be shared with anyone who has the right to know and need to know the information in the report or product.

Law Enforcement Sensitive Information

The second most common SBU label is Law Enforcement Sensitive (LES). It is more restrictive than FOUO because it limited dissemination to anyone in the

[17] For a detailed review of the SBU meaning and how it is defined and used by different statutes and regulations, see: Knezo, Genevieve J. "*Sensitive But Unclassified*" and *Other Controls: Policy and Options for Scientific and Technical Information*. Washington, D.C.: Congressional Research Service, 2006.

[18] U.S. Department of Homeland Security, Management Directive System, MD Number: 11042, *Safeguarding Sensitive But Unclassified (For Official Use Only) Information*. May 11, 2004.

law enforcement community who had the right to know and need to know the information. The additional qualifier was that the recipient had to be a law enforcement employee. One of the reasons for the distinction was because some information that contained Personal Identifying Information (PII) had to stay within the law enforcement community for reasons relating to civil rights and privacy.

While these definitions reflect the intent of the FOUO and LES labels—and because there are no national standards or national policies for the explicit types of information of information that is deemed SBU, agencies at all levels of government began making their own rules and adaptations of rules as they labeled SBU information. It is increasingly common to see a document with both the FOUO and LES dissemination labels, which basically eliminates the original distinctions between the labels.

Agencies provide different interpretations to any given SBU label because there are so few uniform national SBU guidelines. There are no sanctions if SBU information is widely distributed, including to the media, and no guidelines to ensure that the information is secured. Nevertheless, and in many ways, particularly for SLTLE agencies, SBU markings reflected a professional agreement to limit the dissemination of certain types of information.

Many of the problems with SBU dissemination labels and procedures are being remedied during a transition away from SBU and into the new method of marking unclassified sensitive data: Controlled Unclassified Information (CUI).

Controlled Unclassified Information

Among the mandates of the Intelligence Reform and Terrorism Prevention Act of 2004 was the development of policies and practices that would enhance the ability of rapid information sharing among the Intelligence Community, law enforcement, the private sector, and foreign partners. One of the information-sharing obstacles, though, was the lack of consistency in policies regulating SBU/CUI. At the federal level alone, the Program Manager for the Information Sharing Environment observed the following:

> Among the twenty departments and agencies we have surveyed, there are at least 107 unique markings and more than 131 different labeling or handling processes and procedures for SBU/CUI. Even when SBU information carries the same label marking (e.g., For Official Use Only), storage and dissemination are inconsistent across Federal agencies and departments. Because such markings are agency-specific, recipients of SBU information in a different agency must understand the processes and procedures of the originating Federal agency for handling the information, even if their agency uses the same marking. The result is an unmanageable collection of policies that leave both the producers and users of SBU information unable to know how a piece of information will be controlled as it moves through the Federal government and therefore reducing information sharing.[19]

[19] McNamara, Ted. *Statement for the Record before the Subcommittee on Intelligence, Information Sharing and Terrorism Risk Assessment of the House Committee on Homeland Security*, April 26, 2007.

These problems were the basis for establishing a common framework for sharing the information under the new label of Controlled Unclassified Information (CUI). After nearly 4 years of work on developing the new framework, the President issued a memorandum to the heads of all executive departments and agencies in the United States Government to implement the CUI framework:

> The global nature of the threats facing the United States requires that (a) our Nation's entire network of defenders be able to share information more rapidly so those who must act have the information they need, and (b) the United States Government protect sensitive information, information privacy, and other legal rights of Americans. A uniform and more standardized government-wide framework for what has previously been known as SBU/CUI information is essential for the ISE to succeed. Accordingly, this memorandum establishes a standardized framework designed to facilitate and enhance the sharing of Controlled Unclassified Information.[20]

The policies set forth in the Presidential Memorandum for the designation, marking, safeguarding, and disseminating of CUI are mandatory for all CUI originated by the Executive Branch of the federal government and shared within the ISE, regardless of the medium used for its display, storage, or transmittal.

It is important to note that the Presidential Memorandum also encourages the adoption of the CUI Framework by state, local, tribal, and private-sector entities. Frequent consultations with individuals and organizations from these entities during the development of this Framework suggest that there is some support for moving in the direction of a common, or mostly common, CUI Framework. As necessary, departments and agencies may agree with foreign partners to ensure that they protect shared CUI in "a like manner," similar to what is now done for sharing classified information. Of course, this provision applies only to the federal government, not to SLTLE. Presidential Guideline 4 activities address foreign government sharing, including sharing of CUI.[21] Additionally, sharing CUI with the private sector will most likely require some change to an agency's contractual policy, which may include mandating the use of the CUI Framework.

The term Controlled Unclassified Information or CUI is a *categorical designation that refers to unclassified information that does not meet the standards for National Security Classification under Executive Order 12958, as amended, but is (i) pertinent to the national interests of the United States or to the important interests of entities outside the Federal Government, and (ii) under law or policy requires protection from unauthorized disclosure, special handling safeguards, or prescribed limits on exchange or dissemination. Henceforth, the designation CUI replaces Sensitive But Unclassified.*[22] (Emphasis in original.)

[20] www.fas.org/sgp/bush/cui.html

[21] The full text of Presidential Guideline 4 can be found at www.ise.gov/docs/guidance/guideline%204%20-%20sharing%20with%20foreign%20partners.pdf.

[22] Background on the *Controlled Unclassified Information Framework*. (Unpublished background paper.) Washington, D.C.: Executive Office of the President, May 9, 2008, pp. 4–7.

The CUI Executive Agent, based in the National Archives and Records Administration, is responsible for administering all policies and regulations associated with the CUI framework. Among the regulations established thus far are the following:

1. Information shall be designated as CUI if:

    a. A statute so requires or authorizes; or

    b. The head of the originating department or agency, through regulations, directives, or other specific guidance to the agency, determines that the information is CUI. Such determination should be based on mission requirements, business prudence, legal privilege, the protection of personal or commercial rights, or safety or security. Such department or agency directives, regulations, or guidance shall be provided to the CUI Executive Agent for his review.

2. Notwithstanding the above, information shall not be designated as CUI:

    a. To: 1. conceal violations of law, inefficiency, or administrative error; 2. prevent embarrassment to the U.S. Government, any U.S. official, organization, or agency; 3. improperly or unlawfully interfere with competition; or 4. prevent or delay the release of information that does not require such protection;

    b. If it is required by statute or Executive Order to be made available to the public; or

    c. If it has been released to the public under proper authority.[23]

CUI Markings

Marking material as CUI signals that it contains sensitive information and that safeguarding and dissemination controls apply. All CUI will carry one of three markings (See Figure 12-2 for examples).

1. *Controlled with Standard Dissemination:* Information is subject to safeguarding measures that reduce the risks of unauthorized or inadvertent disclosure. Dissemination is permitted to the extent that it is reasonably believed that it would further the execution of a lawful or official purpose.

2. *Controlled with Specified Dissemination:* Information is subject to safeguarding measures that reduce the risks of unauthorized or inadvertent disclosure. Material contains additional instructions on what dissemination is permitted.

3. *Controlled Enhanced with Specified Dissemination:* Information is subject to enhanced safeguarding measures more stringent than those normally required because inadvertent or unauthorized disclosure would create a risk of substantial harm. Material contains additional instructions on what dissemination is permitted.

Figure 12-2: Examples of CUI Document Markings

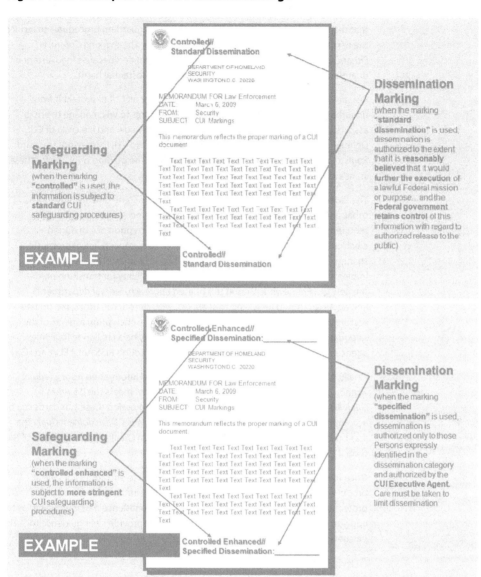

CUI Safeguarding

The CUI background memorandum stated that the marking *Controlled* means that the information is subject to standard CUI safeguarding procedures to reduce the risks of unauthorized or inadvertent disclosure. The marking *Controlled Enhanced* means that enhanced safeguarding is required because inadvertent or unauthorized disclosure would create the risk of substantial harm.

Reasonable safeguarding measures are required for all CUI to protect it from unauthorized or inadvertent release. These measures to will manage the risks associated with the communication, processing, storage, and life cycle of CUI. Defined safeguarding standards will be published in a CUI Framework Standards Registry maintained by the CUI Executive Agents. The guiding principle for these standards is risk management.

The federal government recognizes that it may take some time for state, local, tribal, and private-sector recipients of CUI to implement these safeguarding requirements, particularly the requirements for encryption of CUI during electronic storage and transmission. Because of the importance of promptly sharing CUI, the federal government recommends a phased approach to implementation, which provides the necessary flexibility for transitioning to the new CUI Framework. During this phased approach, federal departments and agencies should be willing to share CUI with state, local, tribal, and private-sector partners that have not fully implemented the encryption aspects of the safeguarding requirements[24] While encryption may be a challenge for some agencies, access to encrypted e-mail is available through RISS.net, LEO, and HSIN.

Finally, for law enforcement agencies to receive CUI information from a federal agency, they must have a privacy policy in place that meets the ISE *Privacy Guidelines*.[25] Fortunately, creating a privacy policy meeting these standards can be accomplished fairly easily by following the *Privacy Policy Development Guide* that was prepared by the Global Privacy and Information Quality Working Group of the Global Justice Information Sharing Initiative.[26]

Once fully implemented, the framework is intended to end confusion about proper access, handling, and control of unclassified information that needs protection. Moreover, the new system will instill confidence that identical rules apply to everyone using the CUI markings and will provide clear guidance to SLTLE partners who are confused by SBU markings.[27]

Summary

At the time of this writing, the transition from SBU to CUI was just beginning[28] and many legacy markings, for example, LES and FOUO, will continue to be used until new policies are put in place. SLTLE agencies should strongly consider adopting the CUI framework for their own products to aid in simplifying the sharing of sensitive information. Agencies should also monitor the CUI office of the National Archives and Records Administration[29] for changes and developments.

SLTLE agencies will encounter these labels when receiving federal intelligence products and it will be useful to know the framework from which they arise. At a practical level, the rule is for law enforcement officers to use good judgment

[24] Ibid.

[25] For detailed information about the ISE *Privacy Guidelines*, see www.ise.gov/pages/privacy-implementing.html.

[26] The Privacy Policy Development Guide and supporting materials are available at it.ojp.gov/default.aspx?area=globalJustice&page=1151.

[27] McNamara, Thomas E. *Annual Report to the Congress on the Information Sharing Environment*, op cit., 2008, p. 36.

[28] The Office of the CUI Executive Agent in the National Archives and Records Administration is located on the Internet at www.archives.gov/cui.

[29] At the time of this writing, a specific web site for the CUI Executive Agent had not been established. Information can be obtained by going to www.archives.gov and using the site's search utility for CUI.

when handling such materials. This does not mean that SLTLE officers may not disseminate this information further unless prohibited from doing so as indicated on the report; rather, the officer should use the information in a manner that meets community safety needs, including disseminating portions of the information to those segments of the community that would benefit from the data contained in the report.

Federal and National Intelligence Resources and Products

A wide range of information systems is available to law enforcement agencies to aid their intelligence function. Some systems are specifically for intelligence purposes while other systems have a much broader customer base but have applications for intelligence. Some systems are classified, allowing limited access to SLTLE, while other systems are designed specifically for wide use by law enforcement officers. Information systems were designed for diverse purposes; therefore, a brief understanding of these purposes can provide insight into their use and applicability.

Some of the resources described in the following discussion are information systems; others are offices or programs that use or provide services through different information systems. Some resources are federal, meaning that they are provided as part of the mission of a federal agency, and still other resources are national, which means they provide services and resources on a nationwide basis although the organization is not a federal agency and in most cases it receives federal funding to provide its service. Because of rapid growth of many of these resources, poor communication, and different perspectives of what is needed, the reader will find there is some duplication of effort.

As a place to begin, resources and systems may be described in six broad categories. Information actually found in some of the categories will overlap a resource in another category. This typology will help provide a perspective of the different types of resources and systems that are available for SLTLE.[30]

1. *Situational Awareness.* Documents and technologies that provide information on threats, incidents, indicators, and other short-term or real-time information needed for planning or operational responses.

2. *Public Records.* Depending on statutes and policies, various types of information collected or recorded by diverse public agencies may be available. Land transactions, driving records, registered sexual offenders, addresses, telephone numbers, and all types of licenses are illustrations.

3. *Criminal Justice.* Whenever anyone has an encounter with the criminal justice system it is going to be in a record. Computer-aided dispatch calls, arrest records, field interview reports, court records, probation and parole records, and institutional corrections records are examples.

4. *Intelligence.* Any records system or network that is explicitly designated to handle intelligence, such as RISS.net, LEO, and the Homeland Security Data Network. (While many of the networks are not exclusively for intelligence, all contain intelligence products.)

[30] Based on: Shaw, Larry. (Inspector, Florida Department of Law Enforcement Information Systems and Technologies. *Presentation at the Bureau of Justice Assistance-Funded Intelligence Commanders' Course,* Norwalk, California, July 2008.

5. *Resource and Communications Systems.* A number of systems have emerged post-9/11 that are explicitly designed to provide diverse types of intelligence resources and/or provide secure e-mail communications for SLTLE. Examples are the NCIRC, the Automated Trusted Information Exchange, and the Federal Protective Service (FPS) information portal.

6. *Open Sources.* The previous chapter addressed open source information as publicly available information that anyone can lawfully obtain by request, purchase, or observation.

Although many information systems can provide support to the law enforcement intelligence function, it is not feasible to include all of them here. This is particularly true when one considers state and local systems that are in use. Rather, the goal is to provide a snapshot of the systems that SLTLE officers across the United States are most likely to encounter, as well as a brief listing of other federal intelligence information systems that they may encounter occasionally. This discussion will help readers acquire an awareness of the different systems available on a national basis so that law enforcement agencies may develop the access they need to best fulfill their intelligence function.

In most cases, the information from the resources and systems in the following discussions will not be classified, but will be SBU/CUI. In all cases, the sensitivity of the information and appropriate safeguarding of the information will be clearly marked.

Department of Justice— Law Enforcement Information Sharing Program[31]

The *Law Enforcement Information Sharing Program* (LEISP) is not an information system. It is a program that addresses barriers to information sharing and creates a forum for collaboration on how existing and planned systems will be coordinated and unified for information-sharing purposes. LEISP delineates guiding principles, a policy framework, and functional requirements that are necessary to facilitate multijurisdictional law enforcement information sharing. LEISP establishes the DOJ's commitment to move from a culture of need to know toward a culture of need to share in which information is shared as a matter of standard operating procedure. Through the strategy, the DOJ also commits to participate as a partner to help bring together the law enforcement community in the common cause of achieving multijurisdictional information sharing.

LEISP sets in motion three implementation tracks: Track I is the DOJ's internal reform initiative, OneDOJ, which will closely coordinate information-sharing efforts within the Department, facilitate sharing of DOJ-held information with law enforcement agencies outside the Department, provide connectivity for sharing of information with the DHS, and allow the DOJ to present a single face to its information-sharing partners. Track II will first incorporate quick hits to leverage existing sharing-technology capabilities and then center on building out the services and technology platforms that will enable the Department to share its information seamlessly. In Track III, the Department will work cooperatively

[31] The information in this section is based largely on: *LEISP: United States Department of Justice Law Enforcement Information Sharing Program.* Washington, D.C.: October 2005. Unpublished report available at www.usdoj.gov/jmd/ocio/onedoj_strategy.pdf.

with its federal, state, local, and tribal law enforcement partners to enhance interconnectivity that allows standard, routine information sharing across all jurisdictions on a national basis.

Currently, the LEISP has five major initiatives:
1. OneDOJ System (formerly the Regional Data Exchange – R-DEx).
2. Law Enforcement National Data Exchange (N-DEx).
3. Joint Automated Booking System (JABS).
4. National Virtual Pointer System (NVPS).
5. Federated Identity Management (FIDM) Pilot Program.

The LEISP plans to implement policies, practices, and technologies to ensure that each component of the DOJ shares information as a matter of routine across the entire spectrum of the law enforcement community at all levels of government. The intent of the program is to ensure that law enforcement information-sharing practices in the DOJ are consistent with the national standards and ensure the protection of privacy and civil rights in all systems that contain PII. Moreover, the program should significantly enhance the amount and quality of intelligence that is shared with SLTLE agencies.

One DOJ (formerly the Regional Data Exchange: R-DEx)

The R-DEx system was developed to ensure that DOJ criminal law enforcement information was available for users at all levels of government so that they can more effectively investigate, disrupt, and deter criminal activity, including terrorism, and protect the national security. R-DEx furthered this purpose by consolidating certain law enforcement information from other DOJ systems, as well as certain state and local law enforcement information, so that it may more readily be available for sharing with other law enforcement entities.[32]

Information in R-DEx includes information about individuals who were referred by the Federal Bureau of Prisons (BOP), the United States Marshals Service (USMS), the Bureau of Alcohol, Tobacco, Firearms and Explosives (ATF), the Drug Enforcement Administration (DEA), the Federal Bureau of Investigation (FBI), as well as individuals referred by certain state and local law enforcement agencies that participate in the R-DEx system. All SLTLE agencies participating in R-DEx had to sign a memorandum of understanding (MOU) with the Department of Justice.

Relying on the basic concepts of R-DEx, including its database, the system has evolved into OneDOJ as the current operational information-sharing system for DOJ. It is hosted at the FBI's Criminal Justice Information Services (CJIS) data center and used to achieve the goals of OneDOJ. The OneDOJ system enables DOJ to meet its internal requirements for effective information sharing across its law enforcement agencies; only DOJ users have direct access to the OneDOJ system. External sharing is accomplished through bilateral partnerships with designated regional, state, or federal sharing initiatives. These partnerships allow non-DOJ users to access OneDOJ data from within their own systems and vice-versa.[33]

[32] *Federal Register*, Volume 72, Number 20, January 31, 2007, pp. 4532–4533, edocket.access.gpo.gov/2007/E7-1567.htm.

[33] www.usdoj.gov/jmd/ocio/leisp/initiatives.htm

The system has two primary operational objectives:

1. To serve as DOJ's system for sharing criminal law enforcement information internally across investigative components.

2. To provide regional criminal law enforcement connectivity for authorized users to conduct federated searches of OneDOJ information. This connectivity will also provide authorized DOJ users with the means to query partner law enforcement information as governed by the respective MOU.

OneDOJ is a DOJ repository for law enforcement information shared with other federal, state, local, and tribal law enforcement agencies through connections with regional information-sharing systems. All DOJ law enforcement components— ATF, BOP, DEA, FBI, and USMS—are sharing information under consistent policy and technical standards. Information shared includes open and closed case documents, investigative reports, witness interviews, criminal event data, criminal history and incarceration information, and identifying information about individual offenders.

Information sharing through OneDOJ with law enforcement outside of DOJ is achieved by interconnecting with regional systems to access DOJ information relevant to their users. As one example, the LInX-NW and ARJIS systems are connected with OneDOJ. This allows, for instance, LInX users in Washington state to access shared DEA case files of the Seattle field office from the LInX user interface. Additionally, the bidirectional nature of the connection allows DOJ users to access state and local information in the regional systems from the OneDOJ user interface.

Interconnection with OneDOJ is accomplished through an open, XML-based, NIEM-compliant standard developed by the DOJ LEISP and its partners. The standard, called LEXS-SR (LEISP Exchange Specification–Search and Retrieval), defines the interface between OneDOJ and regional sharing systems.[34]

Law Enforcement National Data Exchange

The Law Enforcement National Data Exchange (N-DEx) system provides SLTLE agencies with a system for collecting, processing, and disseminating criminal and investigative data for use as a pointer system for nationwide information sharing. Data fields within N-DEx include methods of criminal operation, arrestee/indicator information, victim information, suspect information, and other ongoing criminal and investigative information. The system has adopted the National Information Exchange Model to maximize compatibility for information-sharing. At the heart of success for N-DEx is participation by SLTLE agencies in providing data for the system. Federal agencies may also contribute investigative event data.

All information shared through N-DEx originates from data supplied by data sources from numerous local, state, tribal, and federal systems such as incident reports, arrest reports, case files, booking reports, incarceration records, and criminal histories. These records contain information about entities (people, locations, and items such as weapons and vehicles) and may specify relationships among the entities they contain (e.g., a person lives at a certain address or owns a certain vehicle).[35]

[34] www.usdoj.gov/jmd/ocio/leisp/onedoj.htm

[35] www.fbi.gov/hq/cjisd/ndex/ndex_concept.htm

N-DEx information services correlate data received from data suppliers and apply an analytic process that will proactively notify specific users if certain relationships are discovered. N-DEx data processes will analyze and categorize all information that is entered into the system to address the who, what, when, where, why, and how of law enforcement information nationwide."[36] It will also provide users with a single point of discovery to connect the dots through the N-DEx analytic capabilities. The system's processes will constantly correlate data, even similar data from diverse sources, to provide an ongoing linkage among all known suspects, events, and indicators. When a user conducts a search for a name, for example, the system will automatically link and make available to the user correlations between people, places, and things that he or she did not know.

System development will interconnect the information technology resources housed within the Criminal Justice Information Services (CJIS) Division of the FBI, including the National Crime Information Center (NCIC), Integrated Automated Fingerprint Identification System (IAFIS), and the National Instant Criminal Background Check System's Denial Decision Extract File. It will also define, develop, and connect Federal Crime Reporting data into the N-DEx matrix of information. The system will provide a search capability that will provide law enforcement with a method for querying these repositories in order to link and

---

Requirements for N-DEx Participation

Who can participate?
· Any law enforcement agency can participate.

What are the requirements?
· Agencies must adhere to national standards for efficient sharing of data.

  » National Information Exchange Model (NIEM)

  » Law Enforcement Information Sharing Program (LEISP) Exchange Specification (LEXS)

When can I start?
· Contact the N-DEx program office to develop a strategy for participation. Telephone: 202.324 7126, Fax: 202.324.0920.

How do I start?
· Agencies will:

  » Sign an operational MOU.

  » Identify and map incident/case data to the N-DEx Information Exchange Package Documentation (IEPD).

  » Obtain network connectivity through an existing CJIS wide area network (WAN) or connect over the Law Enforcement Online (LEO.

Why are participation requirements important?
· To provide criminal justice agencies with data standards and suggestions for participation in the N-DEx Program.

Where do I begin?
· The N-DEx IEPD can be downloaded at it.ojp.gov/iepd.

[36] Ibid.

solve crimes as well as the ability to develop crime trend analysis and predictive crime modeling. Connection to the N-DEx System will be accomplished through one of two methods: CJIS WAN or the Law Enforcement Online/Regional Information Sharing System (LEO/RISS).

Joint Automated Booking System

The Joint Automated Booking System (JABS) is an information-sharing initiative for strengthening law enforcement and homeland security activities. The initiative automates the federal booking process and provides a mechanism for rapidly and positively identifying an individual using a fingerprint submission to the FBI's IAFIS. The JABS program is not restricted to DOJ users, but includes other user groups from within the DOJ, DHS, Department of Defense, and the Department of Health and Human Services. JABS added an interagency booking service to provide automated submission of booking packages for federal law enforcement agencies that routinely bring their suspects in for booking. This initiative expanded JABS services to agencies in 11 federal departments outside of DOJ (DHS, Agriculture, Education, Interior, Labor, State, Transportation, Treasury, Veterans Affairs, Housing and Urban Development, and the General Services Administration), as well as the U.S. Postal Service. These agencies can now utilize JABS without having to actually deploy an automated booking station in their offices.[37]

National Virtual Pointer System[36]

For many years, state and local law enforcement envisioned a drug pointer system that would allow them to determine if other law enforcement organizations were investigating the same drug suspect. The DEA was designated by the Office of National Drug Control Policy in 1992 to take the lead in developing a national drug pointer system to assist federal, state, and local law enforcement agencies investigating drug trafficking organizations and to enhance officer safety by preventing duplicate investigations. The DEA drew from the experience of state and local agencies to make certain that their concerns were addressed and that they had extensive input and involvement in the development of the system.

The National Drug Pointer Index (NDPIX) became operational across the United States in October 1997. The National Law Enforcement Telecommunications System (NLETS)—a familiar, fast, and effective network that reaches into almost every police entity in the United States—is the backbone of the NDPIX. Participating agencies are required to submit active case-targeting information to NDPIX to receive pointer information from the NDPIX. The greater the number of data elements entered, the greater the likelihood of identifying possible matches. Designed to be a true pointer system, the NDPIX merely serves as a switchboard that provides a vehicle for timely notification of common investigative targets. The actual case information is shared only when telephonic contact is made between the officers or agents who have been linked by their entries into the NDPIX.

[37] www.usdoj.gov/jmd/ocio/leisp/initiatives.htm

[38] See www.dea.gov/programs/ndpix.htm.

NDPIX was developed for five reasons: 1. To promote information sharing; 2. To facilitate drug-related investigations; 3. To prevent duplicate investigations; 4. To increase coordination among federal, state, and local law enforcement agencies; and 5. To enhance the personal safety of law enforcement officers.

NDPIX has been transitioned and upgraded to the National Virtual Pointer System (NVPS). A steering committee—which included DEA, HIDTA, RISS, the National Drug Intelligence Center (NDIC), the National Institute of Justice, ,the National Sheriffs' Association, the International Association of Chiefs of Police (IACP), and the National Alliance of State Drug Enforcement Agencies—developed the specifications for the system and is overseeing its testing and transition.

Characteristics of the NVPS will include the following:
- Covers all crimes, not just drugs.
- Accepts only targets of open investigations with assigned case numbers.
- Transaction format contains an identifying field for the NVPS Identifier.
- Uses a secure telecommunications network.
- Uses the NDPIX "Mandatory" data elements.
- Single sign-on from any participant allows access to all participating pointer databases.
- Each system provides a user ID and password to its respective users.
- Each system maintains its own data.
- Uniform Crime Reporting or the National Incident-Based Reporting System codes are used to identify type of crime.
- Targets deconfliction for all crimes.
- Will rely on web-based communications.
- Has links with HIDTA and RISS.

This upgrade of the system to the NVPS represents an important development for a comprehensive national pointer system.

Federated Identity Management Pilot

The Federated Identity Management (FIDM) pilot, sometimes known as a single sign-on, now in its second year, is an SBU/CUI initiative funded by the Program Manager's Office of the Information Sharing Environment. The objective is to provide and test an agreed-on standard for authenticating users and remove impediments they may experience while accessing mission-critical data. Benefits include a simpler, more reliable authentication process, thereby providing users with quicker access to data. The U.S. Department of Justice is validating this concept and supporting technologies as they relate to the law enforcement environment and testing specific architecture of the federation believed to be the most appropriate for the LEISP mission.[39]

SLTLE agencies, notably through the Criminal Intelligence Coordinating Council, have been urging adoption of this model. Not only does having an array of different user names and passwords slow the process of seeking information from

[39]www.usdoj.gov/jmd/ocio/leisp/initiatives. htm

different systems, but also users are more likely to use only one or two systems, rather than all that are available because of the cumbersome multiple logons. If users are not fully accessing all available systems, valuable information related to an intelligence inquiry or criminal investigation may not be discovered. While the technology and architecture are in place with the FIDM project, the biggest challenge that remains is related to policy; that is, governing boards of the different systems appear to be reluctant to embrace FIDM as a means of accessing their systems.

Federal Bureau of Investigation Intelligence Initiatives[40]

The Federal Bureau of Investigation (FBI) has stated that to meet its security mission it must gather information and share intelligence with both the domestic law enforcement community and the Intelligence Community concerning all threats, whether from gangs, organized crime, or al Qaeda. As a means to enhance the effectiveness of this responsibility, the FBI developed the Strategic Execution Team (SET).

Through the SET, the FBI is establishing new baseline capabilities for its intelligence process to improve overall performance. The new field intelligence structures and processes have at their foundation the recognition that working seamlessly with SLTLE is essential to protecting America. Law enforcement partners are key customers for FBI intelligence products and the goal is to ensure that those products respond to customer needs.

Integrating Intelligence into the Criminal Programs

After the attacks of September 11, 2001, the FBI shifted resources away from its criminal programs to focus on counterterrorism. During the past few years, as the FBI's counterterrorism capabilities improved and the Bureau grew in size, some resources have been restored to the criminal programs to deal with ongoing threats posed by these groups. During the change process, the FBI recognized the need to develop a capacity to be more predictive and preventive for all crimes within its jurisdiction; that is, in addition to investigating crimes after the fact for prosecution, the Bureau must collect and act on intelligence to detect, disrupt, and dismantle criminal enterprises that pose the greatest threat to society.

While a great deal of progress has been made since 9/11 in developing the FBI's intelligence capabilities, these efforts have focused largely on the national security programs. For many agents working criminal matters, intelligence has been perceived as something done by the other side of the house. A key goal of SET is to change this dynamic to fully integrate intelligence into the criminal programs, to strengthen those programs by making them more intelligence-driven, and ultimately to be one coordinated FBI with a single unified process for intelligence that cuts across all programs.

Impact on Law Enforcement Partners:
- The FBI will provide a more intelligence-driven national and regional approach to criminal investigations.
- There will be an increase in FBI intelligence reports about criminal matters.

[40] The information in this section is based on an internal FBI Report entitled *Implementation of New Field Intelligence Operations: Executive Summary.* April 30, 2008.

Standardize Field Office Structure and Responsibilities

All field offices will be required to have a centralized strategic coordinating component in its Field Intelligence Group (FIG) that will: 1. Help the office fully understand the key threats in their domains and what resources the FBI has to bring to bear on each threat; 2. Ensure that the FBI fully capitalizes on collection capabilities to meet intelligence requirements; and 3. Develop a collection plan to address any gaps.

All field offices will also have a dedicated chief reports officer who will ensure that the office disseminates timely, relevant, and high-quality intelligence to outside partners.

Impact on Law Enforcement Partners:
- There will be uniform structures, positions, and processes across all FBI field offices, making it easier to work with the FBI.

Develop a Domain Management Process

A dedicated Domain Management team on the FIG will pull together information from inside and outside the field office to develop a thorough understanding of the office's territory and the threats and vulnerabilities within. The team will produce the Domain Assessment, a product that takes the synthesized data, adds perspective and context, and recommends specific courses of action. It will answer the fundamental question, "What can we do about it?" The team will also produce a Common Operational Picture, a map representation of the territory, combining open source data on the territory's infrastructure and demographics, and field office data on case subjects, sources, and vulnerabilities.

After creating the initial baseline Domain Assessment and the Common Operational Picture (COP), the team will continuously improve them by identifying what is not known but should be known, i.e., intelligence gaps, and taking action to address them. Domain Management will help FBI managers guide the office's activities and also inform national domain management efforts. It will improve the Bureau's ability to proactively identify threats, manage current investigative activities strategically, and identify new opportunities for information collection and for prosecution.

Impact on Law Enforcement Partners:
- As the FBI develops local, regional, and national pictures of particular threats, particularly criminal threats, the Bureau has committed to share these assessments with law enforcement partners.
- As the domain awareness is developed and continuously improved, the FBI will have better strategic intelligence to share with SLTLE about criminal and national security threats that require attention. If there is the presence of a particular gang or domestic terrorist group, for example, it would benefit local law enforcement to know what trends the FBI is seeing with those groups across the country. It would help local law enforcement know how they are financed, how they recruit, and what their leadership structure looks like. The FBI will develop and share with SLTLE such crime-related assessments.

Develop a Collection Management Process

Collection Management is a formal business process through which the field office's identified intelligence gaps and needs are prioritized into requirements that feed into a comprehensive plan. Elements of that plan are assigned to various squads (and ultimately sources) for resolution. The results are monitored and retasked, as required. Through Collection Management, the FIG will help the field office manage competing demands for intelligence collection, including the need to collect information to further case investigations, to follow threat leads, to conduct liaison and build partnerships, to help meet intelligence requirements from the law enforcement and Intelligence Communities, to complete the COP, to improve the FBI's understanding of a particular issue, and to support regional and national efforts. These requirements will be consolidated and prioritized through a careful balancing of factors, including an analysis of each case, to determine the level of threat represented, national and regional priorities, vulnerabilities and knowledge gaps in the territory and prioritized requirements, and specific requests from SLTLE.

Impact on Law Enforcement Partners:

- Local law enforcement will have a standardized, routine process for submitting, prioritizing, and resolving intelligence requirements.

Enhance Collection

The vast majority of the FBI's intelligence collection occurs in its operational squads. To fully leverage the Bureau's existing source base, the SET plan includes training and information technology tools to increase agents' awareness of priority requirements. Where staffing levels permit, operational squads will be assigned embedded intelligence analysts who will ensure that information collected during the squad's normal course of duties is analyzed and appropriately forwarded to the FIG for dissemination, domain awareness, and/or gap identification.

To further strengthen FBI collection capabilities, all field offices must also have a dedicated team of intelligence special agents assigned to the FIG. These agents will use the full range of appropriate human intelligence (HUMINT) tradecraft and operational skills to develop, recruit, and exploit sources, and leverage relationships with external partners in order to collect information about the most critical gaps. The intelligence special agents will not work on cases for prosecution, but will provide cross-program support, collecting information about counterterrorism, counterintelligence, cyber, and criminal program requirements.

Impact on Law Enforcement Partners:

- Improved information flow between operational squads and the FIG will result in dissemination of more raw intelligence from those squads. The greatest change will be in the criminal programs that historically have not focused on requirements-based intelligence collection.

Enhance Liaison

Recognizing that SLTLE agencies are key eyes and ears in the community, the FBI aslo recognizes that enhanced liaison is a vital component establishing a proactive posture against threats to the U.S. Under the SET plan, the FIG HUMINT squad will serve as the coordinating hub of all field office liaison activities. It will not absorb relationships established in other squads or programs, but these relationships will be centrally coordinated to ensure common messaging and deconfliction of multiple requests for information from the same entity. Some agents assigned to the FIG will serve in an official liaison role and will coordinate with (and in some cases embed themselves with) federal, state, and local law enforcement agencies. They will work to better understand the intelligence needs of SLTLE, leverage non-FBI sources capable of collecting critical information, and make it easier for SLTLE to leverage FBI resources across the entire FBI and the U.S. Intelligence Community.

Impact on Law Enforcement Partners:

- The standardized liaison program will facilitate the two-way flow of intelligence, allowing the FBI and SLTLE to better leverage each other's domain knowledge, liaison contacts, and sources. Local law enforcement will have a single point of contact that will enable each agency to more easily tap into the FBI knowledge base of criminal and terrorist threats.

- Collectively, the FBI will be better positioned to use mechanisms—without duplication or conflict—that provide early warning on the most critical threats.

- The FBI will continue a high level of participation in fusion centers. The intelligence that is gathered will be shared through these fusion centers, as appropriate.

Improve Production and Dissemination

Field offices will improve the quality of their intelligence products through formal training, including basic and advanced training for reports officers. The chief reports officer will provide the necessary technical expertise and oversight to address content and other measures of quality such as technical tradecraft, standardization, and substantive accuracy.

The timeliness of FBI intelligence products will be improved by streamlining the production and approval process, removing duplicative steps and approvals, and enabling direct dissemination from field offices, where appropriate.

To ensure that intelligence products are relevant to FBI customers' needs, Intelligence Information Reports (IIR) will be tied to specific intelligence requirements from the beginning of the production process. Strong mechanisms for receiving feedback will be implemented. New metrics will also assess each field office's throughput, the ratio of IIRs actually disseminated to the Intelligence Community to the total number of IIRs submitted to FBI headquarters.

Impact on Law Enforcement Partners:

- SLTLE will see improvements in the quality of FBI intelligence products. FBI products from across the field will have a uniform look and feel.

- SLTLE will receive raw intelligence reports more quickly.

- More intelligence will be directly responsive to SLTLE requirements.

- SLTLE will see more intelligence reporting originating from criminal squads.

Terrorist Screening Center[41]

The Terrorist Screen Center (TSC) was created to ensure that government investigators, screeners, agents, and state and local law enforcement officers have ready access to the information and expertise they need to respond quickly when a suspected terrorist is screened or stopped. The TSC consolidates access to terrorist watch lists from multiple agencies and provides 24/7 operational support for thousands of federal screeners and state and local law enforcement officers across the country and around the world. The intent of the TSC is to ensure that federal, state, and local officials are working off the same unified, comprehensive set of antiterrorist information.

Since its implementation on December 1, 2003, the TSC has provided the following:

- A single coordination point for terrorist screening data
- A consolidated 24/7 call center for encounter identification assistance
- A coordinated law enforcement response to federal, state, and local law enforcement
- A formal process for tracking encounters and ensuring that feedback is supplied to the appropriate entities.

The TSC created the terrorist screening database (TSDB), a single, comprehensive source of known or appropriately suspected international and domestic terrorists. These data are available to local, state, and federal law enforcement officers through the NCIC. When a police officer queries the NCIC, he or she may receive a notification that the query resulted in the potential match of a record within the TSDB and directs the officer to contact the TSC to determine if it is an actual match. If it is, the TSC transfers the call to the FBI's CT Watch to provide operational guidance to the officer.

Consolidated Terrorist Screening Database

The TSC receives international and domestic terrorist identity records and maintains them in its consolidated TSDB. The TSC reviews each record to determine which are eligible for entry into the NCIC's Violent Gang and Terrorist Organization File (VGTOF) and once the record is entered into the NCIC, it is accessible by state, local, and federal law enforcement officers. If a query by a law enforcement officer matches a name in the NCIC, the officer will be requested, through the NCIC printout, to contact the TSC. The printout also provides the officer with instructions for arresting, detaining, questioning, or releasing the subject. If the TSC determines that the person encountered by the officer is a match with a person in the NCIC/VGTOF file, the officer is immediately connected to the FBI's CT Watch for operational guidance. Depending on the situation, the CT Watch may dispatch a local Joint Terrorism Task Force (JTTF) agent to assist the law enforcement officer. Information that the officer obtained through the encounter is then sent back to the originating agency.

An example will illustrate the TSC's processes. On August 20, 2004, as two off-duty police officers were traveling across the Chesapeake Bay Bridge between

[41] Information for this section was gained from interviews and reviews of various courses, including testimony and press releases at www.fbi.gov/congress/congress04/bucella012604.htm, www.fbi.gov/pressrel/pressrel03/tscfactsheet091603.htm, and www.cia.gov/news-information/speeches-testimony/2003/wiley-speech-62262003.html.

southeastern Virginia and the Delmarva Peninsula, they observed individuals filming the structure of the bridge. The officers reported the suspicious activity to the Maryland Transportation Authority (MTA) who conducted a traffic stop of the vehicle. The MTA officers ran an NCIC check on one of the occupants of the car and learned that the individual may have a record within the TSDB. At the NCIC's request, the officers contacted the TSC and learned that the individual was the subject of the TSDB record. The TSC transferred the call to the FBI's CT Watch who informed the MTA that the individual was an alleged co-conspirator in a significant terrorism case. The FBI arrested the subject on a material witness warrant, and a search warrant executed at the subject's residence turned up valuable evidence. This new level of information-sharing and cooperation among state, local, and federal law enforcement agencies enhances our ability to prevent a terrorist attack within the United States.

Law Enforcement Online[42]

Law Enforcement Online (LEO) is an online service operated by the FBI for law enforcement, first responders, and criminal justice officials. Law enforcement personnel interested in signing up for LEO simply have to fill out a LEO application and submit it to their local FBI office for approval. The LEO site contains the following resources"

- *Topical Focus Area*. Custom web-type pages that provide a secure community area for general information related to the law enforcement profession using text, graphics, audio, and video.

- *Law Enforcement Special-Interest Groups*. Segmented areas with multilevel controlled access for specialized law enforcement groups that have their own members.

- *E-mail*. Provides the capability to send and receive secure e-mail/messages electronically between LEO users and RISS users.

- *Chat*. The ability to have a real-time discussion among users (through a keyboard) on three levels; one-to-one, groups, and the Electronic Academy for presentations or question-and-answer sessions.

- *Feedback*. The capability to survey users for input on various topics.

- *Electronic Calendar*. Provides national, state, and special-interest calendars for posting upcoming dates of interest for conferences, meetings, training courses, seminars, and other important dates.

- *Topical Electronic Library*. An easily accessed repository of a broad range of publications, documents, studies, research, technical bulletins, and reports of interest to the law enforcement community. The library will provide indexed and full-text retrieval capability. Material for this component is expected to come from the entire law enforcement and education communities.

- *Distance Learning*. Online topical learning modules that can be used any time of the day or night at the user's own pace with instructional feedback

In addition, *FBI Intelligence Assessments, FBI Intelligence Bulletins, and FBI Intelligence Information Reports* are available on the LEO web site, as well as other items of interest related to the FBI intelligence program. To obtain access to LEO, contact the training coordinator at the local FBI field office.[43]

[42] The LEO web page is www.fbi.gov/hq/cjisd/leo.htm.

[43] www.fbi.gov/contact/fo/fo.htm

Guardian and eGuardian

The FBI's Guardian system is a federal classified system restricted for FBI use. The system records suspicious activity that is pre-investigation, pre-case, nonintelligence data with a nexus to terrorism.[44] Because Executive Order 13388 requires federal sharing of terrorist threat information with local law enforcement, the FBI is making portions of the Guardian database visible to law enforcement through LEO. The initiative to allow local law enforcement to have access to the system is called eGuardian. Eventually, the eGuardian project will also include a way for state and local agencies to report suspicious activity in addition to reviewing information gathered by FBI agents.

eGuardian utilizes the existing system and its capabilities by filtering classified information. It facilitates the sharing of critical unclassified data stored within the system and enhances interagency threat assessment and coordination, thereby enabling federal, state, local, and tribal law enforcement to obtain, share, integrate, and use the unclassified threat and incident data from Guardian. It also provides incident capture, searching, reporting, and trend analysis capabilities for these agencies.

eGuardian has a robust incident management system, allowing users to create, update, and search incidents. Any number of people, places, vehicles, weapons, or other pieces of information can be added to an incident. Additionally, the system allows users to attach any kind of file to an incident, including documents, images, videos, and audio clips. In addition to incident management, eGuardian offers other capabilities for data analysis, data optimization, and data segmentation as well as a search capacity similar to that of Internet search engines.

Department of Homeland Security
Intelligence and Analysis Directorate

The mission of DHS Office of Intelligence and Analysis (I&A) is to provide homeland security intelligence to the Secretary, the operating components, and headquarters offices as well as to our state, local, tribal, and private-sector partners. I&A, a member of the Intelligence Community, ensures that any information related to protecting the homeland is collected, processed, analyzed, and disseminated to the full spectrum of domestic customers. It provides threat warning, estimative, and alternative analysis. In addition, it also provides intelligence support to infrastructure protection and vulnerability studies. I&A works closely with DHS component intelligence organizations (such as Immigration and Customs Enforcement, Customs and Border Protection [CBP], and others) to ensure that nontraditional streams of domestic information are fused with traditional sources of information from other members of the Intelligence Community to give a complete picture of potential threats to the nation.[45]

DHS has a lead role in providing threat information, situational awareness, and context about nuclear threats to SLTLE as well as private-sector partners. Given the technical nature of nuclear devices and the broad customer base, DHS is providing baseline information on how a field officer might identify components of a nuclear device, differentiate radiological from nuclear devices, training on the

[44] Coleman, Gerry, "Next Generation: CJIS?", *Time System Newsletter* (Wisconsin Department of Justice Crime Information Bureau) 2006-1 (March 2006): p. 1.

[45] Allen, Charles E. *Testimony of the Under Secretary for Intelligence and Analysis before the Senate Committee on Homeland Security and Governmental Affairs: Assessing the Nuclear Attack Threat,* April 2, 2008.

potential effects of a nuclear device, and ensuring that our partners understand the range of effects from a nuclear device. DHS provides this information through unclassified and classified products, as well as secure video teleconferences and in-person threat briefings at state and local fusion centers.

Part of the DHS effort to enhance information-sharing with SLTLE agencies was creation of the Fusion Process Technical Assistance Program Resource Center as a joint initiative between I&A and the DHS Preparedness Directorate. In addition, the program works closely with intelligence and counterterrorism initiatives of the U.S. Bureau of Justice Assistance. The online program serves as a directory of all fusion centers as well as a resource for intelligence-related documents ranging from model policies to lessons learned. It is a dynamic resource available to SLTLE who are registered users of the DHS LLIS web site.[46]

DHS I&A has aggressively developed an intelligence capacity that is consistent with established processes and principles used in the Intelligence Community. Beyond that, I&A has developed new initiatives to increase two-way information-sharing with SLTLE agencies:

- DHS I&A has deployed analysts to many fusion centers at the state and local level across the country. The goal is to have a DHS analyst in all primary state fusion centers. As of this writing, about 35 intelligence analysts had been assigned.

- Trained intelligence reports officers deployed to DHS components provide *Homeland Intelligence Reports* to the rest of the Intelligence Community containing information gleaned from contacts at the borders. I&A has issued nearly 3,000 such reports in the past year, sharing valuable information about transnational threats from the Caribbean and Latin America, sensitive information from ports of entry, and data from people who are given secondary screening or who are denied entry into the United States.

- I&A has raised its visibility with the Intelligence Community, sitting as a full participant in Intelligence Community forums and working hand-in-hand with partners at the Director of National Intelligence, the FBI, and National Counterterrorism Center (NCTC).

  - The I&A has formed the Interagency Threat Assessment and Coordination Group (ITACG) with the FBI, NCTC, and SLTLE. It is located in the NCTC, under NCTC management, but with DHS and FBI senior officers leading it. ITACG officers monitor sensitive databases each day to determine what can be sanitized and sent to state and local partners.

  - I&A contributes to the daily *National Terrorism Bulletin* and *President's Daily Brief* and disseminates joint advisories with the FBI, mostly at the SBU/CUI level, to ensure maximum reach to state, local, and private-sector partners.

  - I&A is establishing a National Applications Office that will use satellite imagery, not only for civil applications, but to support homeland security efforts.[47]

Homeland Security Information Network[48]

The Homeland Security Information Network (HSIN) is a secure, Internet-based system of integrated communication networks designed to facilitate information-sharing between DHS and other federal, state, county, local, tribal, private-sector commercial, and other nongovernmental organizations involved in identifying

[46] Users must first register at www.llis.dhs. gov. Once the user is given access to LLIS, he or she e-mails a request to have access to the Fusion Process Technical Assistance Program Resource Center. www.llis.dhs.gov/channel/channel. do?id=90287.

[47] Allen, Charles E. DHS Under Secretary for Intelligence and Analysis. *Charles E. Allen Address to the Washington Institute for Near East Policy*, Washington, D.C.: May 6, 2008. www.dhs.gov/xnews/speeches/ sp_1210107524856.shtm.

[48] Information in this section is based largely on: *Privacy Impact Statement for the Homeland Security Information Network Database*. Unpublished report of the DHS Office of Operations Coordination, April 5, 2006. www.dhs. gov/xlibrary/assets/privacy/privacy_pia_ hsind.pdf.

and preventing terrorism and undertaking incident management activities. The mission of HSIN is to enhance the communication of relevant information among all applicable domestic security actors regardless of jurisdictional, geographic, or agency boundaries. Additionally, HSIN enables these organizations to maintain voice and data communications with one another during incident management. The HSIN is managed by the National Operations Center (NOC).

The system supports its user community by enabling approved users to research and analyze information with a nexus to terrorism. The database within HSIN is populated with information from: Suspicious Activity Reports from law enforcement, governmental agency, or private-sector security officials; law enforcement bulletins and reports from federal, state, county, local, and/or tribal law enforcement, and relevant information from approved HSIN user's communications. Prior to inclusion in the HSIN, information will be reviewed by NOC personnel to ensure a nexus to terrorism. After a nexus is established, the information is put into categories according to sector, subject matter, geography, and need to know.

Data collected for HSIN focuses primarily on activities, rather than on individuals. It consists of reports about what individuals, either law enforcement or other persons, have observed that is out of the ordinary based on their judgment, experience, and the circumstance of their observation. In most but not all cases, such observations will not include PII, but instead, the facts of a situation. In instances where the observation or incident led to PII being obtained, the information will be logged into the HSIN database, and additional safeguards will be used, including masking the information. The data that included names would be available only to those whose roles authorize them to access and collect such information, primarily law enforcement personnel and the Intelligence Community. Other users, such as private-sector security managers, would be able to access only the activity-based information; private and other sensitive data would be masked. If they have the need for more information, private-sector users will either contact the source entity (such as another private-sector entity) or look to local law enforcement for additional information that they might be eligible to receive.

The HSIN database will collect relatively raw suspicious activity information, which generally is provided by individuals who observe the activities of others and deem that activity suspicious, based on the totality of observable circumstances. While the primary focus of the information will be on activities, the personally identifiable information accepted for retention as part of a particular submission may include full name, address, date of birth, place of birth, citizenship, physical description (height, weight, eye and hair color), distinguishing scars, marks, or tattoos, automobile registration information, watch list information, intelligence information including links to terrorism, any criminal and/or incident activity, the date information is submitted, and the name of the contributing/submitting organization. The system has the capability to analyze data in a manner that identifies potential threats to the homeland or trends requiring further analysis.

The following are among the other capabilities of HSIN:

Communications
- Low-cost, always-on connectivity
- End-to-end encrypted communications

Collaboration/Analysis
- Secure e-mail
- Interactive collaboration tool (real-time text or voice)
- Supports requests for information, exchange, and cross-reference
- Search and link/timeline analysis, map/imagery displays

Information
- Daily, periodic, and ongoing report sharing.
- Suspicious incident/pre-incident indicator data.
- Media studies and analysis.
- Mapping and imaging (national, state, county, city).
- Critical Infrastructure Protection repository.
- Strategic analysis of terrorist threats, tactics, and weapons

A long-term goal of the HSIN is to have seamless connectivity among the different portals that serve the law enforcement and homeland security communities.

Homeland Security–State and Local Intelligence Community of Interest (HS SLIC)

To foster collaboration and share best practices and lessons learned within the fusion center network, DHS sponsors the Homeland Security State and Local Intelligence Community of Interest (HS SLIC). This is a virtual community of intelligence analysts who not only share threat information but also analytic techniques. Its membership has grown significantly and now has members representing 43 states, the District of Columbia, and seven federal departments. An HS SLIC Advisory Board, which includes state and local intelligence leaders, advises the I&A leadership on issues relating to intelligence collaboration between the federal government and its state, local, and tribal partners. Through the HS SLIC, intelligence analysts across the country collaborate through weekly SBU/CUI threat teleconferences, biweekly Secret-level secure video teleconferences, and in a virtual community of interest within a restricted portion of the HSIN-Intelligence platform, to share sensitive information in an appropriately secure and privacy sensitive environment. Members are thus able to post intelligence products so that there is effective vertical information-sharing between the states and the Intelligence Community and horizontally between the states.[49]

National Counterterrorism Center (NCTC)[50]

In July 2004, the National Commission On Terrorist Attacks Upon the United States recommended the establishment of a National Counterterrorism Center (NCTC)

[49] Allen, Charles E. *Information Sharing at the Federal, State, and Local Levels. Statement for the Record before the United States Senate Committee on Homeland Security and Governmental Affairs,* July 23, 2008.

[50] The public NCTC web site is www.nctc. gov.

to serve as a center for "... joint operational planning and joint intelligence, staffed by personnel from the various agencies...." On August 27, 2004, the President signed *Executive Order 13354, National Counterterrorism Center*, which established the NCTC and stipulated roles for it and its leadership and reporting relationships between NCTC leadership and NCTC member agencies, as well as with the White House. In December 2004, Congress passed the Intelligence Reform and Terrorism Prevention Act and, like the preceding Executive Order, among many other reform initiatives, the act prescribes roles and responsibilities for the NCTC and its leadership.[51]

NCTC operates as a partnership of organizations that include the Intelligence Community, law enforcement, and government agencies representative of the U.S. critical infrastructure. The NCTC is responsible for managing integrated meetings with its partners related to all aspects of terrorists' threats, both domestically and abroad. The ostensible purpose for the creation of intelligence centers, including the NCTC, is to bring together the disparate elements of the Intelligence Community having different intelligence foci and missions in order to achieve common intelligence and national security objectives.

A critical part of the NCTC mission is to develop intelligence products related to terrorism threats, including the following:

- Daily analytic products for senior U.S. government officials and the broader counterterrorism community

- A daily accounting of threat reporting and actions taken

- In-depth analytic assessments of the full range of terrorist topics

- Analysis providing alternative views on terrorism issues

- Situational awareness reports of terrorist threats, incidents, and reported plots worldwide

- Alerts, advisories, warnings, and assessments on topics of interest that are widely disseminated to domestic and overseas operators and analysts

- Strategic operational plans integrated and synchronized across U.S. Government agencies, describing specific objectives, department/agency roles and responsibilities, tasks, and activities for counterterrorism.[52]

Consistent with applicable law and direction from the President, the NCTC may receive intelligence pertaining exclusively to domestic counterterrorism from any federal, state, local, or tribal government, or other source necessary to fulfill its responsibilities and retain and disseminate such intelligence.[53]

The NCTC serves as the central and shared knowledge bank on known and suspected terrorists and international terror groups; ensures that agencies, as appropriate, have access to and receive all-source intelligence support needed to execute their counterterrorism plans or perform independent, alternative analysis; and ensures that such agencies have access to and receive intelligence needed to accomplish their assigned activities. Any agency authorized to conduct counterterrorism activities may request information from the NCTC to assist it in its activities, consistent with applicable law and guidelines provided for the provision of, and access to, intelligence. The NCTC enables the sharing of a wide

[51] Masse, Todd. *The National Counterterrorism Center: Implementation Challenges and Issues for Congress.* Washington, D.C.: Congressional Research Service, 2005, p. ii.

[52] www.nctc.gov/about_us/products.html

[53] Program Manager–Information Sharing Environment. *Information Sharing Environment Implementation Plan.* Washington, D.C.: Office of the Director of National Intelligence, 2006.

spectrum of terrorism intelligence and related information among thousands of users in the federal counterterrorism community through its secure web site that operates in separate security domains.[54] While SLTLE agencies have access to this information, for the most part that access is limited and accessible through the fusion centers.

Regional Information Sharing System

The Regional Information Sharing System® (RISS) has been in operation since 1973 providing services supporting the investigative and prosecution efforts of law enforcement and criminal justice agencies. The network was founded in response to transjurisdictional crime problems and the need for cooperation and secure information-sharing among law enforcement agencies.

Today, RISS is a national network comprising six multistate centers operating regionally.

- **Middle Atlantic-Great Lakes Organized Crime Law Enforcement Network.**[55] Delaware, Indiana, Maryland, Michigan, New Jersey, New York, Ohio, Pennsylvania, and the District of Columbia. The center also has member agencies in England, Australia, the Canadian provinces of Ontario and Quebec.

    - 140 Terry Road, Suite 100
      Newton, PA 18940
      Telephone: 215.504.4910
      E-mail: info@magloclen.riss.net

- **Mid-States Organized Crime Information Center.** Illinois, Iowa, Kansas, Minnesota, Missouri, Nebraska, North Dakota, South Dakota, and Wisconsin. The center also has member agencies in Canada.

    - 1610 E. Sunshine Drive, Suite 100
      Springfield, MO 65804
      Telephone: 417.883.4383
      E-mail: info@mocic.riss.net

- **New England State Police Information Network.** Connecticut, Maine, Massachusetts, New Hampshire, Rhode Island, and Vermont. The center also has member agencies in Canada.

    - 124 Grove Street, Suite 305
      Franklin, MA 02038
      Telephone: 508.528.8200
      E-mail: info@nespin.riss.net

- **Regional Organized Crime Information Center.**[56] Alabama, Arkansas, Florida, Georgia, Kentucky, Louisiana, Mississippi, North Carolina, Oklahoma, South Carolina, Tennessee, Texas, Virginia, and West Virginia, Puerto Rico, and the U.S. Virgin Islands.

    - 545 Marriott Drive, Suite 850
      Nashville, TN 37214
      Telephone: 615.871.0013
      E-mail: info@rocic.riss.net

[54] Ibid.

[55] www.riss.net/centers.aspx?9=MAGLOCLEN

[56] www.rocic.com

- **Rocky Mountain Information Network.**[57] Arizona, Colorado, Idaho, Montana, Nevada, New Mexico, Utah, and Wyoming. The center also has member agencies in Canada.

    - 2828 N. Central Avenue, Suite 1000
      Phoenix, AZ 85004
      Telephone: 602.351.2320
      E-mail: info@rmin.riss.net

- **Western States Information Network.** Alaska, California, Hawaii, Oregon, and Washington. The center also has member agencies in Canada, Australia, and Guam.

    - 1825 Bell Street, Suite 205
      Sacramento, CA 92403
      Telephone: 916.263.1166
      E-mail: info@wsin.riss.net

The regional approach allows each center to offer support services tailored to the needs of member agencies, although the centers also provide services and products that are national in scope and significance. Typical targets of RISS-member agencies' activities are terrorism, drug trafficking, violent crime, cybercrime, gang activity, and organized crime. While the RISS network is funded by the U.S. Bureau of Justice Assistance, it is controlled by its member agencies; therefore, state and local law enforcement agencies establish priorities as well as decisions related to services, such as secure client e-mail systems.

Traditional support services provided to law enforcement member agencies from the RISS centers include the following:

- Information-sharing resources

- Analytical services

- Loan of specialized investigative equipment

- Confidential funds

- Training conferences

- Technical assistance.

RISS.NET

RISS operates a secure intranet, known as RISS.NET, to facilitate law enforcement communications and information-sharing nationwide. RISS local, state, federal, and tribal law enforcement member agency personnel have online access to share intelligence and coordinate efforts against criminal networks that operate in many locations across jurisdictional lines. In September 2002, the FBI LEO system interconnected with RISS. In October 2003, the RISS/LEO interconnection was recommended in the *National Criminal Intelligence Sharing Plan* as the initial SBU/CUI communications backbone for implementation of a nationwide criminal intelligence-sharing capability. The Plan encourages agencies to connect their systems to RISS/LEO.

[57] www.riss.net/Centers.aspx?9=RMIN

Automated Trusted Information Exchange

In April 2003, RISS expanded its services and implemented what was initially called the Anti-Terrorism Information Exchange and later changed to its current name, the Automated Trusted Information Exchange (ATIX) to provide users with access to homeland security, disaster, and terrorist threat information. RISS member agencies, as well as executives and officials from other first-responder agencies and critical infrastructure entities, can access the system. ATIX consists of a web site and connected services hosted on the RISS network. It is designed for use by officials from government and nongovernment organizations who are responsible for planning and implementing prevention, response, mitigation, and recovery efforts for terrorist attacks and disasters. The ATIX program serves state, county, local, and tribal government executives; federal government executives and agencies; regional emergency management; law enforcement and criminal justice organizations; fire departments; agriculture; disaster relief; special rescue units; and telecommunication and transportation.

The web site features secure e-mail and information such as DHS bulletins and advisories, terrorist threat-level alerts, advisories from different government units such as the Department of Transportation, and has areas where users can post and share data specific to their occupational communities (e.g., law enforcement, military, emergency services, etc.).

In each community section on the web site, users can establish collaborative electronic conference services, virtual bulletin boards, and live chat rooms. Member groups also create most of the ATIX site's content and bulletin board posts. Each conference has a live chat feature where users can post conversation threads and discuss topics. An on-screen paging function permits users to notify others if they need to shift a conversation to the telephone or to a face-to-face discussion.

ATIX is informative, user-friendly, and an important resource for law enforcement agencies of any size. The site requires access to the Internet through a secure portal to permit communications. To obtain access to ATIX, the potential user must contact the applicable RISS center and request enrollment from the appropriate state coordinator.

Drug Enforcement Administration[58]

Since it was established in 1973, the Drug Enforcement Administration (DEA), in coordination with other federal, state, local, and foreign law enforcement organizations, has been responsible for the collection, analysis, and dissemination of drug-related intelligence. The role of intelligence in drug law enforcement is critical. The DEA Intelligence Program helps initiate new investigations of major drug organizations, strengthens ongoing investigations and subsequent prosecutions, develops information that leads to seizures and arrests, and provides policymakers with drug trend information on which they can base programmatic decisions. The specific functions of the DEA's intelligence mission are as follows:

- Collect and produce intelligence in support of the administrator and other federal, state, and local agencies

- Establish and maintain close working relationships with all agencies that produce or use narcotics intelligence

- Increase the efficiency in the reporting, analysis, storage, retrieval, and exchange of such information

- Undertake a continuing review of the narcotics intelligence effort to identify and correct deficiencies.

The DEA's Intelligence Program has grown significantly since its inception. From only a handful of intelligence analysts in the domestic offices and Headquarters in 1973, the number of intelligence analysts worldwide is now more than 680. DEA's Intelligence Program consists of several entities that are staffed by both intelligence analysts and special agents: intelligence groups and functions in the domestic field divisions, district, resident, and foreign offices, the El Paso Intelligence Center, and the Intelligence Division at DEA Headquarters. Program responsibility for the DEA's intelligence mission rests with the DEA Assistant Administrator for Intelligence.

Legislation and presidential directives and orders have expanded the role of the Intelligence Community and the Department of Defense in the antidrug effort. DEA interaction with both components occurs daily in the foreign field and at Headquarters. At the strategic intelligence level, the Intelligence Division participates in a wide range of interagency assessment and targeting groups that incorporate drug intelligence from the antidrug community to provide policymakers with all-source drug trend and trafficking reporting.

With analytical support from the Intelligence Program, the DEA has disrupted major trafficking organizations or put them entirely out of business. The DEA Intelligence Division also cooperates a great deal with state and local law enforcement and will soon provide intelligence training for state, local, federal, and foreign agencies. This training will be held at the Justice Training Center in Quantico, Virginia, and will address the full spectrum of drug intelligence training needs. The best practices and theories of all partners involved in the drug issue will be solicited and incorporated into the training. Academic programs, the exchange of federal, state, and local drug experience, and the sharing of, and

[58] A number of DEA strategic intelligence reports are available online at www. dea.gov/pubs/intel.htm. For other intelligence reports and related information, contact your nearest DEA Field Office www.dea.gov/agency/domestic.htm.

exposure to, new ideas will result in more effective application of drug intelligence resources at all levels.

The DEA divides drug intelligence into three broad categories: tactical, investigative, and strategic.

1. Tactical intelligence is evaluated information on which immediate enforcement action—arrests, seizures, and interdictions—can be based.

2. Investigative intelligence provides analytical support to investigations and prosecutions to dismantle criminal organizations and gain resources.

3. Strategic intelligence focuses on the current picture of drug trafficking from cultivation to distribution that can be used for management decision-making, resource deployment, and policy planning.

In February 2006, the DEA's Office of National Security Intelligence officially became the 16th member of the Intelligence Community.[59] The designation was necessary because of the DEA's global presence and the fact that terrorists have financed some operations through illegal drug sales. Intelligence Community responsibilities of the DEA are coordinated through the new DEA National Security Branch which is in the Office of Intelligence.[60]

Intelligence Products. Tactical and investigative intelligence is available to SLTLE agencies through local DEA field offices. In addition, intelligence can be shared with SLTLE agencies through secure e-mail. Many strategic intelligence reports are available on the DEA web site.[61] Reports that are law enforcement sensitive"can be obtained through the local DEA office.

El Paso Intelligence Center[62]

The El Paso Intelligence Center (EPIC) was established in 1974 in response to a Department of Justice study that detailed drug and border enforcement strategy and programs. The study proposed the establishment of a southwest border intelligence service center staffed by representatives of the Immigration and Naturalization Service, the U.S. Customs Service, and the DEA. The original EPIC staff comprised 17 employees from the three founding agencies. Initially, EPIC focused on the U.S.-Mexico border and its primary interest was drug movement and immigration violations.

Today, EPIC still concentrates primarily on drug movement and immigration violations. Because these criminal activities are seldom limited to one geographic area, EPIC's focus has broadened to include all of the United States and the Western Hemisphere where drug and alien movements are directed toward the United States. Staffing at the DEA-led center has increased to more than 300 analysts, agents, and support personnel from 15 federal agencies, the Texas Department of Public Safety, and the Texas Air National Guard. Information-sharing agreements with other federal law enforcement agencies, the Royal Canadian Mounted Police, and each of the 50 states ensure that EPIC support is available to those who need it. A telephone call, fax, or e-mail from any of these agencies provides the requestor with real-time information from different federal databases, plus EPIC's own internal database.

[59] Office of the Director of National Intelligence. *Drug Enforcement Administration Element Becomes 16th Intelligence Community Member.* Press Release #6-06, February 17, 2006.

[60] Office of the Inspector General. Audit Division. *The Drug Enforcement Administration Use of Intelligence Analysts. Audit Report 08-23.* Washington, D.C.: U.S. Department of Justice, May 2008. www.fas.org/irp/agency/doj/oig/dea-intel.pdf.

[61] See www.usdoj.gov/dea/pubs/intel.htm.

[62] See www.dea.gov/programs/epic.htm.

In addition to these services, a number of EPIC programs are dedicated to post-seizure analysis and the establishment of links between recent enforcement actions and ongoing investigations. EPIC also coordinates training for state and local officers in the methods of highway drug and drug currency interdiction through its Operation Pipeline program. In addition, EPIC personnel coordinate and conduct training seminars throughout the United States on such topics as indicators of trafficking and concealment methods used by couriers.

In a continuing effort to stay abreast of changing trends, EPIC has developed the National Clandestine Laboratory Seizure Database. EPIC's future course will be driven by the *General Counterdrug Intelligence Plan*, as well. As a major national center in the new drug intelligence architecture, EPIC will serve as a clearinghouse for the High Intensity Drug Trafficking Area's (HIDTA) Intelligence Centers, gathering state and local law enforcement drug information and providing drug intelligence back to the HIDTA Intelligence Centers.

National Drug Intelligence Center[63]

The National Drug Intelligence Center (NDIC), established in 1993, is a component of the U.S. Department of Justice and a member of the Intelligence Community. The *General Counterdrug Intelligence Plan*, implemented in February 2000, designated NDIC as the nation's principal center for strategic domestic counterdrug intelligence. The intent of NDIC is to meet three fundamental missions:

1. Support national policymakers and law enforcement decision-makers with strategic domestic drug intelligence.
2. Support Intelligence Community counterdrug efforts.
3. Produce national, regional, and state drug threat assessments.

The Intelligence Division consists of six geographic units and four specialized units. The six geographic units correspond to the regions of the Department of Justice Organized Crime Drug Enforcement Task Force (OCDETF)[64] program and concentrate on drug trafficking and abuse. The four specialized units include the Drug Trends Unit, the Organized Crime and Violence Unit, the National Drug Threat Assessment Unit, and the National Interdiction Support Unit.

Within the geographic units, NDIC intelligence analysts cover each state and various U.S. territories. Intelligence analysts maintain extensive contacts with federal, state, and local law enforcement and Intelligence Community personnel in all 50 states, the District of Columbia, Puerto Rico, the Virgin Islands, and the Pacific territories of Guam, American Samoa, and the Northern Mariana Islands. NDIC collaborates with other agencies such as the DEA, FBI, U.S. Coast Guard, Bureau of Alcohol, Tobacco, Firearms and Explosives (ATF), the Bureau of Prisons, and the Office of National Drug Control Policy (ONDCP). NDIC is one of four national intelligence centers including the EPIC, the U.S. Department of the Treasury's Financial Crimes Enforcement Network (FinCEN), and the Director of Central Intelligence Crime and Narcotics Center. NDIC also works closely with the HIDTAs and the OCDETF.

[63] See www.usdoj.gov/ndic.

[64] While the OCDETFs are operational entities, not intelligence entities, they are both consumers of intelligence and sources for information collection. For more information see www.usdoj.gov/dea/programs/ocdetf.htm.

Intelligence Products

Threat assessments, NDIC's primary intelligence products, provide policymakers and counterdrug executives with timely, predictive reports of the threat posed by illicit drugs in the United States.

- The *National Drug Threat Assessment,* NDIC's major intelligence product, is a comprehensive annual report on national drug trafficking and abuse trends within the United States. The assessment identifies the primary drug threat to the nation, monitors fluctuations in consumption levels, tracks drug availability by geographic market, and analyzes trafficking and distribution patterns. The report highlights the most current quantitative and qualitative information about availability, demand, production and cultivation, transportation, and distribution, as well as the effects of a particular drug on abusers and on society as a whole.

- *State Drug Threat Assessment* provides a detailed threat assessment of drug trends within a particular state. Each report identifies the primary drug threat in the state and gives a detailed overview of the most current trends by drug type.

- *Information Bulletins* are developed in response to new trends or high-priority drug issues. They are relayed quickly to the law enforcement and intelligence communities and are intended to warn law enforcement officials of emerging trends.

High Intensity Drug Trafficking Areas[65]

The High Intensity Drug Trafficking Areas (HIDTA) Intelligence System has more than 1,500 law enforcement personnel, mostly criminal intelligence analysts, participating full time in more than 60 intelligence initiatives in the 28 HIDTA designated areas throughout the United States. While HIDTA is a counterdrug program, the intelligence centers operate in a general criminal intelligence environment, thereby leveraging all criminal intelligence information for the program's primary mission.[66]

The HIDTA Intelligence System, a core element in the creation and growth of many SLTLE intelligence programs, largely depends on HIDTA program mandates. Each HIDTA must establish an intelligence center co-managed by both a federal and a state or local law enforcement agency. The core mission of each HIDTA Intelligence Center is to provide tactical, operational, and strategic intelligence support to its HIDTA executive board, a group of participating law enforcement agency principals responsible for the daily management of their respective HIDTAs, HIDTA-funded task forces, and other regional HIDTAs. Developing regional threat assessments and providing event and target deconfliction are also among the centers' core missions. These core functions are critical to building trust and breaking down parochialism between and among the participating local, state, and federal law enforcement agencies.

The plan to connect all HIDTA Intelligence Centers through RISS.net was initiated by the HIDTA Program Office at ONDCP in 1999 and completed in mid-2003. The HIDTA Program Office has commissioned interagency and interdisciplinary working committees to develop a national information-sharing plan, focusing on issues relating to legal, agency policy, privacy, technical, and logistical information-sharing matters. HIDTA program and committee personnel are

[65] See www.whitehousedrugpolicy.gov/hidta for HIDTA points of contact.

[66] policechiefmagazine.org/magazine/index.cfm?fuseaction=display_arch&article_id=139&issue_id=11200

coordinating with, and implementing recommendations made by, other information-sharing initiatives such as the Global Justice Information Sharing Initiative and federally sponsored intelligence programs.[67]

Bureau of Alcohol, Tobacco, Firearms and Explosives[68]

The Intelligence Division of Bureau of Alcohol, Tobacco, Firearms and Explosives (ATF) has evolved rapidly as an important tool for the diverse responsibilities of the bureau. Several activities in particular demonstrate the intelligence capability and resources of the ATF.

The ATF, which is now an agency of the Department of Justice, has developed Field Intelligence Groups at each of its 23 Field Divisions strategically located throughout the United States. These intelligence groups meld the training and experience of special agents, intelligence research specialists, industry operations inspectors, and support staff that focus on providing tactical intelligence support for their respective field divisions and their external law enforcement partners. Each Field Intelligence Group works under the authority of a supervisory special agent. The intelligence group supervisors are coordinated by, and work in conjunction with, the Intelligence Division to form a bureau-wide intelligence infrastructure. The Intelligence Division provides indoctrination and training for all Field Intelligence Group supervisors, intelligence officers, and intelligence research specialists.

The ATF maintains intelligence partnerships with the NDIC, EPIC, FinCEN, INTERPOL, the FBI's Counter Terrorism Center, and other international intelligence sources. Furthermore, the ATF maintains an MOU with the six RISSs that represent thousands of SLTLE agencies, pledging to share unique and vital intelligence resources. These external partners are key components of the ATF's *Strategic Intelligence Plan* and the means by which the ATF ensures a maximum contribution to the nation's law enforcement and intelligence communities.

During FY 2000, the Intelligence Division spearheaded the formulation of an MOU with the FBI to collaborate on investigations conducted by Joint Terrorism Task Forces (JTTF) located throughout the United States. This MOU brings ATF's unique knowledge and skills of explosives and firearms violations to the FBI's expertise in terrorism. Among the resources provided by ATF are the online Arson and Explosives National Registry and the Federal Firearms License (FFL) registry.

The Intelligence Division has implemented a state-of-the-art automated case management/intelligence reporting system called N-FOCIS (National Field Office Case Information System). The system consists of two companion applications: N-FORCE for special agents and N-SPECT for industry operations inspectors. Both eliminate redundant manual data entry on hard copy forms and provide a comprehensive reporting and information management application in a secure electronic environment.

[67] As an illustration of the comprehensive and integrated nature of the HIDTA programs and intelligence centers, see www.ncjrs.gov/ondcppubs/publications/enforce/hidta2001/ca-fs.html.

[68] Contact your local ATF Field Office for intelligence products and resources. Offices and contact information can be found at www.atf.gov/field.

N-FOCIS constitutes an online case-management system and electronic central information repository that allows the ATF to analyze and fully exploit investigative intelligence. N-FOCIS epitomizes the strength and unique value of the ATF's combined criminal and industry operations enforcement missions. The Intelligence Division has provided in-service training to many ATF field division special agents, investigative assistants, and inspectors on the use of the N-FOCIS applications. The ATF is planning to expand the N-FOCIS functionality and to integrate N-FOCIS with several key ATF applications including the National Revenue Center, the National Tracing Center, National Arson and Explosive Repository, and the Intelligence Division's Text Management System. This integration plan establishes N-FOCIS as the bureau's information backbone.

The Intelligence Division prepares a wide range of strategic intelligence reports related to the ATF mission that are available to SLTLE. In addition, intelligence is shared with state and local agencies through RISS and the JTTFs. In addition, ATF will readily respond to inquiries wherein SBU/CUI information may be shared.

ATF has also created a series of Regional Crime Gun Centers. The intent of the centers is to integrate gun tracing with ATF intelligence and with the HIDTA Regional Intelligence Centers to suppress gun-related crime.[69]

Federal Protective Service Secure Portal[70]
The DHS's Federal Protective Service (FPS) provides law enforcement and security services to more than 1 million tenants and daily visitors to federally owned and leased facilities nationwide. The FPS protection services focus directly on the interior security of the nation, and require close coordination and intelligence-sharing with the investigative functions within DHS. FPS is a full-service agency with comprehensive law enforcement, response, and communications components.[71]

To support their broad, nationwide role, FPS saw the need to develop a comprehensive online resource to aid in security, threat assessment, law enforcement, and protection of federal buildings, workers, and visitors. From this need, the FPS developed its Secure Portal. The web-based portal supports inter- and intra-agency secure information sharing and collaboration through compartmentalized collaboration tools, document libraries, secure messaging, and community calendars. Custom plug-ins facilitate geospatial awareness of officer safety, homeland security issues, incident reporting, and management of operations.

SLTLE agencies can gain access to the FPS Secure Portal by contacting a local FPS office or going to fps.esportals.net/signup/index.cfm and e-mailing the help desk link for registration.

Financial Crimes Enforcement Network[72]
The Financial Crimes Enforcement Network (FinCEN) brings agencies, investigators, and information together to fight the complex problem of money laundering. Since its creation in 1990, FinCEN has worked to maximize

[69] As an illustration see www.atf.gov/field/newyork/rcgc/index.htm.

[70] fps.esportals.net (Membership required)

[71] www.dhs.gov/xnews/releases/press_release_0154.shtm

[72] See www.fincen.gov.

information sharing among law enforcement agencies and other partners in the regulatory and financial communities. Through cooperation and partnerships, FinCEN's network approach encourages cost-effective and efficient measures to combat money laundering domestically and internationally.

The network supports federal, state, local, tribal, and international law enforcement by analyzing information required under the Bank Secrecy Act (BSA), one of the nation's most important tools in the fight against money laundering. The BSA's record-keeping and reporting requirements establish a financial trail for investigators to follow as they track criminals, their activities, and their assets. Over the years, FinCEN staff has developed its expertise in adding value to the information collected under the BSA by uncovering leads and exposing unknown information contained in the complexities of money laundering schemes.

Illicit financial transactions can take many routes—some complex, some simple, but all increasingly inventive—with the ultimate goal of disguising its source. The money can move through banks, check cashers, money transmitters, businesses, or casinos, and is often sent overseas to become "clean." The tools of the money launderer can range from complicated financial transactions carried out through webs of wire transfers and networks of shell companies, to old-fashioned currency smuggling.

Intelligence research specialists and law enforcement support staff research and analyze this information and other critical forms of intelligence to support financial criminal investigations. The ability to network with a variety of databases provides FinCEN with one of the largest repositories of information available to law enforcement in the country. Safeguarding the privacy of the data it collects is an overriding responsibility of the agency and its employees—a responsibility that strongly imprints all of its data management functions and operations.

FinCEN's information sources fall into three categories:
1. *Financial Database:* The financial database consists of reports that must be filed with the BSA, such as data on large currency transactions conducted at financial institutions or casinos, suspicious transactions, and international movements of currency or negotiable monetary instruments. This information often provides invaluable assistance for investigators because it is not readily available from any other source and preserves a financial paper trail for investigators to track criminals' proceeds and their assets.
2. *Commercial Databases:* Information from commercially available sources plays an increasingly vital role in criminal investigations. Commercial databases include information such as state, corporation, property, and people-locator records, as well as professional licenses and vehicle registrations.
3. *Law Enforcement Databases:* FinCEN is able to access various law enforcement databases through a written agreement with each agency.

FinCEN works closely with the IACP, National Association of Attorneys General, National White Collar Crime Center, and other organizations to inform law enforcement about the information available at FinCEN and how to use the information to attack criminal proceeds.

High-Risk Money Laundering and Related Financial Crimes Areas[73]

High Intensity Financial Crime Areas (HIFCA) were first announced in the 1999 National Money Laundering Strategy and were conceived in the Money Laundering and Financial Crimes Strategy Act of 1998 as a means of concentrating law enforcement efforts at the federal, state, and local levels in high-intensity money laundering zones. HIFCAs may be defined geographically or they can be created to address money laundering in an industry sector, a financial institution, or group of financial institutions.

To implement the goal of concentrating efforts, a money laundering action team will be created or identified within each HIFCA to spearhead a coordinated federal, state, and local anti-money laundering effort. Each action team will be composed of all relevant federal, state, and local enforcement authorities, prosecutors, and financial regulators who will concentrate on the following:

- Focus on tracing funds to the HIFCA from other areas, and from the HIFCA to other areas so that related investigations can be undertaken

- Focus on collaborative investigative techniques, both within the HIFCA and between the HIFCA and other areas

- Ensure a more systemic exchange of information about money laundering between HIFCA participants

- Include an asset forfeiture component as part of its work.

Gateway

FinCEN's Gateway system enables federal, state, and local law enforcement agencies to access online records filed under the BSA. The system saves investigative time and money by enabling investigators to conduct their own research and analysis of BSA data rather than relying on the resources of an intermediary agency to obtain financial records. A unique feature of Gateway is the "query alert" mechanism that automatically signals FinCEN when two or more agencies have an interest in the same subject. In this way, FinCEN is able to assist participating agencies in coordinating their investigations.

Virtually every criminal enterprise and terrorist organization is involved in some dimension of money laundering. The complexities of forensic accounting, often complicated by jurisdictional barriers, reinforces the need for intelligence personnel to be aware of the resources and expertise available through FinCEN.

Essential to effective intelligence is the ability to access and share information readily. A number of resources and systems are available to SLTLE agencies that permit access to federal intelligence products, regional and local intelligence products, current news and events, and secure e-mail. Many resources are available to law enforcement organizations for a minimal, if any, fee. Regardless of the degree of sophistication of a system, it is essential that a law enforcement organization have some form of secure e-mail and access to an SBU/CUI network to receive current advisories that maximize information sharing

[73] See www.fincen.gov/le_hifcadesign.html.

International Justice and Public Safety Network[74]

The International Justice and Public Safety Network (formerly the National Law Enforcement Telecommunication System [NLETS]) was created by state law enforcement agencies nearly 35 years ago as a primary means of integrating data related to traffic enforcement. Since its founding, the NLETS role has evolved from being primarily an interstate telecommunications service for law enforcement to a more broad-based network servicing the justice community at the local, state, and federal levels. It is now a broad-based interstate law enforcement network for the exchange of law enforcement and related justice information. Its purpose is to provide, within a secure environment, an international criminal justice telecommunications capability that will benefit to the highest degree the safety, security, and preservation of human life and the protection of property. NLETS will assist national and international governmental agencies and other organizations with similar missions who enforce or aid in enforcing local, state, federal, or international laws or ordinances.

NLETS is a nonprofit corporation chartered by the states and funded by user fees collected from the membership and managed by a board of directors consisting of state police executives. Primary services include access to key state databases, particularly drivers' licenses and motor vehicle records, criminal histories, and sex offender registries. The system also has access to special databases such as Canadian files, hazardous materials archives, U.S. General Services Administration fleet, immigration records, FAA registrations, NDPIX,[75] vehicle impounds, and import/export files. The system also includes terminal-to-terminal messaging and broadcast capabilities (such as an Amber Alert).

Accelerated Information Sharing for Law Enforcement

The next generation of NLETS is Accelerated Information Sharing for Law Enforcement (AISLE). The intent of AISLE is to accelerate information sharing for the entire U.S. law enforcement community by adopting and deploying XML[76] Web Services technology for interstate inquiries and responses. Like the Global Justice Information Sharing Initiative, it also seeks to promote the common XML standard for law enforcement information systems. Essentially, AISLE seeks to move NLETS completely into the most advanced realms of networking to enhance information sharing.

Operation Archangel and the Automated Critical Asset Management System

While the discussion of resources and systems has largely been avoided, discussion of state and local systems—the Automated Critical Asset Management System (ACAMS)—is an exception. While locally developed, it is becoming a national system with the support of the DHS.

ACAMS is a component of a broader initiative, Operation Archangel, that was developed by the Los Angeles Police Department. Building on local

[74] For contact information and more details, see www.nlets.org/default.asp.

[75] NDPIX is the National Drug Pointer Index, discussed in detail in Chapter 11.

[76] Internet web pages are typically written in Hypertext Markup Language (HTML) which aids in formatting and integrating diverse resources. The second generation is XML, Extensible Mark-up Language, which has all the features of HTML and provides significantly increased searching and comparison characteristics.

responsibilities for protecting Critical Infrastructure and Key Resources (as discussed in Chapter 9), the intent of Archangel is to identify and protect Critical Infrastructure and Key Resources in the Los Angeles metropolitan area. Its purpose is to defend likely targets against catastrophic terrorist attacks, relying on the guiding principle that local agencies are most knowledgeable about their own critical assets. The system was born out of a need to engender interagency/departmental cooperation and coordination to facilitate the strategic application and management of information and resources for the prevention, deterrence, mitigation, and response to critical incidents, including terrorism. Primarily focused on prevention, Archangel has been designed to identify critical threat locations and plan multiagency/disciplinary prevention, deterrence, mitigation and response efforts.[77]

A number of flexible components of Archangel make it a scalable model that is exportable across the United States. The following are among Archangel's initiatives:

- *Identification and Prioritization of Critical Assets*

- *Critical Asset Assessments* using a three-tiered template:

    1. Conducting appropriate vulnerability assessments to determine and reduce a location's degree of vulnerability.

    2. Harvesting detailed location-specific information (i.e., names, phone numbers, floor plans, site postings, etc.) All for use by pre-incident planners and on-scene incident commanders through web-based delivery during critical incidents.

    3. Drafting site-specific, pre-incident security enhancement plans and post-occurrence action plans designed to provide tactical guidance and insight to planners and/or to incident commanders in the field.

- *Critical Asset Assessment Teams* that conduct an on-site threat and vulnerability assessment.

- *Protective Security Task Force (PSTF),* is a plainclothes, low-profile team of personnel specifically trained and equipped with state-of-the-art technology to provide a comprehensive cloak of security to a threatened asset. Primarily, the PSTF will be deployed when intelligence indicates that a threat may be directed at a critical asset and/or event. In the absence of intelligence, the PSTF will deploy to critical assets throughout the area of responsibility, providing low-key but visible enhancements to the resident security measures.

- *Security Officer Terrorism Awareness Course (SOTAC),* is a 4-hour block of instruction designed specifically for the security industry professional to enhance awareness of current terrorist trends and methodologies for attack.

- *Automated Critical Asset Management System (ACAMS).* Archangel has partnered with U.S. DHS to develop ACAMS, a secure interoperable web-based system to manage critical asset information. ACAMS coordinates the following:

    - Critical Asset Inventory and Prioritization Modeling

    - Asset Manager Questionnaires (promotes public/private partnerships)

    - Critical Asset Assessments

[77] www.lapdonline.org/emergency_services_division/content_basic_view/33044

- Site Specific Pre-Incident Security Enhancement Plans
- Buffer Zone Plans
- Building Inventories
- Site Specific Post-Occurrence/Response Plans.[78]

ACAMS also includes any predeveloped response plans for specific incidents[79] and site-specific pre-incident security enhancement plans for use by strategists to prevent and deter incidents from occurring.[80]

Constellation/Automated Critical Asset Management System

The DHS has embraced the Constellation/Automated Critical Asset Management System (C/ACAMS) that is explicitly intended to support fusion centers and other information-sharing partners in support of the DHS mission of protecting critical infrastructure. C/ACAMS provides state, local, and private-sector partners with a set of resources for collecting and managing information related to critical infrastructures and to inject infrastructure information into fusion center analysis. This information, when combined with terrorism threat streams, provides fusion center analysts and private-sector infrastructure owners and operators with a context for understanding risk and to target protection resources against those assets or systems that have the highest risk profiles. Currently, C/ACAMS is deployed to fusion centers across the United States and is used by more than 2,000 state and local infrastructure protection analysts. The data they have collected on more than 38,000 unique infrastructure assets are vital to the national effort to enable prevention, protection, response, and recovery activities.[81]

Law Enforcement Intelligence Unit[82]

Founded in 1956, the Law Enforcement Intelligence Unit (LEIU) is an independent professional association of U.S. and international law enforcement intelligence professionals who gather, record, and exchange confidential information not available through regular law enforcement channels, concerning organized crime and terrorism. It is an association of U.S. and international law enforcement professionals, similar in many respects to numerous other associations serving professionals. LEIU has no staff, other than an executive director, and no capability as an entity to conduct an investigation or law enforcement activity. Each member agency is bound by, and acts pursuant to, local law and its own agency regulations.

The organization is divided geographically into four zones: Eastern, Central, Northwestern, and Southwestern. Each zone elects a chair and vice chair to serve as zone officers. Internationally, LEIU elects a general chair, vice general chair, and designates a secretary-treasurer and a legal advisor who serve as international officers. The international officers, zone officers, past general chair, and two representatives from the Central Coordinating Agency (i.e., the California Department of Justice which houses LEIU data) make up the executive board. The board is the governing body of LEIU and, as such, establishes policy and passes on the admission of all members, and is governed by a constitution and bylaws.

[78] Ibid.

[79] McCreesh, Patrick and Craig Neuman. *Managing for Counter-Terrorism Success in the Los Angeles Police Department.* New York: The Manhattan Institute and Cambridge, Massachusetts: John F. Kennedy School of Government, Harvard University, 2007, p. 9.

[80] Leson, Joel. *Assessing and Managing the Terrorism Threat.* Washington, D.C.: Bureau of Justice Assistance, U.S. Department of Justice, 2005, p. 19. Also see www.dhs/gov/acams.

[81] Allen, Charles E. *Information Sharing at the Federal, State and Local Levels. Statement for the Record before the United States Senate Committee on Homeland Security and Governmental Affairs,* July 23, 2008, 11.

[82] For more information on LEIU see www.leiu-homepage.org/index.html. For contact information concerning LEIU membership, e-mail leiu@doj.ca.gov. LEIU, California Department of Justice, P.O. Box 163029, Sacramento, CA 95816-3029.

LEIU membership is limited to law enforcement agencies of general jurisdiction having an intelligence function. To become a member, an agency head submits a written application. The applying agencies must be sponsored by an LEIU member. Each member agency head appoints an LEIU representative as the contact for the LEIU.

Virtually any kind of information that may be lawfully retained in law enforcement intelligence records may be exchanged as long as the recipient meets the need-to-know and right-to-know standards. It is important to keep intelligence records consistent with legal standards. LEIU is not a computer system where members can make queries; rather, it is a network where information is exchanged between members, albeit in electronic form.

Information Sharing

To submit an inquiry about a suspected criminal to the LEIU automated system, a member agency enters the subject information through a secure intranet that is stored on RISS.net. The subject information includes, among other items, the person's identity, criminal activity, and criminal associates. All information submitted to the LEIU automated file must meet LEIU File Guidelines (See Appendix C) and comply with 28 CFR, Part 23. The submitting agency must certify that the subject meets established criteria, including criminal predicate. The Central Coordinating Agency manages this automated file.

International Criminal Police Organization[83]

The International Criminal Police Organization (INTERPOL) was founded in 1923 to serve as a clearinghouse for information on transnational criminals. It receives, stores, analyzes, and disseminates criminal data in cooperation with its 181 member countries on a 24/7/365 basis in its four official languages (English, French, Spanish, and Arabic). Interpol deals only with international crimes. Its four core functions are to provide member states with the following:

1. *Secure global police communication services.* INTERPOL runs a global police communications system called I-24/7, which provides police around the world with a common platform through which they can share crucial information about criminals and criminality.

2. *Operational data services and databases for police.* INTERPOL's databases and services ensure that police worldwide have access to the information and services they need to prevent and investigate crimes. Databases include information such as names, fingerprints and DNA profiles, and stolen property such as passports, vehicles, and works of art.

3. *Operational police support services.* INTERPOL supports law enforcement officials in the field with emergency support and operational activities, especially in its priority crime areas of fugitives, public safety and terrorism, drugs and organized crime, trafficking in human beings, and financial and high-tech crime. A Command and Coordination Centre operates 24 hours a day, 7 days a week.

4. *Police training and development.* INTERPOL provides focused police training initiatives for national police forces, and also offers on-demand advice, guidance, and support in building dedicated crime-fighting components. The aim is to enhance the capacity of member countries to effectively combat serious transnational crime and terrorism.[84]

[83] The INTERPOL General Secretariat site is www.interpol.int.

[84] www.interpol.int

Criminal intelligence analysts at INTERPOL are uniquely placed to recognize and detect patterns and criminal trends from a global perspective, and have the resources to assist with specific international crime cases.

In the United States, the contact point for Interpol is the U.S. National Central Bureau (USNCB) which operates within the guidelines prescribed by the Department of Justice, in conjunction with the DHS. The mission of the USNCB is to facilitate international law enforcement cooperation as the United States representative to INTERPOL.

When INTERPOL is seeking specific information or seeking a person, it issues a color-coded notice, with each color representing a different type of action from the recipient agencies. While these notices are rarely encountered by SLTLE officers, it is nonetheless of value to be familiar with them should the issue arise.

U.S. law enforcement officers can gain access to INTERPOL reports and make international inquiries through their state point of contact (usually within the state law enforcement or intelligence agency) who will query the USNCB. The USNCB address and web site are: U.S. Department of Justice, INTERPOL, United States National Central Bureau, Washington, DC 20530 www.usdoj.gov/usncb.

Summary

As demonstrated in this chapter, the amount of information and intelligence being generated by federal law enforcement agencies and national law enforcement entities is significant. If that information is not being used, its value is lost. Not only are these resources responsible for making information available to SLTLE agencies in an accessible and consumable form, nonfederal law enforcement must develop the mechanisms for receiving the information and be good consumers of it.

One of the ongoing controversies is the problem of dealing with classified information. This chapter explained the classification process as well as the initiatives that are being undertaken to deal with this issue. One measure is to increase the number of security clearances for SLTLE personnel. The other measure is for the FBI to write intelligence reports so that they are unclassified, but remain as CUI to give SLTLE personnel access.

By gaining access to secure networking (e.g., LEO, RISS.net, ATIX), interacting on a regular basis with the FBI Field Intelligence Group, and proactively interacting with other federal law enforcement intelligence offices, SLTLE can have access to the types of critical intelligence necessary to protect their communities.

A Summary of Selected Intelligence Networks and Applications

A wide and diverse array of information systems that support the law enforcement intelligence function have been discussed thus far.[85] Many other systems exist at the federal level; however, most law enforcement officers will not have access to them unless they are assigned to a fusion center or major urban area law enforcement intelligence unit. Nevertheless, there is value in having a summary knowledge of some of these systems. Those previously discussed in this chapter are not included in the following summaries.

Classified Networks

- *C Local Area Network (Top Secret Network).* This network, commonly referred to as the C-LAN, is used within DHS to communicate Top Secret information with the Intelligence Community. It provides connectivity to the Department of Defense's Joint Worldwide Intelligence Communications System to access, receive, and share intelligence information.

- *Sensitive Compartmental Information Operational Network (Top Secret Network).* This network, also known as SCION, is used to transport top secret counterterrorism data, including intelligence and warning information. It provides an interface with the Department of Defense's Joint Worldwide Intelligence Communications System that allows FBI agents and analysts to exchange Top Secret intelligence information with other members of the Intelligence Community.

- *Federal Bureau of Investigation Network (Secret Network).* Commonly referred to as the FBINET, it is a global-wide area network used for communicating Secret information, including investigative case files and intelligence pertaining to national security. It also runs administrative applications.

- *Homeland Secure Data Network (Secret Network).* Also known as HSDN, this network transmits homeland security data in support of activities including intelligence, investigations, and inspections that are classified at the Secret level. HSDN provides Secret connectivity to civilian agencies and will provide Secret connectivity in the future for civilian agencies currently using the Department of Defense's Secret Internet Protocol Router Network. It is used, for example, to transmit intelligence summaries, secure messaging, and e-mail correspondence.

SBU/CUI Networks

- *Critical Infrastructure Warning Information Network.* Also known as CWIN, the network is used to transmit voice and data on infrastructure protection, communication and coordination, alert, and notification. In the event that a significant attack disrupts telecommunications networks or the Internet, the CWIN will provide secure capability for communications across key government network operations centers, the private and public sectors, and trusted foreign partners. According to the DHS, the CWIN is the critical, survivable network connecting the DHS with the vital sectors that are essential in restoring the nation's infrastructure during incidents of national significance.

[85]The value, use, and application of many of these systems are discussed in: *Information Technology: Numerous Federal Networks Used to Support Homeland Security Need to Be Better Coordinated with Key State and Local Information-Sharing Initiatives. A report to the Chairman, Committee on Homeland Security, U.S. House of Representatives.* Washington, D.C.: General Accountability Office, April 2007.

- *Criminal Justice Information Services Wide Area Network.* Also known as the CJIS WAN, it provides secure electronic connectivity to information on individuals, vehicles, and property associated with crimes or terrorist organizations to state, local, tribal, and federal law enforcement agencies. It is also used to identify individuals from submitted fingerprints and to exchange deoxyribonucleic acid (DNA) information, background-check information, and criminal history information.

- *Customs and Border Protection Network.* Commonly referred to as the CBP Network, it is used to transmit SBU/CUI data related to Customs and Border Protection's support of homeland security functions, such as protecting the nation's borders from terrorists and regulating and facilitating the lawful movement of goods and persons across U.S. borders.

- *DHS Core Network.* Also known as the DCN, the network transmits SBU/CUI data related to the DHS homeland security mission in areas such as customs, border patrol, and intelligence.

- *FBI Unclassified Network.* Commonly known as UNet, this is a national wide area network that provides the FBI with access to SBU/CUI intelligence and law-enforcement sensitive information. It provides bureau agents with access to secure mail and LEO.

- *Justice Consolidated Network.* Known as the JCN, this network transmits fingerprint, arrest records, and other data relating to the investigation and prosecution of crimes and terrorist activities among DOJ components.

- *Justice Unified Telecommunications Network.* This network, also known as JUTNet, transmits SBU/CUI information (such as fingerprint and arrest information) pertaining to the investigation and prosecution of crimes and terrorist activities. In addition, it supports video conferencing and certain Voice over Internet Protocol services.

- *Immigration and Customs Enforcement Network.* Also known as ICENet, this network supports the data transmission needs of the DHS Immigration and Customs Enforcement component. Major programs dependent on this network include the Office of Investigations, the Detention and Removal Office, the Federal Protective Services Office, and the Intelligence Office.

- *Secret Service Wide Area Network.* Commonly referred to as the Secret Service WAN, this network supports the homeland security mission by providing security and protection to our nation's leaders and financial systems

- *Transportation Security Administration Network.* This network, also known as TSANet, is a global network used for security operations, intelligence, and law enforcement information-sharing. It is used to transmit alerts, fingerprints, and information from the Transportation Security Administration's mission-critical applications.

- *ONENet.* A single network using dual carriers to support interoperability and data sharing in all DHS mission areas and between all DHS components. The DHS is deploying ONENet to DHS components and it will consolidate the following seven networks: 1. Coast Guard Data Network Plus; 2. Customs and Border Protection Network; 3. DHS Core Network; 4. Federal Emergency Management Agency Switched Network; 5. Immigration and Customs Enforcement Network; 6. Secret Service Wide Area Network; and 7. Transportation Security Administration Network.

SBU/CUI Network Applications

Bomb Arson Tracking System. Commonly referred to as BATS, this application is a partnership among DOJ, the ATF's Bomb Data Center, and members of the nation's fire and post-blast investigative communities. It provides these organizations with a comprehensive incident-based information-sharing system.

eTrace. The eTrace application is a web-based firearm trace submission system and trace analysis module for use by approved law enforcement agencies. The eTrace application improves the efficiency of the firearm tracing process and provides for the secure exchange of firearms trace-related information between the law enforcement community and the ATF.

Federal Emergency Management Agency Switched Network. This network, commonly known as the FEMA Switched Network, provides support for emergency coordination of federal, state, and local operations, disaster assistance, and government recovery efforts. For example, it is used to provide information about disaster victims and logistics for disasters, in addition to normal business.

Conclusion

If effective information sharing is one of the critical goals of contemporary law enforcement intelligence, then networks and systems are the critical tools to reach that goal. As has been seen throughout this chapter, there has been significant growth in the capability of law enforcement agencies to share information. The growth has been a product of new initiatives following 9/11, the availability of new networking technologies that reduce interoperability conflicts, and the commitment of American law enforcement at all levels of government to facilitate information-sharing processes. These factors are in a dynamic state. Systems and networks will change; therefore, it is incumbent on the intelligence manager to carefully monitor trends to stay current.

Chapter 13:

*Management and Human Resource Issues
for the Intelligence Function*

Management and Human Resource Issues for the Intelligence Function

The basic principles and applications of management—leadership, accountability, span of control, chain of command, labor relations, program evaluation, to name a few—apply to the intelligence function in the same manner as they would apply to any other organizational entity. The extensive literature of police administration and management is a solid resource for these issues when managing an intelligence unit. This chapter will focus on selected issues relating to the development and management of the intelligence function.

While most American law enforcement agencies might not have a formal intelligence unit, they still have an intelligence function to manage. With the increasing symbiosis among federal and state, local, and tribal law enforcement (SLTLE), adoption of the *National Criminal Intelligence Sharing Plan* (NCISP), the growth of networked intelligence information systems, and the responsibility of keeping the homeland secure, virtually every law enforcement agency in the country needs to develop some kind of intelligence capacity. That capacity may be a full-scale unit or one person who serves part time as an agency's point of contact for receiving and disseminating critical information. In some form, an intelligence capacity has become a de facto requirement for American law enforcement agencies. As a result, new intelligence processes for law enforcement present challenges such as the following:

- Reengineering some of the organization's structure and processes
- Developing a shared vision of the terrorist or criminal threat within the agency as well as with the broader law enforcement community
- Participating in intelligence processes and following through with information sharing
- Committing resources, time, and energy to the intelligence function
- Developing a proactive spirit and creative thought to identify "what we don't know" about terrorism and international organized crime
- Developing a culture within the law enforcement agency that is able to think globally and act locally
- Developing a culture of information sharing
- Providing vigilance, patience, and entrepreneurial leadership.

To put these components into operation in a functional intelligence mechanism, SLTLE agencies of all sizes need, at a minimum, fundamental operational components, such as these:

- A person designated as the intelligence point of contact to whom external agencies may direct inquiries, warnings, and advisories, and from whom information and questions may be sent. He or she must have sufficient training to understand the language, processes, and regulations incumbent on the law enforcement Intelligence Community.
- A secure electronic communications system for sending and receiving information that is Sensitive But Unclassified/Controlled Unclassified Information (SBU/CUI). Several systems are available, including Law

Enforcement Online (LEO), the Regional Information Sharing System Network (RISS.NET), Automated Trusted information Exchange (ATIX) (originally the Anti-Terrorism Information Exchange)—some of which are available at no charge to the user. With the growth of the Global Justice Extensible Markup Language Data Model (GJXDM) standard[1], access to these systems will be essential for the most accurate information-sharing.

- Established policies for information collection, reporting, and dissemination.

- Established ability to determine the kinds of information and intelligence that is needed to effectively prevent terrorism and disrupt criminal enterprises. This is a difficult challenge requiring a significant labor investment. Understanding the threats and targets within a community and developing responses to neutralize those threats is essential. American law enforcement must discover the evidence of threats that may be in its backyard.

Beyond these factors, a number of management factors may be considered when developing an intelligence capacity. A common question asked by law enforcement executives and those responsible for developing an intelligence capacity, is "Where do I start?" Providing a succinct response is not easy because the starting place will vary depending on agency size, the chief executive's vision, the geographic location of the jurisdiction, the presence of factors that make the jurisdiction a terrorist or criminal target, and other variables unique to the jurisdiction and agency. The first part of the answer is to provide a list of factors to consider when developing or reengineering the intelligence capacity of a law enforcement agency. The second part of the answer is to develop a Concept of Operations (ConOps) for the intelligence unit to refine how the intelligence function is envisioned to integrate it into the agency's other activities. Finally, attention will be given to selected intelligence management issues.

A Checklist of Considerations in Developing or Reengineering the Law Enforcement Intelligence Capacity

The following is a list of questions and variables to consider when developing the intelligence capacity. Not every factor will apply to every agency, although collectively these factors will give a perspective on the intelligence function as it exists within the organizational environment. The list provides a straightforward perspective of the management responsibilities required to accomplish the task. Many of the factors will be discussed in greater detail later in the chapter. (See also Table 13-1.)

Administration and Management
- The chief executive must have a vision for the role of the intelligence function.
  - What activities are expected of the intelligence function?
    - Clearinghouse of information?
    - Tactical analysis?
    - Strategic analysis/forecasting?

[1] For information about the Global Justice XML Data Model, see it.ojp.gov/jxdm.

- Threat assessments?
- Pointer and deconfliction activities?
- Other? Make sure this is articulated.

- Does the chief executive's vision include incorporating the Intelligence-Led Policing (ILP) philosophy throughout the law enforcement agency?
    - If not, what is the envisioned relationship of intelligence to other departmental activities?
        - This should be clearly articulated by the chief executive.
- If intelligence is one of several responsibilities assigned to one person or unit, what is its priority/relationship to other responsibilities?
- What crimes are to be the focus (i.e., strategic priorities) of the intelligence function?
- Will "all hazards" be included?
- If so, how will it be defined for the intelligence function?
- What outputs and activities are expected of the intelligence function?
- Question: Does the chief executive and/or command staff need to be briefed (i.e., trained) on contemporary law enforcement intelligence?
    - If so, how do you propose to suggest or accomplish this?

- The chief executive must demonstrate commitment and support for the intelligence function.
    - This includes allocation of people and adequate resources.
- Obtain budget parameters.
    - How much funding will be available to establish the intelligence unit?
- Will the intelligence supervisor be organizationally responsible directly to the chief executive or to another commander (e.g., the criminal investigations division commander or operations division commander)?
    - There are advantages to both direct reporting to the chief executive and reporting to another commander.
        - If the intelligence unit supervisor answers directly to the chief executive:
            - Advantage: More direct information flow and operational responses regarding threats.
            - Disadvantage: There may be jealousies among those of higher rank with respect to the intelligence supervisor's access to the chief executive.
        - If the unit is assigned under another division commander:
            - Advantage: It helps shield the unit from criticisms of secrecy, which often becomes an issue.
            - Disadvantage: A filtering effect of critical information can occur.
    - While other advantages and disadvantages can occur, they will be dependent on the culture of the law enforcement organization.

Develop the Intelligence Unit's Infrastructure

- Mission, goal(s), and objectives of the intelligence function must be articulated.
- Develop necessary policies and procedures (See Table 13-1 for a list of areas in which to consider developing policy for the intelligence function. The need for policy will be related directly to the mission, goals, and objectives.)
  - Develop a privacy policy that is consistent with federal privacy guidelines.[2]
  - Develop a policy and procedures for your criminal intelligence records system that is 28 CFR Part 23-compliant.
    - The Law Enforcement Intelligence Unit (LEIU) *File Guidelines*[3] serves as a court-tested model.
    - The criminal intelligence records policy should include:
      - Collection standard of a criminal predicate.
      - Retention guidelines.
        - Temporary files should have a time limit for retaining information and standards for review and purging.
      - Review of records in the criminal intelligence records system.
      - Purging requirements and processes.
      - Dissemination criteria.
      - Nondiscrimination statement.
- Select an office location.
  - Will the unit be colocated with CID, narcotics, organized crime, or other unit?
    - If so, be certain that the physical location will be able to meet the security requirements needed for intelligence records.
  - If the intelligence unit is at an off-site location, it is preferable to have a stand-alone office, not with other businesses.
  - Ideally, the intelligence unit's office will be centrally located.
  - Develop your work environment
    - Get access to intelligence products and networks.
    - Lockable filing cabinets.
    - Dedicated computer.
    - All personnel, supplies, and services necessary to fulfill the vision.
- Purchase or obtain the unit's vehicles
  - Undercover vehicles in a variety of styles and colors.

[2] it.ojp.gov/default.aspx?area=globalJustice &page=1151.

[3] it.ojp.gov/documents/LEIU_Crim_Intell_ File_Guidelines.pdf.

Table 13-1: Sample Issues for Intelligence Unit Policy Development[4]

- Intelligence unit organization, role, and responsibilities
- Intelligence unit staff position requirements, selection, and training
- Privacy policy (consistent with the federal Information Sharing Environment (ISE) *Privacy Guidelines*)
- Intelligence unit records management
  - 28 CFR Part 23 compliant file guidelines (including standards and processes collection, retention, review, purging, and disseminating)
  - Quality control procedures for data and information accuracy
- Handling of SBU/CUI information
- Access, documentation, dissemination, and of use of information form
  - Intelligence records systems (i.e., RISS.NET, LEO, Homeland Security Information Network [HSIN])
  - Contacting other agencies and jurisdictions (i.e., fusion centers, FBI Field Intelligence Group [FIG], and other law enforcement agencies)
  - Contacting International Criminal Police Organization (INTERPOL)
  - Contacting El Paso Intelligence Center (EPIC)
- Types of intelligence products to be produced
  - Marking and dissemination policy for intelligence products
- Intelligence unit reporting procedures and dissemination
- Suspicious Activity Reporting and field interview procedures and reporting
- Classification and security system for the agency and/or intelligence unit
  - Rules for violations of the security system
- Procedures and accountability when operating under a memorandum of agreement
- Intelligence unit processes and responsibilities during critical incidents
- Surveillance operations (processes, documentation, limitations)
- Access to equipment and resources in support of intelligence activities
- Use of criminal informants
  - Guidelines for payments to criminal informants
- Undercover operations in support of the intelligence function
  - Undercover reporting procedure
  - Investigative and undercover expense fund accountability
  - Consumption of alcoholic beverages during undercover operations and surveillance
  - Narcotic simulation during undercover narcotic investigations
- Information release and media policy
- Intelligence unit performance evaluation and review

[4] A number of sample *Intelligence Policy Manuals* are available online at the DHS Fusion Process Technical Assistance Program at www.llis.dhs.gov. In addition, sample policies are available at the National Criminal intelligence Resource Center web site accessible through the RISS.NET portal and LEO. As will be seen, there is a wide variation of structures and approaches to these manuals. Each needs to be tailored to a specific agency's needs, but the samples provide good guidance. In addition, the International Association of Chiefs of Police prepared a document under BJA funding that provides guidance on developing policies and procedures: Orrick, W. Dwayne. *Best Practices Guide: Developing a Police Department Policy-Procedure Manual.* Alexandria, Virginia: International Association of Chiefs of Police, undated.

Staffing

- Select personnel: Intelligence officers
    - Consider languages and education.
    - Consider how the officers get along with other agencies.
    - Consider a past officer/deputy with undercover experience.
    - Consider policing style.
        - A person who is aggressive in making arrests and kicking in doors typically will not be a good fit in an intelligence unit.
        - Personal characteristics most suited to the intelligence unit include:
            - Maturity.
            - Dependability.
            - Works well without supervision.
            - Self-motivator.
            - A team player.
    - In the selection of officers for the intelligence unit, be certain they are able to obtain a security clearance, if required for the position.
        - For law enforcement officers, one of the more common factors that prohibits them from receiving a clearance is poor credit.
    - Consider knowledge of your special needs, such as gangs, computers, surveillance techniques, tactical surveillance equipment, etc.
- Select personnel: Analysts
    - The analyst's position and role should be viewed as a practicing professional of equal organizational stature to officers, not treated as support staff.
    - Desirable characteristics of an analyst include:
        - Highly motivated.
        - Critical thinker.
        - Strong computer skills.
        - Willing to help all with cases.
        - Ability to obtain a security clearance.
- Once personnel have been selected, contact the local FBI office to apply for security clearances for your new personnel[5]
    - In most cases, a Secret-level clearance will be sufficient. The process takes several months.

Training

- Training
    - Get the added training you need to further your strategic plan.
        - Includes training on your specific policies/procedures.
    - Remember, training includes both the intelligence discipline and training on crimes that are the focus of the intelligence unit.
- Ensure that all training meets the standards of:

[5] See www.fbi.gov/clearance/ securityclearance.htm.

- Minimum Criminal Intelligence Training Standards.[6]
- *National Criminal Intelligence Sharing Plan.*[7]
- Conduct a training needs assessment and enroll your personnel in the training they need (Below are examples. Training will be discussed later in the chapter).
  - Training on the discipline and processes of intelligence.
  - Analytic training.
  - Intelligence records management, including 28 CFR Part 23.
  - Analysts will need many other courses to become proficient.
    - Certified Intelligence Analyst certificates.
    - Crime mapping.
    - HIDTA Programs (Analytical Investigative Techniques I and II).
    - FINCEN.
  - Join open-source networks.
- Be certain to monitor the Bureau of Justice Assistance "Criminal Intelligence Master Training Calendar."[8]

Information Management and Information-Sharing

- In light of the chief's vision of intelligence products:
  - Identify the types of intelligence products to produce.
  - Identify the dissemination table of intelligence products.
    - Internal dissemination only?
    - If external dissemination will be included, define:
      - Dissemination criteria (What are the characteristics of recipients who receive the products).
      - Will the Third Agency Rule be applied?
      - Must products be approved for dissemination prior to being sent?
      - What is the mechanism for disseminating products?
      - Will there be an audit trail for disseminated products?
      - What types of products will not be disseminated outside of the agency?
- Select computer databases to store information and intelligence records:
  - Must be kept separate from your agency's regular Records Management System.
  - Must be able to purge records from the system so they are destroyed and not accessible in the future.
  - Secure and audited access to computers and systems.
- Obtain individual computers for your personnel.
  - Analysts need a more powerful and diverse system than needed by officers and deputies.

[6] it.ojp.gov/documents/min_crim_intel_stand.pdf.

[7] it.ojp.gov/documents/NCISP_Plan.pdf.

[8] mastercalendar.ncirc.gov.

- Basic software needs:[9]
    - Word processing program.
    - Spreadsheet program.
    - Relational database.
    - Presentation software.
    - Flowcharting software.
    - Link analysis software.
    - Database reporting/visualization software.
    - Mapping software.
    - Photo enhancement software.
    - Telephone analysis software.
    - Analytic charting.
    - Portable Document Format (PDF) creation software.
    - Security software (virus, adware, spyware software; firewall, and Virtual Private Network [VPN] security).
    - Publication software.
    - Statistical analysis software.
    - Text mining software.
- Budget for analytical tools and commercial databases, including membership in the Regional Information Sharing System (RISS) center and commercial data base search system.
- Full Internet access.
- Stand-alone computer for covert operations.

- Develop a report and intelligence product numbering system.
    - Keep an audit and control log of issued numbers that can be accessed by unit members.
    - Develop a system that easily permits identification of unit, date, and application of the bulletin.
- Organize monthly meetings among all area analysts to discuss and share issues and analytic methods.
- Organize and host a monthly intelligence meeting with other area law enforcement agencies.
    - Meetings should include analysts and officers.
        - Creates a trusting environment with others.
        - Face-to-face contact is critical.
        - Sharing information is critical.
        - Creates a contact list to handle situations quickly.
    - Also invite specific trusted/vetted individuals from appropriate private-sector companies that can assist in your goals, as applicable.
    - Invite federal agencies such as the Joint Terrorism Task Force (JTTF) or Immigration and Customs Enforcement.

[9] Resource: Global Justice Information Sharing Initiative. *Analyst Toolbox. A Toolbox for the Intelligence Analyst.* Washington, D.C.:, U.S. Department of Justice, Global Justice information Sharing Initiative, Intelligence Working Group, November 2006. it.ojp.gov/documents/analyst_toolbox.pdf.

Implementation and Assessment

- Start the process:
    - Test your system and be prepared to adjust it.
    - Identify critical processes and procedures to collect data for assessment.
    - Ask the consumers of the intelligence function if it is working.
    - Seek suggestions for improvement.
- Implement an audit process.
    - Intelligence Guide Audit Model.
    - LEIU Audit Checklist for the Criminal Intelligence Function.
- Strive for continuous quality improvement.

The points in this list are food for thought in developing the agency's intelligence structure. These factors are intended to help identify issues that need to be addressed in planning for the intelligence function. The next step is to integrate these factors into a cohesive vision of how the intelligence structure will actually operate within an agency. The next step, therefore, is to mold these factors into a ConOps.

Developing the Concept of Operations

The Concept of Operations (ConOps) is a user-oriented document that describes the characteristics of a proposed program, initiative, or system from the viewpoints of how staff and users will interact with the proposed initiative.[10] The ConOps is used to communicate overall characteristics of the new organizational entity—in this case, a new intelligence structure—to management, staff, and users. Ideally, the ConOps is prepared in conjunction with a business plan. While the ConOps describes the organization, mission, and organizational objectives from an integrated systems point of view, the business plan describes the proposed system or situation from an investment and process point of view.

The ConOps provides an analysis that bridges the gap between the operational needs and visions and the technical aspects of a functioning organization, in this case, an intelligence unit. The ConOps should also document a program's characteristics and the user's operational needs in a manner that can be confirmed by the user without requiring any technical knowledge beyond that required to perform normal job functions. Management and users, for example, need to understand how the intelligence unit will function and the products it will produce, but do not need to know how to conduct specific types of analysis or access specific systems.

The ConOps documents the visions and expectations of management and users alike without requiring the provision of quantified, testable specifications until later in the system life cycle. The ConOps also provides a mechanism for management and users to express thoughts and concerns about possible issues, strategies, and processes before actual implementation of the system.

The ConOps represents a process for developing a new functional concept of an organizational activity. It seeks to represent the needs of the organization,

[10] To review different law enforcement agency ConOps, after registering for the DHS Lessons Learned Information Sharing (LLIS) system – www/llis.dhs.gov – go to the Fusion Process Technical Assistance Resource Center and search the "channel" for "ConOps."

needs of the users/consumers of intelligence, and embraces lessons learned or best practices of other organizations, all tailored to meet the needs of the law enforcement agency.

Figure 13-1 illustrates the development process. The series of progressive activities, illustrated on the top row, are intended to clarify the operational concept of a new organizational activity, in this case, a new intelligence structure. The bottom row represents functional components required to develop the concept. More specifically, in order to establish goals, one needs to know the intended purpose of the program, which will be strongly directed by the chief executive's vision of the program. This vision must be shared with the staff who will actually develop and operate the program. Once the goals are clear, the ConOps can move forward to develop an intelligence structure that can accomplish those goals.

Figure 13-1: Process for the Development of a Concept of Operations

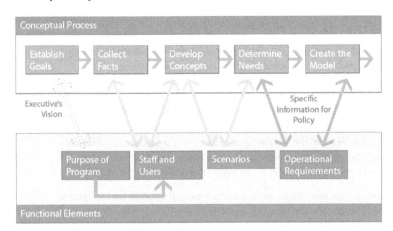

The next conceptual step is to gather information related to the goals, for example, national standards (such as the NCISP and *Fusion Center Guidelines*), lessons learned and best practices from other agencies, legal issues, and other factors that may be specifically idiosyncratic to the jurisdiction. The latter information often has to be gained from staff and potential users of the new (or reengineered) intelligence structure. Based on the collective analysis of these facts, the concept of how the new intelligence structure will work begins to take shape. Once again, two-way discussion with staff and users is essential to ensure that the concept will work. One of the effective mechanisms for testing this is to develop different information-sharing and analytic scenarios to illustrate the concept. For example, if a new Suspicious Activity Reporting mechanism is to be part of the new intelligence structure, different scenarios of how the system would work can be developed with feedback from staff and users on the strengths, weaknesses, and constraints of the system.

By developing scenarios for all aspects of the new intelligence enterprise, specific changes to, or needs for, the system can be identified and built into the concept. These needs will help define the operational requirements for the new intelligence structure to be successful—everything from office space to training to new report forms. Once they have been identified, the final model, represented by the ConOps, can be prepared for review and consideration. The culmination of this process needs to be placed in written form to fully communicate the new operational concept.

Contents of a Concept of Operations

There are different models of ConOps, each of which will always need some degree of adaption to meet the unique needs of a given agency or fusion center. The following model, which is broadly based on a model used by the U.S. Department of Health and Human Services,[11] provides a blending of the more common elements found in a ConOps as used by a law enforcement agency.

> Title Page
> Contents
> Figures
> Tables

1. *Introduction:* Summarize the purpose of the document, the scope of activities that resulted in its development, its relationship to other relevant plans or standards, the intended audience for the ConOps, and expected evolution of the document. Also describe any security or privacy considerations associated with use of the ConOps.

2. *Referenced Documents:* Provide identifying information for all documents referenced within the ConOps document (e.g., NCISP, *Fusion Center Guidelines*, 28 CFR Part 23, as well as legislation, feasibility studies, or any other relevant documentation.)

3. *Current System or Situation:* Describe the intelligence structure as it currently exists. If there is no current intelligence structure on which to base changes, then describe the situation that motivates development of the proposed intelligence unit.

    3.1 Background, Objectives, and Scope

    Provide an overview of the current intelligence structure including, as applicable, background, mission, goals, objectives, scope, and responsibilities for the current intelligence structure.

[11] www.cms.hhs.gov/ SystemLifecycleFramework/Downloads/ ConOps.pdf.

3.2 Operational Policies and Constraints

Describe the operational policies and constraints affecting the operations of the current intelligence structure. Operational policies are predetermined management decisions regarding the operations of the current system, normally in the form of general statements or understandings that guide or limit decision-making activities, but allow for some discretion. Operational constraints are limitations placed on the operations of the current system (e.g., available hours of intelligence unit operation, available number of personnel to work in the unit, networking constraints, etc.).

3.3 Description of Current System or Situation

Describe the current intelligence structure or situation that is simple and clear enough that all intended readers of the document can fully understand it. Provide a graphical overview of the current system or situation in the form of a context diagram, a top-level object diagram, or some other kind of diagram that depicts the system and its environment. The description should include the following, as appropriate:

- The operational environment and its characteristics (e.g., facilities, equipment, computing hardware, software, communications links, personnel, and operational procedures used to operate the existing system)

- Major system components and the interconnection among those components

- Interfaces to external systems or procedures

- Capabilities, functions, and features of the current intelligence structure, including types of products that are produced

- Charts and accompanying descriptions depicting inputs, outputs, data flows, control flows, and manual and automated processes sufficient to understand the current system or situation from the user's point of view

- Cost of system operations

- Operational risk factors

- Performance characteristics, such as speed, throughput, volume, frequency

- Quality attributes, such as availability, correctness, efficiency, expandability, flexibility, interoperability, maintainability, portability, reliability, reusability, supportability, survivability, and usability

- Provisions for safety, security, privacy, integrity, and continuity of operations in emergencies that exert influence on the operation or operational environment of the current system.

3.4 Current Modes of Operation

Describe the various modes of operation for the current intelligence structure (e.g., normal, imminent threat, emergency event, natural disaster) including strengths and weaknesses.

3.5 Current Users and Stakeholders

A user class is distinguished by the ways in which users interact with the current intelligence structure. Include descriptions of both internal and external intelligence users, how these users were identified, feedback from the users, and demands from users to which the intelligence structure is currently unable to respond.

3.6 Current Support Environment

Describe the support environment for the current intelligence structure, including support organizations or units; facilities; equipment; support software; and any other aspect of support. For external partners of the intelligence structure, describe the roles, responsibilities, and if a memorandum of understanding (MOU) is in place.

4. *Justification and Description of Changes:* Describe briefly the shortcomings or limitations of the current intelligence structure or the circumstances that motivated development of a new or modified intelligence structure. If there is no current intelligence structure on which to base changes, then so indicate and provide justification for the new structure.

4.1 Justification of Changes

Summarize briefly new or modified aspects of the intelligence unit's operations, including the types of analysis, products, changes, or modified mission and the reasons for those changes. Changes may be based on new national standards, a new MOU, new strategic priorities of the executive, external funding requirements, legislation, or any of a variety of factors.

It is important to articulate the reasons for change to ensure that the explicit conditions or mandates for the change are being met.

4.2 Description of Desired Changes

Summarize the new or modified capabilities, functions, processes, products, and other changes needed to respond to the factors identified in 4.1. Changes should be based on the current intelligence structure described in Section 3. If there is no existing intelligence structure on which to base changes, summarize the capabilities that a new structure will provide. The description should include the following, as appropriate:

- Capability changes
- Information processing changes
- Product changes
- Personnel changes
- Priority changes
- Partnership changes
- Support changes
- Other changes.

4.3 Priorities among Changes

Identify priorities among the desired changes and new features. Each change should be classified as essential, desirable, or optional, and a reason provided for the classification.

4.4 Changes Considered but not Included

Identify desired changes and new features considered but not included in section 4.2, and the rationale for not including them.

5. *Proposed System or Situation:* Describe the concepts for the proposed intelligence structure that results from the desired changes specified in Section 4. The description should be at a high level, indicating the operational features that will be provided without specifying design details. The description should be of sufficient detail to fully explain how the proposed system is envisioned to operate in fulfilling users' needs and the law enforcement agency's business requirements. The ConOps may contain some examples of typical design strategies for the purpose of clarifying operational details of the proposed system, but should not contain design specifications.

5.1 Background, Objectives, and Scope

Provide an overview of the proposed intelligence structure including, as applicable, background, mission, goals, objectives, scope, business drivers, and motivation.

5.2 Operational Policies and Constraints

Describe the operational policies and constraints affecting the operations of the proposed system. Operational policies are predetermined management decisions regarding the operations of the proposed system, normally in the form of general statements or understandings that guide or limit decision-making activities, but allow for some discretion.

Operational constraints are limitations placed on the operations of the proposed system (e.g., available hours of system operation, available number of personnel to operate the system, computer hardware, and operational facilities constraints).

5.3 Description of the Proposed Intelligence Structure

Describe the proposed intelligence structure that is simple and clear enough that all intended readers of the document can fully understand it. Provide a graphical overview of the proposed structure in the form of a context diagram, a top-level object diagram, relationship to other intelligence entities (particularly as applied to fusion centers), structure within an agency of governmental entity, or some other type of diagram that depicts the structure and its environment. The description should include the following, as appropriate:

- The intelligence unit's environment and its characteristics (e.g., facilities, equipment, computing hardware, software, communications links, personnel, and operational procedures used for the unit's operations)

- Major law enforcement intelligence systems for which access is needed (e.g., RISSNET, LEO, HSIN, National Law Enforcement Telecommunication System)

- Capabilities, functions, and features of the analytic capability including skills of analysts, analytic software, and special skills needed

- Charts and accompanying descriptions depicting inputs, outputs, data flows, control flows, and manual and automated processes sufficient to understand the two-way information flow for the intelligence structure

- Cost of the intelligence structure's operations

- Operational risk factors including civil rights and privacy issues

- Performance characteristics, such as speed, throughput, volume, frequency

- Quality attributes, such as availability, correctness, efficiency, expandability, flexibility, interoperability, reliability, and usability of intelligence products
- Provisions for security, privacy, integrity, accuracy, and continuity of operations in emergencies for the new intelligence structure.

5.4 Proposed Modes of Operation

Describe the various modes of operation for the proposed intelligence structure (e.g., normal, emergency, special threat). The intelligence structure's processes, procedures, and capabilities or functions should be related to each mode, as appropriate, perhaps using a cross-reference matrix.

5.5 Anticipated Users and Stakeholders

Specify the planned user class for the intelligence structure.

A user class is distinguished by the ways in which users interact with the proposed intelligence structure. Factors that distinguish a user class include common responsibilities, skill levels, work activities, and modes of interaction with the system.

In this context, a user is anyone who interacts with the proposed intelligence structure, including analysts, research specialists, reports officers, investigators, management decision-makers, patrol officers, trainers, and perhaps certain segments of the private sector.

5.6 Proposed Support Environment

Describe the support concepts and support environment for the intelligence structure, including partner organizations, facilities, equipment, support software, and the information-sharing environment of the intelligence structure.

6. *Operational Scenarios:* Provide step-by-step descriptions of how the intelligence structure should operate and interact with its users under a diverse set of circumstances (e.g., development of specific intelligence products as a result of a user's request; how Suspicious Activity Reports are processed through the intelligence structure; how and to whom imminent threat information would be confirmed and disseminated). The scenarios should be described in a manner that will allow readers to walk through them and gain an understanding of how all the various parts of the proposed intelligence structure functions

The scenarios tie together all parts of the system, the users, and other entities by describing how they interact, and may also be used to describe what the system should not do. The scenarios can be presented in several different ways: for each major intelligence activity or function of the proposed structure; thread-based, where each scenario follows one type of transaction type through the proposed structure, or following the information flow through the system.

7. *Summary of Impacts:* Describe the anticipated operational and organizational impacts of the proposed intelligence structure on the staff, users/consumers, and management. Also describe the temporary impacts on the staff, users/consumers, and management during the time when the new intelligence structure is being conceptualized, during the development of the structure, while the project is being implemented, and when training is being provided. This information will allow all affected organizations and organizational units to prepare for the changes that will be brought about by the new structure and to plan for the impacts during development and transition to the new structure.

7.1 Operational Impacts

Describe the operational impacts of the proposed system on the users, system developers, and the support and maintenance organizations. The impacts to consider include the following:

- Information-sharing with primary or alternative information sources and/or systems
- Changes in procedures
- Use of new analytic methods and resources
- Changes in quantity, type, and timing of data to be entered into the system
- Changes in intelligence requirements
- New modes of operation based on imminent threats and emergencies
- New processes for responding to user analytic requests
- Changes in the operational budget.

7.2. Organizational Impacts

Describe the anticipated organizational impacts of the proposed intelligence structure, compared with current impacts, on staff, management, personnel, partners, and other users of the intelligence structure.

7.3. Impacts During Development

Describe the anticipated impacts on staff, management, personnel, partners, and other users of the intelligence structure during the development of the new intelligence structure. The impacts to consider include the following:

- Involvement in studies, meetings, and discussions prior to implementation of the new structure
- User and support involvement in testing and review of new processes and methods, including training
- Parallel operation of the new and existing structure during transition.

8. *Analysis of the Proposed Intelligence Structure:* Provide an analysis of the benefits, limitations, advantages, disadvantages, and alternatives and trade-offs considered for the proposed intelligence structure.

8.1. Summary of Improvements

Provide a qualitative (and to the extent possible, quantitative) summary of the benefits that the proposed intelligence structure will provide.

8.2. Disadvantages and Limitations

Provide a qualitative (and to the extent possible, quantitative) summary of the disadvantages and/or limitations of the proposed intelligence structure. Disadvantages might include the need to retrain personnel or change to a new style of information-sharing. Limitations might include products and services desired by users but not included as part of the new intelligence structure.

8.3. Alternatives and Trade-Offs Considered

> Describe major alternatives considered, the trade-offs among them, and rationale for the decisions reached. In the context of the ConOps, alternatives are operational alternatives. For example, using shared or contract intelligence analysts, limiting the intelligence structure to only strategic or tactical analysis, or colocating the new structure with another agency, etc.

Appendixes

Use appendixes to facilitate ease of use and maintenance of the ConOps document. Each appendix should be referenced in the main body of the document where that information would normally have been provided; for example, samples of new report forms or new policy and procedures.

Glossary

Provide clear and concise definitions for terms used in the ConOps that may be unfamiliar to readers of the document.

The ConOps Next Step

As the name implies, the ConOps is intended to describe how the intelligence vision of the chief executive is conceptualized in an operational form; that is, the ConOps translates the vision into a functional model. The intent is to permit stakeholders—staff, users, management, and relevant external parties—to understand the intended dynamics and comment on different aspects of the envisioned operations. Feedback by stakeholders may be used to fine-tune the concept, as long as it stays true to its vision. The next step is to use the ConOps as a road map to implement the new intelligence structure.

Implementing and Managing the Intelligence Structure

As noted previously, the principles of management apply to the intelligence function of an agency just as they apply to any other organizational entity. The following management discussion focuses on selected elements related to the intelligence function. As will be seen, many of the issues in the following discussions will be applicable to preparing the ConOps.

Establishing an Organizational Framework

Just as any other function in a law enforcement agency, organizational attention must be given to the administrative structure of the intelligence function. Administrators and managers must examine these concerns:

- The need for the intelligence function as it relates to strategic priorities of the agency
- How the intelligence structure functions on a daily basis
- Issues of resource acquisition, deployment, and management
- Future agency requirements for the intelligence function.

Properly organized and staffed, the intelligence function serves as an internal consultant to management for resource deployment. It should be designed as an integrated and organic element of the law enforcement organization, not a distinct function. Indeed, this approach supports the effective implementation of ILP. Intelligence defines the scope and dimensions of complex criminality— including terrorism—facing the jurisdiction and provides alternatives for policy responses to those problems. Also important, it serves as a focal point for information sharing and dissemination to maximize community safety.

Some law enforcement agencies have been reluctant to fully develop an intelligence structure—including both tactical and strategic activities—for several reasons. Perhaps at the top of the list is the past abuses and subsequent lawsuits from poorly organized and managed intelligence activities. In many cases, law enforcement executives eliminated the intelligence function to reduce liability and to minimize criticism from persons in the community who did not understand the intelligence role and/or generally opposed law enforcement intelligence for philosophical reasons. Similarly, the need and value of an intelligence function has not been fully recognized by managers who often do not understand that the intelligence function can be an important resource for agency planning and operations. Intelligence analysts, for example, are frequently assigned clerical tasks such as responding to requests to check names or doing a records search of a person's background, in addition to their analytic duties, largely because the manager does not understand the value that is lost to the organization if the analyst does not have the time to devote to his or her function.

As a consequence of several factors, the zeitgeist—or spirit of the times—is now present for American law enforcement to embrace law enforcement intelligence of the 21st century. Many SLTLE agencies have established a legacy of proactive law enforcement through the use of community policing and its activities of problem solving, CompStat, crime analysis, effective internal and external communications, multidisciplinary responses to crime, and a bottom-up approach to operational direction. Moreover, since 9/11, there has been a greater development of resources and training to make intelligence activities more easily adapted and functional. Finally, the law enforcement intelligence function has become professionalized through greater involvement of academic institutions, federal initiatives, and long-standing activities by groups such as the International Association of Law Enforcement Intelligence Analysts, Inc. (IALEIA) and the LEIU.[12]

Chartering an Intelligence Unit

One of the first steps in creating an intelligence structure is to charter the function through the following steps:

- Determine its organizational structural priority and placement
- Allocate resources
- Define its mission and goals
- Establish the unit's authority and responsibility.

[12] For more information about these organizations, see their respective web pages at www.ialeia.org and www.leiu-homepage.org.

A number of publications describe these processes.[13] The current discussion will identify specific points related to the intelligence function.

The creation of an intelligence function should be based on a needs assessment.[14] This includes identifying current intelligence-related competencies of the law enforcement agency and desired competencies. One of the main outcomes of an effective needs assessment is identifying how an intelligence structure can influence the drive toward greater efficiency and responsiveness. Also important, the needs assessment will define personnel and resource needs.

Resource allocation is always a difficult process because it typically involves diminishing one function to develop another. In most cases, the creation of a new unit will not come with a new appropriation of funding to fully staff and operationalize it; therefore, part of the resource allocation process is to determine where the intelligence function fits in the organizational priorities of the law enforcement agency.

The mission of the intelligence function is the role that the unit fulfills in support of the agency's overall mission. It specifies in general language what the unit is intended to accomplish and establishes the direction and responsibility for the intelligence structure for which all other administrative actions and activities are designed to fulfill. Table 13-2 presents a sample mission statement for a law enforcement agency's intelligence unit.

A goal is the end to which all activity in the unit is directed. It is broad-based, yet functionally oriented. Important, too, the goal must be mission-related, that is, accomplishing goals supports the broader mission of the law enforcement agency. Moreover, the goals will give the unit direction in support of the mission. Since the mission of an intelligence unit will be comprehensive and incorporate diverse functions, several goals will be stipulated. The purpose of goals is to not only provide operational direction but to also serve as performance standards.[15] The environment of the community will change over time as will crime patterns and problems; therefore, the law enforcement agency should review goal statements annually and change or revise them to reflect current issues and trends. (Table 13-2 also includes an illustration of intelligence goals for a law enforcement agency.)

Authority is the right to act or command others to act toward the attainment of organizational goals. Operational authority includes decisions that must be made concerning the degree and type of activities the intelligence function may perform without seeking administrative authorization, financial flexibility of the unit to fulfill its objectives, and the degree of direction or precedence the intelligence structure can exercise over other departmental units. These factors have significant organizational implications and must be developed conceptually and stipulated by policy.

Responsibility reflects how the authority of a unit or individual is used for determining if goals have been accomplished and the mission fulfilled in a manner that is consistent with the defined limits of authority. The unit and its members must be held accountable for its charge and administrative mechanisms must be set in place to assess the degree to which the unit is meeting its responsibilities.

[13] Most police management textbooks describe these processes in detail. Perhaps of particular value are publications available from the International City Management Association bookstore.icma.org.

[14] A good illustration of a law enforcement needs assessment and how it can be performed, which includes multiple applications, is: Healy, J.J. *Needs Assessment in a Multinational Context: A Police Training Program*, Chapter 20. Superintendent, International Training and Peacekeeping Branch, Royal Canadian Mounted Police. www.rcmp-learning.org/docs/ecdd1134.htm.

[15] Performance standards are often characterized as effectiveness and efficiency, wherein effectiveness is "Doing the right job," and efficiency is "Doing the job right."

IACP Model Policy on Criminal Intelligence

The International Association of Chiefs of Police (IACP) has taken a proactive role in all aspects of developing a contemporary intelligence capacity in America's law enforcement agencies. The IACP *Model Policy*[16] on criminal intelligence contains a policy statement and procedures that are of particular benefit to a small agency. As in the case of all models, the language of the IACP policy needs to be adjusted to meet the needs of different jurisdictions. Nonetheless, it provides a sound foundation for starting the process.

Table 13-2: Sample Mission Statement and Goals of an LEI Unit

Sample Intelligence Mission Statement

The mission of the Intelligence Unit of the Hypothetical Police Department is to collect, evaluate, analyze, and disseminate intelligence data regarding criminal activity in this city/county and any criminal activity in other jurisdictions that may have an adverse effect on this city/county. This includes providing processes for collating and analyzing information collected by operational units of the law enforcement agency. The Intelligence Unit will furnish the chief of police with the necessary information so that operations units charged with the arrest responsibility can take the necessary enforcement action.

Sample Intelligence Goals

- The Intelligence Unit shall supply the chief of police with accurate and current strategic intelligence data so that the chief will be kept informed of changing criminal activity in the jurisdiction.

- The Intelligence Unit shall provide a descriptive analysis of organized crime systems operating within the jurisdiction to provide operational units with the necessary data to identify organized crime groups and individuals working as criminal enterprises.

- The Intelligence Unit will concentrate its expertise on the following crimes:

  » Islamic extremists in support of terrorism—activities, participants, funding, and logistical support, all of which are of a criminal nature.

  » Domestic extremists in support of criminal acts— activities, participants, funding, and logistical support, all of which are of a criminal nature.

  » Labor/strike activity—monitor and gather strategic intelligence to be supplied to the Operations Bureau with regard to this activity.

  » Organized crime—identify crimes and participants, including new and emerging criminal enterprises.

  » Major narcotics traffickers—provide tactical intelligence and information analysis to the Operations Bureau on persons identified as being involved in narcotics trafficking enterprises.

The Intelligence Unit recognizes the delicate balance between the individual rights of citizens and the legitimate needs of law enforcement. In light of this recognition, the unit will perform its intelligence activities in a manner that is consistent with, and upholds, the civil rights privacy and lawful expressive activity of all persons.

---

[16] www.cops.usdoj.gov/Files/RIC/CDROMS/ LEIntelGuide/pubs/IACP_Criminal_Intel_ Model_Policy.pdf.

Auditing the Intelligence Function

An important tool for managing the intelligence function is to perform regular audits. The audit will provide an accountability mechanism that can help maximize efficiency and effectiveness while verifying adherence to policies and procedures. In addition, the audit can serve as a benchmarking tool to measure changes in performance of the intelligence function which, in turn, leads to continuous quality improvement.

The audit is not only an important management tool; it can also serve as a means of demonstrating accountability to the community. It is a structured method for tracking and measuring critical issues related to the intelligence function and provides assurances that the intelligence function is operating in a manner that is consistent with good management practices and within lawful constraints.

There are different kinds of audits, depending on the needs or issues associated with the intelligence function. In all likelihood, a law enforcement agency should perform diverse kinds of audits, such as the following, on a periodic basis.

- *Financial audit.* To ensure that the expenditure of funds is consistent with policy and allowable expenses, including appropriated funds and grant funds. In addition, if there is an undercover/informant budget, this should be audited on a regular basis.

- *Process audit.* To ensure that all intelligence activities are being performed in a manner that is consistent with the law enforcement agency's internal policies and procedures. This includes not only line personnel but also ensuring that supervisors are adequately performing their supervisory function.

- *Compliance audit.* To ensure that intelligence operations are consistent with law and regulations that are external to the organization, such as 28 CFR Part 23, legal mandates, and grant regulations

- *Outcome audit.* To ensure that the intelligence function is accomplishing its goals and objectives.

- *Service audit.* To ensure that the intelligence function is meeting the needs of its consumers.

The person(s) conducting the audit may be somewhat dependent on the nature of the issues associated with the intelligence function, both internal and external to the law enforcement agency. If no controversies are associated with the intelligence function, an audit by a supervisor should suffice, but if controversial issues are related to the intelligence operations, an external auditor would be preferable. Someone who has recognized integrity, such as a retired judge or a recognized business person who is a community leader, would serve well as an auditor. While the intelligence staff will need to provide the raw information to the auditor, an independent party asking questions, making judgments, and drawing conclusions about performance can serve an important role.

Appendix B is an audit checklist developed by the author and used at law enforcement agencies to ensure compliance with court orders. Appendix C is the Audit Checklist developed by the Law Enforcement Intelligence Unit.

Establishing and Managing Partnerships

The nature of the intelligence function requires that a law enforcement agency enter into partnerships. Critical information is shared through collaboration, typically with other law enforcement agencies, but often with other organizations ranging from the private sector (as discussed in Chapter 9) to nonlaw enforcement government agencies, such as public health, the fire service, or emergency operations. These various relationships have different dynamics related to needs, responsibilities, and limitations on access to information. As such, the parameters of each formal partnership should be articulated in a formal partnership agreement.

Broadly speaking, two types of partnerships are related to the intelligence function.

1. *Users.* Organizations and individuals with which information and/or intelligence products are shared. Users are consumers.

2. *Participants.* Organizations and individuals that provide resources and actively contribute to the intelligence activity, such as a regional fusion center. Participants have a shared responsibility for operations.

A formal agreement is simply sound management because it articulates mutually agreed-on operational provisions related to resource management, clear identification of responsibilities and accountability, adherence to legal standards, and conditions associated with liability. Certainly these agreements apply to a wide range of law enforcement activities or services; however, the current discussion is limited to the intelligence function. While the language varies between states, as a general rule there are three forms of written partnerships:

1. *Memorandum of Agreement (MOA).* Users/consumers of an intelligence unit or system, including a records system, that use the system on an ongoing basis would typically sign the MOA. Essentially, the MOA acknowledges that the user will abide by the rules established for the system or activity, aid in cost recovery, and adhere to legal and accountability standards. Obviously, the character of the activity will dictate more detail. As an example, if one agency's intelligence records system can be accessed by another agency, the user may have to agree to pay a monthly fee, adhere to 28 CFR Part 23, and agree to the Third Agency Rule. Failure to meet these standards would result in ending access to the system.

2. *Mutual Aid Pact (MAP).* The MAP is an agreement that is in place to deal with special circumstances, rather than an ongoing service, and establishes the agreed-on conditions when one agency would provide assistance to another. Often, assistance is reciprocal, except for real costs that may be incurred in extended activities. As an intelligence-related example, two law enforcement agencies may agree to aid each other when conducting a surveillance.

3. *Memorandum of Understanding (MOU).* The MOU is more detailed and involves a partnership in an activity. Essentially a contract, the MOU would specify all obligations and responsibilities and typically share liabilities in the endeavor. For example, if multiple agencies agree to develop a fusion center, the MOU may be a fairly detailed document outlining all aspects of governance, management, structure, funding, accountability, and operations of the center.

A key element to understand is that, regardless of the nature of the agreement, its content and detail is to ensure that all parties understand their obligations. Table 13-3 identifies some of the provisions that may be included in a partnership agreement. While not all of these provisions will be required of every agreement, it is important to have a formal document that clearly defines expectations and responsibilities.

Table 13-3: Sample Provisions for a Partnership Agreement

- Activities
- Civil liability/indemnification
- Dispute resolution
- Funding
- Governance
- Information – access and use
- Information – adherence to 28 CFR Part 23
- Information – dissemination to Third Agency
- Information – entry into a system
- Information – ownership
- Location
- Mission, purpose, goals
- Operating procedures
- Payments and costs
- Personnel assignment
- Personnel evaluation
- Personnel removal
- Physical plant considerations
- Property – purchase and maintenance
- Reports to be prepared
- Security clearances of staff
- Security of information
- Security of the facility
- Time limit/term of the agreement

Sources for Intelligence Management and Resource Trends

Effective management of an intelligence unit requires that the manager be constantly informed of emerging issues, technologies, and trends. This is a difficult process; however, one of the more effective methods is to monitor online newsletters of reliable organizations. Topics can range from emerging issues to best practices to new products and new policy and legislation. As an illustration (not an endorsement), some of the more substantive newsletters include (in alphabetical order) the following:

- Center for Digital Government (three newsletters; one specifically on homeland security) www.centerdigitalgov.com.
- *Federal Computer Week* www.fcw.com.
- Federation of American Scientists: Secrecy News www.fas.org/sgp/news/secrecy.
- Foundation for Defense of Democracies: *Weekly Update* www.defenddemocracy.org.
- *Government Computer News* www.gcn.com.
- *Government Computing* www.kable.co.uk.
- *Government Technology* www.govtech.net.
- *Homeland Security Institute Newsletter*: www.homelandsecurity.org.

- *Homeland Security Update* (DFI International) www.dfi-intl.com.

- *Homeland Security Week* www.govexec.com.

- *Homeland Security Weekly Newsletter* www.homelandsecurityweekly.com.

- PoliceOne.com (*Law Enforcement News*) www.policeone.com/policenews.

- U.S. Department of Justice, Justice Technology Information Network www.justnet.org.

As is the case with any information, and as noted in Chapter 11 on open sources, a newsletter will reflect the agenda of its sponsor. Keeping this in mind, valuable information can be gained for an intelligence manager to remain current on the issues for which he or she is responsible.

Human Resource Issues

Who should perform the intelligence function in an SLTLE agency and what qualifications should that person have? This question is impossible to answer conclusively because it depends on myriad variables tied to the attributes of a given law enforcement agency. The agency's size, jurisdiction, geographic location, the priority intelligence is given, resource flexibility, competing crime and calls for service issues and collective bargaining agreements must be calculated into the formula. Rather than provide for the ideal situation, this discussion will present issues, and guidelines that will enable the law enforcement executive to make an informed decision about options available for staffing the intelligence function.

Staffing

Clerical and support staffing decisions can be made for the intelligence function just as for any other assignment in the agency, taking into consideration professional staff workloads, service demands, nonprofessional work activities (e.g., data entry, clerical work), and budget, among others. The key positions are with the professional staff.[17]

The Intelligence Analyst

The intelligence analyst is a professional who collects various facts and documents circumstances, evidence, interviews, and other material related to a crime and places them in a logical, related framework to develop a criminal case, explain a criminal phenomenon, or describe crime and crime trends. The analyst should have at least a baccalaureate degree and receive training in the intelligence process, criminal law and procedure, statistical analysis, and factual and evidentiary analysis. The analyst should be an objective, analytic thinker with good writing and presentation skills. This is a professional position that should be compensated accordingly. Remember: Executives and managers make important operational and resource decisions based on the analysis of issues; therefore, the best qualified and best trained analysts are essential.

An ongoing issue is whether the intelligence analyst will be sworn or nonsworn. Different agencies use different models, each with its advantages and disadvantages.[18] Those who advocate that the intelligence analyst position would

[17] For more detail, see: Wells, Ian, "Staffing the Intelligence Unit," in *Intelligence 2000: Revising the Basic Elements: A Guide for Intelligence Professionals*, ed. Marilyn B. Peterson, Bob Morehouse, and Dick Wright. Lawrenceville, New Jersey: Law Enforcement Intelligence Unit and the International Association of Law Enforcement Intelligence Analysts, 2000: 53–66.

[18] The *General Counterdrug Intelligence Plan* discusses issues related to human resources in *Section E: Analytic Personnel Development and Training*. While not specifically addressing the issues in this discussion, nonetheless it provides some observations and recommendations that are germane to the issues presented herein. See ftp.fas.org/irp/ops/le/docs/gcip/index.html.

<u>What Characteristics Are Desired in a Good Analyst?</u>

- General factors (modified from Frost, C. and J. Morris. *Police Intelligence Reports.* Orangevale, California: Palmer Press, 1983.)
  - » Impeccable standards of honesty and integrity
  - » A thorough understanding of the concepts of :
    - Intelligence
    - Civil liberties
    - Criminal law enforcement
  - » The capacity to think in a logical and rational manner
  - » Capacity to approach situations from broad and divergent perspectives
  - » The ability to comprehend complex masses of data and communicating its contents to others
- Background factors
  - » Broad range of interests
  - » Developed research ability (library, qualitative, quantitative)
  - » Helpful previous experience (law enforcement, military, security)
- Mental traits
  - » Intellectual curiosity
  - » Rapid assimilation of information
  - » Keen recall of information
  - » Tenacity
  - » Willingness and capacity to make judgments
- Communication skills
  - » Developed writing ability
  - » Skill in oral briefing
  - » Interviewing and interrogating skills
  - » Eliciting information from officers
- Liberal arts skills
  - » Good writing ability
  - » Fluency in a second language desirable
  - » Good knowledge of geography
- Work style
  - » Initiative and self-direction
  - » Effective personal interaction
  - » Disciplined intellectual courage

be best served by a nonsworn employee argue that the nonsworn analyst's characteristics and background may provide a more creative and less restrictive view of data when compared to sworn personnel. Further, a sworn employee is likely to be either transferred or promoted out of the intelligence unit, thereby reducing the unit's overall efficiency. Advocates of having a nonsworn employee argue that the position does not require law enforcement authority; therefore placing a sworn person in an analyst's position may be viewed as an ineffective use of personnel. Finally, the role of an analyst is highly experiential: Over the years, the experienced analysts accumulate a mental repository of names, locations, businesses, and so forth that can be highly useful in an analysis. If this person is a sworn employee who is transferred out of the unit, that accumulated knowledge is lost.

Conversely, opponents argue that nonsworn employees do not have the substantive knowledge and experience for conducting investigations nor do they understand, with the same degree of insight, the life of the street where many intelligence targets live and operate. The analyst builds his or her expertise and knowledge cumulatively throughout his or her work life. Much of this expertise is substantive knowledge and information (persons, crime patterns, locations, and so forth) learned while working on a variety of criminal cases. The analyst needs to view crime problems from the big picture—a picture that is most precisely focused with years of law enforcement street experience.

Other factors not related to the conceptual responsibilities will enter the equation such as the compensation package, collective bargaining agreement provisions, civil service regulations, organizational culture, the candidate pool, and so forth. This is a critical position requiring an effective analytic capability and care should be taken to hire the right person to fit the agency's needs. It should not be, as has too often been the case, an appointment of convenience or a reward appointment to a good clerical person who has worked hard for the department. Professional output from the intelligence unit will occur only if the position is filled by a professional analyst.

Training

The Bureau of Justice Assistance-funded Criminal Intelligence Training Coordination Strategy Working Group conducted a needs assessment of intelligence training in the spring of 2004. Among the findings were the following:

- Training is lacking in all training classifications, but respondents rated intelligence analyst and intelligence manager as the classes most lacking in adequate training. Surprisingly, 62 percent of respondents stated that they are receiving adequate training, but more than one-third (36 percent) indicated that they were not receiving adequate training.

- The majority of respondents cited lack of funding as the primary impediment of training, but respondents also rated as high the difficulty of *finding good trainers, travel and lodging costs,* and *unsure of available training.* Only a handful of respondents selected unsure of appropriate training for personnel as an impediment. *One respondent indicated that, in order to support the tenets of the NCISP, additional training guidelines and opportunities are needed.* Other respondents indicated that training can be sporadic, which dovetails into the need for core minimum standards that can be used consistently nationwide. Other respondents indicated that their agency has not needed intelligence training because they do not have the staff or resources to engage in an intelligence function.[19] (Emphasis in original).

[19] Bureau of Justice Assistance, Criminal Intelligence Training Coordination Strategy Working Group. *Survey of Law Enforcement on Intelligence Training.* Unpublished staff report, 2004.

As a result, the *Minimum Criminal Intelligence Training Standards*[20] were created, and revised in 2007. The standards were designed to "…provide perspective and guidance for the development and delivery of law enforcement intelligence training."[21] The report goes on to note:

> …It is recognized that any type of "standard" can be debated based on an individual's personal philosophy, professional priorities, and life experiences. In order to minimize bias or atypical context, the development process for these standards used a consensual approach reflecting the cumulative judgment of law enforcement intelligence practitioners, managers, executives, trainers, and scholars from all levels of government. The standards reflect the collective judgment of these subject matter experts with respect to the minimum training needed in each noted classification to provide the basic knowledge, skills, and abilities for personnel in each classification in order for them to perform their intelligence duties.[22]

Clearly, intelligence training currently represents the proverbial mixed bag of content, availability, and structure. The content or subject matter of law enforcement intelligence can be divided in two broad categories. The first category is protocols and methodology of the intelligence process. It includes subjects such as information-collection methodologies, laws and regulations associated with intelligence records systems, analytic methods and tools, intelligence reporting structures and processes, and intelligence dissemination. Essentially, these elements constitute the discipline of law enforcement intelligence.

The second category is somewhat more amorphous. Broadly speaking, the category is subject matter expertise. It includes understanding the motives, methods, targets, and/or commodities of criminal intelligence targets. Intelligence researchers and analysts must have subject matter knowledge of the types of enterprises that are being investigated and the context within which these enterprises occur. Whether the target crime is terrorism, drug trafficking, money laundering, or the trafficking of stolen arts and antiquities, the intelligence analyst must be a subject matter expert on the genre of criminality being investigated, both broadly speaking, as well as with the unique facts associated with a specific investigation.

An intelligence analyst working on cases of terrorism by Islamic extremists, for example, needs to substantively understand the distinctions between Shiite and Sunni Muslims, the role of sectarian extremism (notably as related to Palestine), the different Islamic terrorist groups (e.g., al-Qaida, HAMAS, Hezbollah, Islamic Jihad), and their methods, the culture of Muslim nations, different leaders, methods of funding, and so forth. Such substantive knowledge is essential for an analyst to be effective.

[20] it.ojp.gov/documents/min_crim_intel_stand.pdf

[21] Intelligence Training Coordination Working Group. *Minimum Criminal Intelligence Training Standards.* Washington, D.C.: Global Intelligence Working Group, 2007, p. 1.

[22] Ibid.

All training programs currently available contain some aspect of the protocols and methodology of the intelligence process, although most programs for nonanalysts provided an overview of these issues rather than detailed instruction. Fewer programs contained subject matter information for intelligence as part of the training. For those that did provide this information, it was typically because the agency sponsoring the training had a specific jurisdictional responsibility (e.g., the Regional Counterdrug Training Academy's[23] Operational Intelligence course integrates "intelligence concepts" with more specific "drug intelligence indicators").

Training programs continue to emerge on intelligence related topics, most notably funded by the Bureau of Justice Assistance, U.S. Department of Justice, and the Office of Training and Exercise Integration (TEI), Federal Emergency Management Agency, U.S. Department of Homeland Security.[24] Perhaps the best single source for monitoring training programs of all types is through the National Criminal Intelligence Resource Center Master Criminal Intelligence Training Calendar.[25]

[23] www.rcta.org

[24] For example, the Michigan State University School of Criminal Justice has grants from the DHS to offer intelligence training for state, local, and tribal law enforcement agencies nationwide at no cost. For more information see intellprogram.msu.edu.

[25] mastercalendar.ncirc.gov

Table 13-4: Intelligence Training Categories and Descriptions

Training	Description
Awareness	The broadest, most diverse types of intelligence training could best be described as "awareness" training. These programs, which vary in length from 2 hours to 4 days, tend to include information about the intelligence discipline (i.e., definitions, methods, processes, etc.) as integrated with a specific subject matter (e.g., drugs, terrorism, auto theft, etc.). The Bureau of Justice Assistance State and Local Anti-Terrorism Training (SLATT), Federal Law Enforcement Training Center (FLETC), and other groups offer this training throughout the U.S.
Intelligence Analyst	Intelligence analysts training programs have a reasonable degree of consistency in the subject matter topics; however, the hours of training on each topic have more variability. In some cases, the curricula include substantive modules on subject matter: For example, the FBI Center for Intelligence Training program integrates intelligence methods specifically with crimes within FBI jurisdiction. Similarly, Drug Enforcement Administration (DEA) curricula integrates intelligence methods with material on drug trafficking. The most widely used analytic training program is the Foundations of Intelligence Analysis Training offered by the National White Collar Crime Center (NW3C), the International Association of Law Enforcement Intelligence Analysts, and the Law Enforcement Intelligence Unit.
Investigators and Intelligence Unit Researchers	Some intelligence training programs lack the depth of training found in the Analyst curricula, but are more detailed than simply "awareness" training. It appears that the intended audience for these programs is investigators, investigative analysts, or intelligence researchers. In each case, the curricula are similar. Notable among these courses are the 2-week DEA Federal Law Enforcement Analysts Training (FLEAT) course and the FLETC intelligence course.
Executive and Management Issues for Intelligence	Two programs funded by the Bureau of Justice Assistance are in the category: *Criminal Intelligence for the Chief Executive* and the *Intelligence Commanders Course*. In addition, the FLETC offers chief executive training, and an intelligence course at the FBI National Academy is designed for SLTLE enforcement managers.
Specialized Training	This training focuses on a narrow aspect of the entire intelligence process. The best known of these courses is the *Criminal Intelligence Analysis* course offered by Anacapa Sciences, Inc.,[27] that focuses exclusively on the "analysis" component of the intelligence cycle. Other courses that fall into this category are generally software courses such as classes on how to use a particular type of intelligence software (typically either analytic software or databases).

[26] NW3C also offers the course, *Advanced Criminal Intelligence Analysis to Prevent Terrorism*.

[27] Anacapa is a private company. This reference should not be considered an endorsement of the product by the author, the Department of Justice, or any of its components. It is used only as a descriptive illustration.

Categories of Currently Available Intelligence Training Programs

A wide range of programs has been developed on various aspects of law enforcement intelligence. Virtually all were developed before the standards and specifications in the *National Criminal Intelligence Sharing Plan* were established. Table 13-4 describes the five categories of available training programs.

A few law enforcement intelligence training programs serve as core programs because of their consistency and the expertise they offer. A great deal of experience and thought has served as the basis for their development and, as such, they provide models for good practice. For example, the *Intelligence Toolbox* that is offered nationwide by Michigan State University and funded by the Department of Homeland Security, FEMA/TEI, is a comprehensive training program designed to provide a law enforcement agency with all the tools needed to develop a contemporary intelligence capacity that meets all national standards.[28] The following summary descriptions of the most notable programs will provide more insight.

Federal Bureau of Investigation Center for Intelligence Studies[29]

After the terrorists' attacks of 9/11, the Attorney General mandated the FBI to focus on terrorism as its top priority. This necessitated a number of changes in the FBI, including expanding its law enforcement intelligence capability and working closely with state and local law enforcement agencies on terrorism investigations through Joint Terrorism Task Forces (JTTF) and Field Intelligence Groups (FIG). Among the needs precipitated by these changes was a significant broadening of the capacity for intelligence analysis among FBI personnel as well as among state and local JTTF and FIG intelligence staff. The FBI's Center for Intelligence Training, created in 2002 (formerly the College of Analytic Studies) and located at the FBI Academy, offers a range of courses for FBI agents, FBI intelligence analysts, the FBI National Academy, and courses for state, local, and tribal law enforcement.

Drug Enforcement Administration[30]

The DEA has long been recognized for the quality of training it provides through the Intelligence Training Unit of the DEA Academy at Quantico, Virginia. DEA intelligence training focuses on information research and intelligence analysis through the 9-to-10-week (it varies) *Basic Intelligence Research Specialist* (BIRS) program. DEA also offers an advanced intelligence training program as well as specialized programs related to the use of different databases and the classified DEA proprietary intelligence computer system, MERLIN.

Because of the DEA's historic role of working with state and local law enforcement agencies, and the inherent need for intelligence in the Organized Crime Drug Enforcement Task Force and the High Intensity Drug Trafficking Areas (HIDTA), DEA developed its 4-week FLEAT program specifically directed toward state and local law enforcement agencies. The program is offered in different cities throughout the U.S. to enhance the ability of state and local agencies to send intelligence

[28] intellprogram.msu.edu

[29] For enrollment information, contact the training coordinator at your local FBI Field Office. See www.fbi.gov/contact/fo/fo.htm or the FBI Academy www.fbi.gov/hq/td/academy/academy.htm.

[30] For further information on DEA training see www.usdoj.gov/dea/programs/training.htm.

personnel to this tuition-free program. While the program has historically focused exclusively on drug enforcement and money laundering, it is being revised to include a component related to both domestic and international terrorism.

Federal Law Enforcement Training Center[31]

Serving 72 federal law enforcement agencies, FLETC has a massive training responsibility. Predominantly through the Center for State and Local Law Enforcement Training, FLETC offers three courses:

1. *Intelligence Awareness for Law Enforcement Executives Training Program.*
2. *Introductory Intelligence Analyst Training Program.*
3. *Anti-Terrorism Intelligence Awareness Training Program.*

In addition, there is a wide range of other courses related to intelligence and counterterrorism. All information on courses and enrollment is listed on the FLETC web site.[32]

Other Programs and Training Resources

Law enforcement intelligence training continues to evolve, and a number of important initiatives are now underway to deliver improved basic and specialized training at the state and local levels. In addition to the programs described so far, intelligence training initiatives include the National White Collar Crime Center's *Analyst Training Partnership,*[33] HIDTA,[34] and the SLATT[35] program, have both direct and indirect intelligence awareness training.

Beyond these programs, several COPS Office Regional Community Policing Institutes (RCPI) offer a range of counterterrorism training programs, some of which include components of intelligence awareness training. Agencies should contact the RCPI in their region to determine training program offerings.[36]

For a comprehensive view of current intelligence training, including the relationship to the minimum training standards, see *Law Enforcement Intelligence Training: A Mission-Critical Element of Domestic Security* by Merle Manzi.[37]

Intelligence Courses in Higher Education

In recent years, there has been increasing recognition in the academic community of the need for coursework in intelligence that incorporates broad multidisciplinary issues, research, and a philosophical approach to intelligence issues. Increasing numbers of colleges and universities are offering courses and degrees in intelligence studies. Indeed, growth has been so significant that a new organization was formed to represent them, the International Association for Intelligence Education.[38] Most focus on the national security Intelligence Community.

Acknowledging the author's prerogative, there is one higher education program that focuses exclusively on law enforcement intelligence. The nation's oldest criminal justice degree program at Michigan State University (MSU) has offered a cross-listed undergraduate/graduate course entitled *Law Enforcement Intelligence*

[31] FLETC is part of the Department of Homeland Security. For details and contact information see www.fletc.gov/about-fletc.

[32] See www.fletc.gov/training.

[33] This includes the International Association of Law Enforcement Intelligence Analysts, the Law Enforcement Intelligence Unit, and the Regional Information Sharing Systems. For training opportunities see www.nw3c.com/ocr/courses_desc.cfm.

[34] A number of the HIDTA initiatives have intelligence-related training programs. See www.whitehousedrugpolicy.gov/hidta to find an HIDTA office. In addition, the Washington-Baltimore HIDTA often lists a wide range of training programs, including those that are intelligence-related. See www.hidta.org/training/law_enforcement.asp.

[35] See www.iir.com/slatt/training.htm.

[36] To find an RCPI near you, call the COPS Office Response Center at 800.421.6770.

[37] Manzi, Merle. *Law Enforcement Intelligence Training: A Mission-Critical Element of Domestic Security. Intelligence Police Papers Series.* East Lansing, Michigan: Intelligence Program, School of Criminal Justice, Michigan State University, January 2008. intellprogram.msu.edu/resources/policy-papers.php.

[38] www.iafie.org

Operations for approximately 20 years. As a result of a partnership created with DEA, MSU developed a master's degree in law enforcement intelligence and analysis.[39] The degree program, offered completely online, is taught by regular MSU criminal justice faculty members, and is designed as a terminal degree, much like a master of business administration. In addition, MSU offers a certificate program in different aspects of intelligence, many of which are available for academic credit. Clearly, the demand for academic preparation for an intelligence career is a growing market.

Conclusion

This chapter provided an overview of selected issues in the management of the law enforcement intelligence function. As a rule, the application of management principles may be applied generally, regardless of the unit or assignment within a law enforcement agency. The intelligence unit checklist and the ConOps discussion were particularly directed to assist SLTLE agencies to develop or reengineer their intelligence capacity to meet current national standards.

Criminal investigation commanders need to understand caseload differentials for crimes, patrol commanders must know minimum staffing requirements to handle calls for service, and traffic commanders must understand traffic analysis and its application to selective enforcement. It is no different with the intelligence commander. This chapter identified critical substantive elements of the intelligence function that will aid the law enforcement manager to manage this activity more effectively.

[39] www.cj.msu.edu

Chapter Annex 13-1
10 Simple Steps to Help Your Agency Become Part of the National Criminal Intelligence Sharing Plan[40]

1. Recognize your responsibilities and lead by example.

    Recognize the value of sharing intelligence information within your own agency, and encourage the practice of sharing information with other law enforcement and public safety agencies. Use the guidelines and action steps outlined in the *National Criminal Intelligence Sharing Plan* ("Plan") to implement or enhance your organization's intelligence function.

2. Establish a mission statement and a policy to address developing and sharing information and intelligence data within your agency.

    The Plan provides model policies and guidelines for implementing or reviewing an agency's intelligence function. Examples include Criminal Intelligence Systems Operating Policies federal regulation 28 CFR Part 23, the International Association of Chiefs of Police's *Model Policy for Criminal Intelligence*, and the Law Enforcement Intelligence Unit's (LEIU) *Criminal Intelligence File Guidelines*.

3. Connect to your state criminal justice network and regional intelligence databases, and participate in information-sharing initiatives.

    Many states provide access to other government databases, including motor vehicles, corrections, and others. Regional intelligence databases and sharing initiatives promote communication and collaboration by providing access to other agencies' and organizations' investigative and intelligence data.

4. Ensure that privacy issues are protected in policy and practice.

    The protection of individuals' privacy and constitutional rights is an obligation of government officials and is crucial to the long-term success of criminal intelligence sharing. The Plan provides guidelines that support policies which will protect privacy and constitutional rights while not hindering the intelligence process. Implementing and supporting privacy policies and practices within your agency will also reduce your organization's liability concerns.

5. Access law enforcement web sites, subscribe to law enforcement listservs, and use the Internet as an information resource.

    Many web sites on the Internet and others on closed networks provide valuable intelligence assessments and news. Listservs provide instant and widespread communication for investigators, and allow both the receipt and distribution of intelligence information. The Internet provides a wealth of open-source information, including government information and access to private agencies that share with law enforcement.

6. Provide your agency members with appropriate training on the criminal intelligence process.

    Some training models or modules are already found in Internet-based and interactive CD-ROMs, such as the International Association of Law Enforcement Intelligence Analysts (IALEIA), National White Collar Crime Center, and LEIU "Turn Key Intelligence." A listing of available intelligence training sources and specifically scheduled classes is found on the IALEIA Web site: www.ialeia.org. This listing allows individuals to directly contact training source agencies and organizations for more information on classes and schedules.

[40] Bureau of Justice Assistance. *10 Simple Steps to Help your Agency Become Part of the National Criminal Intelligence Sharing Plan*. Washington, D.C.: 2005.

7. Become a member of your in-region Regional Information Sharing Systems® (RISS) center.

    RISS operates the only secure web-based nationwide network for communication and exchange of criminal intelligence information by participating local, state, federal, and tribal law enforcement member agencies. RISS partners with other law enforcement systems to electronically connect them to RISSNET, including High Intensity Drug Trafficking Areas (HIDTA) Investigative Support centers, and other federal and state agency systems.

8. Become a member of the FBI's Law Enforcement Online (LEO) system.

    The FBI's LEO system is a sensitive but unclassified, real-time information-sharing communications system for all levels of the law enforcement community available at no cost to its approximately 40,000 users. LEO provides secure e-mail capability, a national alert mechanism, and access to more than 125 special-interest groups for sharing information by providing access to other networks, systems, databases, and other services.

9. Partner with public and private infrastructure sectors.

    Regular communication with the entities that control America's critical infrastructures such as energy, agriculture, transportation, and shipping is critically important to ensuring the safety and security of the citizens in your community.

10. Participate in local, state, and national intelligence organizations.

    In most areas of the country, there are locally based intelligence organizations that welcome participation from all agencies and are often affiliated with state and national organizations.

Chapter Annex 13-2
Why Law Enforcement Agencies Need an
Analytic Function[41]

1. Helps solve criminal investigations.

    The analytical function develops a variety of intelligence products to assist investigators in detecting, preventing, and responding to criminal and terrorism activities. Analytical personnel initiate inquiries, conduct information searches, and act as a central point for information gathered.

2. Increases the ability to prosecute criminals.

    Personnel assigned to the analytical function develop summary tables, charts, maps, and other graphics for use in a grand jury or trial. Analysts provide factual and expert testimony and organize evidence for presentation in court.

3. Supports the chief executive and the agency's mission.

    By maximizing the analytical function, the chief executive can obtain important information and intelligence to possibly prevent future criminal activities. Personnel can prepare materials to assist in allocating resources; developing budget and resource requests; and preparing departmental reports, investigative briefings, and press releases.

4. Proactively informs law enforcement officers of crime trends and develops threat, vulnerability, and risk assessments.

    The analytical function provides support to tactical and strategic operations. Personnel analyze crime reports, identify crime hot spots, develop crime bulletins and summaries, study serial crime data, and forecast future crime. The analytical function develops proactive intelligence products that assess the potential threats of crime groups or criminal activities and recommends methods to intervene in these threats.

5. Trains law enforcement and other intelligence personnel.

    Staff develop course modules on intelligence and analytic methods and provide awareness and methodology training to agency members, executives, and managers.

6. Assists in the development of computerized databases to organize information and intelligence.

    Personnel within the analytical function help in the development and maintenance of systems that collect, collate, retrieve, and disseminate information. Analytical staff participate in departmental testing and acquisition of investigative, intelligence, and analytical software.

7. Fosters meaningful relationships with other law enforcement personnel.

    Analytical staff interact with other law enforcement agencies and build relationships with peers, allowing them to quickly obtain information and efficiently assist in multijurisdictional or complex cases. Through contact with national programs and professional associations, personnel are able to ascertain national issues that may affect local agencies.

[41] Bureau of Justice Assistance. *Why Law Enforcement Agencies Need an Analytical Function*. Washington, D.C.: Bureau of Justice Assistance, October 2005.

8. Ensures compliance with local, state, tribal, and federal laws and regulations.

   Analytical personnel provide expertise and knowledge in the development of protocols to ensure compliance with local, state, tribal, and federal laws and rules that govern intelligence sharing, privacy, and civil liberties.

9. Provides support to fusion centers.

   Personnel provide support to local, state, or regional fusion centers by performing intelligence services such as crime-pattern, association, telephone-toll, and financial analysis. They create intelligence reports, briefs, threat assessments, and other intelligence products to aid in the prevention and deterrence of crime, including terrorism.

Chapter 14:
Summary, Conclusions, and Next Steps

Summary, Conclusions, and Next Steps

Effective law enforcement intelligence operations are sometimes confusing to understand, frequently controversial, and often challenging to implement. Yet, intelligence operations can be an effective tool for community safety.

Intelligence is *confusing* because many people do not make the distinction between law enforcement intelligence and national security intelligence. Moreover, the term is used generically to describe a wide body of activities, thereby contributing to the confusion. Added to this is the development of the Information Sharing Environment, which is not only changing our information-sharing relationships, but also making the demarcation between law enforcement and national security somewhat more difficult to discern on matters of terrorism. One purpose of this guide was to provide consistent and clear definitions and processes that are accepted by law enforcement intelligence professionals and reflect national standards and initiatives in intelligence to help reduce the confusion.

Law enforcement intelligence operations are *controversial* both because of the checkered history of intelligence activities as well as the concern of many today that in the zeal to prevent terrorism, citizens' civil rights will be abridged. There is no doubt that law enforcement suffered setbacks as a result of lawsuits against law enforcement intelligence practices of the 1950s and 1960s. With those setbacks, however, important lessons were learned that not only set the stage for 28 CFR Part 23, but helped lay the foundation for law enforcement intelligence as a profession. Further controversies face law enforcement today as concerned citizens and civil rights groups, who often do not fully understand the intelligence function, fear that law enforcement agencies will gather and keep information about citizens who have not committed crimes but are exercising their constitutional rights on controversial issues. The lessons law enforcement has learned from public education and community policing initiatives can help eliminate these fears—not only through the practice of ethical policing[1] but also by reaching out to diverse communities to explain police practices, responding to questions, and establishing open, trusted lines of communication.[2]

Intelligence operations are *difficult,* as well. It requires changes in processes and changes in interagency relationships to establish links with different law enforcement organizations and groups to maximize effective information sharing. It also requires a redistribution of resources to make the intelligence function perform effectively and to meet operational and training standards set out in the *National Criminal Intelligence Sharing Plan* and the *Minimum Criminal Intelligence Training Standards.* A change in culture is required for Intelligence-Led Policing to become a reality and a realignment of priorities may be needed to accomplish new goals. There is always resistance to change and always legitimate competing interests that must be weighed.

Finally, law enforcement intelligence processes can be *effective*. Intelligence can help identify threats to a community whether from terrorists, organized crime, or even noncriminal hazards. It takes diverse and often disparate information,

[1] The COPS Office Regional Community Policing Institutes (RCPI) have a variety of training curricula for executives and line officers on different aspects of ethical policing. Agencies should contact the RCPI in their region for training opportunities. For more information about an RCPI near you, call the COPS Office Response Center at 800.421.6770.

[2] The COPS Office sponsored an executive session with the Police Executive Research Forum that examined this topic. The resulting document is a valuable resource: Davies, Heather J., Murphy, Gerard R., et al. *Protecting Your Community from Terrorism: Strategies for Local Law Enforcement. Volume 2: Working with Diverse Communities.* Washington, D.C.: U.S. Department of Justice Office of Community Oriented Policing Services and the Police Executive Research Forum, March 2004. www.cops.usdoj.gov/RIC/ResourceDetail.aspx?RID=168.

integrated into a cohesive package, to provide insight that might otherwise be lost. Increasingly, law enforcement intelligence is more thorough, of higher quality, and disseminated more effectively as a result of cooperative initiatives by the Criminal Intelligence Coordinating Council, the Global Intelligence Working Group, and the Counterterrorism Training Coordination Working Group, as well as various cooperative initiatives in the Department of Justice, notably the Office of Community Oriented Policing Services and the Bureau of Justice Assistance, as well as the Department of Homeland Security (DHS) through the Intelligence and Analysis Directorate, and the Federal Emergency Management Agency through its Offices of Training and Exercise Integration/Training Operations. Similarly, there is a greater emphasis on law enforcement intelligence, punctuated by the creation of the fusion centers, and a renewed spirit of partnership between the FBI and state, local, and tribal law enforcement (SLTLE) agencies that is already bearing fruit. FBI and DHS personnel are working side-by-side with SLTLE personnel in many fusion centers to cooperatively resolve criminal threats facing our communities. The end result of all of these initiatives is to make our communities safer. The investment pays important dividends for protecting our citizens.

Challenges for the Future

When examining challenges for the future, the most effective method is to use a strategic approach that takes a macro view of critical trends and determines their impact on the law enforcement environment. An interesting and relevant study comes from the Intelligence Community as a project from the Office of the Director of National Intelligence (ODNI) that seeks to identify trends that threaten U.S. sovereign principles during the coming decade. The report observed the following:

> [m]any drivers and trends are shaping the future global environment in which the Intelligence Community must operate —demographic and social change, increased economic integration and competition, rapid technological innovation and diffusion, environmental pressures and growing energy demand, broad geopolitical changes, and new forms of governance. Each driver and trend independently produces unique changes and challenges; those points where factors intersect often reinforce and amplify the effects of change and create a series of complex and often unpredictable threats and risks that **transcend geographic borders and organizational boundaries.**[3] (Emphasis in original.)

These same trends that have potential effects on national security will also affect our local communities. At the least, they have an impact on public order and most likely influence major crime trends that are diverse and transjurisdictional in nature.

> The ODNI report goes on to observe:

> To these persistent threats we add a growing array of emerging missions that expands the list of national security (and hence, intelligence) concerns to include infectious diseases, science and technology surprises,

[3] McConnell, J. M. *Vision 2015: A Globally Networked and Integrated Intelligence Enterprise.* Washington, D.C.: Office of the Director of National Intelligence, 2008, p. 4.

financial contagions, economic competition, environmental issues, energy interdependence and security, cyber attacks, threats to global commerce, and transnational crime. Foremost among these challenges is the **blurring** of lines that once separated **foreign and domestic intelligence,** and the increased importance of homeland security. By necessity, we must be involved with numerous new partners in interactive relationships, but we must also **respect and maintain the privacy and civil liberties of all Americans.**[4] (Emphasis in original.)

Thus, like the Intelligence Community, law enforcement intelligence will have increasing responsibility to manage all-hazards types of threats while working in a broadened environment of information sharing. The challenges are not only to learn to deal with these new threats and new disciplines but to do so while ensuring the constitutional guarantees of all people.

These are sobering challenges that we must begin to confront now. The safety of American society cannot wait to react; rather, we must be proactive. This, of course, is difficult to do. The challenges of handling current problems on a much broader scale than ever, while at the same time experiencing proportionately smaller budgets, requires creativity and new ways of solving problems.

While law enforcement and the Intelligence Community have made significant, and necessary, investments in technology, success in the production and application of intelligence relies on people. Law enforcement needs to recognize that the creativity to solve the complex problems of the future will require "the best and brightest" to work in government service. Effective and creative analysis of problems can help lead to interventions and solutions. Not only must law enforcement leaders explore the problems of the future, it must also examine the law enforcement culture of today. Analysts must be compensated and treated as equal professionals in law enforcement organizations. The changes that are required to prepare our organizations must begin now, because the process can be long and challenging. One approach is to use a model the author refers to as R-cubed.

Implementing Change: The R-Cubed Approach[5]

Implementing new intelligence initiatives can be difficult. As a road map to accomplish this, the author recommends a process referred to as "R-cubed": Reassessing, Refocusing, and Reallocating (R^3).

The intent of the R^3 exercise is to provide a framework for organizational change as related to intelligence responsibilities. It requires a critical self-assessment of responsibilities and resources, objectivity absent special interests, realistic perspectives, tactical and strategic considerations of traditional and new policing responsibilities, and methods (including financing) of how all police responsibilities will be accomplished. This is a labor-intensive, difficult process that cannot be rushed and should be inclusive; that is, consideration of the inputs of others—employees, community members, elected officials, other agencies— should be included in the process. Final decisions, however, remain with law

[4] Ibid.

[5] Carter, David L. *The Police and Community.* 7th Ed. Englewood Cliffs, New Jersey: Prentice Hall, Inc., 2000.

enforcement executives to make changes as best determined by their collective judgment of responsibilities, priorities, and available resources. A number of factors may be included in each component of the R^3 exercise.

Reassessing

Examine both current priorities and new priorities for intelligence and homeland security to determine what activities need to be continued to maintain community safety and fulfill the law enforcement mission related to crime, order maintenance, and counterterrorism. This assessment should include consideration of a number of variables, such as the following:

- The number of calls for service received by a law enforcement agency and the ability to handle them.
- Specialization currently in the police department, e.g., gangs, narcotics, school programs, initiatives directed toward senior citizens, traffic, etc., and the true demand or need for each specialization.
- Objectivity is critical because special interests can skew priorities.
- Specialization that needs to be developed, e.g., intelligence capacity, first-responder (including weapons of mass destruction), computer crime/cyberterrorism prevention and investigative expertise, investigative capacity for terrorism, obligation to assign personnel to the Joint Terrorism Task Force, and expertise in all-hazards threats that can effect public safety and public order.
- Resources that can be used to help with police responsibilities of all forms, e.g., police reserves, volunteers, expertise in other agencies, community organizations.
- Objective assessment of threats and potential targets within the community and within the region. The latter includes how multijurisdictional crime and terrorist threats would affect an agency directly and indirectly, including mutual aid obligations.
- Current intelligence expertise and practices, including information sharing, and the need to modify these practices, including adding a private-sector component for critical infrastructure.
- Political mandates from elected officials and/or the community that should not be ignored because expectations and concerns of these groups must be taken into account in any assessment process.

Refocusing

Guided by the results of the reassessment, a department must develop a plan of change that incorporates its new priorities, as appropriate. Virtually all of the department's current tasks will continue in some form, but the amount of emphasis and proportion of resources devoted to those tasks will differ, notably in light of added homeland security responsibilities.

Refocusing first requires the department to establish its new priorities by reassessing and evaluating its responsibilities. From there it can it can refocus on its priorities, if needed. While reassessment involves information gathering and analysis, refocusing is the development and implementation of policy steps to make the changes operational.

Second, each area of responsibility must be weighted (i.e., weight constitutes the amount of emphasis given to each broad area of tasks and determines which area receives the greatest amount of attention.) The author does not suggest that intelligence should be the top priority; indeed, in most police agencies managing calls for service will remain the top priority. Instead, this is a realistic expectation that priorities will change with the addition of intelligence/homeland security and that all responsibilities will be affected to some degree. To determine this realignment, responsibilities and weights must be stipulated.

Third, these changes are actually implemented through the issuance of updated (and new, when applicable) policies, procedures, and orders. Implementation also requires communication and, in some cases, in-service training, to explain and clarify the changes.

Reallocating

Once refocusing decisions have been made, the department must reallocate its resources to meet adjusted priorities. This includes personnel, operating expenses, equipment (from cars to radios to computers) and office space, as needed. There is always the possibility that the department will receive an increased appropriation for homeland security in its budget, but it should not be counted on. If so, most likely it will be only a proportion of actual resource needs. The difficult process of reallocation is a necessity that will produce some alienation and, in all likelihood, political rifts within the organization. Reallocation, therefore, also requires effective leadership to guide the organization and motivate personnel to understand the necessity of the changes and the concomitant benefits to the community.

There is no explicit recipe for change in an organization. This is particularly true with intelligence where a renewed emphasis is given to a process that is largely not understood by most personnel. There is little guidance and, despite the best plans, time will be needed for experimentation. Agencies should take the time to carefully consider all new responsibilities, balance them with legitimate competing demands within the agency, and make a clear step toward adjusting the organization.

Conclusion

As demonstrated throughout this guide, America's law enforcement agencies are facing a new challenge. Throughout the history of policing, challenges have been faced, they have been met with resolute determination, and America has been safer as a result. This new challenge is no different. The intent of this *Guide* has been to help America's state, local, and tribal law enforcement agencies make this journey.

Figures/Tables

Figures

Tables

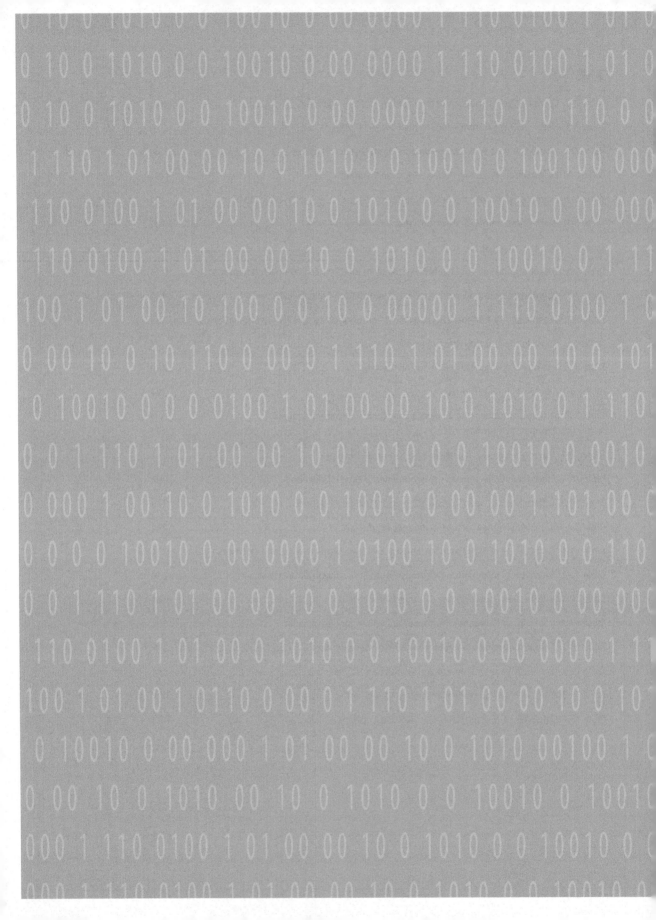

Bibliography/Appendixes

Bibliography

Advisory Panel to Assess Domestic Response Capabilities for Terrorism involving Weapons of Mass Destruction. *Implementing the National Strategy.* Washington, D.C.: RAND Corporation, 2002.

Allen, C. E. *Testimony of the Under Secretary for Intelligence and Analysis before the Senate Committee on Homeland Security and Governmental Affairs: Assessing the Nuclear Attack Threat,* April 2, 2008.

Allen, C. E. *Information Sharing at the Federal, State and Local Levels. Statement for the Record before the United States Senate Committee on Homeland Security and Governmental Affairs,* July 23, 2008.

Allen, C. E. DHS Under Secretary for Intelligence and Analysis. *Address to the Washington Institute for Near East Policy.* Washington, D.C.: May 6, 2008.

American Friends Service Committee. *The Police Threat to Political Liberty.* Philadelphia: American Friends Service Committee, 1979.

Attorney General's Report to Congress on the Growth of Violent Street Gangs in Suburban Areas. Washington, D.C.: U.S. Department of Justice, 2008.

Background on the Controlled Unclassified Information Framework. Unpublished background paper. Washington, D.C.: Executive Office of the President, May 9, 2008.

Baginski, M. Remarks in a keynote address at "Community Policing for America's Future: National Community Policing Conference," Office of Community Oriented Policing Services. Washington, D.C.: June 22, 2004.

Best, R. and A. Cumming. *Open Source Intelligence (OSINT): Issues for Congress. CRS Report for Congress.* Washington, D.C.: Congressional Research Service, December 5, 2007.

Best, R. and H. A. Boerstling. *The Intelligence Community in the 21st Century.* House of Representatives 104 Congress, Permanent Select Committee on Intelligence, 1996.

Bhanu, C. and C. Stone. *Public-Private Partnerships for Police Reform.* New York: Vera Institute of Justice, 2004.

Blackstock, N. *COINTELPRO: The FBI's Secret War on Political Freedom.* New York: Vintage Books, 1975.

Boba, R. *Problem Analysis in Policing.* Washington, D.C.: Police Foundation, 2003.

Boba, R. *Crime Analysis and Crime Mapping.* Thousand Oaks, California: SAGE Publications, 2005.

Bureau of Justice Assistance. *10 Simple Steps to Help your Agency Become Part of the National Criminal Intelligence Sharing Plan.* Washington, D.C.: Bureau of Justice Assistance, U.S. Department of Justice, 2005.

Bureau of Justice Assistance. *10 Ways to Integrate Suspicious Activity Reporting into Your Agency's Operations.* Washington, D.C.: Bureau of Justice Assistance, U.S. Department of Justice, 2008.

Bureau of Justice Assistance. Criminal Intelligence Training Coordination Strategy Working Group. *Survey of Law Enforcement on Intelligence Training.* Unpublished staff report, 2004.

Bureau of Justice Assistance. *Why Law Enforcement Agencies Need an Analytical Function.* Washington, D.C., Bureau of Justice Assistance, U.S. Department of Justice, October 2005.

California Peace Officers' Association. *Criminal Intelligence Program for the Smaller Agency.* Sacramento, California: California Peace Officers' Association, 1998.

Calling Time on Crime: A Thematic Inspection on Crime and Disorder. London, U.K.: Her Majesty's Inspectorate of Constabulary, 2004.

Carter, D. L. *The Police and the Community.* 7th ed. Upper Saddle River, New Jersey: Prentice Hall, Inc., 2000

Carter, D. L. *Law Enforcement Intelligence: A Guide for State, Local, and Tribal Law Enforcement Agencies.* Washington, D.C.: Office of Community Oriented Policing Services, U.S. Department of Justice, 2004.

Carter, D. L. *Law Enforcement Intelligence Operations.* 8th ed. Tallahassee, Florida: SMC Sciences, Inc., 2002.

Carter, D. L. and T. Martinelli. "Civil Rights and Law Enforcement Intelligence. *" The Police Chief,* June 2007.

Chevigny, P. G. "National Security and Civil Liberties: Politics and Law in the Control of Local Surveillance." *Cornell Law Review.* 69 (April 1984).

Christopher S., "A Practitioner's Perspective of UK Strategic Intelligence," in *Strategic Thinking in Criminal Intelligence,* ed. J.H. Ratcliffe, Sydney: Federation Press, 2004.

Clarke, R. V. and J. Eck. *Crime Analysis for Problem Solvers in 60 Small Steps.* Washington, D.C.: Office of Community Oriented Policing Services, U.S. Department of Justice, 2005.

Coleman, G. "Next Generation: CJIS?" *TIME System Newsletter.* Wisconsin Department of Justice, Crime Information Bureau. (2006-1) (March 2006).

Collier, P. M., J.S. Edwards, and D. Shaw, D. "Communicating Knowledge about Police Performance." *International Journal of Productivity and Performance Management* 53(5) (2004): 458–467.

Commission on Accreditation of Law Enforcement Agencies. *Standards for Law Enforcement Accreditation.* "Standard 51.1.1 – Criminal Intelligence." Washington, D.C.: Commission on Accreditation of Law Enforcement Agencies, 2002.

Commission on Terrorist Attacks Upon the United States. *The 9/11 Commission Report.* Washington, D.C.: U.S. Government Printing Office, 2004.

Cowan, P., N. Egleson, and N. Hentoff. *State Secrets: Police Surveillance in America.* New York: Holt, Rinehart and Winston, 1974.

Cryer, D. , Special Assistant to the Director of Central Intelligence for Diversity Management. *Prepared Statement, Hearing before the Permanent Select Committee on Intelligence,* 108th Congress, November 5, 2003.

Department of Homeland Security. Management Directive System, MD Number: 11042, *Safeguarding Sensitive But Unclassified (For Official Use Only) Information.* May 11, 2004.

Department of Homeland Security. National Preparedness Directorate. *Targeted Capabilities List. A Companion to the National Preparedness Guidelines.* Washington, D.C.: U.S. Department of Homeland Security, 2007.

Dillon, D. R. "Breaking Down Intelligence Barriers for Homeland Security." Backgrounder #1536. Washington, D.C.: The Heritage Foundation, 2002.

Dintino, J. and F. Martens. *Police Intelligence in Crime Control.* Springfield, Illinois: Charles C. Thomas, 1983.

Donner, F. J. *Protectors of Privilege: Red Squads and Police Repression in Urban America.* Berkeley, California: University of California Press, 1990.

Elliff, J. T. *Crime, Dissent, and the Attorney General.* Beverly Hills, California: SAGE Publications, 1971.

European Commission. *Report of the Seminar on Public Private Partnerships.* The Hague, Netherlands, 2003.

Federal Bureau of Investigation, Counterterrorism Division. *Terrorism: 2002–2005.* Washington, D.C.: Federal Bureau of Investigation, 2006.

Federal Bureau of Investigation. *The FBI intelligence Cycle: Answering the Questions. A Desk Reference Guide for Law Enforcement.* Washington, D.C.: Federal Bureau of Investigation, July 2004.

Federal Bureau of Investigation. "The FBI's Counterterrorism Program Since September 2001." *A Report to the National Commission on Terrorists Attacks Upon the United States.* Washington, D.C.: Federal Bureau of Investigation, undated.

Fisher, L. E., "Guilt by Expressive Association: Political Profiling, Surveillance and the Privacy of Groups," *Arizona Law Review* 46 (Winter) (2004).

Fourth Annual Report to the President and Congress of the Advisory Panel to Assess Domestic Response Capabilities for Terrorism Involving Weapons of Mass Destruction (Gilmore Commission). IV. Implementing the National Strategy. Arlington, Virginia: Rand Corporation, Research and Development Center, 2002.

Frawley, W., G. Piatetsky-Shapiro, and C. Matheus, "Knowledge Discovery in Databases: An Overview," *Artificial Intelligence Magazine* (Fall 1992).

Friedman, R.S. and F. Peek. "Problem-Based Learning and Problem-Solving Tools: Synthesis and Direction for Distributed Education Environments." *Journal of Interactive Learning Research* 13 (3) (2002) 239–257.

Frost, C. and J. Morris. *Police Intelligence Reports.* Orangevale, California: Palmer Press, 1983.

General Accounting Office. Homeland Security. *Justice Department's Project to Interview Aliens After September 11, 2001. Report to Congressional Committees.* Washington, D.C.: General Accounting Office, Report Number GAO-03-459, 2003.

German, M. and J. Stanley. *Fusion Center Update.* Washington, D.C.: American Civil Liberties Union, 2008.

German, M. and J. Stanley. *What's Wrong With Fusion Centers?* New York: American Civil Liberties Union, 2005.

Global Intelligence Working Group. *Criminal Intelligence for the Chief Executive. A Training Program for the Chief Executive. Glossary.* Washington, D.C.: Global Justice Information Sharing Initiative, U.S. Department of Justice, 2004.

Global Intelligence Working Group. *Fusion Center Guidelines.* Washington, D.C.: U.S. Department of Justice and U.S. Department of Homeland Security, 2006.

Global Intelligence Working Group. *Guidelines for Establishing and Operating Fusion Centers at the Local, State, Tribal and Federal Level.* Washington, D.C.: U.S. Department of Justice and U.S. Department of Homeland Security, 2005.

Global Intelligence Working Group. *Guidelines for Establishing and Operating Gang Intelligence Units and Task Forces.* Washington, D.C.: Bureau of Justice Assistance, U.S. Department of Justice, 2008.

Global Intelligence Working Group. *National Criminal Intelligence Sharing Plan.* Washington, D.C.: U.S. Department of Justice, 2003.

Global Intelligence Working Group. *Privacy Committee Report: Tips and Leads Issues Paper.* Washington, D.C.: Global Justice Information Sharing Initiative, U.S. Department of Justice, 2007.

Global Justice Information Sharing Initiative. *Analyst Toolbox. A Toolbox for the Intelligence Analyst.* Washington, D.C.: U.S. Department of Justice, Global Justice Information Sharing Initiative, Intelligence Working Group, November 2006.

Global Justice Information Sharing Initiative. *Fusion Center Guidelines—Developing and Sharing Information and Intelligence in a New Era.* Washington, D.C.: Bureau of Justice Assistance, 2006.

Global Justice Information Sharing Initiative. *Minimum Criminal Intelligence Training Standards for Law Enforcement and Other Criminal Justice Agencies in the United States. Findings and Recommendations.* Washington, D.C.: U.S. Department of Justice. 2007.

Global Justice Information Sharing Initiative. *Privacy and Civil Liberties Policy Development Guide and Implementation Templates.* Washington, D.C.: Bureau of Justice Assistance, Office of Justice Programs, U.S. Department of Justice, rev. 2008.

Godfrey, E.D. and D. R. Harris. *Basic Elements of Intelligence.* Washington, D.C.: Law Enforcement Assistance Administration, 1971.

Goldstein, H. *Problem-Oriented Policing.* New York: McGraw-Hill, 1990.

Government Accountability Office. *INFORMATION TECHNOLOGY: Numerous Federal Networks Used to Support Homeland Security Need to Be Better Coordinated with Key State and Local Information-Sharing Initiatives. Report to the Chairman, Committee on Homeland Security, House of Representatives.* Washington, D.C.: Government Accountability Office, April 2007.

Government Accountability Office. *Homeland Security: Federal Efforts Are Helping to Alleviate Some Challenges Encountered by State and Local Information Fusion Centers.* Washington, D.C.: Government Accountability Office, GAO-08-35 Homeland Security, October 2007.

Herzog, T. J. *Integrating Correctional Authorities into the Fusion Center Rubric.* Palm Coast, Florida: Corrections Technology Association, 2005.

Homeland Security Advisory Council. *Intelligence and Information Sharing Initiative: Homeland Security Intelligence & Information Fusion.* Washington, D.C.: Department of Homeland Security, 2005.

Homeland Security Council/National Security Council Joint Restricted Deputies Committee Meeting. *Discussion Paper on the Information Sharing Environment,* November 3, 2008.

Information Exchange Package Document (IEPD) for the Suspicious Activity Report of State and Local Entities IEPD. Version 1.01. A joint document of the Program Manager–Information Sharing Environment and the Bureau of Justice Assistance, Office of Justice Programs, U.S. Department of Justice.

International Association of Chiefs of Police. *Criminal Intelligence Sharing: A National Plan for Intelligence-Led Policing at the Local, State and Federal Levels.* Alexandria, Virginia: International Association of Chiefs of Police, 2002.

International Association of Law Enforcement Intelligence Analysts, Inc. *Law Enforcement Analytic Standards.* Washington, D.C.: International Association of Law Enforcement Intelligence Analysts, Inc., and Global Justice Information Sharing Initiative, November 2004.

International Association of Chiefs of Police. *National Summit on Intelligence.* Washington, D.C.: Office of Community Oriented Policing Services, U.S. Department of Justice, 2008.

International Association of Law Enforcement Intelligence Analysts, Inc. *Successful Law Enforcement Using Analytic Methods.* Internet-published document, undated.

Johnson, B. and S. Dorn. "Fusion Centers: New York State Intelligence Strategy Unifies Law Enforcement." *The Police Chief,* February 2008.

Johnson, L. *A Season of Inquiry: The Senate Intelligence Investigation.* Lexington, Kentucky: The University Press of Kentucky, 1985.

Kindsvater, L. C. "The Need to Reorganize the Intelligence Community". *Studies in Intelligence* 47 (1) (2003).

Knezo, G. J. *"Sensitive But Unclassified" Information and Other Controls: Policy and Options for Scientific and Technical Information. CRS Report for Congress.* Washington, D.C.: Congressional Research Service, December 29, 2006.

Koehnlein, B. *The History of the Handschu Decree.* New York: New York Civil Liberties Union, 2003.

Law Enforcement Intelligence Unit. *Criminal Intelligence File Guidelines.* Sacramento, California: Law Enforcement Intelligence Unit, revised March 2002.

Lee, C. "The NYPD Wants to Watch You." *The Village Voice,* December 18–24, 2002.

Leson, J. *Assessing and Managing the Terrorism Threat.* Washington, D.C.: Bureau of Justice Assistance, U.S. Department of Justice, 2003.

Lessons Learned Information Sharing. *Local Anti-Terrorism Information and Intelligence Sharing.* Washington, D.C.: U.S. Department of Homeland Security, 2005.

Lessons Learned Information Sharing. *Best Practices. Homeland Security Intelligence Requirements Process.* Washington, D.C.: U.S. Department of Homeland Security, 2006.

Lilly, J. R. "National Security at What Price?: A Look into Civil Liberty Concerns in the Information Age Under the USA Patriot Act of 2001 and a Proposed Constitutional Test for Future Legislation." *Cornell Journal of Law and Public Policy.* 12(Spring) (2003).

Los Angeles Police Department. *Reporting Incidents Potentially Related to Foreign or Domestic Terrorism. Special Order Number* 11, March 5, 2008.

Loyka, S.A., D.A. Faggiani, and C. Karchmer. *Protecting Your Community from Terrorism: Strategies for Local Law Enforcement, Volume 4: The Production and Sharing of Intelligence.* Washington, D.C.: Office of Community Oriented Policing Services and the Police Executive Research Forum, 2005.

MacLellan, T. *Protecting Privacy in Integrated Justice Systems.* Washington, D.C.: National Governors' Association Center for Best Practices, 2006.

Major Cities Chiefs Association and Major County Sheriffs' Association. *Intelligence and Information Sharing: DHS and law Enforcement.* Unpublished report, 2007.

Martens, F., "The Intelligence Function," in *Major Issues in Organized Crime Control: Symposium Proceedings,* Washington, D.C., September 25–26, 1986, ed. Herbert Edelhertz, Washington, D.C.: U.S. Department of Justice, National Institute of Justice, 1987.

Martinelli, T.J. and J.M. Pollock. "Law Enforcement Ethics, Lawsuits, and Liability: Defusing Deliberate Indifference, " *The Police Chief 67* (October 2000) 10.

Masse, T.M. *The National Counterterrorism Center: Implementation Challenges and Issues for Congress. CRS Report for Congress.* Washington, D.C.: Congressional Research Service, March 24, 2005.

Masse, T. and J. Rollins. *A Summary of Fusion Centers: Core Issues and Options for Congress. CRS Report for Congress.* Washington, D.C.: Congressional Research Service, September 19, 2007.

McConnell, J.M. *Vision 2015: A Globally Networked and Integrated Intelligence Enterprise.* Washington, D.C.: Office of the Director of National Intelligence, 2008.

McCreesh, P. and C. Neuman. *Managing for Counter-Terrorism Success in the Los Angeles Police Department.* New York: The Manhattan Institute, and Cambridge, Massachusetts: John F. Kennedy School of Government, Harvard University, 2007.

McDowell, D. *Strategic Intelligence: A Handbook for Practitioners, Managers, and Users.* Cooma, NSW, Australia: Istana Enterprises, Pty., Ltd., 2000.

McKnight, G. D. "A Harvest of Hate: The FBI's War Against Black Youth – Domestic Intelligence in Memphis, Tennessee." *South Atlantic Quarterly* 86 (Winter 1987): 1–21.

McNamara, T. *Annual Report to the Congress on the Information Sharing Environment.* Washington, D.C.: Program Manager-Information Sharing Environment, 2008.

McNamara, T. *Statement for the Record before the Subcommittee on Intelligence, Information Sharing and Terrorism Risk Assessment, House Committee on Homeland Security,* April 26, 2007.

Modafferi, P. and K. Bouche. "Intelligence Sharing: Efforts to Develop Fusion Center Intelligence Standards." *The Police Chief* 73 (2) (February 2005).

Morabito, A. and S. Greenberg. *Engaging the Private Sector to Promote Homeland Security: Law Enforcement-Private Security Partnerships.* Washington, D.C.: Bureau of Justice Assistance, 2005.

Murphy, W. *Statement by the former FBI Assistant Director, Directorate of Intelligence at the 2007 IACP Intelligence Summit,* Washington, D.C.: November 27, 2007.

Muslim Public Affairs Council. *A Review of U.S. Counterterrorism Policy: American Muslim Critique and Recommendations.* Washington, D.C.: Muslim Public Affairs Council, 2003.

National Advisory Commission on Civil Disorders. *Summary Report.* Washington, D.C.: U.S. Government Printing Office, 1968.

National Advisory Commission on the Causes and Prevention of Violence. *Law and Order Reconsidered.* Washington, D.C.: U.S. Government Printing Office, 1968.

National Advisory Commission on Criminal Justice Standards and Goals. *Police.* Washington, D.C.: U.S. Government Printing Office, 1973.

National Advisory Committee on Criminal Justice Standards and Goals. *Disorders and Terrorism: Report of the Task Force on Disorders and Terrorism.* Washington D.C.: U.S. Government Printing Office, 1976.

National Advisory Committee on Criminal Justice Standards and Goals. *Organized Crime–Task Force Report on Organized Crime.* Washington, D.C.: U.S. Department of Justice, Law Enforcement Assistance Administration, 1976.

National Alliance of Gang Investigators Associations. *National Gang Threat Assessment.* Washington, D.C.: Bureau of Justice Assistance, U.S. Department of Justice, 2005.

National Centre for Policing Excellence. *Guidance on the National Intelligence Model.* London, UK: Association of Chief Police Officers, 2005.

National Commission on the Causes and Prevention of Violence. *Law and Order Reconsidered.* Washington, D.C.: U.S. Government Printing Office, 1968.

National Commission on Terrorist Attacks Upon the United States. *Staff Statement No. 12: Reforming Law Enforcement, Counterterrorism, and Intelligence Collection in the United States.* Washington, D.C.: National Commission on Terrorist Attacks Upon the United States, 2004.

National Commission on Terrorist Attacks Upon the United States. *The 9/11 Commission Report.* Washington, D.C.: U.S. Government Printing Office, 2004.

National Criminal Justice Association. *Justice Information Privacy Guideline. Developing, Drafting and Assessing Privacy Policy for Justice Information Systems.* Washington, DC: National Criminal Justice Association, 2002.

National Gang Center. *Brief Review of Federal and State Definitions of the Terms "Gang," "Gang Crime," and "Gang Member."* Unpublished web document, undated.

National Governors Association. *Policy Position: EC-05. Homeland Security Policy.* Washington, D.C.: National Governors Association, 2007.

National Strategy for Information Sharing. Washington, D.C.: Executive Office of the President, 2007.

Nenneman, M. *An Examination of State and Local Fusion Centers and Data Collection Methods.* Monterey, California: A thesis prepared for the Naval Post Graduate School, 2008.

NIEM Program Management Office. *Introduction to the National Information Exchange Model (NIEM).* Washington, D.C.: NIEM Program Management Office, February 12, 2007.

Office of Intelligence and Analysis. *National Strategy for the Fire Service Intelligence Enterprise.* Washington, D.C.: U.S. Department of Homeland Security, 2008.

Office of the Chief Intelligence Officer. *DHS Intelligence Enterprise Strategic Plan.* Washington, D.C.: U.S. Department of Homeland Security, 2006.

Office of the Director of National Intelligence. *Sourcing Requirements for Disseminated Analytic Requirements. Intelligence Community Directive* 206. Washington, D.C.: Office of the Director of National Intelligence, October 17, 2007.

Office of the Director of National Intelligence. *National Open Source Enterprise.* Washington, D.C.: Office of the Director of National Intelligence, 2007.

Office of the Inspector General. Audit Division. *The Drug Enforcement Administration's Use of Intelligence Analysts. Audit Report 08-23.* Washington, D.C.: U.S. Department of Justice, May 2008.

Orrick, W.D. *Best Practices Guide: Developing a Police Department Policy-Procedure Manual.* Alexandria, Virginia: International Association of Chiefs of Police, undated.

Peterson, M. *Intelligence-Led Policing: The New Intelligence Architecture.* Washington, D.C.: Bureau of Justice Assistance, 2005. NCJ 210681.

Peterson, M. *Applications in Criminal Analysis: A Sourcebook.* Westport, Connecticut: Praeger, 1994.

Peterson, M. et al. *Successful Law Enforcement Using Analytic Methods.* South Florida, Florida: International Association of Law Enforcement Intelligence Analysts, Inc., 1996.

Peterson, M., B. Morehouse, and R. Wright, eds. *Intelligence 2000: Revising the Basic Elements. A Guide for Intelligence Professionals.* Sacramento, California: Law Enforcement Intelligence Unit, and Lawrenceville, New Jersey: International Association of Law Enforcement Intelligence Analysts, Inc., 2000.

Pistole, J. S., Executive Assistant Director, Counterterrorism and Counterintelligence, Federal Bureau of Investigation. *Statement before the House Judiciary Committee Subcommittee on Crime, Terrorism and Homeland Security,* August 23, 2004.

Pitts, D. "Getting the 411." *Fire Chief.* January 1, 2008.

Police Executive Research Forum. *What Is a Fusion Center?* Washington, D.C.: Police Executive Research Forum, 2008.

President's Commission on Law Enforcement and Administration of Justice. *Task Force Report: Organized Crime.* Washington, D.C.: U.S. Government Printing Office, 1967.

President's Commission on Organized Crime. *Final Report.* Washington, D.C.: U.S. Government Printing Office, 1987.

President's Commission on Organized Crime. *Organized Crime and Money Laundering.* Washington, D.C.: U.S. Government Printing Office, 1984.

Privacy Impact Statement for the Homeland Security Information Network Database. Washington, D.C.: Unpublished report of the DHS Office of Operations Coordination, April 5, 2006.

Program Manager–Information Sharing Environment. *Common Terrorism Information Sharing Standards (CTISS) Program Manual.* Washington, D.C.: Program Manager-Information Sharing Environment, 2007.

Program Manager–Information Sharing Environment. *Guidelines to Ensure That the information Privacy and Other Legal Rights of Americans Are Protected in the Development and Use of the Information Sharing Environment.* Washington, D.C.: Office of the Director of National intelligence, September 4, 2006.

Program Manager–Information Sharing Environment. *Information Sharing Environment Implementation Plan.* Washington, D.C.: Office of the Director of National Intelligence, 2006.

Ramsey, T. *Global Maritime Intelligence Integration (GMII) Enterprise.* PowerPoint Presentation. Washington, D.C.: Office of the Director of National Intelligence, May 9, 2007.

Ratcliffe, J. and R. Guidetti. "State Police Investigative Structure and the Adoption of Intelligence-Led Policing." *Policing: An International Journal of Police Strategies and Management,* 2007.

Ratcliffe, J.H., "The Structure of Strategic Thinking," in *Strategic Thinking in Criminal Intelligence,* ed., J.H. Ratcliffe, Sydney, NSW, Australia: Federation Press, 2004, pp. 1–10.

Ratcliffe, J.H. *Intelligence-Led Policing.* Cullompton, Devon, U.K.: Willan Publishing, 2008.

Ratcliffe, J.H. *Integrated Intelligence and Crime Analysis: Enhanced Information Management for Law Enforcement Leaders.* Washington, D.C.: Office of Community Oriented Policing Services, U.S. Department of Justice, 2007.

Reese, S. *State and Local Homeland Security: Unresolved Issues for the 109th Congress. CRS Report for Congress.* Washington, D.C.: Congressional Research Service, June 9, 2005.

Riley, K. J., G. Treverton, J. Wilson, and L. Davis. *State and Local Intelligence in the War on Terrorism.* Santa Monica, California: RAND Corporation, 2005.

Rossmo, D. K. *Geographic Profiling.* Boca Raton, Florida: CRC Press, 2000.

Sagan, Carl. *Broca's Brain: Reflections on the Romance of Science.* New York: The Ballantine Publishing Group, 1979.

Scheider, M., R. Chapman, and M. Seelman. "Connecting the Dots for a Proactive Approach." *Border and Transportation Security.* Washington, D.C.: Office of Community Oriented Policing Services, 2004.

Scott, M.S. *Problem-Oriented Policing: Reflections on the First 20 Years.* Washington, D.C.: Office of Community Oriented Policing Services, 2000.

Shane, J. "CompStat Process." *FBI Law Enforcement Bulletin* 73 (2) (April 2004).

Shaw, L. *Information Systems and Technologies.* Presentation at the BJA-funded Intelligence Commanders' Course, Norwalk, California, July 2008.

Simeone, M.J. *The Integration of Virtual Public-Private Partnerships in Law Enforcement to Achieve Enhanced Intelligence-Led Policing.* Monterey, California: A thesis prepared for the Naval Postgraduate School, 2007.

Statement by FBI Assistant Director Wayne Murphy, Directorate of Intelligence, at the 2007 IACP Intelligence Summit, Washington, D.C., November 27, 2007.

Steigman, J.L. "Reversing Reform: The Handschu Settlement in Post-September 11 New York City." *Brooklyn Journal of Law and Policy* 11 (2003).

Stone, K. *Deploying and Operating an Effective Regional Fusion System: Lessons Learned from the North Central Texas Fusion System.* Unpublished policy paper prepared by the North Central Texas Fusion System, McKinney, Texas, 2006.

Sullivan, J.P. *Terrorism Early Warning and Co-Production of Counterterrorism Intelligence.* A paper presented at the Canadian Association of Security and Intelligence Studies. Montreal, Canada, 2005.

Suspicious Activity Report Support and Implementation Project. *Final Report*. Washington, D.C.: Major Cities Chiefs Association; U.S. Department of Justice and U.S. Department of Homeland Security, 2008.

The Warren Commission. *Report of the President's Commission on the Assassination of President John F. Kennedy*. New York: Barnes and Noble, Inc., 2003 [Originally published in 1964].

The White House. Executive Office of the President. Office of Homeland Security. *National Strategy for Homeland Security*. Washington, D.C.: 2002.

Tomarchio, J. *Focus on Fusion Centers: A Progress Report*. Prepared Statement Before the Ad Hoc Subcommittee on State, Local and Private Sector Preparedness and Integration, Committee on Homeland Security and Government Affairs, United States Senate, April 17, 2008.

Townsley, M., S. Johnson, and K. Pease. "Problem Orientation, Problem Solving and Organizational Change." *Crime Prevention Studies 15*, Monsey, New York: Criminal Justice Press, 2003.

U.S. General Accounting Office. *Security Clearances*. GAO-04-596. Washington, D.C.: U.S. General Accounting Office, 2004.

United States Senate. Select Committee to Study Governmental Operations. *Intelligence Activities: Final Report*. Washington, D.C.: U.S. Government Printing Office, 1976.

United States Senate. Select Committee to Study Governmental Operations with Respect to Intelligence Activities. *Intelligence Activities and the Rights of Americans: Final Report. Book II*. Washington, D.C.: April 26, 1976.

Weimer, D. R. *The Copyright Doctrine of Fair Use and the Internet: Case Law*. Washington, D.C.: Congressional Research Service, 2005.

Wells, I., "Staffing the Intelligence Unit," in *Intelligence 2000: Revising the Basic Elements, A Guide for Intelligence Professionals*, ed. M. Peterson, B. Morehouse, and R. Wright, Sacramento, California: Law Enforcement Intelligence Unit, and Lawrenceville, New Jersey: International Association of Law Enforcement Intelligence Analysts, 2000.

Wortzel, L. "Creating an Intelligent Department of Homeland Security." *Executive Memorandum 828*. Washington, D.C.: The Heritage Foundation, 2002.

Appendix A: Glossary of Terms for Law Enforcement Intelligence

Law enforcement agencies at all levels are working together more than ever to support information sharing. It is important to note that a tremendous effort is under way to streamline intelligence terms to facilitate information sharing. As a result, criminal intelligence terminology is changing. The definitions contained herein are provided from the perspective of law enforcement/criminal intelligence. Further, some words and phrases will have alternative or additional meanings when used in the context of national security intelligence, the military, or business. The definitions are intended to be merely descriptive of an entity, issue, or process that may be encountered by those working with the criminal intelligence function. Definitions may differ according to state statutes or local rules.

Glossary Of Law Enforcement Intelligence Terms

Actionable: Intelligence and information with sufficient specificity and detail that explicit responses to prevent a crime or terrorist attack can be implemented.

Administrative Analysis: The analysis of economic, geographic, demographic, census, or behavioral data to identify trends and conditions useful to aid administrators in making policy and/or resource allocation decisions.

All-Hazards Intelligence: The collection and analysis of information concerned with noncriminal domestic threats to critical infrastructure, community health, and public safety for the purpose of preventing the threat or mitigating the effects of the threat. (Same as Homeland Security Intelligence).

Allocation: Collection and analysis of information that shows relationships among varied individuals suspected of being involved in criminal activity that may provide insight into the criminal operation and which investigative strategies might work best.

Analysis: That activity whereby meaning, actual or suggested, is derived through organizing and systematically examining diverse information and applying inductive or deductive logic for the purposes of criminal investigation or assessment.

Archiving (Records): The maintenance of records in remote storage after a case has been closed or disposed of, as a matter of contingency, should the records be needed for later reference.

Association Analysis: The entry of critical investigative and/or assessment variables into a two-axis matrix to examine the relationships and patterns that emerge as the variables are correlated in the matrix.

Automated Trusted Information Exchange (ATIX): Operated by the Regional Information Sharing Systems, ATIX is a secure means of disseminating national security or terrorist threat information to law enforcement and other first responders through the ATIX electronic bulletin board, secure web site, and secure e-mail.

Bias/Hate Crime: Any criminal act directed toward a person or group because of that person's race, ethnicity, religious affiliation, or sexual preference.

C3: An intelligence application concept initially used by military intelligence that stands for command, control, and communication as the hallmark for effective intelligence operations.

Clandestine Activity: An activity that is usually extensive and goal-oriented, planned, and executed to conceal the existence of the operation. Only participants and the agency sponsoring the activity are intended to know about the operation. Storefront operations, stings, and certain concentrated undercover investigations (such as ABSCAM) can be classified as clandestine collections.

Classified Information/Intelligence: A uniform system for classifying, safeguarding, and declassifying national security information, including information relating to defense against transnational terrorism, to ensure that certain information is maintained in confidence to protect citizens, U.S. democratic institutions, U.S. homeland security, and U.S. interactions with foreign nations and entities.
- *Top Secret Classification*: Applied to information, the unauthorized disclosure of which reasonably could be expected to cause exceptionally grave damage to the national security that the original classification authority is able to identify or describe (Executive Order 12958, March 25, 2003).
- *Secret Classification*: Applied to information, the unauthorized disclosure of which reasonably could be expected to cause serious damage to the national security that the original classification authority is able to identify or describe (Executive Order 12958, March 25, 2003).
- *Confidential Classification*: Applied to information, the unauthorized disclosure of which reasonably could be expected to cause damage to the national security that the original classification authority is able to identify or describe (Executive Order 12958, March 25, 2003).

Collation (of information): A review of collected and evaluated information to determine its substantive applicability to a case or problem at issue and placement of useful information into a form or system that permits easy and rapid access and retrieval.

Collection (of information): The identification, location, and recording/storing of information, typically from an original source and using both human and technological means, for input into the Intelligence Cycle for the purpose of meeting a defined tactical or strategic intelligence goal.

Collection Plan: The preliminary step toward completing an assessment of intelligence requirements to determine what type of information needs to be collected, alternatives for how to collect the information, and a timeline for collecting the information.

Command and Control: Command and control functions are performed through an arrangement of personnel, equipment, communications, facilities, and procedures used by a commander in planning, directing, coordinating, and controlling forces and operations in the accomplishment of a mission.

Commodity (Illegal): Any item or substance that is inherently unlawful to possess (contraband) or materials which, if not contraband, are themselves being distributed, transacted, or marketed in an unlawful manner.

Commodity Flow Analysis: Graphic depictions and descriptions of transactions, shipment, and distribution of contraband goods and money derived from unlawful activities in order to aid in the disruption of the unlawful activities and apprehend those persons involved in all aspects of the unlawful activities.

Communications Intelligence (COMINT): The capture of information, either encrypted or in plaintext, exchanged between intelligence targets or transmitted by a known or suspected intelligence target for the purposes of tracking communications patterns and protocols (traffic analysis), establishing links between intercommunicating parties or groups, and/or analysis of the substantive meaning of the communication.

Conclusion: A definitive statement about a suspect, action, or state of nature based on the analysis of information.

Confidential: *See* Classified Information/Intelligence, Confidential Classification.

Continuing Criminal Enterprise: Any individual, partnership, corporation, association, or other legal entity and any union or group of individuals associated in fact, although not a legal entity, that are involved in a continuing or perpetuating criminal activity.

Controlled Unclassified Information (CUI) : The term Controlled Unclassified Information or CUI is a categorical designation that refers to unclassified information that does not meet the standards for National Security Classification under Executive Order 12958, as amended, but is (i) pertinent to the national interests of the United States or to the important interests of entities outside the federal government, and (ii) under law or policy requires protection from unauthorized disclosure, special handling safeguards, or prescribed limits on exchange or dissemination. The designation CUI replaces Sensitive But Unclassified (SBU). There are three types of CUI:

- *Controlled with Standard Dissemination:* The information requires standard safeguarding measures that reduce the risks of unauthorized or inadvertent disclosure. Dissemination is permitted to the extent that it is reasonably believed that it would further the execution of a lawful or official purpose.

- *Controlled with Specified Dissemination:* The information requires safeguarding measures that reduce the risks of unauthorized or inadvertent disclosure. Material contains additional instructions on what dissemination is permitted.

- *Controlled Enhanced with Specified Dissemination:* The information requires safeguarding measures more stringent than those normally required because the inadvertent or unauthorized disclosure would create risk of substantial harm. Material contains additional instructions on what dissemination is permitted.

Coordination: The process of interrelating work functions, responsibilities, duties, resources, and initiatives directed toward goal attainment.

Counterintelligence: Information compiled, analyzed, and/or disseminated in an effort to investigate espionage, sedition, or subversion that is related to national security concerns. It also is defined as a national security intelligence activity that involves blocking or developing a strategic response to other groups, governments, or individuals through the identification, neutralization, and manipulation of their intelligence services.

Covert Intelligence: An activity that is planned and executed to conceal the collection of information and/ or to conceal the identity of an officer or agent participating in the activity.

Critical Infrastructure: Certain national infrastructures that are so vital that their incapacity or destruction would have a debilitating impact on the defense or economic security of the United States. These critical infrastructures are:

- Telecommunications
- Electrical power systems
- Gas and oil storage and transportation
- Banking and finance
- Transportation
- Water supply systems
- Emergency services (including medical, police, fire, and rescue)
- Continuity of government.

Crime Analysis: The process of analyzing information collected about crimes and police service delivery variables in order to give direction for police officer deployment, resource allocation, and policing strategies as a means of maximizing crime-prevention activities and the cost-effective operation of the police department.

Crime-Pattern Analysis: An assessment of the nature, extent, and changes of crime based on the characteristics of the criminal incident, including modus operandi, temporal, and geographic variables.

Criminal History Record Information (CHRI): Information collected by criminal justice agencies on individuals. It consists of identifiable descriptions and notations of arrests, detentions, indictments, information, or other formal criminal charges and any disposition arising from them, including sentencing, correctional supervision, and/or release. The term does not include identification information, such as fingerprint records, to the extent that such information does not indicate involvement of the individual in the criminal justice system.

Criminal Informant: See Informant.

Criminal Intelligence: The end product (output) of an analytic process that collects and assesses information about crimes and/or criminal enterprises with the purpose of making judgments and inferences about community conditions, potential problems, and criminal activity with the intent to pursue criminal prosecution or project crime trends or support informed decision-making by management. Same as Law Enforcement Intelligence.

Criminal Investigative Analysis: An analytic process that studies serial offenders, victims, and crime scenes in order to assess characteristics and behaviors of offender(s) with the intent to identify or aid in the identification of the offender(s).

Criminal Predicate: Information about an individual or his or her behavior that may be collected and stored in a law enforcement intelligence records system only when there is reasonable suspicion that the individual is involved in criminal conduct or activity and the information is relevant to that criminal conduct or activity.

Cryptanalysis: The process of deciphering encrypted communications of an intelligence target.

Cryptography: The creation of a communications code/encryption system for communication transmission with the intent of precluding the consumption and interpretation of one's own messages.

Cryptology: The study of communications encryption methods that deal with the development of "codes" and the "scrambling" of communications to prevent an unauthorized or unintended party from intercepting the communications.

Data Element: A field within a database that describes or defines a specific characteristic or attribute.

Data Owner: The agency that originally enters information or data into a law enforcement records system.

Data Quality: Controls implemented to ensure that all information in a law enforcement agency's records system is complete, accurate, and secure.

Deconfliction: The process or system used to determine whether multiple law enforcement agencies are investigating the same person or crime. The system provides notification to each agency involved of the shared interest in the case and also provides contact information. This is an information and intelligence sharing process that seeks to minimize conflicts between agencies and maximize the effectiveness of an investigation.

Deductive Logic: The reasoning process of taking information and arriving at conclusions from within that information.

Deployment: The short-term assignment of personnel to address specific crime problems or police service demands.

Designated State and/or Major Urban Area Fusion Center: The fusion center in each state designated as the primary or lead fusion center for the information-sharing environment.

Dissemination (of Intelligence): The process of effectively distributing analyzed intelligence utilizing certain protocols in the most appropriate format to those in need of the information to facilitate their accomplishment of organizational goals.

Due Process: Fundamental fairness during the course of the criminal justice process, including adherence to legal standards and the civil rights of the police constituency; the adherence to principles that are fundamental to justice.

El Paso Intelligence Center (EPIC): A cooperative intelligence center serving as a clearinghouse and intelligence resource for local, state, and federal law enforcement agencies. Primary concern is drug trafficking. EPIC also manages intelligence on other crimes.

Enterprise: Any individual, partnership, corporation, association, or other legal entity and any union or group of individuals associated in fact, although not a legal entity.

Estimate: *See* Intelligence Estimate.

Evaluation (of Information): All information collected for the intelligence cycle is reviewed for its quality, with an assessment of the validity and reliability of the information.

Event Flow Analysis: Graphic depictions and descriptions of incidents, behaviors, and people involved in an unlawful event, intended to help understand how an event occurred as a tool to aid in prosecution as well as prevention of future unlawful events.

Exemptions (to the Freedom of Information Act): Circumstances wherein a law enforcement agency is not required to disclose information from a Freedom of Information Act (FOIA) request.

Field Intelligence Group (FIG): The centralized intelligence component in a Federal Bureau of Investigation (FBI) field office that is responsible for the management, execution, and coordination of intelligence functions within the field office region.

Field Intelligence Report (FIR): An officer-initiated interview of a person believed by the officer to be acting in a suspicious manner that may be indicative of planning or preparing to conduct criminal activity.

Financial Analysis: A review and analysis of financial data to ascertain the presence of criminal activity. It can include bank record analysis, net worth analysis, financial profiles, source and applications of funds, financial statement analysis, and/or Bank Secrecy Act record analysis. It can also show destinations of the proceeds of crime and be used to support prosecutions.

Flow Analysis: The review of raw data to determine the sequence of events or interactions that may reflect criminal activity. It can include timelines, event flow analysis, commodity flow analysis, and activity flow analysis. May show missing actions or events that need further investigation.

For Official Use Only (FOUO): A designation applied to unclassified sensitive information that may be exempt from mandatory release to the public under the FOIA.

Forecast (as related to Criminal Intelligence): The product of an analytic process that provides a probability of future crimes and crime patterns based on a comprehensive, integrated analysis of past, current, and developing trends.

Freedom of Information Act (FOIA): The Freedom of Information Act, 5 U.S.C. 552, enacted in 1966, statutorily provides that any person has a right, enforceable in court, to access federal agency records, except to the extent that such records (or portions thereof) are protected from disclosure by one of nine exemptions.

Fusion Center: The physical location of the law enforcement intelligence fusion process.

Fusion Center Guidelines: A series of nationally recognized standards developed by law enforcement intelligence subject matter experts designed for the good practice of developing and managing an intelligence fusion center.

Fusion Process: The overarching process of managing the flow of information and intelligence across levels and sectors of government.

Granularity: Considers the specific details and pieces of information, including nuances and situational inferences that constitute the elements on which intelligence is developed through analysis.

Guidelines: *See* Intelligence Records Guidelines.

Homeland Security Advisory System: An information and communications structure designed by the U.S. Government for disseminating information to all levels of government and the American people regarding the risk of terrorist attacks and for providing a framework to assess the risk at five levels: Low, Guarded, Elevated, High, and Severe.

Homeland Security Intelligence: The collection and analysis of information concerned with noncriminal domestic threats to critical infrastructure, community health, and public safety for the purpose of preventing the threat or mitigating the effects of the threat. (Same as All Hazards Intelligence).

Human Intelligence (HUMINT): Intelligence-gathering methods that require human interaction or observation of the target or targeted environment. The intelligence is collected through the use of one's direct senses or the optical and/or audio enhancement of the senses.

Hypothesis (from Criminal Intelligence Analysis): An interim conclusion regarding persons, events, and/or commodities based on the accumulation and analysis of intelligence information that is to be proven or disproved by further investigation and analysis.

Imagery: The representation of an object or locale produced on any medium by optical or electronic means. The nature of the image will be dependent on the sensing media and sensing platform.

Indicator: Generally defined and observable actions that, based on an analysis of past known behaviors and characteristics, collectively suggest that a person may be committing, may be preparing to commit, or has committed an unlawful act.

Inductive Logic: The reasoning process of taking diverse pieces of specific information and inferring a broader meaning of the information through the course of hypothesis development.

Inference Development: The creation of a probabilistic conclusion, estimate, or prediction related to an intelligence target based on the use of inductive or deductive logic in the analysis of raw information related to the target.

Informant: An individual not affiliated with a law enforcement agency who provides information about criminal behavior to a law enforcement agency. An informant may be a community member, a businessperson, or a criminal informant who seeks to protect himself or herself from prosecution and/or provide the information in exchange for payment.

Information: Pieces of raw, unanalyzed data that identify persons, evidence, or events, or illustrate processes that indicate the incidence of a criminal event or witnesses or evidence of a criminal event.

Information Classification: *See* Classified Information/Intelligence.

Information Evaluation: *See* Evaluation (of Information).

Information Sharing Environment: A trusted partnership among all levels of government, the private sector, and foreign partners to detect, prevent, preempt, and mitigate the effects of terrorism against the territory, people, and interests of the United States of America. This partnership enables the trusted, secure, and appropriate exchange of terrorism information, in the first instance, across the five federal communities; to and from state, local, and tribal governments, foreign allies, and the private sector; and at all levels of security classifications.

Information Sharing System: An integrated and secure methodology, whether computerized or manual, designed to efficiently and effectively distribute critical information about offenders, crimes, and/or events in order to enhance prevention and apprehension activities by law enforcement.

Information System: An organized means, whether manual or electronic, of collecting, processing, storing, and retrieving information about individual entities for purposes of record and reference.

Intelligence Analyst: A professional position in which the incumbent is responsible for taking the varied facts, documentation of circumstances, evidence, interviews, and any other material related to a crime and organizing them into a logical and related framework for the purposes of developing a criminal case, explaining a criminal phenomenon, describing crime and crime trends, and/or preparing materials for court and prosecution, or arriving at an assessment of a crime problem or crime group.

Intelligence Assessment: A comprehensive report on an intelligence issue related to criminal or national security threats available to local, state, tribal, and federal law enforcement agencies.

Intelligence Bulletins: A finished intelligence product in article format that describes new developments and evolving trends. The bulletins are typically Sensitive But Unclassified (SBU) and available for distribution to local, state, tribal, and federal law enforcement.

Intelligence Community: Agencies of the U.S. government, including the military, that have the responsibility of preventing breeches in U.S. national security and responding to national security threats.

Intelligence Cycle: An organized process by which information is gathered, assessed, and distributed to fulfill the goals of the intelligence function. It is a method of performing analytic activities and placing the analysis in a useable form.

Intelligence Estimate: The appraisal, expressed in writing or orally, of available intelligence relating to a specific situation or condition with a view to determining the courses of action open to criminal offenders and terrorists and the order of probability of their adoption. It includes strategic projections about the economic, human, and/or quantitative criminal impact of the crime or issue that is subject to analysis.

Intelligence Function: The activity within a law enforcement agency responsible for some aspect of law enforcement intelligence, whether collection, analysis, and/or dissemination.

Intelligence Gap: An unanswered question about a cyber, criminal, or national security issue or threat.

Intelligence Information Reports (IIR): Raw, unevaluated intelligence concerning perishable or time-limited information about criminal or national security issues. While the full IIR may be classified, local, state, and tribal law enforcement agencies will have access to SBU information in the report under the tear line.

Intelligence-Led Policing: The dynamic use of intelligence to guide operational law enforcement activities to targets, commodities, or threats for both tactical responses and strategic decision-making for resource allocation and/or strategic responses.

Intelligence Mission: The role that the intelligence function of a law enforcement agency fulfills in support of the overall mission of the agency. It specifies in general language what the function is intended to accomplish.

Intelligence Mutual Aid Pact (IMAP): A formal agreement between law enforcement agencies designed to expedite the process of sharing information in intelligence records.

Intelligence Officer: A law enforcement officer assigned to an agency's intelligence function for purposes of investigation, liaison, or other intelligence-related activity that requires or benefits from having a sworn officer perform the activity.

Intelligence Products: Reports or documents that contain assessments, forecasts, associations, links, and other outputs from the analytic process that may be disseminated for use by law enforcement agencies for prevention of crimes, target hardening, apprehension of offenders, and prosecution.

Intelligence Records (Files): Stored information about the activities and associations of individuals, organizations, businesses, and groups who are suspected (reasonable suspicion) of being involved in the actual or attempted planning, organizing, financing, or commissioning of criminal acts, or are suspected of being or having been involved in criminal activities with known or suspected crime figures.

Intelligence Records Guidelines: Derived from the federal regulation 28 CFR Part 23, these are guidelines/standards for the development of records management policies and procedures used by law enforcement agencies.

International Criminal Police Organization (INTERPOL): INTERPOL is a worldwide law enforcement organization established for mutual assistance in the prevention, detection, and deterrence of international crimes. It houses international police databases, provides secure international communications between member countries for the exchange of routine criminal investigative information, and is an information clearinghouse concerning international criminals/fugitives and stolen properties.

Investigatory Value (of Information): Intelligence or information that is disseminated in the law enforcement community for surveillance, apprehension, or furtherance of an investigation.

Key Resources: Publicly or privately controlled resources essential to the minimal operations of the economy and government.

Key Word In Context (KWIC): An automated system that indexes selected key words that represent the evidence or information being stored.

Law Enforcement Intelligence (LAWINT): The end product (output) of an analytic process that collects and assesses information about crimes and/or criminal enterprises. Its purpose is to make judgments and inferences about community conditions, potential problems, and criminal activity with the intent to pursue criminal prosecution or project crime trends or support informed decision-making by management. Same as Criminal Intelligence.

Law Enforcement Sensitive (LES): Sensitive But Nnclassified information specifically compiled for law enforcement purposes that, if not protected from unauthorized access, could reasonably be expected to 1. Interfere with law enforcement proceedings, 2. Deprive a person of a right to a fair trial or impartial adjudication, 3. Constitute an unwarranted invasion of the personal privacy of others, 4. Disclose the identity of a confidential source, 5. Disclose investigative techniques and procedures, and/or 6. Endanger the life or physical safety of an individual.

Methods: These are the methodologies (e.g., electronic surveillance or undercover operations) by which critical information is obtained and recorded.

Micro-Intelligence: Intelligence activities focusing on current problems and crimes for either case development or resource allocation.

Money Laundering: The practice of using multiple unlawful transactions of money and/or negotiable instruments gained through illegal activities with the intent of hiding the origin of the income, those who have been "paid" from the income, and/or the location of the unlawful income.

National Central Bureau (NCB or USNCB): The United States headquarters of INTERPOL, located in Washington, D.C.

National Criminal Intelligence Resource Center (NCIRC): An Internet web site that contains information regarding law enforcement intelligence operations and practices and provides criminal justice professionals with a centralized resource information bank through which they can access a multitude of criminal intelligence resources to help law enforcement agencies develop, implement, and retain a lawful and effective intelligence capacity.

National Criminal Intelligence Sharing Plan (NCISP): A formal intelligence-sharing initiative, supported by the U.S. Department of Justice, Office of Justice Programs, that securely links local, state, tribal, and federal law enforcement agencies, and facilitates the exchange of critical intelligence information. The NCISP contains model policies and standards and is a blueprint for law enforcement administrators to follow when enhancing or building an intelligence function. It describes a nationwide communications capability that will link all levels of law enforcement personnel, including officers on the street, intelligence analysts, unit commanders, and police executives.

National Security Intelligence: The collection and analysis of information concerned with the relationship and equilibrium of the United States with foreign powers, organizations, and persons with regard to political and economic factors, as well as the maintenance of the United States' sovereign principles.

Need to Know: As a result of jurisdictional, organizational, or operational necessities, intelligence or sensitive information is disseminated to further an investigation.

Network: A structure of interconnecting components designed to communicate with each other and perform a function or functions as a unit in a specified manner.

Open Communications (OPCOM): The collection of open or publicly available communications, broadcasts, audio or video recordings, propaganda, published statements, and other distributed written or recorded material for purposes of analyzing the information.

Open-Source Information (or Intelligence): Individual data, records, reports, and assessments that may shed light on an investigatory target or event which do not require any legal process or any type of clandestine collection techniques for a law enforcement agency to obtain. Rather, it is obtained through means that meet copyright and commercial requirements of vendors, as well as being free of legal restrictions to access by anyone who seeks that information.

Operational Analysis: An assessment of the methodology of a criminal enterprise or terrorist organization that depicts how the enterprise performs its activities, including communications, philosophy, compensation, security, and other variables that are essential for the enterprise to exist.

Operational Intelligence: Information is evaluated and systematically organized on an active or potential target, such as groups of or individual criminals, relevant premises, contact points, and methods of communication. This process is developmental in nature wherein there are sufficient articulated reasons to suspect criminal activity. Intelligence activities explore the basis of those reasons and newly developed information in order to develop a case for arrest or indictment.

Outcome Evaluation: The process of determining the value or amount of success in achieving a predetermined objective. This is done by defining the objective in qualitative or quantitative measurable terms, identifying the proper criteria (or variables) used in measuring the success of attaining the objective, determining and explaining the degree of success, and making recommendations for further program actions to attain the desired objectives/outcomes.

Personal Identifying Information: Any information or data from which a reasonable person may identify a specific individual. When Personal Identifying Information is collected, civil rights protections and privacy standards must be afforded to the document or report that contains the information

Planning: The preparation for future situations, estimating organizational demands and resources needed to attend to those situations, and initiating strategies to respond to those situations.

Pointer System or Index: A system that stores information designed to identify individuals, organizations, and/or crime methodologies with the purpose of linking law enforcement agencies that have similar investigative and/or intelligence interests in the entity defined by the system.

Policy: The principles and values that guide the performance of a duty. A policy is not a statement of what must be done in a particular situation; rather, it is a statement of guiding principles that should be followed in activities that are directed toward attaining goals.

Prediction: The projection of future criminal actions or changes in the nature of crime trends or a criminal enterprise based on an analysis of information depicting historical trends from which a forecast is based.

Preventive Intelligence: Intelligence that can be used to interdict or forestall a crime or terrorist attack.

Privacy (Information): The assurance that legal and constitutional restrictions on the collection, maintenance, use, and disclosure of personally identifiable information will be adhered to by criminal justice agencies. Use of such information is strictly limited to circumstances in which legal process permits use of the personally identifiable information.

Privacy (Personal): The assurance that legal and constitutional restrictions on the collection, maintenance, use, and disclosure of behaviors of an individual—including his or her communications, associations, and transactions—will be adhered to by criminal justice agencies, with use of such information strictly limited to circumstances in which legal process authorizes surveillance and investigation.

Privacy Act: Legislation that allows an individual to review almost all federal files (and state files under the auspices of the respective state privacy acts) pertaining to him or her, places restrictions on the disclosure of personally identifiable information, specifies that there are no secret records systems about individuals, and compels the government to reveal its information sources.

Proactive: Taking action that anticipates a problem or situation, with the intent to eliminate or mitigate the effect of the incident.

Procedural Due Process: Mandates and guarantees of law that ensure that the procedures employed to deprive a person of life, liberty, or property during the course of the criminal justice process meet constitutional standards.

Procedures: A method of performing an operation or a manner of proceeding on a course of action. It differs from policy by directing action in a particular situation to perform a specific task within the guidelines of policy. Both policies and procedures are goal-oriented, but policy establishes limits to action while procedure directs responses within those limits.

Profile/Criminal Profile: An investigative technique for identifying and defining the major personality and behavioral characteristics of the criminal offender through an analysis of the crime(s) he or she has committed.

Protocol (of Intelligence Collection): Information collection procedures employed for obtaining verbal and written information, including on the actions of people, and physical evidence required for strategic and tactical intelligence analysis.

Public Value (of Information): Intelligence or information can be released to the public when there is a need to know and a right to know the information because of the value that may be derived from public dissemination, to 1. Aid in locating targets/suspects and 2. For public safety purposes (i.e., hardening targets, taking precautions).

Purging (Records): Removing and/or destroying records because they are deemed to be of no further value or that further access to the records would serve no legitimate government interest.

Qualitative (Methods): Research methods that collect and analyze information that is described in narrative or rhetorical form, with conclusions drawn based on the cumulative interpreted meaning of that information.

Quantitative (Methods): Research methods that collect and analyze information that can be counted or placed on a scale of measurement that can be statistically analyzed.

Racketeer Influenced and Corrupt Organizations Act of 1970 (RICO) or similar state statutes: Title IX of the Organized Crime Control Act of 1970 (18 U.S.C. Sections 1961–1968) provides civil and criminal penalties for persons who engage in a pattern of racketeering activity or collection of an unlawful debt that has a specified relationship to an enterprise that affects interstate commerce.

Racketeering Activity: State felonies involving murder, robbery, extortion, and several other serious offenses and more than 30 serious federal offenses, including extortion, interstate theft offenses, narcotics violations, mail fraud, and securities fraud.

Reasonable Suspicion: When information exists that establishes sufficient facts to give a trained law enforcement or criminal investigative agency officer, investigator, or employee a basis for believing that there is a reasonable possibility that an individual or organization is involved in a definable criminal activity or enterprise:.

Recommendations: Suggestions for actions to be taken based on the findings of an analysis.

Records (Intelligence): *See* Intelligence Records (Files).

Records System: A group of records from which information is retrieved by reference to a name or other personal identifier, such as a social security number.

Red Team: A technique for assessing vulnerability that involves viewing a potential target from the perspective of an attacker to identify its hidden vulnerabilities and to anticipate possible modes of attack.

Regional Information Sharing Systems (RISS): RISS is composed of six regional intelligence centers that provide secure communications, information-sharing resources, and investigative support to combat multijurisdictional crime and terrorist threats to more than 8,000 local, state, tribal, and federal member law enforcement agencies in all 50 states, the District of Columbia, U.S. territories, Australia, Canada, and England.

Reliability: Asks the question, "Is the source of the information consistent and dependable?"

Reporting: Depending on the type of intelligence, the process of placing analyzed information into the proper form to ensure the most effective consumption.

Requirements (Intelligence): The types of intelligence that operational law enforcement elements need from the intelligence function within an agency or other intelligence-producing organizations to enable law enforcement officers to maximize protection and preventive efforts as well as identify and arrest persons who are criminally liable.

Responsibility: Responsibility reflects how the authority of a unit or individual is used and determines whether goals have been accomplished and the mission fulfilled in a manner that is consistent with the defined limits of authority.

Right to Know: Based on having legal authority, one's official position, legal mandates, or official agreements, allowing the individual to receive intelligence reports.

Risk Assessment: An analysis of a target, illegal commodity, or victim to identify the probability of being attacked or criminally compromised and to analyze vulnerabilities.

Risk Management-Based Intelligence: An approach to intelligence analysis that has as its object the calculation of the risk attributable to a threat source or acts threatened by a threat source. It is a means of providing strategic intelligence for planning and policymaking, especially regarding vulnerabilities and countermeasures designed to prevent criminal acts and a means of providing tactical or operational intelligence in support of operations against a specific threat source, capability, or modality. It can be quantitative if a proper database exists to measure likelihood and impact and calculate risk; it can be qualitative and subjective and still deliver a reasonably reliable ranking of risk for resource allocation and other decision-making in strategic planning and for operations in tactical situations.

Rules: A specific requirement or prohibition that is stated to prevent deviations from policy or procedure. A violation of a rule typically results in an internal investigation and may result in disciplinary action.

SCI (Sensitive Compartmented Information): Classified information concerning or derived from intelligence sources, methods, or analytical processes that is required to be handled within formal access control systems.

SCIF (Sensitive Compartmented Information Facility): An accredited area, room, group of rooms, buildings, or an installation where SCI may be stored, used, discussed, and/or processed.

Sealing (Records): Records are stored by an agency but cannot be accessed, referenced, or used without a court order or statutory authority based on a showing of evidence that there is a legitimate government interest to review the sealed information.

Security: A series of procedures and measures that, when combined, provide protection of people from harm, information from improper disclosure or alteration, and assets from theft or damage. (Criminal Justice Commission, 1995.).

Sensitive But Unclassified (SBU) Information: Information that has not been classified by a federal law enforcement agency which pertains to significant law enforcement cases under investigation and criminal intelligence reports that require dissemination criteria to only those persons necessary to further the investigation or to prevent a crime or terrorist act.

Sensitive Homeland Security Information (SHSI): Any information created or received by an agency or any local, county, state, or tribal government that the loss, misuse, unauthorized disclosure, modification of, or the unauthorized access to could reasonably be expected to impair significantly the capabilities and/or efforts of agencies and/or local, county, state, and tribal personnel to predict, analyze, investigate, deter, prevent, protect against, mitigate the effects of, or recover from acts of terrorism. SHSI does not include any information that is: 1. Classified as national security information pursuant to Executive Order 12958, as amended, or any successor order; 2. Designated by Executive Order 12951, any successor order, or the Atomic Energy Act of 1954 (42 U.S.C. § 2011), to require protection against unauthorized disclosure; 3. Protected Critical Infrastructure Information (PCII) as defined in 6 Code of Federal Regulations (CFR) § 29.2; 4. Sensitive Security Information (SSI) as defined in 49 CFR Part 1520.

Signal Intelligence (SIGINT): The interception of various radio frequency signals, microwave signals, satellite audio communications, nonimagery infrared and coherent light signals, and transmissions from surreptitiously placed audio microtransmitters in support of the communications intelligence activity.

Sources: From an intelligence perspective, these are persons (human intelligence or HUMINT) who collect or possess critical information needed for intelligence analysis.

Spatial Analysis: The process of using a geographic information system in combination with crime-analysis techniques to assess the geographic context of offenders, crimes, and other law enforcement activity.

Statistical System: An organized means of collecting, processing, storing, and retrieving aggregate information for purposes of analysis, research, and reference. No individual records are stored in a statistical system.

Strategic Intelligence: An assessment of targeted crime patterns, crime trends, criminal organizations, and/or unlawful commodity transactions for purposes of planning, decision-making, and resource allocation; the focused examination of unique, pervasive, and/or complex crime problems.

Substantive Due Process: Guarantees persons against arbitrary, unreasonable, or capricious laws, and it acts as a limitation against arbitrary governmental actions so that no government agency may exercise powers beyond those authorized by the Constitution.

Surveillance: The observation of activities, behaviors, and associations of a LAWINT target (individual or group) with the intent to gather incriminating information, or "lead" information, which is used for the furtherance of a criminal investigation.

Suspicious Activity Report: A report and process wherein criminal indicators and behaviors that appear to have a criminal nexus are documented and processed through a law enforcement organization to determine if a crime is being planned, in the process of being committed or has been committed.

Tactical Intelligence: Evaluated information on which immediate enforcement action can be based; intelligence activity focused specifically on developing an active case.

Target: Any person, organization, group, crime or criminal series, or commodity being subject to investigation and intelligence analysis.

Target Profile: A profile that is person-specific and contains sufficient detail to initiate a target operation or support an ongoing operation against an individual or networked group of individuals.

Targeting: The identification of crimes, crime trends, and crime patterns that have discernable characteristics which make collection and analysis of intelligence information an efficient and effective method for identifying, apprehending, and prosecuting those who are criminally responsible.

Tear-Line Report: A report containing classified intelligence or information that is prepared in such a manner that data relating to intelligence sources and methods are easily removed from the report to protect sources and methods from disclosure. Typically, the information below the "tear line" can be released as Sensitive But Unclassified.

Telemetry: The collection and processing of information derived from noncommunications electromagnetic radiations emitting from sources such as radio navigation systems (e.g., transponders), radar systems, and information/data signals emitted from monitoring equipment in a vehicle or device.

Telephone Record (Toll)/Communications Analysis: An assessment of telephone call activity associated with investigatory targets including telephone numbers called and/or received, the frequency of calls between numbers, the dates of calls, length of calls, and patterns of use.

Third Agency Rule: An agreement wherein a source agency releases information under the condition that the receiving agency does not release the information to any other agency—that is, a third agency.

Threat Assessment: An assessment of a criminal or terrorist presence within a jurisdiction integrated with an assessment of potential targets of that presence and a statement of probability that the criminal or terrorist will commit an unlawful act. The assessment focuses on the criminal's or terrorist's opportunity, capability, and willingness to fulfill the threat.

Threat Inventory: An information and intelligence-based survey within the region of a law enforcement agency to identify potential individuals or groups that pose a criminal or terrorist threat without a judgment of the kind of threat they pose. The inventory is simply to determine their presence.

Undercover Investigation: Active infiltration of or an attempt to infiltrate a group believed to be involved in criminal activity and/or the interaction with a LAWINT target with the intent to gather incriminating information or lead information that is used for the furtherance of a criminal investigation.

Validity: Asks the question, "Does the information actually represent what we believe it represents?"

Variable: Any characteristic on which individuals, groups, items, or incidents differ.

Vet: To subject a proposal, work product, or concept to an appraisal by command personnel and/or experts to ascertain the product's accuracy, consistency with philosophy, and/or feasibility before proceeding.

Violent Criminal Apprehension Program (VICAP): A nationwide data information center operated by the FBI's National Center for the Analysis of Violent Crime, designed to collect, collate, and analyze specific crimes of violence.

Vulnerability Assessment: An assessment of possible criminal or terrorist group targets within a jurisdiction integrated with an assessment of the target's weaknesses, likelihood of being attacked, and ability to withstand an attack.

Warning: To notify in advance of possible harm or victimization as a result of information and intelligence gained concerning the probability of a crime or terrorist attack.

Appendix B: Intelligence Unit Management Audit

These audit criteria focus on the management of the intelligence unit. They were developed by the author for use in auditing a police department for compliance with a settlement agreement in a federal civil rights case.

Audit Criteria for the Law Enforcement Intelligence Function Version 2.0

Section A: Meeting National Standards

1. Does the police department subscribe to the tenets and standards of the Global Justice Information Sharing Initiative?
   ☐ Yes   ☐ No

2. Does the police department subscribe to the standards of the National Criminal Intelligence Sharing Plan?
   ☐ Yes   ☐ No

3. Does the police department subscribe to the guidelines for information and intelligence sharing of the Office of Domestic Preparedness Guidelines for Homeland Security?
   ☐ Yes   ☐ No

4. Does the police department subscribe to the guidelines of the Commission on Accreditation for Law Enforcement Agencies (CALEA) Standard 51.1.1 Criminal Intelligence?
   ☐ Yes   ☐ No

5. Does the police department subscribe to the provisions of the International Association of Chiefs of Police (IACP) Model Criminal Intelligence Policy?
   ☐ Yes   ☐ No

6. Does the police department subscribe to the standards of the Law Enforcement Intelligence Unit (LEIU) Criminal Intelligence File Guidelines?

7. Does the police department subscribe to the IACP Code of Ethics or have an articulated Code of Ethics?
   ☐ Yes   ☐ No

8. Does the police department subscribe to the IACP Code of Conduct⁹or have an articulated Code of Conduct?
   ☐ Yes   ☐ No

9. Does the police department have an articulated Statement of Values?
   ☐ Yes   ☐ No

10. Does the police department adhere to the regulations of 28 CFR Part 23 for its Criminal Intelligence Records System?
    ☐ Yes   ☐ No

    a. Does the police department operate a federally funded multi-jurisdictional criminal intelligence records system?
       ☐ Yes   ☐ No

11. Does the police department subscribe to the tenets of the Justice Information Privacy Guidelines?
    ☐ Yes   ☐ No

12. Does the police department subscribe to the tenets for information system security defined in the report, Applying Security Practices to Justice Information Sharing?
    ☐ Yes   ☐ No

13. Does the law enforcement agency subscribe to the philosophy of Intelligence-Led Policing?
    □ Yes   □ No

14. Are defined activities for the intelligence unit designed exclusively to prevent and control crime with no political, religious or doctrinal purpose?
    □ Yes   □ No

Section B: Management issues

1. Has a mission statement been written for the Intelligence Unit?
    □ Yes   □ No

2. Is the purpose and role of the Unit clearly articulated and related to the Police Department's Mission Statement?
    □ Yes   □ No

3. Have priorities been established for the types of crimes the Unit will address?
    □ Yes   □ No

    a. Is any written rationale provided for these priorities?
    □ Yes   □ No

4. Are expected activities of the unit articulated?
    □ Yes   □ No

5. Does the mission statement express ethical standards?
    □ Yes   □ No

6. Does the mission statement express the importance of protecting citizens' rights?
    □ Yes   □ No

1. Policies and Procedures

1. Are there written and officially articulated policies and procedures for management of the intelligence function?
    □ Yes   □ No

2. Have intelligence policies been formed to minimize the discretion of information collectors?
    □ Yes   □ No   If Yes, describe:

3. Is there a policy and procedures on "Information Collection"?
    □ Yes   □ No   If Yes, describe:

2. Management of Information: Definitional Standards

1. Are there standard terms used in intelligence activities that have been operationally defined in writing so that all persons in the department know the explicit meaning and implications of the terms?
    □ Yes   □ No

2. What is the source of the definitions?
    □ NCISP   □ Federal Agency
    □ Mixed   □ N/A

3. Has the department articulated standards for classifying information in the Intelligence Unit?[1]
   ☐ Yes   ☐ No

4. How are those standards monitored and enforced?
   ☐ Superior   ☐ Other

5. Does the department have a system for assessing the reliability of sources that provide information that will be retained in the Intelligence Records System?
   ☐ Yes   ☐ No

6. Are there standardized definitions of the reliability scale?
   ☐ Yes   ☐ No

7. Does the department have a system for assessing the validity of the information that will be retained in the Intelligence Records System?
   ☐ Yes   ☐ No

8. Are there standardized definitions of the validity scale?
   ☐ Yes   ☐ No

9. Does the Intelligence Unit have operational definitions that can be applied to a person under investigation or a series of related crimes where the perpetrator is not identifiable in order to classify the case file as either a "permanent file" or a "temporary file"?
   ☐ Yes   ☐ No

   If Yes...

   a. Are the types of identifying information that should be placed in the file articulated?
      ☐ Yes   ☐ No

   b. Is there a procedure for requiring the articulation of the criminal predicate for the permanent file?
      ☐ Yes   ☐ No

   c. Is there a procedure articulating the conditions wherein a temporary file may be created?
      ☐ Yes   ☐ No

   d. Does the procedure specify a time limit that the temporary file can be kept?
      ☐ Yes   ☐ No

[1]

Priority	Classification	Description	Release Authority
Highest Level	Sensitive	Current corruption case; complex criminality; confidential informants	Deptartment Executive or Intelligence Commander
Medium Level	Confidential	Nonsensitive information through intelligence channels; law enforcement only	Intelligence Unit Commander or Supervisor
Lowest Level	Restricted	LE use but no need for high security	Intell Unit Personnel
Unclassified	Public Access	Information that may be released to public and media	Intell Unit Personnel

  e. Is there an operational definition of "Non-Criminal Identifying Information" and procedures for recording and retaining this information?
    □ Yes   □ No

  f. Are there clear procedures that describe the types of information that should not be entered into the Intelligence Records System?
    □ Yes   □ No

3. Management of Information: Source Documents

1. Does the department have a written directive explaining the different types of source documents that will be entered in the Intelligence Records System?
  □ Yes   □ No

2. What types of source documents are entered into the Intelligence Records System?
  Describe:

3. Does the police department have a written directive that the rationale for each source document entered into the Intelligence Records System must be articulated in a report or notation?
  □ Yes   □ No

4. Management of Information: Data Entry

1. Who is responsible for entering information into the Intelligence Records System?
  Position/Classification:

2. Who supervises the information entry process?
  Position/Classification:

5. Management of Information: Accountability

1. Who is the Custodian of the Intelligence Records System that ensures all regulations, law, policy and procedures are being followed?
  Position/Classification:

2. Is there a person external to the Intelligence Unit who is designated to monitor the Intelligence Records System and related processes?
  □ Yes   □ No   If Yes, Position/Classification:

3. Does the department have written procedures for the retention of records in the Intelligence Records System?
  □ Yes   □ No

6. Management of Information: Retention and Purging of Records

1. Does the retention process adhere to the guidelines of 28 CFR Part 23?
  □ Yes   □ No

2. Does the retention policy and procedure include written criteria for purging information?
  □ Yes   □ No

3. How often does a review and purge process occur?
  Frequency:

4. What is the purge process?
  Describe:

5. Does the purge process include a system review of information to confirm its continuing propriety, accuracy, and relevancy?
   □ Yes   □ No

6. Does the purge process require destruction of the source document and removal of all references to the document to be purged if the information is no longer appropriate for retention?
   □ Yes   □ No

7. What is the destruction process for purged hard copy records?
   Describe:

8. After information has been purged from a computerized Intelligence Records System, is free space on the hard drive and/or specific purged files electronically "wiped"?
   □ Yes   □ No

   a. Are backups wiped?
      □ Yes   □ No

   b. What is the accountability system for purging backups?
      Describe:

9. Does the purge process require the elimination of partial information that is no longer appropriate if the source document is to be kept because the remaining information in the source documents merits retention?
   □ Yes   □ No

10. What is the process for purging partial information from hard copy source documents?
    Describe:

11. Who is responsible for ensuring compliance of the purge process?
    Position/Classification:

7. Management of Information: Personal/Individually-Held Records and Files
1. Is there an intelligence unit policy and procedures concerning the retention of individual notes and records that identifies persons wherein criminality is suspected but is not in either a temporary or permanent file and is not entered into any formal records system or database?
   □ Yes   □ No

   a. How is the possession of personal records monitored?
      □ Yes   □ No

   b. How is the policy enforced?
      □ Yes   □ No

8. Management of Information: Accessing Intelligence Records
1. Is access to the Intelligence Records limited?
   □ Yes   □ No

2. If yes, who may access the Intelligence Records System?
   □ Yes   □ No

3. What security controls exist for accessing computerized records?
   □ Yes   □ No

4. Can the computerized records system be accessed through remote access?
   ☐ Yes ☐ No

   a. If so, what security controls exist for remote access?
      Describe:

5. How are physical records stored?
   Describe:

6. Who grants access privileges to Intelligence Records?
   Position/Classification:

7. Who has access to records?
   ☐ Yes ☐ No

8. Does the police department apply the Third Agency Rule to information that is shared with other agencies?
   ☐ Yes ☐ No

9. What audit process is in place for access to computerized records?
   Describe:

10. What audit process is in place for access to physical records?
    Describe:

11. How are physical records secured?
    Describe:

12. What process is in place to handle unauthorized access to intelligence physical records?
    Describe:

13. What sanctions are in place for a police department employee who accesses and/or disseminates intelligence records without authorization?
    Describe:

9. Physical Location of the Intelligence Unit and Records

1. Sufficiency: Is the Intelligence Unit in a physical location that has sufficient space to perform all of its responsibilities?
   ☐ Yes ☐ No

2. Security: Is the Intelligence Unit in a physical location wherein the entire workspace may be completely secured?
   ☐ Yes ☐ No

   a. Is there adequate secured storage cabinets (or a vault) for (1) documents classified by the intelligence unit and (2) sensitive records storage within the intelligence unit's physical location?
      ☐ Yes ☐ No

   b. Is there adequate security and segregated storage for federally classified documents within the Intelligence Unit?
      ☐ Yes ☐ No

      1. Is that storage accessible only by persons with a federal Top Secret security clearance?
         ☐ Yes ☐ No

3. Convenience: Is the Intelligence Unit in a physical location that is convenient to the people, equipment, and resources necessary to maximize efficiency and effectiveness of operations?
   ☐ Yes ☐ No

10. Tangential Policy Issues: Criminal Informants and Undercover Operations

1. Is there a formally articulated policy and procedures for managing criminal informants?

    ☐ Yes   ☐ No

    a. Is a background investigation conducted and a comprehensive descriptive file completed on each confidential informant?

        ☐ Yes   ☐ No

    b. Are informant files secured separately from intelligence files?

        ☐ Yes   ☐ No

2. Is there a formally articulated policy and procedures concerning undercover operations that apply to members of the Intelligence Unit?

    ☐ Yes   ☐ No

3. Does the police department have a policy on alcohol consumption for officers working undercover?

    ☐ Yes   ☐ No

    a. Does the police department have a policy requiring designated drivers for undercover officers who have consumed alcohol?

        ☐ Yes   ☐ No

4. Does the police department have a "narcotics simulation" policy and training for undercover officers?

    ☐ Yes   ☐ No

5. Does the police department have a policy for the issuance of fictitious identification for undercover officers and the proper use of such fictitious identification?

    ☐ Yes   ☐ No

6. Do undercover officers receive training specifically related to proper conduct and information collection while working in an undercover capacity?

    ☐ Yes   ☐ No

7. With respect to undercover operating funds:

    a. Is there a 1-tier or 2-tier process to approve use of the funds?

        ☐ 1-Tier   ☐ 2-Tier

    b. Is a written report required to document expenditure of the funds?

        ☐ Yes   ☐ No

    c. What is the maximum time that may pass between the expenditure of funds and personnel accountability for the funds?

        ☐ Yes   ☐ No

    d. Is there a regular external audit of undercover funds?

        ☐ Yes (How Often)   ☐ No

Section C: Personnel

1. Is a position classification plan in place that provides a clear job description for each position in the Unit?

    ☐ Yes   ☐ No

2. Is a position classification plan in place that articulates Knowledge, Skills, and Abilities (KSAs) for each position?

    ☐ Yes   ☐ No

3. Is there sufficient hierarchical staff (managers/supervisors) assigned to the Unit to effectively perform supervisory responsibilities?

    ☐ Yes   ☐ No

4. Is there sufficient functional staff (analysts and/or investigators) to effectively fulfill defined unit responsibilities?

    ☐ Yes   ☐ No

5. Is there sufficient support staff (secretaries, clerks) to effectively support the unit's activities?

    ☐ Yes   ☐ No

6. Does the screening process for nonsworn employees of the Intelligence Unit require:

    a. Fingerprint check

        ☐ Yes   ☐ No

    b. Background investigation

        ☐ Yes   ☐ No

7. If the Intelligence Unit has non-police department employees assigned to it—e.g., National Guard analysts, personnel from the state or local law enforcement agencies—would there be a screening process for those persons?

    ☐ Yes   ☐ No   If Yes, Describe:

1. Training

1. What types of training do preservice and newly assigned personnel receive?

    ☐ None   ☐ Some - Describe:

    a. Are newly assigned sworn employees to the Intelligence Unit required to attend 28 CFR Part 23 training?

        ☐ Yes   ☐ No

    b. Are newly hired or assigned nonsworn employees required to attend 28 CFR Part 23 training?

        ☐ Yes   ☐ No

2. What types of training do in-service personnel receive?

    ☐ None   ☐ Some - Describe:

3. Have members of the Intelligence Unit attended any of the following federal government intelligence training programs which are open to state and local law enforcement officers.

    a. DEA Federal Law Enforcement Analyst Training (FLEAT)

        ☐ Yes   ☐ No

    b. FBI College of Analytic Studies

        ☐ Yes   ☐ No

    c. Federal Law Enforcement Training Center (FLETC) Criminal Intelligence Analysis Training Course

        ☐ Yes   ☐ No

    d. National Drug Intelligence Center Basic Intelligence Analysis Course

        ☐ Yes   ☐ No

    e. National White Collar Crime Center Foundations of Intelligence Analysis

        ☐ Yes   ☐ No

    f. Regional Counterdrug Training Academy Intelligence Operations Course

        ☐ Yes   ☐ No

<u>2. Supervision</u>
1. Does supervision effectively monitor adherence to written procedures?
   ☐ Yes   ☐ No

2. Does supervision effectively monitor adherence to guidelines adopted by the department?
   ☐ Yes   ☐ No

3. Are performance evaluations tied directly to the job descriptions?
   ☐ Yes   ☐ No

4. Does supervision effectively monitor the performance of required duties (Including the quality of performance)?
   ☐ Yes   ☐ No

5. Is supervision effectively monitoring personnel to ensure civil rights allegations cannot be made with respect to negligent:
   a. Failure to train
      ☐ Yes   ☐ No
   b. Hiring
      ☐ Yes   ☐ No
   c. Failure to supervise
      ☐ Yes   ☐ No
   d. Assignment
      ☐ Yes   ☐ No
   e. Failure to direct
      ☐ Yes   ☐ No
   f. Failure to discipline
      ☐ Yes   ☐ No
   g. Entrustment
      ☐ Yes   ☐ No

6. Is there effective supervision of the Intelligence Unit throughout the chain of command external to the Intelligence Unit?
   ☐ Yes   ☐ No

Section D: Fiscal Management

1. Is the budget sufficient to fulfill the stated mission?
   ☐ Yes   ☐ No

2. Does the Intelligence Commander have input into the budget planning process?
   ☐ Yes   ☐ No

3. Is there over-reliance on "soft money" to operate the Unit?
   ☐ Yes   ☐ No

4. Are equipment and personnel line items assigned directly to the Intelligence Unit?
   ☐ Yes   ☐ No

5. Is there an established process for reliably monitoring credit cards assigned to personnel?
   ☐ Yes   ☐ No

Section E: Unit Evaluation

1. As a whole, is the Unit effective with respect to:

    a. Providing information to prevent crime?
       □ Yes   □ No

    b. Providing information to apprehend criminals?
       □ Yes   □ No

    c. Effectively analyzing information to identify criminal enterprises, crime trends, criminal anomalies, etc.?
       □ Yes   □ No

2. Are data collected on the following factors and reported in an annual report as indicators of the intelligence Unit's productivity as an organizational entity?

    a. Number and type of analytic products delivered for investigative purposes
       □ Yes   □ No   □ N/A

    b. Number and type of analytic products that led to arrest
       □ Yes   □ No   □ N/A

    c. Assets seized from illegal activities wherein intelligence contributed to the arrest and/or seizure
       □ Yes   □ No   □ N/A

    d. Number and types of strategic intelligence products delivered to the command staff
       □ Yes   □ No   □ N/A

    e. Number of intelligence sharing meeting attended by Unit staff
       □ Yes   □ No   □ N/A

    f. Number of briefings provided by the intelligence staff
       □ Yes   □ No   □ N/A

    g. Total number of queries into the intelligence database
       □ Yes   □ No   □ N/A

    h. Number of permanent files opened
       □ Yes   □ No   □ N/A

    i. Number of temporary files investigated
       □ Yes   □ No   □ N/A

    j. Number of requests for information to the unit from outside agencies
       □ Yes   □ No   □ N/A

3. Are products produced by the Intelligence Unit:

    a. In a consistent format?
       □ Yes   □ No

    b. Easily consumed and used (i.e., understandable and actionable)?
       □ Yes   □ No

    c. Contain timely information and disseminated in a timely manner?
       □ Yes   □ No

    d. Have substantive contact to aid in preventing or controlling crime?
       □ Yes   □ No

4. Given the confidential nature of the information contained in the Intelligence Unit, is there a policy and procedures if a city, county, state, or federal fiscal or program auditor seeks to audit the Intelligence Unit?
       □ Yes   □ No   If Yes, Describe:

Section F: Collection

1. Is there an articulated collection plan for the Intelligence Unit?
   ☐ Yes ☐ No

   a. How often and when is the plan updated?
      ☐ Yes ☐ No

2. Have the following activities been performed by the Intelligence Unit:

   a. An inventory of threats in the region posed by criminal enterprises, terrorists, and criminal extremists.
      ☐ Yes ☐ No

   b. An assessment of the threats with respect to their probability of posing a criminal or terrorist threat to the region.
      ☐ Yes ☐ No

   c. A target or criminal commodity analysis of the region.
      ☐ Yes ☐ No

   d. A target or criminal commodity vulnerability assessment in the region.
      ☐ Yes ☐ No

3. For each identified threat, have intelligence requirements been articulated?
   ☐ Yes ☐ No

   a. If Yes, describe the methods of collection that will be used to fulfill those intelligence requirements.
      ☐ Yes ☐ No

Section G: Technology and Networking

1. Are any members of the Intelligence Unit subscribed members of the FBI's secure e-mail system Law Enforcement Online (LEO)?
   ☐ Yes - All ☐ Yes - Some ☐ No

2. Are any members of the Intelligence Unit subscribed members of the secure Regional Information Sharing System (RISS) e-mail system riss.net?
   ☐ Yes - All ☐ Yes - Some ☐ No

   a. If yes, are the RISS databases (e.g., RISS.gang, ATIX, etc.) regularly used?
      ☐ Yes ☐ No

3. Is the police department a member of the Regional Information Sharing System?
   ☐ Yes ☐ No

4. Is a systematic procedure in place to ensure that advisories and notifications transmitted via the National Law Enforcement Teletype System (NLETS) are forwarded to the Intelligence Unit?
   ☐ Yes ☐ No

5. Are you connected to any state-operated intelligence or information networks?
   ☐ Yes ☐ No If Yes, Describe:

6. Are you connected to any regional intelligence or information networks (including HIDTA)?
   ☐ Yes ☐ No

7. Does the intelligence have access and use the National Virtual Pointer System (NVPS)?
   ☐ Yes ☐ No

8. Is there a formal approval process for entering into a Memorandum of Understanding (MOU) for information and intelligence sharing with other law enforcement agencies or law enforcement intelligence entities?

  ☐ Yes   ☐ No   If Yes, describe the process:
                       Who must approve the MOU?

Section H: Legal Issues

1. Is there a designated person in the police department who reviews Freedom of Information Act requests directed to the intelligence unit?

  ☐ Yes   ☐ No

2. Is there a designated person in the police department who responds to Privacy Act inquiries directed to the Intelligence Unit?

  ☐ Yes   ☐ No

3. Is there a designated person the police department contacts in response to a subpoena for a file in the Intelligence Records System?

  ☐ Yes   ☐ No

4. Does the Intelligence Unit Commander have a legal resource for advice to help protect intelligence records from objectionable access?

  ☐ Yes   ☐ No

5. Does the Intelligence Unit Commander have a legal resource for advice on matters related to criminal procedure and civil rights?

  ☐ Yes   ☐ No

6. Does the Intelligence Unit Commander have a legal resource for advice on matters related to questions of civil liability as it relates to all aspects of the intelligence function?

  ☐ Yes   ☐ No

7. Has legal counsel reviewed and approved all policies and procedures of the intelligence unit?

  ☐ Yes   ☐ No

Appendix C:
LEIU Audit Checklist for the Criminal Intelligence Function

The Law Enforcement Intelligence Unit (LEIU) is the premier organization for law enforcement intelligence. The organization has established a solid reputation for professionalism, objectivity, and promoting intelligence activities that protect the constitutional rights and privacy of all Americans. This checklist was prepared to aid in the professional management of a state, local, and tribal law enforcement intelligence function. Additional materials, including a description of how the checklist was prepared, are available in the original LEIU Audit Checklist document, it.ojp.gov/documents/LEIU_audit_checklist.pdf.

This checklist provides law enforcement executives and senior- to mid-level law enforcement managers with a tool for conducting an audit or evaluation of their agency's criminal intelligence function. Specifically, this audit tool can help an agency ensure that it is carrying out the criminal intelligence function in accordance with applicable laws, regulations, and guidelines. The principles found in the checklist apply most directly to municipal, county, and state law enforcement agencies. Several introductory comments are appropriate.

This checklist should be applied only to criminal intelligence files, not to other types of law enforcement records. Some law enforcement officials fail to make the distinction between criminal intelligence files and other types of law enforcement records (e.g., investigative files). In the law enforcement context, however, these differences are important and must be recognized.

Investigation generally refers to the systematic examination of facts to determine if a crime has occurred and, if so, develop a case for prosecution. Generally, the term "investigative files" refers to information collected in the course of an investigation where there are reasonable grounds to suspect that a person has committed specific criminal acts.

On the other hand, the criminal intelligence process is an ongoing activity, and is not necessarily triggered by the investigation of any specific offense. While investigation tends to be reactive in nature, criminal intelligence is proactive and used to identify and understand criminals operating in a particular area. Once individuals or groups are identified and their habits known, law enforcement authorities may begin to assess current trends in crime and to forecast, and possibly prevent, future criminal activities. Intelligence provides the knowledge on which to base decisions, and select appropriate targets (subjects, criminal groups or businesses) for investigations. Although criminal intelligence may be used to assist in investigations, surveillance operations, and prosecution of cases, it also provides law enforcement agencies with the ability to effectively manage resources, budget, and meet their responsibility to forecast community threats to prevent crime.

Criminal intelligence consists of pieces of raw information that when collected, evaluated, collated, and analyzed, form meaningful and useful judgments that are both accurate and timely. Taking this raw information and turning it into intelligence can be described as a sequential process with multiple distinct phases. Following appropriate planning, the first phase is collection, when raw information is obtained from various sources. Evaluation then occurs, which determines the reliability of the source and the validity of the information. The third phase is collation and involves indexing, cross-referencing, and filing of information. The fourth phase is analysis, which identifies trends, future developments, and case building. The fifth phase is dissemination, which involves the actual dispensing of the intelligence information. A unit that does not complete each of these phases is not a criminal intelligence unit.

Ideally, this checklist is designed to be utilized by senior law enforcement managers who are not directly involved in the day-to-day operations of the agency's criminal intelligence function. This helps ensure that the audit is objective, and accurately identifies the function's strengths and weaknesses. The checklist can also be used as a self-assessment tool by personnel who are directly involved with the agency's criminal intelligence function. This type of effort will help determine if the unit is acting in accordance with the standard practices and procedures established by LEIU.

Historically, criminal intelligence units have experienced problems in the areas of unit operating procedures, collection, collation, and dissemination; this checklist focuses on these areas.

Unit Operating Procedures

1. Does the criminal intelligence unit have a mission statement? If no, go to question 10.
   ☐ Yes   ☐ No

2. Does the mission statement contain a concise, well-defined mandate describing the criminal intelligence unit?
   ☐ Yes   ☐ No

3. Does the mission statement describe the use of the intelligence process in support of the criminal intelligence unit?
   ☐ Yes   ☐ No

4. Does the statement focus toward criminal predicate?
   ☐ Yes   ☐ No

5. Does the statement indicate that the criminal intelligence unit will provide the Chief Executive with criminal information and resulting analysis to counter and control criminal activities?
   ☐ Yes   ☐ No

6. Does the statement identify the criminal intelligence unit's expected results?
   ☐ Yes   ☐ No

7. Is the criminal intelligence unit staying within its mission?
   ☐ Yes   ☐ No

8. Is the criminal intelligence unit assuming work beyond the authorized crime areas?
   ☐ Yes   ☐ No

9. Is the statement reviewed on a periodic basis to insure that it is meeting the needs of the agency/organization?
   ☐ Yes   ☐ No

10. Does the criminal intelligence unit have policy and procedures guidelines? If no, go to question 18.
    ☐ Yes   ☐ No

11. Do the guidelines describe the criminal intelligence unit's operations?
    ☐ Yes   ☐ No

12. Do the guidelines provide the criminal intelligence unit's mission statement?
    ☐ Yes   ☐ No

13. Do the guidelines detail the criminal intelligence unit's methods of operation?
    ☐ Yes   ☐ No

14. Do the guidelines outline the criminal intelligence unit's file guidelines?
    ☐ Yes   ☐ No

15. Do the guidelines establish the criminal intelligence unit's security procedures?
    ☐ Yes   ☐ No

16. Do the guidelines describe personnel responsibilities and assigned duties?
    ☐ Yes   ☐ No

17. Have the guidelines been provided to personnel?
    ☐ Yes   ☐ No

18. Are periodic security updates conducted for intelligence personnel on a regular basis?
    ☐ Yes   ☐ No

19. Is the criminal intelligence unit located in a physically secure location?
    ☐ Yes   ☐ No

20. Are unauthorized persons prevented from accessing the criminal intelligence unit's location?
    ☐ Yes   ☐ No

21. Is access terminated when personnel are on leave or cease to work in an intelligence capacity?
    ☐ Yes   ☐ No

22. Are there guidelines for transferring material to or from floppy disks?
    ☐ Yes   ☐ No

23. Does the criminal intelligence unit have access to the Chief Executive?
    ☐ Yes   ☐ No

24. Does the unit provide the Chief Executive with recommendations?
    ☐ Yes   ☐ No

25. Does the unit provide the agency with valuable strategic and tactical products?
    ☐ Yes   ☐ No

26. Do personnel receive appropriate training?
    ☐ Yes   ☐ No

27. Are there clear lines of responsibility and accountability for the functions of the intelligence unit?

28.   ☐ Yes   ☐ No

29. Is a regular security risk review of the intelligence unit and its systems conducted?
    ☐ Yes   ☐ No

30. Are procedures in place governing the criminal intelligence unit's use of special funds?
    ☐ Yes   ☐ No

31. Is the criminal intelligence unit's mission achievable with the number of assigned staff?
    ☐ Yes   ☐ No

Collection
31. Does a collection effort begin with the development of a written plan?
    ☐ Yes   ☐ No

32. Does the collection plan include a set of information requirements that specifies what data are needed by the agency or investigator (s)?
    ☐ Yes   ☐ No

33. Does the collection plan comply with applicable local, state, and federal statutes and case law?
    ☐ Yes   ☐ No

34. Is the collection plan focused on identifying the nature and extent of criminal activity?
    ☐ Yes   ☐ No

35. Does the collection plan utilize all known available sources?
    ☐ Yes   ☐ No

36. Are the plan's objectives and requirements communicated to criminal intelligence unit staff?
    ☐ Yes   ☐ No

37. Has the Criminal Intelligence Function encouraged the development of a close working relationship between analysts and investigators?
    ☐ Yes   ☐ No

38. Have those assigned to the Criminal Intelligence Function received training in the right to privacy?
    ☐ Yes   ☐ No

39. Does the state in which your agency resides have laws that address the collection of criminal intelligence data?
    ☐ Yes   ☐ No

40. Do the methods used by information collectors fall within legal guidelines?
    ☐ Yes   ☐ No

41. Does your agency have informant guidelines in place? If no, go to question 44.
    ☐ Yes   ☐ No

42. Do these guidelines address informant control and management?
    ☐ Yes   ☐ No

43. Do these guidelines address the maintenance of informant files?
    ☐ Yes   ☐ No

Collation
44. Does the unit have criminal intelligence file guidelines?
    ☐ Yes   ☐ No

45. Is the criminal intelligence unit operating within the guidelines?
    ☐ Yes   ☐ No

46. Are files kept ONLY on individuals who are suspected of being involved in actual or attempted criminal acts; or suspected of being involved in criminal activities with known or suspected crime figures?
    ☐ Yes   ☐ No

47. Are files kept ONLY on organizations, businesses, and groups that are suspected of being involved in actual or attempted criminal acts; or are suspected of being operated, controlled, financed, or infiltrated by known or suspected crime figures?
    ☐ Yes   ☐ No

48. Do files include information that relates ONLY to a criminal predicate?
    ☐ Yes   ☐ No

49. Do the guidelines clearly delineate criteria for determining if information should be entered and retained in the files?
    ☐ Yes   ☐ No

50. Is the information stored in criminal intelligence files evaluated according to source reliability and content validity before it is included in a criminal intelligence file?
    ☐ Yes   ☐ No

51. Is there a clearly articulated system for assessing source reliability and content validity?
    ☐ Yes   ☐ No

52. Is a distinction made between permanent, temporary, and working files along with appropriate retention periods?
    ☐ Yes   ☐ No

53. Is the information stored in criminal intelligence files classified in order to protect sources, investigators, and the individual's right to privacy?
    ☐ Yes   ☐ No

54. Are files clearly marked with appropriate classification?
    ☐ Yes   ☐ No

55. Is information maintained in the criminal intelligence file reviewed for reclassification or purge on a periodic basis to ensure that it is current, accurate, safeguards an individual's right to privacy, and is classified at an appropriate security level?
    ☐ Yes   ☐ No

56. Is information maintained in the criminal intelligence file reviewed on a periodic basis for utility, timeliness, appropriateness, accuracy, and completeness?
    ☐ Yes   ☐ No

57. Do the criminal intelligence unit's purge policies comply with local, and/or state law regarding records retention?
    ☐ Yes   ☐ No

58. Is there a specific staff member(s) who is responsible for purging files?
    ☐ Yes   ☐ No

59. Are procedures in place to govern the storage, handling, and security of hard copy source material?
    ☐ Yes   ☐ No

60. Does the criminal intelligence unit retain hard copies of source documents? If no, go to question 63.
    ☐ Yes   ☐ No

61. Are these documents stored in a safe and secure location?
    ☐ Yes   ☐ No

62. Is access to these documents restricted?
    ☐ Yes   ☐ No

63. Are procedures in place to govern the storage, handling, and security of source material in an electronic database?
    ☐ Yes   ☐ No

64. Is access to the file database restricted?
    ☐ Yes   ☐ No

65. Is a specific employee(s) responsible for controlling automated access?
    ☐ Yes   ☐ No

66. Are automated access audits conducted periodically?
    ☐ Yes   ☐ No

67. Is a record of audits maintained?
    ☐ Yes   ☐ No

68. Is automated access immediately deleted when personnel leave or transfer?
    ☐ Yes   ☐ No

69. Are files adequately safeguarded through back-up and recovery routines, and off-site storage of critical files, programs, and systems?
    ☐ Yes   ☐ No

70. Is the system isolated from other networks or protected by a firewall to restrict unauthorized access?
    ☐ Yes   ☐ No

71. Are files (either hard or electronic copy) indexed in an organized fashion?
    ☐ Yes   ☐ No

72. Is a file locator system in place?
    ☐ Yes   ☐ No

73. Is a particular employee(s) responsible for overseeing the criminal intelligence file system so that it is operating within the guidelines of all applicable laws?
    ☐ Yes   ☐ No

74. Are purged documents destroyed in a secure and appropriate manner according to all applicable laws?
    ☐ Yes   ☐ No

Dissemination

75. Are procedures in place for responding to requests for information?
    ☐ Yes   ☐ No

76. Are records kept of requests for information and responses? If no, go to question 79.
    ☐ Yes   ☐ No

77. Are these records audited periodically?
    ☐ Yes   ☐ No

78. Are there procedures in place governing the methods of enveloping, dispatching, and recording the dissemination of law enforcement sensitive material?
    ☐ Yes   ☐ No

79. Is criminal intelligence information released only to those who have demonstrated a right to know and a need to know?
    ☐ Yes   ☐ No

80. Is there an audit trail to determine who has accessed criminal intelligence files?
    ☐ Yes   ☐ No

81. Has the criminal intelligence unit established a policy prohibiting third-party dissemination?
    ☐ Yes   ☐ No

82. Has the agency identified legal resources that are familiar with criminal intelligence issues and procedures and can adequately represent the agency in legal matters?
    ☐ Yes   ☐ No

References

Audit Factors for the Law Enforcement Intelligence Function. David L. Carter, 2004.

Criminal Intelligence File Guidelines. Law Enforcement Intelligence Unit. Revised in March 2002.

Criminal Intelligence Standards and Guidelines. California Peace Officers' Association, July 2003.

Evaluation Checklists for Intelligence Units. Paul R. Roger. *Turn-Key Intelligence: Unlocking Your Agency's Intelligence Capabilities,* IALEIA, LEIU, and NW3C.

Gang File Audit Checklist. California Bureau of Investigation, Division of Law Enforcement, California Department of Justice, May 2001.

Guidelines for the Criminal Intelligence Function. Dick Wright, Simi Valley Police Department, Revised September 1998.

Intelligence 2000: Revising the Basic Elements; A Guide for Intelligence Professionals. LEIU and IALEIA. Managing Editor Marilyn B. Peterson, Editors Bob Morehouse and Dick Wright, 2000.

National Criminal Intelligence Sharing Plan 2003. Office of Justice Programs, U.S. Department of Justice, Award No. 2000-LD-BX-0003, October 2003.

Appendix D: About the Author

David L. Carter, Ph.D.
Professor and Director, Intelligence Program
School of Criminal Justice
560 Baker Hall
Michigan State University
East Lansing, MI 48824-1118
517.355.6649/Fax 517.355.6646
carterd@msu.edu

David L. Carter (Ph.D., Sam Houston State University) is a Professor in the School of Criminal Justice and Director of the Intelligence Program at Michigan State University. A former Kansas City, Missouri, police officer, Dr. Carter was Chairman of the Department of Criminal Justice at the University of Texas-Pan American in Edinburg, Texas, for 9 years prior to his appointment at Michigan State in 1985. He has served as a trainer, consultant, and advisor for many law enforcement agencies throughout the U.S., Europe, and Asia on matters associated with officer behavior, community policing, law enforcement intelligence, and computer crime. In addition, he has presented training sessions at the FBI National Academy, the FBI Law Enforcement Executive Development Seminar (LEEDS), the International Law Enforcement Academy in Budapest, Hungary; the United Nations Asia and Far East Institute (UNAFEI) in Tokyo; police "command colleges" of Texas, Florida, Ohio, Massachusetts, Wisconsin, and Kentucky; and served at the FBI Academy's Behavioral Science Services Unit, the first academic faculty exchange with the Bureau. Dr. Carter is an Instructor in the Bureau of Justice Assistance SLATT program, author of the COPS-funded publication, *Law Enforcement Intelligence: A Guide for State, Local and Tribal Law Enforcement*, and Project Director for three multimillion-dollar intelligence training programs funded by the Department of Homeland Security. He is an Academic Fellow of the Foundation for Defending Democracies wherein he studied terrorism in Israel. Dr. Carter is also a member of the Justice Department's Counterterrorism Training Coordination Working Group and the Intelligence Training Coordination Working Group. In addition to teaching graduate and undergraduate courses at Michigan State, Dr. Carter is Director of the Criminal Justice Overseas Study Program to England. He is the author or coauthor of five books and numerous articles and monographs on policing issues and is a member of the editorial boards of various professional publications. His most recent book is the seventh edition of the widely-used community relations textbook, *The Police and Community*, published by Prentice Hall, Inc.